The Psychology of
PERSONAL CONSTRUCTS

VOLUME TWO
Clinical Diagnosis and Psychotherapy

The Psychology

of

PERSONAL

CONSTRUCTS

VOLUME TWO

Clinical Diagnosis and Psychotherapy

By GEORGE A. KELLY, *Ph.D.*

THE OHIO STATE UNIVERSITY

W · W · NORTON & COMPANY · INC · *New York*

COPYRIGHT, 1955, BY

GEORGE A. KELLY

ISBN 0 393 9485 5

PRINTED IN THE UNITED STATES OF AMERICA

56789

Contents

VOLUME ONE

VOLUME   TWO

systematic viewpoint. The qualifications and professional
obligations of the therapist are set forth.

Preface to Volume Two

ЛЛЛЛЛЛЛЛЛЛЛЛЛЛЛЛЛЛЛЛЛЛЛЛЛЛ

THIS VOLUME is the second half of what was intended to be a single work. The first volume expounded a new theory of personality. This volume pursues its implications on down to the level of psychotherapeutic technique.

The theory proposed in Volume One is called the *psychology of personal constructs*. It was developed out of a philosophical position called *constructive alternativism*, the notion that there are many successful ways in which man may construe his world and that he is not, therefore, necessarily a victim of circumstances. The volume, also, illustrated the theory's use in a clinical setting involving both diagnosis and therapy. Hence not all that is to be said about techniques remains to be included in Volume Two. Another thing — a repertory of diagnostic constructs for the clinician's daily use was developed in Volume One; therefore that, too, is omitted from Volume Two.

This volume is essentially a clinician's handbook of procedures and techniques. The descriptions being wholly within the framework of the new theory, many familiar terms have systematic definitions which will be strange to the reader. The terms *guilt* and *hostility* are conspicuous examples, but there are many others. The glossary, which is repeated from Volume One, may help the reader.

Volume Two starts with two chapters on the role of the psychotherapist and on certain basic techniques which are more or less applicable to all psychotherapeutic cases. These are followed by two chapters dealing primarily with case-history taking, one on the appraisal of the client's experience and the other on the appraisal of his activities. Next is a detailed outline of steps to be

followed in arriving at the kind of clinical diagnosis which is useful to a psychotherapist. In order for the reader to gain some
idea of how the proposed system of diagnostic axes is applied to
disturbed cases, the next two chapters are filled with illustrative
material.

The last five chapters are strictly cook-book chapters for the
psychotherapist. They have to do with specific techniques for
producing therapeutic movement along the various dimensions of
diagnosis. In general, each section starts with a statement of
the function of the particular type of movement. Then there is a
description of techniques for producing the movement. Next, difficulties or obstacles are mentioned; and, finally, the therapist is
warned of certain hazards to be guarded against.

This volume is not designed as a complete compendium of
psychotherapeutic procedure; that would be a vast undertaking
for anyone. The attempt is to cover only enough of clinical procedure to show how the psychology of personal constructs may
be put to work in the service of people who need psychological
help.

G. A. K.

The Psychology of
PERSONAL CONSTRUCTS

VOLUME TWO

Clinical Diagnosis and Psychotherapy

Chapter Eleven

The Role of the Psychotherapist

⊓⊔

THE FIRST two chapters of this volume have to do with the basic job of the psychotherapist and the general way he goes about it. His task is illuminated in terms of our philosophical position, structured in terms of our theory, and pursued along the systematic lines of the diagnostic constructs proposed in the preceding volume.

A. *Review of the Psychology of Personal Constructs*

1. THEORY AND THERAPY

In the first volume of this book we presented a new theory of personality, together with its philosophical roots. We also took the position that a theory, in order to maintain its respectability, ought to be good for something. This committed us to a lot of writing, for not only were we obligated to expound the theory — an undertaking of no mean proportions — but we were also committed to writing a cook book based wholly on the theory's novel chemistry.

In order to keep the undertaking within reasonable bounds, we chose to ignore, for the time being, the theory's social, industrial, and educational implications — and even its psychological-warfare implications — and develop it, instead, solely in the direction of its clinical implications. Now we address ourselves, in this volume, to the task of developing its diagnostic and psychothera-peutic implications in detail. We shall talk about what the theory is good for.

Before we plunge into this practical development, it will be appropriate to review briefly some of the highlights of our theory, the psychology of personal constructs. The theory is based upon the philosophical position of constructive alternativism, the notion that there are many workable alternative ways for one to construe his world. The theory itself starts with the basic assumption, or postulate, that a person's processes are psychologically channelized by the ways in which he anticipates events. This is to say that human behavior may be viewed as basically anticipatory rather than reactive, and that new avenues of behavior open themselves to a person when he reconstrues the course of events surrounding him. Thus a thoughtful man is neither the prisoner of his environment nor the victim of his biography.

The patterns of man's construction are called *constructs;* and, since each person sets up his own network of pathways leading into the future, the concern of the psychologist is the study of personal constructs. Each personal construct is based upon the simultaneous perception of likeness and difference among the objects of its context. There is no such thing as a difference without a likeness being implied, and vice versa. Each construct is, therefore, dichotomous or bipolar in nature; and, in dealing with a client, the psychologist must frequently go off searching for the submerged poles in the client's thinking.

When a person finds his personal construction failing him, he suffers *anxiety.* When he faces an impending upheaval in his *core structure,* he experiences *threat.* A person who construes the construction system of another person sets the stage for playing a *role* in relation to that person. When he finds himself dislodged from his role, he experiences *guilt.* This has much to do with social organization. *Aggression* is merely the active pursuit of *constructive* experience, but it may be *threatening* to one's associates. *Hostility,* while not necessarily violent, is the continued attempt to extort *validational evidence* in support of a personal construction which has already discredited itself. These are examples of a few of the important constructs which have been developed in Volume One and which are implicit in all that is set down in Volume Two. While it will be difficult for the reader who has not read Volume One to be perfectly clear about the use of terms, this sample may serve to give him some ear for the sound of the language in which this book is written.

2. THE THEORY'S ASSUMPTIVE STRUCTURE

The theory of personality we have called the psychology of personal constructs starts with a basic assumption upon which all else hinges. It is called the Fundamental Postulate. This postulate is then elaborated by means of eleven corollaries. These, also, are assumptive in nature, and they lay the groundwork for most of what follows. While it may be difficult to see the implications of this series of assumptions from a bare recitation of them, it seems appropriate to give the reader an opportunity to see what the statements are, even though his purpose in reading this volume was not to see the theory expounded.

a. *Fundamental Postulate:* A person's processes are psychologically channelized by the ways in which he anticipates events.

b. *Construction Corollary:* A person anticipates events by construing their replications.

c. *Individuality Corollary:* Persons differ from each other in their constructions of events.

d. *Organization Corollary:* Each person characteristically evolves for his convenience in anticipating events, a construction system embracing ordinal relationships between constructs.

e. *Dichotomy Corollary:* A person's construction system is composed of a finite number of dichotomous constructs.

f. *Choice Corollary:* A person chooses for himself that alternative in a dichotomized construct through which he anticipates the greater possibility for extension and definition of his system.

g. *Range Corollary:* A construct is convenient for the anticipation of a finite range of events only.

h. *Experience Corollary:* A person's construction system varies as he successively construes the replications of events.

i. *Modulation Corollary:* The variation in a person's construction system is limited by the permeability of the constructs within whose ranges of convenience the variants lie.

j. *Fragmentation Corollary:* A person may successively employ a variety of construction subsystems which are inferentially incompatible with each other.

k. *Commonality Corollary:* To the extent that one person employs a construction of experience which is similar to that employed by another, his psychological processes are similar to those of the other person.

l. *Sociality Corollary:* To the extent that one person construes the construction processes of another he may play a role in a social process involving the other person.

3. GLOSSARY OF TERMS

FORMAL ASPECTS OF CONSTRUCTS

Range of Convenience. A construct's range of convenience comprises all those things to which the user would find its application useful.

Focus of Convenience. A construct's focus of convenience comprises those particular things to which the user would find its application maximally useful. These are the elements upon which the construct is likely to have been formed originally.

Elements. The things or events which are abstracted by a person's use of a construct are called elements. In some systems these are called objects.

Context. The context of a construct comprises those elements among which the user ordinarily discriminates by means of the construct. It is somewhat more restricted than the range of convenience, since it refers to the circumstances in which the construct emerges for practical use, and not necessarily to all the circumstances in which a person might eventually use the construct. It is somewhat more extensive than the focus of convenience, since the construct may often appear in circumstances where its application is not optimal.

Pole. Each construct discriminates between two poles, one at each end of its dichotomy. The elements abstracted are like each other at each pole with respect to the construct and are unlike the elements at the other pole.

Contrast. The relationship between the two poles of a construct is one of contrast.

Likeness End. When referring specifically to elements at one pole of a construct, one may use the term "likeness end" to designate that pole.

Contrast End. When referring specifically to elements at one pole of a construct, one may use the term "contrast end" to designate the opposite pole.

Emergence. The emergent pole of a construct is that one which embraces most of the immediately perceived context.

Implicitness. The implicit pole of a construct is that one which embraces contrasting context. It contrasts with the emergent pole. Frequently the person has no available symbol or name for it; it is symbolized only implicitly by the emergent term.

Symbol. An element in the context of a construct which represents not only itself but also the construct by which it is abstracted by the user is called the construct's symbol.

Permeability. A construct is permeable if it admits newly perceived elements to its context. It is impermeable if it rejects elements on the basis of their newness.

CONSTRUCTS CLASSIFIED ACCORDING TO THE NATURE
OF THEIR CONTROL OVER THEIR ELEMENTS

Preemptive Construct. A construct which preempts its elements for membership in its own realm exclusively is called a preemptive construct. This is the "nothing but" type of construction — "If this is a ball it is nothing but a ball."

Constellatory Construct. A construct which fixes the other realm memberships of its elements is called a constellatory construct. This is stereotyped or typological thinking.

Propositional Construct. A construct which carries no implications regarding the other realm memberships of its elements is a propositional construct. This is uncontaminated construction.

GENERAL DIAGNOSTIC CONSTRUCTS

Preverbal Constructs. A preverbal construct is one which continues to be used, even though it has no consistent word symbol. It may or may not have been devised before the client had command of speech symbolism.

Submergence. The submerged pole of a construct is the one which is less available for application to events.

Suspension. A suspended element is one which is omitted from the context of a construct as a result of revision of the client's construct system.

Level of Cognitive Awareness. The level of cognitive awareness ranges from high to low. A high-level construct is one which is readily expressed in socially effective symbols; whose alternatives are both readily accessible; which falls well within the range of convenience of the client's major constructions; and which is not suspended by its superordinating constructs.

Dilation. Dilation occurs when a person broadens his perceptual field in order to reorganize it on a more comprehensive level. It does not, in itself, include the comprehensive reconstruction of those elements.

Constriction. Constriction occurs when a person narrows his perceptual field in order to minimize apparent incompatibilities.

Comprehensive Constructs. A comprehensive construct is one which subsumes a wide variety of events.

Incidental Constructs. An incidental construct is one which subsumes a narrow variety of events.

Superordinate Constructs. A superordinate construct is one which includes another as one of the elements in its context.

Subordinate Constructs. A subordinate construct is one which is included as an element in the context of another.

Regnant Constructs. A regnant construct is a kind of superordinate construct which assigns each of its elements to a category on an all-or-none basis, as in classical logic. It tends to be non-abstractive.

Core Constructs. A core construct is one which governs the client's maintenance processes.

Peripheral Constructs. A peripheral construct is one which can be altered without serious modification of the core structure.

Tight Constructs. A tight construct is one which leads to unvarying predictions.

Loose Constructs. A loose construct is one leading to varying predictions, but which retains its identity.

CONSTRUCTS RELATING TO TRANSITION

Threat. Threat is the awareness of an imminent comprehensive change in one's core structures.

Fear. Fear is the awareness of an imminent incidental change in one's core structures.

Anxiety. Anxiety is the awareness that the events with which one is confronted lie mostly outside the range of convenience of his construct system.

Guilt. Guilt is the awareness of dislodgment of the self from one's core role structure.

Aggressiveness. Aggressiveness is the active elaboration of one's perceptual field.

Hostility. Hostility is the continued effort to extort validational evidence in favor of a type of social prediction which has already been recognized as a failure.

C-P-C Cycle. The C-P-C Cycle is a sequence of construction involving, in succession, circumspection, preemption, and control, and leading to a choice precipitating the person into a particular situation.

Impulsivity. Impulsivity is a characteristic foreshortening of the C-P-C Cycle.

Creativity Cycle. The Creativity Cycle is one which starts with loosened construction and terminates with tightened and validated construction.

4. THEORY AND THE PSYCHOTHERAPIST

A theory does not carry much practical weight unless it is rooted in the professional convictions of the persons who use it. This is particularly true in the case of psychotherapists, for they deal most comprehensively with the outlooks of their clients. It is therefore important for us to develop in this volume, first of all, an articulate position regarding the role of the psychotherapist in relation to his client. This position has the same philosophical and theoretical roots as does the psychology of personal constructs. Even our technology is cut from the same cloth. Not all psychotherapists will agree with us, for there are some hair-raising notions afoot about what the psychotherapist ought to do to his clients.

In this chapter we shall attempt to come to grips with varying perceptions of psychotherapy, starting first with the client's, and then developing what we believe to be an appropriate view for the clinician. The view we develop will be one which will sustain the daily use of techniques derived from our theory. We shall also discuss certain general techniques commonly employed in the interview room, regardless of the type of trouble the client is having. Specific and selective techniques come later.

B. Perceptions of Psychotherapy

5. WHAT DOES PSYCHOTHERAPY MEAN TO THE CLIENT?

It should not be considered essential that the client share the clinician's view of what psychotherapy is, either in his particular case or in general. At the outset it is not very likely that the client will hold any conceptualization of psychotherapy other than his own personalized one. If the treatment is successful, a more adequate view of the nature of psychotherapy may emerge as a by-product. In fact, the movement and release of ongoing developmental processes resulting from successful psychotherapy are presumed to be accomplished by means of a revised conceptualization of the whole course of one's life. The client cannot be expected to be able to appreciate this fully at the outset. Indeed, he might be frightened away altogether if the therapist were to convey too literal a view of what psychotherapy is expected to accomplish.

We may remind ourselves of one of our corollaries at this point. The Modulation Corollary states that the variation in a person's construction system is limited by the permeability of the constructs within whose ranges of convenience the variants lie. The client's conceptualization of psychotherapy represents a body of constructs whose permeability determines how extensively he can envision therapeutic change in himself. If the client sees only certain minor adjustments and certain interview-room exercises as constituting psychotherapy, he will not be prepared to essay sweeping changes in his style of life. If one is to move, he needs to have a framework within which that movement may take place. The psychotherapist must, therefore, take the view that he starts with whatever limited conceptualization of psychotherapy the client is initially able to formulate. The evolvement that is psychotherapy itself must first operate within this frame.

But as the client begins to become aware of the sweeping changes that are possible under the aegis of psychotherapy, he develops a far more comprehensive view of what he and the therapist have set out to accomplish. He even discovers that the eventual outcome of therapy is not a fixed state of personal affairs, but rather the reaching of a vantage point in his life's journey from which he can see spread out before him in broad perspective the whole panorama of a life plan. He discovers more. He comes to see therapy as the opening phase of an ever continuing readjustment process synonymous with wholesome living in the years to come. An adequate notion of psychotherapy is therefore a hoped-for outcome of psychotherapy rather than an essential precondition for it.

While it is not necessary for the client to share the clinician's construction of psychotherapy, it is important for the clinician, if he is to play a role in relation to the client, to make an effort to subsume the client's construction of psychotherapy. As we have said before, this does not mean that the clinician must adopt the client's construction of psychotherapy, but it does mean that he must be able to utilize it. To utilize it he must be able to reproduce it with some measure of fidelity. He should also be able to fixate upon the client's construction system within the much more comprehensive perspective which his own system presumably provides. The following types of preconstructions are illustrative of what the therapist may have to deal with.

a. *Limiting psychotherapy by means of the complaint.* While this is not the section in which we propose to deal comprehensively with the analysis of complaints, it is well to point out that a client's complaints reveal something of what he believes psychotherapy can accomplish. They may also reveal what he believes the psychotherapist specifically cannot accomplish. Stating his complaint in the latter terms is sometimes quite important for him. Thus the client's construction of psychotherapy begins to become clear as he trots out the elements, in the form of complaints and descriptions of other people's difficulties, upon which his construction of psychotherapy is formed. The clinician will have to discover how the elements are linked in the various constructs. What elements does the client collect as being amenable to psychotherapy? What elements does he mention in such a manner as to indicate that he specifically excludes them from "treatment"?

Even the complaints which a client seeks to verbalize, however haltingly, are functions of his construction system. Psychological complaints appear to grow on the vines of contemporary discourse. People begin to suffer from "inferiority complexes" after hearing about Adler; they become concerned about their "introversion" after being exposed to Jungian arguments; and they even claim to be aware of their "repressions" after hearing what Freudians have to say about the unconscious. Seen in this light, a conventional personality inventory, in which a person is asked to catalogue his complaints, is a pretty revealing measure of the extent to which a person shares the public mode of discourse in the realm of psychopathology.

It is possible to induce new complaints through the revision of a client's construction system. Some years ago the writer was asked to conduct a brief series of mental-hygiene discussions in a small home-economics class in family life. Incidentally, the class was being used as a control group in Hadley's study of relaxation as a means of preparation for rational psychotherapy. As a point of departure it was arranged to have the class given a specially constructed personality inventory. The inventory, designed by Hadley, was made up in two forms, in each of which half the items were stated in negative form and half in affirmative form. The items which in one form were stated negatively were in the other form stated affirmatively, and vice versa. Half the class was given one form and the other half was given the other form. The ensuing discussions covered, in a generalized way, the personality difficulties which appeared to be most common among members of the class. At the conclusion of the discussions each member of the class was asked to fill out the alternative form of the inventory. Now the number of problems indicated on the second inventory was greater than on the first. This was in contrast with an opposite trend in an inactive control group which was tested in a similar manner.

Had the discussions thrown mental hygiene into reverse? One might be inclined to hypothesize that the discussions had tended merely to raise the anxieties of the students, were it not for the fact that a check on the responses disclosed that the students were saying that, following the discussions, they now felt *less anxious* about the problems which they noted in the second inventory. While this outcome is in the nature of a clinical observation of uncertain generality, and was not reported by Hadley since it was not relevant to his hypotheses, it does suggest that literal complaints can be induced as a function of one's revised construction system. It suggests a number of other things too, but this is not the place to discuss them.

b. *Psychotherapy as an end in itself.* Some clients tend to perceive psychotherapy as an end in itself rather than as a means to achieve an end or as a means of changing something. As psychotherapy becomes more and more fashionable, there is an increase in the proportion of clients who come to the clinic with this point of view. Psychotherapy becomes another one of "the good things": "Other people have their psychiatrists so why can't I?" It is easy for any professional man who attaches considerable intrinsic value to his work to fall victim to this type of thinking. The need to release psychological processes for continuing adjustment may easily be overlooked.

The perception of psychotherapy as an end in itself rather than as a means of generating movement is one of the special types of problems encountered in psychotherapeutic work with those people who are themselves professionally involved with psychotherapy. It may be exceedingly difficult to do effective work with a man who considers psychotherapy in his own case as a way of making himself "legitimate." It can be done, but the psychotherapist may have to be more brutal than he would be in the case of a spontaneous client. When he has finished, he cannot help but wonder what sort of training he has given the budding psychotherapist, whether the outcome will simply be another "psychotherapist" who has a literalistic belief that "psychotherapy is a good thing," or whether he has helped another person to realize his potentialities for continuing readjustment.

c. *Psychotherapy as a way to attain a fixed state of mind.* Closely allied to the view that psychotherapy is an end in itself is the view, also common among many professional people, that psychotherapy produces a fixed or rigidly "healthy" state of mind. The therapist who seeks psychotherapy primarily in order to distinguish more sharply between his own problems and those of the clients he serves may take this view. For him psychotherapy is to provide a kind of fortification against psychological processes which he sees as endangering his proper relationships with his clients. He seeks to protect himself and his clients by fixing his attitudes within a rigid doctrine. As in the ecclesiastical doctrine of apostolic succession, it may be thought to be accomplished through a kind of "laying on of hands." This is not psychotherapy as we would see it, nor does it necessarily provide an adequate protection against improper client-therapist relations.

The outcome of psychotherapy which seeks to produce a rigid state of mind may well be the appearance of the circumspective social mannerisms and the "burned-out affect" that are beginning to become noticeable as generalized characteristics in altogether too many of our professional colleagues who have undergone psychotherapy. In conversation one can sense them trying to hold their hands on all their complexes and grasping for the nearest "sound doctrine" whenever they must pick their way along unfamiliar ground.

d. *Psychotherapy as a virtuous act.* Sometimes clients see psychotherapy as a matter of "doing the right thing" and of being relieved of all difficulties as a reward for their meritorious act. Their transference relations with the therapist are likely to be childlike and superficially obedient. Psychotherapeutic movement is not impossible in such cases, but the therapist is likely to have a number of disillusioning experiences with the clients' "insights" during the course of therapy.

There are, of course, those clients who would like to have psychotherapy cure them "under ether." For them psychotherapy is a kind of magic and the therapist is a kind of magician who waves his psychotherapeutic wand over them. The discovery that therapy can be both painful and exceedingly laborious may lead them to give it up as a bad undertaking.

e. *Psychotherapy as a means of altering circumstances.* Some clients, though the proportion is probably diminishing as psychotherapy becomes better known, expect the therapist to change the circumstances in which they find themselves. Even if they recognize that the therapist does not ordinarily operate in this manner, they expect him to tell them how to manipulate their circumstances without in any way changing their outlook. Some people, in hearing about fixed-role therapy for the first time, guess that it must be a method of manipulating circumstances without reconstruing them. But certainly fixed-role therapy, with its strong emphasis upon seeing things, people, and the self in new ways, is not anything like that. "Just tell me what to do to make my husband love me," a client may say. Even if the therapist decides to operate within this limited conceptualization of therapy, his suggestions will be more effective if they are carefully designed also to enable the client to reformulate her own constructs of what her husband is and of what she herself is.

f. *Psychotherapy as confirming one's illness.* All too frequently clients see psychotherapy as a means of confirming their illness.

It is as if they were saying, "If you take me as a patient it will help me prove that I am sick," or, "Coming here will prove that I am unable to help myself." Sometimes there is vindictiveness in the way a client conceptualizes therapy. The client may think, "Now this will show what a mess my parents made out of me." Of course, the punishment of one's parents and relatives by making them pay the costs of psychotherapeutic treatment or by otherwise inconveniencing them is a well-known neurotic device.

Sometimes the client uses psychotherapy as a means of support against people who are seen as threatening. The client will say, in effect, to the therapist, "I want you to be on *my* side." This happens frequently when parents come in for "help" in solving their problems with their children. They expect the psychotherapy to prove that their parental difficulties are insurmountable.

Then there is the client who says, in effect, "Since my friend got six months of psychotherapy for *her* problems I am sure that *I* deserve at least twelve months for the problems *I* have to face."

g. *Psychotherapy as the proof of the objective difficulty of one's role.* With parents, especially parents of adopted children, the bringing of the child to the psychological clinic often represents a thinly disguised attempt to project their felt inadequacy upon the child. "If my child requires a professional person to straighten him out it will show that I am not necessarily an inadequate parent, even though I could not bear a child of my own and my compensatory adoption of a child did not turn out so very well." Sometimes the adoptive parent sees the child's need for psychotherapy as a justification for "turning him back to the agency" or blaming the agency for passing out inferior merchandise. In any case, the therapist needs to take into account the deep-seated feelings of personal inadequacy which may underlie a parent's seeking psychotherapy for his child.

h. *Psychotherapy as clarification of issues.* There are some rare cases in which the client simply asks for a clarification of his problems. This represents a relatively mature and sophisticated point of view, although, if he insists that all of the problems are external, it need not presage a successful outcome of psychotherapy.

i. *Psychotherapy as drastic movement within one's present construct system.* In those cases where there appears to be surprising readiness for change the therapist may detect an almost fuguelike quality in the client's conceptualization of therapy. While these cases are rare, when they do appear they should be handled with caution lest the movement take place so rapidly that the client loses his perspective. What happens, of course, is not that one rapidly acquires new constructs, but rather that there is a radical shake-up of elements in the old construct contexts. What was seen as black now comes to be seen as white, but the *black-white* construct continues to be operative. Among other things the self is likely to be reconstrued, but within the same construct system. In extreme cases the shift may be accompanied by a deterioration of the construct system tending to make it both constricted and impermeable. Many memories may be frozen out of the context and a partially amnesic state may be the outcome.

j. *Psychotherapy as an environment in which already imminent changes may take place.* Morton's studies provided some clinical evidence that once a client has screwed up his courage to ask for psychological help, some changes of one sort or another can be expected to ensue, regardless of whether or not the help is forthcoming. The very conceptualization of oneself as a psychological client carries with it certain personalized implications which are likely to bring forth a progressive sequence of revisions, major and minor, in one's other conceptualizations of himself. If the treatment is delayed, the client can be expected to attempt, perhaps as never before, certain readjustments on his own. Certainly his complaints tend to change rapidly between the time he first admits that he wants treatment and the time it is made available to him. The seeking of psychotherapy seems itself to be an event of some significance, and it is important for the therapist to make some assessment of what that significance is. As he does so he may find how the client is prepared to conceptualize himself as a patient.

k. *Psychotherapy as the ultimate state of passivity.* There is reason to believe that asking for therapeutic help is so demoralizing in some cases that the client is partly or wholly incapacitated by it. This means simply that psychotherapy is looked upon as destructive of one's integrity. Thus there is an implicit admission of one's feeling of disintegration. The client who casts himself in the role of a helpless patient may see no way to play out his part except by acting as he supposes psychotherapy patients act — with utter despair and helplessness. It is particularly obvious in such a case that the reconstruction of what psychotherapy is is itself one of the initial goals of psychotherapy. This is a problem which is particularly acute in the case of an involuntary patient in a sanitarium or hospital.

1. *Psychotherapy inferred from one's construct of illness.* What psychotherapy means to the client can sometimes be inferred by his general conceptualization of illness. What does it mean to him to be "sick"? The therapist's anecdote about what the client considered to be the opposite of "sick," which was cited in Volume One, is an illustrative example. That client said not to be sick was to be "free." Another client may construe illness as meaning "in need of love," another as "safe," and still another as "rejecting."

In conclusion, we should be careful to point out that, while some of the client versions of psychotherapy may represent special problems for the therapist, they are not necessarily "bad." A client simply is what he is. If he had a perfect outlook on life, the clinical psychologist would be out of a job. What we have been saying about the importance of understanding the client's personal version of psychotherapy is a way of calling attention to whatever comprehensive constructs of change the client may have available as a framework within which to construe change in himself. What kind of readjustments is he able to visualize? Can he see his ideas evolving in any way? Rather than deplore the client's inadequate conceptualization of psychotherapy, we need to understand his own personal construction of change if we are to help him bring about a change.

As we have said before, it is neither necessary nor possible for the client to have a wholly adequate notion of what psychotherapy is in order for the psychotherapeutic series to get under way. Initially the therapist may have to accept almost any one of the illustrative client conceptualizations mentioned in this section. More particularly, it is important for him to discover what it is that he is accepting as a point of departure for himself and his client.

6. THE CLIENT'S INITIAL CONCEPTUALIZATION OF THE THERAPIST

"In what role is the client now casting me?" is a question the therapist should keep continually in mind. The companion question is, "What are the variations which are appearing in his conceptualization of me?" These are not always easy questions to answer. Yet, to the extent that the therapist can answer them accurately, he will be able to judge whether or not the client is ready to find the therapist's counterparts among the people with whom he is in daily contact. Until the client is able to find other people who can enact with similar success the various parts in his revised drama of life, he will probably continue to rely upon the services of the therapist.

From the client's conceptualization of psychotherapy comes the role he expects to play and the role he expects the therapist to play. His behavior as a patient should be seen in this light. He may be bitterly disappointed in the therapist's enactment of the expected role. He may stretch his perceptions of the therapist in order to construe him in the manner he expected to construe him rather than in the manner the therapist seeks to be construed. For example, if he expected a therapist to lay down a set of little daily regulations, he may perceive almost any remark the therapist makes as being in the nature of an admonition. When the therapist disclaims having specified what the client's behavior should be on a certain occasion, it may be looked upon as a refusal to play the proper therapeutic part. The client may then feel lost and insecure in the psychotherapeutic relationship.

a. *The therapist as a parent.* While the nature of transferences is discussed in a later section of this chapter, this is the place to mention certain initial parent-like constructions which the client places upon the therapist. As in the case of all constructions we see the client viewing the clinician through a series of templets accumulated from the past and "tried on for size." Stated in another way, the client applies certain hypotheses to the therapist and subsequently verifies them or abandons them after having tried them out with varying degrees of persistence. One of the more common hypotheses with which a client initially approaches the therapist is that the therapist must surely be like a parent.

Healthy people are continually revising their conceptualizations of their parents and thus, incidentally in a measure, are permitting their parents to revise their own self-conceptualizations. For the therapist, therefore, to perceive that he is being construed by the client as a kind of parent does not necessarily tell the whole story. This is not necessarily equivalent to being perceived as an "authority figure," popular clinical literature notwithstanding. The perceived role of parents varies somewhat from culture to culture, especially the role that parents are perceived to play in relation to older children. It varies from family to family, from sex to sex and, of course, from person to person. The therapist who sees himself as being cast in the role of a parent still needs to discover what the particular "parent" was like whose role he is expected to play. For one thing, is the client seeing him as an adolescent would see his parent or as an infant would see his parent?

If the client looks at the therapist as an infant would see his parent, he may expect the therapist to do a great deal of manipulating of the environment and to spend a good deal of time ministering to his wants. If it is a somewhat older child's attitude which is being projected, the therapist may find that he is expected to extricate the client from difficulties with his companions. A still more advanced view of a parent would set for the therapist a pattern of adviser or dispenser of wisdom.

b. *The therapist as a protector.* While all the ways in which a client may initially conceptualize the therapist might be seen as having their roots in the earliest social perceptions in the family, there are some types of conceptualizations which it is not necessary to interpret as transferences from family figures. The client may see the therapist as a kind of protector, whose job it is to keep him from getting himself into trouble. The alcoholic client may conceptualize the therapist in this way; and the therapist, if he wishes to accept the relationship as the members of Alcoholics Anonymous do, may undertake to begin therapy on this basis. He may find himself bailing the client out of jail and interceding in his behalf in various other ways. The client may even start out by asking the therapist to talk to other members of his family in order to protect him from their harsh judgments.

c. *The therapist as an absolver of guilt.* When the client sees the therapist as one who can relinquish him from the necessity of punishment, the therapist may find himself playing a priestlike role. The client who seeks this kind of adjustment is caught in a construct system which requires him either to conform to some kind of social judgment or to placate the persons who dispense the punishments for his failure to do so. There is a tendency for this kind of person not to reconstrue his approach to life but only to seek some magical way of undoing or avoiding the consequences of what has already been done. Such people usually seek out a clergyman rather than a psychotherapist to play the role they have conceptualized, but every now and then one of them tries to get a psychotherapist to act out the part.

d. *The therapist as an authority figure.* Closely allied to the two preceding views is the view of the therapist as a person who, if obeyed, will reward the client with comfort and relief from anxiety. This, of course, represents an acceptance of a certain kind of authoritarianism. But it is a basic kind. It is the kind that is continually cropping up in gangster rule, in political machines, and in national governments. It is easy for a therapist to accept this kind of relationship and say to the client, in effect, "Just leave everything to me."

This leave-it-to-the-doctor approach is not an uncommon one among medical practitioners and perhaps partially accounts for the fact that, more and more, the medical profession finds itself harried by what it chooses to call "the psychosomatic disorders." The term is, of course, systematically meaningless. "Psychosomatics" utilizes neither a consistently psychological system of explanation nor a consistently physiological system of explanation, but rather makes the gross philosophical error of presuming that certain facts are themselves inherently "psychological" or "physiological," respectively.

The physician who says, "Leave everything to me," creates a kind of authoritarian relationship with his patient which his medical training will not adequately subsume. That is to say, many problems will arise which do not fit in the medical framework. On becoming aware of this inadequacy in his construction system he seeks to remedy the fault by invoking another system — a psychological system — and trying to incorporate it within his physiological system by the linguistic device of inserting a hyphen.

Now some psychotherapists, including a majority of the psychoanalysts, deliberately encourage this kind of authoritarianism, particularly during certain stages of treatment. Many of them consider this attitude on the part of the client to be an essential feature of the transference which is so useful in therapy. If all clients came from homes where this kind of authoritarianism characterized parent-child relationships throughout the years of the child's life, and if all transferences observed in therapy were transferences of parental figures, the position might be well taken. Such is not the case, however. The reader will therefore readily recognize that this essentially authoritarian view of transference is not the one we employ.

e. *The therapist as a prestige figure.* The more impressive the therapist's reputation, his office furniture, and his signs of affluence, the more are certain types of clients drawn to him. A therapist may be viewed by the client much as the possession of a new car would be viewed: the client may try to get the most up-to-date and most expensive-appearing model he can afford.

f. *The therapist as a possession.* Some clients like to feel that the therapist is their very own and treat him very much as a child would treat a new pony or a kitten. They like to feel that the therapist belongs to them, and they suffer sharp pangs of jealousy whenever they see another client walk in or out of his office. For such clients the paying of the therapist's fee is not the persistent reminder that therapy cannot go on forever, as some therapists claim it to be, but rather an act of paying rent on a luxury article. It has about as much effect upon getting a client to get on with his therapy as a fifty-cent slot machine has in getting people to give up gambling.

g. *The therapist as a stabilizer.* Some clients view the therapist as one who will protect them from the threat of a rapidly changing scene. The therapist is seen as one who has sufficient perspective to see beyond the client's immediate troubles and keep him from making frantic and unwise judgments. In a sense, this is a way of seeing the therapist as one who will stanch rather than facilitate movement. The client says in effect to the therapist, "Help me hold still in this seething world."

h. *The therapist as a temporary respite.* Like the client who sees psychotherapy as a temporary state of affairs affording him time to catch his breath, there is the client who sees the therapist as one who grants him a temporary haven against the storm. Such a client usually tells the therapist rather directly and frankly what he expects of him. He may even tell the therapist just what kind of reassurance he expects him to dispense.

Some months ago the writer found a young lady waiting in his outer office at the end of the afternoon. She had come without an appointment and had told the receptionist that she was not greatly disturbed but had felt the need to talk to someone before making an important decision. The writer agreed to see her immediately. During the interview she indicated that she was having to decide between two positions which had been offered her, both of which seemed to be rather attractive. She made it clear that she did not want the writer to try to decide which one she should accept, but said that she just felt like "talking to someone" before making her decision. She told of the death of her husband some months previously, the necessity of her taking a position sooner or later, and the way she had planned to reformulate her life-role pattern. She did not ask the therapist's judgment on any issues, did not complain in the ordinary sense, did not systematically seek to weigh the choice she had before her, and showed relatively few signs of vacillation or ambivalence. While there is no doubt but that she was anxious and might have profited by a more comprehensive type of psychotherapeutic relationship, her initial conceptualization of the therapist seemed to be simply as one with whom she could gain a temporary respite from the difficulties with which she was surrounded. She was, indeed, rather explicit, though tactful, in instructing him not to try to take the initiative in the interview.

i. *The therapist as a threat.* Some clients see the therapist as one who expects the worst of them. As we shall define the clinical construct of *threat* in a later section, this perception on the part of the client is exactly what makes the therapist, or anyone else for that matter, seem to be threatening. It is obvious that "the worst" is a construct which the client has already applied to himself and from which he is trying to escape. He fears that in the presence of a person who "sees through him" he will be enmeshed in an all too plausible construction of himself and have to concede that he still is what he once was.

j. *The therapist as an ideal companion.* Occasionally one finds a client seeking psychotherapy as if he were seeking some ideal person after whom he could pattern his life or who might become an ideal companion. The writer has observed this initial perception more frequently when the therapist is of the opposite sex and perhaps, though not necessarily, of somewhat near the same age. It can also occur in a client who appears to be seeking an ideal parent. The attitude is likely first to be revealed by the client's expressions of curiosity regarding the therapist's personal life, inquiries regarding his health or his mood, or comments regarding his manner or what he does outside the interview situation.

k. *The therapist as a stooge or foil.* Sometimes the client uses the transference relationship as an out-and-out replacement of a normal role relationship with his natural social world. He imposes a rigid set of expectations upon the therapist and insists that the therapist play the parts assigned. He then plays his own part in the manner to which he has become accustomed. The whole exchange is so rigged that it validates itself. This is a case of a person creating a set of facts to validate his constructs rather than testing his constructs against facts as they naturally exist.

As we have seen in defining certain basic diagnostic constructs, this constitutes a basic hostility. Yet, as with other initial attitudes, the therapist may have to accept even a hostile relationship as a point of departure for the therapeutic series.

Occasionally one finds a client who appears to view the therapist as a potential convert to his "system." He views therapy as a matter of finding someone who will see the world in the way he wants him to. As the therapist shows acceptance, which, as we have defined it, is a willingness to see the world through the client's eyes, the client excitedly seizes upon the therapeutic relationship and seeks to exploit it in his own peculiar fashion. This kind of perception, also hostile, is not an easy one to deal with.

1. *The therapist as a representative of reality.* Occasionally a client approaches the therapist in a manner which is conveniently suited to attaining therapeutic goals. This happens when he views the therapist as a representative of reality upon whom he may test out his constructs without suffering devastating consequences whenever his experiments go awry. The interview situation becomes a laboratory in which he may try out social experiments in test-tube proportions. The therapist is asked to play the parts of many other figures as his contribution to the experimental program. He is expected to make himself articulate, and thus to act as a clear-cut indicator of the predictive efficiency of the hypotheses the client seeks to test. He is a validator.

It takes a pretty negativistic therapist to fail to be helpful when he is approached by a client in this manner. Yet, unfortunately, there are a few therapists who are so inept that they will foul up even this promising type of client relationship. When they do so it is usually because they insist upon an authoritarian relationship, rather than a cooperative experimental relationship. Occasionally therapists are genuinely afraid of letting the interview take on an experimental form. They do not trust the outcomes. They lack faith in their own ability to portray reality in a free-flowing situation. Perhaps they even fear the reality which they may represent in the eyes of the client.

7. THE CLINICIAN'S CONCEPTUALIZATION OF HIS ROLE

Comprehensively stated, the job of any psychoclinician is to assist in the continuous shifting of the client's construct system. If the client is psychologically ill, the clinician's understanding of that illness should be in terms of diagnoses that throw light on the paths by which he may become well. We conceive all paths in the domain of psychology as existing in the form of constructs. Even if the client is in psychologically good health, he can retain that healthy condition only if paths of ready movement are left open to him and the surveying of new paths is continually in process. The clinician who comes in contact with a healthy client is nonetheless still concerned with opening up the possibility of continuous change in the client's construct system, for that is always requisite to the maintenance of good health.

The psychotherapist keeps in mind that the changes taking place during therapy should not be the last of their kind. He is concerned with setting the stage for a continuous process of character development extending throughout the client's lifetime. Because of his broad view of the nature of mental health, he does not limit his interest to those changes which can be made evident during the course of therapy. Like the diagnostic clinician, he also is interested in paths for movement opening up long after his formal contacts with the client are concluded.

All movement takes place as a function of some sort of change in constructs. The change may be minimal. For example, a person who sees himself as subordinate in a certain social situation may behave in the passive obsequious ways he has come to collect on this side of the construct. The moment he perceives himself as having been cast in the opposite role — that of an administrative superior — his behavior stands out in sharp contrast. He now demands the passive obsequious behavior on the part of his associates. While his behavior appears to be sharply contrasting, the only constructive change which has taken place is his shifting of himself within the context of the construct by which he has principally governed his behavior. From a psychological point of view one should not consider such behavior contrasts as indicating any more than a minimum of personality development.

Now it may come about that a person, in the course of playing out his "administrative superior" role, may soon find himself confronted with new events and find that his construct is ineffectual in anticipating them. This may lead to his making basic changes in his role-governing construct. These may be far more important psychologically, though they may not be so behaviorally conspicuous, than the changes which were manifest at the moment he was "promoted."

We prefer to conceptualize the role of the psychotherapist quite broadly. It is conceivable that a clinician is operating psychotherapeutically even when he is implementing only such superficial changes as the one described in the preceding paragraph. He may produce such superficial changes in any one of a variety of ways: (1) by creating threat or anxiety, (2) by consistently invalidating the client's obsequious devices, (3) by precipitating the client into a situation in which he perceives himself as "the leader," or (4) by exhortation.

a. *Producing superficial movement by threat.* We have outlined our position on *threat* in Volume One and we have given the reader an idea of what we mean by *anxiety.* Perhaps it is clear that, when we say that the therapist may sometimes conceptualize his role as one of producing superficial movement because of threat or anxiety, we are simply referring to the fact that a person who feels that he has lost his capacity to anticipate events in some way becomes disturbed. When that happens he may attempt a contrasting, though superficial, movement in order to recover his capacity to anticipate. The therapist may, in some cases, legitimately make use of this fact.

b. *Producing superficial movement by invalidation.* When the therapist continually invalidates the client's devices, or the constructs which comprise their psychological core, he may, in some instances, produce superficial movement. Alternatively, he may produce more profound changes in the construct system. The difference in effect is a matter of how the invalidation is presented. If it is presented almost wholly as a matter of current events, including the therapist's personal behavior, not meeting the client's anticipations, the movement is more likely to be superficial. If the client is led to see invalidating evidence over a broad band of experience, he is more likely to attempt basic reformulation of his constructs as a means of achieving movement.

c. *Producing superficial movement by situations.* Superficial movement may be produced by precipitating the client into a situation in which he perceives a contrasting role to be expected of him. If he sees himself as the victim of authority, his behavior may change superficially, though dramatically, if he is placed in a position of authority. If he perceives himself as "cute," his behavior may show a contrast type of change when he finds himself in a situation in which he is obviously "dull."

d. *Producing superficial movement by exhortation.* Finally, as we have said, superficial movement can sometimes be produced by exhortation. Some psychologists go so far as to consider all therapeutic roles which are not "nondirective" as being "directive" and hortatory. When a therapist exhorts a client to change his behavior, he can, at best, expect no more than that the client will attempt movement within the framework of his present construct system. The therapist may choose his words ever so carefully in order to give them just the right shades of meaning, but the best the client can do is to seek the best fit he can find within his own limited repertory of constructs and then act accordingly. The therapist may be surprised at the results. He may accuse the client of not paying close attention. He may believe the client has perversely fouled up his interpretation of the advice offered him. In personal-construct psychology we do not necessarily seek to explain such behavior as an attempt to "undo" the therapist, but more commonly as a failure of the therapist to find or develop an adequate construct within the client's repertory capable of being effectively invoked.

The therapist who attempts to move the client by exhortation is essentially saying to him, "Look, this is what I would do if I were in your place." If the client is able to construe himself as being like the therapist in some way, he may be able to cast himself in the new role. If not, the admonition is likely to fall on deaf ears. This particular kind of exhortation is actually a form of construct formation, in that the client is asked to identify his future self with the therapist and to contrast the two with his past self. The context is thus quite limited; it involves three figures only. The construct formed out of it may not be adequately sustained once the therapist is removed from the situation. If one uses the exhortation procedure at all, it must be in the hope that the client's ensuing behavior will bring him face to face with new experiences which, when handled constructively, will provide adequate contexts for more sustaining constructs. Moreover, this kind of therapeutic effort brings us to the verge of authoritarianism. The authoritarianism, furthermore, becomes viciously destructive of social processes if the therapist also says, in effect, "Look, this is what I would do if I were in your place; but, thank God, I could never be in your place!"

We have been saying that the production of superficial movements within the client's present construct system may be conceptualized by the therapist as a legitimate part of his role. We have discussed four of the methods by which the therapist may produce superficial movement and yet still operate legitimately as a therapist. This, of course, is not the place where we wish to discuss psychotherapeutic techniques in detail, but it has seemed advisable to discuss certain borderland techniques in order to indicate how broadly we conceptualize the clinician's role.

e. *Controlled elaboration.* In a less superficial fashion, the therapist may play his role by helping the client "work through" his construct system in order to bring certain minor constructs into line with the system as a whole. This may lead eventually to a general validation or invalidation of the elaborated system. For example, a client may keep repeating the idea that he would like to have sex relations with his boss's wife. The therapist may help the client by saying, "Let us think through how this would be done and how it would turn out in the end." When the therapist follows this line he is using the method of *controlled elaboration.* The purpose is to make the system — or large sections of it, rather — internally consistent and communicable so that it may be tested out and its validity or invalidity discovered. This is not to say that the only test of the elaborated system is to carry out the overt act of having sexual intercourse with the boss's wife. Quite the contrary. If the construct system can be adequately put into words, it should be possible to test its validity without resorting to such drastic nonverbal experimentation. The therapist's task in a case of this sort is to help the client delineate his construct system in such a manner that it can be tested verbally against reality on a laboratory basis in the conference room. Thus it need not involve the boss, the boss's wife, the boss's children, the client's wife, the client's children, the client's reputation, or the community at large.

f. *Revising constructs.* In addition to producing superficial movement, or seesaw movement, in some instances, and using the method of controlled elaboration in others, the psychoclinician's role is most fundamentally one of helping the client to *revise constructs.* The first two functions do eventually result in some degree of construct revision, since any kind of change in a reasonably alert living being results in setting up a chain of activity through which a continuous evolving of the construction system can be detected. Yet this last function of the clinician's role, setting the stage for an ongoing program of revising constructs, is to be considered central to his job.

g. *Acceptance.* In setting out to help the client revise his constructs the psychoclinician should be prepared to *accept,* for the time being, the client's construction system as it stands. We believe that here is a point of radical departure from the prevailing notion of what the clinician's role should be. Not all of our readers will readily agree that this is such a radical departure. Most clinicians, of course, do try to "understand" their clients. Most of them, fortunately, are sympathetic. And the well-trained psychoanalysts usually try to "empathize" and use their own "preconsciousness" in steering the course of therapy.

The nondirectivists, for example, emphasize the "acceptance" of the client as a person. To them, acceptance means seeing the client as he sees himself or acknowledging the validity of the client's position. Even more basically, they approach therapy from the philosophical position that every person has a right to be and to become anything that he wholly desires. We, too, would like, in principle, to acknowledge the client's right to fulfill his own unique destiny, although we are not exactly sure what is involved when we commit ourselves to such a position. But none of these commitments is identical with what we mean when we say that the psychoclinician should be prepared to accept, for the time being, the client's construction system as it stands.

Our view of acceptance is that it involves not so much the approval of the client's view of himself as it does the readiness to utilize the client's modes of approach — his system of axes, his reference points, his ways of approaching problems. The therapist attempts to employ the client's construct system, though not to be encapsulated by it. This is what we mean by acceptance; and, even though the therapist's version of the system is partially inaccurate, his readiness to seek to use that system meets our criterion.

Now a good therapist must frequently, among other things, be accepting of his client. He should attempt to anticipate events in the way the client anticipates them. He should try to employ the client's vocabulary in thinking about the issues which the client sees himself as facing. He should give words the meanings that the client gives them, rather than the meanings the dictionary gives them, or the personal and professional meanings he has himself customarily given them. He should pay some attention to what he would be compelled to expect in various situations if he were to make his predictions within the same constructive framework the client employs. He should seek a measure of commonality as we have defined it in our Commonality Corollary.

h. *The therapist's overview.* But just as commonality alone is not enough to sustain social progress, so acceptance alone is not enough to sustain therapeutic progress — in any but the simplest cases. The therapist, while trying earnestly to put himself in the client's shoes, does not, in doing so, surrender his own professional overview of the client's problems. He must still seek to subsume a large segment of the client's construction system.

For example, in the case of the man who is fascinated with the notion of having sexual intercourse with his boss's wife, the therapist should try to understand the basic constructs giving rise to such thoughts. He should seek to discover how this particular client structures his world and how that structure in turn leads to the obsessive idea. Perhaps he may find that the client throughout his life has felt safe in the presence of authority only when he was able to ally himself with the woman in the situation. The construct may have been developed by the client at an early age and in the social situation represented by his own family. If this is the way the client's construct system is set up, the therapist may wish to study it in more detail and take into account the more recently added revisions which now are effectively embodied in the system. He then may be able to say to himself, "Ah, now if I should feel this way and then find myself threatened by the authoritative position of this boss, I can see how I too would keep thinking the thoughts that my client thinks." This is acceptance, as we have defined the term.

Now of course the therapist who seeks this kind of understanding does not suddenly dash to the telephone and seek to make a date with his client's boss's wife. Nor does he lie awake nights in unproductive toying with his client's phantasy. He subsumes the construct. He experiments with it ideationally, but he also finds a way to fit it into place within a more comprehensive scheme. He does not fail to perceive that there are better ways of dealing with authority, and that it is possible to establish a kind of relationship with an authority figure which will give a man a more comprehensive and permanent sense of security.

Our illustration is not intended to be a stereotyped explanation of why men have obsessive thoughts. The reader may never run across a case in which the construct system is like the one we have described. We offer the illustration simply to expound the idea that, in addition to an initial acceptance of the client's constructs, the psychotherapist should be prepared to fixate those constructs within a more comprehensive frame, a frame which he himself ought to be able to provide. To do so is to fulfill one requirement of the clinician's role.

8. BASIC APPROACHES TO THE REVISION OF CONSTRUCTS

How does the psychotherapist get the client to form new constructs or to revise old ones? We have said that in some instances he does no more than produce seesaw superficial movement along the dimensions that the client already has, and that the new experiences which will result from such behavioral changes will themselves eventually call for the revision of the system. We have said that another way the clinician plays his role is to use the method of controlled elaboration. This brings about construct revision through testing the internal consistency of the client's construct system, especially when certain ideas are projected into the future. But how does the clinician play his role when he must start from scratch and help the client develop whole new constructs or major revisions of constructs?

For one thing, we have said that the clinician should start out by accepting the client's system in its current form. We have tried to define what we mean by acceptance, using terms which merely suggest operations rather than feelings. We have said that the clinician should be able to go further and to subsume the construct system which he accepts in the client. What happens next?

a. *The therapist selectively adds new conceptual elements.* Whenever one is confronted with new experience, he attempts to fix it within the framework of his construction system. He does this so that he may deal with it predictively — may anticipate it. If his present repertory of constructs does not give him the formula, he casts around for new constructs, perhaps tailor-making them exclusively for the data immediately at hand. If his revision has sweeping implications, he may find himself caught up in it to a degree that frightens him. There are some people who tend to confront themselves with sweeping revisions whenever they face new elements. For them each new experience is deeply disturbing.

Now the therapist must be prepared to add new experience

to the client's life. But he must do so selectively. First he must select new experiential elements which do not fit too neatly into the client's present system. Next he must alert himself to the way the client handles the new elements. If the client attempts superficial movement within his present construct system, the therapist knows that he has not really challenged the construct system but has merely challenged the client's conceptualization of himself within the context of the system. On the other hand, if the client attempts a sweeping revision of the constructs by which the experience is framed, the wise clinician knows that the client is in danger of becoming deeply disturbed as he attempts to put the all-embracing new construct into daily operation. The clinician is therefore on guard against "too much insight" all at one time.

The role of the clinician, particularly in therapy, includes the skillful introduction of new conceptual elements which challenge the client's construction system but which are carefully chosen so as not to precipitate a catastrophic revolution in it. The clinician must be keenly aware of how the new elements he introduces are being handled by the client. He must distinguish between radical but superficial movement in the client and the deeply significant revisions in the construct system which may, if improperly managed, become extremely destructive.

b. *The therapist accelerates the tempo of the client's experience.* All living tends to bring about a continuous revision of a person's construct system. In therapy, not only is the nature of life's experiences carefully controlled by the therapist, but there may be a certain amount of acceleration of life's experiences, particularly during certain stages of therapy. This is accomplished both within the conference sessions and between sessions. The client whose life has been one round of infantile reactions may be treated to a series of experiences which partially re-create the biography of an adolescent. If his life is a perseveration of adolescence, the therapist may confront him with the problems and adventures of young adulthood. It is as if the therapist's role in this respect is to pull the client through the normal succession of life experiences at an accelerated pace.

c. *The therapist imposes recent structures upon old elements.* Every person tends to use older and more infantile constructs in dealing with recollections of elements of experience occurring during childhood. These are the ways childhood events were first structured; the tendency is to keep construing them that way. More recent events — at least, most of them — may be handled in a much more adult fashion. Sometimes, though not always, the therapist may seek to have the client substitute some of his more recent modes of thinking in dealing with the events and figures of his more remote past.

The reconstruction of the past might not be necessary if there were never any danger of the past spilling over into the present. But figures out of the past sometimes materialize in the present; and events long since faded have a way of arising again sharp and clear before our startled eyes. Because we are always prone to see repetitive themes, the stream of life seems to be segmented into events. These events appear to revive themselves and happen over and over again.

If an adult persists in seeing the events of the past through the eyes of his childhood, there is always the possibility that new events, whose similarity to the past is particularly striking, will also be dealt with in a childish fashion. The therapist may forestall this kind of inadequate perception if he takes steps to help the client draw from his repertory of adult constructs in dealing with childhood recollections. Then when an event occurs which bears a striking resemblance to a childhood event, it will not be so likely to invoke an infantile reaction.

In an earlier chapter we pointed out that our approach lays much stress upon the present and the way the client structures it. We noted that our basic system did not lead us to look upon events as causes in any sort of vitalistic sense. We were careful to say, however, that we do not restrict ourselves to an ahistorical approach to psychological problems. We are concerned with a client's past, both because it is the stuff which the client's construct system must have been designed to make sense out of, and because the way the past is now seen is a cue to the way the present is now seen, and a forecaster of the way events which are about to happen will first be seen.

The therapist's role therefore does involve helping the client to apply his most adult thinking to certain selected events of his past, particularly those which may appear to him to repeat themselves. The therapist need not conceptualize this part of his role as eliciting catharsis or as dealing with hidden dynamic forces. The psychology of personal constructs is not what some theorists call a dynamic theory at all. We are simply saying here that the therapist's role includes helping the client to reconstrue certain events and figures of his past because, at some time in his future, the client may think that he has met them again.

d. *The therapist helps the client to reduce certain obsolete constructs to a state of impermeability.* It is not always possible to accomplish the task described in the last section — that of getting the client to reconstrue certain events and figures out of the past. It may be more feasible for the therapist to seek to have the client encapsulate certain ideas so that they will never be used again, except in relation to certain past events and figures. We have already discussed this possibility in an earlier chapter. The therapist may seek to accomplish this function by a careful and limited elaboration of the construct and by the use of time-binding and word-binding techniques. We shall have more to say about these techniques later. It is sufficient to say at this point that the clinician's approach may be to get the client to define the limits of the construct, to tie it firmly to past events and figures which are so unusual that there is little likelihood that their counterparts need be perceived in the future, and finally to wrap the construct up tightly with a word symbol by means of which it can be kept under control. One may think of this as a way of embalming a construct in literalistic impermeability.

e. *The therapist helps design and implement experiments.* Throughout the psychology of personal constructs we have attempted to extend the principles of scientific method to the problems of the individual. Here we extend them to the role of the psychotherapist. The client is in as much need of experimental evidence to verify his newly taken stand as is the scientist. The therapist is keenly aware of this, so he helps the client to survey new data, to reach testable hypotheses by successive approximation, to design experiments without risking too much at one time, and to carry out the experimentation with prudence and courage. The therapy room is a laboratory for the testing of ideas. The therapist even participates in the research himself by enacting the parts assigned to him by the experimental design. And, like any good graduate-school professor, he sets an example of humility in the presence of relevant evidence — an example he hopes the client will follow.

f. *The therapist serves as a validator.* As the client tries out his constructs, old and new, he has an opportunity to observe the reactions of the therapist. From the way the therapist responds, the client draws conclusions as to the predictive effectiveness of his constructs. The therapist is thus, for him, a sample of the social world. The therapist is in a position to validate constructs in the conference room which are validly applicable on the outside. He is also in a position to validate constructs which cannot be utilized by the client on the outside. A negativistic therapist may also invalidate constructs which the client might well find useful on the outside. It is therefore important that the therapist play his role, not only with an acceptance and a generosity possibly rare in the client's interpersonal world, but always with a kind of naturalness and faithfulness to reality which will not mislead the client who uses him as a validator. In a sense, the therapist must play a part as a reasonably faithful example of natural human reactions, rather than one which is superhuman or divested of all human spontaneity. In a sense, the therapist takes the best to be found in human nature and portrays it in such a way as to enable the client to validate his constructs against it. Having identified the therapist's generalization of the acceptable values in human nature, the client may seek them out among his companions.

Thus far in our discussion of the clinician's conceptualization of his role we have not said that the therapist should pass out his own constructs to the client. There is a sense in which the therapist can never quite do this, even if he is disposed to do so. What is likely to happen is that the client translates the words of the clinician into his own construct system. For example, if the clinician tells the client to be "self-confident" the client may look around within his repertory of constructs and decide that the clinician is talking about something the client would be more likely to call "conceited." The client's ensuing experimentation is carried on, not with a new construct, but with the linguistically equivalent construct already existing in his repertory.

Contrariwise, there is a sense in which the therapist's biases must inevitably affect the construction system emerging as the outcome of therapy. The therapist subsumes the client's constructs. He decides what kinds of variation of conceptual elements to introduce into the therapeutic field for the client to make constructive sense out of. He permits the client to validate certain constructs and he sets up the situation in such a manner as to invalidate others. He chooses for experimentation, without always being able to say why he does it, certain tentative hypotheses voiced by the client. His very choice of points at which to clear his throat, nod his head, or murmur acceptance reflects his bias as to what is inconsequential, what is transitional, or what is understandable.

But no matter how inevitably the therapist's biases must affect the course of therapy, they should be used always as subsuming constructs rather than as a ready-made system to be sold to the client as soon as his sales resistance is broken down. The therapist's constructs include constructs of the ways the client can be helped to develop his own system. They are essentially methodological constructs governing the therapeutic relationship, rather than content constructs to be taken over by the client outside or after therapy. The therapist must make sure that he uses his own personal system in this way only. Never should he consider himself a shining example to be emulated by the client. Always he should be skeptical of his work when he finds that his client has entirely ceased to disagree with him in matters of personal outlook. It is to be expected that a client's personal preferences in such matters as religion, entertainment, music, or politics will undergo some variations as a result of the processes set in motion by therapy. But if those changes are all manifestly in the direction of the therapist's preferences, the therapist is methodologically suspect. In such a case it is appropriate for the therapist to question whether or not he has unleashed any continuing life processes by which the client may work his way through the future. Perhaps the therapist has produced only a static type of adjustment. Perhaps the client is about to be abandoned at some psychological camp site along the therapist's own meandering trail.

C. The Psychotherapist's Qualifications

9. THE PSYCHOTHERAPIST'S SKILLS

What we have said thus far might suffice to indicate what we would expect a psychotherapist's skills should be. The following list will therefore be no surprise to the reader.

a. *A subsuming construct system.* By this we mean a system which is primarily methodological and which will therefore permit the therapist to deal with individuals who themselves vary quite widely in their personal construct systems. This does not mean that the therapist should say, "Since all clients have their own personal systems I must have no system of my own and I must approach each client as if he were an utterly new universe." It means rather that he should be able to say, "Since all clients have their own personal systems my system should be *a system of approach* by means of which I can quickly come to understand and subsume the widely varying systems which my clients can be expected to present."

The psychotherapist should have a clear idea of what his system is and should be able to verbalize its specific methodological constructs. If, for example, he uses role playing as a systematic approach to a certain client, he should be able to say explicitly what the approach is designed to do. If he envisions therapy as a procedure for concept formation he should be able to say how he expects to adapt it to the various conceptualization systems with which his clients may unexpectedly confront him.

The psychotherapist should have training in the *utilization* of his subsuming system of constructs. The particular nature of the subsuming system can vary from therapist to therapist. The important requirement is that it should be a subsuming system rather than a rival system and the therapist should be trained in the psychotherapeutic utilization of it in a variety of cases.

b. *Skill in observation.* Alertness and sensitivity to a wide variety of cues is also an important skill in a psychotherapist. From the standpoint of the psychology of personal constructs this skill depends primarily upon two things — a well-elaborated construct system of one's own, and a variety of well-structured experiences. Now this is not to say that a person whose construction system is logically intact is necessarily a better observer. It is the elaboration of the construction system, rather than its logical integrity, that makes it possible for the therapist to pick up a wide variety of cues. By elaboration we mean that the construction system has been extended experimentally to a wide variety of specific applications. For example, one therapist may have a logically arranged system employing the notion of anxiety and yet not be particularly alert to the many little cues by which people reveal their anxiety in everyday life. Another therapist, having a less clear-cut theory of anxiety, may, nevertheless, have elaborated the construct to the point where he may be able to pick up many anxious cues the first therapist overlooked.

The second requisite for skill in observation is a variety of well-structured experience. If the therapist has had several opportunities to compare the confusion exhibited in an acute schizoid condition with the confusion in certain rapidly developing brain-tumor cases, he stands a better chance of being able to detect clinically the subtle differences between them. But he can take advantage of this experience only to the extent that it has been true experience. In Chapter 3 of Volume One we took the position that experience is that portion of the universe which one construes. The increase of experience is a function of the successive revisions of his constructions. It is therefore important that the clinician's contacts with various tumor cases shall not have been merely passive contacts. For the contacts to have added to his experience he must have construed the facts and he must have carefully revised his construction in the light of successive contacts. Thus the clinician makes experience add up to skill in observation.

c. *Use of propositional constructs.* In Chapter 3 of Volume One we also described three types of constructs, classified as to their realms of control. The *preemptive* construct is one which preempts its elements for membership in its own realm exclusively. A *constellatory* construct is one which fixes the other realm memberships of its elements. A *propositional* construct is one which does not disturb the other realm memberships of its elements. For example, when a clinician applies a preemptive construct to a case he may say something like this: "Because this client's symptom is a 'conversion' symptom, organicity is ruled out in this case." If it is a constellatory construct which is applied, the clinician may say, "Since this client's symptom is a 'conversion' symptom it has to involve an Oedipus difficulty." If the clinician were using the notion of "conversion" as a propositional construct, he would say, "Even though this is a 'conversion' symptom, Oedipus difficulties are not necessarily involved nor is an interpretation in terms of organicity necessarily ruled out."

Now if a person were to use propositional constructs exclusively, the structure of his world would have myriads of possible dimensions. If he were to attempt to utilize all of these dimensions at once, he would become hopelessly confused. It is therefore economical for a person to use constellatory constructs in many daily situations. On the other hand, if a person uses constellatory constructs exclusively it becomes difficult for him to recognize or to experiment with any construct which does not fit neatly into a constellation. A clinician who was thus committed to the use of constellatory constructs would not be a good observer. He would necessarily be incredulous of any idea that did not fit neatly into one of his constellations. He would tend to overlook the possible meaning of events and behavior not indexed in his rule book.

The scientist who proceeds by formulating hypotheses, even deductive hypotheses, must have the capacity to consider his hypotheses as propositional constructs. Indeed, that is what they are. When a person ceases to consider his hypotheses as propositional constructs, he falls into the habit of considering them as speculative conclusions instead, and he stops subjecting them to experimentation and to the hazard of invalidation. He ceases to be a scientist.

When the scientist formulates a hypothesis as a propositional construct he says, in effect, "Here is a proposition. Let us act as if it were true. Then we can see if what we expect to happen will actually happen. If it does happen, we will try a related experiment. If it does not happen, our whole world will not collapse as a result; we need then only modify this one proposition. Other truths are not necessarily affected by the outcome of this one experiment." This is the kind of thinking which permits the true scientist to face the outcome of his experimentation with equanimity, while the person whose thinking is stereotyped is frightened at the prospect that some of his constructs will be invalidated. When the scientist performs an experiment, only his hypothesis is at stake. When the stereotyped thinker faces his research data, a whole way of life is at stake.

All of this applies to the clinician and his client. It applies especially to the psychotherapist. Quite often the client cannot afford to experiment with more than one variable at a time. The only way he can do this is to test each construct propositionally: as if it were, for the moment, independent of the other major issues in his life. Unless the therapist helps him take this propositional view, the prospect of any therapeutic experimentation will assume frightening proportions.

d. *Clear construction of the psychotherapeutic role.* We might have expressed this as "courage" or "persistence in the face of threat." A clear understanding of his psychotherapeutic role provides the psychotherapist with much more than courage and persistence, however.

Psychotherapy can be a distressing experience for the psychotherapist as well as for the client. At the beginning of psychotherapy the therapist may feel that there is no reason why this client cannot get well, that a little insight and support is all that is needed to get the client to see the world through the therapist's eyes. As the psychotherapeutic sessions wear on, however, the therapist may begin to lose his enthusiasm. It may seem as though the client does not really want to get well. The client seems to have a consuming need to drag the therapist down into the same depths of despair. This may not be altogether a misperception on the part of the therapist. From the client's point of view, as we have suggested before, the mere presence of a therapist who presumably thinks the client "should know better than to be the way he is" is a threat. The client feels guilty for being a patient. He may therefore try systematically to get the therapist to admit that there is no practical alternative to the pattern of behavior which he has been displaying. Sometimes he succeeds. Then the therapist suffers. So does the therapeutic program. So does the client.

Our definitions of threat and guilt appeared in Volume One. If we define threat in terms of the Landfield hypotheses, discussed in Volume One, we would say a threatening person is one who either exemplifies or expects of us an important pattern of behavior which we have rejected but which is still hauntingly plausible. We may take this as a basis for understanding the nature of the threat a therapist may feel in dealing with certain clients. Perhaps a client will appear to exemplify a construct system, one it would be very easy for the therapist to adopt and put into spontaneous operation. Perhaps the client appears to expect the therapist to behave in a manner which the therapist has only recently, and with considerable effort, outgrown. In either instance the therapist may be threatened by the client and, as a result, behave in an unaccepting fashion. Because the therapist has no adequate subsuming system, he becomes uncertain of his role in the presence of the client and begins to freeze up. He may become rigidly obtuse in handling the client's constructs or he may become unperceptively indulgent in lieu of any real understanding of what the client is saying.

The psychotherapist may find that psychotherapy in certain cases arouses his own feelings of guilt. In the psychology of personal constructs, guilt is understood to be the perception of the loss of one's social role. Like the clinical construct of *threat*, this particular construct of *guilt* was discussed in greater detail in Volume One. When the therapist finds that his construction of his social role in relation to his client is being invalidated, he may become distressed because of the guilt involved. He may find that his relationship to the client is not what he had construed it to be. He may find that the client is using him in ways he had not anticipated or desired. He may then begin to doubt the validity of the part he is playing in the psychotherapeutic drama. If the client appears to be making no progress or to be showing signs of increased disturbance as a result of the psychotherapist's failure to play his role properly, the psychotherapist may feel guilty. The clinician may start casting about for some way to establish a role — any role, psychotherapeutic or otherwise — with the client in order to relieve himself of his guilt.

It would be simple to say that the psychotherapist should number courage and persistence among his talents. But these, as we see them, are more meaningfully perceived as derivatives of a clear construction of one's psychotherapeutic role. Since a role, in turn, is a function of subsuming a part of another person's construct system, this requisite of the psychotherapist is closely related to the first requisite in our list — a subsuming construct system.

e. *Creativity.* Every case a psychotherapist handles requires him to devise techniques and formulate constructs he has never used before. To some extent the ability to do this is a function of the therapist's ability to use propositional constructs. Yet it probably involves more than this. It probably means a readiness to try out one's unverbalized hunches. And it means a freedom from literalism in applying one's construct system. There are sharp limits set upon the creativity of a person whose thinking and activity is so hamstrung by words and symbols that he cannot utilize constructions not encompassed by ready-made sentences and formulas.

Now this is not to say that verbal skill is a handicap in psychotherapy. We are referring here to one's dependence upon words, not one's skill in using them. Creativity implies that one can construe elements as being alike and different in ways which are not logically deduced or, as yet, literally defined. Creation is therefore an act of daring, an act of daring through which the creator abandons those literal defenses behind which he might hide if his act is questioned or its results proven invalid. The psychotherapist who dares not try anything he cannot verbally defend is likely to be sterile in a psychotherapeutic relationship.

f. *Versatility.* Psychotherapy has to be carried out in a wide variety of contexts. One client may spend his hours talking about his life on a farm. Another may tell of the personal humiliation of living in a home without a private swimming pool. Another may have to work out his solutions in the context of a teen-age society. Still another may have to make his therapeutic readjustment work in the unfamiliar closely knit ethnological group to which his spouse belongs. The therapist, in order to help his clients adjust to varying types of situations, must have the capacity for construing a wide variety of events. He should be ready to learn quickly the ethnocentric occupational language of clients from varying walks of life.

The psychotherapist's own experience should have sufficient range to enable him to be sensitive to what is narrowly ethnocentric versus what is psychologically deviant. This does not mean that he must have been a housewife in order to be of assistance to housewives, nor does it mean that he must have been a sheep-herder in order to help a sheepherder. It does mean that he should be able to imagine himself with sufficient vividness in the role of a housewife to be able to sense the difficulties and hidden resources of the housewifely role. It means that he should be able to cast himself in the role of a man in a lonely occupation long enough to explore the means of adjustment which are available to such a person. It means that he will be able to predict what kinds of behavior will be socially validated by other members of his client's primary group and to perceive what kinds of behavior are now being carried out in continuing defiance of the expectations of the group. It means that he will not think of himself as a psychologist all of the time but that he will, during the course of his career, vicariously cast himself in as many roles as he has clients.

g. *Verbal skill.* The psychotherapist needs to be skilled in setting up obscure constructs by means of words. Most psychotherapy, though by no means all, involves communication in terms of verbal symbols. Sometimes the words are more or less exact public symbols of the constructs which the client and the psychotherapist are examining. More frequently the words are symbols of the elements or element-constructs upon which vague new and unverbalized constructs are being formed by the client. In this case the words are used to set the stage for the client's thinking, but they do not symbolize his thinking.

When words are used as the symbols of the constructs which the therapist and the client are examining, it is important for the therapist to be skilled in discovering just what the client's word symbols mean. He needs to be aware of the personalized nature of the client's use of certain words, as well as the personalized nature of the client's constructs. Words are more likely to have personalized or idiosyncratic meanings when they deal with the client's problem areas. Thus a client may use such a term as "tension" in the commonly accepted way when he is talking about a fence wire or a clothes line but in a peculiar manner when he is talking about his sex life. He may use the term "independence" in a way the therapist can readily understand when he is talking about his labor union, but he may be unintentionally misleading when he applies it to his children. In the latter case, for example, it may be discovered that he is describing a kind of familial relationship which might be more meaningfully described as "unrewarded subservience."

Having discovered what the client's word symbols are meant to convey, the psychotherapist's verbal skill is further brought into play when he learns to talk the client's language as well as listen to it. The alert psychotherapist always discovers that certain words and phrases must be used in certain ways with a given client. The more readily the psychotherapist becomes fluent in the client's language, the more likely he will be able to avoid misunderstandings in communicating with him.

In addition to learning the client's personalized use of symbols, particularly as they relate to certain problem areas, the psychotherapist should have a reasonably large and available vocabulary. This, of course, does not mean that he uses a complex vocabulary in dealing with any given client, nor does it mean he uses "big words." It means, rather, that he has an ample store of vivid words upon which he can draw selectively as he develops a vocabulary for dealing with the problems of a particular client. The particular vocabulary that emerges for use with his client may turn out to be quite simple. The point is that it was carefully selected from a large store of words and ideas which the psychotherapist had in reserve.

The psychotherapist's vocabulary needs to be immediately available. As the client progresses in therapy he may show flickerings of insight. The alert clinician will attempt to capture a momentary glimmer with a word — a word taken, perhaps, from the client's own vocabulary, or a word aptly chosen from the psychotherapist's own reservoir. Many a psychotherapist lets his clients drop precious new insights time after time because he is unprepared to attach symbol handles to them so that they may be readily grasped and held. Now this is not to say that the psychotherapist should always bind flickering insights with literalisms. To do so would soon clutter up the therapeutic sessions with more words and epigrams than the client would ever know what to do with. Our point is that the psychotherapist needs to have an immediately available vocabulary from which to draw an apt word or an expression when he needs it in a hurry.

We have been speaking of the use of words as more or less exact symbols of the constructs being examined by client and therapist. As we have already indicated, this is not the most common way in which words are used in psychotherapy. More commonly words are used, both by client and therapist, to set up a field of elements within which a nameless construct can begin to take shape. This, for example, is the way words are ordinarily used in role-playing therapy. The situation portrayed provides a context and elements within it. These in turn can be used by the client, if he is ready, to make constructs. He may be talking about events and portraying fragments of a conversational exchange. What he is saying may, on the face of it, appear to be concrete and incidental. Yet, as he lays out these plain elements in some kind of meaningful order, he may begin to see among them those likenesses and differences which are the vague beginnings of new and useful constructs.

It is not always essential that the elements which a client verbally trots out for consideration be "emotionally charged" or that they represent what some clinicians like to call "clinical material." In formulating new constructs it is sometimes easier for a client to set up the initial formulations of new insights in terms of elements which have not been previously involved in his personality disturbance. Often it is better to shape up a construct in terms of "intellectual," "impersonal," or "nonemotional" elements and then, after it has been established as a principle, apply it to the troublesome features in the client's life. The therapist may even interfere with the formulation of new constructs if he keeps insisting that their models be initially established on the basis of "emotionally charged" material.

There are moments when the psychotherapist is much more a poet than a literalist. The words he uses — and helps the client use — weave a fabric in which the nameless design of a fresh idea can be traced.

h. *Aggressiveness.* In the psychology of personal constructs we make a clear distinction between *aggressiveness* and *hostility*. A person is aggressive if he is active in formulating testable hypotheses and in trying them out to see what happens. If he insists on laying uncollectable wagers or if he procrastinates in looking for validational evidence, he is passive. Aggression may therefore be as much intellectual as motoric.

The psychotherapist should be one who is not afraid to lay wagers which are collectable in the immediate future. He should be one who is disposed to try out his hypotheses and to encourage the client to do the same. This does not mean that he tries out hunches impulsively without first taking care to formulate them into hypotheses. He should have a clear notion of what it is that he is trying out and he should lay his wagers in terms which will get the most valid information with the least risk to the welfare of his client. Without such an experimental attitude toward life and toward therapy it is unlikely that he can hope to do much to help the client develop an intelligently active outlook on life.

10. THE CLINICIAN'S SYSTEM OF VALUES

In connection with any discussion of a clinician's role, whether it be psychotherapeutic or otherwise, the question of explaining the behavior of clinicians, as well as that of clients, naturally arises. What makes a clinician tick? What rewards does he reap? What is his motivation? Why does he continue being a clinician? When may a clinician's motives be questionable? Is the clinician simply "working out his own problems"? Is he striving for power? Is he striving for recognition? Is he a sublimated Peeping Tom? Is he a frustrated authoritarian? Is he an oral incorporator or an anal dissector? Does he work for money? These are the kinds of questions asked by those whose psychological thinking is cast in terms of motivation, reward, reinforcement, hedonism, and the like.

Those whose psychological thinking is cast in terms of ultimates or values ask such questions as the following. What is good therapy? What is adjustment? What are the criteria of mental health? Is the clinician a relativist or an absolutist? What is the clinician striving to accomplish? What are the standards of a good clinician? What should the psychotherapeutic goals be?

a. *Values as a scientist.* The kinds of questions one asks and the types of issues he raises reflect, of course, his systematic thinking. Let us see if we can deal with this area of discourse in terms of the systematic thinking to which we are committed here. In our earlier discussion we emphasized the point that the thinking of the scientist and the thinking of his human subject should be considered to be governed by the same general laws. If the aim of science is usefully construed as prediction, why not try operating on the assumption that the aim of all human effort is prediction and see where this line of psychologizing leads us? In acting upon this proposition we formulated the postulate and corollaries of the psychology of personal constructs. The Fundamental Postulate was that a person's processes are psychologically channelized by the ways in which he anticipates events. We are in the midst of pursuing the implications of this proposition for the handling of clients. Now let us pause, for a moment, and turn our attention from the client to the clinician. Let us ponder the proposition that he too is one of those who is seeking to anticipate events optimally.

b. *Sources of satisfaction.* The psychotherapist's skills listed in the preceding section indicate the channels through which any clinician can derive satisfaction from his work. The subsuming construct system should provide the clinician with a framework within which events in the clinician-client relationship will become predictable. As the clinician develops his skill in observation, the range and variety of his accurate predictions increase. As he learns to use propositional constructs, he finds a way to face his problems one at a time rather than being shaken by overwhelming uncertainties every time an idea is put to a test.

As the clinician gains a clear construction of his own role, whether it be psychotherapeutic or otherwise, his own life takes on meaning and he finds a secure position for his own self in his array of personal values. The clinician's creative skills open to him the possibility of extending his predictive system in the future. Versatility brings new kinds of events within his purview and verbal skill provides him with ways of subjecting his constructs to immediate and frequent validation. It is relatively difficult to test constructs which cannot be verbalized, whether they be the client's constructs or the clinician's. The clinician's verbal skill, if it is carefully used as a means of bringing constructs to test, rather than as a means of suppressing opposing constructs, can accelerate the tempo with which his construct system is developed and guarantee satisfactions resulting from a more comprehensive orientation toward the world in which he lives.

In addition to the direct rewards received by the clinician as a result of the development of his own skills, he acquires satisfactions vicariously through the accomplishments of his clients. In the psychology of personal constructs we see these too as the winning of wagers on life. The clinician as well as the client can count his winnings.

c. *Viewing the client's success.* Sometimes a clinician will feel frustrated when his clients work out solutions to their problems which are unlike those which the clinician would use if he were in their shoes. The implication is that the clinician has staked his own personal system against those of his clients — and lost! Certainly a clinician should not place himself in competition with his clients. To do so is to deny himself any satisfaction from seeing his clients exercise initiative, originality, and independence. The clinician should stake only his clinician's role on the outcome of his clinical efforts, not his whole philosophy of life. The clinician's role is basically a set of subsuming constructs which provide latitude for embracing a great variety of personalized systems in a great variety of clients. Thus a client's success may be seen by the clinician as a validation of his clinician's role, but not necessarily as a validation of his whole personal system.

Occasionally a clinician is genuinely threatened by a client's apparent success with a particular mode of adjustment. For example, a clinician who has only a precarious hold on his own heterosexual adjustment may be threatened by a client's apparently successful decision not to seek marriage. The client's successes may offer a too ready validation for constructs which the clinician finds dangerously plausible for his own personal life. Again this is a situation in which the clinician should not try to stake his whole personal system on the outcomes of his client's experimentations. It is only the clinician's role — as a clinician — which is to be validated or invalidated by the results of clients' ventures.

d. *Clients' constructs as clinicians' values.* Our emphasis upon the personal nature of the constructs by which people work out their adjustments amounts to a set of values for the clinician. The clinician who can accept the fact that people can quite properly work out their problems under a wide variety of systems is in a position to experience success as a clinician more frequently than is the person who counts as successful only those solutions which are reached by means of a standard formula. We are here saying that the clinician should value and derive satisfaction from a wide variety of personalized solutions on the part of his clients. We are advocating that the clinician try a psychology of personal constructs and that he let it govern his system of values in relation to his practice as a clinician.

All of this adds up to various ways of saying that a clinician should treat his clients' construct systems as one treats propositional constructs. The demonstrated validity or invalidity of one person's system should not be taken as *necessarily* affecting the validity or invalidity of other persons' systems — including the clinician's own system. Each client's system is treated as a relatively, though of course not wholly, independent proposition.

In the broadest sense we are restating here the philosophy of constructive alternativism. In a narrower sense we are describing the value system of the clinician as a kind of liberalism without paternalism. The clinician is not only tolerant of the varying points of view represented in his clients, but he is willing to devote himself to the defense and facilitation of widely differing patterns of life. Diversity and multiple experimentation are to be encouraged.

11. FEES AND VALUES

It seems appropriate to discuss the matter of fees within the framework of the topic of the clinician's system of values. There are many clinicians who insist that the paying of fees for services is an essential feature of psychotherapy. The reason is variously stated. Some claim that the mounting cost of a psychotherapeutic series puts the client under pressure to make something out of the treatment as soon as possible. Others describe the charging of fees as a way of bringing the psychotherapy within the value system of the client: as a result the therapist will be taken more seriously. Still others say that the client who pays a fee for the services he receives is less embarrassed by his unsocial behavior toward the clinician — after all, the clinician is being paid! It is also said to make it easier for the client to discontinue therapy without feeling that he owes the clinician further "gifts of clinical material": the client feels less beholden to the therapist.

Granted that the assessment of fees may have any or all of these effects in certain cases, let us consider the further effects that such

a blanket policy may have. The cost of fees is usually a burden which is shared by other members of the client's family. Fees paid by a father cannot be spent for his children's education. Prolonged treatment demanded by a daughter may represent for her a very drastic means of retaliation against her parents. The guilty feelings toward one's failure to subordinate himself to the therapist, which are supposedly absolved by the payment of fees, may be more than replaced by guilty feelings for having depleted the family exchequer. All of these are effects which may interfere with therapy in a considerable proportion of cases.

It is this writer's observation that many clinicians use their fees punitively. Some of them appear to gain considerable satisfaction from charging a client who rejects them by not keeping his appointments. Others are willing to take a great deal more abuse from a client who pays a high fee than from one who pays the minimum scale or no fee at all. Only recently the writer had called to his attention an instance in which the therapist was personally upset because a client, whose financial difficulties had led to the omission of fees in her case, began to cancel appointments. The therapist had done a good job and the client was only showing a healthy attempt to be independent; yet the therapist felt rejected, unrewarded, and annoyed with the client. Perhaps the charging of a fee would have helped this particular therapist resolve his "countertransference" problems, but there is no reason to believe that it would have helped the client.

It is not uncommon for a clinician to behave quite differently toward "top scale" clients. This is a fact which has to be taken into account in reckoning human relations. Clinicians are human too. But let us recognize that this is a problem relating to the unique value system of a given clinician and not necessarily one relating to the inherent nature of psychotherapy.

It is practically impossible to build a differential fee scale which will make the cost of therapy approximately of equal burden to all clients. The fifty-dollar-an hour fee charged some clients may represent far less of a burden than the one-dollar-an-hour fee charged others. The motivating effect of fees is therefore practically impossible to control on a blanket policy basis. If it is to be utilized as a basic psychotherapeutic measure, it needs to be just as carefully evaluated in each individual case on the basis of a thorough understanding of the personal psychological structure, just as one would evaluate any other particular psychotherapeutic measure in an individual case.

Frequently, in psychotherapy, the clinician is confronted with the task of helping the client build a system of values on some basis other than that of barter or monetary exchange. Many clients have difficulty in making personal adjustments because they have no approach to life except by a kind of continual bargaining or trading with other people. They trade with their children by giving toys in exchange for good behavior. They trade favors with their friends. They exchange dollars for prestige. They may even come to value what they receive wholly in terms of its monetary cost.

The psychologist, because he operates within a psychological rather than an economic framework, cannot allow himself to be caught up in such a system of values. As a psychologist he is committed to a more comprehensive viewpoint with respect to human relations. If he makes his fee system the universal basis of his psychotherapeutic relations, he abdicates this more enlightened position at the outset. One cannot always insist upon a monetary exchange as the primary basis of his relations with his client and at the same time hope, as a therapist, to represent values which transcend crass materialism.

We have been talking about the clinician's making fees *a universal basis* of his relationships with his clients. Now we must recognize, just as surely as we recognize the personal nature of constructs, that there are some clients whose own value systems are basically materialistic in nature. Moreover, we have already indicated that it may be necessary to initiate therapy on the client's own terms. When one is confronted with a client whose particular construct system is such that he will not incorporate therapy into his life unless he pays money for it, there may be good therapeutic reasons for charging an appropriate fee. In order to be therapeutically effective the initial fees may in some cases need to be whoppers! But, whether the fee is large, small, or absent altogether, the therapist should not allow its local value to contaminate his own comprehensive system of values.

We have also been talking about the clinician's making fees the primary basis of his relationships with his clients. Now of course we do live partly within an economic system. The psychologist does not ordinarily believe that we must live wholly within it nor does he believe that it is healthy to attempt to do so. Yet, because some of the necessities and conveniences of life are bound up with our economic system, it is necessary that a reasonable proportion of the clinician's services be financially rewarded. Fees assessed under this necessity are for the welfare of the clinician, not the client. Let us make no mistake about that!

What about the client who drags out his series of psychotherapeutic interviews without making much effort to profit by them? Is not a mounting bill for professional services just what he needs? Not necessarily. When a therapist finds that his client is not making enough effort toward recovery, he has a great variety of anxiety-producing devices upon which he can draw. His employment of anxiety at this stage should always be carefully chosen and measured with respect to the case at hand. To depend blindly upon a fee system which obviously affects clients differentially but indiscriminately, according to their economic means and their family relationships as well as according to their psychological disposition, is unnecessarily crude and unprofessional.

12. PROFESSIONAL OBLIGATIONS

This is not the place to attempt a comprehensive description of all the types of professional obligations the psychologist assumes by virtue of his calling. There are, however, certain types of professional obligations which are appropriate to discuss in the light of the systematic position which we have taken. At this point our discussion is intended to be illustrative rather than definitive.

a. *Claims and client expectations.* When a client comes to a psychologist for assistance, he usually, though not always, believes there is a chance that he can be helped. The psychologist, in accepting him as a client, necessarily concurs in this hope. Yet it is generally agreed that it is unethical for the psychologist to make any unwarranted claim for his services. But what if the client's hopes are unwarranted? Does the psychologist have a professional obligation to say that he does not share those hopes? What about the stand we have taken to the effect that the clinician may need to accept the client's version of therapy at the outset?

Here the psychologist's systematic position gives him a firm ground upon which to stand. Since he is a scientist, in the sense we described in our theoretical exposition, he is a dealer in probabilities rather than inevitabilities; he casts his eye toward the future in terms of hypotheses rather than in terms of destinies. He can express his proper scientific position by some such simple statement as the following: "Now let us see what we can do," or, "When I have come to know you better, perhaps I can be of help to you." There is nothing unethical about a clinician's sharing a client's hopes; what is unethical is for the clinician to express those hopes as certainties or to misquote the odds to his own advantage.

The whole problem of what the psychologist shall allow his client to believe is vastly larger and more complicated than the foregoing discussion might imply. Perhaps the little we have said, within the context of our theoretical position and this particular chapter on the psychotherapist's role, is a sufficient guide to what we would say if we were to pursue the topic in detail. Moreover, what we have said with primarily a clinical situation in mind applies equally appropriately to the industrial psychologist's relation to his client, or to any professional psychologist's obligation to those whom he serves.

b. *Medical collaboration.* Psychologists frequently have to face the matter of their obligation to obtain the professional collaboration of other disciplines in certain cases. Some even take the extreme position that a psychologist should always have medical collaboration. Conversely, it is quite rare for a physician to seek psychological collaboration, although, from the standpoint of the welfare of the patient, psychological collaboration for the physician is probably more generally useful than medical collaboration for the psychologist. Moreover, the popular interpretation of pain is such that a patient himself is more likely to take the initiative in obtaining medical assistance than in obtaining psychological assistance. Occasionally a psychologist makes the mistake of treating a client psychologically when he might better be treated wholly or in part from a medical point of view. In the writer's experience this is a mistake which is made quite as frequently by psychiatrists in private individual practice, perhaps because they rely too much upon their own remote medical background. On the other hand, hardly a day goes by in a physician's practice when he does not treat a client medically who might better be treated wholly or in part from a psychological point of view.

In dealing with this problem it is quite appropriate for us to go back to the basic fundamentals in our philosophy of science. It will be recalled that the psychology of personal constructs is a particular theoretical orientation toward the psychological construction of life. Psychology is one of the many systematic ways of construing life. So is physiology, upon which medicine is based in part. Psychology and physiology are not separate regions of fact with some sort of boundary between them. They are simply two different ways of construing many of the same things. They are not to be considered as "bordering" on each other or as being "joined" any more than should physiological facts be considered as inherently different from psychological facts. It is not meaningful to speak of psychological and physiological facts as existing "side by side." Nor is the relationship between psychology and physiology clarified at all by invoking such truisms as "the whole person."

Now we must recognize that, while psychology and physiology are different systems for construing the same things and not different things assigned to different systems, each of these systems tends to work better with some facts than with others. We have called the group of facts which seem to yield most meaningfully to psychological construction those which fall within psychology's *range of convenience*. But it would be misleading to call them "psychological facts." Psychology has no lien on them simply because it can construe them meaningfully. Similarly for physiology. And similarly for medicine.

Now when a psychologist comes up against a group of facts (symptoms) in his client which fit very neatly into his psychological system, he should not assume therefore that these facts are "psychological facts" and hence none of the physician's business. Perhaps they can be construed even more meaningfully within a physiological system. Moreover, even if they can be construed more meaningfully within a physiological system, the psychological construction is not one whit invalidated by that coincidence.

The question of when to seek professional collaboration from a physician is a very practical one. One cannot answer it merely by tagging the facts in a case as "psychological" or "physiological." The probable outcomes of psychological and physiological methods of treatment should be used as the more practical basis for seeking medical collaboration. Suppose a psychologist has a client with hypertension symptoms. A psychological construction of the apparent facts may fit ever so neatly; but so may a physiological construction. Now the question is: is this a case for the psychologist or for the physician, or is it a case which neither should attempt to treat alone? The really important question to ask is: what can each of these two types of practitioners do for the client and what is likely to happen to the client if either or both of them fails to do anything? The answer to that question should make clear the answer to the practical question of when each discipline should seek the professional collaboration of the other.

c. *Breaking relationships.* During the course of therapy the therapist and his client may develop a kind of relationship which cannot be broken suddenly without leaving the client in a disorganized state. While this type of client dependency can be controlled somewhat, it cannot be avoided altogether. Moreover, there are occasions when a client is encouraged to "go out on a limb," from his own point of view, in order to accelerate the therapeutic process. If the therapist discontinues the relationship in the midst of such adventuresome experimentation, he may leave the client in the lurch. For one thing, a client's exploratory behavior is likely to be accompanied by a good deal of perceptual distortion. The therapist cannot prevent this, although he should stand by to deal with it and to correct it as soon as it appears. If he leaves the client in the midst of a phase of therapy involving considerable exploration, he may leave the client a victim of accentuated perceptual distortions or a victim of confusion during the attempts to make some new sense out of his experience. The therapist should plan both his therapy and his vacations with this professional obligation in mind. He should also keep in mind the same considerations in discontinuing his cases altogether, and in turning them over to other therapists. Careless handling of the transference relationship between client and therapist may easily make the whole therapeutic series add up to gross injury rather than assistance for the client.

d. *Conveying information about a client.* Different people may construe the same facts in quite different ways. The clinician must therefore be particularly careful not to reveal facts regarding his clients to people who might misconstrue them. Even "professional" status is no guarantee that an informee will not injuriously misconstrue information conveyed to him by a professional colleague. It is particularly easy to make the mistake of improperly disclosing information when a clinician is talking to a parent regarding his child. The relation of a parent to a child is a complicated one and may involve some areas in which there is marked perceptual distortion. The therapist should always keep in mind that any information he gives a parent regarding his child should be handled as a therapeutic interpretation to a client and not merely as an objective fact. When a parent asks for an "I.Q. Test" for his child, the well-trained clinician never accepts the client on that basis solely. The referral should always be at least as broad as "a psychological examination" or "a psychological appraisal." When the clinician discusses the results of the examination with the parent, he is professionally obligated to make sure that he knows what kind of construction is likely to be made upon his report before he attempts to communicate it. This is just as important a safeguard in dealing with a parent as it is in dealing with a client who has come for help for himself.

Certainly no psychologist can permit himself to write "to

whom it may concern" clinical reports. To do so is to ignore the widely variant and personalized nature of people's ways of construing facts. All clinical reports should be addressed to a known person, if possible, and, if not, to a specific professional group, such as the staff of a reputable clinic, whose biases are reasonably well known and who will, in turn, respect the confidentialness of the report. Ordinarily one does not send the same report to a parent that he sends to a teacher, nor the same report to a teacher that he sends to a physician. He may omit from the physician's report items relating to the child's education which might be misconstrued by a pedagogically untrained person. Details from psychological tests, such as I.Q., item spread, and so on, he should mention only to other psychologists, except as he has a personal acquaintance with those who may read the report or as he may use the detail within a well-elaborated context where its meaning is not likely to be misconstrued.

The clinician's files should, of course, be kept locked and all records safely protected from unauthorized readers. While psychologists generally do not enjoy the legal right of "privileged communications," a proper professional relationship to a client demands that his communications with his psychologist be treated as confidential. Perhaps the law will eventually recognize de juris what is de facto a humanitarian principle.

Ordinarily a client should have control over the reporting of the results of his psychological examination. Even though it may appear to the clinician that the client's best interests would be served if the clinician talked to the client's wife or to a legal judge about certain things that he knows from his clinical contacts, the clinician is obligated not to do so unless he is authorized by the client or unless the client is grossly unable to make a rational decision in the matter. Even if the client authorizes the clinician to disclose certain information regarding himself, the clinician may find that he cannot do so because other people's welfare may be involved. It would be improper for a therapist to reveal what a client had said during therapy regarding his extramarital escapades when that information might adversely affect the social relationships and peace of mind of the client's children or other members of the client's family. Furthermore, the client is not always a good judge of what others may misconstrue. The client may feel that his life is an open book, but others may read that open book in a way that the client would find quite surprising.

For example, the writer recently had in a class a student who talked quite glibly about his dreams and was eager to report aloud what constructions he placed on Rorschach plates and TAT cards. Now one might say that this was no more than an underlying exhibitionism coming to the fore. But, on the other hand, there is no doubt that the student would have been shocked and anxious if he had known how transparent some of the remarks he let fly appeared to the more informed members of the class. The writer felt that he had a professional obligation to shush the student, even though the student was quite eager to elaborate his remarks in embarrassing detail.

e. *Obligation to administrative superiors.* Frequently a clinician finds himself a part of an administrative organization in which the interests of the client and the interests of the organization appear to come into conflict. For example, a student may be referred by the dean of a university to the psychological clinic which is also a part of that university. The dean may then request that the psychologist submit periodic reports on the progress of the student and advise whether or not the student should be permitted to continue his course of study. Now ordinarily a client stands the best chance of readjustment if, in his relations with his therapist, he has a maximum latitude of action open to him. If the therapist, however, is administratively placed in a position of constricting the client's activity, even though that constriction may eventually be one which the client might want to impose on himself, the therapist cannot offer a full professional service to the client.

In practice, the difficulty of a clinician's working in an administrative setup is not usually as great as it might at first appear. It requires, first of all, that the clinician take some time to interpret his work to the appropriate administrative officers. It can then be made a matter of agreement just how much the clinician will be asked to participate in administrative decisions which will limit clients' freedom of action. Once this has been decided, the clinician can make clear to each client the exact extent to which he expects to participate in administrative decisions affecting his case. Now the clinician may not like the position he has been asked to assume. He may find that he is expected to be more of a personnel psychologist than a clinical psychologist. But a psychologist should always know what is expected of him anyway, even if he does not want or intend to play the part.

The role of the psychotherapist involves keen alertness to what the client expects from psychotherapy and the initial acceptance of a wide variety of client misperceptions of what psychotherapy is. It involves subsuming the client's personal constructs and at the same time accepting them. It involves a set of professional values that makes the life of the clinician worth living for its own sake. Finally, it involves certain ethical obligations that transcend mere legal status. It is for the person whose role is basically structured in this way that we propose the procedural devices which are described in the ensuing sections of this book.

Chapter Twelve

The Psychotherapeutic Approach

⊓⊔⊓⊔⊓⊔⊓⊔⊓⊔⊓⊔⊓⊔⊓⊔⊓⊔⊓⊔⊓⊔⊓⊔⊓⊔⊓⊔⊓⊔⊓⊔

THIS IS the second of two introductory chapters which outline broadly the scope and methodology of psychotherapy.

A. Basic Techniques

1. SETTING UP THE RECONSTRUCTIVE RELATIONSHIP

Our conceptualization of the role of the psychotherapist carries certain important implications regarding the kind of personal relationship he allows to develop between himself and his client. The therapist plays a versatile role. On one occasion he may enact the part of a father, on another that of a teacher, and on another the part of a child. He is frequently a portrayer of social reality to the client, who, in turn, tries out psychological experiments of test-tube size in the laboratory of the conference room. It does not do for the therapist to become rigidly "typed" in any one of his parts. He must be prepared to respond to his client in a great variety of carefully chosen ways. The client must be given an opportunity to cast the therapist in whatever dramatic parts his reconstructive adventures require.

If the psychotherapist conducts himself in such a manner as to become an intimately known person and a sharply delineated personality for the client, he is handicapped in his reconstructive role. He then comes to play only one part out of the many that the client may need to have portrayed. The likelihood of the client's developing a *primary transference* upon the therapist rather than *secondary transferences* (terms which are defined explicitly in a later section) is markedly increased. Primary transference results in undiscriminating dependence upon the therapist, more difficulty in terminating the therapeutic series, and a constriction in the range of experimentation which can be tried out in the interview room.

In taking this stand for the therapist's personal ambiguity we are aligning ourselves somewhat with the classical position of psychoanalysis. We are also partly in agreement with the client-centered therapists. We are in much less agreement with those whose view of personal-relationship therapy leads them to exchange expressions of feeling with their clients. We do not, however, see our stand as a denial of the value of "warmth" in one's relations with his clients. The therapist can be "warm" and responsive to the client without confiding in him. The therapist should reserve the capacity, as the situation requires, of being like the ink blot in a Rorschach Test — that is, interpretable by the client in a variety of ways. He can be perceived as a loving figure during one interview without specifically defining himself that way. In another interview he can be perceived as starkly realistic without permanently casting himself as a heartless person. Thus he reserves the capacity to play a series of parts in the sequence of social experiments which constitute the client's psychotherapy.

This view leads the therapist to avoid social contacts with his client outside of the therapeutic situation. It means that he tells his client relatively little about himself, his likes and dislikes, his interests, his family, his recreation, and his experiences. Some clients try to develop an intimate relationship with their therapists by inquiring about such matters, but the therapist is well advised to avoid the kind of relationship that would thus be set up. The therapist should usually avoid physical contact with his clients, too much hand shaking, back patting, dancing, and so on. This is as important in dealing with children as in dealing with adults. Conversations outside of the therapeutic situation should be kept at a minimum. Formal relationships, as when the client and therapist are colleagues, visiting in each other's homes, contacts with other members of the therapist's family, all may interfere with the therapist's playing his role with proper versatility.

The therapist should also avoid, as much as possible, contacts with other members of the client's family. Certainly attempting to treat two members of the same family simultaneously results in the limitation of the ways the therapist can be construed by each of his clients, and hence may interfere with the course of therapy, particularly at certain crucial points. For example, when a therapist is seeing both husband and wife it is almost inevitable that each of them will become more guarded in what he tells the therapist. Because the husband knows that his wife regards him as a brute, he hesitates to express his aggressive feelings toward his wife, lest the therapist, having heard the wife's interpretation, jump to the conclusion that the husband is indeed overtly cruel to his wife. The wife, knowing that her husband has probably told the therapist about a quarrel they had last week, will distort her account of the episode so as to make the therapist punish the husband and validate her own part in the enactment.

There are similar difficulties when the therapist sees both parent and child. The child tends to cast the therapist as an ally of the parent. The parent, on his side, dreads the relationship that is springing up between the therapist and the child and may take steps in the home to make the child fear the therapist. It is not uncommon in such situations for the parent to threaten the child with the therapist by saying, for example, "Doctor Blank will be disgusted with you when he finds out what you said to me today." Or the parent may say, "Doctor Blank and I are going to see that you stop talking like that." Of course, this may happen even when the parent is not being seen therapeutically.

2. THE CLIENT'S RELATIONSHIPS TO OTHERS

What we have been saying should not be construed to mean

that the client should not have many intimate or individualized relationships in his life. Nor does it mean that such relationships do not play an important part in his psychotherapy. Indeed, the therapist usually seeks to help the client formulate wholesome close relationships with other people. The task of therapy is often facilitated by persons other than the therapist. As the client develops relationships outside the therapeutic situation on terms which permit him freedom of movement, his opportunities for making therapeutic progress simultaneously on many fronts are greatly increased.

The therapist should always consider as suspect the progress of a client when it appears to be based solely upon the insight and social relationships of the conference room. The client should develop his interpersonal resources outside the conference room and the therapist should not necessarily be disturbed if he finds that his functions are being taken over by a variety of the client's friends. Therapy certainly is not properly confined to a conference room, even though the relations between therapist and client may be so confined. Nor is the therapist the only person who should be permitted to play a rehabilitative part in the client's life.

a. *Helping others through the client.* Frequently the therapist must set up the therapeutic situation with an eye to the readjustment of certain other persons in the client's personal-social milieu. He may hope to accomplish this through the agency of the client. The client's therapy in such a situation thus involves, in part, his learning how to deal with a particularly distressing interpersonal relationship. In fact, the therapeutic goal may involve trying to produce more movement in some other member of the client's family than in himself. This is the kind of situation that develops when one does therapy with a parent in order to assist a child who is in greater need of that assistance than the parent is.

The writer has also had experience with the converse situation: where the parent was more greatly disturbed but where it appeared that more could be accomplished by assisting the child to make an effective effort to reorient the parent than by working directly with the parent. From this point of view psychotherapy can be seen as a means of dealing with a group involving two or more people. The person who is designated as a client is not necessarily the most disturbed person in the plot, nor is he necessarily the one who is responsible for "causing" the difficulty; rather, he is the one who appears to hold a present key to the situation. An interesting fact is that therapy is not a process reserved solely for those who are personally disturbed nor for those whose behavior causes disturbance among others. In its broadest sense psychotherapy is the approach to readjustment of persons singly or in groups through whatever avenues are open.

b. *Illustrative case.* A few years ago the writer had a teen-age girl brought to him on the initiative of a neighbor of the girl's family and with the concurrence of the girl's teachers. The girl was a senior in high school and was in line to become valedictorian of her graduating class. She had decided to drop out of school during the spring semester because, as she expressed it, she could not face the prospect of giving the valedictory address, nor could she face the criticism that would be heaped upon her by her family if she refused to give it. Throughout high school her teachers had found it advisable to make concessions to her anxieties by not requiring her to recite in class.

The girl was the oldest of a large family of north European extraction. From the accounts furnished by the neighbor and the girl it appeared that not only did the family retain its patriarchal form of control but the father's authority was greatly indulged and greatly feared in the household. All conversation between other members of the family was carried on in whispers or stopped altogether when the father was within earshot. The children were warned before the father's arrival home. While it seemed that he rarely expressed himself and spent most of his time withdrawn behind a wall of silence, the mother was said to live in terror of his criticism. Throughout the writer's development of the case he failed to learn of any evidence of physical cruelty or excessive verbal abuse on the part of the father.

On arrival at the clinic the girl showed marked motor disturbances. She showed choreiform movements of the arms and legs, her face was unusually mobile and contorted as she spoke or listened, she exhibited irregular tics of the neck and shoulders. Her thinking was clear, however, and her verbal responses showed both originality and appropriateness. After the first few minutes of the interview she was able to elaborate the less acute phases of her problem somewhat spontaneously.

Her verbal description of her father was trite and showed no trace of manifest empathy with him. Her construction of other members of her family was also somewhat impermeable and barren in comparison with her conceptualization in general. Her formulation of life-role constructs for herself was almost altogether blocked.

Now, in a case like this, it is possible to consider any one of several points as the focus of the disturbance. The mother might well be considered to be the one whose outlook has been most responsible for letting the unhealthy situation develop. It might be said that it was she who taught the children to fear their father and who isolated him completely from the circle of their affection. On the other hand, it might be said that the father was the one who was most in need of change. He had failed to establish a wholesome interpersonal relationship with the members of his family and he appeared to be accepting the role of a tyrant.

If one were a disciplinarian he might say that the focus of the difficulty was in the teachers who pampered the girl's shyness. From the standpoint of cultural anthropology one might say the crux of the difficulty was in the contrast of cultures represented in the family's life space. Or again one might see the girl herself as the primary locus of the disturbance and point out that the mechanisms she was using were essentially hostile and passively destructive.

We chose to consider the girl herself as the point upon which therapy would make contact with the situation. She was available. She was ready to readjust. She was capable of good communication with the therapist. She had congenial social contacts outside the home which she could use to validate a revised construction system. We chose to develop the therapeutic goals, not in terms of further self-criticisms or self-insights, but in terms of gaining new types of responses from the father, and in terms of reinterpreting the father to other members of the family, particularly to the mother. Informal role playing and verbalizations of hypothetical interpretations of the father were used extensively during therapy. The therapeutic developments permitted the girl some new perspective regarding herself, but this was never designated as the primary goal of the conferences. A variety of social experiments involving the father were designed for execution in the home.

Progress in the case appeared to be quite satisfactory in relation to the therapeutic goals. There was external corroboration of the fact that the father's behavior in the presence of his family changed significantly. The girl felt that she had rediscovered her father. She decided to continue in school. She graduated and took a job away from home. Her psychomotor symptoms diminished to the point where they were not conspicuous.

This case is cited as an example of one in which the psychotherapeutic situation is set up with an eye to the readjustment of individuals other than the client as well as to the assistance of the client herself. The therapist limited his face-to-face interpersonal relationship to one person, although he was dealing with several people. The client and the therapist made test runs in the conference room, but the validating experiences for the client took place between conferences, and in relationship with other people. The therapist did not attempt to develop a full-blown father-daughter relationship with the client; rather, that relationship was developed concurrently between the real father and the daughter. While there were times when the client appeared to be somewhat dependent upon the therapist, particularly as she attempted measures which seemed to leave her vulnerable to the criticism of her father, for the most part she seemed to remain relatively independent of the therapist as a single essential figure in her life. Thus the therapist, as a person, was able to drop out of the picture and leave the client free to continue normal life explorations into the ever intriguing complex of interpersonal relations.

3. MULTIPLE APPROACH

Sometimes a reconstructive situation is set up with several individuals playing the parts of therapists with respect to one case. This may take the form of *multiple therapy*, where each therapist performs a similar type of service, but with such differences as their viewpoints and skills impose. It may take the form of *total-push therapy*, which is a kind of departmentalized approach to the client, each therapist undertaking to function in relation to the client in a prescribed way. In an institution, for example, the occupational therapist, the recreational therapist, the educational therapist, the psychiatrist, the nurse, the attendants, the chaplain, the physiotherapist, and others may put on a twenty-four-hour-a-day campaign to accomplish certain therapeutic goals. This type of therapy may be employed with outpatients too, although it is more difficult to keep the client on the move when he is an outpatient.

Multiple therapy appears to make greater demands upon the client's capacity to reconcile seemingly conflicting points of view. It has the advantage of permitting the client to relate himself in a variety of ways to his therapists. And yet a single therapist who is versatile and maintains himself as a flexible figure in the client's environment should be able to achieve the same results without adding to the client's confusion.

Total-push therapy shows much promise for those clients who are unable to organize their behavior around the verbalizations of the conference room. With each therapist carrying out a prescribed program there is less danger of confusion. The program is expensive during the period it is in operation; but, when compared to the cost of protracted treatment, it appears to offer marked savings in therapists' time. When such a program is attempted, each therapist-contributor should participate both in planning and in progress conferences with the other therapists.

The therapeutic goals should be clearly stated in writing. Landmarks of progress or regress should be listed in advance so that each therapist may be on the lookout for certain expected developments and may alert the others when these begin to show. Each therapist who handles clients in a group situation should have a summary sheet for each client to which he can refer frequently in order to refresh his memory as to what it is he is attempting to accomplish at a particular stage of the total-push therapy.

4. PHYSICAL ARRANGEMENTS

Most psychotherapy is conducted in an interview room. The room should be free of distractions, although, during the war, it was found that it was possible to conduct intimate interviews with some measure of success even in the midst of the confusion of a large room. The main thing is for the client to feel that he has the interpersonal situation defined, that he is not being made the object of other people's curiosity, and that he is not under the pressure of social expectancies which are extraneous to the interview situation. Thus it may be that a client being interviewed in the midst of a scurrying mass of people may feel that the interview is more private than would one who was being interviewed behind an eight-foot semipartition on the other side of which inquisitive secretaries were pretending to work. Distraction is not merely a matter of the volume of noise or the number of people within sight; rather, it is a matter of the potential field of interaction of which the client is aware.

a. *Recording.* It is becoming a common practice to record interviews electronically. With the advent of wire and tape recorders in homes and schools, much of the resistance that clients once offered to such recording has been disappearing. The microphone should be inconspicuous but not necessarily concealed. If the recording machine is in the interviewing room, it too should be inconspicuous but not necessarily concealed. Even if a client fully accepts the idea of having his interview recorded, he is likely to be distracted by a conspicuous microphone standing between himself and the therapist, by the dials and whirling wheels of a wire recorder, or by the idea of a microphone so cleverly concealed that he cannot find it.

The therapist may introduce the idea of recording by saying, "I am going to record some of the things we say to each other so that I can go back over each interview and study it carefully. Otherwise, I would have to sit down each time and write detailed notes from memory. If you don't mind, I will not bother to record everything — just the parts that I feel I need to go back over and make sure that I understand. The microphone is over there. And the recorder is here. There is nothing much to see. Now would you tell me about how you felt when you first decided to come to see me," and so on.

By proceeding directly to the main point of the interview, rather than making an emphatic point of the recording, the therapist tends to put the recording in proper perspective. Later on, after the therapy is under way, he can raise the issue of how the client first felt about the recording. This might be considered a part of the task of getting the client to interpret the interview situation.

b. *Room arrangement*. The therapist's desk, as well as the rest of the room, should be relatively free of nonessential gadgets. Papers and letters should be out of sight, for they point up the private life of the therapist. For the same reason, pictures of the therapist's family or professional friends should not be displayed. The telephone should be hushed or the bell disconnected altogether. There is some justification for doing all therapeutic interviewing in a special interviewing room rather than in an office, where the accouterments of one's other activities are likely to be in evidence.

The room should be acoustically treated and as free as is possible of street noises. In most psychotherapeutic interviewing the voices drop to a very low intensity level, particularly as crucial material is discussed. The therapist will not ordinarily notice this, for his voice tends to fall with the client's. With some types of recording equipment it is necessary to turn up the gain after ten minutes, and again after thirty minutes.

Under these conditions street noises are likely to be picked up and appear as unexpectedly distracting on the record. The use of carpeting and the liberal use of drapes helps the situation. Wooden Venetian blinds help control street noises. Even if a microphone is not used, the acoustical treatment of the room will make a significant contribution to the effectiveness of therapy. The microphone, when used, should be placed so that both speakers are well within its pickup angle. The recording of psychotherapeutic interviews is an unusually difficult matter. Experienced sound engineers who have never had specific experience with this type of recording are usually amazed at the difficulties they encounter.

This writer definitely prefers to have a desk or table between the client and the therapist for most types of interviewing. Since the interview is a verbal exchange, the attention of the client and therapist should be mainly upon each other's faces. If the acoustics of the room permit, there should be considerable distance — six to eight feet — between client and therapist. Both client's and therapist's chairs should be comfortable — the client's to avoid distraction, the therapist's so that he may portray a relaxed posture with which the client can empathize. A comfortable chair is one in which the client may comfortably assume a variety of postures; it is not one which is comfortable for one posture only. The client should be able to lean forward, slide down with his head resting upon the back of the chair, or turn aside and away from the therapist. A footstool which the client can manipulate easily adds to the variety of postures which he can assume. The client's chair should face at right angles to a line between himself and the therapist. This permits him either to face or to turn away from the therapist. The door should be kept closed and the therapist should make sure that it is not opened inadvertently during an interview. A client with tears streaming down his cheeks does not respond well to being exposed to the view of others, either through a suddenly opened door or through a door with a glass panel.

c. *Special equipment.* We have been discussing a reconstructive situation which primarily involves interviewing. Some therapy is conducted in rooms with special equipment. Therapy with children frequently involves the use of play equipment such as sand tables, large building blocks, paints, clay, dolls, miniatures of adult objects, etc. Group psychotherapy with adults usually involves the use of a conference-size table. Group psychotherapy with children requires provision for children to withdraw from the group activity as well as to participate in it.

Where parents are to be assisted in understanding their nursery-school-aged children, there should be one-way screen facilities with a sound pickup which permits the parent to observe his child's behavior and to hear what is going on. It also requires some provision for the parent to analyze the child's behavior in the group on some sort of check-list schedule, and facilities which permit a clinician to help the parent in using the schedule.

Of course, occupational therapy, recreational therapy, and the like require special equipment. The general principle to be followed in equipping a special therapy room is that the room should have maximum versatility and that a great variety of supplies and equipment, while stored out of sight, should be instantly available to the therapist if he should need them during the course of a session. Certainly, the activity which is carried on in a special therapy room should not be viewed as a series of formal exercises; it is better conceived as a means of nonverbal formulation and communication of the client's personal constructs. The equipment and materials are to aid the client in expressing something. If, in the midst of a session, he has something to express which can best be expressed by finger painting, the alert therapist will ordinarily want to make that means of expression immediately available to him rather than wait until the next day "because Tuesday is finger-painting day."

The therapist needs to be particularly careful about keeping his appointments. Clients who have some psychoanalytic sophistication will interpret tardiness and cancellation as evidence of the therapist's "resistance" to or "rejection" of the client. Other clients may actually feel the rejection although they may not have a rationale for it. When appointments are canceled, it is usually essential that a substitute appointment be immediately designated so that the client will be able to maintain an orientation toward the therapeutic series and its relation to his everyday decisions. It is not unusual for a client to make rash decisions when he feels himself cut loose from his therapist without knowing when his next appointment is likely to be.

5. CONTROLLING INTERVIEWS

The specific technique which a therapist uses should be chosen with regard for the particular case to be treated. The psychology of personal constructs, because of its emphasis upon the individuality and variety of ways different persons have of construing their worlds, also implies that the ways of assisting people may vary quite widely. With regard to psychotherapeutic technique in general, then, we are mainly concerned with the ways in which the therapist can maintain with a client a relationship providing for maximum flexibility and change of pace. What we have to say about the more differential use of psychotherapeutic techniques will be discussed in later chapters.

a. *Planning interviews.* The procedures of planning therapy are discussed in a later chapter. It is sufficient to point out here that each interview needs a measure of planning if the therapist is to play his role effectively. If the therapist is exploring autistic material, he is not required to plan his interviews in great detail except to consider the amount of loosening of conceptualization the client is able to stand at the current stage of therapy versus the amount of structuring the client is ready to attempt, the kind of material from previous interviews that may be interwoven into the interpretations at this point, and the tentatively formulated constructs currently being explored. If the therapist is using role-playing techniques, for example, he may need to spend a good deal of time planning the situations to be utilized and considering how they may be made to provide an effective setting for testing out constructs, both old and new.

How rigidly should one adhere to his plan for an interview? The therapist will want to give some thought to what probably should not be allowed to happen as well as to what ought to happen. As the treatment program gets under way, the therapist will gradually become aware of special danger areas where the client is not yet ready to explore. In his planning of interviews, such areas can definitely be marked out of bounds. Thus the therapist enters the interview room with two kinds of guideposts in mind: what he thinks might be a good thing to have happen, and what he will definitely try to avoid. If, as frequently occurs, the client takes off in an unexpected direction, the therapist can freely alter his plan as to the former, without trespassing on the latter. The real danger of too flexible planning is that it may fail to take account of the client's limitations.

How does the therapist know how flexible to be in a given case? In the early interviews, and especially in diagnosis, this is a difficult question. In general, the therapist has to depend upon the best formal test results he can lay hands on, upon subtle cues in the client's behavior, and upon his own well-digested experience as to where certain topical discussions are likely to lead. But later in the therapeutic series, the therapist can apply two kinds of criteria: his painstaking plot of danger areas, and his tested ability to predict what this client will say.

The plotting of danger areas will have been made from the therapist's experiences in previous interviews in which he and the client burned their fingers, and from inferences of a less direct nature. On the other hand, the ability to predict the client's behavior is a more general criterion, and, if used correctly, an excellent one in any practical situation.

When we speak of an ability to predict the client's behavior, we are talking about *differential* prediction. For example, the therapist may predict that tomorrow instead of continuing his discussion of his wife's housekeeping, the client will turn to his childhood home life. This would be differential prediction. It would not be differential prediction if the therapist could only guess that the next interview will be like all the preceding ones. When the therapist is to do a fair job of predicting how his client's behavior will differ from interview to interview, he can afford to be more flexible in his moment-to-moment handling of the client.

b. *Occasions calling for special interview plans.* It is a serious mistake, and one often made, to assume that everything of therapeutic significance happens in the therapy room. Clients talk about their problems outside the room, even when admonished not to do so. But even if they do not explicitly confide in others, they tend to experiment at the preverbal level of communication. And the results of such experimentation carry therapeutic implications, even though the therapist may condemn them as invalid.

If the client is about to go on a vacation trip, or has just returned from one, if he is about to be visited by his parents, his children, or his ex-wife, the therapist will note that something therapeutically important is likely to go on outside the interview room. He may wish to set the stage for the inevitable experimentation, or to review its factual outcomes. For example, if the client is about to meet some new and difficult situation, the therapist will probably avoid loosening techniques, such as recall of dreams and phantasies, in the interview immediately preceding. The same precaution may be employed when the client is about to try out some new and precariously held insights in an old situation where familiar role expectancies threaten to engulf him.

The general rule is to avoid both loosening and probing in the interview immediately before a break in the chain of appointments, or before any important extramural experimentation. (The functions, techniques, obstacles, and hazards of loosening and probing are discussed in greater detail in a later chapter.) This means planning the interview around more concrete material, such as everyday facts, events, and explicit ideas.

A similar rule applies to post-break interviews. The reason for applying it is somewhat different, however. Much may have happened since the therapist last saw the client. What the therapist remembers from the last interview may not be especially relevant to the client's present state of mind. For example, the client may now be hostile and anxious in a way the therapist has never seen him before. He may have reformulated his problems and the solutions he envisions for them. He may feel guilty because, during the holiday, he experimented in ways he thinks the therapist will disapprove of. Indeed, the chances are very great that he has done some experimental confiding. If, within this framework, the therapist returns to routine probing or loosening, as if nothing had happened, he may open up the client's system to confusion, just when there is much new material to be set in order. It is much better if the therapist starts the post-break interview by sitting back and saying, "Well, I suppose a good deal has happened since our last conference."

c. *Spacing interviews.* The interval between interviews in part governs the therapist in deciding how much disorganization he can impose upon the client. If the interviews are a week apart, the client who is capable of minor experimentation only will be handicapped. Such a client needs frequent contact with the person who helps him formulate his hypotheses. On the other hand, the therapist may wish to lengthen the interval between interviews, so as to put him on his own and make him do some of his own interpreting of his daily experiences.

d. *Length of interviews.* Therapists, and the writer is no exception, are frequently tempted to prolong interviews beyond the usual forty-five minutes or hour in cases in which the client comes from a distance and is unable to appear as frequently as would normally be required. Yet the client's readjustment tends to come about by fits and starts. The new constructs that he formulates do not spring to life full blown and ready to be put to use. The therapist who thinks that they do has simply not been aware of the subliminal signs which have probably been flitting around in the conference series for some time. During the course of an interview the therapist is lucky if he can bring into momentary focus only one or two new ideas which have meaning for the client. Most of what is said is background. A long-drawn-out interview tends to confuse the client and cause some items which would be sharply focused in a shorter interview to lose their identity in a welter of words.

For most purposes a forty-five-minute interview is adequate. If the therapist makes his appointments at one-hour intervals, this allows him time to dictate a few notes and to collect his thoughts for the next interview. Group-psychotherapy sessions, and some play-therapy sessions with children who are capable of sustained attention, can be scheduled for as much as two hours' duration. Contrary to what some therapists may expect, role-playing sessions with a single client can be quite strenuous and should not be prolonged. The role-playing episodes should ordinarily be quite brief and the therapist should not underestimate the amount of material with which a client is confronted in a few moments of an enactment.

e. *Keeping notes on interviews.* The more clients a therapist has to handle simultaneously, the more carefully he needs to keep his notes up to date. It is easy to confuse what one client has described with a similar incident reported by another client. The records should be brief enough so that the notes of the previous interview can be scanned very quickly before the start of another interview. A dictation machine at the therapist's elbow is a great help. If he records his interviews electronically, he can add his summary by dictation as a final paragraph on the same disk after the client has left. The summary can be typed and the full sound transcription be left on the disk and filed in the case folder. The summary of the interview, since it is written primarily for the therapist himself, can be written at a high level of abstraction — that is, in terms of the therapist's own system rather than in the concrete terms one would use if he wished to allow others to make their own inferences regarding the psychodynamics.

The summary should indicate where the therapist believes the client now is with respect to the anticipated course of therapy, material which should be explored later, and predictions as to what the client will do in the interval before the next conference. This latter point is of real significance within the psychology of personal constructs. If the therapist is able to "call the shots" on his client, he can be reassured that he is developing a fairly adequate construction of the case. If he misses, or if he can make only the most general types of predictions, he should proceed with caution until he has a better understanding of what he is dealing with. In the language of the psychology of personal constructs, the therapist should test his subsuming system with respect to the client by making his predictions with sufficient precision so that they will stand or fall according to what the client does.

f. *Initiating the interview.* Having decided what general type of interview he wants to conduct for the day, the therapist should initiate the interview with that in mind, rather than let matters take their own course at first and then try to change the type of interview. For example, if the client has been cluttering up the interviews with a lot of "yesterday I got up and brushed my teeth" type of material, the therapist may well set the stage for the interview by saying at the outset, "Today I would like to have you lay aside all of the everyday happenings of the type that you and I have been discussing and turn our attention to the kinds of things that are hard to put into words. For example, you might try relaxing in your chair for a while. Then you might tell me how it feels to be 'relaxed'." In another instance the therapist may be eager to check his client's reaction to the sequence of interviews. He may say, "In our last interview we were talking about the general topic of crises and how they affected one. Do you remember? . . . Now could you tell me how you felt after that interview — what you thought about?"

There are, of course, many different types of interviews and many different ways of initiating them. What we have to say here is simply that the therapist should start with a planned interview and not expect that he can always convert the interview into the type he wants after having once let it get out of hand.

g. *Terminating the interview.* In therapy an interview does not take up where the last one left off. The client goes on living between interviews, a fact which is easy for the therapist to overlook. The state of mind in which the therapist leaves his client at the end of an interview is the initial point in a chain of behavior leading up to the beginning of the next interview. If the client is confused at the end of an interview, he may make frantic efforts to resolve his confusion in the ensuing hours. If he is suddenly enthusiastic about his latest reinterpretation, he may review it later and decide that he has made a rash judgment.

If the confusion involves a new concern with his own unworthiness, he may resolve it by means of suicide. If the client goes away feeling that he has not told the therapist all that he wanted to tell him or all that he ought to tell him, he may spend some of the next few hours planning what he wants to say in the next interview. The client's state of mind at the end of an interview is therefore not at all static, but is a momentary heading toward a new sequence of psychological events.

Since the interview room is a place where the client is given greater opportunity for spontaneous expression, it becomes a special kind of social laboratory with its own set of rules and expectancies. It sometimes helps if the therapist is careful to maintain a therapeutic type of relationship throughout the time he and the client are in the interview room, and refuses to discuss the client's personal problems outside the threshold of the room.

Some clients try to take up the forepart of the therapeutic hour with pleasantries and then, when the time is up, insist on drawing out the interview by lingering at the threshold. Sometimes we call this "threshold therapy." There are several devices by which an interview can be terminated other than by shoving the client out the door bodily. Most therapists use a clock which is well placed so that the client and therapist can both see it. The therapist can make a regular practice of terminating his interview by noting the time of the next appointment and entering it on his calendar or appointment book. He then can rise and open the door for the client to leave. He can pretend to ignore clinical material which the client presents after that point. Or he can acknowledge it with minimal noncommittal remarks followed immediately by reference to the next meeting. If he does not record his own appointments, he can mention the time of the next interview and then ask his secretary to come in to verify the opening and to record the next appointment in the appointment book. From this point on the terminating procedure is relatively easy. One device is to have the secretary ring a buzzer when the hour is up. If the client does not leave, the secretary can be instructed to enter the room herself a few moments later and announce that the next client is waiting or remind the therapist of the next item on his calendar. If a therapist is positive in his handling of the in and out of interviewing-room behavior, he will be able to handle most of his clients smoothly. If he tries to do therapy outside the interviewing room, he can expect to accumulate more than his share of dawdlers, slow starters, crisis howlers, and telephone sitters.

h. *Controlling interview tempo.* The therapist needs to be able to change pace at will. On some occasions he should be able to let the client fumble for words or ideas without appearing to be impatient. On other occasions he should be able to keep the client responding to a barrage of questions without appearing to be cross-examining. When the slow tempo is used, it is ordinarily designed to enable the client to seek structure for elements which are not easily construed or to seek words for constructs which have no immediate or precise symbols. When the rapid tempo is used, it is ordinarily intended as a way of getting many new elements into the picture without emphasizing their over-all structure or their meaning. It may also be used as a means of controlling anxiety. In the latter case the client is kept so busy manipulating verbal symbols and responding to the kaleidoscopic questioning that he has little opportunity to build up a case of the "sobs."

Interviews do bog down. When they do it is not always necessary to take corrective steps immediately; but, when a corrective step is taken, it can frequently take the form of a change in pace. A client who has been prattling can be told to keep still, relax, and think about the one thing he would most like to have said when he thinks back upon the interview tomorrow. Later he can be asked to state his thoughts by means of single isolated words rather than in sentences. Another way is to ask him to summarize the real meaning of all that he has said so far in the interview. It is probably valuable in certain cases to play back the sound recording of certain interviews, or earlier sections of the same interview, in order to give the client an overview of himself in action. We have not yet explored this procedure sufficiently to be able to say what all its limitations and advantages are.

An interview that has been going too slowly, with the client struggling for words or indulging in thoughts which he cannot even begin to express, can be speeded up after the therapist has decided that enough time has been spent at the slower tempo. He can initiate a rapid interchange of conversation at a level that the client can handle. Most clients can handle recent incidents, such as those occurring within the last few hours, at a fairly rapid pace. What is said about such recent happenings is not necessarily superficial. It may express the client's status more accurately than a summarization of his present feeling and outlook could.

When this emphasis is placed upon specific items, the therapist, of course, has to work a little harder to infer just how the client is putting the material together. If the material seems to be sorted by the client into a rather clear pattern, the therapist can venture to express the generalization which is being applied — subject to the client's approval, of course. Alternatively, the therapist can say at the close of an artificially speeded-up passage of the interview, "Now what do the things you have been telling me about really mean to you?" Sometimes the client can structure the meaning of a limited array of elements — for example, the facts he has been reciting — when he is unable to cope with the larger context in which he bogged down in the earlier part of the interview.

Changing tempo is, of course, not the only way of getting a client to broaden or narrow the scope of his immediate perceptual field. It is, however, often required for the skillful control of a psychotherapeutic sequence. The psychotherapist should therefore develop versatility in its use.

i. *Controlling guilt and dependency.* We have defined the concepts of *guilt* and *dependency* in the preceding volume. When a client engages in what some systems would call "catharsis," or the spilling of emotionally laden material, we would emphasize the fact that the listener is placed thereby into a particular kind of transference perspective by the client. The guilt, as we have pointed out, is the awareness of the loss of one's social role. The client who seeks to assuage his guilt by confessing either his wrongdoings or his childishness throws himself upon the mercy of the listener in the hope that here is someone who will help him restore his role status. It is almost inevitable that it will be impossible for him ever again to deal as an adult with the listener or with him in a detached fashion.

On the listener's part it should be a rule of thumb never to encourage a guilt-laden dependency on the part of anyone unless he is prepared to undertake a continuing responsibility for the person's welfare. Moreover, the psychotherapist should not be too eager to listen to this type of outpouring on the part of his client, revealing as it may be. Frequently, the most helpful thing the therapist can say to a client is, "Perhaps this is something which you should tell me at a later time — when you have come to understand the therapeutic relationship between us better." It is even possible for a therapist to precipitate a psychotic episode by "opening up" a case prematurely.

6. THE PSYCHOTHERAPIST'S MANNER

While all of us depend a great deal upon words for the communication of explicit ideas, we also depend upon other cues to give those words their particular inflections of meaning and value. Sometimes one is unaware of what he conveys by means of his gestures and manners. Those who interact with him may make some astonishing interpretations of his attitude. The psychotherapist should learn how his manners are interpreted by his clients and should cultivate manners which will make him generally acceptable and effective in his relations with them. Sometimes this involves a good deal more than managing his muscles. Sometimes his manner betrays a deeper hostility which his clients sense, even though they cannot quite put their finger on it.

Often the therapist's colleagues can help in this connection. In a properly structured situation it is possible to ask one's colleagues what their initial reaction to him was, and to discover from their answers what feature in his behavior accounted for their reaction. Another approach is to ask one's colleagues to observe his facial expression and posture during a discussion and then attempt to infer what his thoughts and attitudes were. Regardless of whether or not they are correct in their inferences, what they think they see is what one has actually "communicated." Certainly one gets only the more superficial reactions by this procedure, but these are worth considering seriously. The responses to the therapist's unintentional expression of deeper personal attitudes may suggest, of course, that the therapist himself should undergo a psychotherapeutic series.

Manners are closely associated with cultural variations. They are probably also closely associated with the changing cultural scene. But the latter variations are not so much of a problem for the therapist, since he operates in only one decade at a time. For the most part his clients do too, although there are times when one senses that he has picked up a client who rightfully belongs to a bygone generation. It is appropriate for the therapist to attempt to adjust his manners somewhat to the cultural expectations of the group from which his client comes.

a. *Posture and gesture.* During almost any type of interview the therapist should appear to be physically relaxed and mentally receptive. He should sit in his chair as if he expected to be there for a long time, not crouched as if he were about to spring into action. When he wants the client to formulate his ideas into words, he should not look as if he were seeking the first opening to interpose his own remarks. He should not catch his breath at the end of each of the client's sentences, nor should he heave a sigh at the end of each difficult passage in the interview. His breathing should be regular, and appropriate to the kind of therapeutic part he is playing.

The therapist's gesture pattern should be predominantly of the accepting type. Rhythmic and autoerotic gestures should be kept at a minimum. Sweeping gestures, gestures indicating pity or deprecation, and gestures indicating self-assertion should be rarely used, if at all. Slight gestures and nonverbal vocalizations may be used to indicate understanding, suspended judgment, or uncertainty as to what the client means, and to offer an implicit invitation to the client to elaborate what he has just said. Certainly any gesture pattern that is equivalent to throwing up one's hands or grasping his aching head and moaning, "My God, what have you done now?" is likely to militate against successful treatment.

b. *Voice and speech.* The therapist's voice should not be offensive to the client. This does not mean that the therapist should seek to produce a melodious sound pattern such as some public speakers try to affect. More important is that the therapist develop a responsive voice: changing his speech rhythm to suit a situation or the client's speech, adjusting the modulation to the mood of the moment, indicating both stability and sympathy, keeping the volume almost on a par with the client's voice, except when leading into a transition of one type or another, and always indicating that understanding is of more concern to the therapist than rhetoric. The therapist's choice of language should be as colorful as the situation will permit without being offensive. The choice of the colorful expression is dictated by the need for clarity rather than by the need for emphasis.

Much of the language of therapy is in incomplete sentences, especially as far as the therapist is concerned. The well-timed hesitation in the formulation of a sentence gives the client a chance to fit his personal construction into the pattern which the structure of the therapist's sentence initiates. As soon as the therapist has learned the client's language well enough to be sure that he can use it correctly, he should utilize it for purposes of communication in therapy sessions. Until he learns the vocabulary, he may ask the client to supply a great many of the key words in all of the important sentences he seeks to formulate.

c. *Signs of impassivity or overcontrol in the therapist.* While it is important that the therapist always appear to be "shockproof," some therapists assume such an impassive manner that the client is unable to use the therapist's response as a means of checking his hold on reality. Basically this impassivity or "overcontrol" (of the self) is due probably to the therapist's fear that his own personal maladaptations will be communicated to the client.

From our point of view the therapy room is a laboratory in which experiments are performed. For the therapist to put on an immobile mask is equivalent to making the client do his experiments blindfolded and to giving him no opportunity to observe the social results of his tests. Rather than showing no response, it is our position that the therapist should be prepared to show a wide range of carefully selected responses. Certainly the therapist should not be undisciplined and self-indulgent in his response pattern. He needs to be a highly disciplined person. But if this means that he has completely suppressed his response pattern, his effectiveness with clients is likely to be diminished. The inscrutability of the therapist is highly related to the incidence of clients' breaking off therapy at the points where they feel personally insecure.

d. *Laughter.* It is all right for the therapist to smile or even to laugh in therapy. The general rule is never to smile as broadly or laugh quite as loudly or as long as the client does. One can never be too sure as to what is lying at the other end of the construct which the client is invoking with his laughter and how quickly the client will reconstrue himself at that opposite end. Humor is closely associated with quick movement and reversed construction. The client's use of humor should always put one on the alert for the construct avenues along which movement is so sudden. The therapist should never let his own laughter dull his wits.

e. *Age of the therapist.* In most instances clients initially respond better to the therapy situation if they perceive the therapist as being older than themselves. In general, therefore, the therapist should gauge the behavior which his client observes or hears about to a level of maturity which the client can respect. Yet it is surprising how effectively a young clinician can, in the long run, deal with an older client if he conducts himself as a good psychotherapist and does not overconcern himself with the age differential between himself and his client.

7. TEACHING THE CLIENT HOW TO BE A "PATIENT"

The preliminary instructions one gives a client depend upon

the type of therapeutic relationship to be undertaken. But whatever the type of relationship, the task of teaching the client how to be a "patient" — that is, how to respond to the therapeutic situation — involves much more than the recitation of a formal charge. In longer therapeutic series it may take months to teach the client how he should respond to the therapeutic situation in order to get the most out of it. The therapist should not become impatient during this stage in therapy and should consider this teaching to be an essential feature of his job.

Ordinarily, though not always, the therapist must first listen to the complaint before he attempts to define the therapeutic relationship. At some point, before too much has been said, he must take steps to indicate to the client what may be expected in the developing relationship. If the client is a child, this may be done "nonverbally" — that is, by letting the child "test the limits of the situation." When we say "nonverbally," we do not mean that speech is not used, only that the situation is not abstracted and defined by means of symbols of the whole. We mean that words are used semeiotically rather than semantically, that is, as signals of the therapist's forthcoming reactions rather than as symbols of the therapeutic opportunities and limitations.

With adults it is possible to employ words with more regard for semantics and less for semeiotics, though in therapy one can never take it for granted that words, by their mere sounds, will magically invoke meanings that are beyond what the client is prepared to comprehend. It is one thing to use words as symbols of the contextual elements out of which the client causes a new construct to emerge; it is quite another to expect a "symbol" itself to give birth to the construct which it may only later come to represent.

The writer recalls a client who was having difficulty with interpersonal relations largely because the constructs of *personal acceptance, tolerance,* and *intimacy* were closely constellated. Her friends variously construed her behavior as "too personal," "her own needs projected into her perceptions of others," or "overdependent," although she was generally well liked. The writer attempted over an extended psychotherapeutic period to help her develop, among other things, a functional construct that might be described as "respect for personal integrity and individuality." Such a dimension of thinking had implications both for the way the client construed herself and for the way in which others might be construed. It was only after a long period of therapy and some trying personal experiences that the construct began to take shape. The client, a brilliant professional woman, and an unusually able verbalist, could only express it at first by saying awkwardly, "I'm beginning to see that people just are what they are. They can't help it. They must be what they must be. I never knew what you meant by 'respect' before. I talked as if I knew what it meant but all the time to 'respect' someone was a little like being afraid of them." Her development of the construct was, of course, much more complicated and involved many more intermediate steps than this simple account might imply. The point to be made here is simply that even with a highly literate person such a commonly used word as "respect" could not invoke a construct which had never been adequately formed as a personal dimension of life.

While keeping clearly in mind that a verbal symbol will not invoke a personal construct which does not exist, the therapist may, nevertheless, make some attempt to structure the therapeutic situation semantically. He may say, for example:

"Probably as we talk about these problems it will gradually become clear to both of us that they are related to some things that have been bothering you for a long time. For that reason it is a little difficult to tell just how long this series of conferences will have to last before you discover just how to deal with your troubles. Let me tell you a little about what to expect.

"In the first place I think you will find that these conferences are quite different from anything you have had experience with before. Sometimes you will be telling me very frankly about how you feel about yourself or about other people. Sometimes it will be hard to find the words for what you are thinking. Lots of times you will say things here that you would not think of saying on the outside. Don't be upset by any of this. Treat this room as a kind of special place. What you say here will not be held against you. We are here to help you, not to criticize you.

"Now if you are like most people who go through a series of conferences like this, you will find yourself changing your mind back and forth about things quite often. Sometimes you won't know for sure just where you stand. We expect that. The main thing is for you not to make any final decisions during this series of conferences that you cannot withdraw from later. Don't, for example, decide to get married, sell your house, or go into debt during the course of these interviews. Keep an open mind about such things for a while.

"Another thing, don't talk to anyone else about what you have discussed in these conferences. If you do that you will be led into saying things and making decisions that you are almost sure to regret later on. For the present, at least, I want you to be free to change your mind about the things you discuss here. You may be too much embarrassed to do that if you have already stated what you thought was your point of view."

There are some cases in which it is not desirable to stress the insularity of the therapeutic situation as we have in the illustration above. Among children and young adolescents may be cases in which the therapist hopes that the client will talk more freely with his parents, even to the extent of discussing some of the interview material. He should not invite that type of discussion too soon in the interview series or without knowing how the parents will respond to the child's unaccustomed frankness.

At some stage in the early part of therapy it may be necessary to make some statements about the client's assuming the initiative in reorienting himself. The therapist may say:

"You realize, of course, that all of your life you are going to be facing new experiences. That is what makes life interesting. Nobody can ever tell you in advance just what these experiences are going to be and exactly what to do when you meet them face to face. In the final analysis only you can make your decisions. The same is true as regards the problems you are going to deal with here. I am not here to solve them for you. Even if I could solve them for you it would not be good for you to let me. Only you can find the right answers;

and, once you have found them, only you can put them into practice. I shall help you all I can, but you will have to take the matter of your own recovery in hand."

The task of getting a client to loosen his conceptualization and express autistic thinking is frequently long and tedious. Why this is necessary in many cases is a topic to be discussed in a later chapter. Yet because it is so frequently a part of the task of teaching the client how to become a patient, it is relevant to discuss the technique here.

The client can be urged to talk about those ideas which seem difficult to express. He can be told that he should not try to decide what is important and what is unimportant but rather try to put into words those ideas which come to mind for no apparent reason at all. A client may protest, "This seems silly," or, "I can't see why I should be thinking about this." If the therapist is seeking a loosening of conceptualization he may respond by saying, "I know, but those are the kinds of thoughts I have been talking about. Try to put them into words." The therapist may also say, "Let us see where your thoughts lead you when you just let them go." He may also say, "Don't try to make sense, just let your mind wander."

The therapist may also teach the client to give vent to his loosened conceptualizations by breaking into any chain of the client's associations which appears to be too tightly organized. He may also, as we have indicated in an earlier section, say, "But what does all this mean to you? How does it make you feel? What other experience does it vaguely seem to resemble?" Or he may say, "Suppose the incident you are describing had never happened. How would your life be different?" Again he may interrupt the recitation and say, "Now let us stop right at this point. What kind of person were you when this was taking place?" He may invite confabulation by saying, "You have told me how things actually were. Now tell me how they might have been if they had, perhaps, happened to someone else." The client may even be asked to make up a story built upon the same incidental material.

Sometimes a client will "intellectualize" at a very abstract level but the therapist wishes to have him express ideas which are not necessarily less abstract but which are less structured. He may say, "Since our last conference you may have thought about some of the things that might have come up in the last conference or which might come up in this conference. Perhaps you thought of some things which you were glad did not come up or which you hoped you would not have to talk about. . . . Let's talk about them."

Physical relaxation is an important aid to conceptual loosening. With some clients it is profitable to spend a considerable proportion of a series of interviews teaching them how to relax, muscle by muscle, and limb by limb. They then can be told to let their minds relax in an analogous way — not to think intensively about any one thing. They may be told, if they find themselves thinking about one thing, to break the chain of associations and think about something else. It may be helpful in this stage if the therapist does not ask them to express their thoughts, but rather checks on the loosening simply by asking such questions as the following from time to time: "Is your mind wandering now? Does it seem as though your thinking does not make any particular sense?" Sometimes the very necessity of communicating with the therapist makes a client resort to overstructuration and hence to limit his communication to those more superficial constructs which are not so difficult to put into words. It may be even more important for some clients to be taught how to think loosely than it is to get them to express their loose thinking.

It should be pointed out that a client may become frightened of the therapeutic relationship if he is permitted to go too rapidly and come face to face with anxiety-producing material before he is able to handle it. In such cases the therapist may wish that he had spent more time helping the client to develop his side of the therapeutic technique before having to deal with too much meaningful therapeutic material. From the standpoint of personal-construct theory, the therapist should be much more interested in how the client is prepared to deal with "clinical material" than he is in turning the stuff up into consciousness.

Throughout this chapter we have tried to emphasize the fact that the purpose of therapy is not to produce a state of mind but to produce a mobility of mind that will permit one to pursue a course through the future. Now here we are saying that pursuing a course through a therapeutic sequence requires preparation too. It also requires teaching the client mobility of mind. Indeed, the psychology of personal constructs, by the very nature of its Fundamental Postulate, lays great emphasis upon optimal anticipation as a basic principle of life. We have said that therapy should serve an anticipatory function. Now we are saying that the client should be helped to take therapy itself in his stride by being taught how to be a "patient."

B. Palliative Techniques

8. REASSURANCE

Reassurance is a simplified superordinate construction placed upon the clinical situation. It is communicated to the client so that his behavior and ideas will temporarily appear to him to be consistent, acceptable, and organized. It is never more than a temporary expedient. The therapist should never use it in an attempt to bring about far-reaching results. Yet it does have its place in therapy, just as a sedative has its place in medical practice.

In an earlier section of this chapter we discussed the nature of *acceptance*. We described it as a function of the clinician's conceptualization of his role rather than as a therapeutic technique. The accepting therapist tries earnestly to put himself in the client's shoes, but at the same time seeks to maintain a professional overview of the client's problems. This means that in accepting the client the therapist makes an effort to understand him in his — the client's — own terms, and that, also, he subsumes a major portion of the client's construction under his — the therapist's — own professional constructs.

Now acceptance may provide a background for the discriminating use of the techniques of reassurance and support. It may give the therapist an opportunity to judge when reassurance is desirable as a temporary expedient. His professional overview may permit him to formulate some form of superordinate or summarizing statement that will temporarily stabilize the client's conceptualization. The superordinate construction which is communicated to the client is not necessarily an expression of the therapist's own subsuming construction of the client's viewpoint. Indeed, it rarely is. If the client were able to handle the latter type of statement, there might be no need for him to continue in therapy. He would already think about his problem the way the therapist does. What the therapist uses as reassurance is the proverbial string and baling wire. It keeps things together until a more substantial structure can be built.

Now and then a client finds his construction system badly shaken. If too much appears to be giving way all at once, the therapist may decide to employ reassurance. This means that he takes the initiative and superimposes a systematic construction of the events at hand. This tends temporarily to stabilize the client and to permit him to keep his own personal constructs intact and operative. Of course, if the superimposed systematic construction does not provide a comfortable place for the client's badly shaken constructs, the effect is anything but reassuring. For example, if the client is suddenly and disruptively disillusioned regarding his parents, the therapist is scarcely reassuring when he murmurs, "Well, your parents are probably human just like other people." He is more reassuring if he says, "Well, you have known your parents for a good many years. Let's not suddenly decide that everything you have believed about them is completely wrong." This latter is what we mean by superimposing a construction under which the client's personal constructs may temporarily remain intact and operative.

Reassurance is a temporary way of reducing anxiety. Anxiety is defined in the glossary (see Chapter II). For our purposes here it is enough to use the term in its popular sense. Anxiety, as we see it in relation to therapy, is not necessarily bad. It is like pain. It can be disruptive or it can be informative. The therapist must know how to use anxiety and to keep it under control. Reassurance is one of the means of reducing it temporarily.

a. *Hazards in the use of reassurance.* Reassurance can backfire. If one reassures his client by saying that things are not going to turn out badly, and then things do turn out badly, the client loses faith in the therapist's ability to reflect reality. The result is that the client is reluctant to test out his constructs against the therapist's reactions. The laboratory of the conference room ceases to be used as a place where valid experiments are conceived and performed.

It should always be recognized that reassurance tends to operate as a confirmation of the client's symptom and of his maladjustive mechanisms. Just as it provides a frame within which the client's constructs can temporarily remain operative, so it tends to perpetuate the use of those constructs, some of which may constitute the basis of the client's difficulties. If the task of therapy were always to disrupt the use of faulty constructs as soon as possible, one might say that reassurance should never be used. However, the task of therapy is to prepare the client for achieving long-range goals, and not simply to perform surgery on his misconceptions. It may then be temporarily advisable to encourage him to retain his symptom. Reassurance is one way of doing this.

Too much reassurance tends to develop a kind of relationship between the client and the therapist that makes the client overly dependent upon the therapist and unable to use him as a representative of a wide variety of people. The therapist tends to become fixed as a figure and the therapeutically undesirable condition we choose to call *primary transference* tends to develop. Transference is discussed in a later section of this chapter.

b. *Ways of reassuring.* There are various ways of providing reassurance, some of which are less likely to produce the unfavorable reactions we have been discussing than are others. One simple technique is the prediction of outcomes. Of course, if the therapist makes sweeping predictions, he puts himself in the position of ladling out a palliative medicine indiscriminately. If he wishes to measure out his reassurance and confine its effect to a definite period of time, it is better for him to predict how the client will feel between the present conference and the next, or over the week-end. The therapist may say, "You have been on the verge of dealing with some rather fundamental problems. You may find your moods fluctuating somewhat more than usual be-tween now and the next conference. This is to be expected. While you may be uncomfortable at times, I don't believe it will be more than you can handle." This type of reassurance is less prejudicial to the eventual reconsideration of the client's con-structs than a more sweeping one would be.

Just as the prediction of outcomes has a reassuring effect, so the postdiction of outcomes tends also to have a somewhat re-assuring effect. For example, the therapist may say, "I would guess that the last few days have been a little rougher than usual for you. Am I right?" The fact that the therapist can make either predictions or postdictions indicates to the client that the therapist, at least, has an over-all frame of reference within which the client's turbulent mental life must make some sense. This suggests that his behavior and ideas have some measure of consistency, acceptability, and organization, and permits him to go on using the constructs upon which they are based without feeling that his whole world is coming apart.

The therapist can provide a generally reassuring atmosphere by accepting all new and anxiety-laden clinical material offered by the client as if it were not wholly unexpected. If the thera-pist treats what the client confides as something that might rea-sonably be expected under the circumstances, the client tends to be reassured and tends to go on to complete the story. The thera-pist may say, "Yes, I know some of the ways things do turn out. Tell me: how did they turn out in your case?" Certainly the therapist can upset most clients by appearing to be surprised or shocked at what they have to say.

It should also be said that structuring the interview situation tends to have a reassuring effect. Similarly, the therapist's man-ner as expressed by his voice, gestures, and posture may be reas-suring.

A popular but hazardous mode of reassurance is the use of value labels. The therapist may say, "That is good," or, "You were quite right," or, "He was in the wrong, I would say." Like the other forms of reassurance, this puts the client in a spot where he cannot restate his position with respect to the valued construct without appearing to have been wrong, inconsistent, or out of step with the therapist. The client should be free to readjust interpersonal relationships in the therapy room as rapidly as new insights require. The therapist should, therefore, be quite careful about all use of value labels; they tend to create a rigid state of affairs. This is not to say that the therapist ordinarily rejects the client's use of value labels. On the contrary, he normally accepts the client's values, but he tries to make clear that this is at the level of acceptance, not necessarily at the level of concurrence.

c. *Creating "resistance."* It is possible to create "resistance" by the use of reassurance. Clients are frequently ambivalent about their complaints, being uncertain either as to which end of a given construct continuum they wish to station themselves or which construct dimension they wish to invoke. The therapist, in seeking to comfort a client, may find that he has put the client in the position of having to live with the point of view he has just expressed. That may be threatening.

For example, a client may complain bitterly that he has been misunderstood all his life. The therapist may seek to reassure him by saying that no one can hope to know anyone else completely but that that does not mean he was not affectionately regarded by the people with whom he was intimately associated. But let us suppose that in making his complaint the client was working up to the point where he could express the contrast pole of his construct of not being understood. Suppose that he was getting ready to say, "I have never understood the people who were close to me and it is about time I started doing it." This is an example of a possible implied opposite in the client's personal construct system. If this does happen to be the submerged end of the client's construct, he is covertly invoking it when he goes into his tirade about not being understood. Now the therapist, in seeking to give him reassurance, actually succeeds, not only in throwing him back into the clutches of his old conceptualization, but also in making it seem unnecessary that he now come to understand those who are close to him.

One should always keep in mind the experimental nature of the therapeutic process. When a client launches into a tirade, he may be considered as conducting an experiment with a form of behavior. Now the experiment may be one which he has repeated ad nauseam, but that does not mean that he is anticipating exactly the same results that he has been accustomed to getting. The therapist, in reassuring the client, or even in agreeing with him, may discourage the client's hopes that there can ever be any new outcomes of his experiment or that there are any alternative ways of construing his situation.

The point we wish to emphasize is that reassurance can make a client feel trapped. He may feel that there are no alternatives, that he cannot solve his problems — he can only be comforted in his failure to solve them. The therapist's sympathy may indicate to the client that the therapist himself sees no alternative save "to grin and bear it." Just as it may be very disturbing to a student of mathematics to come to his instructor for help on a problem and receive only approval of the unsuccessful methods he has already tried and comfort for his failure, it may be just as disturbing to a person seeking to solve a psychological problem to receive a similar treatment from his mentor.

Reassurance probably always operates to slow up the immediate therapeutic movement. In this sense we may say that it tends to create a kind of resistance. There are times when this is desirable. Reassurance can also constitute a threat. It may threaten the client with the possibility that he can never find any solution to his problems, that what he has been saying and doing, after all, do make the only sense that can be made out of life.

d. *Reassurance by reinstating a symptom.* There are occasions when the therapist may reassure a client by helping him temporarily to reinstate a symptom or defense. A number of years ago a student therapist working under the writer's direction was dealing with what might be called a "psychosomatic" problem. The client was a high-school girl with an orthopedic disability of long standing. The onset of the disturbance could not be determined precisely. The difficulty had appeared at one time to be structural, and a highly reputed orthopedic surgeon had once operated on the girl's hip. In her senior year at high school she was referred for psychological examination and treatment. She was judged by her teachers to be an excellent student; but the attitudes of her parents, particularly her father, were judged to be a hazard to her personal and vocational adjustment. It was understood that her father was threatening to keep her from completing her senior year and from carrying out her plans to enter nurses' training.

After a period of psychotherapy with the student therapist, the girl was judged to have made excellent progress. It had also become evident that her limp had at one time had a great deal of psychological meaning to her and had been the source of a number of important "secondary gains." It seemed to the writer at that time that the therapy had probably alleviated the childhood need for the symptom and that the perseveration of the symptom might be explained wholly on the basis of what might now be called "functional autonomy," after Allport. (Incidentally, the writer no longer sees this as a useful construction of that case.)

It was decided to countersuggest the symptom. The therapist reviewed with the girl the meaning the symptom had had in her life and suggested that with her new outlook the symptom had lost its utility and might well be allowed to disappear. The therapist suggested that the next day the girl should wear a low-heeled pair of shoes and that the limp would probably disappear altogether. The next day, for the first time in as long as the girl could remember, she was able to walk freely and without the limp. The change was clearly observable. There was no observable trace of asymmetry in her gait. The girl was pleased beyond measure and very grateful. The psychotherapy sessions were continued regularly, however, because it was felt to be important to follow closely the repercussions of our psychotherapeutic venture.

A few days later, immediately following a session with the client, the student clinician asked for an emergency appointment with the writer. The girl had told of a phantasy regarding the telephone lines she could see outside the window of her room. She imagined them to be lines of communication that led across the sea and enabled some people in the Orient to keep in touch with her. The girl's manner of describing the phantasy left some real doubt as to her hold on reality and suggested that it approached a true delusion.

It was decided immediately to "give her her symptom back"! The next day the therapist listened to her relate more "paranoid" material. The therapist suggested that she should "not go too fast in getting rid of her limp," that "such things" were hard to get rid of all at once. Immediately the girl started limping again and the "paranoid" material subsided and did not return. Within a few weeks the orthopedic symptom gradually disappeared. The case was followed for two years. The last report was that the girl was doing well in nurses' training, and that her adjustment seemed to be adequate.

This case illustrates how the retention or the restoration of a symptom may have a reassuring effect. It permits the current constructs to remain intact and operative. The case also illustrates an important compensatory relationship between "paranoid" and "hysterical" reactions, a point we shall want to develop in detail in a later chapter.

e. *When to use reassurance.* When should a therapist use reassurance? First of all, he should use it only when he is willing to accept the slowing up of therapeutic movement which goes with it. It can be used when the therapeutic movement is too rapid and threatens to leave the client without a basic structure upon which he can depend.

Secondly, reassurance can be used as a temporary preventive of fragmentation. The reassured client tends to keep his constructs intact even though they are not particularly adequate and he is not particularly happy with them.

Thirdly, reassurance can be used to encourage the loosening of conceptualization. This may seem to be the opposite of the effect we have just mentioned. What we mean is that the reassured client is freer to express those looser constructs which govern his life. He is probably less inclined to fragment his basic constructs in order to do so. The reassured client is less likely to complain, "This seems silly," or, "I don't dare let myself think that way."

In the fourth place, reassurance may be used to control anxiety between sessions or during a period of suspended sessions.

In the fifth place, reassurance may be used as a temporary expedient during the course of an interview to keep an important chain of associations from being broken.

Finally, it may be used during temporarily traumatic situations.

Always it should be used minimally and in calculated amounts. The therapist should remember that it is "cheap medicine" and likely to be "habit forming."

9. SUPPORT

Support is a broad response pattern on the part of the therapist which permits the client to experiment widely and *successfully*. Nearly all therapy should involve the therapist's being responsive to the client. However, the therapy is supportive only if the client is allowed to have *successful* outcomes to his ventures with the therapist. Support means, then, not only receptiveness of the client's overtures, but also some degree of validation of his anticipations. It is a technique which becomes possible through the therapist's acceptance of the client. Support does not trap the client in his own construct system in quite the way reassurance traps him. The client is not told that he is right before he even has a chance to experiment. Rather, the therapist responds to him more or less in the manner the client appears to expect him to respond. This does not necessarily mean that the therapist verbally agrees with the client.

For example, the therapist, instead of saying, "You are absolutely right" (*reassurance*), may respond by saying, "I think I am beginning to understand what you mean. Let me see if I can put it into my own words without losing the meaning." Or the therapist may say, "You have been very critical of me today but there is no reason why you shouldn't be critical of me if you want to." Or the therapist may simply say, "I think I can see your point of view." All of these remarks suggest not only that the client is being accepted in his own right, but also that his exploratory attempts at communication are getting positive results. There is a minimum of implication that the client's way of looking at things is the only way of looking at things or that the therapist agrees with the client. Moreover, the therapist is not responding in terms of certainties or making firm predictions of outcomes.

In using support techniques the therapist accepts the client's dependency patterns of behavior. Even this can be threatening to a client, though not so likely to be so as in the case of reassurance. Support is also a means of helping the client recognize his own dependency patterns as he sees them exhibited in the therapy sessions. As he finds how he uses his support, he may be able to see more and more what he has been expecting of others in his personal-social milieu.

Support may arouse guilt feelings in the client as he initially construes his dependency. The problem is not that clients have dependencies — all of us depend upon some things — but rather that the maladjusted person may be depending upon things the way a child or an invalid depends upon things. The client as he begins to construe his dependency may see himself as exiled by his manner of depending and hence as a guilty person. The relationship of guilt to exile is an important point developed in the preceding volume.

The supported client may feel caught between the feeling of interpersonal dependency and the prospect that his overdemanding relationship to the therapist may lead to exile.

Support requires that the therapist develop an ever expanding repertory of response patterns in order to meet the demand of the clients whom he wishes to support. It is difficult for the inexperienced clinician to give support to all clients, primarily because his repertory is restricted. He does not know enough affirmative answers; he cannot exhibit all the responses his clients anticipate of him.

a. *Support techniques.* One of the simplest support techniques is for the therapist to keep his appointments promptly. The client who needs support is keenly sensitive to the therapist's tardiness or to the cancellation of appointments. He resents the fact that he is dependent upon the therapist and he resents the fact that he is disturbed by the therapist's tardiness. He berates himself for being upset, reminds himself that he has no right to expect the therapist to be on time to the minute, and then feels guilty because he feels that he *has* no right to the therapist's attention and that the therapist is probably teaching him a needed lesson in letting him cool his heels.

Another support technique is for the therapist to recall clinical material at appropriate times. A client who needs support tends to feel it when the therapist shows that he remembers something the client told him weeks before and apparently considered worth remembering. To a client this is a way of responding to him affirmatively.

It is supportive when a therapist demonstrates that he can construe events correctly within the client's own construction system. By "correctly" we mean as the client would construe them. This means that the therapist not only is accepting the client by responding flexibly to the client's attempts to communicate, but also that he is supporting the client by responding in the way the client anticipated or hoped that he would. Support provides the client with some degree of evidence of the plausibility of his constructs. It makes them appear to have some predictive potency. Subsequent experimentation may prove them invalid or in need of modification; but, by offering support, the therapist gives his client enough confidence in his constructs to put them to test.

It is not always necessary to support a client's constructs in order to get him to put them to a crucial test. Sometimes it is enough that the therapist be able to construe the way the client does. The willingness to do so is acceptance. The act of construing within the client's own system is one of the therapist's main functions in the whole experimental process which comprises therapy. Those clinicians who approach therapy via learning theory may be concerned that the therapist's use of the client's construction system may serve to "reinforce" it rather than to "extinguish" it. Let us say, rather, that the therapist, by restating the system from which the client's own experimental hypotheses may be deduced, helps the client set up the hypotheses which he is to try out in therapy. Thus it becomes easier to see what it is that he is daily testing against reality, and to determine precisely what it is that has been invalidated if he gets negative results. In this respect the therapist is like the adviser of graduate students who helps them formulate their hunches systematically and, from the systems, deduce hypotheses which may be staked against the fortunes of experimentation.

The therapist may support his client by making immediate adjustments to changes in the client's construction system without emphasizing the disparities that arise. One of the insecurities that may disturb a client is the feeling that he is beginning to express inconsistent viewpoints. He may putter around through several conferences before letting himself express the new point of view which has been brewing in his mind. Here is where the reassuring and supporting therapist may have his chickens come home to roost. If the therapist has already endorsed and validated the client's now obsolescent point of view, the client may feel foolish and unstable in expressing a new one. At this point further support may be called for. If the therapist readily adapts his responses to the new point of view so as to give the client affirmative evidence, he can be supportive at this point. If his evidence is to be effectively supporting, it must be provided in a framework which does not immediately emphasize the contradictions in the client's thinking.

The therapist can be supporting if he helps the client verbalize his new rationale, or if he helps him verbalize the superordinate rationale under which his constructs are governed. The therapist should always be cautious lest he overstate the rationale and carry it too far beyond where the client is ready to go. This is a failing of overeager therapists. Always the new verbalization suggested by the therapist should be kept at a bare minimum. It should be stated no more than a sentence at a time with the client elaborating and documenting each sentence before the therapist ventures the next one. When the therapist attempts to express the client's vague thoughts in new words, he is always on shaky, but often profitable, ground.

The therapist is supportive when he is compliant with the client's wishes. Yet it should be clear that this form of support may often retard the client's progress.

A therapist who provides services for his client is supportive. If the therapist makes arrangements for the client to join a group, get a special examination, find a tutor, have a traffic ticket canceled, get out of jail, have his wife visit him in the hospital, get his children into a new school, or if he performs any one of a variety of services, he puts himself in the position of support. While some of these may be no more than normal courtesies, the therapist should always be aware of what they imply for the therapeutic relationship.

Like reassurance, support may sometimes be used in anxiety cases. The writer believes it is particularly applicable to certain anxiety cases in which somatic disturbances are also evident. It applies, of course, only to certain phases of the therapeutic treatment; usually the beginning phase and just after transitions. Clients having somatic symptoms without verbalized anxiety are not necessarily candidates for support until they reach the stage of therapy when verbalized anxiety begins to be manifest.

b. *Uses of support.* Support may be used preliminary to helping a client understand his dependency strivings. As he enacts the part of a dependent person in the therapeutic relationship, he provides himself and the therapist with data on how his dependency is structured. Having accepted the support of the therapist, the client should be in a good position to see just what use he makes of support. Sometimes a therapist may support a client ad nauseam. The client gets fed up. He wins so often that he becomes bored with the game, and begins to explore more independent patterns of life. At this point the therapist can help the client structure the situation as it has been and develop new constructs by which to structure situations in the future.

The therapist may use support to stabilize a situation. For example, the situation in a home may be such that the client is likely to make frantic efforts to solve his problems and may thereby precipitate new social difficulties which he cannot handle. The therapist may take supportive steps to keep the client's household together until the client is able to manage the situation by himself. The therapist may also use hospitalization of the client as a means of supporting him. The hospital may meet his daily requirements and provide him with the needed validating experiences.

The therapist may provide support in the therapy sessions so that the client will not need to attempt radically new approaches on the outside in his effort to find a predictively effective system. The client may thus be saved from bringing down new problems upon his head. Later, of course, he must experiment, but the therapist can help him formulate his hypotheses and experimental designs more realistically before the client's whole social world is turned into a laboratory for radical ventures.

Support may be used as a preliminary basis for helping the client revise his role-construct repertory. If the client finds that some of his constructs are supported, he may be able to deal with the people around him with greater equanimity. This means that he may be better able to reconstrue his associates without "his own needs getting in the way." Not only that — he may be better prepared to formulate altogether new dimensions in which to construe them.

The use of support should be limited to cases or to phases of treatment in which the client cannot otherwise handle all modes of reality or, more specifically, cannot take unexpected events in his stride. For such a client, support minimizes the negative results growing out of his experimentation. As in the case of reassurance, support is an available technique largely to the degree that the therapist accepts his client. Also, as in the case of reassurance, support should be localized, conservatively measured, and not allowed to form an addiction.

C. Transference

10. TRANSFERENCE AS A CONSTRUCT

The concept of transference is an important feature of orthodox psychoanalytic theory. While transference is not conceived of in quite the same way within the psychology of personal constructs, there is enough similarity to encourage us to attempt to use the same word for our corresponding concept. Much of what we have to say regarding the use of transference, as indeed much of what we have already said about therapeutic technique, has been said by those who approach therapy from the standpoint of psychoanalysis. This is not to say that psychoanalysis and personal-construct theory are equivalent in a practical sense. The writer sees the differences both as systematically fundamental and, frequently, as quite practical.

To the extent that all construing is deductive, we find that a person, in staking a prediction on the future, must lift a construct from his repertory and use it to determine the nature of his bet. This is essentially a transferring process. The construct may not fit and he may lose his bet, but the point is that the construer has drawn an available construct from his store and used it as a basis of action.

Suppose the prediction is imperfect. What happens next? He may make another bet using the same construct. He suspects that the construct may be right but that he has not yet applied it on a long-term basis. Perhaps he has expected success in too short a cycle. Alternatively, he may take a brief look at the situation and try making a bet on the basis of another construct drawn from his available repertory. These are essentially deductive procedures.

Construing has its inductive phase too. Our gambling construer may hesitate, following his first failure, and take a close look at the elements which he collected by means of the construct he has just used. These elements are constructs too. For the time being, let us say that they are constructs of a lower order — more concrete, if you will. He labels the elements deductively, just as he originally tried to label the situation as a whole. But now he may try to regroup the elements. He may have the beginnings of a new construct there. Undoubtedly he has tried to employ the broad principles of more permeable constructs in formulating his new construct inductively. Thus, even his new construction has both its inductive and its deductive aspects. To begin with, the construer transferred — or applied — a construct which seemed specifically to fit the situation. He deduced his bets. They failed. Now he has attempted to tailor-make a construct to fit the situation; but he has applied — or transferred — a more permeable superordinate construct in doing so.

It may be apparent by now that the notion of transferring, in its broad sense, is an essential feature of the psychology of personal constructs.

a. *Transference and the therapist.* Now what does the client do when he is confronted with the therapist? He lifts a construct from his repertory and goggles at the therapist through it. What does he see? To answer that question in detail is to construe *transference.* The answer may not be easy, yet the therapist must frequently seek to find it. Perhaps he may be threatened when he finds it. He may even dread the first look at himself through his client's eyes. For what he discovers the client is seeing from behind a figured but semitransparent construct may bear a haunting resemblance to a recently banished self-perception.

Transference, as the term is reserved for use in psychotherapy, is based upon role constructs rather than constructs in general. It has to do with one's perceptions of persons who perform parts in cooperative social enterprises. It refers to the way one attempts to subsume the constructs of others. In psychotherapy it represents the client's bid to subsume parts of the construct system of the therapist and thence to play in a role relationship with him. Unless the client makes an effort to construe the therapist by transferring role constructs upon him, the therapist is scarcely able to exemplify any aspect of reality in the hope of having it meaningfully interpreted.

While the therapist is continually being subjected to construction by the cooperative client, he is also continually extricating himself from the client's constructions. He extricates himself from those constructions which are not generally useful to the client. In the process of doing so he seeks to have the construction patterns changed. He must also extricate himself from some useful constructions in order to make himself available as material for other useful constructions. It is correct to say that the therapist enacts a series of carefully chosen parts and seeks to have the client develop adequate role relationships to the figures portrayed.

Often the client perseverates in viewing the therapist in a fixed way. He may do this just as he persists in seeing other persons in a particular way. The therapist sees the client "acting out" the part the perception calls for but finds himself baffled when he attempts to get the client to formulate the perception in terms which allow it to be put to test.

To summarize this passage we may say that the therapist is always looking for transferences, trying to get them formulated as testable hypotheses, designing experiments, and confronting the client with negative as well as positive results, upon the basis of which the transferences may be abandoned and replaced. Transferences, and the constructs which they employ, are then both means and obstacles in the therapeutic process.

Sometimes the therapist feels the client is acting in an unfriendly manner. This may be called "negative transference," but the term is not particularly meaningful psychologically. It may mean one of several things. It may mean that the therapist feels threatened by the client. This can be explained by either of Landfield's hypotheses — the expectancy hypothesis or the exemplification hypothesis — as described in Volume One. Again, it may mean that the client is employing devices which ensue from his perception of the therapist as one from whom the necessities of life must be wrung by force. Finally, the behavior of the client may indicate that he now sees the therapeutic situation as one in which the "negative" construct can safely be brought to light. The therapist has been successful in producing a laboratory situation which enables the client to invoke such a construct. At last the client brings his delinquent construct into the laboratory, alive and kicking, for a preliminary test. Here is what the therapist may have been looking for. This is it — in the flesh. The client does not merely talk about the construct in terms of some polite superordinate construction; he actually perceives in terms of the construct and he acts out its implications. Indeed, he may not be able to haul it into the laboratory in any other way, for its word handles may be loose. The symbolization may be expressible only in terms of verbal acts and not in terms of name words.

Whatever the source of the client's unfriendly behavior, the therapist must frequently face it in the conference room if he is to deal with all of the client's constructs which have a bearing upon the client's life adjustments. He should be no more disturbed by it than he is by any "emotional" behavior. As Raimy is fond of pointing out to his student clinicians, emotion is to the psychologist what blood is to the surgeon. Because unfriendly behavior is, for some clients, incompatible with a continuing personal relationship, the therapist may find that the expression of constructions involving unfriendliness comes quite late in the therapeutic sequence. Because these constructions are explored last, they may be followed by marked improvement. This is not to say, as psychotherapists frequently claim, that "negative transference always precedes improvement." It does in certain clients, but by no means does it in all.

b. *Transference and constellatory constructs.* One of the features that makes transferences difficult to handle is their tendency to be based upon heavily constelled constructs. (Constellated constructs are those which tend to define the realm memberships of their elements.) Another way of putting this is to say that, because of his client's transference, the therapist soon finds himself cast into the form of a highly elaborated and vastly prejudicial stereotype. Once the therapist is seen as a "father figure," for example, he, as an element in the construct, finds that his realm membership with respect to a great number of other constructs has become fixed. The fact that he is "a father" makes him a lot of other things that he does not bargain for. The more he invites the client to act toward him as he would toward a father, the more he puts himself in the way of being construed in this constellatory manner. The more confidence he accepts, the more he gets treated according to the stereotype.

Here is a point from which "just a good friend" counselors may take an important warning. To accept confidences is to invite a heavily constellated set of transferences from one's confidant. Having accepted them, the would-be good friend finds himself cast in an inflexible part, against which the confidant acts out a primitive role. The confidant may learn nothing new about his own mode of perception, the "good friend" loses patience and seeks to escape, and the confidant chalks up another rejection in a cruel world. As we have suggested before, a good rule is not to accept confidences from anyone unless one is prepared also to accept both the stereotyping which will ensue and the complicated responsibilities involved in finding a solution.

The kind of construction one employs in making a transference depends upon the apparent needs of the situation. One does not ordinarily have to pull a very elaborate construction out of his repertory to deal with a street-car conductor or a postman. Our business relations with such persons are ordinarily quite simple. But if one is to have a street-car conductor or a postman as a personal friend, he will have to pull a much more elaborate templet out of his hat.

c. *The Bieri-Lundy effect.* What happens when a person is confronted with the task of construing another person in a rich and meaningful way? Bieri and Lundy have provided us with the beginnings of some experimental evidence on the subject. Bieri had a group of university students interview each other in pairs. He hypothesized that, after a brief period of interaction, each person would construe the other as being more like himself than he had at the beginning of the period. He was able to demonstrate the effect after only twenty minutes of interaction, ten minutes on each of two topics. This convergence may be called the *Bieri effect.* Interpreted within the psychology of personal constructs, it may be said that the person, when first confronted with a stranger, may construe him by means of fairly simple conventional forms. Then, when a much richer source of cues must be employed to keep up a running conversation, the person next turns to the most available elaborated system: his construction of himself.

Lundy, after following the Bieri study through its later stages, hypothesized that the Bieri effect would reach a maximum fairly early in a series of interactions and then would be followed by a reversal of the trend. He predicted that in a group-psychotherapy situation the Bieri effect would reach its maximum after one week (two sessions), and then the perception of others would diverge from the perception of self and reach a maximum after another two weeks. His predictions were confirmed. This phenomenon may be called the *Lundy effect*. Moreover, Lundy's control group, a group practicing typing in the occupational-therapy department of a hospital, showed the Bieri effect, but at a much slower rate. The convergence reached a maximum after three weeks. This, Lundy had not hypothesized, but the outcome fits well into the rationale of the psychology of personal constructs if one takes account of the fact that even typing involves some amount of interaction in the group.

An understanding of the Bieri-Lundy effect throws light upon the way in which transferences may be evoked. We do not yet have evidence as to what is being converged upon in the Lundy phase of the effect. It may be the construction that the person has from some intimate figure of his family — his father or mother. We do not yet know what kinds of intercommunications accelerate the effect or whether, indeed, verbal intercommunication is essential to the production of the effect. This and many other interesting problems arising out of the notion of transference and the theoretical position of the psychology of personal constructs are awaiting experimentation.

11. TRANSFERENCE OF DEPENDENCY

a. *Systematic interpretation of dependency.* From time to time we have noted that constructs are not always verbalized. A person may collect certain elements and respond to them predictively without being able to say what the basis of their similarity appears to be. The construing process may be said to govern all forms of behavior, verbal and nonverbal, "conscious" and "nonconscious." When the notion of the construct is given this broad an interpretation, we can even apply it to those so-called "physiological" processes which are associated with nutrition and physical protection. To be more precise, we may say that we can apply a psychological construct to some of those facts which also lend themselves to physiological interpretation.

Now there are certain constructs which relate both the processes of nutrition and general survival to the lives of persons. For the young child the fact of having food is associated with the fact of having mother. The two are collected by means of a construct.

The child may not have a word for it, but he utilizes the construct. Similarly, the child construes other persons in relation to his survival. The constructs by which certain persons are construed by the child in relation to his own survival we shall call *dependency constructs*.

Dependency constructs collect both persons and a particular kind of event under the same rubric. They are not role constructs, as we have defined role; but they do, in a measure, govern interpersonal relations. They are probably put to use by the child long before he is able to do the subsuming which is an essential feature of role construction. Normally they are greatly modified as one develops the acumen and insight into the reactions of others which make role playing possible. They are not easy to verbalize.

Persons vary in their dependency constructs and in the kinds of dependency transferences they place upon their therapists. The therapist should not expect to find that all clients depend upon him in the same way or make the same demands of him. He may find that one client expects him to furnish quite a different set of "necessities" from those expected by another client.

A child's dependency constructs are relatively impermeable. That is to say, he sees himself as having only one mother who can supply him with food, only one father who can provide shelter, or, at most, only one family upon which he can depend. As he grows older he finds other sources of food and shelter. His dependency constructs tend to become more permeable. He can allow himself to be dependent upon other people too. And he is more and more discriminating in his allocation of dependencies. He depends upon one person for one thing and upon another for another.

Furthermore, as the child grows older his dependency constructs tend to be less preemptive. The construct of mother becomes less of a pigeonhole for the person whom he construes as mother. He slowly comes to place her on other dimensions and to allow her degrees of freedom in his construction system. This is a step toward ceasing to see himself as wholly dependent upon a given person and, instead, seeing the dimensional lines of his dependency extending through others. Then he can begin to depend upon various people in appropriately various ways.

What we have said is that the child starts out with a relatively impermeable and preemptive set of dependency constructs. When he operates under such constructs he puts demands upon those who fall into their contexts. When he becomes older the same demands are considered by his associates to be excessive. He modifies his dependency constructs. He makes them more permeable. That permits him to depend upon persons other than his parents. He makes his dependency constructs less preemptive. That permits him to relate himself to people in other ways. He begins to develop role constructs. That permits him to depend upon the persons who want him to depend upon them, and for the things which they are willing to supply.

b. *The practical assessment of the client's dependency.* When a psychotherapist becomes the target of transferences, he may find that some of them involve dependency constructs. He may find that they are unverbalizable and still in their immature state. That means that his client construes him preemptively, impermeably, and inarticulately. It means that the client responds to him as if his life depended upon it. The response may be cloying or aggressive, compliant or resistive, appealing or demanding, but always it is urgent. In fact, the urgency with which the client appears to construe the therapist is the surest single clinical sign that dependency constructs have been invoked in the transference.

Sometimes psychotherapists invite dependency transferences and then resent what they get. If the therapist takes the stand that "he is the doctor," that "he knows what is best for the client," he leaves himself wide open for being construed as an authoritarian father. He gets scrutinized through a set of constructs that are impermeable, preemptive, unverbalized, and urgent. He may like his status for a time, but he is likely soon to feel that he is not making any progress and that the client is at fault. An interim dependency transference of this type can serve a useful purpose if, through it, the client can be helped to observe it, verbalize it, and test its validity. The client may then be able to work out something better to take care of his dependencies. But if the therapist refuses to grow up along with the client, and continues to insist upon being construed as "the doctor," the client is faced with the alternatives of construing the therapist either as the father to his infantilisms or as a stuffed shirt. Fortunately many clients guess the truth of the latter alternative and get well.

Dependency is not, in itself, an unhealthy state of affairs. Society is based upon a complicated system of interdependencies. The problem, as far as psychology is concerned, is how one's dependencies are conceptualized. Who gets what from whom? Must one's necessities always be wrung from certain other people directly or from "the government," or may one, through cooperative enterprise, extract necessities from the nonpersonal world? Is slavery the only effective form of cooperative society, or may people play cooperative roles in a social process through understanding each other? We believe that dependencies can be handled through adult role relationships which are based on mutual understanding and which generate an ongoing social process. This is the civilized alternative to the sort of infantile dependency which makes people submit to a paternalistic control in order to survive.

12. COUNTER DEPENDENCY TRANSFERENCE

The client is not the only one who goggles. The therapist looks at the client through the transparencies with which he is personally equipped. If the therapist is well trained, he has an adequate repertory of subsuming constructs which permit him to deal with his client in a strictly professional way. If he does not have such a repertory, or if he does not choose to use it, he is thrown back upon other resources for construing his client. The result may be no better than that which has been forthcoming from all of the client's other social contacts — contacts which have thus far failed to be of help.

The therapist who cannot adequately construe his client within a set of professional constructs runs the risk of transferring his own dependencies upon the client. The client is then seen preemptively — that is, as an undifferentiated whole person without multidimensionality or continuity with other persons. He is seen impermeably — that is, as the one and only of his type, or as belonging to a categorically limited group. He is seen by means of a construct or constructs which are unverbalizable for the therapist — that is, by constructs which cannot be formulated into hypotheses and put to test. Finally, he is perceived with an urgency which stems from the fact that the therapist's own dependencies are at stake. Needless to say, the situation is more likely to result in the therapist wanting to marry or adopt the client than it is in the client's being able to improve his own construction system.

We have already mentioned another type of stalemate that may result from the therapist's inability to utilize an adequately subsuming set of professional constructs. This is the stalemate that occurs when the therapist views the client as being like himself. In order to play a role in an ongoing social process — and therapy is such a process — one must, in the language of our Sociality Corollary, have a subsuming construction of those with whom he is conjoined in that process. Commonality is not enough. Commonality, as defined by the Commonality Corollary, is no more than a basis for people's duplicating each other's psychological processes. For the therapist to be able only to duplicate his client's constructions is to participate in a *folie à deux*.

But the failure of the therapist that results from his being unable to rise above commonality in his relationships to his client's constructs is not what we mean by counter dependency transference, although both represent a failure of the subsuming professional construct system. Counter dependency transference is probably much more serious, since it may lead to more than a stalemate: it may lead to complications from which the therapist may not be able to extricate himself. The failure to rise above commonality strikes all therapists from time to time. By being reasonably alert they can detect the difficulty and take measures to overcome it, perhaps by a restudy of the client's case or by staffing it with other therapists. The counter dependency transference is likely to be inaccessible to the therapist, since it is not easily verbalizable and since he may feel that he does have a subsuming approach to the client.

There are those who maintain that the only effective preventive of counter dependency transference is for the therapist himself to undergo a thorough analysis of his own dependencies. If such an analysis makes the therapist more mature in the handling of his dependencies, it probably does contribute to his handling his clients with more respect for their personal systems. Too often, however, what is rationalized as prophylactic self-insight is no more than indoctrination with a rigid construct system which is imposed upon all clients with all the intolerance of a father who persistently, though patiently, sets about "larnin' his kids."

It is important for the therapist to do two things: first, maintain a permeable, nonpreemptive set of professional constructs within which the case is carefully construed; and second, make maximum use of the client's own personal constructs within the subsuming system. The first preventive requires thorough professional training, including the development of an organized and meaningful set of diagnostic constructs. The second preventive requires a point of view similar to the one we have attempted to develop in the psychology of personal constructs. It requires the therapist to look upon his client's views with respect and not as targets for indoctrination. It requires that the therapist help the client to develop his own system with whatever originality the client can muster. The therapist should not allow himself to become an advocate of dogma. He should be a teacher who respects the adventuresome thinking of his students and helps those students formulate their ideas and put them to test. These are the preventive measures against counter dependency transference as one would undertake them under the psychology of personal constructs.

How can a therapist detect counter dependency transference in himself? One of the ways is to note when he finds his thought turning to the client. Does he find himself thinking about his client when his spirits are low? Does he find himself recalling certain fragments of the interview over and over without any attempt to structure the material in terms of professional constructs? Does he find himself responding to the "gifts" the client brings in the form of little compliments or quotations from what the therapist has said in previous interviews? Does he find himself wanting to block the overtures the client makes toward other persons? Does he resent the advice that other persons give his client? Does he find himself wanting to limit sharply the experimentation the client attempts outside the interview room? Is he annoyed by the client's "resistances"? All of these are possible indications that the therapist has allowed himself to become unduly dependent upon his client.

13. PRIMARY AND SECONDARY TRANSFERENCE

Let us turn back to the kind of transference the client places upon the therapist. Ordinarily, the kind of perception the therapist can best utilize is one in which the client applies a varying sequence of constructs from the figures of his past. This we call *secondary transference*, since the therapist is himself merely incidental to the client's perceptions, and the constructions placed upon him by the client are lifted directly from former experiences. The therapist, or a part of his behavior, is collected as another element in the context of each construct. For example, the therapist is seen as "authoritative" like Father, Old John B., Superintendent Savage, Colonel Jenks, and so on. Then he is seen as "passive" like Mother, Aunt Penelope, Sissy Sam, and so on. Next he is seen as "intelligent" like Big Sister Sonya, Professor Tittlebaum, Percy d'Arta, and so on. Each construct that is "tried on for size" is permeable to other figures. Its validation or invalidation has significance for the manner in which the client will approach, not only the therapist, but other persons outside the conference room. The therapist can use the transference as a basis for reorienting the client's constructions of other persons. He can play varying parts and thus enable the client to develop a versatile capacity for role relationships with different kinds of people.

Now what happens when the client construes the therapist preemptively? (A preemptive *construct*, as defined in Volume One, is

one which preempts its elements for membership in its own realm
exclusively — for example: "If this person is a tyrant, he is *nothing but* a tyrant — not a citizen, not a victim, not a fugitive — only
a tyrant.") The therapist becomes "typed" in his part. No longer
can he cast himself in a variety of supporting roles. The play must
always be written and enacted to fit his identity. Therapeutic
movement may appear to take place within the therapy room,
but no really new approaches appear to be tried outside of the
therapy room. What the client learns he generalizes to other behaviors of the therapist but not to other people. The conferences
become intimate, but not meaningful in outside social relationships. The behavior of the client in relation to the therapist tends
to become stabilized. The client's construction of the therapist is
elaborated, perhaps with great spontaneity and originality, but
there is not the day-to-day reversal of stand or the experimentation with wholly new constructions of the therapist's part. The
elaboration takes place in the direction of learning more details
about the therapist and fitting them into place. What the therapist says is taken as context material for constructs of the therapist
as a unique person, not as a part of a context containing outside-of-conference-room elements also. In simpler language, the client
puts together what the therapist has said with what else the therapist has said and not with what other people have said. As new
constructs are formed, the documentation tends to be in terms of
material which has already been mentioned in the therapy room,
as if the client were saying, "Look, see how I am beginning to
understand what *you* mean," but not saying, "Let me tell you
what I have just found out about what *I* mean." The client
"types" the therapist, and his typological approach does not help
him adapt his social role to other persons any more than the
typological approach in social philosophy has led people to adapt
themselves to each other with mutual respect for each other's individuality.

The personal identification which we have been describing may
be called *primary transference*. It stands in contrast to the more
productive type of transference which we have called *secondary
transference*. The therapist becomes a primary figure realm and

the client becomes "attached" to him in a dependent way that offers little opportunity for resolving the relationship. Along with this personal identification one finds that the client is tending to show dependency transferences. The client may "fall in love" with the therapist, not as another figure in a world populated with potential lovers, but as the one person who alone comprises the whole population realm of his dependency constructs. The constructs undoubtedly stem from the past, but they are applied in a relatively unvarying manner and are elaborated in an organized fashion with respect to the therapist's behavior, his presumed interests, his background, and his daily life. The therapist finds that he himself is the latent topic of the interview and that the client is no longer primarily concerned with himself or the other figures of his personal-social milieu. The alert therapist will note that the client is beginning to use the second personal pronoun with increasing frequency, or that he is beginning to use the therapist's name in a personal manner.

Now the therapist may have only himself to blame. He may have confided in the client. He may have cited his own personal experiences in an attempt to bring additional material into the interview room. He may have allowed himself to become a member of the client's social group. He may have entered into business relations with the client or some member of the client's family. He may simply have engaged the client in too many conversations outside the interview room. He may have expressed personal opinions about matters on which the client also had personal opinions. His biography or his recreational behavior may have become known to the client in such detail that he has begun to emerge as a fixed personality in the view of the client. He may simply have responded in unnecessary detail to the client's invitation to furnish information about himself.

All of this may mean that the client is beginning to form an impermeable construction of the therapist. The therapist is about to become a "one and only" person in the client's life rather than a flexible supporting character whom the client can cast in varying parts. The way the therapist is seen appears to be a way which will always remain specific to the therapist, and the types of relationships the client is developing with the therapist may never be tried on anyone else. The therapist is himself the symbol of this emerging impermeable construction.

a. *The client's manipulation of the therapist.* Frequently it is possible to detect the forming of primary transference by the client's seeking to invoke the therapist's counter dependency transferences. Does the client seek to make the therapist dependent upon him? Does the client respond to what he appears to think are the therapist's personal wishes?

There are some therapists who accept this type of construction and seek to utilize it. The writer is quite skeptical of the wisdom of allowing this type of relationship to develop to any great extent. It tends to limit the variety of experiments the client can perform in collaboration with the therapist. It tends to prevent the client from using the lessons learned in the therapy room when he goes outside and faces other persons. What he learns tends to be specific to the therapist and not applicable to others; it is seen as relevant to the therapy room but not outside it. It catches the client up in a dependency transference which he cannot construe adequately, for all the verbalizable elements are bound up in the therapist himself and the dependency cannot be seen as an abstraction from different figures. The moment the therapist attempts to help the client to sit in judgment of what is going on, all of the elements of the primary transference construction are involved. It is difficult enough for the client to sit in judgment of himself when so many of the elements being judged are inherent in the one who is judging. It is even more difficult to sit in judgment when the therapist, who ought to be seen as sitting beside the client in sober judgment also, is himself the sole representative of the type of figure being judged. In addition to all of these handicaps there is the danger that the therapist, because of the pandering nature of primary transference, will become involved in counter dependency transference and the whole therapeutic process will break down.

b. *Generalization in primary transference.* In an earlier chapter we discussed the relationship between the idiographic and nomothetic approaches. We indicated that, while we could agree with the psychological phenomenologists and assign an important place to generalization within the realm of the individual, we were quite sure that some data must be lifted from the realm of the individual and construed nomothetically — that is, in a realm comprising many individuals. One of the essential features of the psychology of personal constructs is that it sees this principle, as well as many others, as being just as applicable to the needs of the client as to the needs of the scientist. The client must eventually be able to make nomothetic constructions. To the extent that his new constructions stop with an idiographic generalization of the therapist, his readjustment stops at the threshold of the therapy-room door.

Primary transference or personal-identification constructs tend to be impermeable to the collection of other persons into the construct context. They thus limit the client's conceptual development as regards his relations with other people. But personal-identification constructs tend to be permeable with respect to additional information regarding the therapist. The realm of the therapist therefore becomes a rich field for spontaneous elaboration and for the pursuing of exciting interests. The client is "simply thrilled" by the therapist. He finds the therapist fascinating and endlessly entertaining. He may even think of his therapist as walking by his side throughout his daily comings and goings. And he may even "talk to the therapist" when he is alone.

Personal-identification constructs tend to have an effect on whatever social-identification constructs the client uses to construe the therapist. The effect is to construe the therapist as the contrast or "unlike" figure in the context. The client has difficulty in seeing anyone as being like the therapist in any way. The therapist's behavior is unique and not seen as being like that of other persons.

c. *The phenomenologically oriented therapist.* Therapists can get themselves into the same fix as regards personal identifications that clients do. The phenomenologically oriented therapist who admits no public or subsuming professional constructs into his system, but who insists that "every client is unique in every way," can get involved with his client in an unproductive series of "lovely personal relationships." He incurs an additional hazard if he makes a counter dependency transference in his effort to construe the client in some meaningful way. Too often the clinician with this type of orientation is wholly dependent upon "me and thee" constructs. He may end up by providing the client with an adjustment that is no more than a "me and thee" adjustment.

14. CONTROL OF TRANSFERENCE

When the therapist accepts a transference of dependency constructs, and then continues with construct loosening or dislodging measures, he may put his client in a helpless position. Because the therapist is utilized as the symbol of an unverbalized stabilizing structure, his continuing presence becomes essential to continuing personal organization. The therapist is supportive in the sense in which we have defined support. More than that, he is supportive, not merely because of any particular thing that he says or does, but simply because he is there. He is the sole symbol of an organizing purpose for which there are, at the moment, no adequate word symbols.

Another way of saying the same thing is to note first that when a client loosens his conceptual structure or starts to replace some of it he becomes, for the time being, somewhat unstable and vulnerable. He vacillates. He resolves his constructs into actions uncertainly and tentatively. He is unsure of himself. He mixes enthusiasm with equivocation. He gives his old constructs "one last try." The organization of his whole system is somewhat shaky.

Now in most cases a client has enough sense not to let the therapist "make him over" too fast. He does not accept "insights" until the superstructure of his personality has been shored up sufficiently to stand the weakening that comes with remodeling. But let us suppose that the therapist allows the client to transfer his dependencies to him. He allows the client to treat him like a parent. He supports the client. He implies that everything may safely "be left in the hands of the doctor." The client makes the investment of his personal securities. Let us remember also that these investments are of preverbal origin. To a large extent they are constructs which were formed before the client was old enough to put verbal handles on them. They have been in use ever since, and there has been no occasion to "put them in writing" or assign to them the ordinary verbal symbols. The physical presence of another person may have been the only symbol they have ever had or ever needed — that is, until the therapist came along. Now this never-before-verbalized dependency system is transferred upon the therapist. The therapist's admonishments and reactions become operating features of the dependency system. More than that, the therapist is now the *symbol* of the dependency system. His very presence means that the dependency investments of the client are being protected.

The client who has invested his dependencies in the therapist is temporarily shored up. God is in his heaven and the therapist is in his swivel chair! Now the client is again invited to loosen his conceptualization — to think and talk in the same way that he dreams. He is asked to test certain long-cherished beliefs in the white light of reality. But now he feels safe. His dependencies are well protected. He starts the ticklish task of renovation. Ah! Now is no time for the therapist to go on a vacation! This is a moment when the client would be greatly embarrassed if he were caught with his constructs down.

The implications of this kind of reasoning, together with the clinical observations which are structured by means of it, are that the therapist must be quite cautious about the kind of transference relationship he establishes with a client, even though some kinds of transference may appear to make the client more cooperative. The therapist should accept only those forms of transference which in the exigencies of the situation appear reasonably safe. He should take into account the possibility that the therapeutic sequence may have some unavoidable breaks in it. He should not ask the client to loosen or tear down more than can be replaced in a reasonable length of time. He should seek always to maximize the client's own external resources as an ultimate protection against collapse during the course of reconstruction. He should keep as alert as possible to the amount and kind of investment the client has entrusted to him. He should note its verbal availability, for that is a key to how completely the client may withdraw his investment when the therapist shows signs of insolvency. He should note the tendency toward personal identification in the client's transference. In short, the therapist should keep as close track as possible of the whole transference situation and should always consider its nature in relation to any possible break in the continuity of his relations with the client. Certainly the nature of the transference situation takes precedence over unpaid bills in determining whether or not the therapist shall hold the next interview. This is nothing short of a basic ethical principle.

a. *Transference cycles.* The client's use of constructions which are transferred upon the therapist appears to go in cycles. The writer is not sure that this observed phenomenon is one which would be clearly deduced from the theoretical position of the psychology of personal constructs. But it is a readily observed phenomenon when one approaches his clients with the point of view this system implies. The client confides in the therapist. In doing so he lays out, for the therapist's examination, certain constructs. He does not always lay out everything, at least not intentionally. During a given cycle of transference it appears that the client elaborates, examines, and tests certain role constructs. He makes use of the therapist — may even be quite dependent upon him for a time. Yet upon the completion of each major reconstruction of a construct area the transferences made upon the therapist appear to become superficial again. Dependencies appear to be reduced as far as the therapist is concerned. The client treats the therapist more as he would another person in his personal-social milieu. We would say that this marks the closing of a *transference cycle.* It also marks the point at which discontinuation of the therapeutic relationship is most feasible.

As the therapist observes the completion of each transference cycle he must consider whether or not he wishes to start another one, and, if so, what kinds of transferences he will invite. Some therapists think of these transference cycles as based on the "depth" of the "clinical material" involved. If the term "depth" has a reasonably precise personal meaning to the therapist, this kind of professional conceptualization may suffice to enable the therapist to keep the situation under control. We prefer to measure this "depth" in terms of the specificity of the words used by the client in expressing his anticipations of what he expects to happen in the therapeutic situation. If he is utterly inarticulate in generalizing what he expects of the therapist, and is able to use words only as remote signals of what he must be expecting of the therapist, the transference cycle may be expected to be relatively long and tortuous. In predicting the length of the transference cycle, however, two other factors should be taken into consideration: the nature of the therapeutic approach the therapist expects to use during the cycle, and the age of the client.

If the therapist tends to use a method of substituting whole new prefabricated constructions, as in fixed-role therapy, rather than "analyzing away" old rickety structures, the cycle may be greatly shortened. This method can be used only if the prefabricated structure is erected, so to speak, side by side with the old structure, and not substituted for the old structure until it has become functional. This side-by-side erection is accomplished in fixed-role therapy by the device of *enactment,* or "play acting" with an artificial identity, and with great care being taken at the outset not to imply that the new structure is eventually to replace the old.

In the case of a child, the transference cycles are more likely to be short, even though they involve constructs which are not wholly expressed by verbal symbols. In the case of an older adult the transference cycles involving constructs at a given level of verbal symbolism are tremendously lengthened. Even the difference between a twenty-year-old and a thirty-year-old client is quite marked.

b. *Termination of the transference cycle.* The beginning clinician is likely to be disturbed by his first experience with a good healthy termination of a transference cycle. The client calls up and asks if the therapist thinks it would be all right if he omitted the next conference and then came the time after that on schedule. The client points out that he has a great deal of work to do and that he would appreciate some rearrangement of the schedule which will give him more time in which to accomplish it. The therapist notes that the work mentioned by the client is work which is relatively new, desirable, and on which some progress has already been made. Again, the client may admit that he "has been so busy that he has not thought much about the last conference." The therapist notes that the activities have indeed been reasonably well organized, although he may also have the feeling that his own curiosity regarding why the client has been behaving the way he has has not been completely satisfied. The client tends to use summarizing statements in the conference. He says things like, "That situation had me all worked up a few weeks ago when I came to see you; but now, well, er, the situation hasn't changed particularly, but it certainly looks different to me now." The client's expressions of urgency seem to be transferred from issues which could not be solved in the form they were once stated to issues which can be solved in the form they are now expressed.

All or any of these clinical signs may, in conjunction with other evidence, be taken as indicating that a transference cycle is coming to an end. The interviews should not be abandoned immediately, however, for the client should have an opportunity to feel that the interviews lasted a little longer than he himself felt the need of them. A good rule of thumb is *either to plan a new cycle or to terminate the series with the second conference after the first clear sign of a transference break.* Obviously, if the break is to be made there should be no probing, loosening, or negative validating during the last three conferences. Ordinarily, also, the last conferences should be double or triple spaced — for example, a week or ten days apart instead of twice a week. The last conference should always be short, preferably not more than fifteen minutes. If it appears that the last conference must be continued for an hour, at least one more terminating appointment should be made. It should always be understood that the client is free to request a further appointment if he wishes. If the transference cycle has been terminated properly, there is much less likelihood of a further appointment being necessary if the therapist leaves the door open in this manner.

Sometimes the therapist must find ways of speeding up the termination of the transference cycle, even though he has allowed himself to become committed to a type of transference cycle which would normally take a very long time to resolve itself. If this is his plan, he will, in the first place, have to abandon his concept-loosening techniques during the therapeutic interviews. These techniques are discussed in greater detail in a later section. The therapist also must ordinarily shift to current material rather than dwell upon the client's childhood memories. He should deal with lower levels of abstraction, local events, social techniques, plans for the week ahead, and so on. He should shift to constructions which involve other people and things rather than those with respect to which the client broadly characterizes himself. He should express himself in more highly structured sentences, should formulate issues in the same language each time they are mentioned, and should let the client's explorations take place outside the therapy room rather than inside. He should not try to be so much a representative of reality himself but should point the client to the outside representations of reality. Negative validation should be avoided as much as possible, though that may be difficult to accomplish. In general, support should be reduced to a minimum; but, perhaps paradoxically, reassurance can be given in limited amounts as long as dependency transferences are not invited thereby. In general, role playing seems to help bring a transference cycle to a close, though the types of roles selected and the problems proposed in the situations have a great deal to do with what the effect will be. Fixed-role therapy appears to be an excellent and safe way of bringing a transference cycle to a close in time to meet a deadline.

c. *Controlling primary transference.* When a therapist finds himself caught up in a personal-identification type of transference, he should take definite and positive measures to resolve it immediately. There are two techniques. The first is for the therapist to assume a rigid, perseverative, and repetitive pattern of behavior. This has the effect of cutting down sharply on the opportunities provided the client for spontaneously elaborating the construction system he has built in the realm of the therapist. Instead of having the thrill of seeing his favorite character in a new story each time he visits the therapist, he finds that he sees only the same movie and listens to the same sound track he experienced the last time. The therapist becomes stereotyped in his formulations and interpretations. He repeats himself regardless of the "gift" of clinical material which the client brings him. He shows no new ability to understand what the client is trying to say, although in this type of situation the client is not ordinarily trying to communicate much.

The second method is not quite so drastic. It involves the use of free roles and counterroles. This technique is described in greater detail in a later chapter. The therapist forces the client to play opposite, not the therapist, but other persons whose parts the therapist enacts. The therapist, in a sense, leaves the room and the client finds himself confronted with other characters lifted from his normal world. There is no chance to elaborate his construction of the therapist as a person; the therapist is not there. Instead, now his mother is there. Next it is his father who enters the room, his teacher, his boss. Always he is forced to depend upon constructs which apply, not to the therapist, but to the people with whom he really needs to work out an adjustment. When the parts are reversed the client is forced to work spontaneously within the most plausible rationale he can muster regarding the person he is portraying, while sitting opposite him is — not the therapist — but a version of himself. This procedure tends to cut off the elements which the personal identification type of transference must feed in order to stay alive.

d. *Conclusion.* We have attempted to delineate the role of the psychotherapist and his basic approaches within the systemic position of the psychology of personal constructs. While we have gone into some detail regarding psychotherapeutic techniques, this chapter has not been intended as a cook book for domestic psychotherapists. When we have described techniques in detail, it has been primarily in order to illustrate what we consider the basic functions of the psychotherapist to be. After all, there is much to be learned about psychotherapeutic techniques; and probably, eventually, much to be unlearned — including, possibly, some of the items we have been asserting with a high level of confidence. Moreover, a further pursuit of the implications of our theoretical position shows promise, we think, of bringing to light a great many more possible and useful techniques. As we stated in our philosophical position which preceded our statement of the Fundamental Postulate in Volume One, one of the important criteria of a good theory is its fertility. Let us hope the psychology of personal constructs will continue to be as fertile in the therapeutic field as the first fruits would suggest.

Chapter Thirteen

The Appraisal of Experiences

⎍⎍⎍⎍⎍⎍⎍⎍⎍⎍⎍⎍⎍⎍⎍⎍⎍⎍⎍⎍⎍⎍⎍⎍⎍

AMONG PSYCHOLOGISTS, and many others, personal experience is commonly regarded as the inexorable determiner of the individual man's destiny. But we view the role of experience quite differently, as we have explained in the preceding volume. In this chapter we will present detailed schedules and outlines for use in eliciting case-history material to be structured in the light of the client's deep-seated personal outlook.

A. Culture and Experience

1. THEORETICAL VIEW OF EXPERIENCE

Clinicians have generally taken either one or the other of two contrasting stands on the matter of appraising the client's experience. Those who see him as the product of those events which have transpired in his lifetime are likely to spend a good deal of time taking his "case history." They may spend even more time trying to figure out whether this or that actually happened, or whether the client just thinks it did. Their write-ups are likely to be long and anecdotal.

The other view is that the only thing that matters is what the client thinks now. The past lives in him only in terms of attitudes, problems, and shortsightedness toward the future. Clinicians who take this stand look at the client's case history only to get a better idea of how he behaves on various occasions, and not to see how circumstances molded him. Some of them do not bother with the experience record at all.

Our view differs from both of these. In part we agree with the latter group that the present is what counts most and we refuse to look upon the client as a lump of matter shaped by the happenings of the past. But we are nevertheless interested in the case history, particularly as the client gives it to us himself. From our theoretical point of view his outlook is important. And what he remembers and how he remembers it tend to reveal that outlook. Even if he gets his facts crossed up, it is revealing to explore the crossed-up perception.

There is a further point. From the standpoint of the psychology of personal constructs one also has some interest in the chronicle of events in the client's life, whether he tells us about them or not. These events are the validational evidence against which he won and lost his wagers, against which he tested his personal constructs. They are the checkpoints he had to use in charting the course of his life. To understand what they actually were is to get some notion of the ranges of convenience of the client's constructs, what the system was designed to deal with, one way or another. Moreover, many of these events will have to be given some stabilizing interpretation in the new construct system produced under therapeutic intervention.

Certain common features of one's social surroundings are often described as his *culture*. It is important that the clinician be aware of cultural variations. Yet, from our theoretical view, we look upon the "influence" of culture in the same way as we look upon other events. The client is not merely the product of his culture, but it has undoubtedly provided him with much evidence of what is "true" and much of the data which his personal construct system has had to keep in systematic order.

All of this has been discussed in greater detail in Volume One of this book. The only reason for mentioning the viewpoint here is that it has a lot to do with the way this chapter, and the one following it, may be read. We shall be talking about detailed case-history outlines and illustrating problems with records of client experiences. It will be easy to forget that we are concerned with such information primarily because *it is validational material for the client.*

2. THE CLIENT'S CULTURE AS HE SEES IT

A Scottish friend of the writer's once twitted him about his American accent, but he was incredulous when it was pointed out that he had an accent of his own. It is much easier to see culture as a factor in the lives of persons having a partially unfamiliar background than it is to see it in our own lives or in the lives of those whom we really know well. Knowing a person well, even though he may have been reared in an alien society, tends to make a cultural interpretation of his behavior seem artificial and mechanistic. This happens among friends, and it is particularly striking to a therapist as he begins to understand his client.

The Role Construct Repertory Test, described in Volume One, may give the clinician a view of how the client's culture looks to others when seen through the client's eyes. Our theoretical view would lead us to be more concerned with this personal view of culture than with an inventory of the folkways which comprise it. Of course, when the culture is viewed uncritically through the client's eyes, it does not look like anything distinct or unusual. Yet when we look at it critically through his eyes, we can see interesting cultural features.

Following is a sample protocol elicited by the Repertory Test. Perhaps it will serve to illustrate what we mean. Because the culture from which this subject came is probably unlike that most familiar to the reader, the cultural features may be conspicuous. They were not, of course, conspicuous as such to the client.

The test was administered to this particular twenty-one-year-old male university agriculture student in the Self-identification Form. It was given in sequential order, a procedure which tends to test the limits of one's repertory.

Overlooking many of the interesting features of this protocol — the constriction, the asymptotic striving, and the situational

TABLE 9. Role Construct Repertory Test Protocol,
Self-Identification

Harold Styller

Sort	Figures	Construct
1	Self (S) Interesting Person (24) Successful Person (23)	S and 23 farmers, 24 lives in town.
2	Self (S) Successful Person (23) Intelligent Person (22)	All three live on a farm. 22 is different in that he runs a fruit farm and is a teacher. S and 23 are interested in dairy farming.
3	Self (S) Intelligent Person (22) Pitied Person (21)	S and 21 are of same age. 22 is older. S and 22 have college education while 21 was resistant to attending high school.
4	Self (S) Pitied Person (21) Rejecting Person (20)	S and 20 have college education, while 21 was reluctant to go to high school.
5	Self (S) Rejecting Person (20) Disliked Companion (19)	S and 19 are interested in farming. 20 is interested in teaching and graduate school.
6	Self (S) Rejected Person (19) Liked Companion (18)	S and 19 want to farm. 18 doesn't.
7	Self (S) Liked Companion (18) Disliked High-school Girl (17)	S and 18 are in college. 17 isn't. S and 18 would feel their own community was higher on the social ladder than 17's community.
8	Self (S) Disliked High-school Girl (17) Disliked High-school Boy (16)	S and 16 took army physical exam together.
9	Self (S) Disliked High-school Boy (16) Liked High-school Girl (15)	S and 15 are in college.

10	Self (S) Liked High-school Girl (15) Liked High-school Boy (14)	S and 15 are single. 14 is married.
11	Self (S) Liked High-school Boy (14) Difficult Neighbor (13)	S and 14 are in college. 13 is a teacher.
12	Self (S) Difficult Neighbor (13) Liked Neighbor (12)	S and 12 are farmers. 13 is a teacher.
13	Self (S) Liked Neighbor (12) Difficult Colleague (11)	S and 12 are farmers. 11 is a city person.
14	Self (S) Difficult Colleague (11) Liked Colleague (10)	S and 10 are in school yet. 11 has graduated.
15	Self (S) Liked Colleague (10) Sister (9)	S and 10 are single. 9 is married.
16	Self (S) Sister (9) Brother (8)	S and 8 are single. 9 is married.
17	Self (S) Brother (8) Father (7)	S and 8 would attack a problem — go right after it — while 7 would debate about it for an indefinite length of time.
18	Self (S) Father (7) Mother (6)	S and 6 wanted to make money work for us. Wanted money for what it was worth. 7 always felt insecure no matter what amount of money was present.
19	Self (S) Mother (6) Liked Boss (5)	5 and 6 are capable of taking hold of a job and bossing it good. They have confidence in themselves and can use someone else's money to run a farm. I don't feel I'm capable of doing it.

20	Self (S) Liked Boss (5) Disliked Boss (4)	S and 5 have college education. 4 does not.
21	Self (S) Disliked Boss (4) Girl Friend (3)	S and 4 talk restaurant business for hours. (Inquiry) 3 and 4 are nimble and quick. I'm a little bit on the slow order.
22	Self (S) Girl Friend (3) Disliked Teacher (2)	S and 2 have college education. 3 does not.
23	Self (S) Disliked Teacher (2) Liked Teacher (1)	1 and 2 are teachers. (Inquiry) That's all.
24	Self (S) Liked Teacher (1) Interesting Person (24)	1 and 24 have a tendency to jump around from one kind of a job to another.

nature of the constructs used — let us look merely at what it implies regarding the cultural controls operating in this subject. Perhaps we can see that it is not so much that the culture has forced conformity upon him as it is that his validational material is cast in terms of the similarities and contrasts offered within and between segments of his culture.

Only on the nineteenth, twenty-third, and twenty-fourth sorts does the subject fail to identify himself with one of the two other figures. This tendency to construe himself as being like other people need not necessarily indicate strong cultural identification, but it certainly sets the stage for it. The twenty-fourth sort is particularly interesting because it suggests a little wistfulness for the kind of escape the "liked teacher" and the "interesting person" seem to be finding. Also bearing out this interpretation are the other two sorts in which the subject places himself outside the emergent construct pole. In the nineteenth sort he expresses a feeling of inadequacy, and in the twenty-first he describes the other two figures as nimble and quick and himself as slow. Are these his momentary efforts to find some new place for himself?

Sixteen of the twenty-four sorts are based on constructs in which farming, teaching, or the amount of one's education is involved. The heavy stress upon socially structured identifications — occupation and education — suggests that his life is held firmly within a construct system manifest to him mainly in terms of the groups to which he sees himself belonging. His use of education in his repertory and his prestige construct on the seventh sort suggest the class-level consciousness that one associates with heavy-handed cultural control within his system.

It may be difficult to follow this notion of culture as a validational system of events. And it may be even more difficult to reconcile with the idea of cultural control what we have said about man not being the victim of his biography. The cultural control we see is one which is within the client's own construct system and it is imposed upon him only in the sense that it limits the kinds of evidence at his disposal. How he handles this evidence is his own affair, and clients manage it in a tremendous variety of ways.

Since cultural control is a matter of construing, we always find it operating, as in the case of the subject in our illustration, in terms of the similarities and contrasts perceived within the person's milieu. He certainly cannot structure his life in terms of a contrast, none of the elements of which are perceived by him. Nor can he structure his life in terms of similarities, without the contrasts necessary to give them differential meaning.

The clinician who fails to understand the operation of cultural controls, as well as the ways of the culture itself, often misjudges his clients' anxieties. The client sees apparently irreconcilable events the clinician overlooks. Sometimes this happens because the clinician, although he is aware of cultural homogeneities, is unaware of their heterogeneities. He assumes that his client goes swimming along in a smooth stream of cultural and neighborhood expectancies. Yet this is rarely true. Perhaps if it were there would be no science of psychology.

3. PROCEDURES FOR IDENTIFYING THE CLIENT'S CULTURE

By identifying the client's distinctive culture groups the clinician can make a quick appraisal of the validational systems operating in the case. One of the most commonly used culture groupings is the socio-economic class — "upper class," "middle class," "lower class," and so on. This is actually based on a particular system of social values, and the thinking which it embodies has attained considerable political significance during the past two centuries. Actually, from the standpoint of the psychology of personal constructs, this classification system has limited value only. The system does throw light upon the tools which people employ in their living: houses, vehicles, wealth, institutional memberships, personal services, and so on; but it throws comparatively little light upon the way the people of the different classes strike off the dimensions along which living can be evaluated. The system does throw light upon the privileges which people believe they enjoy, but it does not indicate the more important psychological fact of what the person considers a privilege to be, independently of whether or not it opens any real doors for him. Finally, it does throw light upon where the person pinpoints himself on certain social construct scales. But again, it does not take adequate account of the fact that the scales themselves are important variables and are not particularly well categorized by the terms "upper class," "lower class," and the like.

Most clinical psychologists try to employ the notion of socio-economic classes to give them some idea of the client's freedom of movement or the resources which might be utilized in bringing about his rehabilitation. To be sure, one's economic status determines what treatment he can afford to purchase, how far he can travel to escape from his neighbors, and the time he can take away from wage earning in order to reorient himself. But again, as we have attempted to point out before, freedom of movement is first of all a matter of one's dimensioning of life; no matter how much he pays for railroad fare, one cannot move along a psychological track which for him does not even exist.

The simplest approaches to the identification of a client's socio-economic class are the following:

a. In urban communities the district in which one's residence is located provides the basis for making the first approximation of one's socio-economic class membership. In most cities these districts have been identified for purposes of psychological study, polling, and market research; and the charts can be employed by the clinical psychologist who wishes to know more about the socio-economic classification of his client.

b. In highly industrialized and commercialized communities, the occupations of the client and members of his family provide some clue as to his socio-economic class identification. In these areas one's rank in the organization in which he is employed is also an identifier of his socio-economic class.

c. In less urban, less industrialized, and less commercialized communities, socio-economic status is more accurately identified by real-estate ownership and freedom from regular working hours.

d. Income, not merely wages, is, when it can be known, one of the most accurate indicators of socio-economic class membership. It becomes a more accurate indicator when the income of relatives, especially those who live in the same community, is also taken into consideration.

e. When a home visit is feasible one may use one of the assessment outlines which have been developed by sociologists. The estimated value of the house, and the nature of its furnishings and accommodations in relation to the number of people who live in it, can be used as bases for assessing socio-economic class membership.

f. A less obtrusive way of identifying socio-economic class membership is through an inventory of the periodical literature which is used in the home.

g. One of the most popular modern ways of identifying socio-economic class membership is by the automobile one drives. The label is frequently misleading, but it has become so commonly accepted that its validity may be increasing as people find it effective to use this means to exhibit their choice of the class with which they wish to be identified.

Instead of spending too much time on identification of socio-economic class membership, however, the clinical psychologist is usually better advised to turn his attention to the ethnic groupings with which the client is identified. This is more likely to give some inkling of the kinds of constructs governing the client's life. The following represent some simple labels of ethnic groupings.

a. *Racial and national extraction.* The recency of immigration of the client or his family, the country of origin, the culture group, if any, represented by the race, and the types of racial or national communities in which the family has lived are all important indicators of the ethnic controls which affect a person's personal constructs. Judgments based on these facts must be tempered by evidence of cultural marginality in the individual client.

b. *Migration routes.* Within this country the migration routes are important indicators of cultural identification. The layman's approach to the identification of the culture from which a new acquaintance comes nearly always includes some inquiry as to where he came from and where his folks came from. The places where relatives live, and the routes taken on vacation trips, also provide some indication of the cultural attachments of a client.

c. *Retirement plans.* The place where a person hopes to go when he retires is sometimes a very meaningful clue as to what cultural identification he wishes to make for himself and the ethnic group in which he feels most comfortable.

d. *Complaint.* A client seeking help of a clinician frequently expresses his cultural identification directly in his complaint. For example, a premedical student who complains that he cannot concentrate is immediately suspected by the clinician of being under parental pressure to achieve the social status of a professional man. A young client who complains that he is losing his religious faith is likely to be expressing a conflict aligning group cultural expectations on one side and recent experiences on the other.

e. *Church membership.* Since religion tends to emphasize extensive controls over persons' lives, church membership may give some indication of the kinds of controls imposed by the culture. It is not easy to determine the effectiveness of the controls and the extent to which the client has used religious group expectations as validators of his own personal constructs.

A clinician should not be misled by the fact that a client appears to reject the cultural controls to which he is heir. Although a person may say, "As a child, I once believed this was bad; I now perceive it as good," he has not necessarily changed the coordinates he uses to plot his course of action. One should not assume that a construct has evaporated or lost its potentiality for control just because a person has shifted some of the elements in its context, or because he has reclassified the construct, as a whole, within his system of good and evil. A person who has rejected his early religious upbringing may still be just as much under restricted paths of thinking as he ever was. A revolt which fails to strike off new dimensions or create new contrasts, whether it be a revolt of an individual or of a nation, provides no new freedoms and leaves man following the old ways of life under new labels merely and in subservience to new masters with new names. To understand this point is to understand the *why* of the theory of the psychology of personal constructs within a philosophical system of social values.

4. CULTURE-DEFINING PROCEDURES

Frequently the clinician finds it most profitable of all to make some direct assessment of the cultural-experimental determinants of personal constructs. This usually has to be done on a concrete level, since it is practically impossible for a person to describe his own culture as a culture. It is like trying to express a construct within a context in which there are no contrasting elements. One cannot form a construct out of likenesses only, nor out of differences only. The person who has lived always under one type of cultural control will find it most difficult to express that control as a special construct. Not only do the words fail him but the similarity and contrast which are basic to conceptualization simply do not emerge in his thinking.

There are fifteen lines of concrete inquiry which can be used to obtain definition of a client's cultural-experiential background.

a. *The client's descriptions of other people.* The Rep Test provides some indication of how the client reflects group expectations upon the human figures in his environment. As he describes other people in more informal ways he also reveals how he and his peers expect members of his own cultural group to behave.

b. *The client's description of strangers.* Some notion of cultural controls and expectations can be obtained by eliciting from the client descriptions of people whom he identifies as strangers. In a sense this is a way of getting the client to describe his culture by saying what it is not. The descriptions of the strangers should not, of course, be taken as useful or accurate delineations of their characters; they are useful only to the extent that they throw light upon the client's perception of his own culture.

c. *The client's descriptions of ne'er-do-wells.* Within every culture there are grounds upon which people are rejected from the group when their behavior becomes unacceptable. The ways in which people lose caste or "jump" the culture are interesting and useful clues to the real nature of the cultural controls which operate in an ethnic group. While some clients find it difficult even to speak of such outcasts, it is possible in most cases to get illuminating descriptions of such persons.

d. *The client's description of "peculiar" people.* Some forms of the Rep Test make use of a figure entitled, "A person with whom you have worked who was hard to understand." The handling of this figure tends to test the limits of the subject's construct system. A similar testing of the limits of the person's culturally determined construct system can be accomplished less formally in an interview situation. If the "peculiar" person is similarly seen by the client and the client's neighbors, the clinician may infer that the constructs offered by the client are characteristic of the ethnic group.

e. *The client's descriptions of "bad company."* The notion of what is bad company is characteristically of ethnic origin. Since the descriptions of bad company tend to include many negative statements, the contrasting affirmative statements tend to be descriptive of the ethnic expectations. Of course, the clinician has to ask for concrete illustrations of what the "bad company" does and what it does not do.

f. *The client's definitions of career or life-role success.* Again, the illustrations are effective if they are couched in terms of named people and descriptions of actual accomplishments. The historical hero figures of a culture, while probably distorted to fit the cultural expectations, throw a great deal of light upon ethnic controls.

g. *What the client cites as evidence of prowess.* Fighting, for example, is characteristically cited as evidence of prowess in some ethnic groups, while in others it may be taken as evidence of outcast behavior.

h. *Frustration and anger reactions.* The client's descriptions of what people characteristically do when they are disappointed or angry may throw some light upon ethnic expectations. Does the disappointed person get drunk, write a poem, beat up his wife, plunge himself into his work, or join the Foreign Legion?

i. *How quarrels are patched up.* Here the role of the family and the types of concessions which are considered to be ethnically acceptable throw some light upon the freedom of readjustment permitted by the group. Face saving is very much an ethnic affair.

j. *Mating behavior.* The client's descriptions of courtship activities and conjugal patterns of behavior may help the clinician understand some of the important ethnic constructs which may underlie personal conflicts.

k. *Humor.* Jokes tend to reflect the trend of the times more than the stable characteristics of a culture. Nevertheless, the joke may indicate what elements of a system of cultural control are under reconsideration. If we consider the joke, under the psychology of personal constructs, to be an unexpected but neat reconstruction of an event, the joke which is popular at the moment may indicate rather clearly what element of social control is open to reevaluation.

l. *Folklore.* One of the standard approaches to understanding what ethnic controls are like is the study of folklore. Stories, particularly those which are stabilized and defined by retelling by different people in the same way, tend to embody the beliefs, aspirations, and controls of a culture group. The stories told the client in his childhood by his parents or the stories which he remembers having been told and retold in his community will throw useful light upon the cultural controls which operate upon him. In American culture the "western" movie or "horse opera" is highly expressive of our beliefs, aspirations, and controls.

m. *Topics of group conversation.* The client may reveal those constructs which come to him by virtue of his ethnic identification by describing the topics of conversation which have appeared in the groups to which he belongs. The Personal Role Form of the Rep Test uses this approach, when the subject is asked what a certain group of figures would do and what they would probably talk about.

n. *Other group activities.* The clinician should be alert to group activities of various other sorts not mentioned above. They may throw additional light on the client's culture.

o. *Personal conflicts expressed by the client.* Many of the conflicting problems described by a client, especially an adolescent who is meeting new cultural expectations, patently reveal the nature of the culture system in which he has been reared.

From the standpoint of the psychology of personal constructs it is important to keep in mind that the study of the client's culture is a study of the validators against which he must have tested his repertory of personal constructs, or which are potentially available to him for testing new constructs along the way. The purpose of the inventory is this — and simply this!

Just as we have insisted that man is not necessarily the victim of his biography, we would also insist that man is not necessarily the victim of his culture. Having taken this view we, as clinicians, approach the client's culture in a somewhat novel way. We do not stop merely with labeling, nor even with a descriptive study of each client's culture. Rather, we continue on to discover what has emerged in the client's construct system in conjunction with those cultural validators which have been gratuitously available to him.

B. Personal Experience

5. THE ANALYSIS OF A PERSON'S COMMUNITY BACKGROUND

The foregoing paragraphs have suggested ways of assessing cultural factors in relation to personal constructs. We suggested lines of inquiry designed to form a basis for such assessment. Frequently, however, the assessment of cultural influence cannot be made so directly. The clinician must approach that topic through the analysis of his client's community experiences. He must first employ a description of the community at a popular level of abstraction. He must then seek information in terms which his informant finds compatible regarding the client's relationship to the community. The more psychological and sociological levels of description have to be attempted later, after the facts are in.

There are six lines of inquiry the clinician can follow in eliciting information regarding his client's community. The same lines of inquiry can be used to make a supplemental inquiry regarding the client's particular neighborhood in the community. If the client has moved about, it is important to bring out the similarities and contrasts in the various communities in which he has lived, since these are the elements out of which he has had to form important social constructs.

a. *Description of the population.* The size of the population of the community, particularly the trading area, is usually the first point covered. The racial and ethnological composition of the population comes next, followed by such descriptions of the community and neighborhood groupings as the informant is able to provide.

b. *Description of community economics.* The industrial and commercial basis of community life should be described. If the population is principally composed of wage earners, the employing agencies should be described. For example, one should be particularly careful to describe the specific characteristics of an employing agency when it employs a large proportion of the community's wage earners. The company policies in such an instance will represent a peculiar and probably unfamiliar pattern of cultural influence. The conditions of unemployment and longevity of employment should be considered. Attention should be given to the problem of retirement in the community, for it affects the pattern of emotional stability in the homes and the crowding of households with aged parents and relatives. Seasonal and unstable features of the community economics should be noted.

c. *Transitions in the community.* If one is to understand the effectiveness of cultural control in the community he must be aware of the transitions which are taking place. A community in transition, or a migratory social group, poses particularly difficult problems of social-construct formation, particularly for its children. Transitions, such as a sudden influx of added popula‑ tion, are usually accompanied by conflict and controversy, irritants both for children and adults, which may throw the residents back upon simpler and more primitive social constructs in their dealings with each other.

d. *Religious organizations and mores.* Religious sects and denominations frequently represent the characteristic cultural controls which operate in the construct systems of a group of people. As we have indicated before, the cultural control represented by a religious group is not limited to its formal membership. A rebel may be as much influenced by the construct system within which he seeks to exhibit contrasting behavior as is the conventional person who abides by the approved similarities which his construct system identifies for him. The store-front mission and bar next door to it do not necessarily represent sharply contrasting construct systems; more likely they represent merely reidentifications of a few elements of similarity and contrast within commonly accepted construct systems. Therefore, the clinician who seeks to understand cultural controls may often find out as much about the construct systems of "nonchurch" people when he studies the religious mores of the local church as he does about the construct systems of the "church" people. One does not necessarily change his construct system significantly when he joins or rebels against an organization.

Some religious groups impose extensive taboos upon the behavior of their members — abstention from eating of certain kinds of food, the restriction of Sabbath activities, prescription of everyday dress, limitation of recreation, self-abnegation, church contribution and attendance, manner of speech, taboos against birth control, and refusal to use medication, to mention only a few. These taboos are important in understanding the personal construct systems of persons who live in communities where they are extensively observed, not only because of the restrictions they tend to place upon specific forms of behavior, but also because of the difficulties they may interpose in the establishment of role relationships. Moreover, it is a serious mistake to consider all religious taboos as strictly "spiritual"; many of them are as thoroughly "materialistic" as anything one can imagine. Some of them throw a major emphasis upon organizational control and the authority of officials. All of them throw light upon the patterns of guilt and anxiety feelings that a resident in the community may fall heir to.

e. *Schools and educational patterns.* Communities differ considerably in the proportion of public income they are willing to use in the support of the public schools. The states differ, of course, in the relative amount of support that schools receive from local and state taxation. States and communities vary greatly with respect to the proportion of children in their populations. The educational traditions and group expectancies differ tremendously from community to community. The proportion of young people who go to college in a small city where ample college facilities are located is likely to be several times the proportion going away to attend college from remote communities whose residents are relatively immobile.

The salaries paid teachers provide a more certain indication of the community's educational convictions than the amount invested in school plants. The educational level and tenure of teachers is also an important variable in the evaluation of educational tradition in a community. It is usually quite easy to check up on the number of teachers who have been able to make a life career out of teaching in the local school. The use of private and parochial schools in the community should also be checked. The extensive use of private schools is likely to be associated with high barriers between social classes and with many personal anxieties about one's socio-economic class membership.

A more detailed discussion of procedure for evaluating the influence of the school appears in a later section.

f. *Recreational resources.* The clinical psychologist needs to make a quick survey of the recreational resources of the communities from which his clients come. Public resources, such as parks, playgrounds, swimming pools, zoos, public gardens, etc., can easily be checked. Organizations and recreational programs, not always implicit in physical facilities, require more careful checking. The activity of youth organizations should be studied: Scouts, YWCA, the extracurricular recreational program of the schools, church youth groups, settlement-house programs, summer camps, summer and winter playground programs, sports training, clubs, etc. The adult recreational pattern should also be studied: women's organizations, lodge and labor-union programs, church activities, adult educational activities, bowling and baseball leagues, dance spots, skating rinks, taverns, sporting clubs, etc. One approach is to make a list of the recreational activities in the community which are feasible for a given client at a given time. Such an approach is frequently revealing. It may indicate that, although there are many activities going on in the community, there is none suitable for a given retired man at the hours or within the distances which would be convenient for him. It may indicate that there is no program suitable for an adolescent girl whose parents work in the evening, and so on.

6. OUTLINE FOR A BRIEF PSYCHOLOGICAL APPRAISAL OF A SCHOOL

It is possible in an hour or two of time for a clinical psychologist to make an appraisal of a school situation which will be of considerable help to him in dealing with any of the children who experience that situation. Of course, an exhaustive survey of the school would probably require more time and training than he is likely to have. If the school is visited during school hours, the psychologist should arrange his appointments with the principal and two or three teachers in advance. One or two classrooms and the playground can be visited for fifteen-minute intervals, and the principal and teachers can be interviewed for fifteen minutes each. Since the information he obtains will presumably be used in connection with his work in individual cases, it is not necessary for him to attempt to determine the extent to which the school is "good" or "bad"; but rather he should get some notion of what it would be like to attend it, what cultural validations of personal constructs the school appears to provide, and what readjustive resources may be mobilized in the treatment of the child.

a. *Playground and building.* By the time he reaches the doorway, the psychologist may have had an opportunity to observe what traffic-safety provisions have been made, such as the use of the schoolboy patrol, the presence of a police officer, and the type of traffic-light protection provided in the area. If school buses are used, he may get some idea of their state of repair and the type of driver employed. All of these reflect the community's concern for the children's safety, and possibly its general concern for the children as persons.

Playground activity can be observed before school "takes up." With a little experience a psychologist will become aware of marked differences between playgrounds. Equipment, segregation of boys and girls, crowding which makes it impossible for one group to play a game without interfering with the activity of another group, supervision and the manner in which it is exercised, evidence of taunting, appearance of organized or constructive play, number of isolated individual children or isolated pairs, behavior around the drinking fountain and toilets — all can be observed in a very few minutes. Snatches of conversation can be noted and classified. Easily noted is the balance of derogatory as against supportive remarks such as, "That's all right," "Okay," "I'll fix it," "Come along, Bill," etc.

b. *The classroom.* The bulletin board may be observed, since it gives some idea of the activities which are functioning as contrasted with those which are merely "on the books." In the classroom of an elementary school the displays give some idea, not only of the quality and variety of work which is accomplished in the room, but, more importantly, of the degree to which the spontaneity and originality of the individual child is accepted, and the proportion of children in the room whose work receives this type of recognition. With a little experience one can develop a "nose" for pupil-initiated-and-developed projects versus adult hobbies. One should also make note of the remarks and notations which the teacher has placed on individual pieces of work: they give some idea of the kind of relationship she establishes with her pupils. The variety of materials used — art paper, paints, stickers, colored pins, cloth, wood, electrical wire, tools, and so on — gives some idea of the resources which are placed at the disposal of the children for carrying out creative work. The relative emphasis upon verbal and artistic forms of expression may be noted. The psychologist should observe whether or not projects appear to be in progress. Sometimes a classroom exhibit is no more than "window dressing," rather than a display designed to enable children to study and appraise their own individual and group accomplishments.

Excessively large classes are the bane of nearly every teacher's professional life. Unless a psychologist appreciates this problem his interprofessional relations with teachers are likely to be strained; indeed, probably more misunderstandings between psychologists and teachers develop around this one point than around all the combined systematic differences in the two disciplines. In considering a teacher's ability to individualize her work with pupils there are three closely interlocking factors which must be considered, in addition to her understanding of children: the size of the class, her familiarity with the curriculum of the grade or grades she must teach, and the teaching resources and materials immediately available for her use.

The writer was once much impressed by a rare demonstration of the use of teaching resources in the Glasgow [Scotland] Provincial Training College. A teacher was successfully handling some sixty elementary-school pupils at about four different grade levels, *with individual syllabi for each pupil!* She was, of course, thoroughly familiar with her teaching resources and she had a great many of them at her finger tips. In fact, if the writer recalls correctly, there were two walls covered with shelving on which were all kinds of teaching materials, outlines, explanations, illustrations, equipment, exercises, source materials, and so on.

A psychologist visiting a classroom can quickly appraise two of the important interlocking factors in the individualization of instruction by noting the number of children in the room and the variety of teaching materials available. For the most part, the teaching materials which are actually used will be dog-eared, stacked within reach of the children, and not covered with dust. In a fairly large class, the number of library or source books lying out on desks or work tables with the appearance of having been used recently gives a fairly good indication of the usage of such materials.

The furnishing of a room gives some idea of the kind and variety of activities which can be successfully carried out. A room which is versatile will have movable furniture, tables, work benches, racks, bookcases, and the like. Visual aids, including projectors, charts, models, displays, diagrams, and so on are not hard to locate. The lighting may be poor; it usually is. A simple test is to attempt to read the second hand on one's watch in the darkest corner of the room. Reading distances may be bad. Children tend to be nearsighted as compared with adults. The observer, while taking account of this fact, may attempt to read the blackboard and charts which the pupil is expected to read from the back of the room. Reflections which interfere with reading the blackboard can be checked. When entering the room the observer can simply check reflections on the blackboard, usually from the right front seat position. In rooms where the light fixtures are hung low both the reflections and glare seriously interfere with vision.

c. *Classroom behavior.* Classes vary widely in their reaction to the presence of a visitor. In fact, one can get some fairly accurate notion of the frequency with which a class has been visited by its reaction to the observer. When both children and teacher show signs of self-consciousness it is probably an indication of a lack of constructive parental interest and participation in the program of the school. The spontaneous friendliness of the children, as contrasted with formalized "politeness," gives some idea of the classroom-centered morale of the group.

The responsiveness of the children to the teacher's suggestions and to each other's suggestions can be noted. If they are responsive to the teacher, and not to each other, one may suspect that cooperativeness has not become a generalized pattern of behavior. If they are responsive to each other but yield only grudgingly to the teacher, one suspects that the social organization of the class excludes the teacher, and perhaps all adults and people who are dissimilar to themselves. Conversations between pupils throw light upon the social climate of the group.

If there are evidences of defensiveness or bullying in the verbal exchanges, one may interpret the findings as throwing light upon the social expectancies against which a child in the room must seek to defend his integrity as an individual.

Voice modulation is, to some extent, a measure of the freedom of movement open to a member of a group. High pitches or pitches rising with the passing of time or with the discussion of a topic indicate that the freedom of movement is seen as a function of one's aggressive efforts. Modulation should show some response to the topic of interest; a perfectly uniform or flat pattern of modulation indicates a feeling of being restrained and perhaps a feeling of submissiveness. It is not too hard to distinguish a modulation pattern which varies from sentence to sentence or from topic to topic from one which appears to be a function of the social situation and rises steadily with the passage of time or the presence of other people.

Tension and relaxation in the classroom can be noted. Children show their tensions in different ways. Absence of movement is not necessarily an indication of relaxation, especially in a harshly disciplined social situation. Again, just as one looked for modulation in the voice or in the appropriate rising and falling of pitch in relation to content, one can look for the appropriateness of the motor behavior, in general, as evidence of relaxation. If a child's motor behavior tends to be wooden — that is, each member moves independently of the movements of other members — even though he is active, one suspects an interfering state of tension. If his motor behavior shows coordination throughout, even in shifting his position in his seat, there is reason for believing he is relaxed. Frequently tension will be revealed by "explosive movements." These are jerky, sometimes almost choreiform, movements that can be observed in some children when they are tense and overstimulated. For example, a sudden movement of the leg which appears to be almost involuntary, or a lateral movement of an arm which appears to be unrelated to the readjustment of posture or to the performance of the task at hand, may be considered explosive.

So-called mannerisms may be noted. Nose picking, twitching,

hair twisting, scratching, grimacing, face rubbing, nail biting, sucking, rocking, tapping, lip licking, blinking, scowling, pushing a pencil along the cracks in a desk, pencil chewing, excessive use of erasers, rolling a pencil or other object between the fingers, paper tearing, scratching nail polish from nails, grunting, momentary breath holding during the performance of a task are all signs suggesting that the appetitive strivings of the child are partially unsuccessful. Under rigid disciplinary control they may disappear, though clinical experience with children seems to indicate that when the child is not in the presence of the disciplining agent they reappear to a marked degree.

Evidences of the effectiveness of cooperative efforts in the classroom may be noted. Children working together with some indication of spontaneous cooperation can be observed. One should note also whether this cooperation is under the heavy hand of personal leadership or whether it appears to involve the enactment of cooperative roles based upon mutual understanding of each other, whether it rests on implicitly understood or explicitly stated objectives and methods. The cooperative formulation of objectives can sometimes be noted, although that is not easy to discover during a brief visit. The pursuit of an adult's objectives rather than children's objectives can frequently be detected in the joint efforts of a group.

One should look for initiative and independence within the cooperative pattern of the group. The immediacy with which a child undertakes a task of his own choosing, his spontaneity in solving a problem by his own method rather than by the stylized method of his teacher, the tendency for appropriate action to follow immediately upon the idea or the verbal expression, are all signs of initiative, though they may also be accompanied with explosiveness. The extensive seeking of "permission" to do simple things like sharpening a pencil, speaking to another pupil, or leaving the room to go to the toilet or to get a drink, or hesitancy in starting a job or in performing simple acts, or circumlocutions in speech are indications of the extent to which initiative has been subordinated to regularity in group behavior. Initiative can also be revealed by signs of independent study on the part of the children. Children using source materials, teaching aids, special equipment, and so on without being directed to do so, indicate that they have taken some initiative in accomplishing the learning tasks of the class, and have probably relieved the teacher of a good many chores in that connection.

d. *Interviewing the teacher.* The interview with the teacher should be designed to enable her to indicate the nature of her own construct system, especially as it relates to the expectancies which it subtly imposes upon the children who must adjust themselves to her social presence. The teacher may be asked to describe the problems she faces and some of the children she has in her room. From the way in which she sets up the coordinates one can come to understand what her pupils must try to incorporate into their experience. Along what kinds of continua does she plot them? Does she see children as ambitious or lazy, gentle or cruel, quiet or noisy, cooperative or stubborn? If so, these are the lines of freedom of movement along which her construct system permits her pupils to move themselves back and forth as they seek to adjust to her expectations. It is less important that she see her children as predominantly ambitious or as predominantly lazy than it is that she has plotted her children with respect to this type of construct as a whole.

Again we emphasize this theme in the psychology of personal constructs! A child put under pressure will try to move along the constructive lines which are clear to him, though he may not move in the direction the teacher wants him to. The psychologist should listen carefully to the constructs the teacher uses and consider what directionalities they provide for the adjustment efforts of the children under her supervision.

From a careful interview with a teacher one may determine the kinds of problems with which she feels unable to cope. In general, these are expressed as descriptions of children's behavior at a relatively concrete level, without apparent ability to relate these concrete behaviors to more comprehensive constructs. The teacher who cannot see certain concrete behavior as fitting into a larger scheme or pattern, or who can fit it only into a construct which provides her with no latitude of behavior for herself, is having real psychological difficulty. The psychologist should listen carefully to see what kinds of behavior and what children are described by the teacher at a concretistic level only. Sometimes this type of description is called "objective," but objective descriptions which are not subjected to construction cannot be dealt with adequately. This is conspicuously true of the teacher, though it is a fundamental point in all human relations. The constructive interpretation of children's behavior, especially when that behavior is seen as emanating from their own constructs, is much the soundest basis for a productive role relationship between a teacher and her children.

Sometimes a psychologist can discover whether or not a teacher has established for herself a basis for a role relationship by asking her directly how she thinks certain children feel and what their outlook is. If she can anticipate what a child would say in a certain situation and how he would relate his response to other facets of his outlook, she may have a basis for relating herself to him by construing him in a manner which will help him to readjust, even though she does not describe him in flattering terms.

The use of punishment may usually be taken as evidence of a breakdown in role relationships. If the psychologist can discover the teacher's reasons for punishing, and what is the mode of punishment, he may gain some notion of the points at which a teacher's construct system fails to provide her with a structural approach to her relationships with children. It is not particularly helpful to condemn a teacher for using punishment; that smacks of punishment itself. It is probably expecting too much to anticipate that all teachers will avoid punishment or punishment equivalents in dealing with situations which they cannot understand. In fact, the teacher who claims that she never uses punishment has probably developed an intricate system of punishment equivalents, such as social rejections, personal deprecations, sarcasms, or painful guilt-evoking mechanisms, which may be just as cruel and destructive of self-respect as those measures which are literally defined as "punishment."

e. *The teacher's orientation toward records.* One particularly important approach to a teacher's construct system is through her understanding of psychological test results. Some teachers reject or ignore altogether psychological test results as being irrelevant to the construct systems which they use in their professional relationships with pupils. Others look upon tests as indicating what their own level of responsibility is: if a child is stupid they should not be held responsible for accomplishing anything with him, if he is intelligent they are guilty if they fail to make him act as an intelligent person is supposed to act.

A very common view among teachers, but one causing all kinds of unnecessary misery, is that the purpose of a test is merely to point an official finger at the child's faults. They pounce upon any low score with great delight, as if it were a blackhead or a pimple, and refuse to let the child budge until his fault has been "remediated." High test scores are ignored, and yet these may point to the very resources a more perceptive teacher would mobilize to achieve the same end.

Then there are the teachers who take test results quite literalistically. In this they share the attitudes of some psychologists, for whom the virtues of objectivity can be attained only through literalism. The psychologist should come to know the extent to which a teacher is aware of the kinds of test variation that can be explained by cultural handicap, her awareness of the possible inadequate clinical training of the examiner, her appreciation of the type of test given, her appraisal of the circumstances of testing, and her awareness of the interval between testing. All these are indications of her versatility in dealing with her pupils.

School personnel records vary widely in their usage. The way to check to see what bearing they have upon the lives of pupils is to ask the classroom teacher what the personnel record shows regarding certain children in her room. No matter how good the record system is it cannot have much bearing upon the everyday life of children unless the important facts it records are known to their teachers. Some teachers and administrators take the view that personnel records should not be made available to teachers on the grounds that each child can thus start with a clean slate when he faces a new teacher. There is merit to this point of view, particularly if teachers tend to evaluate their children primarily in terms of "good" and "bad." However, the teacher who can restructure material — in other words, can exercise judgment — will come to understand a child better the more she knows about him.

One of the most important checks on a teacher's orientation toward her work with a given child is to ask her when she thinks the child will leave school and just what she thinks the school can best accomplish for that child during the specific number of months which appear to remain to it. Sometimes teachers are shocked to discover how fast time is running out and sometimes they are able to say very little about what is the functional relationship between what they are seeking to accomplish for the child now and what they believe he will be doing five years from now. A teacher's ability to project a child's life role into the future is an important measure of her own role relationship to him.

The psychologist can ask to see samples of reports given to parents. From such reports he can judge the effectiveness of the communication that the teacher attempts to establish with parents. He can also judge what kind of material the teacher considers relevant to the evaluation of a child's progress in school. Sometimes teachers' reports to parents are in the nature of complaints. Sometimes they point out specific approaches which the parents might attempt in dealing with the child's problems. All too frequently they are intended to placate the parents and make them less of a problem for the teacher. One common technique in a series of reports during a school year is to make the first report highly critical, then to report progress, and finally, at the end of the school year, to report glowing success. This may be a status-maintaining effort on the part of the teacher.

Some teachers make home visits during the early part of the year. Their reports of such home visits throw some light upon their construction of the problems they face in dealing with the child as a member of a particular household.

A teacher will frequently volunteer descriptions of the ways in which she deals with particular problems. A brief description of the kinds of remedial procedures she finds useful for children with certain subject-matter deficiencies, and the measures she uses for sight-saving or hard-of-hearing adjustments, throws light upon her versatility and flexibility. A good opening question is, "Do you know whether or not there is any child in your room who is hard of hearing?" In general, a teacher who can sharply contrast the individual needs of certain children in her room can take the group problems in her stride.

f. *The principal's outlook.* In the interview with the principal, the curriculum and the schedule of school activities are good starting points. Course offerings, including those of vocational and recreational significance, together with the functions the courses particularly serve in the local school community, can be discussed with regard to their local function. It is always important to check to see what proportion of children is affected by each type of extracurricular activity. The proportion of pupils participating in athletics, dramatics, clubs, and musical activities is often distressingly small, though the number of activities in which certain children are involved may be excessively large. The formal schedule of activities should be checked against the actual schedule of activities. A formal schedule which has lapsed into disuse is a sign of declining morale.

The administrator's awareness of sororities, fraternities, and social cliques among students and teachers can be tapped. These limited groupings may, in a small school, diminish the effectiveness of the program as a whole. In a large school, where the social grouping is too unwieldy otherwise, the presence of formalized subgroupings may be a necessary condition for the establishment of adequate social relationships. The nature of the whole subgroup arrangement in a school is an important topic for psychological evaluation.

The relation between marks and privilege is a worthwhile topic. Sometimes children are allowed to take industrial-arts courses or to participate in athletics only if they achieve certain marks in their "academic" work. Such a system may defeat the most worthwhile purposes of industrial arts and athletics and create such a superficial and legalistic attitude toward "academic" work that the whole system suffers. A child's misadaptation to academic work may be the most urgent reason for making industrial-arts training available to him, and the difficulties which keep him off "the team" may be the very ones which cry loudest for team identification.

Special programs undertaken by the school can be investigated briefly. What does the school do about crippled children in the community who cannot get to school? What is done about children with rheumatic fever who must stay out of school for months at a time? What is done about mentally retarded children? Under what conditions is a young child assigned to a room for individualized instruction? What is the nature of that instruction? What kind of teacher is given the job of teaching there, and what, for the child, is the usual outcome of such an assignment?

One check that speaks volumes for a principal's orientation toward the pupils in her school is her knowledge of what has happened to the children who have left the school during the preceding year, either by graduation or by dropping out. The age at which children customarily leave school in relation to the maximum age of compulsory attendance is an important fact to know, both from the standpoint of the administrator and from that of the psychologist who is to work with children who come under the school's expectancy system. The occupational pattern that the majority of the school's pupils can be expected to follow should be known to the principal.

Personnel records can be examined. The principal can be asked what kind of administrative decisions make use of the records. The school's policy regarding access to the personnel records should be discovered.

The use of teacher staff conferences should be checked. It is extremely helpful if the psychologist can attend one of them. Are administrative matters discussed exclusively or are professional problems dealt with? Can the teachers "staff a case" in any comprehensive way? What kinds of professional decisions are made in staff conferences and what follow-up is customary?

What participation in the control of the school is actually exercised by the parents of children in the school or by the pupils themselves? To what extent are policy matters initiated by parents or pupils? Are student-government organizations used merely for police functions?

Finally, as in the case of understanding the teacher, the administrator's own construct system is the most important ultimate topic of investigation. It will be manifest throughout the discussion of the foregoing topics. The adjectives which are used and the topics upon which stress is laid, or from which elaborations ensue are important for the psychologist to note. The administration's constructs represent the cultural expectancies which operate as validators for an individual pupil's constructs; they open up the channels of movement for him within the culturally accepted network.

7. THE ANALYSIS OF A PERSON'S CURRENT COMMUNITY
INTERPERSONAL RELATIONSHIPS

While we have already discussed the analysis of a person's community background as it might be described more or less objectively by various observers, the study of a person's community experience would not be complete unless we attempted to see that background at the neighborhood level through the eyes of the person himself. Who are the people with whom he lives? With which one does he identify himself? What are his interpersonal activities? How does he give these interpersonal relationships the structure and coloring that make them into a vivid experience? The viewpoint of the psychology of personal constructs encourages us to seek this personal level of interpretation in order to provide a more scientific means of making psychological predictions.

a. *Language group.* In a community where there are different language groups the language in which a person speaks most spontaneously and feels most comfortable is a clue to his group identification. Sometimes a person seeks to disidentify himself with his language group, not because he is uncomfortable in

his intragroup relationships, but because the label makes him
feel uncomfortable in his relationships with other groups. In
such a case the psychologist may make the mistake of taking
his protestations of disidentification at face value. The more
clearly the client perceives the psychologist as a member of an
outgroup of a type with which his relationships are jeopardized
by his own private group identifications, the more difficult it
is to gain access to his interpersonal relationships in the community.

The successful pursuit of an inquiry into a person's allegiances
requires that the psychologist be seen as accepting of the client's
identification and that the client not identify him closely with a
rival group. The danger is not so much that the client will refuse
to name his group, but rather that he will strive to express attitudes toward his group which he believes to be acceptable to
the psychologist's group. It is not uncommon for a white interviewer to have a colored client speak disparagingly of his own
group as "Niggers," when a deeper analysis indicates that he is
using a version of the common and effective colored man's social
device of contemptuous compliance in dealing with a white man.
A Jewish client may broadly refer to his fellows as "Kikes"; but
the term may, in some instances, have more significance as an
indicator of his social perception of the interviewer than of his
real attitude toward the group. Language groups present the
same hazards.

Sometimes a person seeks to disclaim his membership in a
language or cultural group because he is threatened from within.
As was pointed out in an earlier section, the psychology of personal constructs has a special contribution to make to the notion
of *threat*. Threat is internal. Threat, as we have defined it, is an
altogether too plausible way of seeing things. If this way were
adopted, it would have far-reaching disruptive implications. Usually threat is related to "movement," or to the development of
one's psychological construct system; thus, a threat is that which
confronts us with the possibility that we have not really made any
progress, that we are still children, that we have not really extricated ourselves from the past, that we have not really rid our-

selves of undesirable characteristics, that our efforts have come to naught. When threat is viewed in this way, it is not too difficult to see how identification with one's culture group could be construed as threatening. Especially is this true if one sees his culture group as static or stagnant while the main stream of events seems to flow rapidly past it. But more of this later!

In conducting an interview designed to reveal a person's current interpersonal relationships, one should be alert to the "we's" and "they's" as indicators of the client's feelings of group membership. As the client talks about activities that he has observed, or about groups in general, these two pronouns and their equivalents are the main source of information regarding the client's group identifications.

b. *Organizations.* The names of the organizations, formal and informal, to which a client belongs are an important item of information. Their type reveals the kind of cultural control to which he submits himself. Their variety reveals the range of seeking for a sense of belongingness. Their number reveals the intensity of the striving for cultural identification and rectitude. The exhibition of emblems, stickers, lapel pins, honorary fraternity keys, and so on throws light on a client's need to identify himself publicly with a group.

It is important to ascertain the client's interpretation of the structure and functions of the organizations he joins. The psychologist may be in for some surprises. If the client starts by verbalizing only the euphemisms, in terms of which many organizations announce their purposes, it may require some skillful interviewing to discover how he values his membership cards.

After interviewing has progressed to a point where communication is spontaneous, the psychologist can inquire into the client's perception of his own acceptability or unacceptability within certain groups in the community. The rationale he offers to explain his perceptions may be considered as a general perceptual pattern the client fits to various other life situations. These may, in turn, throw considerable light upon the way he digests all social events into nutritive experience. It is also important in this same connection to see what groups he himself considers acceptable and unacceptable. This can then be matched against the acceptances and rejections he sees as emanating from others. The discrepancy can then be taken as a measure of the client's manifest sense of community insecurity.

The psychologist can add to his understanding of the client's experiential field by analysis of the community disputes in which he becomes embroiled. To what pressure organizations does he belong and to what extent does he identify himself with the objectives of these organizations? A person may belong to a veterans' organization, for example, primarily because of the personal identifications offered. He may not actually be an intentional endorser of the rigid politico-economic line along which it exerts pressure. Such a person sooner or later finds himself involved in community disputes, even though, at first, he is not aware of them. Inquiry can be made as to the campaigns — charity, political, public improvement, etc. — in which the client has participated. Campaigning can become a way of life, a formula for accomplishment which tends to blind the chronic campaigner to all other forms of achievement. Lawsuits and family disputes, including divorce suits, may show up important features in the pattern of interpersonal relationships. "Trouble with the law" is a handy phrase for making inquiry regarding involvement with the police.

A look at social obligations a client wrestles with throws light upon the way he structures his social world. When the client is overwhelmed by these obligations he usually resorts to complaints about fatigue or makes profuse excuses for failure to keep appointments. Among members of certain groups the strain of meeting social obligations is the principal reason for "needing" a trip to the mountains, the lakes, the beach, or some other psychological Shangri-La. Social obligations include, not only the obligation to entertain social or business associates, but also the felt obligation to attend "important" meetings and make appearances where appearances count. The lives of some people are completely caught by the ruts of felt social obligation. An understanding of a person's construed social obligations throws light not only upon his daily pattern of behavior, but also on his insecurities and his latent feelings of guilt. This relationship to guilt may be understood more clearly in the light of what the psychology of personal constructs has to say (in Volume One) about the nature of guilt and its relevance to group membership.

c. *The figures inhabiting the client's world.* Having investigated a person's group identifications one may, with profit, turn to the figures inhabiting the person's social world. While the Role Construct Repertory Test makes some use of this approach, it is profitable, in cases where time permits a thoroughgoing study of a person's experience, to make an inventory of the people with whom the individual must live. What kind of people are they? Who are they? How does he describe them? Even with a child client it is important to discover who the adult neighbors are and what their attitudes toward the child appear to be. Some children grow up in a community in which the only accepting adults are their own parents. And some, of course, are even more isolated from adult society.

In general, two kinds of community figures can be investigated: those who just happen to be there and those who are more or less chosen as companions. The former includes neighbors, classmates, and working colleagues. The latter include playmates, cronies, and people spontaneously described as "friends." The conditions under which a figure is moved from the status of "neighbor" to that of "friend" are important variables in the social-adjustment pattern of a client. The psychologist can discover those conditions by taking the case of one or two persons who are described as "friends" and asking the client to tell how they came to be so regarded.

The identification of figures in the interpersonal-relationship pattern can be approached sociometrically, if time is limited. The sociometric technique developed by Moreno, Jennings, and others lends itself primarily to the study of group dynamics, but it can be adapted to individual case study by specifying the variety of nominations to be made by each individual. An attractive form of the technique has been developed by a University of California group and is known as the "guess who" technique.* The Naval Aviation Psychology Group headed by Jenkins during World War II developed a "nominating" technique which is also sociometric in form, but which lays great stress upon the "reasons" for the nominations and the time and place at which the nominations are obtained. With children the "guess who" technique can be amplified to include both the "guess who" question and a "how do you know" question. The former requires the child to select his figure within the system of constructs laid down by the examiner; the latter permits him then to reveal the personal constructs which really determine his choice. To some extent this combination is the approach used by the Role Construct Repertory Test: first a structuration in terms of prescribed role-title constructs — for example, "successful person," "intelligent person," and so on — and then the invitation to formulate and express personal constructs.

Finally, the analysis of a person's current interpersonal relationships can be approached by asking him to describe those relationships in terms of activities. What does his group do? What does each do *in the presence of* the others? What does each do *with* the others? What does each characteristically do as a result of being the kind of person he is? Here is a chance to get four kinds of direct evidence which throw light upon the client's understanding of the feelings and thinking of the group members, and therefore on his role in the group.

The client's recreational pattern of behavior can be analyzed. It may involve active group participation or, as in the case of a spectator at a football game, little more than congregate behavior. Does his recreation involve role relationships? What is the nature of the roles he plays with sufficient spontaneity to give them

* The original *Guess Who Test* is credited to H. Hartshorne and M. A. May in 1929. The copyright was granted to the Institute of Educational Research, Teachers College, Columbia University. It is an extension of Hartshorne's and May's "portraits device" which, in turn, stems from the *Characters* of Theophrastus. Thus it is possible to trace this technique of sociometry, as many other modern techniques can be traced, back to Greek Classicism.

personal value as recreation? What kinds of insights do these role-type recreational activities reveal? If he enjoys participating in team sports, to what extent is his team play indicative of his understanding of the sensitivities and personal values of the other players. Does his description of his participation indicate only that he shares their delight in competition, in defeating, in winning, in acclaim, and in exhibitionism?

8. THE ANALYSIS OF A PERSON'S EDUCATIONAL EXPERIENCE

The psychological appraisal of a school has already been discussed. Now let us consider the appraisal of a school in relation to an individual case and with an eye to the assessment of a person's whole educational experience. In a clinical interview program it may be preferable to deal with both of these topics in the same interviews; but here, for the purpose of clarity, the topics are dealt with separately. In clinical practice there are usually three informants who provide the information relevant to the analysis of a person's educational experience: the client himself, a teacher, and a parent.

a. *The teacher's complaint.* The interview with the teacher should ordinarily start with a request for a statement of what the teacher considers to be the client's problem. While this involves essentially an analysis of complaint, a topic dealt with at length in a later chapter, it may here be considered as a feature in the social expectation system within which the client must develop his role. Actually there are three ways in which a teacher's statement of a pupil's problem may be considered: (1) as a first approximation of a psychological formulation of the client's problem, (2) as a complaint or statement of the teacher's problem upon which she herself seeks help as a client, and (3) as the teacher's attitude or expectation to which the client must work out an adjustment. The reality of a teacher's complaint should never be considered independent of the reality of the teacher herself. It should always be kept in mind that the teacher's statement of the client's problem, while important and real, should always be kept identified with the teacher; it is a statement of her personal construction of the client's situation.

For example, a teacher may describe a child's problem as "laziness." The clinician should never therefore, say to himself, "The child's problem is laziness." Rather, he should say, "The child's problem is construed by the teacher as 'laziness'." The clinician may then find that his job is to help the teacher deal with what she calls "laziness" as it is incidentally associated with her pupil, or he may decide that his best contribution is to help the teacher reconstrue the problem as belonging to another construct in her repertory — for example, "frustration" — or he may attempt a concept-formation job on the teacher and help her formulate a new construct, say of "depression," to replace "laziness" altogether.

Finally, the clinician may say, "This child is having to get along with a teacher who construes him as lazy." This is the sense in which we are particularly concerned with a teacher's statements about a pupil's problems in this chapter. This is the sense in which a teacher's complaint becomes a fact to be considered in the analysis of a person's experience.

The point we have tried to make here in interpreting a teacher's "diagnostic" statement is a fundamental one which applies to other things the teacher may say regarding the child, his school record, his attitudes, his appearance, his family, his vocational prospects, or his history. Still more generally, it applies with equal force to what anyone else may say about the client. As we shall see in a later chapter, it applies even to what a person says about himself. In fact, what we have just said is a statement of a principle of clinical practice — not a wholly new one to be sure, but one which can quite obviously be derived directly from the theoretical position of the psychology of personal constructs.

b. *Basic questions.* There are seven types of questions which can be used in eliciting a teacher's (or anyone's else for that matter) complaint and obtaining its initial elaboration.

1. Upon what problems do you wish the clinic to advise you?
2. When were these problems first noticed?
3. Under what conditions did these problems appear?
4. What corrective measures have been attempted?

5. What changes have come with treatment or the passing of time?
6. Under what conditions are the problems most noticeable?
7. Under what conditions are the problems least noticeable?

The object of this line of initial questioning is to get a statement of the problem in terms which, as much as possible, reflect a picture of the problem in a fluid rather than in a static condition. In other words, the clinician seeks the most permeable construction of the problem which the teacher is able to give. Fixed or concretistic statements, whether expressed by clients or by the people with whom they live, are a common but major obstacle to clinical work. The above questions therefore first attempt to put the problem on a time line. (It is no mere euphemism to refer to time as the great healer.) The next attempt is to get an elaboration of the problem in terms of circumstances that may no longer exist or which might be altered; next to see it in terms of treatability; and finally to see the problem as yielding, in some measure, to changes in other variables. The terms in which a problem is defined, rather than the problem itself, frequently determine whether or not it can be solved. It is the clinician's job to elicit statements of complaint in a form which makes it optimally amenable to correction.

c. *Orientation of the school toward a particular child.* What kind of role do you expect this child to play during his lifetime after he leaves school? Where do you anticipate that he will live? What general type of vocation is it most reasonable to expect he will follow? These questions, and others like them, help set the stage for understanding the school's relation to a child's experience. Again the approach is in the perspective of time.

How many years do you estimate that the school has left during which it can prepare this child for the kind of life you expect him to live? As you see it, what is it reasonable to expect the school to accomplish during that time? Which of these objectives is being particularly pursued at the present time? In what courses or subjects relating to these objectives is this child enrolled? What are his reactions? These questions represent an attempt to ascertain the school's awareness of the objectives of its program in relation to the time dimension or the child's emerging life role.

What kind of avocational life do you anticipate for this child? What sorts of things do you expect him to take an interest in — to consider worthwhile and worth striving for? What kind of neighbor do you suppose he will be? What kind of recreational interests do you think it most likely that he will pursue? What recreational training is he now receiving? It is not difficult to discover how realistic a teacher is in anticipating a child's adult interests. If the expectancies with which she surrounds him are within adaptation range of his expectancies regarding himself, she may be of assistance to him in experiencing school as truly educative; otherwise, he may experience school as another one of the numerous obstacles which he must surmount in order to attain maturity.

What features of his training for his life role do you see as already having been mainly accomplished? How was it done? The emphasis is still on movement and change. A teacher who sees a child as changing, even though she may make strenuous demands on the child, is not as likely to damage his ability to make future adjustments as is a teacher who casts the child in a fixed part in which there is no conceptualization of life-cycle changes. The former teacher surrounds him with the vibrant expectancies of open-ended constructs, the latter embalms him in impermeable ones. In the language of our Modulation Corollary, variation in a person is a function of the permeability of the constructs which govern his experience.

What roles do you see this particular child's parents playing in his education? What is the nature of their interest? Is it in terms of marks and educational prestige, or are they genuinely interested themselves in the subject matter? Do they attempt to do supplemental teaching? How does it work out? Do you find that you can collaborate with them successfully in the education of their child? It is a common experience for a child to become caught in the cross-currents of expectancies arising in his school and in his home. It is not easy for a teacher to adjust her program so as to enable the child to experience both school and home in a consistent and meaningful manner. This is a problem which is by no means confined to elementary schools or even to secondary schools. In fact, it may be said generally that education, by its very nature, is frequently experienced as in conflict with the home and other less self-consciously progressive institutions.

In assessing the part the school plays in a person's experience one should not overlook the more conventional items which go into an educational history. When did he enter school? Where? Who were his teachers? What marks did he make during the successive years and what changes in patterns of marks appeared? Did he "pass"? Did he change schools? How did he adjust to the new school situations? Where did he develop the greatest enthusiasms? What subjects is he taking? Why? What is his "major"? Under what conditions has he changed it? What difficulties is he experiencing? What remedies have been attempted?

What is the client's own vocational aim? How does it stack up with the parent's wishes and their own residual unfulfilled ambitions? How does it relate to the school's vocational aim in his case? What supplementary vocational experience is the school providing in the way of excursions, round-table discussions, library materials on vocations, etc.?

What are the client's avocational interests? Which of them have been noted by the school? What ones have been utilized, either for their motivational value or for the framework they provide for seeing the relevance of various "academic" subjects? In what avocational activities does he participate? Is his opportunity to receive such avocational training dependent upon his ability to eliminate competition, as is usually the case in training in athletics, rather than on the basis of his need?

It is important also to ask many of these same questions of the parents and of the client himself. The viewpoints may differ; but, taken together, they sketch the outlines of the picture of the client's field of educational experience and the way in which the school has succeeded, either in opening new vistas for him or in slamming the door on youthful enthusiasms and aspirations.

9. THE ANALYSIS OF A PERSON'S DOMESTIC RELATIONSHIPS

Perhaps the most important social expectancies giving definition to a person's experience arise in the home. It is almost im-
perative that any adult play a true role of one sort or another in
his home; otherwise the members of the family are likely to become dispersed or, if not dispersed, the family, at best, fails to
become an effective and developing social group.

The description of the component and ancillary members of
the household is the usual point of departure. Their ages, financial interdependencies, vocational pursuits, work and sleep patterns, the assignment of "own rooms" and bedfellows, and their
characteristic activities should be described. Their attitudes and
complaints against each other, as well as toward the client, should
be surveyed briefly at least. If the client is a young child, the
overtness of family members' expressions of feeling toward one
another should be understood. In what ways and how frequently
is affection expressed between members of the household? In
what ways and how frequently is tension or conflict expressed?
If there is conflict, what version of that conflict is offered the
younger children, and do they accept that version? Do members
of the household seek allies among other members of the household in their disputes? Does the mother customarily seek the
alliance of the father in criticizing the child? Does the father
try to cast the mother rather than himself in the role of the child's
critic? Do parents seek the alliance of children in their disputes
with each other? Do parents compete with children for the affection of each other? Are disciplinary decisions immutable, or
are they subject to discussion and revision? What is the basis of
revision? Is it usually on the basis of feeling only, thus carrying
with it the implication that the original decision was a matter of
feeling and that all unpleasant decisions are forms of personal
rejection? These are the types of questions by which the social
interactions of the household group can be elaborated and analyzed.

What is the attitude toward property in the household? Must
all belongings be shared or may a child have the security of a

"very own" toy, room, pet, or time of day? How does the child or wife receive his share of the family income?

What has been the occupational history of the family? Where have they lived? How steadily has the breadwinner been employed? What occupational shifts has the breadwinner attempted?

What has been the history of family separations? When did they occur? Why? What adjustments did the children have to make? Have there been deaths, divorces, and remarriages? What was the household like during the advent of the other spouse? What explanations were offered the children? What lingering attachments do present members of the household have for former members of the household?

What tensions appear between the family and neighbors? What forms of extrafamilial maladaptation are evident? What catastrophes have befallen the family? What explanations or constructions are now used to explain those catastrophes?

What is the nature of the family's religious participation? What religious identifications did the parents have before their marriage? What measures were taken to reconcile religious differences? Are those measures still acceptable? What religious indoctrination is attempted with the children? How overt is the religious participation? What personal functions appear to be served by the religious identification or participation? Is it maintained largely out of custom and maintenance of the family identity? Does it provide a feeling of comfort? Are there status factors apparent? Does it have philosophical roots?

What taboos are exercised in the home and what rationale is used to support them: foods, games, cards, dancing, parties, Sabbath activities, use of the family car, smoking, drinking, certain companions, dates, etc.?

What is the nature of the family organization and control? Is it patriarchal, matriarchal, anarchical, or democratic? Who controls finances? Who controls children's behavior? Who formulates occupational plans? Who manages the buying of household necessities?

What appears to be the basis for family cohesion: division of labor, community of recreational interests, community of vocational interests, affection, financial security? With whom does the family exchange visits? How near do relatives live and what is the pattern of relationship with them? What languages are spoken in the home? What kinds of things are dealt with in one language, as contrasted with the language used in dealing with other things? What is the recreational pattern of the members of the household? What literature is available in the home? What radio and television programs are listened to? What musical instruments are played in the home?

What is the family's financial status? Is it ample, enough for security, irregular, temporarily low, involving serious indebtedness, requiring public assistance? Is it inadequate for food, shelter, clothing, medicine, entertainment, education? What has been the family reaction to financial reverses? Has it been to keep the reverses from becoming apparent to the neighbors or relatives? Have the parents tended to withdraw from social relationships? Have reverses been accompanied by serious anxiety, excesses in entertainment, excesses in spending, excesses in drinking, by irritability, dependency or parasitic attitudes, or by cynicism, disillusionment, and espousal of radical socio-political schemes or ideologies?

10. THE ANALYSIS OF A PERSON'S FAMILY HISTORY

Most clinicians, particularly those with a medical background, place great store in the family history as a source of important information about the client's plight. Yet the psychology of personal constructs, by its very nature, leads the clinician to view this information as something to be examined through the client's eyes, and to consider its intrinsic value as quite limited.

While this has been a chapter dealing with inventories of the client's experiences, we have endeavored, throughout, to convey the theme that the client is not the victim of these experiences, but that he is, at worst, victimized only by his limited ability to interpret them. We have said it this way: man is neither the prisoner of his environment nor the slave of his biography. What he constructs out of his circumstances, no matter how fateful they may be, is still, in the final analysis, a structure of his own making.

But if man is not the victim of his own biography, how much less apt it is to claim that he is the victim of his ancestors' biographies. Still, it is difficult for one of limited outlook to disidentify himself wholly from the ways of his family, even though separated from them both in time and space. One usually plays a role. The fact that Great-grandfather Ezekiel was strung up as a horse thief does not necessarily make one light-fingered, but both the fact and the man may call for construing. The incident may even be related to one's friends as evidence of one's own common and earthy relationship to a complex society.

But does all this mean that Great-grandfather Ezekiel etched his character into the generations who followed him? We think not. We prefer to believe that Great-grandfather Ezekiel's record is merely used to prove something; that it serves essentially as a validator. Indeed, it is quite unlikely Ezekiel the Fourth has retained any of his ancestor's impulsive attraction to strange horses.

Consider another, more poignant illustration. Suppose a female client's mother committed suicide following a menopausal depression. The suicidal *tendency* may not be congenital in the client, but the suicidal *event* looms in her memory as a conspicuous and potential validator for any depressive theme that may scurry across her mind. The real danger is that the suicide may serve to prove something. The therapist who deals with this case needs to be especially alert to any personal constructs which might fall back on this kind of proof.

There is a special practical or institutional reason for the clinical psychologist's involving himself occasionally in a detailed family history. If he works in collaboration with physicians, he may wish to accumulate the kind of evidence that makes sense to them. If the history seems to them to point to problems needing medical treatment, the psychologist may enlist their active collaboration by citing it. Thus with physicians working within their framework, and the psychologist functioning within his, the client stands a better chance of getting well. This assumes, of course, that the physicians' approach will not be so conceptually preemptive that it rules out any concurrent psychological construction of the case.

With our viewpoint on family histories thus made explicit, let us turn to the method of outlining historical information. The writer prefers to lay out a kind of chart, sometimes on an accountant's large analysis pad. Along the left-hand side the first names of grandparents, parents and their siblings, and the client and his siblings can be listed in order of birth. Across the top, at the heads of the columns, can be listed such items as age, age at death, cause of death, etc. Conspicuous items of disease history can be entered in a "disease" column by use of symbols or abbreviations. Other columns can be used to record the marital status of each person, number of children, and the perceived economic, social, and personal standing of each individual in the family group. The record of handicaps, institutionalization, schooling, and occupation may be mentioned. The kinds of persons whom the relatives married may be indicated.

Throughout the interviewing on family history the psychologist should be especially perceptive of the validating effect the family history may have in the thinking of the client.

11. SUMMARY

We have dealt with the kinds of information usually sought out by clinicians. But we have tried to keep all historical and circumstantial facts in the perspective of our systematic position. We have looked for available *validators* rather than implacable *causes*. We have dealt with facts as personal constructs; and the constructs, in turn, we have envisioned as avenues of movement which the person opens up for himself through the bewildering tangles of his life's events.

Chapter Fourteen

The Appraisal of Activities

WE CONTINUE with inventories of the client's experiences, with the emphasis now placed upon his more overt activities.

A. Spontaneous Activity

1. THE CONCEPTUALIZATION OF SPONTANEOUS ACTIVITIES

The psychology of personal constructs has far-reaching implications in the field of spontaneous behavior, motivation, and interests. In our discussion of the concept of mental energy in theory design we pointed out that the notion of "energy," or of "stimulus," or of "motivation," had originally to be invoked as soon as men had allowed themselves to become committed to the assumption of a basically static universe. Later we attempted to show how the Fundamental Postulate of personal-construct theory avoided this necessity by embodying the notion of movement and action in its assumptive structure. The being we start with is already alive and kicking — we do not have to invent anything to "motivate" him! When we describe his "interests" we are calling attention to the directions his activities take, rather than to the amount of pressure behind them.

Our postulate puts us in an interesting position regarding such issues as spontaneity versus control and play versus work. First of all, we are in the position of assuming that all activity is spontaneous, in that it stems primarily from the nature of the person rather than from the nature of the extrapersonal world. Second, we assume also that all activity is controlled, in that it is lawful and ultimately predictable. How can we reconcile these two views? Basically we have already done so. In our discussion of determinism and free will we pointed out that these two abstractions were primarily functions of the framework within which they are perceived. Freedom is what one sees when he looks at a construct in its superordinate aspect. Determinism is what one sees when he turns the other way and sees how the construct is subordinated to more far-reaching considerations. Mathematically it is like the concept of the independent and the dependent variables in an equation; the independence and the dependence are functions of the equation in which the variables are arranged, not concrete features of the variables themselves. What is an independent variable in one equation may be a dependent variable in another, and vice versa. Similarly, what is free in one equation of human behavior may be determined in another; and what is determined in one behavioral equation may be construed as free in another.

The same kind of reasoning applies to spontaneity and control in human behavior — also to leisure and work. In a sense, one always does "what he wants to" — if we reach high enough in placing the level of the "wanting." In a sense, also, one always does "what he has to" — if we look at his behavior in its subordinate aspect. The distinction between work and play becomes a matter of one's putting his finger on the *level* of the control which operates rather than trying to determine the *amount* of control which is involved. The study of interests becomes the study of the whole range and variety of one's psychological processes, and not merely the study of a special class of activities. Since one is dealing with range and variety, the study of interests involves the understanding of the broader, more generalized, or permeable constructs under which a person's psychological processes are organized.

By this line of reasoning we reach the position that the analysis of spontaneous activities is properly the seeking of an individual's permeable personal constructs. It leads us to say that the pattern of one's interests reveals those areas in which his construct system appears to him to operate effectively and thus even suggests where he may be judged by others to play an effective part in the economic and social operations of society. The use of the Strong Vocational Interest Blank is an illustration of this approach. In the psychology of personal constructs the problem of motivation resolves itself into the problem of the alignment of tasks with a person's permeable constructs or into the more substantial problem of developing permeable constructs which have broad and obvious implications for the kinds of work society needs to have done.

a. *Permeability of constructs.* In analyzing spontaneous activities the psychologist should keep in mind that apparent freedom and versatility are signs that the functioning constructs are organized within a permeable system, and that therefore the field of fact covered by those activities is being extensively elaborated by the person observed. The psychologist who, from the standpoint of personal-construct theory, watches a child at play sees a person who is elaborating his field of experience under the regnancy of the most permeable constructs which are available to him. For example, the fact that a child can play with that which frightens him indicates that he is still in the process of elaborating that particular field of experience, and that he may work out some new solutions to his fears. When he ceases to be able to play with his fears, the implication is that his constructs in that area of experience have become impermeable, rigid, and perseverative, and that his fear is approaching the status of a phobia.

Since psychological processes are interpreted in personal-construct theory as continually evolving, it follows that one's activities tend to be more elaborate and extensive in those areas where the regnant constructs are permeable enough to permit evolution and elaboration. Just as the analysis of spontaneous activities indicates where such optimal conditions for evolution exist, so we may expect that in those areas where the optimal conditions do not exist there would be found relatively little activity. People do tend to avoid activity in those areas where their construct systems seem to them to have become rigid and not to permit further elaboration. This, then, is the way inactivity is interpreted in this theoretical system. The notion of "laziness" as a kind of willful passivity is thus translated into the terminology of personal-construct theory as the outcome of impermeable thinking. As "laziness" it never was a psychologically productive notion anyway!

Our position regarding spontaneous activity permits us to formulate a rational explanation of why children, and adults too, appear to seek danger and discomfort. Neither self-preservation theory nor hedonistic theory has been able to handle this problem satisfactorily. Psychoanalytic theory, a double-ended version of hedonistic theory, handles it by postulating the instincts of Eros and Todestrieb, thus bracketing all kinds of behavior while defining none. The explanation of danger-seeking and discomfort-seeking behavior, which the psychology of personal constructs offers, is that it is an elaboration of one's psychological system in an area where the regnant constructs are permeable enough to permit such elaboration. In simpler, though somewhat looser language, spontaneous activity, even though it involves danger and discomfort, indicates where a person's areas of richest experience lie.

b. *Utility of constructs.* While we have explained spontaneous activity as the elaboration of one's experiential field under the aegis of permeable constructs, it may be profitable to approach it from another level of description. Let us explain it from the standpoint of utility. According to our Choice Corollary, a person chooses for himself that alternative through which he anticipates the greater possibility for extension and definition of his system. One may, therefore, select a part of the world about him and deal especially with it, rather than some other part, simply because he can. In other words, one tends to choose what events he will elaborate upon because they appear to be amenable to treatment. Thus the man who spends his leisure hours listening to a sports broadcast sees that as a closely interrelated series of happenings which he can anticipate without utter bafflement, but which is not so monotonously repetitive that it does not invite any extension or definition of his prediction system. His construct system.

in the area of that sport, is not so rigid, as a result of guilt and other protective devices, that he cannot tinker with it, nor is it so ineffectual that he can only feel baffled and confused at each new turn of the game. One does control his field of perception in order to keep it within predictable and fertile limits.

There is another way of looking at the utilitarian value of spontaneous activity. It helps a person to recover his poise after working in an area where his elaborations have thrown him off balance. The man who enjoys the broadcast of the ball game may have been working all week as a clerk. As a clerk he must check figures and items and leave nothing to chance. Of course, from our point of view, his working as a clerk is, in a sense, just as spontaneous as his listening to the ball game. He may see an interesting pattern of developments and intriguing surprises unfolding in his world of figures or he may see his life being elaborated by his role as the wage earner in his family.

But his elaborations in the field of his daily "work" may carry with them evolving implications regarding himself as a person. He may, in effect, ask himself, "Does all this mean that I am a 'drudge,' a 'fuddy-duddy,' an 'old man'; that there is no world outside the world of clerical items in which I have spent my working week?" For this man, listening to the ball game may permit him to revalidate his superordinate constructs, particularly those regarding his age and virility status, after he has been cast for a week in the part of a meticulous clerk.

The classical Greeks would have seen it as an instance of *catharsis*, through which the natural wholeness of the man was restored. Personal-construct psychology thus uses a conceptualization of recreative activity which somewhat parallels the Greek notion. Contrariwise, it does not employ any close parallel to the psychoanalytic notion of "catharsis." The psychoanalytic notion of "catharsis," as it has actually been developed, has much more in common with the more primitive notion of "exorcism."

There is a slight variant of the explanation offered in the last paragraphs, a variant throwing some light upon spontaneous activity. People frequently feel that, in the course of the evolution of their construct systems, a part of their field of experience is getting out of hand. That elaboration of one's construct system taking place in recreational activity may be a way of bringing an area of experience back under the regnancy of one's effective construct system. This comes a little closer to the current psychoanalytic use of "catharsis."

The clinical psychologist, whose primary concern with a person is necessarily psychotherapeutic, takes careful account of those phases of a person's activity which appear to be spontaneous — that is, those whose organizational control is not immediately apparent. He seeks to understand that organizational control and thus comes to understand behaviors as not being free acts exclusively, even though they may be unconventional or antisocial. Only in this way can he come to understand fully why his client behaves the way he does and what changes in behavior, resulting from therapy, are most likely to be extensively and spontaneously elaborated, rather than literalistically and dutifully performed at the behest of the therapist.

For similar reasons, the clinical psychologist concerns himself with the client's autistic thinking — his phantasies, his dreams, his fanciful perceptions. That is where the permeable constructs in his system hold sway. Here is his rationale for "doing things on his own." Here is the framework of "emotional insight."

When a teacher complains that her pupil is "lazy" and the psychologist encourages her to observe what the child does while he is being "lazy"; when a social worker complains that her client is "shiftless" and the psychologist suggests that she observe and describe the persistence and ingenuity with which he maintains his indigent status; when the psychiatrist complains that his patient is too "passive" for therapy and the psychologist urges him to delineate the variety of ways in which the patient utilizes his "passivity"; when a fellow psychologist describes his subject as "unmotivated" and one urges that self-expression be more carefully observed — all of these are examples of the application of the psychology of personal constructs to the analysis of spontaneous activities. Our point of view lays great stress upon listening thoughtfully and open-mindedly to the client to see what he is trying to tell us. Similarly, it lays great stress upon observing his spontaneous activities to see what he is trying to do. Rousseau might have called it "education," Reik might call it "listening with the third ear," Gregg might say it meant "listening to the babblings of nature rather than cross-examining her," some would call it "swimming in the patient's unconscious," and Fenichel might call it "steering close to Charybdis." But whatever the figure of speech, the thoughtful analysis of his client's spontaneous activities is one of the basic arts of the clinician.

In summary, let us say that what we have tried to convey in the foregoing paragraphs is the idea that the analysis of spontaneous activities should lead us to an understanding of the basically permeable constructs. Since we have assumed (Modulation Corollary) that change hinges upon the more permeable aspects of one's system, the clinical psychologist, who must always be primarily interested in the client's capacity for psychotherapeutic change, observes spontaneous activities in order to discover the permeable constructs in his client's system. In fact, it might be said that one of the distinguishing characteristics of the clinical psychologist is his concern with spontaneous activities and the permeability of constructs.

2. THE DESCRIPTION OF SPONTANEOUS ACTIVITIES

Spontaneous activities, like most other types of activities, tend to fall in cycles: diurnal, hebdomadal, monthly, seasonal, and life. It is therefore important, in studying recurrent spontaneous activities, to take time samples which tap the person's experience systematically. A number of years ago Lehman and Witty studied the interests of children by making an inventory of what they did during a whole week. Their approach was an example of time sampling which spanned the variations that occurred within the day or week. It is also an example of the study of experience in order to show how a person's psychological life is structured.

If the study of spontaneous activities is made through verbal inquiry, it is possible to make an inventory of all the topical activities in which a person has engaged during a day, particularly a fairly complete compilation of what he remembers having thought about, then to extend the outline to the week, using broader topics and seeking new topics of the broader variety. For example, the client may mention a letter he has written during the day. The psychologist, after learning that the letter was considered by the client to have been long overdue, can ask about other letters written during the week and further overdue tasks which the client feels are pending. Similarly, topics appearing in the weekly cycle can be cast in a more general form and investigated in a seasonal cycle.

As might be inferred from our theoretical position, the psychologist should, throughout his inquiry, pay particular attention to the way in which the person interprets his experience. Does he feel that he has frittered away his time? Does he feel that he has accomplished or demonstrated something? Is the task incomplete? Was the opportunity to do what he did a kind of deserved reward? Did it compensate for something? Is he ashamed of it? Is he looking forward to the opportunity of doing it again? Was the spontaneous behavior appropriate to the situation? What, in the client's mind, constitutes appropriate behavior for the kind of situations in which he found himself? If he had a stiff drink, what, from his point of view, constitutes an appropriate occasion for a stiff drink? Was he frustrated? Was he frightened? Was he feeling socially dull? Was he feeling isolated? Did he think he was in danger of being perceived as unfriendly? Did he "celebrate"?

It is possible to approach personal constructs through the analysis of spontaneous activities, without depending upon the person's verbal explanations. The sequence of activities, and the situations in which they are carried out, indicate with some measure of clarity the personal constructions which must underlie them. Thus, a person who usually works a crossword puzzle while he defecates reveals something about his construction of experience which he probably could not put into words. It may be as meaningful to find out *when* a person does certain things as it is to find out *what* he does and *why* he says he does them.

The analysis of spontaneous activities should include a description of the topics and developments of one's conversations during the time sample. The remembered portions of these conversations are important residues. The analysis should include, also, his physical movements from place to place, his pacing the floor, his sleeplessness, his times of eating, his isolating of himself from his family, and so on.

The way a person's spontaneous activities are adjusted to the presence of other people is important. The contrasts between behavior shown in the presence of people and in solitude, or between that shown in the presence of one person and that shown in the presence of another, should be drawn. Is the person's behavior characteristically socially participant behavior, spectator behavior, or solitary behavior?

What is the nature of one's creative efforts and what productions does he have to show for them? Samples of creative efforts — poems, drawings, photographs, doodling, letters, diagrams, finger painting, handcraft, and so on — can sometimes be put into the case record, where they can, in relation to other material, be interpreted as revealing certain personal constructs governing the client's life. Where samples are not available, descriptions can be entered in the record. One's hobbies and collections should be noted. Everyone collects items in a manner which is somewhat characteristic of him, even though he may not consider them to be "collections" or "hobbies." Sometimes one can approach this topic by asking, "What are some of the things you have trouble throwing away?" One may also inquire about the art forms one uses in self-expression. The choice of the art form can be important, but the way in which one actually uses the art form for expression is even more significant.

It is important for the clinician to be aware of the tools which his client requires for implementing his leisure-time activities. A person whose recreational rehabilitation requires tools which have been suddenly taken away from him may suffer severely from the constricting effect. The writer recalls a client whose husband's pre-Depression income was reported to be about $20,000 a year from selling an expensive make of automobile. The reduction of the family to pauperism during the 1930's appeared to affect the client's psychological adjustment in various ways, but particularly because she could no longer go to the races. A person's recreational dependency upon equipment which may no longer be available to him, or which may later become un-available to him, reveals a kind of impermeability in his construct system which must be taken into account, regardless of the specific complaint of the moment.

In examining the equipment resources available to a child for play, the psychologist should take into account the flexibility of the child's equipment for experimentation with various solutions to problems, both personal and mechanical. At a certain age, blocks are more useful for experimentation than are more complicated toys. A toy which can be tinkered with permits more extension of one's construction system than one which must always be construed in the same concretistic way. Some toys can be dealt with either concretistically or constructively. A doll, for example, may be treated by a boy as an inflexible "thing," while, in the hands of an imaginative and experimentally minded girl, it may become a pliable element in formulating a great variety of social and role constructs. Incidentally, it is not surprising, considering the play of girls, that they come earlier to an understanding of certain kinds of interpersonal relationships than do boys.

One's dependence upon the presence of other people, or upon certain people, for successful recreational activities should be noted. Sometimes there appears to be a marked constriction of spontaneous behavior when one is alone. Sometimes the behavior is markedly less spontaneous when one is with other people. Sometimes one finds a client who feels that he has no spontaneity unless he has a gallery of spectators to applaud his performance. It is important, therefore, to know, not only *what* one's general dependence upon social presence is, but *who* it is that one is dependent upon.

It is a simple matter to make an inventory of the client's spontaneous reading habits. The psychologist should be careful not to judge them, however, merely in terms of "good" and "bad" literature. The themes, the levels of abstraction, and the field of fact subsumed are more important considerations in analyzing this type of spontaneous activity.

The relation of spontaneous activity to the nature of one's vocation should be considered. Where there are no harmonizing constructs to tie the two together, the vocation stands to become a threat, or at best to become a stagnant area of development. If a person is to develop himself successfully in his vocational line, he must show some spontaneity — or, in the language of personal-construct theory, some permeability — in that area.

In this same connection, the level of abstraction and the appearance of permeability should be noted in the analysis of any spontaneous behavior. In fact, the principal purpose of analyzing spontaneous behavior is to come to understand one's client's permeable constructs, under which further elaboration of his psychological life can be anticipated and exploited.

3. OUTLINE FOR THE OBSERVATION OF A CHILD IN A GROUP

Successful psychological observation of a child's spontaneous behavior, when he is construing himself as a member of an active group, requires considerable skill and practice. One needs to be fully familiar with his own system for categorizing behavior and quick to recognize the various kinds of activity which belong in the various categories. Even if one uses shorthand notes or dictates into a recording machine a running account of what he observes, he is likely to have trouble keeping up with everything that goes on.

a. *Steps.* The first step is to decide, in the light of the activity which is to be observed, what time-sample intervals are to be employed. When a child in a relatively quiet classroom is to be observed, the periods may be as long as five minutes. When he is on a crowded and poorly supervised playground, one may have to divide the time into thirty-second intervals in order to capture the rapidly shifting patterns of behavior.

The next step is to describe the setting in which the activity is to be observed — place, time, social setting. The group from which subsamples will be drawn during the course of the observation period should be defined, together with its ostensible purpose for assembling.

In each time interval the setting of the child's behavior should be described in three ways: (1) the topic of the activity — including topic of conversation, (2) the group composition, and (3) the movement. The topic of the activity is simply the name of it as a group activity, and does not necessarily include a description of the purposes of the activity, from the standpoint of the individual child who is being observed. Since the topic of conversation is frequently different from the topic of activity, it is desirable to list it additionally, although, of course, one might argue that the topic of conversation might be more truly representative of the real purpose of the activity, as, for example, in the case of a ladies' sewing circle.

The group composition should be described in terms of the persons comprising the focal subgroup, the participant subgroup, the spectator subgroup, and the abandoned subgroup. The focal subgroup is composed of those whose activities appear to be most representative of what the group is doing; they are those who are "on the beam." The participant subgroup is the somewhat larger circle of persons whose activity is a part of the general group movement which takes place. The participant subgroup includes the focal subgroup. The spectator subgroup is a separate group composed of those who have no part in initiating or carrying out the topical activity, but who are obviously paying attention to what is going on. The abandoned subgroup is composed of those who have quite recently been members of the group, but who have effectively withdrawn or have been rejected, even from spectator status.

The movement of the group is described in terms of the changes in the topic of activity. What is abandoned? What is added? Are the changes progressive — that is, inferrable from previous activities — or are they kaleidoscopic?

The next task is to keep a running record of the individual child's position with respect to the group composition, and to describe the way in which he maintains that position. Does he make a bid for membership in the focal or participant subgroups? In doing so, how does he represent himself? — as a dominating leader? — as a pitiable person? — as an initiator of topical movement? — as an assistant? What kind of figure does he portray himself to be? What kind of adult figures or approach patterns does his behavior suggest? What constructs of himself, his companions, and the group is he "trying on for size"?

b. *The child's anticipations.* What we are saying here is what we might be expected to say, in the light of our theoretical position: that psychological processes move in the direction of anticipation. In terms which express our point of view, but which are by no means original with the psychology of personal constructs, "All behavior can be construed as anticipatory in nature."

It would follow from the observer's notation of the personal constructs which the child appears to be using to relate himself to his group that the observer would have to note next the outcomes of the child's anticipatory efforts. It is mandatory that we consider the analysis of experience, with which this chapter is primarily concerned, as showing us the kinds of criterion evidence against which the child's tentative constructs are validated. Do his anticipations work out? Do his companions respond in the way *he expects?*

It is much more important that the psychological question be stated in this form than in terms of whether or not his efforts meet with resistance or whether or not he is rejected by the group. The latter type of question commits us to the prior assumption that what the child is seeking is a membership in the group which is analogous to the memberships of other individuals. From this point of view, if his efforts do not achieve this end, we must presume that he has had a "failure" experience and that he must "learn" something from it. But anyone who has observed children's behavioral explorations extensively is likely to be impressed as much by the fact that children often do not "learn" from such experiences as by the fact that sometimes they do. Pete, the little brat, may not be a "happy" child, but he cannot fail to note with a certain amount of glee how neatly his anticipations work out when he plays his part in the accustomed way. Considering the kinds of social constructs he is using, the evidence the group furnishes him is confirmatory to his expectations and validative for his constructs. Pansy, the crybaby, may not be a "happy" child, but the response to her histrionic act usually comes up to her expectations and sooner or later provides her with indisputable evidence that her infantile constructs still work *the way she expects them to.* Both Pete's and Pansy's spontaneous activities, in or out of a group, may well be considered as elaborations of the permeable and regnant constructs which they have found so useful in ordering their unhappy but somewhat orderly worlds.

Certain kinds of observations throw light upon the permeability of the constructs under which a child is laboring. If we consider the appearance of spontaneity as evidence of the regnancy of permeable constructs, we may make our observations first under the more familiar rubric of "spontaneity." It is no accident that a child who is stiff-legged in a certain kind of social situation tends to structure that situation "by the book" because he has no flexible and generalized approach to follow. The observation of voice modulation — the spontaneous rising and falling of pitch — and the observation of secondary inflection — the manner of stressing and spacing syllables which is not prescribed by the language — are keenly observed by the perceptive clinician. Any interference with this kind of spontaneity is commonly interpreted by clinicians as an indication of "stress," or "rigidity," or "latent hostility." From our position we would use the intervening construct of "impermeability" in making a generalized interpretation of the behavior. The term is not antithetical to the more common interpretive clinical concepts. Motor behavior — gait, posture, gesture, expression; speech behavior — quality, vocabulary, quantity, modulation, inflection; activity level — distracted, over-stimulated, quiescent, explosive, precipitate, hesitant as-if-knuckle-rapped; role behavior — reflecting the constructs of others, elaboration of others' ideas, implementation, questioning, explaining, interpreting one child to another: all are important types of behavior for observation when one wants to understand how flexible and utilitarian are the constructs under which a child is operating.

4. OBSERVATION OF THE CHILD IN THE FAMILY GROUP

What we have been saying about the observation of the child

in a children's group applies equally, if not even more meaningfully, to the observation of the child in his own family group. A much needed, but rarely used, clinical facility is a laboratory living room where the family group can be asked to spend an hour or two together under the observation of a psychologist. The equipment of the room can be varied in order to implement various kinds of domestic activities. Better still, of course, would be a home, which could be adapted so as to be a reasonable facsimile of that with which the family group was familiar, thus giving the group a chance to participate in a greater variety of activities while under observation.

A device which works out surprisingly well in psychological clinic practice is the home visit, arranged in advance with the parents and embracing the hours from just before the father returns from work on a week night until after the child has retired. This time sample is sufficiently representative to be extremely useful in understanding the nature of the child's domestic experience and the kind of conceptualization of interpersonal relationships which it tends to validate. To be sure, neither parents nor children can be expected to behave precisely the way they normally behave when "company" is not present; but again, the psychologist who is aware of the cues of spontaneity can detect much of what is being performed naturally under the regnancy of permeable constructs and what is being performed stiff-leggedly under "manners."

Even in the testing of infants, particularly those who are being given tests in boarding homes prior to adoption, it is valuable to take such a time sample, and perhaps precede it with a check test of the child to compare with another test given earlier in the clinic. The nature of the visual and auditory stimulation given the child in his crib, the part he plays in the expectancies of the boarding-home parents, and so on give some idea of what opportunities he has had to develop his own anticipatory behavior and their relation to his performance on the test.

Regardless of what a parent does or does not do during the period of the home visit, the discerning psychologist can discover something of what the parent means to the child *by what the*

child appears to expect him to do. If the child is loud and insistent in his demands upon the parent, it may be interpreted to
mean that the parent has made some attempt to avoid acceding
to such requests in the past. If the child accedes to each personalized request of the parent without taking issue, this may be
taken as indicating that the child sees the parent as hopelessly
adamant in making such requests.

As in the case of observing a schoolroom, the clinician can
make some judgment of the disruptive effect his visit has upon
the customary activities of the different members of the household. Does this appear to be a family which is used to having
the neighbors drop in for a visit? His observations may lead him
to believe that the household routine is normally so rigidly maintained that his presence, or the presence of any outsider, is a
major disruption. He may infer, in such a case, that readjustments in the household organization constitute major threats to
the construct system by which the household is maintained. He
may also get some idea of the pliability of the family, or the
possibility that it is a capricious validator of the child's personal
constructs regarding interpersonal relations.

Observation of the home may give some indication of what
must be the nature of the customary daily activities — reading,
hobbies, social activities, valued achievements, religious devotion,
and so on. The tools of living are likely to be in evidence.

Put these observations together with what is obvious regarding
the parts the different members of the household play in relation
to each other, and the observant psychologist can find much in
the situation which will enable him to be helpful. Moreover, he
is likely to find the experience surprisingly pleasant.

5. THE PSYCHOLOGICAL SIGNIFICANCE OF VOCATIONAL CHOICE

A vocation can be looked upon, both as a system of ready-made
constructs, and as a system of validators. Viewed in either way,
it has far-reaching implications for one's approach to life, implications including much more than the assigned workaday
duties and the size of the paycheck. We may say that a vocation
is a certain field of experience. If, then, we define experience as

a set of construed events, or as the compass of fact which has fallen within a given man's purview, we may see how his vocational choice exercises a selective effect upon his experience. It affects both the constructs he uses to bring certain ranges of fact within his purview and the kinds of evidence against which he is likely to check the validity of his anticipations. It seems appropriate, therefore, that we discuss the matter of vocational choice in a chapter which is concerned with gaining access to personal constructs through the analysis of experience.

a. *An area of permeable constructs.* While persons vary markedly in their reactions to their own vocations, it can be said, in general, that one's vocational field is one in which his constructs have considerable permeability. Each day's events, while possibly appearing to be quite concrete and repetitive to an outsider, can not only be put neatly into place, but can be subjected to reevaluation as the vocational construct system evolves under the aegis of permeable constructs. A person's vocation is an area in which he ordinarily has many constructs which are permeable enough to permit a considerable amount of successive evolving to take place. To understand a person's vocational choice is, therefore, to know something about the kinds of change which he may be prepared to make — always a crucial issue with the psychotherapeutically oriented psychologist. The permeable constructs under which a person's vocational thinking is spontaneously elaborated can frequently be invoked directly by the therapist as he seeks to help his client reconstrue some other part of his experience.

Too often a therapist fails to make use of a client's vocational constructs. In some cases it is because the therapist is not willing to take the time to learn them. In others it is because he is so dogmatic in his outlook that it does not occur to him that the client's own construction system may be quite as adequate as Freud's to embrace the necessary "insights."

A vocation is not only an area of experience which lends itself to elaboration but it is also an area of experience which ordinarily does not overtax one's tolerance of ambiguity. One can frequently see in a given person's spontaneous choice of vocation, or of a course of study in school, his seeking of a happy compromise between what is challenging and what is safe. The selection may be something which is excitingly new, but not so strange as to be confusing. One person may choose to major in mathematics because it permits him to explore in the realm of answers which are generally "right," and yet does not disturb his brittle relations with people or pose unexpected problems to his conscience. Another person may choose to build a house because that occupation permits him to elaborate his ideas of design just enough to make life interesting, yet always protects him against the disquieting suspicions of self-inconsistency: a house is so palpably whole when it is finished! A third person may choose to set himself up as a salesman, because, in this manner, he can explore a variety of ways to snuggle up to people, yet he can always have at hand the validating evidence of success or failure in terms of "sales." In gaining access to personal constructs through an analysis of vocational experience, one should always take account of the compromise between adventure and security the vocation represents for the client.

Of course, when we say that a vocation is an area of experience in which there are permeable governing constructs, and that it may also be seen as one which does not overtax one's tolerance of ambiguity, we are really saying the same thing. Our Modulation Corollary equates the two by committing us to the position that a person's tolerance of incompatibility is limited by the permeability and definition of certain superordinate aspects of his system.

Occasionally one sees in a vocational choice an attempt to encapsulate the area of activity which is necessary for the earning of one's livelihood, or for the appeasement of one's family. Encapsulation cuts down the job's interference with the areas of one's real spontaneous interests. In such a case, the daily work is something to be finished and forgotten the instant the whistle blows. This is a difficult pose to maintain. Sooner or later one is likely to find himself unable to restrain the impulse to give his job a little personal twist, like the king in Shaw's *The Apple Cart* who could not resist the temptation to wink when he read the speeches which his ministry had prepared for him.

b. *An area of validation.* A vocation may be looked upon as a system of validating evidence to which one's daily anticipations are repeatedly subjected. A person will tend to construe life in the way in which it can best be anticipated, and the check points which he uses to see how accurate his anticipations have been are pretty well defined by his occupation and by his fellow workers. It is difficult to get a person to make sense out of a new construct when it does not help him to predict what will happen on the job or to anticipate what his colleagues will say. Recognition of the system of validators to which a person's vocation commits him is an important step in the therapist's decision about what new ideas should be developed by his client. It is not realistic to expect an enlisted soldier to get much practical utility out of the idea of the universal brotherhood of man when he cannot get by with treating either his officers or his enemy like brothers. It is not realistic to expect an employee in a highly regimented system to be able to find validating evidence for the idea that free expression of everyone's convictions is a wholesome approach to life, when the only convictions he sees accepted are those of his employer. If he does lay hold of the idea at all he may try to restrict the privilege to people who agree with him, or even seek to destroy all those who exhibit "free" expression which is contradictory to his own "free" expression.

One's conceptualization of oneself and his role is an important factor in the choice and maintenance of an occupational identification. If the father figure is representative of what adulthood means to the young man, he may be able to see clearly no pathway to adulthood except that which leads through his father's vocation. This is not to say that he idolizes his father or that his relationship with his father is a happy one. It is to say what we have said before, that constructs are channels of freedom of movement, and therefore that the father figure, representing a major construct in the young man's life, stands as the most clearly marked guidepost to the future. Other figures may also point the way to adulthood, and it is not surprising that many a man starts down the pathway leading to a particular vocation because some person familiar to him gave the vocation clarity and plausibility.

A vocation is one of the principal means by which one's life role is given clarity and meaning. Hence it serves as a stabilizing support against chaos and confusion. Most occupations, though by no means all, have clear-cut implications for one's career and hence help one visualize and anticipate with equanimity one's middle age and declining years. A vocation also helps one define his role in day-to-day situations, for it carries with it certain standard interpretations of other people's motives and the social obligations he owes to persons both in and out of his occupational group.

One's occupation may carry with it implications regarding those social relations entirely extrinsic to the duties involved in the occupation. Many a young man has had the medical profession wished on him by his frustrated mother, who visualized a doctor as the man with the cleanest hands, the whitest collar, the glossiest car, and the greatest self-assurance in town.

Frequently a vocational choice is based on the most clearly perceived elements in a situation, as well as upon the most clearly perceived and exemplified over-all vocational patterns. Being confronted with certain particular facts and issues out of which he must make some sense, many a young man has built for himself a career in business which was not visualized as a lifetime vocation when he started out. Thus, comparatively minute details of a vocational activity may occasionally involve the young adult in an over-all pattern he did not initially envision for himself.

Students of occupational adjustment have discovered that one of the most fruitful approaches to their field is the study of why people abandon their occupations. One's original choice of occupation is likely to be based upon some misperceptions of its nature, but his abandonment of the occupation is based upon fuller knowledge of what it entails and how well his construct system enables him to cope with it. The personal-construct psychologist is therefore inclined to adopt this same emphasis in the study of vocational experience, and the interpretation of it in terms of personal construct systems. The study of job satisfaction, the use of the exit interview, the analysis of training failures, the establishment of job retraining programs, the development of industrial counseling programs in connection with personal difficulties arising in relation to one's job, all offer means of understanding personal constructs through the analysis of vocational experience.

B. Structural Interpretation of Experience

6. APPRAISAL OF THE BIOGRAPHICAL RECORD

The biographical record may be viewed in five different ways. First of all, it may be seen as factual material out of which a person has had to make some kind of sense at some time in his life. Second, it reveals something of what the person's construction system must have been in order to account for his behaving in certain ways in the past; hence it suggests the kind of thinking and behavior to which he may have recourse if his present way of life suddenly becomes invalid or unpredictive. In the third place, it indicates the kinds of social expectancies with which the person has been surrounded, and hence the kinds of validators with which he has had to check his construct system. In the fourth place, the biographical record, as selectively remembered and personally construed by the individual, throws important light upon that which, most of all, is of concern to the psychologist: the presently operating construct system. Finally, the record may be seen as something which will have to be rationalized by the client in connection with any therapeutic reformulation of his concept of his life role.

It is to be noted that, while we have pointed out five ways in which the biographical record is important to a psychological understanding of the individual, we have not included the one justification which is most popularly offered by clinicians for examining it. We have intentionally avoided saying that the raw events of the past have themselves *caused* the individual to become the person that he is. Events may be the mile posts in reference to which the individual's progress is timed, yet it is the *con-*

struing that weaves impersonal events into personal experience.

a. *Birth.* The points usually stressed are: date of birth, mother's age, pregnancy period, duration of labor, type of delivery, mother's health before and after birth, evidence of early injury to the child, difficulty in initiating breathing, convulsions, infections, fevers, early feeding difficulties, and measures taken to correct early injuries and difficulties.

b. *Maturation.* The following landmarks of rate of development are usually noted: age of learning to sit alone, appearance of first tooth, discontinuation of breast feeding, discontinuation of bottle feeding, walking, use of sentences, bowel control, bladder control, holding a cup, holding a spoon, dressing self, lacing and tying shoes, discontinuing regular nap, discontinuing sleeping with parent, playing with children of own age, playing organized and competitive games, and reaching puberty. Other landmarks may be more significant, but it is harder to get reliable statements regarding them.

c. *Care.* Illnesses should be noted, together with the age at which they occurred, the severity, the duration, the maximum fever temperature and its duration, and the medical care used. The following may be recorded: frequency of routine visits to a physician, nurse, and dentist; frequency and amount of medication administered at home; hours of retiring and rising and their regularity; frequency and regularity of bowel movements, urinations, washing, bathing, and eating; variety of foods eaten, number of quarts of milk used in household per week in relation to the numbers of children and adults. One may inquire regarding the presence and proportions of fruit, fresh vegetables, meat, sweets, and cooking fats in the child's diet. What about the manner of serving meals? Are they served regularly? Are they served hot? Served in a family group? Accompanied by criticism and rigid discipline?

In evaluating the foregoing part of the biographical record the psychologist should keep in mind the five interpretive approaches which were listed at the beginning of this section. The information listed above under the heading of "birth" may have certain physiological implications which, in turn, may be subjected to one or more of the five types of biographical interpretation. It may also indicate what the advent of the child must have meant to other members of the family and the kinds of expectancies with which the child must therefore have been surrounded in his early years. When the biographical record is obtained from the mother, for example, it is obvious that the psychologist who is thinking in terms of personal constructs will make a considerable effort to elicit and understand what the events meant to the mother and, perhaps, attach even more importance to that than to the objective accuracy with which the events are reported. In a sense, the events which a mother remembers and reports may be considered to be the arguments which she assembles in defense of her perception of her child. It is therefore important to see what her construction of those events is. It is a serious clinical mistake to ignore her account of what happened just because it is inaccurate.

For similar reasons one's own account of his birth may be an important consideration in the explanation of his personal constructs. The oft retold story of how he came into the world becomes in later years one of the pivotal points about which a person's thinking revolves. It is customary to make the conditions of one's birth both the symbol and one of the fundamental elements in the construction of one's own life role, and in the construction of the life roles of others. Note, for example, the meaning that a child attaches to being his parents' "own" child versus being adopted, the position given historically to hereditary "rights," or even to the religious significance attached by certain Christian sects to the legitimacy and cleanliness of circumstances under which Jesus was born.

The maturational record generally indicates how the child came to rely upon his own resources. It indicates what kinds of independence he found valid at different stages in his life. This is not to say that the earlier a maturational landmark is reached the more adequate is his approach to life. The proper differentiation and gradual allocation of dependency enables one to develop a more adequate way of construing one's world.

For example, the student who maintains a kind of "dependent" relationship until relatively late in life learns more about what to depend upon. He may thus become more "independent" of those material tokens his erstwhile "self-reliant" playmates cannot get along without.

The care record can be used, not only to gain an idea of the status of the child in the family, but to indicate the controls or regular day-to-day validators against which one has had to check his anticipations. In a previous chapter we have attempted to describe the "deterioration" of constructs and the accompanying reduction in the level of awareness with which they are utilized. The care record gives one an idea of what constructs have operated and are probably still operating, even though they have now been reduced to a low level of cognitive awareness.

d. *Behavior problems.* The biographical record should indicate what behavior "problems" have occupied the attention of the parents and of the person himself. The psychologist should again be careful to keep in mind that it is quite as important to see the behavior "problem" as throwing light upon the construction system of the perceiver of the problem, whether the parent or the now grown child, as it is to see the "problem" as evidence of maladjustment. As the respondent elaborates the "problems," the perceptive psychologist may learn as much about the constructive systems which are operating in the present as about those which have operated in the past.

In making the inquiry regarding the biographical record of behavior problems, the psychologist will develop his questioning along the lines already discussed briefly in the preceding chapter dealing with the analysis of a person's educational experience. The topic is more fully discussed in a later chapter. The age at which the "problem" appeared, the circumstances — at least what are interpreted as relevant circumstances by the respondent — the conditions under which the problem was least noticeable, the conditions under which the problem was most noticeable, the corrective measures attempted, and the changes associated with the corrective measures or the passage of time should be explored.

e. *Interpersonal relations.* The history of the client's companions and how they are perceived by him, and how they were perceived by other members of the family, is an important part of the biographical record. The controls over interpersonal relationship which were imposed on the child should be investigated. The degree of intimacy involved — for example, in a sex relationship — the kinds of activity shared, the manner of reaching agreements in joint activities, and the manner of terminating the companionship should be detailed. The descriptive terminology now employed by the client in referring to these companions should be examined, just as they are examined in interpreting the Role Construct Repertory Test protocol. Included in this section should also be the record of what sex information was given, the manner in which it was given, the circumstances, and the controls imposed in connection with this type of interpersonal relationship.

f. *Education and occupation.* These aspects of the biographical record have already been discussed.

7. HEALTH AND EXPERIENCE

The clinical psychologist is concerned with the health of his client. He is concerned, not only because of broad professional and humanitarian interests, but because health has a specific kind of bearing upon the psychological evaluation of his client. Just what is the nature of the psychologist's concern about the health of his client? This is a question about which considerable tension has arisen between clinical psychologists and certain medical groups.

a. *Psychology vs. medicine.* The controversy has arisen largely out of the confusion which must inevitably result when one seeks to construe a set of events solely within one conceptual system. The philosophical principles involved in this problem were discussed in various sections of the first chapter. There is a difference between construing a set of events *wholly* within one scientific system and construing them *solely* within one scientific system. In the former case, one seeks to embrace each and every event of the set within the unifying system. This does not mean that each event cannot also be construed in another system. When one construes events *solely* within one conceptual system, he assumes that the events are the property of the system. Such a position violates the basic tenets of the modern philosophy of science. The physician violates scientific principles when, hearing that a person has a pain in his chest, he assumes that the case therefore *belongs* to him. The clinical psychologist is similarly confused when he agrees that, since the pain is medically construed, he has no responsibility for construing it psychologically also. Both views stand in clear contrast to the position we have described as constructive alternativism.

There is also a more subtle confusion which interferes with the interprofessional relations of the clinical psychologist and the physician. It arises out of the notion that physiologically construed facts are more "real" than psychologically construed facts. The latter are sometimes even said to be imaginary. Since physiologically construed facts are more "real," the problems which are formulated in physiological terminology are thought to be more urgent and to require attention "first."

Now it is true that the physiological approach tends currently to be more concretistic than the psychological approach. In part, that is due to the greater current stability of the physiological system. As we have said before, there is a tendency of a system to deteriorate, with unchallenged and repeated use, toward impermeability. That has happened in the field of medicine. But that is incidental to the interprofessional controversy and does not necessarily argue either for the priority of the physiological issues in dealing with a client or for the abandonment of the physician's approach on the grounds of its conceptual rigidity and its apparent philosophical obsolescence.

b. *Legitimate separation of professional functions.* While this is not the place to deal extensively with the problems of interprofessional relations, it should be said that the physician does, on other grounds, have a legitimate claim to priority in dealing with complaints of certain types. There are complaints with which the physiological, chemical, and mechanical approaches have proved consistently efficacious — at least the complaints are altered as a result of the application of these approaches. Where psychological approaches can make no equivalent claim to efficacy it would seem most economical to approach those particular problems *first* by applying the system in which there appears to be the greater promise of therapeutic change.

But while the physician sometimes has a legitimate claim to priority in dealing with a given client, the psychologist has a no less legitimate claim to any bit of information from which he can make important psychological inferences. In simple language that means, for example, that a psychologist should be free to test a client's reflexes if he is to construe the results psychologically. This is not to say that the psychologist, in doing so, is making a "neurological" examination, or even part of a neurological examination; he may still be working within a strictly psychological system. When a psychologist tests and observes behavior in this manner he should be careful not to mislead either himself, the neurologist, or the client as to the nature of his examination.

c. *Health and validation.* The discovery of truth is greatly affected by where one has to look for it and the kinds of experiments he is able to perform. A person who is seriously crippled cannot look for truth on the football field, and a child who is restricted to his bed by illness does not discover exactly what happens when you give a playmate a solid sock on the jaw. The ill or unhealthy person does, however, have a special field of validating evidence placed at his disposal as a consequence of his illness. With it he may verify constructs which, for others, must always remain unclear.

To describe a person's health from a psychological point of view is to describe the facts against which he must validate the pattern of his daily living and the implements with which he must explore his world. The child who is deaf misses the shades of meaning which are conveyed by intonations of the voice, and thus may appear to be obtuse in his interpersonal relationships. The adult who becomes deaf misses them also but he has learned that they are there, and, in his attempts to sense them, he has to rely overmuch upon the projection of his construction system.

The child who is malnourished does not learn what might otherwise be learned regarding the attainment of long-range goals. His attempts at putting forth sustained effort are continually interrupted by short cycles of rest and agitation. He may indeed appear apathetic, and in some instances even patient, but that is because of the repetitive nature of his psychological processes. Figuratively, he cannot leave his body long enough to go away and actively explore other areas of interest. The starving adult is not likely to be found assuming a firm long-range position in such matters as free enterprise, democracy, socialism, or communism. Similarly, the psychological correlates of many types of physical illness can better be explained as *adjustments to the illness* rather than as "psychosomatic" symptoms. In the terms of the psychology of personal constructs, the person must gear himself to his illness, and the optimal way he has found for doing it is commonly called a psychological symptom of the illness. This is an important viewpoint in looking upon problems of health. We see it as a far better structured approach than the eclecticism known as "psychosomatic medicine."

d. *Health and dependency.* There is a special way in which health is related to psychological experience. In childhood one's relations with his parents are partly determined by his dependency upon them for meeting physical needs. The parent is stronger and he can lift the child over obstacles. The parent provides food which the child could not otherwise obtain. The parent protects the child from physical danger. In addition to these functions, there are, of course, more complicated functions such as affection and teaching which are performed by the parent. Considering, for the moment, only the parent's assistance in meeting physical needs, we can see that the child comes to see his relationship to the parent as a *dependent* one. The parent is the immediate validator for the child's testing of his construct system. As Courtney suggests, the parent is himself a kind of solution for the young child's problems. The child sets up his system to predict the parent. He may establish a role for himself in relation to the parent by attempting to subsume or understand the parent's way of looking at things.

As a child becomes older, he is able gradually to establish and validate for himself a more independent pattern of activity as far as his relations with his parents are concerned. This is not necessarily accompanied by any diminution of his role relationships with his parents; indeed, he may come to play a much more comprehensive and helpful role in relation to his parents as he becomes more independent of them. He becomes comparatively independent of them because his dependencies are distributed elsewhere.

When a person becomes ill or handicapped, many of the old dependency patterns must be reactivated. The parent, wife, nurse, or doctor becomes the validator for a large share of the constructs with which the person must order his daily life. In psychoanalytic terms, "the ego is weakened."

Now this is not necessarily a destructive thing. There are times when the reactivation of the old dependency patterns, and the setting up of a set of validators for which these simple types of anticipatory systems are adequate, will stabilize the client psychologically. There are cases in which the medical treatment of an ailment has accomplished more psychologically for a client than it has physiologically. As a hospitalized patient the client's difficulties in formulating his role and his guilt disturbances resulting therefrom may disappear, because his pattern of life has become clarified and more effective for dealing with what is at hand. In psychoanalytic terms, "the demands of reality have been simplified."

With some clients, however, the dependency pattern upon which the illness throws them is inadequate. The psychological disturbance which results from the attempted treatment of the physically construed illness may be more disruptive than the illness itself. We have all seen this happen in the case of older people who have been demoralized by the kind of dependency relationship which they were required to establish as a consequence of their presumed helplessness.

We have been talking about persons whose ill health has forced them to return to childlike dependency patterns. There is also the problem of the child whose ill health has, from an early age, required the use of certain dependency patterns long beyond the point where he would normally replace them. There is also the child whose parents behave as if the child were in ill health, and thus continually offer validation to his constructive exploration of his world only when he casts himself in a dependent relationship to them. Ill health, and particularly the child's and his parents' perception of ill health, therefore, become important data for a psychological interpretation of a person's life.

e. *Adjustment to ill health.* The adjustments that arise out of ill health are sometimes utilized in psychotherapy. Simulated ill health — hospitalization, reactivation of dependency patterns, even the temporary perception of "symptoms" — are all devices which, if properly used, may help a client construe his world in a more adequate manner. We shall have more to say on this topic in a later chapter.

Each "physiological" disorder requires a somewhat characteristic pattern of anticipatory adjustment. Each disease characteristically withdraws certain validators from the immediate experience range of the person and substitutes certain others. Each handicap invites its own characteristic dependency pattern. Each symptom calls for a typical psychological construction. Even though a person may follow a commonality pattern in the psychological construction of his ill health, the pattern is worked out by him on his own and must involve a characteristically personal approach. It is not contradictory to say that a psychological adjustment to ill health is characteristic both of the ill health and of the client.

We have already mentioned the regression to older dependency patterns as part of the adjustment a person makes when he becomes physically helpless. The regression involves more than the reinstatement of old dependencies. There is a tendency for disease to be accompanied by a reactivation of other older systems, at least during the earlier stages of the illness. This comes about because the person, in seeking to reconstrue the world which has become altered by illness, must experiment with sweeping revisions of relatively great generality. The only alternative approaches which are sufficiently general to fit his new situation, and yet which are in his repertory and thus immediately available to him for "trying on," are those more comprehensive constructs which have at one time been operative and "valid" but which have since been tentatively abandoned.

This regression to earlier modes of conceptualization, often accompanying a sudden major illness, need not crystallize. With a reasonable number of tools and a reasonable variety of validating evidence in his immediate experience range, a person can reconstrue a new pattern of life which is both appropriate and mature.

In studying a person's psychological construction of organic conditions one can learn a good deal from the way organs and sensations are used as elements in the context of constructs. The hand that an amputee no longer has may become constructively linked with lost opportunities, deprivation experiences, sexual impotency, and various other elements coming to his attention. The victim of stomach ulcers may apply highly discriminative constructs to foods and the sensations associated with them. In the Draw-a-Man Test (Goodenough) or the Draw-a-Person Test (Machover) he may focalize his efforts upon elaborating the midriff or perhaps avoid the job of drawing the stomach altogether because it is "too difficult." Or he may simply criticize the completed drawing as "not being right around here" (pointing to the stomach or esophagal region).

The careful psychological study of how certain organs and sensations are construed is an important way to arrive at an understanding of a client's more generalized approaches to life. The psychologist may occasionally arrive at a helpful understanding of marital adjustment by discovering how his client construes sex organs. He may understand a woman's intensive preoccupation with the color scheme in her home if he learns how she construes graying hair. He may uncover perversion constructs by seeing how lips are construed. He may come to appreciate a client's feeling of guilt if he learns what interpretation has been placed upon a birthmark. He may spend a great deal more time helping a client to reconstrue the fact that he has had syphilis than the physician spends in remedying the physiological symptoms.

Just as an element is used as a symbol, or as the sine qua non of a construct, so may an organ, a sensation, or a symptom be used as the symbol of a construct. When a client talks about the pain in his chest he may be expressing in his own language a far more comprehensive construct than the psychologist at first suspects. It has long been recognized that the affected organ in what is commonly called "conversion hysteria" is utilized symbolically, even though it may be chosen according to the principle of "somatic compliance" — that is, was somewhat physiologically disturbed anyway and thus was a plausible locus of a conversion symptom. The symbolic use of a symptom is nowhere better illustrated than by the following account by Poch, which only recently came to the writer's attention.

A patient was complaining, as he had done during numerous therapy interviews before, about the trouble he was having on his job. "The same old trouble" was cropping up on this new job; namely, frequent headaches and trouble with his eyes. It was so bad yesterday that he couldn't bring himself to go to work at all.

These complaints had become very familiar in therapy by this time. The therapist had used them in many ways to carry discussion into a variety of areas. This time, however, the therapist suddenly became aware that the patient was saying repeatedly: "I'm sick. . . . I'm sick. . . . I'm sick. . . . " Realizing that this must have some significance for the patient which had as yet not been explored, but having exhausted the usual non-directive attempts at eliciting the meaning for the patient of his illness, the therapist asked this time: "What's the opposite of 'sick'?" The patient promptly replied: "Free." This came as a surprise to the therapist, who was expecting "well," or "healthy," or some similar term.

This new information opened up a whole new channel for discussion with the patient, by way of which it became possible to bring the patient closer to a recognition of *his use* of illness as a security operation.

8. THE CLINICIAN'S STRUCTURIZATION OF EXPERIENCE IN A CASE

We have laid a great stress upon the way a client structures his experience. That is understandable, in view of our theoretical position. But does this mean that the clinician's own personal structurization of the client's experience is not important? By no means! For seeing the client's experience as being structured by him in a characteristic way is itself a clinician's way of structuring experience. The problem, of course, is to help the clinician structure the client's structurizations. The clinician must interpret the client's experience, not merely his activity.

Now basically this is to say that the clinician should establish for himself a true role relationship to his client. And it is to be remembered that in the psychology of personal constructs a role relationship is defined in a special way. It is not enough that the clinician be able to think *about* the client's actions or even at times to think *like* the client; he must be able to *subsume* the client's thoughts. That means he must be able to say to himself, "Now this is the way I would anticipate that the client would see this thing. I infer this, not merely from sampling his perceptions, for as far as I know he has never dealt with this specific thing before, but from my knowledge of his repertory of constructs upon which he would have to draw if he were confronted with this situation." In the language of our earlier chapter, the clinician's relation to his client is not based merely upon the Commonality Corollary but also upon the Sociality Corollary. The effective clinician is not the client's twin brother who acts like him, talks like him, and thinks like him. He is the client's teacher who can *anticipate* his behavior, not merely imitate it, and therefore can act as the client *would act,* not merely as the client *has acted.* The clinician then can also turn around and act in contrast to the way the client would act. Finally, the clinician can reconcile and differentiate the two courses of action by subsuming, under some more permeable constructs, the constructs which governed them.

Now this is not to say that only a clinician who establishes a comprehensive role relationship with a client can serve psychotherapeutic ends. As we have indicated before, a client may get himself straightened out by coming in contact with a "therapist" who offers himself up as an example through expressing personal views on sundry matters more or less related to the client's complaint. The client, in the course of understanding the "therapist," works out a plan of action. The therapist helps the client by offering himself to the client as an unwitting example. The client profits from the experience, but not in the way the therapist intended.

The clinician's construction of a case proceeds by successive approximations. He uncovers many facts about his client before he begins to discover the personal constructs with which the client orders those facts within his system. It is therefore essential that the clinician have a ready-made ad interim set of constructs to bind the facts revealed in the case record until such a time as he is able to construe them in the light of the client's personal system and, in turn, to subsume the system in terms of a comprehensive psychological point of view. For clarity's sake we have distinguished between the clinician's ad interim binding of the facts and his eventual organization of the record into a well subsumed system, comprising the client's personal constructs. The former we call *structurization* and the latter we call *construction.*

The clinician's construction of a case is that formulation which permits him to see the client in perspective— past, present, and future. His structurization throws light only upon the past and the present and has very little predictive or anticipatory utility. The structuristic approach to psychological problems is represented historically by the approaches of Wundt and Titchener. The constructive approach, to the extent that it is in contrast, is perhaps best represented historically by the French school of psychopathology of the late nineteenth century and by its Freudian outgrowth. Both approaches, as we incorporate them into the psychology of personal constructs, bear a relationship to the British associationistic movement which will have scarcely escaped the reader who has followed our discussion up to this point.

The frame of reference for the psychiatrically trained reader is the terminology of "descriptive" versus "dynamic." While we have made it clear that we want to avoid the implicit assumptions ordinarily implied by the term "dynamic," the formulation of a case in terms of "psychodynamics," rather than in terms of "descriptive psychopathology," is an illustration of one way of making a construction of a case rather than a structurization of it.

Now this is not the place to make a final statement of how to go about completing the clinician's construction of a case. That comes later. It is certainly not the place to make definitive statements as to what the construction of a given case must be. The whole gist of our theoretical discussion is to the effect that that can be accomplished only in relation to a particular client. At this point all we can do is offer a way for the clinician to structurize his client's experience. That means suggesting ways in which the facts can be temporarily bound together until some later moment when the clinician's construction of the client's *personal system* makes the whole picture spring to life. As the clinician who has worked in intensive long-term psychotherapy knows, when that time comes the facts in the case record begin to stand out in vivid detail and the pattern of the client's life can be seen extending far into the future's distance.

9. COLLECTIVE TERMS FOR THE STRUCTURIZATION OF EXPERIENCE DATA

The following terms are proposed for use in the ad interim stages of dealing with factual material in the client's experience record. For the most part they do not represent the kinds of constructs which are utilizable during the course of therapy. They do not have high predictive utility for the future. They are not *prognostic*, not even *diagnostic* in the sense we have reserved for that expression. They are certainly not *personal constructs* except for the purely incidental fact that they are the writer's. They are simply formal *collecting terms* under which the data comprising the record of experience can be tentatively assembled. Some of them represent levels of generality and utility different from that of others. Some of them are scarcely psychological, though their use serves a temporary psychological function for the clinician.

Validators is the systematic construct for describing the kind of generality chosen for this ad interim structurization of a case. That is simply to say that the following terms refer to the kinds of events the person has had to anticipate. While the terms do not describe his personal construct system directly, they do indicate what that system has had to deal with and they offer some indirect evidence as to how its dealings must have been accomplished.

The following terms may be used as section headings in the presentation of a case in a staff conference which is preparing to take up, from the start, the problem of the diagnostic planning of therapy. They may also be used in the interagency reporting of detailed case records.

a. *Figure matrix.* Under this heading one may place information from the experience record regarding the *kinds* of people the individual has known intimately. The individually characteristic ways in which the people known to the client have worked out their interpersonal relationships and their life spans can be collected into *figure constructs* by the psychologist and then, in turn, assembled under the rubric of *figure matrix.*

b. *Cooperative relationships.* Under this heading is collected information from the experience record which indicates that the client has played identifiable parts in constructive social processes. This permits the psychologist to hypothesize that the client has developed a role type of relationship with the other people involved in the social processes. Whether he actually has or not is a matter to be verified from a more intimate study of the client's personal constructs. Indications of the effectiveness of role relationships can be assembled under this rubric.

c. *Characterizations of the client.* Under this heading are collected the various bits of information regarding the manner in which the client is described by the people with whom he must live. Whether they are "right" in their characterizations of him is less important than the fact that he must continually validate his construction of himself against the image which he sees reflected in their eyes.

d. *Externally imposed group identifications.* Under this heading is collected information regarding how the client is seen by others in terms of membership in various collections of people. This is not to say that he sees himself identified in the same way that he is identified by others. It is to say that, somehow, he must account for the fact that he is continually being perceived as a member of certain groups. Again it is a matter of *validators.* Frequently the easiest solution, from his own point of view, is to admit that he actually is a member of a certain group and to start using the construct system that the group uses. That permits him to anticipate, in a reasonably stable fashion, the behavior of his parents as well as that of teachers, bosses, cops, and snobs. He may even take great delight in spiteful obedience to their misperceptions.

e. *Areas in which the client is incorporated or alienated.* Under various appropriate subtitles one may collect those evidences of the client's incorporation or alienation by others. By *incorporation* we mean the willingness to see a person as like oneself. By *alienation* we mean the unwillingness to see a person as like oneself. This concept of *incorporation-alienation* is a little tricky to apply. It is to be noted that incorporation, when defined in the way we have chosen to define it, does not mean the absence of criticism. Nor does it mean that other people imitate the client by adopting his ways. It is not quite the same as identification or empathy with the client; rather, it is more of a projective phenomenon. It does not necessarily involve acceptance or the readiness to play out a role relationship with a person.

May incorporates John if she seeks to understand him in terms of herself. She may scold him, as she scolds herself, or as she feels that she should be scolded by others, but still she incorporates him if she sees him as like herself in various important ways. She may fail to play a role in relation to John because of her failure to attempt to subsume his construct system. She may even feel threatened by him. But if she sees him as like herself, she, in the sense of this structurization construct, *incorporates* him. He is one of her kind. She is willing to work on the idea that John is really like herself, even though he is somewhat hard to understand at times. She elaborates her construction of John along the lines of her construction of herself.

Perhaps another person, Maybelle, alienates John, in that she does not pursue the possibility that John is like herself. She may "like" John. She may exploit him effectively. She may temporarily please him. Yet she does not make him one of her kind; and this is what we would call alienation.

In collecting information from the experience record regarding the client's areas of incorporation and alienation we should take into account (1) the *groups of people* who are ready to see him as somewhat like themselves and (2) the *areas or ways* in which they are ready to see him as somewhat like themselves. In this way we can see the potential validators of the client's construct system in terms of the way his associates look upon themselves.

For example, if a group of graduate students in psychology look upon Lemuel as possibly being a psychologist, and start to experiment in their social relations with him as if he were one, they are incorporating him. They are incorporating him into the areas bounded by whatever they believe to be characteristic of their occupational group. We may say, then, that Lemuel has a particular area of incorporation which is bounded by these graduate students in one dimension and by their conception of themselves in another dimension. This means that he has a number of potentially "right" answers waiting for him if he will only behave in the way these graduate students think they behave.

f. *External patterns of conflict and solution.* While the clinical psychologist is eventually concerned with the problems his client construes for himself, he may collect intermediate information by discovering the patterns of conflict and solution of conflict which are exhibited in the client's social milieu. Presumably the client must experience these external patterns in some subjectively valid way. As he experiences them he may be able to construe them so as to disentangle himself. If he does, he may experience them without coming to use them as prototypes for his own pattern of behavior. That is not easy. It is much more likely that he will become enmeshed in any externally imposed patterns of conflict and will seek solutions along the lines local custom dictates. For example, if he finds himself in a society which defines some of its issues in terms of a conflict between white people and colored people, he will be hard pressed to keep from dealing in terms of the same dichotomy and employing the same methods of solution customarily used by one or the other of the two groups.

g. *Thematic repertory.* Just as in a clinical analysis of the Thematic Apperception Test one attempts to discover the underlying thema in the stories told by the subject, so may one also look for thema in the social world which surrounds the subject. What are the family stories? What is the community folklore? What epic tales are told? What are the life-span patterns that are most clearly represented to the client as he looks about him? It is against these that he must somehow make his own story plots appear to be plausible. If the play is written by his culture group, how can he interpret his own part in order to fit into the plot?

h. *Symbolic system.* Under this rubric are collected items of information starting with the language background of the client and including various other symbolisms: religious, nationalistic, architectural, institutional, proverbial, epigrammatic, and so on. This provides a key to the way a person is likely to construe his world when he is reduced to the use of literalisms. It also indicates what common verbal resources may be available for use in therapy.

i. *Climate of opinion out of which complaints arise.* Even a complaint is likely to be a somewhat conventionalized thing. When it was ladylike to faint, people who wanted to be ladylike fainted. When the writings of Jung became known in American educational circles, many teachers began to act more consistently like introverts. When the work of Adler was imported, people began to complain of inferiority complexes. In certain rural areas, children who do poorly in school are said to have "worms." In certain urban areas and in certain strata of society, children are described as "insecure," while neither the term nor the proto-type symptom is very likely to be found in other places. In certain sophisticated groups, people complain about their "in-hibitions." A family that has "headaches," "gas on the stomach," "the blues," or "high-strung nerves" provides ready-made "symp-toms" for its members to have when anything vaguely goes wrong. That is not to say that nothing is really amiss when a person complains of one of these symptoms. What we are emphasizing is the climate of opinion in which certain types of complaints tend to flourish.

j. *Versatility.* Collected here is the evidence from the ex-perience record which indicates the *range* of activities in which the client has engaged or about which he has done considerable thinking. This will enable the clinician to make a tentative estimate of the client's freedom for experimentation and the lengths to which he has gone in order to find solutions for his problems. It also provides some useful information regarding the context for therapy, that is, the areas from which both the client and therapist may draw in seeking illustrative material to facilitate their communication with each other.

k. *Biographical turning points.* This refers to another kind of versatility. In the experience records of some clients there is clear evidence of changes in their courses of action. These may indicate — though not necessarily — changes in the superordinate construction system. The presence of such inflection points in the biographical record suggests the client's capacity or readi-ness for making further marked changes in himself. They suggest, not only the capacity for therapeutic movement, but also the capacity for psychological "breaks." The manner in which the changes have taken place indicate the manner in which further changes may be expected to take place. The biographical rec-ord, studied carefully with reference to a time line, will show a great deal more than it will if it is composed merely of an aggregation of facts which are not distributed according to their chronology. The therapist who sees his client in a time perspective is likely to find him both more acceptable and more plausible.

1. *Physical resources.* Collected here are the physical resources which may be brought into play in helping a client solve his problems, as well as the physical resources upon which he has become dependent. These range all the way from toys, for a child, to wealth, for an adult. They include not only personal property but also the resources of the community — playgrounds and schools to laboratories and business opportunities.

m. *Social resources.* Collected here are the people who can help in the over-all rehabilitation of the client, as well as those whom he currently uses in working out his problems.

n. *Personal resources.* In this collection are such items as vocational skills, intellectual ability, knowledge areas, health, reputation — including credit standing, for example — physical attractiveness, youth, and other personal attributes which may figure in the development of a readjustment pattern.

o. *Dependencies.* This overlaps the three preceding resources terms but relates primarily to those resources upon which the client appears to have been so dependent that his whole pattern of life would be seriously interrupted if he were to lose them. A mother may be one of a child's principal resources, even though she may appear not to be a very reliable mother. Because he has no substitute and he is dependent upon her, he may cling to her with a tenacity which surprises the observer who thinks that the child "should" abandon the mother as a bad job. There is an old story which has always impressed the writer as quite relevant to this point. It has to do with a man who lost his status as a musician because "his monkey died."

p. *Supportive status.* Here are collected those items which indicate how and in what manner the client is seen as necessary to the lives and comfort of other people. Who is dependent upon him? In what way is he seen as supportive? The facts collected under this rubric are likely to be conspicuous validators which the client will have difficulty ignoring when he starts to check his efficiency in anticipating the events of everyday life.

The conclusion of this chapter finds us with many of the most significant applications of the personal-construct point of view yet to be described. Having taken the stand that we have, we could not be expected to attach any more than intermediate importance to the analysis of experience as such. The clinical constructs which have been used to bind together the material in this chapter are not the kinds of personal constructs which are considered to be of salient significance in the psychological construction of life. All we have been able to accomplish in this chapter is to provide a kind of outline by which the clinician may become aware of the matrix of events which his client has had to anticipate. This has been a discussion of validators, not the constructs which are validated.

Chapter Fifteen

Steps in Diagnosis

THIS IS a strictly methodological chapter having to do with routine steps to be followed in arriving at a diagnosis which, in turn, will point the way to treatment.

A. A Systematic View of the Major Clinical Issues

1. TRANSITIVE DIAGNOSIS

From the standpoint of the psychology of personal constructs, diagnosis is properly conceived as the planning stage of client management. Our basic philosophical position, which we have chosen to call "constructive alternativism," assumes that there are many ways in which the same facts may be construed and that it is therefore impractical to claim that what events naturally are dictates the one and only way in which they may be accurately construed. Rather, we have taken the view that the reality of events permits many alternative and useful constructions to be placed upon them. In deciding just which construction to employ, we need to be guided by what we want to do about the events as well as by their reality.

The psychology of personal constructs proceeds from the assumption that the clinical psychologist wants to help his clients. It therefore sets up an approach which is designed, not only to embrace the realities of the client's life, but also to point out those avenues along which the client and the psychologist may proceed toward a solution of the client's problems. This is the approach which follows from our philosophical position of constructive alternativism, and from the series of psychological assumptions which have been stated in our basic postulate and its eleven corollaries. An important feature of such an approach is that clinical diagnosis should be construed as the planning stage for client reconstruction.

So that it may be kept clearly in mind just how we approach diagnosis, we are using the term *transitive diagnosis*. The term suggests that we are concerned with transitions in the client's life, that we are looking for bridges between the client's present and his future. Moreover, we expect to take an active part in helping the client select or build the bridges to be used and in helping him cross them safely. The client does not ordinarily sit cooped up in a nosological pigeonhole; he proceeds along his way. If the psychologist expects to help him he must get up off his chair and start moving along with him.

In the preceding chapters we have proposed some diagnostic constructs which are designed to help the psychologist meet this particular kind of responsibility. As we have indicated before, these constructs define the more important ways in which the client can change, and not merely ways in which the psychologist may distinguish him from other persons. The diagnostic dimensions are avenues of movement as seen by the therapist, just as the client's personal constructs are potential avenues of movement as seen by the client. Transitive diagnosis is, therefore, based on a dimensional system of axes and transitional states.

Much of the reform proposed by the psychology of personal constructs is directed toward the tendency for psychologists to impose preemptive constructions upon human behavior. Diagnosis is all too frequently an attempt to cram a whole live struggling client into a nosological category. Among psychiatrists this approach is frequently labeled as Kraepelinianism. Among psychologists it is often called Aristotelianism. These terms are themselves preemptive labels which tend to do injustice to two great contributors to psychological thought.

In the writer's opinion, one of the many great contributions of psychoanalytic thinking is its development of a system of "psychodynamics" to replace the nosological systems of the day. Psychoanalysis permitted the clinician to see that there was something going on in the client; that he was not merely a misshapen lump of matter. To be sure, in making this contribution, psychoanalysts, particularly Freud and his disciples, reached far back into preclassical thinking for their model. Psychoanalytic thinking is shot through with anthropomorphisms, vitalisms, and energisms that are only a few short steps removed from primitive notions of demoniacal possession and exorcism. Yet rooted as it is in this way, the psychoanalytic construction of man presents him as a warm, living creature, albeit a relatively helpless one. At least it does not portray man in the stony form of a classical Grecian statue.

Like psychoanalysis, the psychology of personal constructs also registers its protest against nosological diagnosis and all the forms of thinking which distract our attention from the fact that life does go on and on. If a clinician wishes to free himself of the restrictions of fixed nosological pigeonholes, he must start examining clinical situations with an eye for the practical potentialities. In transitive diagnosis the clinician, instead of preoccupying himself with the question, "In what category should this case be classified?" immediately addresses himself to the question, "What is to become of this client?" He attempts to formulate the decisive issues at the outset and forthwith directs his diagnostic examination toward resolving them. Eventually, of course, he makes a temporarily preemptive construction of the case in the manner described in the preceding chapter. After all, he must do something with the case. He must decide whether to send him to this ward or that ward, whether to undertake outpatient treatment or not, whether to approve his university schedule or not — whatever the situation calls for. Thus, transitive diagnosis is not an end in itself, but rather, the development of a plan for a client's management. The plan involves more than what some clinicians construe as "therapy" or even "treatment." It includes everything which is done for the client's welfare.

While much progress has been made recently in the clinical applications of psychology, the variety of practical measures likely to be taken in behalf of a disturbed person is still distressingly limited. It is particularly limited in neuropsychiatric hospitals, where there is almost always a shortage of staff and, though not quite so often now, of imagination. The next few years will undoubtedly see clinicians choosing treatment measures from a much bigger bag of tricks. Even with this anticipated extension of the clinician's repertory, the number of alternative courses of action which are feasible in a case will still be finite. In a very practical sense the limited number of action alternatives in a given case will continue to determine, in a practical manner, the diagnostic issues at stake.

2. OUTLINE OF THE CLINICAL ISSUES

Following is a tentative list of the practical issues which arise when one considers a client from the standpoint of the psychology of personal constructs and attempts to make what we have characterized as a transitive diagnosis. The issues at the beginning of the list are essentially at a descriptive level and are therefore framed within the common patterns of perception of psychological observers. One does not have to adhere strictly to a particular psychological viewpoint in order to report them consistently. The issues at the middle of the list require a greater scientific sophistication. The final issues require therapeutic training on the part of the psychologist who resolves them.

I. Normative formulations of the client's problem.
  1. Description of the manifest deviant behavior patterns (symptoms).
  2. Description of the correlates of the manifest deviant behavior patterns.
  3. Description of the gains and losses accruing to the client

through his symptoms (description of validational experience).

II. Psychological description of the client's personal constructions.

1. The client's construction of what he believes to be the problem area.
2. The client's construction of what others believe to be the problem area.
3. The client's construction of his life role.

III. Psychological evaluation of the client's construction system.

1. Location of his areas of anxiety, aggressiveness (or spontaneous elaboration), and constriction.
2. Sampling of the types of construction he uses in different areas.
3. Sampling of his modes of approach to new problems to determine how he customarily resolves anxiety.
4. Determination of his accessibility and levels of communication.

IV. Analysis of the milieu in which adjustment is to be sought.

1. Analysis of the expectancy system within which the client must make his life role function.
2. Assessment of the socio-economic assets in the case.
3. Preparation of information to be utilized as contextual material in helping the client reconstrue life.

V. Determination of immediate procedural steps.

1. Physiological construction of the available data.
2. Other professional constructions of the available data.
3. Evaluation of the urgency of the case.

VI. Planning management and treatment.

1. Selection of the central therapeutic approach.
2. Designation of the principally responsible clinician.
3. Selection of adjunctive resources to be utilized.
4. Designation of the responsible clinician's advisory staff.
5. Determination of the ad interim status of the client.
6. Setting of dates or conditions under which progress reports will be reviewed by the advisory staff.

The six issues can be stated colloquially as six questions:

1. Exactly what is peculiar about this client, when does he show it, and where does it get him?

2. What does the client think about all this and what does he think he is trying to do?

3. What is the psychological view of the client's personal constructs?

4. In addition to the client himself, what is there to work with in the case?

5. Where does the client go next?

6. How is the client going to get well?

B. *Issue One: Normative Formulations of the Client's Problem*

3. DESCRIPTION OF THE MANIFEST DEVIANT BEHAVIOR PATTERNS (SYMPTOMS)

The clinician first sees the client through the eyes of society. He applies a normative yardstick. The client, by normative standards, appears deviant. The clinician sets out to elaborate the client's problem. The first step is the description of the manifest deviant behavior patterns. Now what constitutes deviant behavior?

a. *The clinician's behavior norms.* The use of the concept of "deviant behavior" suggests that the clinician must have a set of behavior norms to use as a base line for his judgments. Such norms do not exist, at the present writing, in any statistical or scientific sense. Except in certain limited areas, they exist only as unstandardized totalized impressions in the minds of experienced clinicians. The psychological job of replacing them by collecting and classifying normative data along the base lines of human behavior has yet to be done. Until that job is done and such norms are established, each individual clinician will have to estimate these base lines as best he can. If he has had an intimate experience with a wide variety of persons, he can work them out satisfactorily enough. At this moment no definition of "norms" that could be written here can, for the reader, take the place of such experience.

b. *Deviation from the ways of the primary group.* While recognition of what is deviant in human behavior is now wholly a matter of wide and balanced experience in the individual clinician, there are some checks which the clinician can apply in making his judgments. Does the client's behavior represent a significant deviation from the ways of his normal primary group (family, neighborhood, and other face-to-face circles of which he is a functioning member)? For him the path of normalcy is one which has been trodden down by his friends, not the one on which his clinician beats out a particular daily route. In dealing with people from isolated regions, or from minority ethnic groups, the clinician may easily mistake ethnically consistent behavior for psychopathological symptoms. For example, a clinician with a New York City background believed he had detected a "withdrawn schizoid" tendency among Kansans with whom he associated, while a clinician with a Kansas background was impressed with the number of "character defectives" he observed in a limited sample of New Yorkers.

c. *Incompatibility with own norms.* Does the client's behavior show incompatibility with his own norms? The deviant nature of some clients' behavior is not clear except by contrast with what they were like at some previous time. What was this person like six months ago or six years ago, is a type of question the clinician should keep in the background of his thinking during the diagnostic phase of his clinical contacts.

d. *Common interpretations.* Is the client's behavior inconsistent or unpredictable under commonly used systems of interpretation? This may seem like an irrelevant yardstick. It may seem as though the failure of a system to predict behavior or make it appear consistent with nature should be charged to the system and not to the behaving person. Yet our various psychological systems do tend to explain the common modes of behavior, and when it appears that a person's behavior is not explicable in terms of any of the common systems, the chances are that the behavior is itself truly deviant.

If a person laughs when our psychological system would lead us to expect that he would weep, there is some evidence of deviant behavior in that fact alone. We could call this laughter the "symptom of emotional inappropriateness" and say there is a "schizoid process" going on.

This kind of classification of behavior leads us into curious bypaths. If we say that inappropriateness or unpredictability is an essential feature of the behavior that helps define schizophrenia we are saying, in effect, that schizophrenia is anything which we do not understand. If we really understood why a client laughed, his laughter would not be unexpected. If we understood his point of view, the behavior could not appear to be emotionally inappropriate. Thus, when we say that a person's behavior is emotionally inappropriate, we are likely to be saying simply that we do not understand him. We certainly do not make him any more understandable when we reify our own confusion and call it a symptom of the client's.

This is the kind of confused thinking which we wish to avoid in expanding the psychology of personal constructs. What we have said is simply this and no more: a good check on the deviancy of a client's behavior is to note whether it is predictable under the commonly used systems of interpretation. If it is not predictable, the chances are that the behavior is unusual. But to say that behavior is "unusual" is not to make it explicit or predictable; that is where we came in!

e. *Frequent abandonment of adjustment patterns.* Another cue to deviant behavior, in general, is a history of frequent abandonment of adjustment patterns which have been attempted. Has the client tried many different jobs, launched himself in various careers, abandoned several marriages, resigned from numerous enterprises. In a way, this is the same as the criterion of deviation from his own norms. Yet his norms, in this case, have a wide standard deviation.

f. *Distinction between what is deviant and what is transparent.* The clinician should be careful to distinguish between what is truly deviant and what is merely transparent. Sometimes inexperienced clinicians are inclined to consider behavior abnormal because the "lower-order impulses" which appear to lie back of it happen to be particularly easy to detect. Clinicians who are particularly adept in tracing aggression or homosexual tendencies, for example, may be inclined to classify as deviant all behavior in which they can see those factors plainly.

Depending on his working system and his skill in using it, the clinician may see "primitive" impulses in much of everyday human behavior. He may also, if he wishes, detect "civilized impulses." He may see either type of impulse through an overlay of socially acceptable behavior. Yet this does not necessarily mean that the client is pursuing a highly deviant course of behavior. He may be behaving quite normally. He may deviate only in the fact that he does not try to "cover up."

From the standpoint of the psychology of personal constructs, the "low-order impulses" such as "rage and sexual lust" are not necessarily any more fundamental than are "high-order impulses" such as "ambition and altruism." Both pairs of constructs are designed as subsuming constructs and may be used by the clinician as such. A clinician chooses his constructs according to what he wants to accomplish. If he wants his client eventually to see himself as behaving like a child, he may himself choose to use diagnostic constructs which are particularly adapted for construing a child's behavior. He can then say to the client, "Look, a child does this and this and this. So do you. You don't want people to notice your behaving like a child, now do you?" If the clinician eventually wants his client to deal with his problem in terms of constructs which are particularly fitting for describing adult behavior, he may use such constructs in his own thinking about the client. It is not merely a question of "discovering" the client's motives; it is also a question of how the clinician can most effectively choose from among *constructive alternatives.*

What a clinician sees in a client is a function both of the client and of the clinician. This does not mean that the observation of deviant behavior is a wholly arbitrary matter. But it does mean that there are many ways in which a given client's behavior can be seen as deviant and many ways in which it can be seen as normal. Our choice of ways to see the client is best determined by what we want to do about him. Just because it is easy for us to see "primitive impulses" peeping through his proprieties, it does not follow that he is exhibiting deviant behavior. It may be more a matter of our own readiness to construe behavior in primitive ways.

g. *Deviation in the way of complaining rather than in the content of the complaint.* A clinician should always be alert to the possibility that there is more that is deviant in the complaint which appears on the client's registration sheet than there is in the content of the complaint itself. A complaint is itself a form of behavior. It may be deviant behavior. Consider two possibilities. Consider first the complaint that has been lodged by the client's relatives or by his employer. Without exception, the clinician should view this as a measure of the demands being made upon the client as well as a description of his manifest behavior.

One time a twelve-year-old foster child was brought to our clinic with the complaint that he was lazy. Elaboration of the complaint revealed that his foster parents considered him lazy because he was dilatory in digging up all the cactus in a 200-acre pasture. Further inquiry revealed that this two-months' after-school task had been assigned to "pay back" the cost of bringing him back from X City, where he had been picked up after running away to see his younger sister from whom he had been separated by the breakup in his natural family.

Consider, secondly, the complaint which has been verbalized by the client himself. The clinician should always keep in mind that what the client says, as well as what he does, is part of his behavior. For example, a client may complain that he lies awake all night. A checkup shows that he sleeps like a baby. This does not mean that there is no deviant behavior. His *report* of sleeplessness is itself the deviant behavior.

Whenever a clinician records complaints or case-history information, he should be very careful to indicate both the source of the information and the circumstances under which it was obtained. The writer is painfully aware of the many times he has heard clinicians describe the mothers of their clients as "dominating" and "indulgent" without indicating who made the observation. Usually it has turned out that the description was offered by the client's husband or by a sibling, or had even been accepted uncritically from the client. The clinician overlooked the fact that the problems of early marital adjustment tend to make the husband see himself as competing with a mother-in-law who seems unusually "dominating" or "indulgent." Similarly a sibling, who is likely to feel some competition with the client, finds it easy to construe his mother as "indulgent." Clinicians who accept this kind of thing at face value, rather than in terms of the personal constructs of the people who are talking, are likely to be misled.

h. *Data for description of the manifest deviant behavior.* The following sources usually provide the basic data for the description of the manifest deviant behavior patterns.

1. The nominal complaint.
2. The client's description of his own behavior.
3. The initial "status examination."
4. Medical, military, school, and employer personnel records.
5. Observations of reception and ward behavior.
6. The client's family.
7. Other associates.

A lay description of deviant behavior is likely to characterize the clinician's first contact with any new case. It is easy to become impatient listening to complainants give drawn-out recitations of anecdotes of the client's behavior. Yet, properly explored and elaborated under careful questioning, the complaint provides the core for the psychological description of deviant behavior patterns. The complainant may be either the client himself, a relative, an occupational associate, or some other person who has had direct contact with the client.

Second in the usual order of availability is the client's description of his own behavior. This may not be stated in the form of a complaint. That may require a session of exploratory questioning under optimal conditions of rapport. The client's statements and behavior under inquiry may have two kinds of signal value: (a) factual meanings, such as where the client has been, what he did yesterday, and so on, and (b) subjective meanings, such as the kinds of places where he *says* he has been, what he seems to *think* he did yesterday, and so on. Both kinds of signal value are important; the first because it may describe behavior which has taken place, and the second because it suggests the content of the client's present perceptual field.

The third source of information on deviant behavior is the initial "status examination." This examination, which varies from clinician to clinician, usually involves an abbreviated appraisal of the client's behavior, including the client's statement of complaint, his temporal and spatial orientation, a brief check of intellectual functioning, observation of speech and mannerisms, observation of amount of activity, and an estimate of social responsiveness. All too frequently the initial status examination is administered rapidly under poor conditions of rapport. The results may give the clinician a distorted view of what the client's behavior would be under normal conditions. A careful examination of the other sources of information on deviant behavior will prevent the clinician from overinterpreting the status examination.

Next in order of availability is likely to be personnel records. In terms of the currently used nosological systems these records provide some indication of the deviant nature of the client's behavior. It is difficult, however, to "read back" behavior from the nosological category which has been assigned to the case. In other words, it is much easier to take a description of behavior and classify it nosologically than it is to take the nosological term and, from it, visualize the behavior of the client.

Personnel records may have usefulness beyond the disease names which they list. The client's history of duty assignments, hospitalizations, reenlistments, and ratings provides a behavior record which is likely to be more useful than the record of disability assessment at a separation center.

In the fifth place, hospital-ward behavior (in the case of hospitalized patients), if systematically observed and recorded, may provide an important source of information. Here is a field of research open to psychologists interested in time sampling of manifest behavior. With properly developed instruments designed to fit their construct system, and with a minimum of training, attendants can compile a great deal of useful data.

Much depends on the kind of ward in which the patient is placed. In a ward where social stimulation is at a minimum and the only social values recognized are inaction and untroublesomeness, the patient's meaningful behavior is reduced to a minimum. Under such conditions the observation of ward behavior has minimal possibilities. On the other hand, where a premium is placed upon affirmative behavior rather than upon negative acquiescence, the manifest behavior of the patient becomes a rich source of information regarding his psychological life. Games and occupations, both individual and organized, self-care and self-enhancement, opportunities, socialized duties, and purposeful activities all serve to enrich the meanings of the patient's ward behavior. In an outpatient clinic it should be possible to convert the patient's period of waiting in front of the admission desk for an appointment to a period of meaningful activity worth observing, recording, and evaluating, as a part of the clinical examination.

Of course, the client's family and household constitute a sixth source of information regarding his behavior and the development of his symptoms. Members of the client's family usually fail to see the deviant behavior as a gradual development but are inclined to report it as wholly of recent origin or as the result of a recent situation. For example, it is common for the family to claim the client is reacting to a disappointment in love. They may fail to recognize that in his romance the client did not behave normally from the outset. His own deviant courtship behavior may indeed have been a partial cause of his disappointment. Despite the characteristic aberrations of the family's observation, they can, under the proper type of questioning, furnish useful information regarding deviant behavior which cannot readily be obtained elsewhere.

One should keep in mind that the interview with members of the client's family and with other associates may throw light upon issues which are not strictly a matter of assessing deviant behavior. As in all clinical interviewing, the clinician should be sensitive to his informant's personal involvement in reporting the client's behavior. What the clinician gets is a report of how his client affects this particular associate. He also gets some idea of what resources and expectancies have to be reckoned with in planning for the client's social readjustment.

i. *What is manifest behavior?* Stripped to its lowest terms behavior may be considered merely as motor action. At one time the behavioristic school of thought in psychology insisted that all observations of behavior should be confined to what could be construed in physical and chemical terms. For example, they said that speech should be observed as a phenomenon of muscular contractions and that any report of the content of one's speech could not be considered as a scientific observation. This approach had the advantage of placing observers on a common ground of agreement, since the simple physical and chemical construction systems which were employed were widely shared by different observers.

At the other extreme are those who immediately relate all their observations to an elaborate theoretical structure which is not widely shared. For example, instead of saying that a client has been biting his nails the clinician may report that he has observed "oral masochistic behavior." Or a client who refers to his clinician in scatological terminology may be reported to have exhibited "anal aggression."

Ordinarily the clinician should report his observations of manifest deviant behavior in terms which are commonly understood. As much as possible he should allow the reader of his report to reformulate these observations in terms of his own professional system. If a clinician uses such terms as ambivalence, anxiety, uncooperativeness, compulsiveness, and so on in describing the manifest deviant behavior patterns, he has already biased the report to such a degree that another clinician, who does not share his professional point of view, cannot reconstrue the observations in another system.

Now it must be recognized that some personal bias is unavoidable. In fact the clinician who has no basis of pertinence does not know what to look for. More than that, he does not even know what he has seen! What the clinician should do is first describe the manifest deviant behavior in terms of common biases. After he has done that, he can venture into higher and more specialized levels of interpretation.

For example, it may seem to the clinician that a client is show-ing "anxiety." In such a case the supporting behavior should be detailed first — for example, crying during the interview, vocal and lip tremors while discussing certain topics, alterations of the breathing pattern, speech content, and so on. These are observa-tions upon which most of us might be expected to agree. Having cited these observations the clinician may then wish to refer to the likelihood of there being an anxiety pattern associ-ated with certain topics or occasions. At this point he is launching out into an interpretation growing out of a particular systematic point of view.

A good general rule is for the examining clinician to impose his own special systematic bias upon the data only after he has re-corded a precise account of the client's deviant behavior in com-monly understood terms. His record of observations should thereafter prove serviceable to the reader who might be inclined to place another type of professional construction upon them — for example, psychoanalysis or field theory.

j. *Elicitation and description of the complaint.* The complaint with which the clinician is introduced to a new client rarely pro-vides a scientific statement of the clinical issues at stake. It is, however, an extremely important datum which deserves more attention than it usually gets. An analysis of its content and the manner in which it is formulated throws important light upon the complainant's basic framework of ideas. If the complainant is the client, the analysis should reveal his basic "manner of understanding," within which any reconstruction of his thinking about his problem must take place. If the complainant is some-one with whom the client must eventually work out an adjustment, the analysis of the complaint material will show the clinician what the client is up against.

(1) The complaint is the layman's formulation of the clinical issues. It is usually a poor formulation. The fact that the client has come for help attests to the fact that it has opened no avenues to a happy solution. The verbatim complaint may therefore reveal both the locus of the maladjustment and the reason why the complainant is unable to see a solution.

By having the client carefully elaborate his complaint, the clinician may come to understand the conceptual processes within which the personal maladjustment is developed and maintained. By having a representative member of the client's society elaborate his complaint, the clinician may come to understand the conceptual process within which the social maladjustment is developed and maintained.

Modern sound-recording devices, such as magnetized wire and tape and embossed plastics, have opened a vast new area of inquiry into the psychological nature of maladjustive and readjustive processes. They now make profitable a much more detailed analysis of interview data. Verbatim protocol of complaints which have been carefully elicited and faithfully recorded may be subjected to such modern analytic procedures as the "conceptual matrix method" or the "A/V word count." Clinicians' "case notes," on the other hand, are obviously not too well suited to such analyses.

Hearing out a complaint is also one of the best methods of establishing rapport, and thus of anticipating a cooperative therapeutic relationship. It is not enough merely to listen to a client until he stops talking. He may run out of words long before he runs out of feelings he wants to express. Nonthreatening questions, both specific and unstructured, along the lines which the client (or informant) himself believes important, may aid the establishment of rapport and the conviction that everything of importance is being taken into account. Questioning the client is, then, much more than a simple matter of extracting objective information.

(2) There is a language of complaint, as the experienced clinician soon learns. It is made up partly of an empirical communication system and partly of a highly subjective communica-

tion system which may tax the clinician's philological talents. He must listen as if learning a new language without a textbook or a translator. Once he has learned the client's language of complaint he must find a way to translate the client's complaints and place them in the record. The clinician in reporting complaints may first report protocol verbatim and second say, "After establishing communication with the client I believe I have learned that what he is trying to say is . . . "

Since a complaint may often be viewed as an expression of failure in the enactment of a role, it partly describes the expected social and personal patterns with respect to which the client has failed to plan his role. A disturbed client is always deviant *with respect to something*. He misfits either the pattern of his society or the pattern he conceives for himself. The clinician should listen to his complaint so carefully that he can infer patterns of society and self with respect to which the client has come to be seen as a misfit, either through his own eyes or through the eyes of others. With the complaint viewed as a statement of recognition of the breakdown of an attempted role, the clinician may, through the study of the complaint alone, make a preliminary appraisal of the restructuration in concepts of role which must necessarily precede readjustment.

k. *Temporal patterns in the deviant behavior.* Prediction of behavior is largely a matter of extrapolation; but, to the extent that the behavior is cyclical or follows a well-known accumulative pattern, predictions may be made from a careful analysis of the temporal sequence which has already been made manifest.

There are typical cues to a history of emotional crises. "Psychosomatic" disturbances are usually evidence of a series of emotional crises and are predictive of future emotional disturbances. Reluctance to make plans or to establish new personal relationships may, in some cases, indicate that the client has been frequently "burned" and is unwilling to risk further affective investments. The man who has lost interest in his work and "drags his feet" immediately causes the experienced clinician to look for the point where he lost his initiative and became unable to channel his aggressiveness. The problem of hostility or guilt may or may not be involved.

The clinician should look for periodicity in the deviant behavior. Does the deviant behavior repeat itself? At what intervals? With what variations? The clinician who cannot detect periodicity in the deviant behavior should begin to doubt the adequacy of his own abstraction of the case. Nearly always there is *some way* in which the present deviant behavior is like behaviors which have occurred again and again in the client's life. Perhaps the earlier behaviors were not considered deviant at the time they appeared. Perhaps they are not the kinds of behaviors which the clinician is accustomed to recognize as deviant even now. The task of detecting the recurrent phases in the client's life is a real task in concept formation for the clinician.

The clinician should be aware of diurnal cycles. It is not enough to know that the client felt suicidal yesterday. The clinician should know the time of day when the client felt suicidal.

The clinician should elicit phase descriptions of the deviant behavior. What is the sequence of behaviors and moods from one corresponding phase point to the next? Sometimes it is possible to explain deviant behavior in terms of what immediately precedes it in the phase and then to break up the deviant behavior by altering the sequence of events of which a phase is composed. More often, a variety of behaviors have to be taken into account and treatment undertaken which deals with the phase as a whole.

Nearly always it is a good plan for the clinician to draw a line on a piece of paper and mark off the years of the client's life along it. The salient events and the history of deviant behavior can then be noted along the line so that they can be seen graphically. The line should be extended into the client's future and some entries made which are relevant to what may normally be expected of him later. In this manner the clinician may be able to see the client in a better time perspective. Not infrequently he discovers, through using this device, features of the case which had previously escaped him.

4. DESCRIPTION OF THE CORRELATES OF THE MANIFEST DEVIANT BEHAVIOR PATTERNS

Since the clinician has a concept-formation task on his hands when he attempts to formulate a transitive diagnosis, it is important that he not limit his attention to the specific elements which he or the client structures in terms of the complaint. The clinician should deliberately look for other elements to construe along with the manifestly deviant elements. If he fails to do so, he may be able to make no more progress than the client has in reaching a constructive formulation of the problem.

a. *The cultural context.* The clinician should keep himself clearly aware of the cultural context in which the deviant behavior arises, and in relation to which it takes on its particular deviant coloration. This is not to say that "culture determines psychopathology" — that is a meaningless generalization! But an awareness of the cultural context may enable the clinician to piece together certain facts and arrive at a meaningful construction of the case which goes beyond what the client has been able to develop.

b. *The personal-social context.* The clinician should be aware of the particular figures who people the client's world. Here, too, he may find new elements which may be put together with facts from the story of deviant behavior. Out of the combination may come a meaningful reconceptualization of the client's problems.

c. *Threat concomitants.* Even though we have used the term "transitive diagnosis" to indicate a kind of diagnosis which is oriented toward doing something about the client's condition, the psychology of personal constructs is not a "dynamic" theory in the ordinary sense. The term "stress" also sounds like a "dynamic" term. Without buying "dynamism," however, we can say simply that stress is a matter of being aware of potential threat. If a father finds himself in a position where the course of events may force him to reconstrue himself as an unfatherly parent, he may be under stress, and the events may be perceived as threat.

The clinician should look for the stress concomitants in a client's life, both past and present. What reconstructions were thrust

upon him or are about to be forced upon him? Against what expectancies did he have to maintain himself? Sometimes it is possible to see the deviant behavior as a direct adaptation to the
stress to which a client has been subjected.

d. *The occupational pattern.* The occupational history of the
client, together with the history of his occupational aims, his
abandonments of occupational aims, and his outright occupational
adjustments and failures, need to be described as a part of the
correlational material. The subjective values the client attaches
to the occupational record may throw additional light upon his
deviant behavior.

A number of years ago the writer was asked to examine a
high-school boy aged about sixteen. His teachers, principal, and
superintendent reported that he seemed unmanageable. He would
talk loudly in the classroom to any other student at any time
about any topic that seemed to interest him. He seemed to have
a complete disregard for the customary restraints. He would
walk in and out of the classroom as he pleased, go downtown to
shoot pool, interrupt conversations, and generally ignore all regulations. His teachers found him rude but not particularly hostile.
If he was interested in a topic he might ask to talk it over with
a teacher at length. Altogether, it seemed to add up to his placing
a very low value on most of what the school was attempting to
do and a genuine unwillingness to let himself take the school's
program seriously.

The boy's father had died when he was about ten and his
mother, true to folklore, had taken in washing to help make ends
meet. The school had dealt with him intelligently and sympathetically. There had been a concerted attempt to establish personal
relationships and to seek to enable him to express the problem
as he saw it. Perhaps it was because of this enlightened approach
that his deviant behavior was not markedly mixed with hostility.
However, he remained inarticulate regarding his problem.

The diagnostic efforts of the writer yielded initial results simply
because he followed a routine procedure, such as that proposed
in this chapter. Asked about his vocational plans the boy said he
had none. Asked further about what his vocational aspirations

had been when he was a child he replied that he had wanted to be an airline pilot. Further questioning revealed that he had placed great stock in that occupational goal and that somehow it had become fixed as a part of his personal adjustment to his father's death and the changes in domestic life which ensued. The payoff came when he was asked why he had given up his ambition. His "front" was completely swept away, and he told how suddenly one afternoon about two years before everything had gone up in smoke. His physician, in the course of an examination, had told him that his vision would never meet the requirements for a pilot's license and that he was foolish even to think about it. Now, of course, this bit of information and his sharing of this confidence could not be expected to bring about any miraculous cure, nor did it even furnish a fully comprehensive picture of how the boy had painted himself into that particular corner. It simply helped the clinician to formulate a dynamic type of diagnosis which had some implications as to what might be done, not merely implications as to what kind of "case" the boy was.

e. *The domestic pattern.* As in the case of the occupational pattern, the domestic pattern of behavior should routinely be explored so as to bring the deviant behavior into perspective. As one does this, the deviant behavior is likely to appear less and less deviant and more and more plausible. This is a course the clinician must take, and yet there lies a trap waiting for him at the end of it. The client may begin to appear so utterly plausible that the clinician sees no problem to be solved, save that of "the society which made him this way" or of the "mother who projected her own neurosis upon him."

One has only to look about to see the numerous writers who, after pursuing a clinical career with individual clients, came up with sweeping criticisms of what exists outside the arena of their own activity. A clinician who has done nothing but work with individual clients decides that what is wrong really lies within the area of the sociologist. Or he may conclude that the trouble is "mothers" or "momism." If he works with mothers, then he sees only really deviant behavior as residing in *their* mothers, and so on and on. This is the trap that one is likely to fall into as a result of coming to see the groupwise deviant behavior as normal within the context of the client's biography.

What the clinician must plan to correct is not the behavior which is implausible or irrational, but the behavior which he has come to see as plausible and wholly rational. There are many clinicians who cannot do this. They think that what is plausible and rational is therefore "true" or "realistic." They see no alternatives to what is "true" or "realistic." Not fully realizing that there are such things as alternative truths and alternative realities they are unprepared to help their clients find psychological solutions for personal problems.

Yet fully realizing that there is this trap waiting for him at the end of his exploration, the psychodiagnostician should continue his search for the patterns of behavior, in the context of which the client's deviant behavior looks less and less deviant. Having looked at the occupational pattern, he routinely looks at the domestic pattern. What has been the history of the client's domestic life and of the personal attachments which he has formed, used, and broken? In the language of the psychology of personal constructs, what have been the changing contextual contents of his dependency structures? Furthermore, what has been the history of the client's domestic and personal-affective aims? What has he thought he wanted at various stages of his life history? Also, the clinician should know the history of adjustments and failures in the broad area which we call "domestic." What have been the cycles, what sequences are involved in the phases, in what phase of his cyclical pattern is the client now?

5. DESCRIPTIONS OF THE GAINS AND LOSSES ACCRUING TO THE CLIENT THROUGH HIS SYMPTOMS (DESCRIPTION OF VALIDATIONAL EXPERIENCE)

The psychology of personal constructs invites the clinician to see the client's gains and losses in terms of validating and invalidating experience and in terms of the freedom to acquire such experience. Validation is experienced when one perceives that he has correctly anticipated an event. An event which is rewarding for one person is therefore not necessarily rewarding for another. The second person may have experienced the event as a complete surprise.

Does this mean that people never like surprises? Not at all. A surprise that opens up a field where one can see many new predictions as coming true is likely to be welcomed, even though it involves momentary confusion. A surprise which opens upon illimitable chaos is always to be avoided.

From the standpoint of the psychology of personal constructs, it is not practical to try to catalogue events as intrinsically rewarding or as intrinsically punishing. Nor is it psychologically meaningful to describe some outcomes of a person's trials as intrinsically reinforcing. The reward which inheres in an event is primarily a function of how that event is construed and predicted by a given person. Nowhere is this more apparent than in the field of clinical psychology, where one frequently finds clients who collect their rewards in unusual ways and who appear to find genuine satisfaction in what most of us would like to avoid at all costs.

In setting the stage for diagnosis, one needs to make some analysis of the client's experience. Since we have devoted a whole chapter to this topic, there is no point in discussing it in detail here. That this experience must have validational implications for the client follows from our systematic position. We are interested in what has happened to the client, not merely because it happened and may happen again, but also because, in happening, it must have confirmed or upset the client's expectations.

At the outset all one can do is begin to list the client's experiences which are most closely associated with his deviant behavior and to interpret the losses or gains which those experiences might normatively be expected to provide. One can look for the compensation demands and the formal disability claims the client has made. One may look for equivalences between his symptoms and the love which was otherwise unavailable to him. One may see in his hostilities the control over the course of events which might otherwise get completely out of hand. His anxiety may keep him at home. His expressions of guilt may prove that he is still aware of his role responsibilities.

Yet each of these gains may be made at the cost of losses on other fronts. He may have had to accept some guilt along with his hostility. His freedom to explore for new validational experience is often paid for with anxiety. He may have been able to open one area of life to spontaneous elaboration only by constricting himself with respect to other areas. In transitive diagnosis the clinician seeks a preliminary normative overview of these gains and losses in relation to the client's symptoms. He follows this up in a later stage with a more intimate appraisal of these gains and losses in the light of the client's personal constructs.

C. Issue Two: Psychological Description of the Client's Personal Constructions

6. THE CLIENT'S CONSTRUCTION OF WHAT HE BELIEVES TO BE THE PROBLEM AREA

It is important to understand the client's viewpoint. The best place to start is with the immediate problem which brought him to the clinician. Even though the client is upset by a discussion of his problem area, the clinician will ordinarily establish a better relationship with the client if he does not evade the issue. The discussion of the problem area may be quite brief, perhaps only a sentence or two, but if the relationship between client and clinician is to be a profitable one, it is important for each to be as candid with the other as circumstances permit. Even in dealing with children it is important that the clinician give each child a chance to come to grips with the fact that he has been brought to the clinician for a specific reason. As far as the writer is concerned, this procedure is so basic that it constitutes an ethical requirement in clinical practice.

The client should be invited to say what he believes his problems are. The clinician who privately disagrees with him and lets it go at that makes a serious mistake. From the standpoint of psychology of personal constructs the statement of the client is, by definition, a true formulation of the problem. However, it is not the only true formulation, for there are levels of formulation, and the client's level of formulation may not be the most fruitful one.

We have already discussed at some length the matter of accepting the client's initial formulation of his problem, of the clinician, and of the psychotherapeutic process. That discussion appears at the beginning of the chapter on the role of the psychotherapist.

7. THE CLIENT'S CONSTRUCTION OF WHAT OTHERS BELIEVE TO BE THE PROBLEM AREA

Not only should the client be permitted to make a formulation of what he believes to be his problem but he should always be given an opportunity to give his version of what others believe to be the problem. This, too, is an ethical consideration and a useful step in diagnosis.

Every clinician tends to be biased by what he hears. A parent tells him that her child will not eat breakfast. The clinician labels the problem as a feeding problem and plans to probe the child's core constructs. If it occurs to him to find out what the child thinks about this breakfast matter, he may find that the mother expects the child to eat cold fried eggs left over from the evening before. He may also discover some other interesting things which are relevant to a psychological understanding of the situation.

8. THE CLIENT'S CONSTRUCTION OF HIS LIFE ROLE

This is where the analysis of self-characterization comes in. Whether this is based on a self-characterization which is written, as were the self-characterizations discussed in an earlier chapter, or upon an impromptu oral self-characterization, the response of the clinician is essentially the same. The clinician should assume, for the time being, the attitude which we have called "the credulous approach." He should use the techniques of overlay, inflection, and topical analysis. He should look for antecedents and consequences, generalizations and specifications, conceptual lapses, retractions, qualifications, and appendages.

But more than a self-characterization is in order here. The

clinician should make himself aware of how the client construes his own biography, what meanings he attaches to the salient events of his past, indeed what he considers to be the salient events of his past. Again, as we have so often cautioned before, the clinician should not assume that the events of the past have inexorably herded the client along a path of life. As always, the clinician should keep in mind that his client is bound only by the consistent interpretations he places upon his experience. What is the thread of meaning upon which the client strings the events of his life? How will future events be added to his string? What is his conceptualization of his life role?

Since a role is a course of activity played out in the light of one's interpretation of other persons, a clinician cannot understand a client's conceptualization of his life role without learning something about how he construes other people. This is where a type of instrument such as the Role Construct Repertory Test comes in. A skillful analysis of the client's Thematic Apperception Test protocol also throws light upon his construction of his life role. The strictly thematic type of analysis, originally proposed by Murray, gives the clinician some indication of how the client can string together the events of his life. The figure type of analysis, which most clinicians have come to employ — perhaps because it is easier — gives the clinician some idea of what kinds of persons populate his world. It is in relation to such persons that he acts out his life role in each separate scene. It is in relation to his thematic apperceptions that he develops his life role from scene to scene.

D. Issue Three: Psychological Evaluation of the Client's Construction System

9. LOCATION OF THE CLIENT'S AREAS OF ANXIETY, AGGRESSIVENESS (OR SPONTANEOUS ELABORATION), AND CONSTRICTION

As we have pointed out before, there are two levels of understanding a client. The first is seeing the world through the client's eyes, the second is seeing the client's construction system from the vantage point of a psychologist. The first level of understanding permits the clinician to understand the client sympathetically and to communicate with him. The second permits the clinician to join with the client in a true role relationship and, together with him, make progress which the client cannot accomplish alone.

This does not imply that the psychologist must be a superior person. Subsuming another person's construct system does not require a more elaborate construct system nor even, in a strict sense, a better one. It requires only that we have constructs whose contexts are composed of elements, those elements, in turn, being the constructs of other persons. In fact, the writer has observed some psychotherapists whose construct systems seemed quite mediocre work out helpful role relationships with clients whose construct systems seemed far more intricate and intellectually meaningful. In spite of their limitations the psychotherapists were able to subsume parts of their clients' construction systems and provide the overview that was necessary in order to be therapeutically effective.

Locating the client's areas of anxiety, aggressiveness, and constriction is a matter not merely of describing the client's construction system but of evaluating it psychologically. Here is where the psychologist uses his own professional constructs. The previous chapters represented the beginning of a clinician's repertory of professional diagnostic constructs.

It is relevant to mention three types of psychological construction in particular at this point. First, there is our old friend "anxiety." While the term has been redefined within the system of the psychology of personal constructs, the seeking of these areas is by no means novel to our system. Few modern clinicians will doubt but that a good diagnosis involves a search for the areas of a client's anxiety.

The seeking of the areas of aggressiveness is more often overlooked. Not only are they a clue to where the client can work out his own problems, but it shows the clinician how the client can be expected to operate when he does open up his constricted areas as a result of therapy. When he starts out, the clinician has no sure way of knowing just how the client will contrive eventually to solve his most perplexing problems. Every successfully treated client solves them differently. The best single preview is provided the clinician when he looks at the areas where the client is currently working out problems — in other words, the areas of aggression or of spontaneous elaboration. He may also examine the problems and solutions which the client has already worked out. Here the clinician can examine the working models of the devices which the client will probably utilize when he starts to straighten things up in his present problem areas.

Location of the client's areas of constriction is like observing the eye movements of a person reading a letter; the passages he can read only a word at a time are the ones where he is likely to lose his perspective. When the clinician runs across an area of discourse in which the client must figuratively put his finger on each successive word, he can be sure that he has located an area of constriction. We have said that constriction occurs when a person narrows his perceptual field in order to minimize apparent incompatibility in his construings. It can be seen in the perseveration in brain-injured adults, in the circumstantiality of certain senile persons, and in the legalistic thinking of certain compulsive neurotics. Each of these types of clients, of course, employs constriction in a somewhat different way.

There are other types of professional interpretation of the client's personal construction system which can be applied during the diagnostic or treatment-planning stage of client management. One can look for suspension, comprehensive constructs, core constructions, guilt, and so on. Diagnosis cannot, of course, tell the whole story. A complete psychological evaluation of a client's construction system, if ever made at all, would have to come at the conclusion of a long period of comprehensive psychotherapy.

10. SAMPLING THE TYPES OF CONSTRUCTION THE CLIENT USES IN DIFFERENT AREAS

A client may use loose construction when dealing with people and tight construction when dealing with money. He may show guilt in his relationships to his family, hostility in his relationships to his employer, preemption in his relationships to foreigners. It is not practical to try to seek out all the areas where these particular types of construction are used, as we have suggested in the case of anxiety, aggression, and constriction. It is practical to sample a few areas of the client's life and see in greater detail just how effective his conceptualization is in each of them.

11. SAMPLING THE MODES OF APPROACH

The clinician samples the client's approaches to new problems to determine how he customarily resolves anxiety. This is pretty much a matter of investigating further the areas in which the client is able to engage in aggressive spontaneous elaboration. We have defined anxiety quite broadly. From our point of view, a continuing life-adjustment process involves continual dealing with anxieties in manageable amounts.

Most psychological tests which have been devised in the past half century will throw some light on this issue. The intelligence test sets up relatively novel problems for the subject to solve. The scoring is usually in terms of whether or not the subject gets the "right" answer. It measures his intellectual efficiency; and, if it is administered by a skillful clinician, it may throw some light on how the client arrived at his answers. This, in turn, throws light upon what may be expected in the way of efficiency and novel approach once the client gets his personal problems verbalized at the level of an intelligence-test question.

But not much of therapy is likely to be conducted at the verbal level of an intelligence test. The clinician may find it more meaningful to fall back upon less explicitly formulated questions. He may observe the client's construction of a Rorschach set of ink blots, his drawing of geometric forms, or his grouping of a number of miscellaneous objects. In each of these test situations the client may be seen as resolving bits of anxiety created for him by the ambiguity of the test item. The psychologist is interested in how he resolves each bit of anxiety, for that may be the way in which he will have to resolve the lingering anxieties which brought him to the clinic for help.

12. DETERMINATION OF THE CLIENT'S ACCESSIBILITY AND HIS LEVELS OF COMMUNICATION

An important feature of diagnosis is the determination of the client's capacity to work with a therapist. For example, some clinicians make a considerable point of determining whether the client should work with a man or woman therapist. This may be important in some cases, particularly ones where an extreme type of dependency relationship must be acted out. More basic, however, is the question of whether or not the client and the clinician can ever be expected to speak the same language or to communicate with each other by any sorts of semeiotic devices. Will the client confide? Can he use words? At what level of abstraction does he pitch his communications? Can he act out his major constructions in the therapy room as well as talk about them? Will he seek to validate his predictions against the responses of the therapist? If the answer is no to any of these questions, then the therapist is likely to have a rough way to go.

Psychoanalysis emphasizes the importance of "ego strength and accessibility" as a prerequisite for successful psychotherapy of the psychoanalytic type. Usually the psychoanalysts think of "ego strength" mainly in terms of "contact with reality." While we do not attempt to employ the notion of "ego" in the psychology of personal contructs, what we are saying here is roughly parallel to what a psychoanalyst would have to say if he allowed himself to be pinned down to something approaching an operational definition of "ego strength" and "contact with reality."

There are, however, some important practical differences between our position and that of classical psychoanalysis at this point. Some psychoanalysts emphasize the ability to verbalize "emotional" material. They take a dim view of "acting out." Yet they often call for "emotional insight." While we, too, consider words as extremely useful in psychotherapy, our position is that that which is considered by the analysts as "emotional" is often better understood merely as that which is not word-bound.

The person who is anxious cannot completely verbalize his

anxiety; if he could he would no longer be anxious. Of course, he can demonstrate his anxiety in part by means of words, sometimes a torrent of words. But the words are the loosely held elements in the seething pot of his anxiety. The word symbols which would give those elements structure and continuity are yet to be found. Indeed the structure and continuity must themselves first be found.

The personal-construct psychologist is willing to accept a client whose verbalizations in the area of his anxiety are quite inadequate and who has no means of expression except to "act out." We emphasize the acting out of roles in human relationships and we utilize "role playing" as a legitimate procedure in psychotherapy. Even at the conclusion of a successful course of therapy the client may not be able to say what has happened to him. He may be able to talk *about* it, but still be inarticulate as to what it *was*. We hope, however, that he has achieved structure where once there was anxiety and that his new structure is stabilized by means of some portable symbols which are not necessarily verbal in nature.

E. Issue Four: Analysis of the Milieu in Which Adjustment Is To Be Sought

13. ANALYSIS OF THE EXPECTANCY SYSTEM WITHIN WHICH THE CLIENT MUST MAKE HIS LIFE ROLE FUNCTION

It is a mistake to assume that a psychologically healthy person can immediately adjust himself happily to any kind of situation. Adjustment can only be achieved in relation to something. It makes a difference what one has to adjust to. Diagnosis is not complete until the clinician has some understanding of the milieu in which adjustment is to be sought. This position represents a departure from the common notion that diagnosis involves an analysis of the client only. From our point of view, diagnosis is the planning stage of client management. Therefore, *both* the client and his milieu must be understood.

In our chapter on personal experience in a social setting we pointed out the effect upon a person of having his associates expect certain things of him. Usually this means that a person gets along better if he does what is expected of him. Adjustment is not quite as simple as this, however. Many highly conforming people end by having troubles which are an outgrowth of their conformity. If one's conformity is achieved through excessive constriction there comes a time when he is unable to demonstrate the aggressiveness or initiative that his associates expect of him. Yet one can make an adjustment, as we pointed out in our earlier chapter, which is essentially nonconforming. But he has to know what it is that he is not conforming to if he is to get validating results from his ventures. If he has a pretty clear idea of what his neighbors expect of him, he can pretty well anticipate their gasps and grunts. He may have, for this reverse kind of adjustment, a wide and well-structured field open to spontaneous elaboration. But whether the person conforms or rebels, he can validate his life role only if he conceptualizes what those associates, with respect to whom that role is enacted, expect of him. Without that conceptualization his life role will rapidly become chaotic.

The diagnostician must take account of the expectancy system within which the client must make his life role function. Is it one to which the client can comply without undue constriction? Is it one against which the client can successfully rebel? Can he understand it well enough to do either? If he rebels, will he find closed to him those fields of spontaneous elaboration which he is best prepared to explore — for example, the fields of material luxuries, parental protection, sex, and so on?

In this connection the clinician who considers hospitalization for a client should take into account, not only the urgency of the case, but the effect that hospitalization may have upon the client's morale. The hospitalization may break the client by diverting all his aggressive tendencies. It may make it impossible for him ever to achieve self-respect again. It may also force him to face a set of community expectancies upon his return which may be more difficult for him to handle than are those which now cause him difficulty. Perhaps the hospitalization itself will be easy for him to adjust to. Then the clinician must face the question of whether or not the further elaboration of the client's dependencies through hospitalization may make it impossible for him ever to revise them properly. The clinician may need to ask the same questions regarding a course of outpatient psychotherapy. Sometimes the family and community expectancies make it inadvisable to undertake a protracted series of psychotherapeutic interviews. This whole question of the expectancy system within which the client must make his life role function is one to which clinicians have customarily given too little consideration. From our point of view, it is one of the crucial issues in diagnosis itself.

14. ASSESSMENT OF THE SOCIO-ECONOMIC ASSETS IN THE CASE

Here we refer to the socio-economic resources which may be utilized by the client, not those which can be exploited by the clinician. It is important to know whether or not the client has a family who will stick by him through a period of difficulties. Or will his wife desert him if he shows that he needs psychotherapy? Will a child's community accept him as worth rehabilitating? In many communities, perhaps in most, the maladjusted child is not considered worth rehabilitating. In this connection, one is reminded of the midwestern state which spent more per head improving the livestock on its institutional farms than it spent per patient on those farms.

The clinician should know whether or not the client can bear the financial burden of protracted treatment. Can the client accept hospitalization or go on a vacation without experiencing guilt through loss of his legitimate social role? In some cases the economic unrealism of the clinician's recommendations exceed even the unrealism of the client's symptoms.

There is no doubt that a client who has an established family which is determined that he must be rehabilitated, who has financial resources, who has influential friends, who has acquired effective social techniques, who has high-prestige vocational training and skills, who is physically intact, and who is young and attractive is a better psychotherapeutic risk than one who has none of these assets. The clinician is not necessarily losing sight of his humanitarian objectives when he recognizes this fact. Furthermore, the clinician should not hesitate to put any of these assets to use in the client's interest. The fact that another client does not have these assets, or that the clinician himself does not have them, does not put them out of bounds for psychotherapy.

15. PREPARATION OF INFORMATION TO BE UTILIZED AS CONTEXTUAL MATERIAL IN HELPING THE CLIENT RECONSTRUE LIFE

Since psychotherapy is largely a matter of concept formation — a point which is to be developed in a later chapter — transitive diagnosis requires that the clinician mobilize a considerable array of items relating to the client's life which can be sorted out in meaningful ways during psychotherapy. It is helpful, for example, for the psychotherapist to know at the outset that his client is familiar with the history of political thought during the eighteenth century, even though that fact may not be directly related to the client's psychological difficulties. This information can be used in two ways. The facts with which the client is familiar may be arranged together with other experiences to form new and useful constructs. To use the analogy of the concept-formation test, the clinician may acquire a ready-made inventory of appropriate psychological objects for the client to sort in new arrays. Secondly, the alert therapist may find occasion to invoke some of the client's historical concepts in helping him build analogous social concepts with which to guide himself in the twentieth century. Essentially this means that the clinician may find preformed constructs already available in the client's repertory, constructs which need only to be made more permeable to the experiences of everyday life.

F. Issue Five: Determination of Immediate Procedural Steps

16. PHYSIOLOGICAL CONSTRUCTION OF THE AVAILABLE DATA

Part of the task of diagnosis is to determine the order in which the diagnostic steps should proceed. As in all clinical work, one arrives at a diagnosis by successive approximations. If a client comes into the office threatening homicide and suicide before the night is out and revealing a specific plan for accomplishing both acts, the wise clinician makes a partial and tentative diagnosis on the spot and takes preventive measures. Perhaps he sees that the client is put under custody. Perhaps he seeks immediate consultation with other professional people. Certainly he does not invite the client to come back a week from Tuesday, in the event he is still alive.

The clinician with psychological training should be prepared to place psychological construction upon the facts of a client's case. The clinician with physiological training can also place physiological construction upon some of those same facts and thus, in addition, mobilize some other facts which the psychologist would ordinarily overlook or ignore. It is helpful if each specialist has some idea of what facts are most likely to be given meaningful construction by the other. This is not always possible. The psychoclinician is ordinarily the more alert of the two as regards the possibility of a meaningful construction of the data by the other.

Does this mean that diagnosis should determine whether the client is a "psychological case" or a "medical case"? Not at all! The client is himself neither psychological nor medical. He is his own uncommitted self. This is a point we have made several times before. Here we are concerned with a practical diagnosis. We have the task of determining what is to be done about the client. The fact that a client has a cerebral lesion does not make him a medical case exclusively or even necessarily predominantly. Nor does the fact that he is anxious about the effect his example may have upon his children make him a psychological case exclusively nor even necessarily predominantly. The issue is always how can he be helped, not who can see the most that is wrong with him.

The psychoclinician frequently finds that it is profitable for a medical clinician to construe the facts of the client's record, perhaps to look for additional facts, and often to make an examination of the client in person. This is no guarantee that the physiological construction of the client will be exhaustive. Many physicians are quite unskilled in picking up cues other than aches and pains. What the psychoclinician has to do is take what steps he can to see that the available data are physiologically construed, even if he has to do it himself. From the physiological construction of the case certain immediate procedural steps may be shown clearly to be in order.

The psychoclinician frequently finds himself in the position of having to decide how soon a client should be seen by a physician. Even more frequently he has to decide what medical specialty should be called upon first. This does not mean that he is in the best systematic position to select a medical specialist; it means that the practical exigencies of the situation may require that he make a specialty referral on the spot. Ordinarily a psychologist who found a man wandering the streets at night in a highly confused condition would refer him to a psychiatrist rather than to an obstetrician or a neurosurgeon. Yet the man's problem might possibly be such that either the obstetrician or the neurosurgeon would turn out to be the person who could be of most help to him.

17. OTHER PROFESSIONAL DISCIPLINES

We have been speaking of a physiological construction of the case. There are other professional disciplines which can throw their own special kind of light upon the facts. The educator may construe many of the same facts that the clinical psychologist and the physician construe. In addition, he can dig up some important ones that the other two would overlook. He may draw some unique and important conclusions as to what immediately needs to be done. Likewise, the social worker. Likewise, the clergyman. Likewise, the attorney.

18. EVALUATION OF THE URGENCY OF THE CASE

Treatment facilities are not always immediately available. One of the unpleasant tasks of any clinician is the determination of how long treatment can be postponed or of whether, in the light of other urgent cases, it can be forgone altogether. Sometimes, as we have already hinted, immediate steps must be taken to protect the client and others. This, too, is an essential step in transitive diagnosis.

G. *Issue Six: Planning Management and Treatment*

19. SELECTION OF THE CENTRAL PSYCHOTHERAPEUTIC APPROACH

This is, of course, the central issue to which the other five issues are merely preliminary. Transitive diagnosis is not complete until a plan for management and treatment has been formulated. The treatment can proceed on several fronts. There may also be psychotherapy of the individual interview type. There may be orientation sessions for the client's family. There may be groupings of the client with other clients or with other persons in his community. At the same time there may be occupational guidance. There may be recreational supervision. Some of these may be closely integrated with the central psychotherapeutic approach; most of them, at best, will be no more than loosely integrated.

Later chapters contain illustrative descriptions of psychotherapeutic designs. Each design is likely to be modified in the light of the information available regarding the case and in the light of the therapeutic resources which can be conveniently mobilized. Our discussion of the role of the psychotherapist indicated that we conceive psychotherapy as involving a great variety of procedures and skills. So widely may these vary from case to case that a procedure which is used predominantly with one client may never be used in precisely the same way with another. The particular fixed-role sketch in fixed-role therapy is an example. Some of the construct-loosening devices which are described in a later chapter would be another example. Not all psychotherapists will agree with the writer on the matter of re-using devices. Psychoanalysis tends to use loosening devices with all clients. Client-centered therapists appear to use the nondirective approach with all clients whom they accept for treatment, regardless of any differential diagnostic evaluation.

There is a sense in which personal-construct psychology, in accepting a wide variety of psychotherapeutic procedures, is eclectic. The theoretical grounds upon which the varying procedures are accepted do not, however, represent eclecticism. There is no particular objection to eclecticism implied by this.

It is interesting to note, in passing, that when eclecticism is itself systematically formulated it loses its eclectic flavor.

One of the reasons the psychology of personal constructs provides room for a greater variety of psychotherapeutic approaches than does psychoanalytic theory or the self-concept theory, upon which client-centered therapy is based, is that it is not so exclusively a *clinically induced* theory. A theory which was originally contrived, as were these two great contributions of psychoanalysis and client-centered therapy, to tie together a wealth of clinical and psychotherapeutic observations is more likely to set limits upon the approaches which it countenances. The great deductive theories in psychology — the Hullian and Tolmanian learning theories — and the field theories are less likely to set limits on how the client is to be approached; but, on the other hand, neither do they provide one with a means of discriminating between the therapeutic approaches to be used with different clients. The great eclecticist, Adolph Meyer, who did view psychotherapy as embracing a great variety of techniques, may have been in the midst of formulating a truly comprehensive clinically derived theory — we will never know. Since his position regarding psychobiology has never been systematically formulated, his true legacy may be forever lost.

a. *Size of the client's investment.* In choosing the central psychotherapeutic approach, the first consideration is always the size of the investment the client should make. Psychotherapy takes time that the client might spend in other pursuits. It takes attention away from the client's work, his family, his recreation. It usually takes funds that would otherwise be spent in support of a family. It frequently plunges the client or his family deeply into debt. It often puts a temporary strain on the client's interpersonal relations. His wife is likely to find him unpredictable and aggressive. So may his children. If other members of the family are in poor mental health, the clinician should be extremely cautious in choosing the therapeutic approach lest he precipitate a crisis in the lives of those who are dependent upon the client.

Against these costs the clinician should weigh both the benefits that the client might obtain and the degree of likelihood that they can be obtained. He must also weigh the risks of the client's becoming disorganized as a result of therapeutic efforts. The client may commit suicide if the therapist misjudges the situation. He may divorce his wife or cease to support his family. He may develop an undesirable dependence upon the therapist and not be able to terminate the psychotherapeutic sequence satisfactorily. He may become less imaginative and less creative in his work. While none of these outcomes is what one ordinarily expects of psychotherapy, they are real risks and the diagnostic clinician must recognize them as such when he recommends a central psychotherapeutic approach in a case.

It is very difficult to determine in advance how long a psychotherapeutic sequence will last. In the case of fixed-role therapy it is possible to come nearer making an estimate of duration than it is in most other types. Group psychotherapy can usually be conducted in such a manner as to meet a predetermined termination deadline. In general, the role-playing techniques keep the client in sufficient contact with his environment to enable him to terminate at almost any predetermined time and still profit from the psychotherapeutic experience. If the therapist goes in for construct-loosening procedures, he is likely to commit his client to a long series. If he spends much time with the client's early history, he is likely to increase the client's investment considerably. Early-history items are likely to be bound up with preverbal constructs of a dependency nature. Such constructs are less accessible and more difficult to modify. If a therapist opens up this area to anxiety, he lets the client in for a long reconstruction job.

Difficult as it is for the diagnostic clinician to make a precise determination of the duration of therapy, he should, nonetheless, make the very best estimate he can. If the client cannot reasonably invest in a drawn-out psychotherapeutic series, the clinician should recommend one of the approaches which is more likely to permit an earlier termination. On the one side of the balance is the size of the client's investment and the risk of an unfavorable outcome; on the other side is the nature of the client's problem and the probable outcome if no psychotherapy were to be attempted or if a superficial approach were to be used.

b. *Accessibility and level of communication.* In choosing the central psychotherapeutic approach, the clinician should take account of what he has learned about the client's accessibility and level of communication. At what level of cognitive awareness are the problems which the clinician sees in the client? Will it be profitable to attempt to get the client to put some of his preverbal and core constructs into words? In what ways can the client best express himself? As a result of this kind of consideration the clinician may decide to recommend a type of psychotherapy which involves a minimum of verbal communication. He may recommend finger painting and clay modeling, or he may recommend a situational change, such as a change in employment or a planned occupational-therapy sequence.

c. *Type of transference.* The clinician must also consider the type of transference relationship which can best be used. Will it be profitable to involve the client in extensive dependency transference? Should the client be invited to construe the therapist in terms of core constructs? What kinds of constructions should the client be invited to place upon the therapist? Should the therapist allow himself to be cast in the role of a parent figure? If the therapist is to be a "parent," how young a "child" is the client to be allowed to be?

The diagnostic clinician should make some preliminary estimate of the amount and kinds of support and reassurance to be employed. Simply to say, as is frequently said at the conclusion of staff conferences, that the therapist should assume "a generally supportive relationship in this case" is not enough. The areas of support need to be mentioned. As we attempted to show in our more detailed discussion of reassurance and support in an earlier chapter, either of these comforting techniques can backfire and cause the client damage.

As we indicated in a previous chapter, the primary or personal-identification type of transference should ordinarily be avoided in psychotherapy. Yet there are cases in which considerable personal identification of the therapist is unavoidable, and there are cases in which the client is unable to experiment successfully with a therapist who is a *type* of person rather than a *unique* person. In deciding what amount of personal identification should be permitted, the clinician pretty well determines where and under what circumstances the therapist will allow the client to come in contact with him.

d. *Threat.* The central therapeutic approach needs to be determined in the light of the transitional conditions which the client is able to deal with. We discussed the transitional constructs of *threat, fear, anxiety,* and *guilt* in Volume One. The diagnostic clinician needs to consider the threat implications of the central therapeutic approach he recommends. If the approach requires the client to assume a childlike role in relation to the therapist, or if it requires him to play the part of a person who is abjectly dependent upon his family, the threat may be more than he can bear. It may lead immediately to widespread disorganization and to anxiety, constriction, delusions, or to any one of a number of undesirable adjustments. Also, if the client is asked to discuss or recreate a picture of an earlier self, he may be threatened deeply.

e. *Fear.* Fear, too, must be considered. The client may be frightened by what his employer may do if he finds that the client is seeking psychological assistance. He may lose his job. He may be permanently cut off the promotion list. Even if there is no fear associated with the act of going to a psychotherapist, the client's circumstances may be such that he will be afraid to experiment with new ideas during the course of psychotherapy. If he tries anything new, or if he allows himself any degree of spontaneous elaboration, he may figuratively get his throat cut. A client who lives in a highly regimented situation — as, for example, an enlisted man in the military forces, a prisoner, or a patient in a traditional state hospital for the insane — is likely to experience real fear as soon as he starts to respond to certain types of psychotherapeutic treatment.

f. *Anxiety.* The central psychotherapeutic approach should be chosen with regard to the client's anxiety also — both the anxiety he exhibits at the time of diagnosis and the kind of anxiety the therapeutic approach characteristically creates. A client who shows widespread anxiety may have to be given support in the areas of his anxiety before any of his constructions are put to crucial test. The effect of invalidation may be to spread the anxiety more widely. He may then be forced to fall back upon the most primitive and infantile constructions in order to deal with the enveloping events of the present.

Some types of psychotherapeutic approach characteristically create anxiety. A form of psychotherapy which emphasizes what some psychoanalysts call the "first law" is bound to create considerable anxiety from the outset. That so-called law is that "the client shall report everything that comes to mind and withhold absolutely nothing." The client who allows himself to be caught in this type of regimen soon experiences a feeling of helplessness. Like a child, he must confess everything. If he is operating under a childlike construction system, he may actually be stabilized by the regimen and his anxiety be reduced thereby. If he is more adult in his outlook the confessions may swamp him with anxiety before he is able to manage it. From the standpoint of the psychology of personal constructs, the "first law" of psychoanalysis is an exceedingly dangerous precept when applied indiscriminately. Certainly the diagnostician should make a careful appraisal of the client before recommending a course of psychotherapy which involves any such precept.

g. *Guilt.* Psychotherapy can cause guilt. A client under treatment may find his role status slipping away from him. He may find that he is no longer doing his job. He may find that he has no social function. In an effort to maintain his role he may turn to the psychotherapist and attempt to work out a role relationship with him exclusively. He may seek to justify his existence wholly in terms of what he can do with and for the therapist. With some clients, particularly with some children, this means of prevention of guilt is acceptable. With others it may mean simply that the therapist has been unwise in using a therapeutic approach which robbed the client of a feeling of usefulness.

This point must be kept in mind particularly when dealing

with the aged. As people pass the prime of life they are likely to feel less and less useful. They have an awareness of loss of role. That awareness is, by definition under the psychology of personal constructs, guilt. If the therapist puts the aged person under a therapeutic regimen which requires him to be skeptical of his whole life role from beginning to end, the therapist is likely to end up with an extremely helpless person on his hands.

h. *Loosening.* Loosening of a construct tends to lessen its effectiveness in the precise structuring of a situation. Yet it may make the construct more permeable and, hence, applicable to new elements. Again, loosening may lead to new anxiety and may spread confusion to new areas. Now this calculated confusion may be just what the therapist wants in order to set the stage for some sort of therapeutic transition. Still, the anxiety may get out of hand. The client may loosen up all around, the chaos may seep into all the cracks and corners of his life, and the therapist may end up treating a full-blown schizophrenic patient.

In deciding how much loosening to hazard, the clinician should take into account the client's superordinate structure. Here we are back to our Modulation, Fragmentation, and Organization Corollaries. A client who has a fairly permeable over-all construction of his life role can stand a lot of loosening without becoming functionally schizoid. But a client who does not attach very much purpose or meaning to his life had better not be subjected to too much structural loosening, lest he collapse.

i. *Elaboration of the complaint.* Selection of the central psychotherapeutic approach requires some decision as to what the therapist should do about elaboration of the complaint. Should the client talk about "his problem"? Should he talk about his past? Should he talk about his future? Should he talk about his day-to-day doings? Or should he just talk? Some clients want to talk about nothing except what they consider to be their problem. Others want to avoid it as much as possible. Therapists who approach therapy from the point of view of learning theory tend to emphasize the elaboration of the complaint and then to follow that by a search for ways of getting new reinforcements in the client's life. In fixed-role therapy there is little elaboration of the complaint and almost all of the discussion is centered upon how the client may currently construe his interpersonal relations. It may very well be that the client should not be encouraged to elaborate his complaint. The therapist may need to dilate the client's perceptual field before attempting to reconstrue the area of complaint. Again it may be that the therapist wishes to constrict the perceptual field — for example, by hospitalization — so that smaller bits of the complaint area will be opened to anxiety at one time.

j. *Finding validation.* The diagnostic clinician must give some thoughtful attention to the question of how the client is going to find validation of the new constructs which are to emerge as a result of therapy. A good healthy construct can be hatched in the incubator of the conference room, but it will not grow to maturity unless it gets out and scratches. The therapist cannot expect to be the sole validator of new constructs, although some therapists attempt to assume that omniscient role. Actually the client is going to have to see if his new constructs meet the test of reality outside the interview room. What realities will he have available? If he has no one save other hospitalized patients to use for reality testing he may get some erratic and badly biased returns. If he has only members of a family who continue to cast him in an inflexible part he may get little response to his new performances. One of the important considerations in therapy is the opportunity for the person to discover that the new constructions he places upon life are actually workable. Without that opportunity he is not likely to respond, even to the most skillful of psychotherapeutic interviewers.

k. *Areas to be opened to elaboration.* The diagnostic clinician should give some attention to what areas should first be opened up to spontaneous elaboration. In psychoanalytic terms this is somewhat equivalent to opening up the ego to aggression. Our definitions of aggression and hostility are somewhat different from those employed by psychoanalysts, however. Ordinarily aggression and the resultant spontaneous elaboration are first explored in the interview room. Almost immediately following, they are likely to be explored outside the interview room. Then there may be trouble. But that is a form of trouble the therapist cannot wholly avoid, nor should he always avoid it even if he can. Sometimes the client first tries out his aggression outside the interview room. Then there is likely to be real trouble.

Keeping all of this in mind, the diagnostician should make some preliminary appraisal of the situation and suggest what areas should first be opened up to aggression and spontaneous elaboration. He must, of course, keep in mind the wave of guilt that may sweep over the client as a result of expressing himself aggressively. In the case of the so-called neurotic depressions, this deadlock between guilt and initiative may hold up therapeutic results for months on end. In such a case, particularly, the diagnostician must consider most carefully just where the therapist should first try to open the door to initiative.

1. *Submerged ends.* The diagnostician who has listened carefully to the client will be aware of some constructs that have what we have called *submerged ends.* He will be aware of the fact that the submerged ends represent potential directions the client's overt actions may take. With this in mind he will want to make some initial determination of when, if ever, the submerged ends should be exposed. What regnant constructs need first to be established? What reconstruction is most feasible for dealing with the elements now bound in the submerged ends? What central psychotherapeutic approach will be most suitable for dealing with the submerged ends in proper order?

20. DESIGNATION OF THE PRINCIPALLY RESPONSIBLE CLINICIAN

If the client is being diagnosed in a situation involving teamwork among a group of clinicians, the designation of the principally responsible clinician is the next step. The principally responsible clinician is normally the one who is in most intimate contact with the client; serious difficulties almost always develop in the treatment when he is not. The principally responsible clinician is sometimes considered to be the only one who is the client's psychotherapist, although it should be clearly borne in mind that all clinicians who organize their efforts directly toward the rehabilitation of the client are, in some manner, performing psychotherapeutic functions and are therefore psychotherapists. In this sense everything that is done to and for the client may be considered to have psychotherapeutic implications.

Aside from the matter of administrative availability, the choice of the principally responsible clinician usually hinges upon two considerations: (a) understanding of the reconstructions which are needed in the case, and (b) compliance with the transferences which may best be utilized during the course of therapy. The clinician need not be familiar with the case at the time he is designated. His skills and competencies should be well enough known to his colleagues to enable them to judge whether or not he is the man for the job. Some clinicians are known to be better in dealing with obsessive-compulsive clients, others are known to handle schizoid clients well, and others do their best work with anxiety cases.

But more than assigning a clinician to a case on the basis of the Kraepelinian diagnosis, the matter of constructions should be taken into consideration. A clinician who tends to plunge his clients into childlike forms of dependency should not be assigned to a case in which the client must maintain adult-like dependency relations. A clinician who is confused by abstract verbalizations should not be assigned to a client who must reorganize his permeable constructs.

Since the client must try many of his questionable constructions on the therapist for size, it is important that the therapist be one upon whom such transferences can be made. He should, then, be a reasonably compliant figure, in the sense that he will let the client see him in the guise of figures from the client's personal-social milieu. This may not be wholly a matter of the attitude of the therapist. The therapist may simply have physical characteristics which make it easier for the client to see him in the ways the client needs to see his therapist. The sex and age of the therapist may be taken into account. Sometimes it is desirable to change the designation of the principally responsible clinician as therapy progresses and the client is ready to make new transferences. Ordinarily, however, this kind of shifting is not necessary if outside social resources are properly used.

21. SELECTION OF ADJUNCTIVE RESOURCES TO BE UTILIZED

In the case of a hospitalized patient it is important to mobilize as many adjunctive resources as the hospital can provide and the patient can use. Hospitals are naturally sterile, from a psychological point of view, regardless of how well staffed they may be. Adequate therapy requires full use of their resources, yet many clinicians lack the comprehensive training and the professional overview necessary to enable them to make full use of the resources in a modern neuropsychiatric hospital, much less make full use of the more comprehensive resources in a community.

a. *Dealing with minor problems too.* The clinician's concern for the principal difficulties faced by a client should not prevent him from recognizing the cumulative over-all effect of dealing with the client's minor problems too. The client may need minor medical attention. A hernia may need mending. He may need dental attention. His glasses may need to be replaced. He may need a prosthetic device such as a hearing aid. If so, he will certainly also need training in how to use it. Many prosthetic programs fail because this fact is overlooked.

b. *Occupational therapy.* In a hospital the therapist should make full use of that group of adjunctive services which are sometimes called "corrective therapy," but which, more recently, are grouped under "physical and mental rehabilitation." The fitting and training in the use of prosthetic devices is sometimes included in this group. Physiotherapy in its variety of forms belongs here. Occupational therapy in its many forms is included. The occupational therapy may include formal exercises for restoring the function of a particular muscle group or it may set up tasks of a semirecreational or semioccupational nature which accomplish the same purpose.

Occupational therapy may be diagnostic. The patient may find it a means of expression, whether it be in terms of finger painting, woodworking, typesetting, or scrubbing floors. If the tasks are carefully assigned, or if they are freely chosen by the patient, and if they are thoughtfully observed, the hospital staff may learn much about the patient's construct system which is not apparent in the interview therapy room. As we have said before, words are not the only symbols of constructs. Indeed, the more basic constructions that we place upon life are frequently not symbolized by words at all. A therapist should keep close track of the developments which occur in his patient's occupational therapy. It is a good plan before each interview to make a quick check of the patient's latest finger painting, his latest clay model, his latest work plan.

Occupational therapy is also therapeutic. A client who cannot communicate well in terms of words may quite appropriately be treated with occupational therapy as the central therapeutic approach. The occupational therapist can observe new constructs emerging, and can introduce new elements which, if embraced, will give the new constructions appropriate range and permeability and provide the client with facilities for validating them. It is a mistake to assume that constructs are sharply divided between those which have to do with physical things and those which have to do with mental or social things. A client who loves to pound nails, dig holes, or grease machinery is likely to be using constructs which govern his relations with people as well as his relations with things. As the client's activity and modes of approach to these tasks change, his relations with other people are almost certain to change perceptibly. This important fact can be used as a basis for bringing about genuine therapeutic changes in the client's interpersonal relations.

In a somewhat less fundamental sense, occupational therapy is therapeutic because it involves the client in a series of constructive interpersonal relations with his occupational therapist, and with the other clients who share his interests. Therapy usually requires that the client establish his relationships with other people on the basis of cooperative undertakings rather than on the basis of domination and submission or on the basis of minimum insularity in a minimum space.

The activities of group psychotherapy can encourage the feeble beginnings of cooperation for the sake of a common undertaking. That cooperation must naturally be based upon role constructs, those constructs which help the client to interpret the behavior of the other person.

We have mentioned the Bieri-Lundy effect in interpersonal interactions. At first the client may have no basis for engaging in a cooperative role relationship with his fellow clients or with his occupational therapist, save to concede gradually that they may be like himself. Later he begins to discriminate and finds that people who are not like himself can still be plausible people with whom he can collaborate.

Occupational therapy can be educative. The client may learn skills which will enable him to get along better both vocationally and avocationally. This is not to say that education does not also include aiding the development of an understanding of other people, as does therapy. We refer merely to those more formalized understandings which enable people to get along in the world. A client may learn to typewrite. As a result he may be able to do the creative writing in his spare time which means so much to his general feeling of well-being. He may also learn to typewrite in order to earn a living at a type of job where typewriting is useful.

We may even consider occupational therapy as a diversion. This may seem like a negative value, but there are instances when negative values are appropriate. A patient who is traumatized by his first hospitalization, or one who has to face an inevitable disaster, may find that the diversionary activities of occupational therapy will cushion the shock.

c. *Recreation.* Most hospitals provide programs which are broadly recreational. They include sports, music, entertainment, preparation for and participation in festivals, and recreational reading. The reading can be set up as an important feature of the therapeutic program. Sometimes the reading facilities and program are organized under what is called "bibliotherapy." Some therapists are able to work out with the client a course of readings which has important therapeutic implications.

It is often claimed that music can be utilized therapeutically by all clients. So far, research undertaken along this line has failed to verify the claim. There are some clients who appear to make good use of music as an adjunctive approach to their problems. Group music programs such as bands and orchestras do seem to be helpful. Dancing and dramatics programs can also be used adjunctively.

d. *Dilation.* One may look upon the adjunctive approaches to psychotherapy as providing dilation of the client's perceptual field so that the new constructs which he forms will not be too constricted and impermeable. It makes a great deal of difference when a hospital puts on a program of getting patients out of their pajamas and bathrobes into street clothes and out of their wards onto the grounds or on errands. The more patients are encouraged to move around, the wider their psychological horizons are likely to be. The hospital is, of course, the often mentioned "protective environment," but it can also become a prison for the mind where the disturbed patient can eventually become socially incapacitated.

The clothes that patients wear makes a difference in their social behavior. A man in a ragged pair of pajamas does not pull himself up to his full psychological height, but a man in a freshly pressed pair of trousers often tries to enact the part the costume calls for. A woman whose hair is unkempt is usually a miserable creature and anything but charming in her manner, whether she is a patient or not. A permanent wave, costume jewelry, hose, and a little attention may not make her well, but they will make her behave differently. Moreover, the change is usually for the better and it usually provides a far better background for making therapeutic progress in the interviewing room.

There are additional ways of dilating the patient's perceptual field. If patients are always greeted in the hall, just as professional people are always greeted in the hall, if they are always encouraged to speak to each other, if they are introduced to each other as one would introduce guests in a home, if they are generally treated with respect, they will be less likely to show the constriction which is the dread contagion of so many neuropsychiatric hospitals. The program of the Red Cross Gray Ladies may also be utilized in avoiding constriction. They may take groups of patients into town for a movie or for shopping. They may help them maintain correspondence with their families and aid in a thousand other ways in keeping the patients "in contact."

e. *Community participation.* Even with hospitalized patients the general resources of the community may be employed. Community recreational facilities may be used. Some local organizations are accessible to patients. Educational resources can sometimes be tapped. Local industry may provide employment for some patients as they leave the hospital. Social agencies in the patient's home community may help take care of his family and, through cooperation with the hospital's social-work department, help maintain the patient's functional identification with his community.

The hospital itself is a community. Many community functions can be maintained by the patient group. A newspaper can be published, and frequently is. Concerts can be prepared and given. Some group problems can be discussed and solved. Mutual-interest groups can be organized. Friendships can be formed. Personal plans can be made and discussed with fellow patients. Educational programs can be carried out. Vocational training can be given and utilized in the hospital community.

Guidance can be obtained on a professional basis. This guidance involves much more than being told what job to seek. It can include the obtaining of comprehensive occupational information, the study of community facilities for training, avocational pursuits, and family living. The guidance services may also include training in social skills, particularly those which will be needed for reentry into the home, community, and job. Sociodrama may be used in this connection.

Good psychotherapeutic planning of adjunctive approaches will usually also include the services of the chaplain, the nurses, the attendants, and members of the patient's family who have particular skills or who stand in important relationships to the patient. Psychotherapy is largely a matter of mobilization of resources along lines which bear directly upon a patient's psychological problems. It involves far more than waiting for next Tuesday's office appointment with the patient.

f. *Resources for the nonhospitalized client.* We have been talking about the mobilization of adjunctive resources for the hospitalized patient. The resources available to the nonhospitalized client are more abundant, more complex, and more difficult to mobilize. The school in the community, for example, is a complicated agency with an immensely varied program, often including adult-educational offerings. Churches are also relatively complicated. Neither is likely to have a program which is specially designed for meeting the needs of disturbed people. Social-welfare agencies are usually easier to enlist for adjunctive treatment. Industrial organizations, commercial organizations, and some fraternal organizations have programs which may meet, in part, the adjunctive needs of a client. A client who has been employed in a large industrial organization may have available to him the personnel and counseling services of that organization. There may also be nursing and legal-aid services available. The district nursing service or the county public-health nursing service may be available to help the client or members of his family who are incapacitated. There are likely to be arts and crafts groups, including Little Theater, an organization which, more frequently than most people realize, incidentally provides adjunctive therapy for people having difficulty in enacting their life role or sex role.

One should not overlook the fact that adjunctive therapy for the client is often a matter of setting up the wholesome living situation for his family that he is unable to provide himself. Consider the use of the public playground. If the client's therapist helps make sure that the client's children use the playground, not only will the children be better taken care of, but the client will be relieved to know that this part of his family obligation is being discharged. Moreover, his children may be less irritating to him if their own adjustment is more satisfactory.

A similar principle holds with respect to other members of the client's family. The more the clinician can do to help the client's family understand how to deal with the client, the more he can do to keep their morale at a high level, and the more he can do to mobilize the family resources in general, the better results he is likely to get in dealing with the client. This does not mean that all therapy should be situational. It does not mean that the therapist should necessarily do what some clients seek to have him do — manipulate the family so that it will conform to the client's demands. It simply means that therapy can usually be more successful if it pushes forward on a broad front.

22. DESIGNATION OF THE RESPONSIBLE CLINICIAN'S ADVISORY STAFF

Ordinarily a therapist can do a better job if he has an advisory staff with whom he can discuss his work with a given case from time to time. Therapists who have worked too long without seeking professional collaboration on their cases are likely to develop blind spots and questionable habits of work. Members of the advisory staff should ordinarily be clinicians who are responsible for some of the adjunctive therapeutic approaches being used in the case. They are in a position to make independent observations of the client.

An interdisciplinary advisory staff can sometimes, though not always, be used to an advantage. All too frequently the interdisciplinary approach breaks down because it is not truly interdisciplinary, but rather a hierarchy of technicians with different titles working in an identical disciplinary framework. The client is not actually seen from the point of view of two or more theoretical systems. Each technician makes his particular set of categorical observations but the interpretations are all structured with the same bias. This is not an interdisciplinary approach.

In order to have a true interdisciplinary approach, one has to start first with a basic philosophical orientation toward the nature of truth. The epistemological position of all of the collaborators should be that knowledge is a matter of the construction that one is able systematically and consistently to place upon phenomena. They must agree that all contemporary construction systems have an ad interim status only, and that the disciplines which collaborate have status as different disciplines primarily because they employ different construction systems. This agreement need not be explicitly verbalized as long as it is implicit in the attitudes of the participating staff members.

The status of staff members as representatives of independent disciplines does not rest upon a division of the phenomena which each is permitted to observe. To make that kind of division is to fall into the trap of preemptive and wholly primitive reasoning. If the interdisciplinary approach is to be seriously attempted, it should be upon a basis of full appreciation of the fact that two mutually inconsistent interpretations of a case may both be "right" and, furthermore, that the future may prove both of them to be "wrong."

Now a group of clinicians, each representing a different discipline, may describe a case in an amazing variety of ways. What then happens to the client? If one of the clinicians is labeled "the boss" or the representative of the "senior profession" — for example, the psychiatrist — the upshot is likely to be that there is no true interdisciplinary consideration of the needs of the client and that all decisions are made within the framework of "the boss's" favorite set of constructs. This is an authoritarian way of reaching an action decision — and authoritarianism has had a long and dismal history in man's social organization. The only trouble with this kind of approach is that the thinking which stems from other premises is stifled when it is cut off from validating experience. This objection to authoritarianism is a fundamental one. It argues ultimately against authoritarianism in any type of social organization, not merely in the organization of a professional clinical team.

But again, what happens to the person whose problems are waiting to be solved while the different disciplines are each trying to escape the authoritarian control of the others? Again we refer to our C–P–C Cycle — circumspection, preemption, control. As each disciplinary representative presents his construction of the case, the members of the team should seek to deal with the constructions propositionally. This means that the case is seen not only multidimensionally but also multisystematically. Each team member attempts to follow the separate constructions presented by the others. This propositional thinking permits the clinicians to deal with the case *circumspectively*.

Then comes the question of what to do — what action to take. In large measure, this means accepting the version of the case which seems best to order the facts, which seems most clearly to indicate what the therapeutic alternatives are, and which opens a plausible path to the most desirable outcome. This is the preemption phase of the C–P–C Cycle. The ensuing decision to take action is the final or *control* phase of the cycle. The teamwork, of course, breaks down if none of the clinicians is able to follow the systematic presentations of the others. In that case there is nothing for it but to resort to authoritarianism. Indeed, wheresoever communication breaks down there is nothing for it but to resort to authoritarianism.

The principally responsible clinician should have an advisory staff which is in contact with the case by means of the adjunctive psychotherapeutic approaches, which is truly interdisciplinary, and with whom he can communicate well enough so that he will not have to resort to authoritarianism. It takes a lot of professional man-hours out of the week but provision should be made for regular, even though brief, consultation with the advisory staff.

23. DETERMINATION OF THE AD INTERIM STATUS OF THE CLIENT

This involves a decision which can be revised later but which is properly a part of the transitive diagnostic procedure. The client should be protected and the decision should be on the conservative side, as far as his alternatives are concerned, if it is possible to determine what the conservative side is.

24. SETTING OF DATES OR CONDITIONS UNDER WHICH PROGRESS WILL
     BE REVIEWED BY THE ADVISORY STAFF

In an earlier chapter we pointed out that a therapist should check his understanding of his client by continually testing his ability to predict what the client will do. The therapist who cannot distinguish clearly between what his particular client will do and what would be expected of other people in general may well question his understanding of the case. This criterion of the understanding of a therapist for his client is very much in line with our systematic position in the psychology of personal constructs. Again we are placing our emphasis upon generally effective anticipation of events.

Our systematic position might also be expected to affect what we would have to say about diagnosis. In fact, it does! Effective diagnosis is a matter of making some reasonable predictions as to what the client will do under different circumstances and then proposing to create that set of circumstances which will lead to the client's doing what we think he generally ought to do. Like all predictions, they should be made within a reasonable time cycle. We should not have to wait until the millennium to find out how far off we were. If we do, we shall not learn much! In diagnosis, then, we should indicate what we think will happen, how it can be made to happen, and when to check up to see if it has happened or not. Transitive diagnosis is a matter of a clinician's "sticking his neck out." Clinicians should be encouraged to stick their necks out in making predictions, although they should show exemplary professional caution in deciding what to do with the client.

The clinician can make two types of predictions. He can say that he expects a given crisis to occur by a specific date and that the case should then be reviewed. Or he can say that if and when the client begins to show a given type of behavior it will be time to review the case and perhaps change the diagnosis. Both of these call for some preliminary estimate of the dates or conditions under which progress reports will be reviewed by the advisory staff. Setting up such mile posts is an important feature of transitive diagnosis.

Chapter Sixteen

Disorders of Construction

ᒐᒥᒐᒥᒐᒥᒐᒥᒐᒥᒐᒥᒐᒥᒐᒥᒐᒥᒐᒥᒐᒥᒐᒥᒐ

Now follow two descriptive chapters. The reader will want to see how representative types of psychological disorders can be structured in terms of our proposed set of axes, instead of being pigeonholed in conventional nosological categories. While the original presentation of these axes took them up one at a time, we will now illustrate how they can be used together as a multi-dimensional system to describe the plight and plot the treatment of the disturbed client.

A. *Introduction*

1. DIAGNOSTIC CONSTRUCTS DO NOT NECESSARILY DENOTE DISORDERS

The psychology of personal constructs is designed around the problem of reconstruing life, but it is not a system built upon psychopathology. The diagnostic constructs proposed in Volume One and reviewed at the beginning of this volume are designed to be relevant to various personal construct systems, regardless of whether or not the persons are sick or their constructs inappropriate. The problem of disorders of construction is therefore considered separately in this chapter and in the one which follows it.

The discussion of disorders is arranged according to the diagnostic dimensions which are principally involved. As might be expected, any disorder is likely to involve more than one dimension. The discussions are illustrative and should not be taken as an attempt to catalogue a group of disease entities. Our approach to psychological disturbance is altogether in terms of dimensions rather than in terms of entities.

The brief sketches of therapeutic approaches are also intended to be illustrative rather than definitive. It seems to us that the treatment of psychological disorders is not a matter of nostrums but a matter of drawing plans in outline only and then adjusting techniques to the particular characteristics of the client and to the special skills and limitations of the therapist.

2. WHAT IS A DISORDER?

From the standpoint of the psychology of personal constructs we may define a disorder as any personal construction which is used repeatedly in spite of consistent invalidation. This is an unusual definition, as psychological thinking ordinarily goes. At first glance it may seem as though we have cut the ground from under a major premise of psychology — that readjustment inevitably follows upon failure. But let us point out that we have not laid down such a premise; we have not said that invalidation necessarily causes revision of one's personal construction of life. What we have assumed in this regard is carefully expressed in our Organization, Experience, Modulation, and Fragmentation Corollaries.

A personal construction system is an organized thing. The failure of one part of it does not necessarily lead immediately to a replacement of that part. Before replacing a part the person is likely to take a look at his whole scaffolding to see how much useful structure is in danger of collapsing. Thus, even an obviously invalid part of a construction system may be preferable to the void of anxiety which might be caused by its elimination altogether.

We may approach the problem of what constitutes a disorder at a very simple and practical level. *We may say, simply, that the goal of psychotherapy is to alleviate complaints — complaints of a person about himself and others and complaints of others about him.* Some psychologists will not be very happy with this definition. Clinical psychologists are always being pressed to make some definitive statement of what ultimate value they pursue in their work. Such a statement would have to be pitched at the level of a religion or a philosophy, not at the level of a system of psychology.

What we have attempted to do here is to pitch our discussion at two levels. Our definition of a disorder is pitched only at the level of our psychological system — the psychology of personal constructs. Our statement of the goal of psychotherapy is pitched at a phenomenological level — the complaint, whatever its grounds. Except for constructive alternativism, we have not tried to formulate a complete philosophical system of values.

A word about our definition of the goal of psychotherapy is in order here. We said that the goal of psychotherapy is to alleviate complaints. But this does not mean either that the person who complains or the person who is complained about is necessarily the one to be worked over. The psychologist, as we have suggested before, turns his attention to that point which offers the greatest likelihood of producing results in the future. He does not necessarily turn his attention to the cause of the complaint. If the cause is in the past, looking backward at it may not undo its damage. If the offending person is inaccessible or intransigent, the best therapeutic approach may be elsewhere.

From the standpoint of the psychology of personal constructs, psychological disorders can be traced to characteristics of a person's construction system. There may be other bases of explanation but this is the one that seems most profitable. If such an explanation will adequately cover the facts, we shall at last have arrived at a vantage point from which the treatment of psychological disorders may be seen as plausible. One can do something about a person's construction system. On the other hand, if we are bound to explain disorders in terms of the past, treatment can be accomplished only by turning the clock back or by tediously canceling out each old experience by overlaying it with a new one.

The reader will recognize in the above paragraph a recurrent theme which has been appearing more or less regularly from chapter to chapter. It is not original. It is at least as old as the

Christian religion. It is embodied in the notion that repentance or "rethinking" is a better way of correcting mistakes than atonement is. Rethinking (or reconstruing) seems to be a more likely way of avoiding the same mistakes in the future. As we see it, the classical transition in thinking from the notion of *atonement* to that of *repentance* has its parallel in the life of the individual client who is helped by the therapist to substitute *reconstruction* for *compensation*.

Another way of emphasizing the same point, although it may be an oversimplification, is to say that a man may not now choose his past but he may select his future. If we concern ourselves with his past it is because, and only because, the way he has been behaving is often a rough guide to how he has been approaching his future. It is often a good idea to see what particular kind of mischief he has been up to. While the psychology of personal constructs has little of the scope of a philosophical or a religious system, there are, in a few instances, interesting points of congruency, such as this one.

In an earlier chapter we pointed out our preference for using diagnostic constructs which did not primarily represent preemptive classes of persons but represented, rather, coordinate axes with respect to which the various behaviors and behavior trends of individual persons could be plotted. This was to say that we preferred to construe people propositionally rather than preemptively. For purposes of convenience we have no objection to construing groupings of people in a constellatory manner — for example, by occupational, socio-economic, or even racio-cultural groups — although we recognize in such stereotyping the danger of constricted thinking about individuals who are perceived as members of the artificial groupings.

For example, it is often considered the mark of a sophisticated clinician that he considers all of his clients in terms of the culture groups to which they belong. Yet, in the final analysis, a client who is to be genuinely understood should never be confined to the stereotype of his culture. For the clinician the cultural approach should never be more than a preliminary step in the understanding of his client, the first in a series of approximations which bring the client into sharp focus in a complex matrix of basic psychological dimensions.

We feel pretty much the same way about the commonly used, and frequently useful, nosological categories of neuro-psychiatric disorders. To start out by describing a client to a fellow clinician as schizoid is pardonable. But for a therapist to continue thinking of his client primarily as a schizophrenic is unprofessional. No client should continue looking like a stereotype to an alert therapist who works with him day after day.

For the most part it is misleading to think of a disorder solely in terms of a disease entity. That makes one dependent upon a published catalogue of "disorders." If a client's construction does not fit one of the official categories, his actual difficulties are likely to be ignored.

The failure of the disease-entity type of thinking is not so obvious in the area of physiology as it may be in the area of psychology or — even more clearly — as it is in the area of sociology. In the area of physiology the healthy or "nondis-ordered" conditions are more or less obvious. We come in daily contact with a few "healthy" people. We have healthy moments ourselves. Disorders are somewhat easier to see. In the social area we have less contact with people operating in markedly different social groupings. Our vision of what is socially disordered is clouded by our being aware of so little that is not similarly disordered.

Yet even in the physiological realm, where we seem to have daily contact with a wide variety of states of health, our vision may be distorted. Who knows what perfect health is or could be? Most of us live in a world of high blood pressure, gastric ulcers, and spring colds. Is there any other world? Perhaps some day we shall see.

There are some who say that the essential nature of a psychological disorder is the failure of the client's "insight." The client who lacks "insight" is in a state of disorder. From the point of view of the psychology of personal constructs this definition does not make much sense. Does the clinician mean that the client has no structure? That is preposterous. It takes some kind of structure to keep one's symptom alive. Even the symptom of anxiety is maintained with some kind of structure. Does the clinician mean that the client who has a disorder is one who misunderstands his situation? That makes a little more sense. What is the essential difference between understanding? Today's understandings so often turns out to be tomorrow's misunderstanding. Is the client who disagrees with his therapist benighted, confused, resistant, and repressed? Does he have health-giving "insight" only when he comes to construe his world with the same biases his therapist has? The view of the psychology of personal constructs is that the gray dawn of a more enlightened age may reveal them as both wrong. Let us hope it will not reveal the therapist to be more wrong than the client was.

But let us return to our question: what is a disorder? It is not explained simply as the inevitable outcome of any past which happens to be unfortunate. It relates to one's present stance as he faces the future. It is not a conventionalized category. It should be construed propositionally rather than preemptively or constellatorily. It makes no sense to try to define it either as the absence of structure or as unorthodoxy. Rather than attempt to give it such a categorical definition we have suggested simply that it represents any structure which appears to fail to accomplish its purpose.

This is an extremely flexible definition. Appear to whom? What purpose is *its* purpose? What is failure? The answers are: anybody; anybody's; and whatever you like. In other words, we are content to let "disorder" mean whatever is ineffectual from the viewpoint of the client, from the viewpoint of his therapist, from the viewpoint of his stuffy neighbors, from the viewpoint of history, or from the viewpoint of God. Perhaps the proper question is not *what* is a disorder but *where*, and the therapist's question is not *who* needs treatment but *what* needs treatment. Can we live with such a definition?

Yes. Only we must keep in mind that we are working with a definition that is both provincial and heuristic. And now let us stop worrying about it!

It is not practical to attempt to catalogue all the typical psychological disorders — even if he could, who would have the stomach for writing that kind of cook book? What we propose to do here is to take our system of coordinate axes — called diagnostic constructs — and do some illustrative plotting of cases with respect to them. The reader will need to keep in mind that our axes are not altogether orthogonal, although, when it is appropriate, we are free to deal with the different properties of persons in a truly propositional manner. We shall order our approach in terms of the different axes, first taking up dilation and constriction and some of the disorders which are most conspicuously reflected in terms of that dimension. In turn, we shall discuss disorders which illustrate extremes in each of several other diagnostic construct dimensions.

B. Dilation

3. DISORDERS INVOLVING DILATION

It is probably abundantly clear at this point that the system of dimensions or diagnostic constructs which we have proposed is not a nomenclature of diseases. For example, *anxiety* is not a psychological disorder, but simply a harbinger of change. The change may or may not result in disorder. *Guilt* is not of itself a psychological disorder. It is a form of social disidentification which may represent either exile or emancipation. So with *dilation*. For one client it may be the way he got himself into difficulty. For another it may be the most promising approach to recovery. One person may look into the heavens at night and contemplate the uncounted stars, the mystery of the universes beyond our own, and the patient procession of infinite time. From that experience he may gain serenity and poise. Another may look into the same sky and see invaders from Mars, flying saucers spewing out fire, or the ominous heralds of doomsday. For the one the dilation brings into play the superordinate constructs beneath whose reaches the swirling events of everyday life become tiny eddies in a placid stream. For the other the dilation brings him face to face with a chaos with which his superordinate constructs cannot cope. Is dilation then a disordering process or an ordering process? It all depends.

a. *Illustration of the abandonment of constructs governing a dilated field.* Consider a person who once, perhaps as a child or adolescent, leaned heavily upon a belief that God could be inveigled into complying with all his requests. Suppose he had developed a dilated field with respect to this construction. God would take care of *all* his requests. Suppose the construction, as well as being one imposed upon a dilated field, is also a *tight* one — for example, God's compliance is perceived both literally and specifically. Now suppose that, through testing and invalidating evidence and perhaps through other developments as well, this religious structure is abandoned. The person is left with a considerably dilated field.

Let us suppose that the formidable task of reconstructing the person's dilated field is postponed or, perhaps, is undertaken on too small a scale. As the person confronts a succession of major issues in his life, he finds himself without the capacity to construe them satisfactorily. He attempts to make great generalizations with little ideas.

But what other remaining bases does such a person have for construing adult issues? Obviously he must use certain preverbal dependency constructs, since these are the only ones with sufficient range of convenience. There is nothing else to use and here he is with a dilated field on his hands. He attempts to work out his problems in terms of constructs which are of even longer standing than the ones he has abandoned: preverbal constructs which once governed his infantile relations with his parents. He still wheedles to satisfy his day-to-day wants; except that now he wheedles his associates instead of God or his parents.

Such a person avoids testing his solutions to current adult issues in terms of impersonal facts. He looks only for the "don't you love me" facts. Actually he is not prepared to face any clear-cut invalidating evidence, for that would call for revision of a large portion of his construction system. He is not ready for such revision, for, in terms of our Modulation Corollary, the impending variation in his construction system, being necessarily subordinate to something more permeable, cannot be worked out.

Those permeable aspects of his system which might once have given him over-all stability have been abandoned. Perhaps they were so tightly drawn that they would not have worked anyway. He is not in a position where he can afford to stake his adult thinking on the outcome of a practical experiment. Instead, he snuggles up to people, whimpers, panders to their whims, indulges his own, and generally postpones his psychological maturation.

Such a person is not necessarily immobilized by his lack of a suitable working superordinate system. He may do a lot of thrashing about. But his experiments are not designed to get definitive results. The only thing that he is testing is his preverbal construct that some people are indulgent and others are not. He may now express it by saying that some people are "accepting" and others are "rejecting." It means the same thing. He looks for the "accepting" people.

Actually, as far as adult issues are concerned, the person can be seen to be procrastinating a good deal of the time. He is not in a position to experiment because he is not in a position to make revisions that the results of the experimentation would call for. He cannot take such revisions in his stride because he has abandoned — and has not replaced — the superordinate structure with which his dilated field was once held together. His world would really collapse in a heap of anxiety if he had suddenly to abandon either the little structures which he has recently erected or the one remaining superordinate structure of parent-like indulgence.

Such a person as we have described does not wholly avoid anxiety. As he looks at his dilated field, he gets anxious because he has no structure to force it all into an orderly array. Every time he skims too close to invalidating evidence bearing upon his construct of "indulgence-rejection" he gets anxious, because it threatens to make him abandon another major line of defense. In therapy he may be anxious as he lays some of his other preverbal constructs on the line for testing. Moreover, if he sees the therapist as likely to reinstate some of the abandoned religious structure he may be threatened, in the sense in which we have defined *threat*.

b. *What if the field had not been so dilated?* Now what might have happened in this case if the person had not had such a dilated field? For one thing, the problems of adult life would probably be less complex. The person would have to take fewer things into account in construing his issues. He could get by with the use of more mechanical constructs. He could add his sums by counting on his fingers, look up his words in the dictionary to see how they were spelled, apply his rules of thumb, beat out his little daily round, and generally adjust himself to a world of limited radius. The fact that he could no longer see God as granting him his petulantly vocalized wishes would not be so important, because his wishes would remain relatively simple and limited in number. He could revise his constructs about how to obtain things for himself under the aegis of his remaining superordinate constructs, which, though less permeable and more limited, still might be permeable enough to hold sway over the reconstructions that daily living demands of him. Such revisions as he might be likely to undertake could still be contained.

Another outcome of having a less dilated field — although we are essentially saying, in different words, the same thing as we did in the last paragraph — would be that there would be a smaller area left vulnerable to anxiety, by the abandonment of the religious structure. The person's confusion would be relatively less, simply because there would be relatively little stuff lying around to make a clutter. A simple way of putting it is to say that he would not be greatly upset by deciding that God was not going to shell out, because he had not ever thought of much to ask God for anyway.

4. DILATION WITH LOOSE CONSTRUCTION

The person who develops a dilated field in early life may have no way of spanning that field save by loose construction or by increasing the permeability of many of his early constructs. The development of a comprehensive construction system, with the permeable constructs at the top and mostly in superordinate positions, is a big job. A child whose field is prematurely dilated may be compelled to keep on using constructs which ordinarily would long ago have been closed out and made impermeable or which would have been abandoned altogether. Now his childlike constructs must be made or kept permeable in order to contain the flood of new experience. When, at last, these constructs are abandoned, he already has more on his hands than he can handle in disarray. He finds a void of anxiety opening up. If his field had been less dilated there would have been less necessity for increasing the permeability of his childlike constructs and less confusion on the occasion of their abandonment.

The anxiety and threat which a dilated client of this type shows may easily be taken as a sign of a paranoid structure; the client appears to be threatened on so broad a front. He is threatened by certain people who add their weight to the evidence against the effectuality of his *indulgence-rejection* construct. There are moments at which the dilation is suggestive of delusions of grandeur. But the client does not necessarily show the other characteristics which are supposed to be diagnostic indicators of "paranoid" tendency. Of course, the writer has no objection to one's defining the term "paranoid" in any way he wishes. In fact, he would have no systematic objection to one's pinning a "paranoid" label on the type of case which has just been described. Considering the other things which are supposed also to be characteristic of the "paranoid" case, however — systematized delusions of persecution, incurability, and so on — such a label would likely be misleading to the reader.

a. *Dilation with loose construction and undifferentiated*

dependency. Let us look a little deeper into this type of case. Is there not a faint odor of magical thinking the closer one comes to the client? Consider his manner of dealing with his world. To be sure, the person no longer prays to God with a shopping list in his hand. Nor does he write letters to Santa Claus. But what about the way he expects indulgence to solve his problems for him? Is that not a kind of magical thinking? It is! We may wonder how it originally operated.

Most infants and young children get what they want from their parents. Many parents like it that way. They get a big boot out of being the sole suppliers of their children's wants. Some of them encourage their children to try to get the moon for a plaything. But the children are not encouraged to try to get it by means of their own organized efforts. Rather, the children are encouraged to try to get it from their parents. Perhaps the parents set an example by operating that way between themselves. "Don't do it yourself; entreat me to do it for you" may be the essence of family interpersonal relationship between adults as well as between adults and children.

A child reared amid such social expectancies is likely to find out a lot more about how to entreat than he finds out about how to get moons. The outcome is likely to be a kind of thinking which clinicians commonly call "magical thinking." It starts with a belief in the omnipotence of the parents. The child brings the magical powers of the parents into play by making the proper incantations. Thus he too becomes "omnipotent." As he begins to realize that his parents are actually impotent in some areas he makes his incantations to more "powerful" agents: "God," "society," then "the Communist Party"; finally, possibly, a "psychologist." His approach is not necessarily a fault of the agency but is rather a fault in his use of the agency.

When the case arrives at his doorstep, the psychologist is likely to find himself looked upon as a pretty potent being. The client may see him as having hypnotic powers. The client may alternately be threatened by him or seek to become his disciple. The psychologist may enjoy this state of affairs until he finds that he is supposed to produce results. Then he may become annoyed at having his impotence discovered. Eventually he may try to throw the client "out on his own." In the interim, he is likely to keep mumbling something to the client about "insight into dependency needs," a phrase which will not mean much to a person who knows of no other ways to invest his dependencies.

5. TREATMENT OF A TYPE OF DILATION

There are several ways in which a psychotherapeutic program can be designed for a person of the type we have described. The design will, of course, need to take into account a good many more factors than we have listed, but we shall not bother to mention all of them here.

One way to deal with such a case is to start by accepting whatever omnipotency transferences the client is inclined to use for construing the therapist. At the same time the therapist may control the threat by making it clear that he will not use his supposed omnipotencies for making the client over into something he does not want to be. This step has some hazards, for it puts the relationship on a cafeteria basis — the client will get nothing that he does not ask for. Soon the client starts bringing detailed shopping lists to the interviews: "I lack this," "Help me get that," "Give me a whole basket full of those," "I must know how to do this — and no later than Tuesday!"

a. *Indiscriminate "insights."* Each new construction that is developed in the interview room is likely to be applied to a dilated field. "That makes *so much* sense," the client will say. "My Great Aunt Penelope was that way. Mother certainly was. Oh, I see, it is like making deductions on your income tax. And wouldn't you say that kind of thinking has influenced the recent strike in the steel mills? Oh, and I can think of so many times I have made that mistake. Perhaps this is real important — one time when . . . " and so on. This is the I-see-it-all-now type of reconstruction that can be expected in an overdilated field. Each interview is likely to produce a whole set of "fascinatingly new insights" which are smeared on the client's life picture with sweeping strokes and gaudy colors. Yet all of this kaleidoscopic shifting appears to be pretty much confined to the interview room and is actually subordinate to the stabilizing preverbal dependency construction with which the client views the therapy relationship. Knowing no other way to deal with the necessity for change, the client is essentially making incantations to Psychology.

The psychologist will have to wade through all this "insight" and help the client establish little islands of intact and workable structure. Thus the remaining seas of confusion or anxiety are broken up into something of more manageable size. The client can be made aware of his dilation and his propensity for "world-shaking insights." At this stage of therapy it will probably do more harm than good to confront him with his magical thinking and the possibility that his whole preverbal dependency system ought to be abandoned. Such a turn of affairs might very well precipitate a psychosis. He needs the preverbal system, inappropriate as it is, as a permeable, comprehensive, superordinate structure beneath whose stabilizing sway new reconstruction on more limited scales can be experimentally tried out.

b. *Attacking manageable areas.* When the psychotherapist has broken up the oceanic expanses of potential anxiety into areas of reasonable size, he may start taking more aggressive steps to get the client out onto dry land. There are two interrelated phases that must be articulated during this stage of treatment. The one has to do with the development of a new comprehensive superordinate construction system or "system of values." The other has to do with the verbalization, testing, and eventual occlusion or abandonment of the preverbal structure upon which the client's prior readjustments had been hinging. If the latter phase is pursued to the exclusion of the former, the therapist will have a confused and anxious client on his hands, one who may be too anxious to make any further experimental investments. If the former phase is pursued to the exclusion of the latter, the therapist will find himself involved in an endless series of erudite intellectual discussions with a client who still wheedles when he gets anxious and wants something desperately.

This is the stage of treatment which taxes the psychotherapist's skill and perspicacity. It may also be the stage of treatment where he finds that he must settle for something less than optimal results. The new superordinate system should be verbalized so that it can be readily subjected to occasional test and periodic revision throughout the client's life. It has to be worked out experimentally during the period of therapy. The client should actually do things which are reflected by the proposed new system of values. He should give the system a good trying out.

c. *Use of anxiety.* Along with the experimental development of a new superordinate system the therapist will have to take steps to help the client test his old system. If he fails to do this, he may find that the client does not have enough anxiety in the interview room to cause him to look for any alternative solutions to his problems. In order to get results the therapist must keep in mind the principle that the anxiety in the interviewing room must often exceed the anxiety outside the interview room. Otherwise the interview room becomes a haven and nothing more.

An attempt should be made to make the old system verbal. This attempt may not always work. But if the client can verbalize his dependencies upon his parents and his transferred dependencies upon the therapist, he can more readily start testing them. Are these dependencies the ways to get things done, to anticipate life's sequence of events?

d. *This is a special case only.* The technique for accomplishing the kinds of therapeutic goals required in this and other types of cases are a topic for another chapter. Our purpose here is to give some idea of the kind of reasoning about a case which follows from the systematic point of view of the psychology of personal constructs.

Furthermore, the type of case we have used to illustrate dilation is by no means the only type of case involving dilation.

Dilation is not a name for this type of case. Not only that, our illustrative case has obviously required plotting with respect to a number of other dimensions in our diagnostic construct system.

Since our approach to psychological disorders is in terms of dimensions rather than in terms of a catalogue of diseases, we are obviously not going to attempt the Herculean task of describing all the types of disorders which involve dilation, nor all those which involve any one of the other dimensions. Dilation is a good thing if one has the construction system to handle it. If the over-all construction system is shaky, there is likely to be a big crash.

6. DILATION AND THE MANIC SYNDROME

Consider the type of client who is likely to be called "manic." Usually he too is the kind of person who assays sweeping generalizations with little ideas. If the ideas are too bizarre, the diagnostician will have to clutch for some such descriptive term as "schizo-manic" or "excited schizophrenic" in order to pigeonhole the case. The excitement the manic shows represents a kind of unmodulated spontaneous elaboration. He goes free-wheeling down an incline of ideas. To use a colorfully mixed metaphor which is attributed to a certain California politician, "He grabs the bull by the tail and looks the matter squarely in the face." Of course, he does not know which way the bull is headed, but that does not keep him from an adventuresome but near-sighted testing of reality.

If the manic goes through a depressive phase, the ultimate effect of some dilation without adequate structure may be evident. The client makes a frantic effort to constrict his field. Spontaneous elaboration is sharply curtailed; the client has difficulty making the decisions required in the ordinary routine of living. The effort to cut his field down to manageable size by constriction is not successful. He still has moments when he is overwhelmed by the immensity of the problems before him.

The depressed client may be hospitalized. That helps him constrict his field. His anxiety may therefore diminish as he finds that he is no longer compelled to face that for which he has no adequate structure. He may appear to "recover." He may be released from the hospital. A few days later, faced with a suddenly dilated field, he may commit suicide — a definitive act of constriction.

Clinicians like to point out the "oral-dependency" nature of the person who has manic-depressive tendencies. The infant's omnivorous oral explorations suggest an attempt to incorporate everything within his grasp. The infant's dilation of his field and his attempt to use his mouth as a universal prospecting tool are conspicuously noticeable. The therapist is struck by what appears to be the same outlook on the part of certain clients, including some of those who are "diagnosed" as "manic-depressives."

Consistent with the point of view of the psychology of personal constructs, particularly the view regarding dimensions rather than traits, it seems as though the behavior of the infant, and of certain adults, might better be projected on a dimension of *dilation*. What has happened is that the person's exploration has outrun his organization. In order to make the readjustments that his far-flung horizons call for, he must rely upon the preverbal dependency structures which once stood him in such good stead in infancy. The "orality" is what keeps him together. It is what was left after the other comprehensive structures proved inadequate. He is not sick *because* he is oral, nor *because* he has dilated his field, nor *because* he lacks comprehensive structure; he is sick only in terms of the combination of all three.

In addition to orality there is also the matter of guilt in some depressed clients. Considering the manner in which we have defined guilt, one would not necessarily expect to find it in all clients who show dilation-constriction shifts or even in all those who are suicidal. Depending on what one considers to be the observational referents of guilt, this inference from theory seems to be supported by clinical observation. Guilt might be expected particularly in cases where the dilation-constriction cycle is in the areas of interpersonal relations.

Dilation is sometimes observed in cases which are diagnosed as "paranoid." The elaboration of the persecutory theme with its component of surreptitiousness often leads the construer far afield. The theme is highly permeable. Immediate testing of the construct of persecution is forestalled by the notion that other people would not disclose their true attitudes no matter what overtures were made toward them. With such a comprehensive and permeable construct at hand it is quite easy to go ahead and dilate one's whole perceptual field, especially as it relates to interpersonal reactions. The classical "delusion of grandeur" is sometimes the outcome. There is also a guilt component to be considered here too, but let us deal with that matter later.

C. Tightening and Loosening

7. DISORDERS INVOLVING TIGHTENING AND LOOSENING OF CONSTRUCTS

The revision of constructs is not always easy to accomplish. It usually starts with the invalidation of a part of one's construct repertory. This stage in the revision sequence may follow a dilation of the field of elements. If that dilation presents no new elements which cannot be handled satisfactorily by familiar constructs drawn from his repertory, about all that happens is that the constructs used may be seen as having increased permeability. If, however, the dilation presents the person with a situation he cannot handle, he can do one of three things. He can live with his anxiety for a time; he can crawl back into his shell for a time; or he can immediately start doing something about his constructs. If he crawls back into his shell he is using constriction, a device which enables him to postpone the revision of his constructs. The procedure is also a concession that his constructs are impermeable, that, while they fit the sorts of things he had previously found them useful for, they are not applicable to his newest venture.

Suppose the person starts to revise his constructs. He can expect some clutter about his household while the process is going on. This means anxiety. A semblance of organization can be maintained, however, if he has some superordinate structure to his life which is permeable enough to deal in a general fashion with the strange and unruly elements for which he is seeking some precise structure. Again we refer to our Modulation Corollary. The permeable structure of his "long-range goals" — his life-role structure, his philosophical position — keeps him from collapsing in complete anxiety.

From this point on there are several courses open to him. He may use circumspection. This involves the use of propositional constructs, several of them at a time. Out of this multidimensional approach he may be able to evolve some simpler structure, some clearer picture of what it is that he is dealing with.

This approach has its analogue in the clinical approach the psychologist uses in attempting to revise his construction system. The psychologist's case is viewed from several angles simultaneously. Out of the multidimensional structure the psychologist devises a more economical construct or group of constructs.

We may also say that the circumspective approach has its analogue in factorial-analysis procedure. A variety of test observations is made. Then the factorial structure is reduced to a smaller number of vectors. Finally, the vectorial structure is rotated to bring it into closer alignment with familiar vectors.

The person who has set out to revise his constructs may proceed in another manner. He may start by loosening his present constructs. They may not fit his new situations precisely, but he uses them anyway and considers his results as rough approximations. His constructions are irregular, somewhat inconsistent, and variable. He is not precise. His thinking has a dream-like quality to it. He tolerates ambiguity and yet still proceeds as if he were construing his world in a manner which is good enough for practical purposes. He thinks of his predictions as being true "in the main," "approximately," "in a sense," or as being "something like" the truth.

This kind of thinking also has its analogue in statistical methodology. The correlation coefficient is an example. The relationship between two variables is not precisely stated as it would be in a formula of the type the physicists like to use. The prediction formulas are not reversible and one accepts ambiguity in terms of "regression." Yet out of loose thinking may come new precise conceptualization, provided the person is able to pull himself together again.

a. *Facing life with nothing but tight constructions.* Reconstructing frequently calls for the alternate loosening and tightening of one's constructs. The type of psychotherapy which seeks to make basic revisions in a client's construction system requires a delicate touch in articulating these two processes. As we have already said, Fenichel aptly and poetically describes it as "steering between Scylla and Charybdis." If construing is tight, one runs the risk of being shattered on the uncompromising rocks of reality. If it is loose, one may be spun around endlessly in the whirlpool of fantasy.

Consider the person who faces the changing scene of life with nothing but tight constructions. Every prediction, every anticipation, must be precise and exact. Every element which he construes must fit the context of its construct without any possibility of being questioned. There are no loose fits which might let anxiety seep in. The whole structure is designed to be anxiety-tight.

Now why would a person try to build this type of unventilated structure? The answer, both from the standpoint of our theoretical position and from the standpoint of clinical observation, is that he does not have the permeable type of superordinate structure that would enable him to anticipate life otherwise. Without his vast array of precise little formulas his world would collapse in anxiety.

But life presents a changing scene. The person's formula making has difficulty keeping up. Repeatedly, his anticipations fail to materialize. He must start discarding constructs. Anxiety finally takes over in spite of all the elaborate little preventive measures he has taken. Now he can either resort to preverbal comprehensive structures or he can constrict. The extremes of these alternatives represent the well-known choice between psychosis and suicide.

8. TREATMENT OF THE TIGHTENED CONSTRUCTIONS

With this type of client, psychotherapy may be tedious but not necessarily unfruitful. The transferences placed upon the therapist are, of course, likely to be legalistic and literalistic. Usually the therapist tries to develop, instead, a generalized construction of the therapeutic situation which will temporarily stand in lieu of a suitable comprehensive superordinate system. It may be necessary to constrict the client's field, perhaps by temporary hospitalization or by narrowing down the client's daily beat. When anxiety does appear, though not before, the therapist may be supportive. For the therapist to try to be supportive before the anxiety is accepted by the client is likely to be either futile or vigorously rejected. This is because the client is not yet ready to face the futility of his modes of construing.

After the therapeutic relationship is established as a bridge which spans the unpredictable vicissitudes of life, the therapist should turn attention to the basic therapeutic undertaking. That is to help the client develop an outlook which will enable him to grow and to establish a program of continuous construct revision. Ordinarily this stage starts with a course of training in how to loosen one's conceptualization. The client's response is likely to be strangely inept at first. It may be weeks before the client can respond in a satisfactory manner. Gradually some of his fantasy life and his capacity for creative and poetic thinking is restored to him. The techniques for accomplishing this therapeutic objective are discussed in a later chapter.

One of the principal hazards of therapy is that the loosening will produce extensive anxiety. A person of this type will see loose constructs as much like no constructs at all. If the loosening takes place on too wide a front, or if it is applied to an area where the reserve structures are vulnerable to invalidation, the client may suddenly be confronted with a vast amount of anxiety with which he must deal drastically. For example, if the therapist keeps harping on conceptual loosening, he may find that the client gets loose with respect to all of his daily affairs. Not only will such a client behave in a bizarre fashion but the therapist will be unable to maintain communication with him. Again, if the therapist opens up a particular area, such as that of the sex role, he may find that his client "panics" and falls back upon reserve structures which are harder to deal with than was the original brittle structure. Tight structures tend to be impermeable also, and any attempt to loosen them up in the hope of making them more permeable should be made with a wary eye toward the kinds of issues involved. The ultimate danger is that the client, suddenly overwhelmed with anxiety or perhaps faced with an explosively dilated field which the therapist did not count on, will either constrict or resort to preemption and hostile behavior.

After the client has learned to loosen his construction, the therapist has the task of showing him how to tighten up the newly formed constructs which may arise from the loosened old ones. This involves verbalization and experimentation. The weaving back and forth between tightness and looseness is difficult for this type of client to learn. It is like teaching an imitator to be an inventor or an exceedingly stuffy person how to be an imaginative organizer.

Next, the therapist must open areas to aggressive exploration. The client always experiments, of course, but at this stage the therapist seeks to encourage experimentation on a broad front. Here the client and the therapist, considering the breadth of the constructions involved, are somewhat dependent upon the accident of circumstances. It may take weeks or months to accumulate the kind of validational experience which will weigh the evidence in favor of the new construction.

Finally, the therapist has the task of getting the client launched. The temporary relationship which was established at the beginning must be spontaneously abandoned by the client in favor of the new superordinate structure. This may involve quite a struggle on the part of the client. Over and over he asks himself what *really* keeps him going, his new perception of his life role or his relationship to the therapist. As he starts to experiment with the idea that it is not the therapist, he stands a chance of demonstrating to himself that he no longer needs his temporary moorings.

In this sketch many of the complications which variously arise in psychotherapy are left out. Psychotherapy with this type of case is rarely simple. One is likely to find himself dealing with intricate guilt reactions, extensive preverbal constructions, confusion between aggression and hostility, sex-role troubles, unusual distributions of dependencies, literalistic regnancies, submergences, suspensions that come and go as the client makes successive revisions of his system, and, finally, the exigencies of the client's daily life, upon which he must depend for validational experience. Never, literally never, does the therapist work through all of the complications that could possibly be attributed to the case. He ignores all that he can. He is still likely to have his hands full in dealing with the rest.

9. OTHER WAYS OF TREATING TIGHTENED CONSTRUCTION

There are other general approaches which can be used in dealing with a case such as that we have described. If the problem does not appear to be too severe, the therapist can go lightly in establishing the initial relationship. This will simplify the termination procedure. But it means also that he must go ever so lightly in the matter of construct loosening. Instead of dealing primarily with the problem of the tightness in the client's construction, he turns to the problem of making the tight constructs more permeable. He accepts the client as a literalistic person and makes very little effort to change that. Rather, he attempts to extend the range of applicabiliy of the formulas which the client has already acquired. This program of therapy does not greatly increase the hazard of anxiety for the client, since everything is kept screwed down tight and only the basic weakness of the structure is likely to cause a breakdown. The therapy itself puts little additional strain on the system.

Still another therapeutic approach can be built around the idea of controlled constriction for the client. The client is given vocational and social guidance which, if followed, will keep his world cut down to manageable size. He can choose to live amidst an expectancy system which will not be so likely to change and which, like himself, is built upon a tight system of constructs. The occupational duties can be explicit, the protocol for interpersonal relationships can be well defined, the table of organization and the lines of authority can be posted on the wall, and the system of etiquette can be detailed and traditional. The client can order his life by means of a kind of psychological dictionary. A well-established seniority system in the organization where he works may even protect him from the disruptive effect of receiving an untimely promotion on his job.

There are still other approaches to therapy in the type of case we have discussed. Moreover, there are many other variations of psychological disorder which involve a tight construction system. It would be a mistake to assume that we have presented, or even tried to present, a plan of therapy which is applicable to all cases which show an unusual degree of tightness.

10. DISORDERS INVOLVING LOOSENING

Next consider the type of person whose constructs are mostly loose. The inferences he makes vary from occasion to occasion. The looseness may tend also to make the constructs comprehensive, since the variation in the construction encourages the inclusion of a variety of elements. Because his personal constructions are loose it is difficult for the clinician to keep up with him. The clinician who tries to be accepting, who attempts to establish commonality as one of his levels of understanding, keeps missing his predictions regarding the client's behavior. Each time the clinician applies the basic check of psychological understanding — the check of whether or not he can predict what the client will do in novel circumstances — he is blocked. The clinician may develop considerably more anxiety than the client does.

Now this is not to say that the client is operating wholly without relevant structure. A live person *never* operates wholly without some kind of personal structure. To assume that he does is to assume that human nature, unlike nonhuman nature, is unlawful. The psychologists who make that assumption confound their own scientific position.

Nor is it to say that the client is at a point where the situation he faces seems to him to be relatively unstructured. If that were the case we would rather call his experience anxiety. If he were anxious, rather than loosened — the two conditions are sometimes intermingled — he would vacillate from construct to construct, fall back upon preverbal constructions, and generally show the clinical signs of anxiety — weeping, incomplete exploratory movements, repetition of obvious errors, diffuse and uneconomical sallies into the surrounding world, short-sighted and abortive efforts, alternations of independence and dependence in the transference relationship, etc. But let us suppose, for the sake of our illustration, that he is not anxious, even though, from a therapeutic standpoint, we might prefer that he were.

The loosening may be, for this client, actually a protection from anxiety. In a basic and long-range sense, anxiety is what we all seek to resolve. This is an extension of our Organization Corollary — each person characteristically evolves, for his convenience in anticipating events, a construction system embracing ordinal relationships between constructs. Anxiety, representing a personal failure to find structure by means of which events can appear to be optimally construed either now or in the future, is the state of affairs from which we have assumed that a person seeks escape. By loosening his constructions the person makes a kind of rubber-sheet templet to his experiences. His constructions can now be stretched to fit almost any kind of validational evidence. No matter if he does appear to miss his predictions; he can always take the stand, "That is *practically* what I said." Thus he escapes, for the time being at least, the chaos of anxiety.

a. *Looseness in psychoanalysis.* The psychoanalytic theory of personality is commonly viewed by sophisticated students of scientific theorizing as having itself the characteristics of looseness.

Psychoanalytic hypotheses are often called "rubber hypotheses." Since rubber hypotheses can always be stretched to fit any kind of evidence, they run no risk of falling with the evidence; they lack the brittleness required of the hypotheses which are to be tested in an experimentally oriented scientific system. This is probably psychoanalysis' most vulnerable point.

But there are some substantial advantages in loose or "schizoid" thinking other than the temporary avoidance of anxiety. Loose construction permits one to make rough sketches of his world rather than having to draw, in turn, each precise line. It permits one to "tolerate ambiguity." Indeed, it prevents one from appearing to be wholly ambiguous. It represents an approximation or an asymptote to a more precise construction. It therefore lends itself to clinical usage, as psychoanalysis best lends itself to clinical usage, wherein one arrives at understanding through successive approximations. More than that, loose thinking may be propaedeutic to creativity and inventiveness. It is not surprising, therefore, that many artists and inventors have appeared to be schizoid in their thinking. Nor is it surprising that psychoanalysis should have proved to be the most fertile of all of the personality theories thus far devised.

b. *Direction of movement with respect to loosening.* But while loosening of construction may lend itself to the successive approximation that is the soul of creativity and is the basic artistry of the clinical method, it does not always lead in this shining direction. It may go in reverse. The loose construction may get looser and looser and the predictions less and less proximal. The person may not be able to pull his constructions together into a clean-cut prediction. He may arrive at nothing that he or others can put to rigorous test. He may thus save himself from anxiety but in doing so he may take himself out of circulation.

Let us come back to our loose-thinking client. It is important to know in what direction he is moving with respect to the axis of loosening. Will he keep getting looser and looser until he is ultimately chased by anxiety into social oblivion? Or does he recover from moment to moment? What is his range of action on the loose-tight scale? Can he follow a Creativity Cycle? Is he always loose in some areas and tight in others or can he start with loose thinking and come back through successive approximations to tight thinking about the same things? Does his loosening enable him to revise his tight thinking or does he, when he recovers from loosening, always end up with the same brittle construction? If this latter is what always happens, we can look for the shattering of anxiety to take its eventual toll.

11. LOOSENING AND WITHDRAWAL

We have hinted that our loose-thinking client may carry "a diagnosis of schizophrenia." Whether he actually does or not will depend upon the point of view of the local clinician. In mental-hygiene team settings, where psychological tests are used, particularly concept-formation tests, and where the clinical psychologists who use them are alert to problems of conceptualization, the official psychiatric opinion is likely to be that "there is a schizophrenic process involved." In other settings the diagnosis of "schizophrenia" is likely to be pinned on a client for other and various reasons.

Some clinicians are particularly sensitive to "the withdrawal features" of the case. They may base "a diagnosis of schizophrenia" largely on that. We have already pointed out that loose personal construing is hard for another person to follow. Commonality, which is, in part, preliminary to sociality and role relationships (cf. the Commonality and Sociality Corollaries), is difficult to establish. It is therefore not surprising that the loosened thinking of the client will have taken him out of circulation. People feel unhinged themselves — they get anxious — when they talk to him. So they avoid him! His thinking isolates him. The withdrawal is dictated by the failure of communication and the resultant breakdown of role relationships.

As the person more and more finds himself outside the orbits of social interaction, he discovers also that he has less and less access to validational material of an interpersonal nature. He cannot check his understanding of other persons for two reasons; first, because his constructions are not rigorously formulated in testable form and second, because his friends avoid him. From the standpoint of the psychology of personal constructs, we would have to see his withdrawal as one of the likely outcomes of loose thinking. Withdrawal would not, however, represent as clear-cut a basis for understanding the client as would the dimension of tightness-looseness.

One should be careful not to depend too much on reverse logic. Clinical inference depends a great deal upon reverse logic anyway and the clinician should be particularly aware of the logical fallacies into which he is likely to fall. Reverse logic is an occupational hazard of the clinician. Consider the logic in the present problem. If we grant that a loose thinker may find himself outside the orbit of society, does it necessarily follow that the "withdrawn person" is a loose thinker? No. For this reason the biographical record or the social history of a client frequently leads to diagnostic conclusions which are different from those reached on a clinical or casual interview basis; and both, in turn, may be different from those based on formal psychological testing. The client with a history of withdrawal may not appear to be either loosened or withdrawn in the free clinical interview. Or the client who reveals withdrawal, both in his social history and in the clinical interview, may not appear to be loose in his response to formal psychological testing. There are other bases for social isolation as well as loosened construing.

a. *Cultural tolerance of loose construction.* Consider another factor in the relation between loosening and social withdrawal. Commonality of thinking is one of the bases of culture grouping. We have built this idea into the assumptive structure of our theory. The Commonality Corollary expresses the idea that to the extent that one person employs the same construction of experience as another he may duplicate the other person's psychological processes. Now what happens if both persons use similar, though loose, constructions in the same area? These people have similar constructs in the sense that they lead approximately to the same conclusions.

Of course, one loose construction is only *approximately* the same as another for it is only *approximately* the same as itself from time to time. The communication between two persons who both employ the similar loose construction will not be as precise as will the communication between two persons who employ similar tight construction. Yet each loose thinker is tolerant of the other's ambiguity because it is approximate to his own. Neither needs to be made anxious by the other. Neither needs to avoid the other in order to maintain his poise. In such a case, then, loose conceptualization does not lead inevitably to withdrawal.

Whether or not loosening leads to withdrawal depends upon the cultural milieu in which the loose thinker must operate. Not only is this a conclusion one can reach by theoretical deduction from the postulated structure of the psychology of personal constructs, but it is entirely consistent with widely shared clinical observations. Clients whose personal constructs would quickly isolate them from effective membership in the cultural group to which the clinician belongs may, because they happen to live in a community of like-minded people, not show the history of withdrawal their "schizoid symptoms" would normally lead one to expect. The ethnocentric clinician will be puzzled by this. The cosmopolitan clinician will not be surprised.

Take, for example, the loose thinking that, in part, characterizes most religious doctrines. Taken out of its cultural context some of this religious conceptualization is enough to make a clinician's hair stand on end. If he is not aware of the cultural stabilization and insulation provided such thinking in the client's society, he may wonder how the client can possibly continue to be "in contact." The next day, when the clinician finds that one of his most trusted professional colleagues is a devout member of the same sect, he may even begin to wonder about his own sanity. Failure to understand the tricks that culture can play thus lead to many a distorted clinical misjudgment.

Yet while, in the context of a freely interacting culture grouping, loose thinking may be confined to limited areas of experience and may not lead to "withdrawal symptoms," the clinician must remain alert to what may happen when the client must look for validational material in a society which has a different set of expectations. The client's original culture identification may not save him from "schizophrenia" in this latter setting. Nor can a marriage of convenience with the new culture necessarily enable him to adapt himself to its expectations. It is for this reason that many religious sects find it necessary to settle down in tight little communities. Such is a way of preserving their sanity.

b. *Withdrawal because of cultural identification.* But to return to our problem of reverse logic! We have pointed out that cultural containment may keep the loose thinker from showing the expected withdrawal signs. Let us point out also that one's cultural identification may lead to a withdrawal which does not stem from loose conceptualization. If one is inept in construing members of an alien culture he may himself withdraw in order to avoid anxiety. Perhaps his ineptitude stems from certain tight constructions practiced by his own sect. He may, for example, be firmly convinced that people with a certain type of speech accent are ignorant and basely motivated. He may therefore withdraw when he finds himself engulfed in a group of persons whom he cannot predict with regularity according to this formula. His withdrawal may turn into a rout when he recognizes that there is taking shape in his experience with them a new psychological outlook that strikes at the roots of his tightly drawn system of values. That is *threat.* His tightness rather than his looseness is the basis of his withdrawal symptoms.

c. *The client's development.* Now to return again to our client. We have said that he is loosened in his construing. We have said that the looseness may tend to make his constructions more comprehensive. Let us suppose, in this particular case, that it actually has had that effect. The looseness now spreads to many areas of his life. We have said that his looseness makes his thinking and behavior hard for others to follow. We have pointed out that, with the exception of cultural containment, the breakdown in commonality may lead to "withdrawal symptoms" — only the withdrawal may often better be understood as a rejection by his associates who get anxious when he is around. Now that he is cut off from the sources of validational evidence for his role constructs, as well as for many of his other constructs, his constructive elaborations can be subjected only to limited testing.

On and on he goes! More and more, his superordinate structure emerges on the basis of inadequate validational evidence. More and more he becomes an outcast. His behavior looks more bizarre than ever. Finally he is led, mumbling and grimacing, up the clinic steps.

12. TREATMENT OF THE LOOSE AND WITHDRAWN CLIENT

First of all, the clinician has the task of re-establishing contact. This is a two-way proposition. The client must bring himself into contact with the clinician and the clinician must bring himself into contact with the client as well. This is the first chock against the client's solipsistic runaway. It may be too late or the clinician may not have the time or the skill to slip this first chock into place. Yet until the client is ready to accept the clinician or some other person as a validator of his personal constructions, it is not reasonable to expect him to bring his constructions into line with society's demands.

Establishing this contact depends on meeting two conditions: (1) the clinician must be able to construe the client well enough to establish a role for himself in relation to the client, and (2) the clinician must become predictable to the client so that he may reasonably become a figure which is well within the ranges of convenience of the client's role constructs. If the clinician understands what the client is expecting of him he may behave in such a way as to make it possible for the client, in turn, to anticipate the clinician's behavior. Thus he may hope that the range of convenience of the client's constructs, whatever they are, may be extended to include him. With this foot in the door of the client's psychological household he stands some chance of throwing the weight of validational evidence one way or another.

Let us suppose that the clinician makes his first bid toward getting himself included in the context of the client's dependency constructs. The client finds that he can and must take the clinician's behavior into account if he is to sustain himself. The clinician may manipulate the client's circumstances so that this discovery is facilitated. The client's nonsocial anticipations of his own private world can be intentionally jeopardized. Electroshock may do it (though heaven forbid that we should add another theoretical explanation to the list of those which seek to explain "what EST really does"). At the same time the client's dependence (if any) upon people can be consistently verified. If the clinician succeeds in this step he may have an infantile person on his hands but he has nothing as simple as the development of a child to cope with. The client's field is far too much dilated, and the realm of possible social experience far too much distorted, for the clinician to visualize the therapeutic process from this point on out as following the analogue of childhood development.

a. *Facing the client's loose construing.* At this point the clinician comes face to face with the difficulty which originally caused the client's withdrawal — the loosened comprehensive construction system. It may be a dirty gibe to say so, but he is in a position which is strikingly analogous to that of the experimentalist who tries to get a psychoanalyst to test and revise his elastic constructs on the basis of experimental evidence.

How can the clinician get his loosely conceptualizing client to accept negative evidence as negative? Obviously, he cannot accomplish this until he has found a way to get the client to make some firm bets. But there is difficulty at this turn of the road too. What is the client staking when he makes what looks like a firm bet? Can we tell from the symbols he uses, from the verbal rationale expressed in connection with his expectation? We need to know. If he is staking one of his more comprehensive constructs on the outcome of his prediction, the clinician may be responsible for plunging him into widespread anxiety if the bet is paid off in negative evidence. The crucial question is always: what will the client do if he finds that he has been wrong? Will he constrict? Will he decide that the clinician, and all that goes with him, is unpredictable and not worth expecting anything of anyway?

In general, the clinician should not attempt to make the client's comprehensive constructs explicit at this point. The client, now presumably "in contact," can mouth the word symbols and even formulate some fairly testable hypotheses, but he cannot adjust himself to negative evidence yet. If the clinician ventures to give him negative evidence at a comprehensive level at this stage, constructs, words, and bets all go loose in the face of anxiety. This turn of events may be exasperating, yet it is better for the client than sudden constriction to the point of suicide. When the psychologist stoops to pick up the pieces he finds that all of his carefully cast word symbols have crumbled and no longer carry precise and testable meanings. The ensuing interviews may be a nightmare of abstruse psychological jargon that may make the clinician wonder, in his more cynical moments, if he himself has the faintest idea of what he is talking about. Even worse than that, the client may go to another therapist of differing persuasion and start sounding off about what he learned from the first clinician, a turn of events which is bound to have profound and fateful repercussions in the clinician's professional community. The writer speaks from experience, both in the role of the first clinician and in the role of the second.

b. *Watching for dilation.* But let us suppose the clinician successfully manages the delicate situation and proceeds cautiously to rebuild the client's construction system by tightening up a nut here and backing off a screw there. Now he must watch for a too sudden dilation of the field. That might call for a reinstatement of the loose but necessarily comprehensive construction system.

As therapy proceeds, the clinician must choose the points at which the personal-social milieu can be expanded to include relatively unpredictable people. To be sure, the client may have been in contact with other hospitalized patients all of the time, and, to be sure, they would have been relatively unpredictable. Yet he should not have been too closely interdependent upon them if he is to make his tentatively reconstructed prediction system workable. It is when he must rely upon the erratic behaviors of supposedly "well" people that his newly formed prediction system is put under strain. The clinician will have to help him build his interpersonal world person by person, figure by figure.

c. *Vestiges of tight construction.* There is a difference between the looseness of construction which characterizes one whose thinking has always been loose and that which characterizes one whose thinking was once more tightly organized. The latter exhibits fragments of tightly drawn constructs. Some of these have been preserved by blocking off restricted areas of experience. The constriction enables the person to preserve the constructs; but, in doing so, it reduces them to a state of triviality.

This kind of delimited thinking, which is a residual of the days when the person's structure comprised a better combination of tightness and comprehensiveness, is illustrated in a patient's "blocking" in order to get good form perceptions out of the Rorschach ink blots. The looseness and poor form that result when one tries to go beyond the boundaries of safe ground is illustrated by the "position response" which some clinicians consider as a definitive sign or "stopper item" for "schizoid thinking." In "blocking," the subject constricts his field by some definite gesture, saying, for example, "Here, just this [holding his hand over the rest of the blot]! I see a dog's head in just this much of the blot." The gesture makes the constriction obvious and shows it to be a device actively imposed in order to limit the perceptual field. Presumably the "blocking off" enables the subject to deal only with that which can be tightly construed. Without the setting of such artificial limits upon what is to be construed, the subject's construing may loosen up to the point where he says "Well, I suppose all this must be the dog's tail over here."

"Why?" the examiner asks.

"Simply because it is at the opposite end from his head."

"Does it look like a tail?"

"Well, no — er — yes; not because of its shape, I suppose, but *because of where it is* [position response]."

When a clinician deals with a client whose tight constructs were once more comprehensively applied, he may be misled by the verbal symbols. The words may at first appear to stand for constructs having both wide utility and precise meaning. But as the clinician comes to understand the client better, he discovers that when the constructs are used precisely they apply only to a narrow range of experience, and that when they are used comprehensively they lose their precision. Yet the constructs are of such a nature that one would presume that they could have come into play originally only if the client needed something which carried both precision and range.

Take, for example, a client who uses the term "sturdiness." At first it seems that the client has here a construct of reasonable precision and comprehensiveness. He applies it both to people and to objects. It must therefore have comprehensive range. In his conversation he refers to an ottoman as an object which is definitely sturdy and to a card table as something which is definitely not sturdy. That makes sense. He refers to John Jones as one who is definitely sturdy and to Pete Smith always as one who is not sturdy. The clinician's judgment of these two particular individuals confirms the client's construction of them. Yet it may develop that the ottoman is "sturdy" because "a person can stand on it and if he falls he will not fall far." The card table is "not sturdy" because "if the client fell off it he would fall far enough to hurt his sore leg." John Jones is "sturdy" because "he talks loud and one who talks loud enough usually holds up the person who is on his side of the argument." Pete Smith is "not sturdy" because "he usually disagrees with me."

The present triviality and circumstantiality of a construct which must once have had some measure of comprehensiveness and tightness begins to become apparent to the clinician. Yet, within separate and limited ranges, the construct still carries the marks of precision. The ottoman, from which, if one fell, one would not fall far, is relatively broad for its height. So are other objects which are "sturdy." If one stood on higher objects having similar proportions, his fall would be more likely to land him on top of the object instead of on the floor. One is not so likely to hurt a sore leg. The reasoning is peculiar but, within a limited range of objects, represents a fairly precise facsimile of what physicists and most of the rest of us might call "the inherent stability of an object."

The client may also "have the word" on John Jones and Pete Smith. John Jones may be outspoken and have developed the habits of frankness and integrity which may be facilitated by outspokenness. The person who shares John Jones's position may empathize by feeling "sturdy" in the face of a yapping argument. Pete Smith may disagree with the client and with everyone else, including himself. One cannot feel "sturdy" around him, no matter on what side of the argument he may be temporarily aligning himself. Again, the reasoning is peculiar and private, yet suffices to give the client an evaluation of John Jones and Pete Smith which is substantially equivalent to the way another person would appraise the sturdiness of these two individuals.

But what will happen when the client applies his personal construct of "sturdiness" to two other people? Will he continue to construe them in terms of what they do to him, as he has in the case of the ottoman, the card table, John Jones, and Pete Smith? Will he come up with a facsimile of the "correct" answer? He may, but let us not bank on it! As long as he is tethered with a short rope, he may be able to conform to most of society's expectations; but if he is turned loose on the open range, his thinking may go galloping away beyond anyone's reach. The therapist who attempts to dilate his field for him may therefore make a serious mistake.

When a client's loose thinking includes vestigial islands of high-level thinking, and his spontaneously used verbal symbols correspond to those used by society for high-level communicable ideas, we then suspect that there is a progressive loosening of conceptualization in the case. When the looseness is general, when the construction is relatively preemptive, and when the words are either concretistic or used self-consciously as intellectual noises, we suspect that we are not dealing with a progressive disorder. In the former case, some clinicians like to toy with a diagnosis of "schizophrenia" and in the latter case they are inclined to call it "feeblemindedness" and let it go at that.

d. *Applying the notion of "schizophrenia."* If we must have a diagnostic construct of "schizophrenia," let us not assume that it must be of the same order as the construct of manic-depressive psychosis or the construct of conversion hysteria. Schizoid thinking — that is, marked loosening of conceptualization — may occur with many other disorders, or it may occur by itself.

Viewed in this fashion we may consider that "schizoid" thinking takes place, on occasion, in almost anyone; that it is characteristic of transitional stages in one's mental development; that it is even characteristic of the transitional stages in solving an ordinary problem; that it appears in the course of creative production; and that it may appear to some degree in any far-reaching readjustment. The loosening of "associations," the uncritical reporting of thoughts, and the general demands of psychoanalytic therapy call for the client to indulge in "schizoid" thinking, though the wise therapist will try to keep the situation in hand.

"Schizoid" thinking has sufficient pliancy to make so-called creative thinking possible in some instances. Since the development of new ideas requires some loosening of the old, creative thinkers must go through a "schizoid" stage in formulating their ideas. Yet if one's thinking remains "schizoid" all the time, he will never be able to develop a new concept with sufficient clarity to communicate it and devise it to his heirs as a part of the cultural inheritance. If, out of "schizoid" looseness one may formulate a tentative new structure, a structure which may subsequently be tightened up, he may end up with a creative achievement. But we have been calling it "schizoid" and "schizophrenia." Let us be more precise. Let us call it "looseness" and consider it as a dimension rather than as a disorder or a class of people. Then we may tighten our own constructions, and be more comprehensive — and more creative, too!

13. LOOSENING AND GUILT

Several paragraphs back we spoke of withdrawal symptoms as a social consequence of loose thinking. We pointed out that a person is likely to be rejected as a functioning member of a group because of his loose and unfathomable ideas. As he finds that his construction of life has the effect of isolating him from membership in his group, he may find that, from his own point of view, he no longer has a role to play. His former companions have become unfathomable to him, just as he has become unfathomable to them. This is loss of role. In a personal sense, it is what we have defined as guilt.

If a person could ignore his loss of role by constriction, he might also be able, thereby, to avoid his guilt and its implied paralysis of all the elaborative processes that make life worth living. Some persons do this. The loose-thinking person who constricts his field may not be aware of his loss of role and he may therefore stand a chance of saving himself from guilt. He creates his own monastery! Behind its high and encompassing walls he plays a new role. He is no longer guilty. He belongs again!

It is a matter of clinical observation that the so-called withdrawal symptoms do interact with the guilt symptoms which clients show. Withdrawal, or loss of contact through the looseness and unpredictability of one's thinking, sets up a situation which a client can handle in one of two ways. He can constrict his field, thus appearing more uninterested than ever in what others think and do, or he can remain aware of what is going on around him and of the fact that he may have lost his role. In the former case he retires to his corner. In the latter case he must either feel guilty or place some construction upon his interpersonal relationships which makes it appear that he is still a very important figure in the social interactions which are going on around him.

The psychotherapist who keeps confronting his loose-thinking, protectively constricted client with a dilated field without first assuring him of a role can expect guilt reactions. If he keeps pressing for dilation without structure and without role, he may expect the client to erect his own new defenses against the mounting guilt. Those defenses are likely to be in the nature of a "paranoid" role. If that happens, the psychotherapist can next pin a label of "paranoid schizophrenia" on his client, a diagnostic feat which is really of little consequence.

D. Core Constructs

14. DISORDERS INVOLVING CORE CONSTRUCTS

A core construct is one which governs a person's maintenance processes. When a client expresses physical complaints his core constructs are likely to be involved. But more than that, his communication of his complaint may also imply that dependency is also involved. From his point of view his core structure is ailing and he needs help. The clinician should realize, of course, that the construction of the problem, as expressed in the complaint, is not necessarily the construction that he, the clinician, can most profitably work from. The client's personal complaint is simply the best construction the client can bring himself to express to the clinician.

From the viewpoint of the psychology of personal constructs, dependency is something that everyone has. Some persons envision their dependency as involving only certain other persons who directly provide them with food, shelter, and the other palpable things upon which life obviously depends. Other persons, more mature, see their dependency as involving a much wider range of people and objects. They also discriminate between what dependency can be placed here and what dependency can be placed there. Thus their core system has many roots which tap many different sources of sustenance.

The so-called "psychosomatic symptoms" may, in some cases, represent the expression of dependency constructs as well as core constructs. Clinically they appear as if they were something which the client requires just as urgently as he requires sustenance and safety. We infer that he must personally construe them in just that way. Yet, like much of one's dependency construing, the construction is preverbal and therefore not easily communicated.

We should hasten to say that one's "psychosomatic symptoms" are not necessarily themselves the elements which are lumped under the dependency constructs. They may be; they may not be.

The vomiting of a client with peptic ulcer may not itself be a love-seeking gesture. It certainly does not look much like a food-seeking gesture either. It looks much more like a stomach-saving gesture. The chances are that the vomiting is an outgrowth of other gastrointestinal gestures made much earlier and over a protracted period of time. It may have been that they were personally construed as expressions of dependencies. The person who must abandon his stomach's normal program of activities in order to sustain himself is likely to hear from his stomach later on. The symptom is not what he bargained for; it is what he got.

In another client the symptom itself may be a dependency gesture. From the client's point of view, little girls who vomit may get taken care of. The client gags, feels a lump in her throat, and puts on a vomiting act. The urgency of the situation is so great that she has no other means at her disposal for taking care of her dependency.

The so-called "psychosomatic symptoms" can be found both in cases of loose thinking and in cases of tight thinking. In the loose-thinking "schizophrenic" they are likely to appear simply as incessantly vocalized galloping complaints. For him one thing is pretty much like another anyway. The symptoms of the "hysteric" are acted out with histrionic embellishments. It is thus that he uses his preverbal constructions to build a relationship with his doctor or anyone else who enjoys having people dependent upon him. The tight-thinking "compulsive" — for example, the migraine client — has symptoms which seem to catch him unawares. They spill out of his meticulously constructed filing system and cause him no end of surprise, annoyance, and anxiety. Unlike the "hysteric," he can neither enjoy his symptoms nor build a relationship upon them. He lacks the over-all approach to his dependencies which a suitable superordinate system might provide him. His dependencies, being less explicitly formulated, find no place in his system of intellectually neat pigeonholes. He is therefore always surprised to find how they keep cluttering up his household.

Many times "psychosomatic symptoms" can be brought under

control simply by establishing a well-selected type of dependency relationship between client and therapist. The loose-thinking client who complains of a different ache each day may be allowed to have his dependency demands upon the therapist met in other ways. This shifting of dependency behavior may or may not be therapeutically profitable. In order to be successful, therapy must tighten some constructions, establish a reasonable set of role constructs, and let the client acclimate himself gradually to the psychological out-of-doors. Ultimately, most of his dependencies should become verbally explicit for him and should take into account a greater variety of resources. The simple elimination of "psychosomatic symptoms" is not a very profound psychotherapeutic objective, especially in a client who depends upon a wide range of loose constructs anyway.

The elimination of "psychosomatic symptoms" in a construction system which is largely based on tight but poorly subordinated constructs is often difficult. In such a case it is somewhat more appropriate to consider the elimination of the symptom as a real mile post to be reached in the course of therapy. We have already sketched illustrative procedural steps one may take in dealing with disorders involving tight construction.

The elimination of "psychosomatic symptoms" in the person who attempts to use them to build a role relationship with the therapist is likely to be dramatic, just as everything else such a person does is likely to be dramatized. If the therapist attempts to countersuggest a symptom, he may find that the client sees him as he would a rejecting father. If he indulges the symptom, he may find that the client is insatiable.

Always the clinician must be alert to the submerged ends of the role-building constructs of the "psychosomatic" client. Therapy is largely a matter of helping the client deal with these submerged ends. After the client realizes what he is embracing by means of his constructs, the therapist can go deeper and deal with some of the preverbal constructions which are causing the client difficulty in developing his role.

15. DISORDERS INVOLVING PREEMPTION

Sometimes it is said that the appearance of symptoms in certain cases represents the operation of a mechanism called "conversion." The classical symptoms of "hysteria" are frequently called "conversion symptoms" and, together with the presumed processes underlying them, are entitized as a disease known as "conversion hysteria." The conversion process which is presumed to take place is visualized in slightly different ways by different writers. One way is simply to see the case as representing a psychological problem or conflict converted into a physical problem or conflict. This may be further perceived to be a series of one-to-one substitutions of terms in an equation which leaves the form of the equation itself unchanged but which disguises its content from the person and from his associates. By converting the terms the person "unconsciously" protects himself from the humiliation that a public or "conscious" admission of his problem would bring upon him. The term "conversion," rather than "transference," "replacement," or "substitution," is used to indicate that neither the problem nor its solution undergoes any substantial change; only the elements are translated into physiological terms.

Some psychoanalysts — for example, Fenichel — place a more "dynamic" construction upon "conversion." They see it as a transformation of "libido" from one physiological form to another, a transformation which changes its psychological guise. As far as this writer is concerned, it is at this point that such "dynamic" reasoning becomes hopelessly entangled in Cartesian or Leibnitzian dualism.

Freud, while he envisions cathexis as involving points of contact between the reality which he likes to construe physiologically and that which he likes to construe psychologically, is, nonetheless, able to describe conversion without resort to dualism, anthropomorphism, or vitalism. On occasion he does so. In his book *The Problem of Anxiety*, he says that in order to "explain the hysterical seizure, one needs only, indeed, to look for the situation in which the movements in question were a part of the behavior appropriate to that situation." This suggests that the conversion is not necessarily a conversion of what is psychological into something else that is physiological, but rather a process the clinician can see as a translation from one set of psychological terms to another set of psychological terms.

Here is an important point about conversion. The client translates his problem from terms which *for him* are "psychological," into terms which *for him* are "physiological." He thinks that makes a different problem out of it. He is able to think so because he is a dualist. If he were not a dualist the disguise would not work. Conversion is therefore characteristically a disorder of culture groups whose thinking is dualistic.

The person who uses dualistic thinking and the conversion mask usually has little difficulty in finding companions who will accept his disguise. Physicians are an easy mark — up to the point where they decide that the client is "a psychiatric case" and therefore obviously not "a medical case." When the once appreciative physician pulls that flip of construction, the client is immediately faced with a suddenly crumbling personal structure. He is likely to become extremely anxious and resort to desperate measures, perhaps even self-inflicted bodily injury, in order to reestablish his position. He may commit suicide, although, rather than take measures which lead to such an absolute constriction, he is more likely to try to act in such a manner as to elaborate the "organicity" of his case.

But just because the client is dualistic in his thinking is no reason for the clinician to be dualistic all the way up through his subsuming construction of the case. The clinician can appreciate the dualistic thinking of his client, empathize with it, and still construe it all psychologically. The kind of thinking which we choose to call dualistic is indeed a phenomenon of life. It is real enough in its own right. Yet we can construe a person's thinking as dualistic without resorting to dualism ourselves. Let us therefore do so. Let us see if we can avoid "conversion hysteria" ourselves.

What about the term "conversion"? Does it represent a concept appropriate to the systematic position of the psychology of personal constructs? Or can the phenomena which it subsumes better be abstracted in other ways which are more consistent with the theory? Actually, the term is suggestive of the way personal-construct psychology looks at certain disorders. It is a tossup whether we should attempt to use the term or not. The reader can call the toss.

The essential feature of the conversion mechanism is that the client construes certain phenomena of his intimate life to be "physical" and "obviously therefore not psychological." This is, of course, the kind of construction which we have chosen to call *preemptive:* "If this is a spade it cannot therefore be anything but a spade." He elaborates his problem, not in terms which one might interpret as being basically psychological, but in terms which appear to him to be wholly "physical." The perspicacious clinician sees the portrayal of the "physical" elements of the problem as an "acting out" of a "psychological problem." Is this "conversion"? No, not really! But the client acts as if it were. It is like the game of "peek" one plays with an infant. The infant closes his eyes and acts as if he cannot be seen. The client hides his own eyes and thinks his clinician sees only what he sees — nothing! It is as simple as that!

Chapter Seventeen

Disorders of Transition

⊓⊔⊓⊔⊓⊔⊓⊔⊓⊔⊓⊔⊓⊔⊓⊔⊓⊔⊓⊔⊓⊔⊓⊔⊓⊔⊓⊔⊓⊔⊓⊔

THIS IS the second of two chapters in which illustrative cases are plotted against the system of axes stemming from our theory of personality.

A. Aggression and Hostility

1. DISORDERS INVOLVING AGGRESSION

Our manner of defining *aggression* permits us to construe it independently of *hostility*. Aggression refers to the degree to which a person involves himself in spontaneous elaboration. It means that he takes steps which lead somewhere. It places him on new ground, confronting him with new experience he would not otherwise have, dilating his field in certain anticipated directions, bringing him face to face with new problems to be solved, exposing him to new anxieties to be resolved, and generally accelerating the evolvement of his construction system.

Hostility, on the other hand, need not involve aggression. It may, for example, involve constriction by one's trying to put himself or someone else "out of the way." It refers to one's inability to live with the results of his social experimentation. A person who attempts a marital relationship (aggression) which results in a state of affairs he cannot manage may become hostile. He is likely to express his hostility toward the person with whom he entered into the experimental relationship. The same is true of an extramarital sexual relationship which produces results the person cannot live with. Yet the hostility, when it develops, perhaps as the consequence of an earlier aggression, need not involve further aggressive behavior. The hostile person is in a bad spot, may be blocked, may constrict himself, yet do nothing aggressive to invite new experience. Perhaps the only course of action he sees open is so drastic that he cannot allow his aggression to express itself in that direction.

a. *Aggression as a solution for hostility.* Aggression is often the most promising solution for hostility. The trick is to channelize the aggression. This means the development of appropriate two-ended constructs. The drastic alternatives which seem, under the client's system of constructs, to be the only other choices open to him must be replaced by reconstruing the situation in more discriminating terms. Thus new possible courses of action are charted. The client may then embark on aggressive ventures which will eventually place him upon tenable ground and relieve his hostility.

In order for aggression to be a solution for hostility it must deal with the relevant elements, not simply be aggression for aggression's sake. The psychology of personal constructs leads the therapist to attempt to do many of the same things he would do under the aegis of other psychological systems. Here, however, it parts company with systems which use the notions of catharsis or stimulus generalization to provide drainage for hostility. Hostility is not a commodity which must be disposed of somehow, nor is it an aura which surrounds experience. It is rather a relative state of affairs having to do with the construction of a certain area of experience. It has to do with personal construing. It requires solution, not drainage.

b. *Aggression and interpersonal relationships.* Aggression arises when one involves himself in spontaneous elaboration. The person himself is an element which is construed and reconstrued. Core constructions may not be involved but peripheral constructs are. The person keeps placing himself in varying relationships to other people, to other things, to time, and to place. He makes himself a ubiquitous element in his "working through," continuously realigns himself, puts himself in a new "spot," seeks a new

minor vantage point. The elaboration may involve role constructs, but it need not. In fact, the person in his elaboration may
develop his detailed reconstructions of himself without much
regard for the thinking of other people. Other people are, somewhat more likely than not, dealt with, not so much as people with
viewpoints which require understanding and as phenomena
which have their natural place in the scheme of things, but as
objects which can and must be manipulated. Aggression, then,
sometimes leads one to pursue a course of action which is not
based on an understanding of other people, hence may represent
an ignoring of role or a failure to elaborate one's role.

The tendency of aggressiveness to lead one to elaborate his
own position without regard for role relationships is not inevitable. It arises simply because the development of role relationships requires understanding of other persons' construing and
such understanding requires time — time which the impatient
aggressive person is often not willing to spend. The aggressive
person, then, barges ahead and elaborates his position without
waiting to see how his associates respond. He runs the C-P-C
(Circumspection-Preemption-Control) Cycle with relatively little
emphasis on the circumspection phase of the cycle. If he involves
himself or his group in the cycle without misconstruing his role
too badly, he may successfully play the part of a leader. If he
badly misconstrues the thinking of the members of his group, he
may continue to play a role, in the sense in which we have defined
role, but his aggressive behavior may well place him in the position of an outcast, as far as the other members of his group are
concerned. It is indeed a very short jump from the position of
leader to the position of outcast — much shorter than the jump
from spectator to follower. The nature of aggression helps to
explain why.

Yet, as we have indicated, it is possible to be aggressively concerned with the elaboration of one's role. This aggressiveness is
usually the kind one seeks to have the client demonstrate as a
result of therapy. It may be difficult because the client's aggression may previously have found its most fertile field in the realm

of objects and statuesque human figures. The elaboration of role relationships may seem to the client to be a flimsy undertaking. Rather, he may be inclined to relate himself to people by shifting, developing, and reconsidering his own position with respect to theirs. It may take skillful therapy to make it seem worthwhile to him to deal with other persons' understandings rather than with their positions.

Clinicians frequently speak of clients as "having difficulty with authority relationships." What we have been saying about disorders involving aggression is relevant here. The person with "authority problems" aggressively seeks to elaborate his field. He is too impatient to be able to learn to deal with people as *persons*. Instead he deals with them as *figures*. He involves himself. He construes his relationship to other people as a matter of "social position," in terms of "status variables," by means of "class concepts," in the light of "subculture norms," rather than in terms of their unique identities and their personal viewpoints. He plays a *part* in relation to them, but it is not so much what we would call a *role*. It may be that the more aggressively he explores the area of group "dynamics" and interpersonal "relationships" the more he adapts himself to *position* and the less he adapts himself to *persons*. It may soon become apparent to others and to himself that he "has difficulty with authority relationships." But it may not be in relation to the authority dimension only that his aggression leads him into difficulty; it may be in relation to any of his other construct dimensions which are based upon the *positional construing of human figures*.

2. AGGRESSION AND GUILT

Aggression, as well as hostility, may lead to guilt in a variety of ways. If a person feels that his intellectual explorations are not accepted by the group, he may also feel that his role is jeopardized. In the system of the psychology of personal constructs that is the threat of *guilt*. The guilty adventurer may then seek to reestablish a role on the basis of his being misunderstood and persecuted by selfish and hostile people. It is relatively easy for an aggressive person whose adventuresomeness leads him into deviant paths to develop a "paranoid" role as an alternative to the experiencing of guilt.

Aggression may eventuate in guilt because it may lead to misadventures in elaborating one's role constructs. The novel role relations one aggressively seeks to establish may collapse. Aggression in the area of role relations may thus lead quite directly to guilt.

Aggression may invite guilt in some clients, not so much because their ideas seem too novel to be accepted, or because they perform hazardous experiments with their roles, but because they feel that aggression itself miscasts them. For them to be aggressive at all is to feel themselves out of character. Being out of character, they perceive themselves out of their proper role as dutiful and conforming pople. It would seem as though they conceived their role to be one of suspended animation. Their condition is like a psychological paralysis or a "psychic ataxia" which is maintained by the peril of guilt.

3. PSYCHOTHERAPY IN AGGRESSION-GUILT COMPLEXES

Psychotherapy in cases where aggression appears to invite guilt is, as one might expect from the psychology of personal constructs, first directed at maintaining a minimally adequate role for the client. If the client is a genius, the therapist tries to keep the guilt under control by helping the client pursue some courses of activity which are based upon an effective homespun understanding of certain persons. This occupation maintains role. Having such a role, the client may avoid the guilt that might ensue from discovering that in the pursuit of his fantastic ideas he cannot possibly hope for any inspirational basis in the thinking of his friends. It is truly difficult for a genius to play a role while working at being a genius.

Where the danger of guilt stems from aggressive exploration of one's role, the therapy can take another line. The client can be encouraged to try out his ideas in symbolic form or in small experimental quantities. Just as the manipulation of symbols in a mathematical formula may give one an answer that would otherwise have to be obtained at the risk of dire consequences, so clients can be helped to explore novel role relationships by means of abstract words and logical forms. Doing this may save them from the drastic alteration of the field that might result from the use of more concrete symbols and acts. If the role relationships cannot be adequately explored by means of symbolic manipulation only, the experimentation may be confined to certain frank discussions in the therapy room. The level of frankness may be such that it could not be used outside the therapy room without starting a prairie fire.

Where aggression itself seems to the client to be a violation of his role, the therapist may as well settle down to a long hard winter. The winter may be followed by a summer and another winter or two. Treatment will require some delicate articulation of anxiety and support together with continuous vigilance against constriction trends. Even after the client ventures to explore new areas in the interview room, it is likely to be a long time before he risks his role by aggressive exploration outside the interview room. When he does the therapist may well hold his breath. The client's friends are likely to be so shocked that he will interpret their behavior as rejection. He may come back to the interview room saying that he is ashamed of himself.

4. DISORDERS INVOLVING HOSTILITY

In distinguishing hostility from aggression we have indicated that hostility represents inability to cope with the outcomes of one's social experimentation. Hostility carries with it the implication that the mess in which one finds himself is of his own making. The discomfiture one feels is a form of anxiety. But it is a very special form. The disorganization and chaos of anxiety is not so formless that one cannot see in it the outcome of his own prior decisions. Moreover, one's construction of the situation is clear enough to lead him to predict that matters are likely to get worse if left to run their course. Further and more sweeping confusion may seem inevitable. One seeks some way to stop the clock, to undo what has been done, to alter the circumstances which he created, to ward off anxiety of epidemic proportions, to break the chain reaction he has unleashed, and to make further circumstances conform to his thinking, now that it is too late to make his thinking conform to circumstances. He seeks to force nature to yield what he expects, and in response solely to those incentives which he has already chosen to offer her.

We have defined hostility as being in the social realm. Yet there is a counterpart of hostility which can be directed against things as well as persons. It is interesting and sometimes amusing to see the counterpart of hostility directed against things. A hostile young child may crush a toy in attempting to force it to do what he has anticipated for it. A less hostile child may examine the toy more carefully and attempt to fix it or find a different use for it. It is similarly amusing — or distressing — to see some graduate students express hostility in their research. They sometimes try to force the data to conform to their hypotheses without changing the experimental procedure. The work of the applied scientist is often popularly described as if it were a series of hostile acts: "So-and-so *wrested* from the soil a new source of food," "Whosits *forced* the atom to give up its secret." These are grossly misleading descriptions of scientific behavior.

Hostility in the field of human relations is an all too familiar sight. Human nature is not only complicated but is also multi-faceted and subject to progressive, though orderly, change. One's ventures in the field of human relations are likely to yield surprising results. Yet human nature is still nature. It is no less natural than the behavior of cattle, of bees, of plants, of rocks, or of minerals. It is somewhat easier for a person to be hostile toward another person than it is to be hostile toward a piece of rock; our experiments with persons yield such unexpected results. Some of our attempts to win friends and influence people threaten us with chaotic outcomes. We make desperate efforts to make the original investment pay off, rather than try another complicated experimental procedure. A hostile parent will restrict or injure a child who does not produce the kind of action the parent thought he was motivating. Or the parent may take punitive action against a child who does not pursue the career that the parent has been daydreaming about. Yet it is no more rational for one to be hostile in the realm of human nature than it is to be hostile in nature's other realms of minerals and vegetables.

We must continue to be careful to distinguish between hostility and aggression. To the extent that well-placed aggression may stem from hostility the hostility may be propaedeutic to progress. The trouble with hostility is that it always attempts to make the original investment pay off. It is unrealistic. Aggressive elaboration may enable one to find new ways of getting expected results. Aggression may then be more adaptive than hostility.

a. *Hostility may produce results.* Yet hostility may yield, as a secondary result in the field of human relations, the very outcomes which were unrealistically anticipated by the hostile person. It comes about in this way. The hostility is perceived by the hostile person's companions. They decide to manipulate him by providing him with the outcomes he originally sought. They let him think that his original investment is paying off when actually it is his importunity which is paying off. The hostile person learns nothing. He is kept from discovering how wrong he was. He is consigned to ignorance. When, later, he comes against other associates who will not bother to toss him palliative results, his world is more likely than ever to break down into a shambles of anxiety. The tragedy of hostility in the world is not so much that people are hostile, or even that their hostility leads them to destroy those who ignore the incentives they offer, but that there is so much willingness to indulge the hostile person's whims. Such indulgence leads the hostile person down a garden path bordered with flowers of appeasement. At the end of the path there is a wilderness of confused human relations for all.

b. *Aggression sometimes elicits hostility.* Aggression in one person may elicit hostility in another. The aggressive person is restless and overeager. He keeps exploring. If his aggression is manifested in the area of interpersonal relationships, other people find themselves involved in his experimental ventures. His continual "ad-libbing" and shifting of the scenery confuses the other players. The situation is unexpectedly dilated for them. The straightforward cues they give are not picked up. They look foolish. Their anticipations go awry. Rather than revise their anticipations they seek to force the aggressive person to validate them. This constitutes hostility on their part. In an effort to make the development conform to the original script, the hostile person may attempt to impose constriction upon the aggressive person.

It is a psychological fact of considerable significance that people who go around aggressively dilating other people's fields are likely to find themselves the targets of hostility. This is the crux of many social conflicts. From the standpoint of the psychology of personal constructs, it is this basic principle of interactive relationship between aggression and hostility which accounts for the phenomena which, under other psychological systems, are described traitwise as "intolerance of ambiguity" or "the authoritarian personality." As we have already claimed, and hope to have demonstrated partially, the psychology of personal constructs is more concerned with interactive psychological principles than with traits, types, or groupings of persons.

c. *Dilation and hostility.* In terms of principles, we would be led to expect that some people would be made hostile by the incessant dilating activities of others. This is not merely a matter of conflict between "liberals" and "reactionaries." So-called "liberal" people can become just as hostile and reactionary as the owner of a complicated holding company ever does when it is proposed that the grounds for their "tenure" be broadened to take account of more factors. If a person's hostility is to be avoided, dilation should never be forced upon him too far ahead of his enlightenment, else he will feel that he has stumbled into a room with no walls, no dimensions, no shape, and no illumination. The fact that he had been leaning against the door will make him feel even less kindly toward the person who opened it before he was ready.

d. *Does aggression always follow hostility?* The hostility one feels may not lead to aggressive action nor even to aggressive investigation. Hostility is a matter of being unable to accept the results of one's social experimentation. If one redesigns his experiment the hostility breaks up into aggression. If he modifies the conditions only slightly and continues to try to wring confirmation of his hypotheses from the data, most of the hostility remains. If he makes no concessions to reality and refuses to re-examine the situation, his burden of hostility will be very great. The hostile person always hopes to prove that he was right in the first place. The action he takes, if indeed he takes any, is likely to be taken on a small front with very little consideration for the broader aspects of the situation. Sometimes he just sits and feels hostile — determined that somehow he must be right even though he has obviously gotten himself into an intolerable mess.

Sometimes hostility fails to break up into aggression because of the way the situation is construed. The person sees that his choice of a course of action has brought about an intolerable state of affairs. He then starts to reexamine his choice. What is the principal construct dimension? To what alternative course of action does it point? Does not the alternative also point to chaos; or to guilt through loss of role — or through "loss of face"? How can he then take aggressive action when all roads lead alike to a confusion of his own manufacture?

Perhaps this will help to explain why the hostile person does not necessarily beat up his neighbors. He may keep on trying to get them to conform according to his original formula — or he may beat himself in order to force conformity to the only law of self-control he knows. Hostility is not a force which is turned inward or outward. It is a condition. Sometimes the measures one takes to resolve the condition are disturbing to the neighbors. On the other hand, if nothing is done to resolve the condition, the neighbors may say, "What a sweet soul. She always makes a point of seeing good in everyone. She must have just *worked* herself into a nervous breakdown."

e. *Resolving hostility.* The use of plastic materials is both a folkway and a therapeutic way of converting hostility into aggression. Clay modeling is an example. One's social experiments have gone awry. He cannot tolerate the results. He is not yet prepared to reconstrue the persons with whom he lives. Somehow they must be made to validate his expectations. Part of the solution lies in making figurines of people, and in making them so that they do conform to his expectations. The clay is only partly plastic to his wishes, but it is more plastic than his neighbors are. Having partly verified his original anticipations through his anthropomorphized figures and objects, the person becomes a little more able to tolerate chaos. The clay modeling is not itself the solution to the person's hostility but it does set the stage for reconstruction. The therapist may now be able to start the reconstruction process on a limited scale.

Primitive peoples may use a similar device as an expression of their hostility. The crosscurrents of culture may cause their social experiments to end up in frustration. The channels of aggression are cut off. How can they people their world with a race of human beings who conform to their expectations? A partial answer is to make images or dolls which will represent their inscrutable neighbors but which, unlike their neighbors, will yield to manipulation. Thus their social experiments are *validated in effigy*. The hostility is partly replicated. "People" — at least their effigies — do behave in the accustomed ways. A fitful voodoo composure is restored.

5. CLINICAL APPRAISAL OF HOSTILITY

From the point of view of the psychology of personal constructs hostility has four important features.

First, the situation in which the person finds himself is intolerable. It is chaotic. It is fraught with anxiety.

Second, it is perceived by the person as an outcome of his own social experimentation.

Third, the person perseverates by seeking to have his original anticipations confirmed by some means short of a genuine reexamination of his basic premises. *The hostile person seeks appeasement rather than understanding.*

Fourth, hostility may sometimes be alleviated or resolved by aggressive exploration. The exploration may be on a narrow front and amount to no more than an attempt to force the facts to appear to conform to expectations. In that case the persons who are expected to conform may feel the whiplash of hostility and the hostile person may feel some measure of relief. The exploration may be on a broader front and may turn up workable alternative courses of action which will lead, in turn, to more interpretable outcomes. In that case the person's hostility may be entirely resolved.

Perhaps our rather lengthy discussion of hostility will help to make it clear that the clinical detection of hostility is not a simple matter of noting the client's aggressive or injurious behavior toward other people. The clinician first notes whether the client has backed himself into a corner and then whether the client sees his plight as an outcome of his own decisions. The clinician then looks to see whether or not there is any aggression, and, if so, what areas it opens up to exploration.

Consider the case of a person who shows symptoms of headaches, dizzy spells, weeping, and sleepiness. Suppose the symptoms follow upon social circumstances in such a manner that the clinician believes an explanation in terms of psychological constructs will provide a better basis for treatment than an explanation in terms of physiological constructs. Suppose that the client has always sought to conform to his parents' wishes but that recently he has had reason to question the wisdom of that course of action.

The clinician looks first for the anxiety. Does the client feel that his world is confused and chaotic? If so, he meets the first criterion of hostility. Next, the clinician checks to see whether or not the client sees his state of affairs as the result of his own dutiful behavior. He may or may not blame his parents. The essential point is not so much whether he "blames" his parents for his own action but whether he sees that it is his own action that has precipitated the confusion. Let us suppose, in this case, that the client does not dwell upon his parents' responsibility for his impasse, and that he infers that his own actions have led him into it. The client now meets the second criterion for hostility.

The clinician will now look further for evidences of hostility. Does the client still seek or hope to have his original dutifulness pay off? Does he demand or expect to be "rewarded" for his dutiful behavior, even though he can now see that it was not realistically designed to achieve genuine psychological results? In other words, does the client seek to falsify the outcomes of his experimentations so as to vindicate himself? If the client is disposed to demand "an E for effort" type of reward rather than reexamine the basic premises on which his dutiful behavior has been based, the clinician can check him as meeting the third criterion of hostility.

Finally, the clinician examines the client's aggression. Let us suppose in this case that the client does not aggressively explore any of the alternatives his personal system of constructs might reveal to him. He just sits on his original anticipations and hopes they will hatch some day. There is no indication that the hostility is being dissipated. The clinician can now judge that the client exhibits the fourth feature of hostility.

Our definition of hostility does not coincide with the popular notion of what hostility is. This case in particular is not one which would be popularly labeled as hostile. On the other hand, a skilled and psychoanalytically oriented clinician would be likely to have his attention immediately drawn to the hostile features of the case. He would probably arrive at his diagnosis via the psychoanalytic concept of "reaction formation." A behavioristically oriented clinician might not use the notion of hostility at all, or he might withhold a diagnosis of hostility until it could be shown that the client was acting destructively toward someone.

a. *Origin of symptoms.* But what about the symptoms in the client whom we have described — the headaches, the weeping, the dizzy spells, the sleeplessness? These have two bases. First, they represent the client's falling back upon a second line of defense in the face of the confusion that his more socially oriented experimentation has led to. He invokes dependency. He construes his situation in terms of stark survival. His core constructs are applied. His interpretation of the situation in which he finds himself may not be a happy one but it provides some measure of structure and freedom from anxiety.

In the second place, the symptoms represent a last-ditch effort to vindicate his dutifully filial stand. These are the kinds of behaviors which will win him his "E for effort" reward if anything will. They represent an abortive effort to compel his parents and his associates to conform to his expectations — not by understanding them and adjusting his expectations to their personal outlooks, but by threatening them with confusion and anxiety, with loss of parental role and guilt.

b. *Rewards vs. solutions.* This is perhaps as good a place as any to discuss briefly the difference between psychological "rewards" and psychological "solutions." The difference is much like the difference between "reinforcement" as used by many learning theorists and "validation" as used in personal-construct theory. The hostile client whom we have described has regressed to the point where he is looking for rewards for his investments rather than solutions to his problems. The eventual outcome is likely to be just as dismal for him as it is in the case of a scientist who makes a similar substitution of values. A reward is not an answer to a problem. Most healthy people would rather achieve answers than rewards.

Consider an intellectually aggressive child. He tries to build a toy. After he has put in so many hours of work, his father decides to "reward" him by buying him a factory-made toy of the type he was trying to build. If the child is psychologically healthy, the father is likely to find him the next day working away at the original toy. In spite of the father's unhealthy interference, the child is still looking for solutions rather than rewards.

But suppose the child had developed a hostile equivalent. Let us suppose that he had gotten himself into an impasse in his explorations with the homemade toy. Let us suppose he had ceased to explore the situation aggressively. He sits and imagines that his original plans will somehow pay off. He waits for them to hatch. Such a child is much more likely to accept a reward, since he has already stopped looking for a solution. When faced with a parallel social situation on another occasion, the father is likely to find that he is expected to appease the child's hostility rather than help him solve his problems.

Yet, by and large, reward and the appeasement of hostility are not the prime motives which underlie human behavior. Even in the most hostile person they are, at most, only stopgaps. The basic psychological process always moves in the general direction of evolving an optimal system for anticipating events. The acceptance of appeasement, in lieu of forecasting knowledge, is a compromise which temporarily protects the integrity of the system as a whole during the evolving process. That and no more!

By accepting the postulate that a person's processes are psychologically channelized by the ways in which he anticipates events, the psychology of personal constructs bases its position upon a system of *solutions* rather than upon a system of "rewards," "appeasements," or "reinforcements." It grants, however, that these solutions may be highly personalized solutions, that they are subject to the person's peculiar construing. It grants, also, that one's seeking of realistic solutions in one area will not necessarily cause him to risk the whole structure he has created for solving problems in all other areas. The anticipatory system as a whole is frequently preserved at the expense of retaining an obviously faulty part.

6. APPROACH TO THE HOSTILE CLIENT

Therapy in cases of hostility is a complicated and difficult matter. The therapist is dealing with a person who has come to seek appeasement for his distress rather than a solution for it. He is likely to judge the effectiveness of the therapeutic program outlined for him, not in terms of the new answers it promises to provide, but in terms of the concessions it promises to make. He expects the real world to yield to his anticipations rather than to be its natural self. He is not looking for the correct way to forecast the future so much as he is looking for the future to align itself with the forecasts he has already made.

The client looks at the therapist in this light too. He expects the therapist to align himself with what he has determined the therapist shall be. When the therapist fails to conform, the client may reveal his basically hostile attitude in a variety of ways. He may throw an ash tray at him, he may publicly disparage the therapist's competence, or he may simply continue to express disappointments in what the therapy is accomplishing and talk about vague feelings of wistfulness and emptiness.

The therapist needs to keep in mind, also, that when he is dealing with a hostile client he is dealing with one who perceives his difficulties as the outcome of his own social experimentation. We have insisted that this condition be considered a part of the definition of hostility. The client has burned his fingers. He is therefore reluctant to experiment further in the area in which he has been burned. This fact adds to the therapist's difficulties in prompting psychotherapeutic movement.

Now here we come against an interesting characteristic of hostility. The client, because he has been burned and because his social experimentation in a certain area has ended up in an intolerable state of confusion, attributes his confusion *to the elements* with which he was dealing rather than *to the way in which he dealt with them.* To some extent this is true of all psychologically disturbed people — they tend to blame their difficulties on the elements or the "facts" rather than on the constructions they have placed upon these facts. When we realize that the hostile person is doing this too, it throws new light upon what we may expect in therapy. The hostile person insists that it is the elements 'which must be recalcitrant rather than his own thinking. Since many of his elements are people, he sees them as recalcitrant. Of course, he realizes that his own experimentation got him into difficulty, but he feels that the hazard lies in the people with whom he allowed himself to get mixed up. He thinks it is the people who are dangerous, not his construction of them. Thus he sees his difficulty as arising out of his ill-considered experimentation with inherently dangerous elements.

The two clinical features of the hostile person — his seeking of appeasement rather than solution and his reluctance to experiment further in certain areas — are the primary considerations the therapist must take into account in designing the therapeutic program. Basically, the program has to produce aggression. Of that much we can be reasonably sure. What progressive steps should be followed is still problematical. Our thinking thus far would lead us to suggest that the best way is to open a sequence of selected areas to aggressive exploration, one at a time. The writer has had some success with this approach, although it often takes too long to carry out the program. Furthermore, if one miscalculates the extent of the hostility, he may find that he is opening up new areas where there is more hostility than he expected. He may then have to do so much appeasing that the client's interim adjustment is jeopardized.

a. *A first step.* One approach is to start by attempting to encapsulate the area of hostility — and hence the area in which some measure of appeasement is to be practiced. The therapist may attempt to confine the hostility to certain topics which are discussed in the therapy room only. This may not seem possible, if the client has already gotten himself into difficulty as the result of experimentation outside the therapy room. What the therapist does is try to confine *the chaos that the client feels* to certain topical areas and not take any steps which would lead the client to feel that he has gotten his *whole* life into a mess. He may do this, in part, by getting the client to designate certain people and certain situations in relation to his hostility rather than have him perceive at the outset that he is hostile to all people and in all situations.

Having roped off an arena of hostility, the therapist may make certain concessions within its boundaries. He may be particularly careful to conform to the client's expectations by keeping his appointments promptly, by listening always to what the client has definitely planned to tell him, by observing certain items of protocol that the client seems to demand. The purpose of this step is to clear away some of the initial confusion in the area where a major readjustment is eventually to be accomplished.

b. *Second step.* The next step is to start introducing some opportunities for aggressive exploration which will not be too likely to end in anxiety. Ordinarily, this is first done in the therapy room. The therapist may point out that he is responsive to what the client does and that the client can experiment with the therapist's reactions in various ways. If the hostility has not immobilized the client too much he may be able to express himself aggressively to the therapist in talking about certain persons with whom he has failed to establish an expected type of relationship.

This aggressive talk is itself a kind of aggressive experimentation in which the therapist is, in a measure, a figure representative of the persons talked about.

The therapist should not overlook the fact that he is himself involved when he listens to the client's tirades. His response is important. If he appeases or appears to share the client's attitude toward the offender, the client may be reassured, but he may also find his aggressive exploration unprofitable. If the therapist retaliates or represents the offender's point of view, the client may collect some useful validating evidence. If the client is not ready to face such behavior on the part of the therapist, he may subside and discontinue his attempts to experiment with reality, or he may start to engage in even more frantic and ill-conceived aggressive explorations.

During this stage, the therapist needs to be alert for guilt which may result from the client's aggressive explorations. If the client feels that he steps out of his role in expressing himself aggressively, he may experience guilt and find it necessary to take such protective steps as constriction or the adoption of a "paranoid" role. Guilt, by the way, is an ever present hazard in psychotherapy. Whenever the therapist cannot tell what is happening, he should try looking at his client guiltwise.

c. *Generalization of "insight."* If therapy is "deep," there will come a time when the therapist will expect the client to see that his hostility is more widely diffused than he realized when it first began to come to his attention during the early weeks of treatment. If the therapist is impatient to pass this landmark, he may wake up some morning to find that his prize therapy case has ended up in suicide or in a psychotic break. The time when a client realizes that his hostility is widely diffused should always coincide with a time when he has a workable alternative outlook on life.

d. *Effects of therapy on the client's associates.* Since the resolution of hostility is through the development of aggression, the client's family and close associates are likely to have a rough time of it during certain stages of his therapy. To a large extent, this depends upon the way the therapist handles the program. If the therapist urges the client to become active in his elaboration before he is able to place his interpersonal relations on a role basis, he may exhibit some violent or vindictive symptoms. His demands for appeasement are likely to convince members of the family that the therapy is doing more harm than good. The therapist can ease the situation somewhat by employing interpretive techniques in order to help the client put his relations on more of a role basis.

If other members of the family are also under treatment, the situation may involve additional hazards. The writer recalls an instance of a man and a wife, each of whom was under psychotherapeutic treatment. Both cases involved hostility. The wife had a female therapist and the husband had a male therapist. The wife's therapist attempted no encapsulation, opened the case immediately to aggression, failed to provide a clear matrimonial role structure, and allowed the hostility to be seen as diffusing wide areas of the matrimonial relationship. The husband's therapist did not or could not open his case as rapidly to aggressive exploration. By the time the husband was ready to venture some tentative experiments in the area of marital relationships he found that the only responses he could get from his wife were those which demanded appeasement from him. He constricted with suicide.

7. HOSTILITY IN THE THERAPIST

It is easy for the therapist to develop true hostility toward members of the client's family. Consider the definition of hostility. The hostile person is unable to live with the results of his social experimentation. He seeks to validate his original anticipations through a demand for appeasement rather than through adjusting his construction of the situation. He sees the hazard as inherent in the elements rather than in his construction of them. A therapist can very easily fall into exactly this kind of hostility trap.

Now the therapist performs what is essentially a social experiment when he undertakes therapy. His struggles are often ineffectual or unexpectedly prolonged. He sees that his social experimentation with the case is leading him into an impasse. He is unable to extricate himself from the chaos his therapeutic efforts have led him into. Instead of going all the way back to the beginning and reexamining his whole plan of treatment, he starts demanding his own "E for effort." He wants to validate his bad bets by the appeasement route. So he says it is society which will not let his client get well. He decides that society should be forcibly altered. Or it is the client's mother — or the client's lingering image of her — that will not yield to the "insights" the therapist is so sure are correct. Hence "mothers are bad things and something ought to be done about them." As in all cases of hostility, the frustrated therapist starts to see the hazard as inherent in the elements which he has been unable to construe successfully rather than in his construction of them.

It is at this point that the training of a therapist as a scientist rather than merely as a practitioner should prevent a destructive breakdown of therapy. The scientist always accepts his data as natural responses to the questions his experimental design has actually posed. He does not become annoyed with his data! If he fails to get the answers he expects he reexamines both his expectations and the experimental procedures upon which his expectations were based. He is careful not to get himself into the position of demanding that nature appease and vindicate him. In short, the scientist is certain to get into difficulty the moment he becomes hostile. To be sure, scientific literature is replete with the records of scientists who did become hostile, but that hostility tends to occur after the climax of their careers when the onward march of science has begun its inevitable reconsideration of what yesterday this particular scientist demonstrated was "true."

The scientifically oriented therapist does not rail at human nature, either in its social-organization aspects, its parenthood aspects, or its biological aspects. He does, however, seek to bring about improvements. He could scarcely be in the therapy business if he did not. But he seeks to bring about changes which are based on understanding rather than on blame. He accepts human nature as nature. He does not allow his fumbling therapeutic efforts and theoretical investments to cause him to end up in a morass of hostility. He remembers that he is a scientist, not merely a practitioner, priest, boss, or businessman. He maintains a profound respect for the truth of human nature, as well as for other truths not so persistently underfoot.

B. Anxiety, Constriction, and Guilt

8. DISORDERS INVOLVING ANXIETY

We have defined anxiety as the awareness of the failure of structure in a situation. Not only has the anxious person realized that his particular predictions have fallen short of validation, but he knows that his construction system is failing him. The situation seems to call for a new system — one which he does not have available.

Sometimes the anxiety has to do with situations which are expected to arise in the future. A person may see clearly enough where his construction of the present situation is leading him, but at the end of the road he apprehends a situation in which there will be nothing but confusion. He is anxious. His structures seems to be failing from the long-run point of view. If he perceives that his core structure will also succumb to the approaching confusion, his anxiety will be more widespread and his defensive efforts will be more frantic.

If one wished to state negatively the new position of the psychology of personal constructs regarding motivation, he might say that human behavior is directed away from ultimate anxiety. One would have to go further and say it is directed away from the *perception* of ultimate anxiety. Indeed, one would have to write in a number of qualifications. But there is no need here to try to develop our theoretical position from a negative point of view. Even if we did, we could not hope to arrive at the same inferences which follow from a positively stated postulate.

Yet it is helpful to look, from time to time, at the negative end of our basic psychological construct of life. We see a person behaving in a peculiar manner. Why does he do such preposterous things? According to our Fundamental Postulate and its corollaries he must be evolving his psychological processes toward what he construes to be an optimal anticipation of events. Yet, at the moment, we cannot see how he can possibly be elaborating his field or evolving a more comprehensive construction system.

Let us vary our approach and look at the opposite end of our Fundamental Postulate. To what is his behavior an alternative? What would he feel that he had to do if he were not to do what he is doing? Between what two basic courses of action is he, from his own point of view, choosing? With what anxiety is his alternative course of action fraught? These questions may lead us to an explanation of his behavior.

a. *The necessity of choosing between two "somethings."* The anxious person is frequently told by his friends to "stop worrying." If it were possible to order our lives according to the concepts of classical logic, we might happily choose between "worrying" and "not worrying." But life goes on. Psychologically we cannot choose between a "something" and a "nothing"; we have to choose between two "somethings." To tell a person simply to "stop worrying" is not to offer him a real alternative to his present course of action. Instead, one has to tell him to "start" something which will alleviate his confusion. One may say to him, "The way to stop worrying is to constrict: confine your attention to what is going on here and now." Or one may say, in effect, "The way to stop worrying is to leave it all to me: be dependent." Or one may say, "Dilate your field: look at the big picture — the stars, your life as a whole; see how much sense it makes; rely upon the stable superordinate and comprehensive constructions you have of those things; all of these little worries will then seem insignificant." The only trouble with this last type of admonition is that here may be precisely where the person's construction breaks down; he may not have a usable superordinate system for handling a dilated field.

b. *How common is anxiety?* There is a sense in which all disorders of construction are disorders involving anxiety. A "neurotic" person casts about frantically for new ways of construing the events of his world. Sometimes he works on "little" events, sometimes on "big" events, but he is always fighting off anxiety. A "psychotic" person appears to have found some temporary solution for his anxiety. But it is a precarious solution, at best, and must be sustained in the face of evidence which, for most of us, would be invalidating. A "normal" person also lives with anxiety. He keeps opening himself up to moderate amounts of confusion in connection with his continuous revision of his construction system. He avoids collapse into a total chaos of anxiety by relying upon superordinate and permeable aspects of his system.

Does a person ever completely succumb to anxiety? The answer is no, not as long as he is alive. Always his psychological processes follow in the patterns of some personal construction. His patterns may be obscure to the observer. His constructions may waver. He may dilate or constrict to the point of destruction. But always there is some patterning of his behavior, some personal construction involved. Even his anxiety is structured, in some measure, as he becomes aware of his inability to cope with a stream of events that seems to have turned into a cataract.

9. APPRAISING ANXIETY

The clinician has to appraise anxiety by observing the measures which appear to have been undertaken in order to control it. Anxiety cannot be observed directly. Even weeping is best viewed as a device for avoiding anxiety rather than as an element of anxiety. In the language of some psychologists, we may call it an "operational referent" of anxiety, but we have to be careful not to assume that weeping is therefore implicit in all anxiety. Weeping is often the expression of a childlike dependency construction. In the face of anxiety the person falls back upon a secondary line of defense: he cries like a child. If he is hostile his crying is a bid for appeasement. If he is simply without a variety of resources among which he can distribute his dependency, he may be laying his whole dependency upon the one person before whom he cries or who he expects will learn about the crying later.

If a clinician wants to establish a dependency relationship between his client and himself, he will ordinarily let his client weep in one of the early interviews. In accepting the weeping the clinician is in effect saying to the client, "I will take care of you as if you were a child." If the client accepts and sticks with construction of his patient-role, he is likely to be considerably relieved of his anxiety. But where he and the clinician go from there is quite another matter.

a. *Weeping in the anxious hostile client.* The clinician who encourages the weeping of a hostile client gets himself even more deeply involved. Not only must he take care of his client's maintenance needs by fitting himself into the client's core construction system; he must validate all of the client's bad bets — he must conform, he must appease, even in peripheral matters. This is not to say that a hostile client should never be allowed to weep; it means only that there are important consequences which the therapeutically oriented clinician cannot afford to ignore.

b. *Does crying help?* Is weeping ever an adequate solution? Does it really help "to cry it out"? Sometimes it helps; sometimes it makes matters worse. A person whose role relationships are collapsing in anxiety may sometimes, through crying, reestablish a role for himself on a more dependent basis. In effect, he goes back to a childhood construction and reapproaches his problem. He starts all over again by making the assumption that he does have friends who are like parents. This may not be a bad assumption. It may lead him into more fruitful avenues of exploration than he had previously been able to find. He finds a person who will accept his weeping. There is one person at least with whom he can get along. He looks for others who are somewhat like him. Soon he may find himself among people whom he can call friends.

But suppose the person must test out each candidate for friendship by weeping on his shoulder. His test for friendliness is altogether too rigorous. It suggests hostility. He will soon find that there are many people who are disinclined to wheel him through life in a perambulator. The person who first encouraged his habit of gregarious weeping, and who then abandoned him, may not have done him a favor.

If the anxiety is situational, and not chronic, the acceptance of weeping in a one-shot interview may be beneficial. It may reinstate the client's customary composure and help him avoid making intemperate decisions which may prejudice the outcome of his dealings with the problem. If the anxiety involves confusion in role relationships, the weeping may be the occasion for the client to experience the beginning of a satisfactory role relationship with people who are somewhat like the therapist. This is not likely to happen in one interview only, but sometimes it does. If the client is hostile, the acceptance of weeping is likely to do more harm than good, unless the therapist is willing to follow through with an extended interview program which is both patient and realistic.

c. *Anxiety and impulsivity.* Sometimes anxiety can be inferred from the way a person explores his field. In his eagerness to replace confusion with structure the person often seeks quick solutions. His anticipation cycles are shortened. He performs short-range experiments, collecting his validational evidence at the very earliest moment. This gives his behavior an appearance of randomness. Actually it is not random, for if we are to take a scientific stand with respect to these matters we have to operate on the assumption that, somehow or other, behavior is always structured, never random.

The attempt to resolve anxiety by means of short-sighted experimentation can be clearly observed in certain performance-test behavior. Suppose we have an anxious child working on a form board. Suppose he is attempting to relieve himself of anxiety as quickly as possible by using short anticipation cycles. He grabs a handful of blocks, dumps them on top of the board, rubs and presses them down in the hope that they will fit. Or, if he is only a little more circumspect, he will rapidly select, try, and discard separate blocks before he has had time to consider each block in all of its relevant aspects. He keeps repeating his futile efforts, coming back to the same block time after time and trying to fit it into a certain recess. He does not accumulate his validational evidence systematically. His inability to tolerate anxiety even temporarily makes it difficult for him to design an effective set of experiments leading to the solution of his problem. In the language of our Modulation Corollary, he is sharply limited by the lack of sufficient permeability of the relevant superordinate aspects of his system.

People show their anxiety by using short anticipation cycles in other areas of life. The person who gambles in order to make money, the person who becomes intoxicated in order to readjust his social role, the person who flits from job to job in order to achieve a successful career, all may be revealing an underlying anxiety which they cannot tolerate long enough to work out a better-designed sequence of experiments.

d. *Anxiety, dilation, and constriction.* Sometimes the clinician may infer anxiety from the client's dilation. If the client, when confronted with invalidating evidence, suddenly dilates, it may be his way of looking for additional elements which, if added to the profusion of elements before him, may somehow provide a key to the situation and enable him to regain structure. To the observer this may seem like distractibility. Yet, from the client's point of view, it is actually a frantic search for structure by finding new elements — that is, by dilation.

Sometimes the clinician can infer anxiety from the constriction the client shows. If the constriction is limited to certain areas and to certain occasions the clinician can be reasonably sure that he is dealing with an anxiety phenomenon. The phenomenon of "scatter" on the Wechsler-Bellevue scale or of "spread" on the Stanford revision of the Binet scale can often be interpreted as the result of this type of localized constriction. The examinee, having certain areas of anxiety, may have used constriction in those areas to contain the anxiety. When he is tested in those areas, he shows a lack of versatility and an inability to take into account more than a few features of the situation at one time. In other areas, where anxiety is less of a problem to him, he may show a competence which is less cramped.

Poor performance on a digit-span type of test is taken by many clinicians as a sign of anxiety. It can be explained either in terms of an invasion of competing ideas preventing the examinee from remembering the digits read to him, or in terms of a self-crippling constriction adopted by the examinee to prevent unwanted elements from entering his perceptual field. To the extent that it is the latter, it may be an indication that the examinee is using constriction to protect himself from the ravages of anxiety. To the extent that it is the former, we may interpret it to mean that the client is still performing a diffused series of impulsive experiments in an attempt to solve his problems in the anxious area. His efforts to solve his problem are distracting him. But whether we interpret lowered performance on the digit-span test as distraction or as constriction, the chances are very good that it reveals a kind of local anxiety.

10. ANXIETY AND THERAPEUTIC MOVEMENT

Perhaps our discussion has sufficed to indicate that movement with respect to almost any of the diagnostic dimensions we have proposed may be attempted by a person who is seeking to escape from anxiety. As we have indicated before, we could interpret all human behavior as running away from anxiety. But to take that stand would be to seek to develop a system of reverse psychological explanations. We would end up with a psychology of escape, and the most obvious solution to all of our problems would be nirvana. From where this writer sits, humanity does not appear to be heading in that direction. Anxiety is universal among mankind, however, and people generally escape it, not by scampering away in any direction they happen to be facing, but by probing for better ways to anticipate the future.

Just as people naturally try to deal with anxiety by attempting movement along almost any one of the avenues mapped by our system of diagnostic constructs, so the therapist may deal with anxiety in a great variety of ways. He may encourage weeping and its implicit invocation of the client's dependency constructs. He may encourage short-range experimentation in order to help the client find a little structure here and a little structure there. He may encourage dilation. By taking more elements into account, the client may find that he can invoke a more comprehensive structure to tide him over his period of greatest anxiety. The therapist may encourage constriction. Hospitalization would be an example of a constricting approach to anxiety.

The therapist may encourage loosening of construction in order to make the client less sensitive to invalidating evidence. The client with loosened construction does not need to abandon a construct every time he finds that it does not quite work out; he still considers it a good enough fit to retain in his armamentarium. The therapist may encourage tightening of certain constructs, so that the client may regularize his predictions. He may encourage circumspection in order to help the client see that a situation may be viewed from a variety of constructive angles. He may encourage preemption in order to help a client find grounds for taking needed action. In fact, therapy is rarely a matter of unidirectional action; it usually involves a composite or chessboard approach to its objectives.

11. DISORDERS INVOLVING CONSTRICTION

Constriction is a form of isolationism applied on an individual, rather than on a national, scale. It may represent the psychological basis of isolationistic thinking on a national scale too, but for the moment let us not try to define it in sociological terms. Constricting movement, like other forms of movement, may, if one wishes, be viewed as an avoidance of anxiety. That is the negative way to understand it. If one wishes to view constriction positively, he can see it as a way of making one's world manageable by shrinking it to a size he can hold in his own two hands.

A person finds that he knows more than he can understand. That is an anxiety-provoking state of affairs. It constitutes a "problem." He tries to solve his problems by keeping himself ignorant of any further knowledge until his understanding can catch up. He may even try to ignore some of the things he already knows, a neat trick if he can get by with it, but rarely a successful way of avoiding anxiety indefinitely. This is constriction.

a. *Diary of a "stuffed shirt."* It is perhaps easiest to observe some of the disorders involving constriction by looking at certain persons' careers. A high-school boy finds that his teachers and textbooks keep throwing facts in his face which he cannot comprehensively organize or understand. His efforts at spontaneous elaboration fail to yield new structure. His elaboration becomes less and less spontaneous. He looks forward to the time when he can leave school and deal only with those matters to which he is able to attribute meaning.

When he does leave school he is likely to lead a much constricted life for a period of time. He may concern himself with only the most obvious local events. He may take the best-paying job he can find without regard to its career limitations. It may be a temporary job or one which he can manage only while he is young and strong. If he is an athlete, he may take a job which employs him on a campus where he can be a football hero. Yet the constricting movement may already be taking place. As times goes on, more and more things may be excluded from his perceptual field. His list of things which he has decided "do not count," and which he therefore chooses to ignore, grows longer and longer. Only certain people are "important." Only certain ideas are "worth having." Only certain enthusiasms are "normal." Only certain forms of entertainment are "natural." Only certain viewpoints should be expressed in public. All else is "silly" and ought to be abolished. Not only has the person constricted his own field but, sooner or later, he is likely to start trying to constrict the field of his associates, his neighbors, and eventually his fellow citizens.

When movement, both in the direction of constriction and of hostility, occurs, the person may present a particularly difficult problem of social adjustment both for himself and for his associates. Hostility implies that the person has carried out some social experimentation which has gotten him confused. He still wants his original bets validated. He demands appeasements. He uses constriction to reduce the range of confusing elements with which he is confronted. Yet he finds that he has projected himself into a group of associates who have relatively dilated outlooks. Instead of the appeasement which he demands, they keep thrusting new facts, new issues, and new ideas upon him to shatter his constriction and add to his confusion. Now, in order to get his appeasement, he may seek to constrict the fields of those from whom he demands it.

b. *Parental constriction.* A parent may combine hostility with constriction in dealing with his children. His social experimentation with marriage and parenthood may have created a state of affairs which is confusing for him. His original expectations prove to be ill-founded. Instead of reconsidering his expectations, he becomes hostile and demands that his wife and children somehow validate his misconceived original expectations. He wants appeasement. But he also partially manages his own anxiety by means of constriction. He stops taking the family out in the evenings. He refuses to discuss any but the narrowest range of topics with them. He tolerates fewer and fewer changes in the household routine. When his children threaten to dilate his field by bringing new elements into his situation — their friends, for example — he attempts to make them constrict also.

c. *Constriction and hostility.* A person may combine hostility with constriction in his community and socio-political life. His early adventures into the realm of socialized thinking and community responsibility may have gotten him into deep water. Perhaps he expected to become a political leader and a wealthy man, and expected to achieve that goal by following a certain biographical pattern. But let us suppose that his original anticipations failed to materialize. He may discover that he is generally regarded as an untrustworthy character and as improvident in financial matters. He is fully aware that he got himself into his present mess. The situation is intolerable, yet he is unwilling to reconsider the biographical scheme he originally set out to follow. Somehow he must wrest from the situation the public trust and the wealth which he originally demanded. All this adds up to hostility.

But suppose he constricts also. He starts disregarding elements of his situation. He narrows his political perspective and concentrates on certain elements only. He campaigns on the basis of one or two issues and one or two kinds of facts only. He makes short-sighted financial deals. He starts thinking solely in terms of cash values. All other issues and facts are ruled "out of bounds." This constriction, together with his hostility, may make him a community or even a national problem. In order to compel his constituency to make good his original ambition he may try to constrict its field also. He may try to ban certain competing products from the markets. He may try to gag those who disagree with him. He may become able to see or to express only the most limited, and therefore often misleading, portions of the truth. He may refuse to allow anything to be seen in perspective. Thus he uses his constriction, not only to keep his own world shrunken to the dimensions of his mind, but he attempts, by forcing his fellow men into the same cramped quarters, to wrench from them an appeasement of an ill-conceived ambition.

d. *Constriction and preemption.* Constriction is often accompanied by preemptive thinking. In fact, if we disregard the different levels of construction involved, we may say that constriction and preemption are the same. The constricting person says, "I will consider these elements and none other." The preempting person says, "There is only one way to look at these things and there is none other." The constricting person limits the number of elements in his field; the preemptive person limits the number of constructs which he will apply to each of the elements in his field. If we consider that elements are, in turn, the constructs of still other elements which are subordinated to them, we may say that constriction amounts to preemption in one's thinking about the subordinated elements. If we can consider that the one construct which is singled out for preemptive use is itself a narrow selection from a number of potential constructs, we can say that preemption amounts to constriction in one's use of superordinate constructs. It is therefore not surprising that the person who shows constriction and refuses to attend to more than a few selected elements may also be preemptive and allow himself to apply no more than a few selected constructs to those elements.

12. CONSTRICTION IN "INVOLUTIONAL MELANCHOLIA"

Consider the case of a client whose use of constriction to control anxiety has been moderate but progressive over a period of years. Perhaps it is a woman in her late forties. Throughout her life she has tended to meet confusing circumstances by placing further limits on her range of activities. Gradually she has restricted her interests to the home and the care of her family. Her reading of the daily newspaper, for example, has gradually shifted from the front page of Section A to one of the inside pages of Section B where the neighborhood news is published. More and more, she has confined her reading to wedding announcements and obituaries. She goes downtown less frequently. Intimate friends who moved away have not been replaced. More and more, she has left all major decisions to her husband.

Now she finds herself with more constriction than she bargained for. Her children have left the home and become self-sufficient. Menopause is upon her. Her bodily processes are irregular and somewhat unpredictable. She has few areas left to her where she can engage in spontaneous elaboration of her constructive system. She finds herself faced with confusion — anxiety — even in those constricted areas to which she had withdrawn for security. What shall she do? Shall she constrict further? Where? There is nothing much left to constrict except in the areas covered by her core structures. She seems to be faced with the alternatives of anxiety or constricting illness — perhaps suicide.

a. *Electroshock.* Electroshock therapy is frequently used in such cases. The results are often beneficial, at least temporarily so. There are, of course, many hypotheses regarding the psychological and physiological implications of electroshock therapy. To a large extent, as one might expect, these hypotheses are derived from the varying and mixed theoretical points of view held by different clinicians.

The hypothesis that follows most directly from the viewpoint of the psychology of personal constructs is that electroshock has, by and large, a constricting effect on the client. There is partial amnesia. There is a sudden constriction of the whole perceptual field, followed by a rapid redilation of the immediate field but a slower dilation of the more remote field. The client recovers consciousness, not to face the wide world which confronted him an hour or so before, but a shrunken world comprised largely of the here and now. In this respect the regaining of consciousness following electroshock is different from an awakening following sleep. The morning following the constriction of a night's sleep may provide a few minutes of awakened relief, but the dilation is rapid and soon the awakened sleeper is faced with all the confusion and anxiety that were his lot on the night before. As we see it, the therapeutic effect of EST is primarily in the way the person redilates after the constriction caused by the shock. From this point of view it is quite important to control the redilation psychotherapeutically.

Suppose our client is brought to the sanitarium by her husband. She weeps. She shows diffuse and active signs of anxiety. She complains that she has nothing to live for, that her life is a hopeless failure. She shows the evidences of her customary constrictive remedy for problems of anxiety, although now, of course, the anxiety is out of hand again. Its extent seems to call for a final step toward total constriction, a step which, fortunately, she is hesitating to take.

The psychiatrist first administers sedation. This has an immediate effect, even if sleep does not result. The rest period may have some tendency to restore the regularity and predictability of bodily processes. It therefore alleviates anxiety in the area served by her core structures. But, in this particular case, let us suppose that wakefulness following sedation brings on the flood of anxiety again.

Suppose our client is now "diagnosed" as a case of "involutional melancholia." This, of course, is a diagnosis at the classification or *preemptive* level and does not represent the kind of *transitive* diagnosis at a *propositional* level which we have proposed in the preceding chapter. The psychiatrist decides to employ electroshock therapy.

Now the constriction is sudden and affects bodily processes which were not constricted by the sedative. There is an ensuing dilation which is considerably slower than the constriction. The dilation opens up the bodily processes to core construction sooner than it opens up other areas of the client's psychological field. Comprehensive structures which once had wide ranges of convenience now have only relatively narrow ranges of convenience.

Peripheral elements drop out of the picture. The client may be able to solve certain problems which fall squarely within the range of convenience of one of her constructs, but she has difficulty attending to problems which have to be solved by remote analogy. Her superordinate constructs tend to be less permeable. In a sense, her thinking becomes more practical, materialistic, concretistic, less widely applicable to new experience, and more constricted. For example, a quarrel which she had with her younger sister when she was fifteen years of age is now remembered simply as an event which happened and not as an important bit of evidence bearing on the issue of whether her whole life is worthless or not. The meals served her are simply meals to be eaten and not a sign that she is a burden on society. She may be uncertain what day of the week it is and only mildly amused that the matter has slipped her mind. She does not take as an indication of hopelessness her minor memory lapses in forgetting whether she has two or three grandchildren. The part of her field which she considers it essential to construe remains relatively constricted and well organized, mainly under her core construct system.

b. *Continued shock treatment.* Suppose the shock series is continued. More and more, peripheral elements are screened out of her perceptual field. More and more, she relies upon core constructs and dependency constructs. The psychiatrist may choose some point in the constricting series to try to establish "contact" for psychotherapy. Such evidence as we have from research conducted by Albrecht seems to indicate that the attempt should ordinarily not be delayed past the tenth shock. The longer the psychotherapy is delayed, the less available become the constructs which need revision and the less available become the elements which should play a part in the reconstruction of the client's superordinate life role.

But the constricting effect of electroshock therapy does not produce a permanent state of affairs. The time may come when new events pile up with such insistence that again the client is unable to manage her anxiety and may see only total constriction as a solution. Her previous series of treatments may have done little to help her establish a structure which could be expected to impose order upon the vicissitudes of the ensuing years. Structure fails. Again things start happening to her which she cannot adequately anticipate. The next psychiatrist in line now makes his diagnosis. All too frequently he, too, will decide that what she needs is — electroshock therapy!

13. CONSTRICTION IS SOMETIMES VALUABLE

As with other diagnostic constructs proposed for use in connection with the psychology of personal constructs, constriction is not necessarily a "bad" thing. There are times when all of us need to constrict our field in order to maintain composure. The psychology of personal constructs itself represents an attempt to deal with an intentionally constricted field — the field of human psychology. It is not proposed as a complete philosophical system but rather as a "miniature" system — and one to be used only temporarily at that! We have constricted our field, as far as psychology is concerned, to a size which we think we may be able to handle. We hope to devise constructs which may embrace this limited field within their ranges of convenience. Elements which fall outside this field we choose to treat with constructs which are outside our particular psychological system.

The point we wish to make is that constriction may sometimes be used to solve problems but that, in doing so, it may let issues accumulate which will eventually threaten a person with insurmountable anxiety. Constriction is one of the axes with respect to which we plot the position and movement of a person's psychological system. There are, indeed, some disorders in which displacement with respect to constriction is most conspicuous. We have attempted to illustrate our use of this dimension by citing illustrative material involving disorders of this type.

14. DISORDERS INVOLVING GUILT

In the section of a preceding chapter which dealt with the diagnostic construct of *guilt,* a passing reference was made to guilt in certain primitive culture groups. Keeping in mind our definition of guilt as the awareness of dislodgment from one's core role structure, we mentioned the fact that sometimes the tribesman who breaks taboo, and thus dislodges himself from his core role, may not be able to sustain life. There are records of outcasts who soon die, apparently as a result of the loss of their core role.

If the whole truth were known, it is likely that we would learn that the sustenance of life in the face of extreme guilt is difficult in any culture group, including our own. It is difficult, not only because it interferes with the adequate distribution of our dependencies, but also because it interferes with the spontaneous elaboration of all our psychological processes, including the so-called "bodily" processes. Our constructions of our roles are not altogether superficial affairs — masks to be put on and taken off for the sake of social appearances only. Our constructions of our relationships to the thinking and expectancies of certain other people reach down deeply into our vital processes. Through our constructions of our roles we sustain even the most autonomic life functions. There are indeed *core role structures*.

Since guilt, as we have defined it, represents dislodgment from one's core role structure, we could scarcely expect guilt not to be related to "physical" health. Strictly within the psychological realm one might transpose the Biblical saying, "The wages of sin is death," into "The wages of guilt is death." It is genuinely difficult to sustain life in the face of guilt. Some people do not even try.

a. *Danger in assigning the agency for creating guilt.* Because guilt is such a powerful destructive agent there is great danger in letting the means for making people feel guilty rest in the hands of hostile persons. The hostile person, as we have said before, wants his original viewpoint validated even if the whole world has to be changed around to fit his prejudices. He is basically a reactionary person who wants man's ideas to stand pat and nature to be made to conform to them. Suppose he becomes the spokesman for a societal group. Members of the group construe the thinking of the group through construing his thinking. Thus they develop their roles.

But let us remember that he is also a hostile person who feels that somehow his social experimentation usually ends up in a mess, believes that it must be the world's fault, not his. Instead of reconsidering his stand, he demands appeasement of his original views. He condemns "deviationists from his party line," whether it be the party line of "Communism" or of "American-ism." If he has the means to excommunicate members of his group, he may effectively use their vulnerability to guilt in order to obtain appeasement for himself.

No one is capable of taking a wholly independent stand against such tyrants if his core role is really jeopardized. He is almost sure to "confess," whether he is an involuntary drug addict at a Soviet trial, a penitent whose life and livelihood is completely enmeshed in the hostile demands of his priests, a "regular" U. S. Marine whose behavior has been interpreted as disloyal to his unit, or a child who has been told that he must choose between the ways of an affectionate but hostile parent and an unknown world of freedom. To give a person control over the means of making others feel guilty is, in some respects, equivalent to giving him control over life and death. In fact, ordinary death is less threatening to people than is the total loss of their core role.

b. *Hostility and guilt.* If a person feels guilty for what he has done, and yet considers no alternatives, we can expect him to become hostile. He demands reinstatement of his core role. Instead of perceiving the unreasonableness of his own demands he feels that others are making unreasonable demands upon him. He sees other people as behaving or thinking in a hostile man-ner. The persons whom he sees making unreasonable demands upon him are likely to be those with respect to whom his role is structured. Because the trouble started with guilt, we assume that it is his original core role that he wants validated and that he will accept nothing short of appeasement from those whose construction systems were subsumed in it.

Suppose a child is reared in such a manner that he considers he has more in common with his mother than with his father. Suppose his role is structured on the ground that his mother is one to be identified with and his father is one to be sought. Suppose he uses these figure interpretations as the bases of transferences to other social situations. Soon he is identifying himself with women and seeking the indulgence of men. Let us suppose that this pattern is substantially interwoven among other core role constructs; he sustains himself by maintaining this basic outlook.

As the child grows into adolescence, he finds that he has missed the point in his interpretation of his sex role. He finds himself dislodged from his adult core role as a result. With this realization comes guilt. But let us suppose that more than this has happened. Let us suppose that the intolerable situation in which he now finds himself seems to be the outcome of his own social experimentation. Let us suppose that he sees no remaining ways of experimentation open to him. He has now become, and will forever be, a "homosexual" person. He is not prepared to reapproach the problem with the idea that the eventual outcomes could still be different.

Now the stage is set for hostility and the demands for appeasement which inevitably follow. People must be compelled to accept him in the role, as he originally construed it, and not in the alien part of a homosexual outcast. In order to elaborate his core role in its original form he may see monstrous plots being hatched against him. People are stubbornly refusing to behave as people should. Thus the original core role is bolstered by the addition of "paranoid" features and the hostility continues to extort appeasement from a society that "ought to have stayed put."

Therapy in a case of this sort has, in the past, generally been considered unusually difficult. There seems, however, to be much more optimism among therapists in recent years. There has also been a marked increase in the tendency of clinicians to diagnose cases in terms of this general type of psychodynamics. Thus the optimism may be a function of the greater tendency to apply the "homosexual to paranoid" interpretation to cases which would have been considered treatable anyway.

c. *Therapeutic approach to the "paranoid" case.* The most

promising approach seems to be via dependency constructs. The client is placed in a position where, in order to take care of even the simplest needs of food, water, and shelter, he must, moment by moment, be dependent upon some person or some small group of people. Along with this regime conversion symptoms have to be encouraged. They will tend to appear anyway. Thus the client is thrown back upon core constructions which involve only the simplest types of subsuming of other people and hence, only the simplest types of role constructs.

Of course, preverbal types of role constructs are involved. The client establishes a relationship which is so childlike that the notion of adult homosexuality is inapplicable, and so dependent that the notion of maintaining himself against a hostile society is obviously untenable; if it were true, he could not live the day out. Guilt, too, is managed. The client has his role restored. To be sure, it is a childhood role and looks more like a diaper than a pair of pants — but, at least, it is not a skirt.

With the client ensconced in this type of core role, and the therapist in a position to become a principal figure in the relationship, the next phase of therapy can begin. The task is to develop a set of constructs both permeable and comprehensive. Permeability is necessary if the constructs are to be used to embrace events which cannot now be foreseen; comprehensiveness is necessary if the client is to construe a masculine role with sufficient latitude to cover some of his established "effeminate" interests and experiences. The therapist should remember that the client's construction of his life role must embrace both the future and the past as well as the present. Any client needs some rationale to justify his biography. The future must not catch one entirely unawares. Even the client's present — his wholly dependent present — needs to be construed within the revised comprehensive structure.

With a revised superordinate structure which is both permeable and comprehensive, the therapist can encourage the client to broaden the range of his experimentation. Dependencies can be seen as being gradually distributed but not as being abolished. The new permeable structure should enable the client to face minor incompatibilities and change without his bogging down in anxiety, guilt, or hostility. He should be free to make revisions when he finds that one of his social experiments gets him into trouble. It should no longer be necessary for him to sit and demand that the world make his experiment turn out successfully. He should be freed from the notion that he is the prisoner of a host of little biographical anecdotes. He should come to realize that it is his direction of movement which now determines his life's course, and not the record of his past.

C. Dependency

15. DISORDERS INVOLVING UNDISPERSED DEPENDENCY

We have not used "dependency" as one of the principal axes in our diagnostic construct system. Within the diagnostic construction system of the psychology of personal constructs it has somewhat more of a subordinate status. It is treated more like a phenomenon. Of course it is not absolutely a phenomenon; it is still a construct.

Perhaps our view of dependency can be made clearer by an illustration. A child is commonly said to be dependent, and an adult is said to be independent. A child has to have people wait on him, while an adult appears to be able to fend for himself. But is an adult really less dependent? It seems to us, rather, that it is a matter of how one's dependency relationships are distributed. For the most part, adults are highly dependent upon a complex society made up of many people. They also grow to be dependent upon possessions, resources, and services which are of no particular concern to a child.

Sometimes it appears that the more "successful" a person becomes the more dependencies he has, because he thinks he "needs" things to survive which previously he could get along without. If an adult did not show some tendency to keep his dependencies and to spread them around, there would probably not be the emergence of societies, economic systems, cultural inheritances, and so on, which is the mark of the human species. Those societies which have been characterized by efforts to train their children to be wholly independent — and hence usually selfish — have survived no better than those which squandered their resources in short-sighted efforts to satisfy dependencies.

An adult wants more things. He roams farther afield to get them. He seeks them from more people. He taps a wider range of resources. He develops role relationships in order to distribute his dependencies. He seeks to satisfy one need here and another there. He discriminates between his dependencies and then disperses them appropriately. Thus, with respect to any one person, he is indeed more independent than he was with respect to his parent when he was a child. But, taking all his interpersonal relationships into account, he has a wide range of dependencies as well as resources for meeting them. It seems to the writer, therefore, that it is likely to be misleading to emphasize *dependency* as an axis along which people vary from time to time and from person to person. Rather, it seems as though we ought to throw the emphasis upon variation in the *dispersion of dependencies.*

a. *Indiscriminate dependency.* Some persons do not disperse their dependencies in a discriminative fashion. Instead of trying to get some things from some people and other things from other people, they try to get everything from everybody. They go around looking for a replica of "mama" and they want multiple copies. The associates from among whom the person seeks a lot of "mamas" may, at first, find the relationship warm and pleasing, but later become exhausted from taking care of the "baby" and then start to accuse him of having insatiable "dependency needs." To make matters more complicated, the person may have considerable hostility in his make-up. His social experimentation has not been turning out so well. About the only social experimentation he is willing to continue to carry on is his search for more whole "mamas." Now his more sophisticated associates will accuse him of exhibiting "oral aggression."

The difficulty with a client of this type lies in his failure to elaborate the field of his dependencies. As he grew up he increased both the permeability and comprehensiveness of his dependency constructs. But he failed to elaborate the constructs so as to develop some subordinate incidental bases for his social relationships. He thus failed to develop the capacity to have any relationship which was both satisfying and casual. For a friend to serve as a friend he must be used extensively to procure everyday nourishment and services, must be confided in, must be generally embraced, or even slept with. The dependency relationship must be comprehensively construed; if not, it seems to fail him altogether.

It may seem as though a client of the type we have described has really dispersed his dependencies. But that is not quite so. He probably looks far afield for someone upon whom he can unload all of his dependency at once. In the course of his wandering and the inevitable succession of rejections and "one-night stands" he does cover a lot of territory, but the dependencies themselves are never adequately dispersed. He is still looking for a whole "mama." He is not really elaborating his dependencies; he is only seeking someone who will satisfy them en bloc.

16. THERAPEUTIC APPROACH TO UNDIFFERENTIATED DEPENDENCY

The therapist who deals with a case involving undifferentiated and undispersed dependencies will always be wise to look for hostility too. Hostility is a characteristic of a person who demands appeasement rather than reappraising his approach. The person who has failed to disperse his dependency and deal with much of it in terms of incidental constructs, instead of comprehensive constructs, is probably one who has found it impossible to live with the natural results of his experimentation. Instead of revising his anticipations so that they will conform to plausible results, he demands that the results conform to his anticipations. With a hostility factor to be considered, the course of therapy will necessarily be somewhat altered.

a. *Approach through documentation only.* One may approach the case from either of two therapeutic angles. He may attempt to produce "insight." This involves documentation of the undifferentiated dependency by the recollection of many incidents in the past. As the evidence mounts, the client is gradually brought to recognize that his behavior is thoroughly childlike. Even his relationship to the therapist, accepting as the therapist may be, looms up as another instance of his childlike dependency. Dependency, and all the many behaviors which the term abstracts, becomes a serious threat. It begins to look to the client as if he might never be able to exist as an integral person.

When the problem of undispersed dependencies is approached in this manner, there is a real danger that the client will attempt to move without making the proper discriminations. What the therapist hopes for, of course, is that the client will become more like an adult. That is a reasonable hope, provided that the client has a clear picture of what the adult reactions are. But if his outlook is still that of a child, his model of adult life will be seen through a child's eyes. Instead of discriminating between his various dependencies and the various ways they can be met through proper role relationships, he is likely to try to deal with the whole matter of dependency all at once. He may then become as ruthlessly "independent" as an adult appears to be in the eyes of a hostile child.

The client sees that everything he does adds up to a dependency reaction, but he may not see how his dependency reactions can be separated out from each other and conceptualized along with role relationships. He sees only that he is confronted with the threat of never being able to grow up. The only course of action which appears to be open to him is to reverse his field and dash in the opposite direction. This means taking action along the dependency axis *as he sees it*. Obviously if he has been too "dependent" he must become "independent" instead. So he starts to do what he thinks independent people do. He accepts no gifts that might obligate him. He avoids entangling relationships. He is beholden to no man. He takes what he wants from anyone who has it, *provided* that he does not thereby obligate himself!

The real danger, therefore, in approaching the problem of undispersed dependencies by getting the client to generalize all of his behavior as "dependent" is that he will move drastically toward what he construes as "independent" behavior and will fail to form the role relationships which are such an important part of healthy adult life. Since the client's construction of how needs are satisfied is not basically changed, this amounts to a continuation of the client's demands for appeasement — hence we have real hostility on our hands, coupled with the client's childlike version of "independence." The therapist may not be pleased with this outcome of his therapeutic efforts.

b. *Approach through limited experimentation.* But suppose we approach the client's dependency problems in a somewhat different way. Suppose we help the client to experiment with ways of meeting particular needs, first in the therapy room, later in his personal-social milieu. Suppose we help him set up minor experiments with social relationships on the basis of peripheral rather than core constructs. Instead of leading him first to the conviction that he is altogether a childlike person, let him discover that *some* of his particular wants can be met *in certain new ways.* As therapy progresses, the mounting conviction that he has been seeking to satisfy his dependencies in a childlike way will not find him lacking the tools for meeting his wants in more adult ways.

c. *Panic following the interpretation of "dependency."* New "insight" can be extremely threatening. It may throw a client into a state of panic. By "insight" we mean the comprehensive construction of one's behavior. A client who is rapidly brought to the point where he sees that much of his life's behavior can be generalized as hopelessly childlike is likely to go into a state of panic unless he has first been provided with tools and experience which will enable him to experiment with better ways of meeting his needs. A good rule for the therapist to follow is never to urge a client toward a new comprehensive construction without first making sure that the client is able to do something about it.

In psychotherapy there is always some risk of producing panic. Most experienced psychotherapists are aware of the panic that may follow upon a person's reconstruction of himself as "homosexual." The sex construction is so permeable that once one applies it to himself comprehensively his whole life is affected. When a male client is brought face to face with the fact that his whole manner of life is more like that of a woman than that of a man, he is likely to go into a panic state. This type of panic is, of course, well known and frequently observed by clinicians. The "paranoid" reactions which commonly follow upon this type of "insight" are also a matter of everyday observation.

But panic is not limited to cases of sudden "insight" into one's own "homosexual" ways of behaving. Panic can be produced by any sudden new comprehensive construction which enmeshes the person in a web of circumstance before he has been given the tools for making his escape. A client who is confronted with an interpretation of "dependency" may become panic-stricken. The plausibility of the interpretation makes it impossible for him to ignore it. The comprehensiveness of the construct completely engulfs him. His lack of social tools for exploring alternative modes of behavior leaves him helpless. He may have nothing left but his faith in the therapist and his daily contact with him to ward off a collapse.

d. *The hazard of overgeneralization in therapy.* Comprehensive "interpretations" and "insight" acquired in advance of exploratory techniques are always hazardous in therapy. We have mentioned the risk of such constructions in cases involving "homosexuality" and dependency. We might also mention the risk of comprehensive constructions of hostility itself. The client who suddenly realizes that nearly everything he has done and thought can be construed as hostile may be badly shaken unless the therapist has first been careful to see that the client has developed ways of behaving which are nonhostile. The sweeping generalization in psychotherapy may be dramatic and stimulating to the therapist but it should never be undertaken without first making sure what the client's alternatives are and how able he is to pursue them.

e. *Problems of treatment.* Let us return specifically to the treatment of disorders involving undispersed dependency. Ordinarily the therapist has difficulty in persuading the client to design and execute experiments having to do with moderate amounts of differentiated dependency. If he suggests that the client develop a relationship with a certain new acquaintance in order to meet some particular aspect of his own dependency, the client may foul up the experiment by trying to throw himself into the arms of the new acquaintance. The new acquaintance is likely to be flabbergasted. The client may return to the therapist and say, "See, I'm still mixed up." Or again, the client may refuse to make any use of the potential relationship. He may say, "That person just does not appeal to me." What the therapist then has to do is to bring out more clearly during the therapy sessions the different and varying *aspects* of the client's dependency. It is certainly hazardous to develop merely a comprehensive construct of dependency; that produces anxiety only, or perhaps even panic.

But then suppose that, even after the client has made some progress in differentiating his dependencies inside the therapy room, he still hesitates to experiment outside the therapy room. In terms of our model of "every man his own scientist" he continues to be an armchair speculator rather than becoming an experimentalist. This is the point where the therapist can put a little anxiety to good use. He can let the client see his dependency as involving him with the therapist ad nauseam. The client's undifferentiated dependency upon the therapist can be made a little clearer to him. The dependency can be accepted by the therapist. The world within the therapy room can become more and more constricted and the world outside the therapy room more and more confused. At first the client may appear to be losing ground. He may become so utterly dependent upon the therapist that he can scarcely lace his shoes without the therapist's advice. Since the therapist has already made sure that the client knows what can be done about some of his dependencies, he does not hesitate to make it clear to the client just how dependent upon the therapist he is. Ordinarily the therapist does not reject the client's dependency; that is more likely to make the client pack up his whole dependency kit and move to another stand. What he ordinarily does is accept the client's dependency, make clear how some of it can be met elsewhere, and then let the client discover the crippling effect of his present relationship to the therapist.

Throughout the treatment of the undispersed dependency case the therapist must keep clearly in mind that it is not dependency which must be eliminated, but rather the differentiation and appropriate distribution of dependency which must be achieved. For a client to become dependent upon the therapist is not in itself an unhealthy development. What is unhealthy is for the client to be unable to depend upon anyone else. The task of therapy is to enable the client to differentiate between his dependencies, to wrap them up in small packages so that they may be appropriately allocated and distributed among different people. In developing a variety of dependency relations he may learn also to play a variety of roles and to give as well as take in adapting himself to the dependencies of other persons. To do so is to be civilized. To do so is to be psychologically mature.

D. "Psychosomatic" and "Organic" Problems
17. DISORDERS INVOLVING "PSYCHOSOMATIC" SYMPTOMS

The psychology of personal constructs is essentially a miniature system rather than a pluralistic or interactionary system. It accepts, and is specifically designed for, a limited range of convenience. That range can be roughly located as that of human psychology. Throughout our discussion we have tried to maintain the position that the natural phenomena of our universe owe no exclusive loyalties to any one system — that a phenomenon which is psychologically interpretable is not necessarily therefore any less interpretable in a physiological system. It makes no sense to us to say that "the mind and body interact." The person under observation just goes on being himself and we can look at him through our psychologist's spectacles, or through our physiologist's spectacles, or, if our eyes will stand the eclectic strain, through both.

But we are propounding a psychology of personal constructs. We therefore recognize not only the constructive nature of our own approach to the real phenomena of our universe, but we recognize that other people also have their characteristic approaches.

As far as we are concerned, the personal construct systems of other people are real phenomena even though they may misrepresent real phenomena. Their interpretations may be in error, but they truly exist as interpretations. With respect to psychosomatics, we ourselves may be neither dualists or interactionists. But other people may be! A client thinks of his "mind" and his "body" as "interacting." That is his personal construction. We accept it as his personal construction. We need not accept it as ours, except as we attempt to subsume his system within our own. It makes no sense to us to say that "the mind and the body interact," but it may make sense to the client, and the client's construct is something we wish to understand.

When we find that our client has symptoms not readily explained under a physiological system, we may turn to a psychological system to find their explanation. (Incidentally, we might be more effective as clinicians if we routinely applied both psychological and physiological systems at the outset rather than applying one only after the other has been shown to be inadequate. But that is another controversy.) When we turn from a physiological system to a psychological system to find an adequate explanation of our client's behavior, we should be prepared to understand how the client himself sees the relation between "mind" and "body." Quite frequently the difficulty is seated in the client's own dualistic thinking. Perhaps, for him, what is mind is *not body* and what is body is *not mind*. Moreover, the *mind-body* construct may be applied preemptively by him. That would mean that what is "mind" can hardly be construed except in ways that are "intellectualized," and what is "body" can hardly be construed by him except in ways that are "mechanical." He cannot construe his facts comprehensively except as he goes back to the easiest forms of preverbal thinking. Only at that primitive level may we find that the "mind" and the "body" were not preemptively separated.

a. *Basis of the inaccessibility of certain "somatic" symptoms.* From the point of view of the psychology of personal constructs, then, the inaccessibility of certain "somatic" symptoms, in persons suffering from psychological conflict, stems from their dualistic thinking. Of course, dualistic thinking is characteristic of our culture. Be that as it may, the dichotomy is personally perceived and the client may not have constructs of sufficient comprehensiveness to bridge the gap. But more than this, the *mind-body* construct is applied preemptively. Even if the client admits that there must be some relation between his "symptoms" and his "conflicts," he is not necessarily relieved by this admission. The dichotomy is still there. It separates his whole world. He may be able to bridge it with only the most childlike constructions — constructions involving such undifferentiated dependency and helplessness that he is threatened or made guilty at the very prospect of invoking them.

The therapist's task is to help the client develop permeable comprehensive constructs which he will not be ashamed to use and which will enable him to go back and pick up the threads of relationship between "mind" and "body." These relatively new constructs may themselves be "preverbal," in the sense in which we have used the term. That is to say that, while they obviously were not altogether formulated before the client had words, they possess the nonverbal characteristics of those constructs which were formulated before the client had words.

b. *Levels of symptom formation.* It is sometimes said, by way of explaining "psychosomatic symptoms," that the person has three levels of expression: (1) an ideational level, (2) an aggressive level involving rage, flight, and fighting and often accompanied by cardiovascular symptoms, and (3) a regressive level involving helplessness, dependency, and preparatory responses and often accompanied by gastrointestinal disturbances. The further inference is sometimes made that the last of these levels is the most difficult to treat. Such experience as the writer has had does not confirm this inference.

The "ideational" level does involve verbalized constructs of a somewhat more superordinate and permeable level. The client who comes to the clinician with disturbances of ideas is, of course, more likely to do a lot of verbalizing, to talk at higher levels of abstraction, and to apply his constructs readily to new situations. But this very fact may make him a really tough nut to crack. It may be hard to get his constructions down to an experimental level. He may insist on philosophizing rather than hypothesizing and experimenting.

The "aggressive" level may involve considerable impulsivity. The therapist may find that he has a rocky way to go. The client may keep involving himself in difficult social situations which have the ultimate effect of constricting his field of elaboration. This level may be characterized as one in which there is considerable alternation of the client's response. He tends to throw himself from one end of a construct dimension to the opposite end. His thrashing about may represent a frantic attempt to produce therapeutic movement. His importunity may get him into further trouble.

The "regressive" level may represent a spastic attempt to go two ways at once. It is difficult to deal with because therapy must first help the client to differentiate between the two ways (or more) that he is trying to go. Because such cases require the therapist to do much of his work on a nonverbal level, many therapists are discouraged with such cases before they start. But the task is not necessarily any more difficult than with the client who has "ideational" symptoms. A person whose system is largely preverbal, but not too loose, may not resist treatment as much as one whose constructs are "nailed down" with words. The therapist simply has to deal with interpersonal relationships rather than word symbols. He needs to be able to enact varying parts as if he were a child's playmate. He needs to be able to do role playing skillfully and sympathetically. He needs to be aware of the therapeutic effectiveness of genuine role relationships, both for himself and for his client.

A large proportion of psychological disorders involve some kind of "psychosomatic" symptom. We could say the same thing another way; a large proportion of physiological disorders involve some kind of "psychosomatic" symptom. A still more sophisticated way of expressing the same point is to say that the phenomena of human behavior can mostly be construed both psychologically and physiologically. We have no specific illustrative treatment sketches to offer for "psychosomatic" disorders, since the term "psychosomatic" has no precise meaning within the structure of our system. We suggest that, instead of allowing himself to become wholly preoccupied with the client's "physiological" symptoms per se, the therapist also seek the answers to his questions in the personal construction system within which the symptoms arise.

18. DISORDERS INVOLVING ORGANIC DEFICIT

In recent years, psychological tests have been used extensively to diagnose conditions of organic deficit. For the most part, such tests rely upon two fairly well documented facts: (1) that in cases of organic deterioration or injury some broad types of psychological functions are disturbed more than others, and (2) that the physiologically handicapped person tends to constrict his field of spontaneous elaboration. The former fact refers to greater loss of memory for recent events, retention of vocabulary and certain language skills, even after problem-solving ability has been sharply impaired, and retention of certain formalized social skills long after social sensitivity has been blunted. The latter fact refers to "rigidity," "perseveration," and general ineptitude in changing the course of one's thinking. The client exhibits behavior which may be characterized as "clutching his marbles."

Some clinical psychologists add a third type of "organic sign" to the cues by which "organicity" is diagnosed. If the client produces speech or projective-test content referring to organic impairment, there seems to be some increased likelihood that he in fact has such impairment. From the standpoint of the psychology of personal constructs, we would say simply that he expresses constructs whose range of convenience is typically concerned with certain "physiological" content and that this suggests his areas of recent spontaneous elaboration.

Actually, all of these critical characteristics of the organically deteriorated person stem from the fact that he must now reconstrue himself in a constricted world, using as his point of departure the constructs which were once richly documented, and gradually substituting for them constructs dealing with new content and with new and limited ranges of convenience. What the diagnostic clinician observes is a reconstruction process during the course of its transition. He observes the relatively greater facility with old constructs, the constriction of the field of spontaneous elaboration as the client gropes to find himself, and, lying about, the evidences of the specific materials out of which the client is trying to develop an appropriate revised personal construct system.

The therapeutic task is to help the client along with his reconstruction job. It calls for developing constructs which will bridge the past, the present, and the future, even though, for this particular client, the events of these periods may seem markedly different from each other. The new constructs which emerge must ordinarily be heavily documented from the past. The life role must be firmly established.

For example, in attempting to assist an elderly person psychotherapeutically it is extremely important that the significance of his earlier life be carefully preserved and enhanced. This is in sharp contrast to the psychotherapeutic treatment of a young person, whose past is often discounted and who is invited "to start all over again." The elderly person must, of course, reconstrue, for the course of events in which he is caught up requires some radical readjustments; but the events of his past cannot be safely ignored or wholly replaced by the insecurities of the present. The therapist must help him develop a sense of personal history and destiny that will enable him to see his life role as something far more than the little daily orbit he taps out with his cane.

One of the features of construction which is commonly observable in "organic" and aged cases is the use of deteriorated constructs. A deteriorated construct is one which has become relatively impermeable. For example, a person may use such terms as "liberal" and "reactionary" in describing facets of his social world. Such a term as "liberal" might be expected to embrace a considerable variety of new faces and experiences; it sounds like a permeable construct. But the alert clinician may note that, as the term is used by a certain elderly client, it does not seem to have the permeability that its dictionary meaning might lead one to expect. As the clinician further studies the personal construct system of his client he may find that the context of "liberal" has been closed out, that the age of "liberalism," like the age of miracles, is dead. It is like going to a meeting of the Daughters of the American Revolution expecting to find oneself in the same kind of company that attended the original "Boston Tea Party." This type of deterioration in construing is characteristic of senility in the individual, just as it is characteristic of senility in a society.

The "organic picture" in psychodiagnostics is not limited to cases in which there is demonstrable organic pathology. Rather, it is a picture of attempted reconstruction which may ensue from other handicaps as well. Any person who begins to find himself beyond his depth with a deep-seated feeling of inadequacy may show the so-called "organic" picture. The psychodiagnostician will have to distinguish between him and the true "organic" case by means of more subtle cues. For example, if the constriction exhibited at the moment is more marked than the case history would lead one to expect, the clinician suspects that he is dealing with something immediate and acute. If there is a discrepancy from hour to hour, the clinician may be inclined to suspect a toxic disturbance. If the constriction is highly selective and indicates the tight operation of some superordinate construction, the clinician is more likely to look for a "psychological" handicap or trauma. The clinician should therefore be careful not to consider the client's constricting behavior as directly revealing an organic pathology in a manner analogous to the way the appearance of blood reveals a wound. Rather, it is better to consider the constricting behavior, together with other behavior characteristically observed in "organic" cases, as the client's own attempt to make an adjustment to his changing situation.

E. Control

19. DISORDERS INVOLVING CONTROL

We have defined control as an aspect of the relationship between a superordinate construct and the subordinate constructs which constitute its context. The way the subordinate constructs are subsumed determines the way in which they may operate, just as the way a person construes determines the way in which he behaves. In a sense, then, all disorders of construction are disorders which involve faulty control.

We have further described the Circumspection-Preemption-Control (C–P–C) Cycle, by means of which a person prepares himself to take definitive action in a given situation. We have pointed out that control involves the choice of an alternative and that the choice of the alternative is determined by that side of the construct which appears to provide a better opportunity for further elaboration. (Choice Corollary)

Sometimes a clinician observes his client behaving in regularized ways which make it appear that there is *more* control operating than in the case of another client. This is misleading. From the standpoint of the psychology of personal constructs, all behavior may be seen as controlled, just as all behavior can be seen as natural and all nature seen as lawful. What makes one person's behavior seem more controlled than another is the way it is subsumed by overriding construction. The "controlled" person performs long-cycle experiments; the impulsive person indulges in short-range experimentation. Both must bow to the outcomes of their experiments sooner or later. Both control their behavior through superordinate construction systems.

Sometimes a person's behavior can be seen as regular, purposeful, and consistent and yet altogether so inimical to the welfare of others that it must be construed as pathological. The clinician must realize that in dealing with this type of case he is dealing with highly permeable superordinate constructions and with long-cycle prediction formulas. He cannot expect this type of client to be swayed by means of little ideas or simple interview-room experiments. The client may use anecdotes to illustrate his own constructions, but he will not be likely to change his control system as the result of having anecdotes cited by the therapist. He simply does not make such short-term wagers.

This type of client may be very baffling to the therapist, largely because the therapist never gets to see the faulty superordinate constructs laid on the line for examination and experimental test during the course of a single interview. Even if the person is not what one would ordinarily call "psychotic," he may be a very baffling person with whom to establish a role relationship. Perhaps his behavior is organized under a set of religious constructs which seem utterly primitive and magical to the therapist, and the person seems inaccessible to psychological treatment. The therapist is unable to think of any tests which will be sufficiently comprehensive to lead the person to reexamine his religious principles. Whatever new experience is introduced during the course of therapy is too readily subsumed and too easily brought under control of the superordinate construction causing all the difficulty.

The same difficulties are faced when nations try to work out role relations with each other. For example, little demonstrations of good will do not have much effect upon leaders basically indoctrinated with the 1955 political and social philosophy of the Soviet Union. Its leaders have so clear-cut a view of the course of events leading to the future that they cannot be swayed by border incidents or by sporadic demonstrations of determination on the part of those who differ with them. Like the systematized paranoid patients, such political zealots are not likely to shift from their pathological position until certain crucial experiments have been designed and executed. The hope of civilized mankind is that the experimentation will not include all-out war.

With those who are not so basically indoctrinated, however, a consistent policy of good will and liberal tolerance may serve to validate their more friendly interpretations of our motives. The task of the therapist (or the socially responsible nation) is to keep the client (or disturbed nation) actively experimenting with the relationship. He seeks to have the client put his superordinate construction to test, a test that will definitely yield results of one sort, if the construction is correct, or results of another sort, if the construction is in error. The therapist says, in effect, to the client, "This is what you have been assuming to be true; let us perform a reasonable experiment which will come out one way if it is true and another way if it is not."

As in all cases of psychotherapy, the therapist should be alert as to what alternatives will confront the client if his experiment turns up negative evidence. What alternative does the client have to his view of pervading hostility? What will there be to take the place of communism in the Soviet Union if the present regime is discredited? Will it be anything more than another kind of serfdom with only the manners and dress of the masters changed? In the client, whose interpretation of a hostile world is clearly invalidated, will there be any alternative left, save a chaos of anxiety or a schizophrenic fragmentation? It may be necessary to make sure that the client has certain role relationships and tentative structures to fall back upon as soon as the crucial experimentation is over. These stand-by structures may be of the dependency type, as we have suggested before; or they may be of the fixed-role type; or they may be of the occupational type. But whatever type they may be the therapist should always, before prodding his client to jump, make sure that there is something reasonably firm to land on, that there is a suitable basis for *control*.

In dealing with a disorder of control the therapist must, as in other problems, subsume the construction system which is faulty. If the control is of the long-cycle variety we have been describing, the therapist (or the socially responsible nation) must understand the personal construct system with which he is dealing. That means, of course, that he must understand it sympathetically and insightfully, not simply condemn it as something abhorrent and unthinkable. Rarely have therapists (or nations) exercised far-reaching influence over their clients (or fellow nations) by condemning them, instead of thoughtfully studying their beliefs and customs.

20. DISORDERS INVOLVING IMPULSIVITY

We have defined impulsivity as a form of control which is preceded by a relatively short period of circumspection. The person looks at his problem from a multidimensional point of view for a short time only. Or perhaps he scarcely sees it in terms of more than one dimension. Then he preempts, thus settling upon the issue. Then he makes his elaborative choice and goes into action.

Consider the client who shows impulsivity in his sexual behavior. When confronted with a sexually stimulating situation he is able to consider it multidimensionally for a brief time only. In a moment or two the matter is brought to the issue of whether he shall attempt sexual intercourse or not. The elaborative choice, the choice that seems to offer the greater possibility for further exploration, seems to lie in the direction of having intercourse rather than avoiding it. He swings his behavior under the control of this construction and acts accordingly.

There may be a number of antecedent reasons for his behavior. It may be that sex for him has always been oversimplified. He may not be able to see it in terms of more than one or two dimensions — either you have intercourse with a girl or you leave her strictly alone. Or the only real basis for association between people of different sexes is to select sexual partners. If the issue is so simple there is no basis for circumspection. Preemption takes place almost immediately. The person need pause only long enough to decide whether pursuing his sexual object offers greater promise of elaboration than not pursuing it.

Now we see this type of behavior in an individual whose own sex role has not been satisfactorily developed. Persons of the opposite sex may be puzzling to him. The intersexual role relationships that other people seem to enjoy may seem to be exasperatingly elusive as far as he is concerned. How can he solve his problem? Obviously he must take some kind of action. But if he knows of only two things to do with a girl — either have intercourse with her or leave her alone — the elaborative choice will clearly appear to him to lie on the side of having intercourse. It is not surprising, then, that we frequently find impulsive sexual behavior in persons who are not too clear as to their own role relationships to persons of the opposite sex.

The difficulty may go back to childhood days. The relationship between the parents may have been one which was difficult for the client to understand. It may have been one which threatened his own childhood role, perhaps produced guilt. Within his own personal construct system the relation between man and wife is undimensional and not well elaborated along a variety of construct dimensions. He seeks to correct the deficiency by acting along the only dimension he can clearly perceive. That makes him appear to be impulsive, not only to the therapist, but to others who are in a position to observe his behavior closely.

It should also be borne in mind that the impulsive person's sexual behavior is frequently, though not always, oversimplified within the limits of the sex act itself. He may not be able to coordinate his sexual behavior with the impulses of his sexual partner. The relationship may prove to be far from satisfying for either of them. Furthermore, it may be accompanied by hostility as in desperation he seeks appeasement rather than natural validation of his exploratory hypotheses. Then his behavior takes on the features of rape.

Whereas one person may impulsively seek to perform the sex act, another may just as impulsively seek to avoid it. The person who avoids it is not showing more control; his control is simply exercised in another direction. The person who impulsively extricates himself from a sexually potent situation may not be doing so because of any high moral standards or any superordinate construction of his life role. He may simply find the prospect suddenly repulsive. His C–P–C Cycle may be just as short as that of the person who attempts to seduce every woman he meets. In his case also, the circumspection phase of the cycle is shortened by his oversimplified construction of how men and women relate themselves to each other. He too may see it as primarily a matter of having sexual intercourse or not having sexual intercourse. The only difference between him and the other person is that he makes his elaborative choice at the other end of the construct dimension.

a. *Difficulty with the circumspection phase of the C–P–C Cycle.* Thus far we have spoken of impulsivity as a function of a one-track mind — at least a mind that runs back and forth along one track in a certain area of experience. The circumspection phase of the C–P–C Cycle is shortened simply because the person's construction of the situation is so simple that he quickly runs out of angles from which to view it.

But the circumspection phase may be shortened for another

reason. Let us go back to our Modulation Corollary. A person's tolerance of incompatibility is limited by the permeability and definition of certain superordinate aspects of his system. Suppose a man finds himself in the company of a woman. There are many angles to the situation. But the more he looks at the situation from the various angles, the more confused he becomes. He becomes acutely aware of the incompatibilities that are arising. He becomes anxious. He has no superordinate construction of sufficient permeability and definition to provide stability during his elaboration of the interpersonal relationship. His role as he perceives it is not superordinate to the situation.

Suppose the person is a student psychotherapist dealing with his first female case. Suppose he is not sufficiently grounded in psychological principles to be guided by them through the confusion of his shifting relationships to his client. He becomes anxious. He seeks to resolve the anxiety by preemptively construing the situation, by casting it into a single issue. The result is a foreshortened C-P-C Cycle and an *impulsive* decision.

The decision may be to give the client an inspirational lecture, to translate all the client has said into a dimension that makes sense for the therapist but not for the client, to recoil from her and refer the case to someone else, to "bring her into line" in an essentially hostile manner, or even to seduce her. Any of these steps may represent an attempt to escape anxiety by quickly bringing the situation to a point of issue. Any of them may represent impulsivity.

b. *Difficulty with the preemption phase of the C-P-C Cycle.* The impulsivity may arise out of difficulty with the preemptive phase of the C-P-C Cycle. A person may have difficulty in reducing a multidimensional problem to a crucial issue. When he seeks a crucial issue or preemptive construct it may seem that it never quite subsumes the other construct dimensions in terms of which his problem is structured. He then chooses his issue more because it is something he can act upon rather than because it seems to be crucial. This is like the person who looks for his lost wallet under a lamppost because there is more light there than at the place where he dropped it. His decision may follow upon either a short or a long circumspection phase and thus the cycle, as a whole, may not, in every instance, meet our definition of impulsivity. His impulsivity is like that of the man who, cheated at poker, exclaimed, "Certainly I knew it was a crooked game; but it was the only poker game in town!" Clinically this type of impulsivity may be discerned by the doubts and reservations which accompany the client's ill-conceived plunges. The circumspection is not wholly replaced by preemption even though the client preempts the issues and chooses sides.

c. *Difficulty with the control phase of the C-P-C Cycle.* The impulsivity may appear to lie in the foreshortening of the control phase of the C-P-C Cycle. Having decided upon the issue and having made his elaborative choice, the person may appear not to bide his time sufficiently to act in the most effective manner. He considers his target circumspectively, takes careful aim, but pulls the trigger at the wrong time. Actually this type of impulsivity arises out of the person's inability to distinguish between the major issue which has been preemptively chosen and certain operational issues which still need to be considered circumspectively. When he decides what he is going to do he does not give enough attention to choosing the appropriate time and place. The operating issues are lumped with the major issues and a preemptive decision taken with respect to all of them at once. This kind of impulsivity is often experienced during the active experimentation phase of psychotherapy when the client, having reduced his problem to certain meaningful issues in his life, makes the mistake of walking out of the room and taking action on the sidewalk.

21. PSYCHOTHERAPY IN CASES OF IMPULSIVITY

Psychotherapy with disorders involving impulsivity may cause the therapist a lot of headaches. Some therapists prefer to undertake it in an intramural situation only. If the impulsivity arises out of the one-track mind, the therapist will need to provide for protected elaboration of the relevant construct within the therapy room or within the sanitarium. If the impulsivity represents an attempt to escape anxiety as quickly as possible, the therapist will need to take steps to protect the client from anxiety and guilt. The latter is particularly difficult in an intramural situation because hospitalization itself tends to dislodge a person temporarily from his social role. Gradually the therapist will need to rebuild a reasonable system of superordinate structure which will increase the client's tolerance of incompatibility and thus permit him to deal circumspectively with a variety of conflicting issues without becoming upset.

If the client's impulsivity stems from his difficulty in choosing a suitable preemptive issue, the therapist may have to spend some time helping the client to delineate the action implications of various "insights" which arise during the therapeutic discussions. Again, this may call for "role playing" and "acting out" within the protective walls of the therapy room. Once the client discovers that he can act in a variety of ways as the situation demands, he can be more choosy about his preemptive constructions. This phase of the therapy may appear to be extraneous to the central issue, as the therapist sees it, but it should always be borne in mind that a client needs to feel that he can act in a variety of ways before his final choice of a single way to act takes on any personal significance. A person who feels that he has no choices also feels like an automaton. His Hobson's choices reflect no personality development. A man who does not know how to do wrong cannot lay claim either to morality or to great strength of character.

If the impulsivity arises out of the tendency of the client to do the right thing at the wrong time, the therapist will have to help the client develop his social techniques. In a hospital situation the various social-activity programs may be utilized. Outside the hospital or with an outpatient, the therapy may involve considerable discussion of incidents occurring between sessions and the detailed planning of day-by-day social experiments. As this technical experimentation goes on, the client and the therapist may discover some superordinate constructions, likely of the hostility variety, which are interfering with the learning of the daily lessons. The technical experimentation can usually be continued after this is discovered; but, for a time, relatively greater emphasis will have to be placed upon superordinate-concept reformation. The daily experiences can be used partly as documentation and validational evidence for the new structure. Historical evidence can also be used to piece out the new construct contexts.

22. DISORDERS ARISING OUT OF THE CONTENT RATHER THAN THE FORM OF PERSONAL CONSTRUCTS

In our illustrative survey of disorders and our brief sketches of therapeutic designs we have thus far confined ourselves to the dimensions proposed in our chapter on diagnostic constructs. It would be a mistake to assume that all disorders are disorders of dilation, constriction, anxiety, preemption, impulsivity, and the like. Quite frequently the client's difficulty arises out of the intrinsic meaning of his personal constructs rather than out of the general form which they have assumed. A person who believes that punishment expunges guilt is likely to punish himself. If he is hostile he will extort compliance with his construct from other persons too. If a middle-aged woman believes that she will not be loved by her husband after menopause, she will act as one faced with the loss of love. If a person is convinced that the flesh and the spirit are antithetical, he will make decisions on the basis of that dichotomy — and the decisions may cause trouble. The therapist should be concerned with what the client construes to be taking place as well as the form of his constructs.

Some therapy can be undertaken and successfully concluded without the therapist's being concerned with the type of diagnostic construction we have been talking about. The task in such cases is to give information, to introduce new constructs which reorder the construct contexts, and to help the client to reconstrue what has been going on. Moreover, a therapeutic program of social experimentation can be designed to invalidate old constructs and validate new ones without the therapist's having to be greatly concerned with such matters as anxiety, hostility, or guilt. There is such a thing as education for mental health, and the therapist should not be rigid in his belief that the only important learning takes place on a couch. It is a good thing to remember that the great ideas by which men have liberated themselves have not been acquired from psychotherapists nor were the values of those great ideas depreciated when the original teachers of them neglected to assess a professional fee.

Chapter Eighteen

Elaborating the Complaint

⎍⎍⎍⎍⎍⎍⎍⎍⎍⎍⎍⎍⎍⎍⎍⎍⎍⎍⎍⎍⎍⎍⎍⎍⎍⎍⎍⎍

THE LAST five chapters of this volume are technical discussions of psychotherapy as it is planned and pursued along our theory's diagnostic axes. The first of these chapters starts with what confronts the psychotherapist at the beginning of his contact with his client — the complaint.

A. The Nature of Elaboration

1. PSYCHOTHERAPY AS AN AID TO RECONSTRUCTION

The psychology of personal constructs and the philosophy of constructive alternativism upon which it is based lead one to view psychotherapy as a reconstruing process. Within these two frameworks we see man not as the victim of his past, only the victim of his construction of it. To be sure, his past cannot be altered. Operationally speaking, its unalterability makes the past what it is, and its pliancy makes the future what it is. As for the present, man can divert some small part of the stream of events upon which he is borne. Moreover, he can navigate over broad latitudes if he has a mind to. Nature, inexorable as she is, is not half so intransigent as our thinking about her. And it is only a knuckle-headed outlook that makes the past seem to adults to be so implacable, the present so self-evident, and the future so fateful.

Our view, then, is that there is nothing in the world which is not subject to some form of reconstruction. This is the hope that *constructive alternativism* holds out to every man and it is the philosophical basis of the hope that a psychotherapist holds out to his client.

a. *"Slot" movement.* In our chapter on the role of the psychotherapist we included a section on the clinician's conceptualization of his role. We pointed out that superficial movement could be produced by sliding the client back and forth in his construct slots. For example, a client who sees people as distinguished from each other principally in terms of "kindly" versus "hostile" may be encouraged to shift himself from "kindliness" to "hostility" or vice versa. This type of therapeutic movement amounts to no more than a shifting of one of the elements in the construct context — in this case himself — from one side of the construct dimension to the other. Sometimes this kind of superficial movement is worth seeking; but, as every clinician should know, it is all too likely to end up in seesaw behavior: the client is "kindly" as long as things are going well, then he turns to "hostility," then back again, ad infinitum. Let us call this type of reconstruction *contrast reconstruction.*

b. *Controlled elaboration.* The second type of reconstruction discussed in the section dealing with the clinician's conceptualization of his role was described as *controlled elaboration.* It is a way of bringing about reconstruction through clarification. This amounts to a reorganization of the hierarchical system of one's constructs, but not essential revision of the constructs themselves. The client is helped to work through his construct system experimentally by verbal as well as by other behavioral actions. He deals essentially with the subordination-superordination features of his system. He brings his constructs into line with his system as a whole. Essentially he works on the internal consistency of his system rather than attempting to make outright replacements of constructs. For example, the person who sees himself as "kindly" in a "kindly-hostile" dimensioned world may be helped to discover just what incidental constructs and behaviors are "kindly" and what ones are "hostile." Thus his system becomes clearly delineated whereas once it was sketchy, his superordinate constructs are tightened, and he becomes a person of greater integrity — though not necessarily a "better" man.

c. *Formation of new constructs.* The third and most basic type of reconstruction which may take place in psychotherapy is that which changes the reference axes against which the events of life are plotted. By judiciously introducing new elements into the client's field of experience, the therapist may so change the content of the construct contexts that the axes of the client's system are rotated. The same words may be used to symbolize the constructs, but the meanings may have been subtly changed in the course of psychotherapy. For example, the client who lumps humanity as either "kindly" or "hostile" may be brought to the point of seeing that some behavior which is constricting and repressive is the sort of thing he has been calling "kindly" and some elements which are straightforward and reliable are the sort of thing he has been calling "hostile." As this revision of contexts begins to take place, the "kindly-hostile" axis begins to rotate with respect to the rest of his system. As far as his own behavior is concerned, he sees himself confronted with alternatives which have somewhat different behavior implications. In a given situation to which the construct is applied, his *elaborative choice* will be affected. And once he has made his choice, the repertory of behaviors falling under that choice will, in turn, be revised.

The therapist may help the client accelerate the tempo of his experience. He may precipitate him into situations in which he can be expected to "mature." This is, of course, also a matter of adding new elements, but it is principally a matter of giving the client more new elements to deal with, rather than a matter of judiciously selecting new elements in order to rotate his axes or force him to contrive new constructs. For example, the client may be encouraged to take a job or enter a social situation in which the "nonkindly" people are not "hostile" but only disinterested and objective.

The therapist may help the client impose new constructs upon old elements. The new constructs may be tentatively originated as *incidental* constructs. But once formed, they can be made more permeable and their range of convenience gradually expanded until the client is able to use them to replace certain obsolete *core* constructs. For example, the therapist may help the client develop the notion that certain behaviors of people can be distinguished on the grounds of "objectivity vs. selfishness." At first this is no more than an *incidental* construct and can be used by the client to distinguish only between a few specific figures which seem relatively detached from himself. Later he may be able to apply it to more familiar figures; and, last of all, he may be able to apply the construct to his own behavior, past and present. At this stage of the game there is a reasonable chance that he can incorporate the new construct into his *core* system. Because it has proven to be a better basis for anticipating life than the old personal construct of *kindliness-hostility*, he may begin to make his life's choices in terms of the alternatives the new construct provides instead of in terms of the old dichotomy.

d. *Reduction of constructs to impermeability.* One of the most interesting approaches to construct revision is the reduction of obsolete constructs to a state of impermeability. As the writer sees it, this is essentially what the general semanticists propose as the basic approach to psychotherapy. Thinking is made more and more specific to its elements. Constructs are tightened and given sharply limited ranges of convenience. Our client who lumps his associates as either "kindly" or "hostile" may be urged to see only certain people as "kindly" or "hostile" — these and no more. Or better still, he might be urged to see only certain past behaviors of these people as "kindly" or "hostile" — these and no more. As far as other people and other behaviors of these same people are concerned he would be assisted in applying another construct such as, for example, "objective-selfish."

2. PSYCHOTHERAPY IS A FORM OF EXPERIMENTATION

The psychotherapeutic approach of the psychology of personal constructs is experimental. The whole system is built upon the modern science model. Constructs are hypotheses. Prediction is the goal. Systematization extends the range of anticipation.

Experiments are performed. They are carefully designed to yield definitive results. Only small samples are committed to experimentation at a time. Abortive undertakings are avoided. Hypotheses are revised on the basis of empirical evidence. Hostility is avoided, for the scientist seeks to learn from nature rather than extort from her a confirmation of his prejudices.

All of this is embodied in the approach of a psychotherapist to his client. The psychotherapist helps the client design and implement experiments. He pays attention to controls. He helps the client define the hypotheses. He helps the client avoid abortive undertakings. He uses the psychotherapy room as a laboratory. He does not extort results from his client to confirm his own systematic prejudices nor does he urge his client, in turn, to seek appeasement rather than knowledge. Finally, he recognizes that in the inevitable scheme of things he is himself a part of the validating evidence which the client must take into account in reckoning the outcome of his psychotherapeutic experiments. The client, in experimenting with the old *kindly-hostile* construct and the new *objective-selfish* construct, must see those bits of evidence which the therapist's own varying behaviors provide as fitting more neatly and meaningfully into the *objective-selfish* dichotomy.

In summary, we may say that psychotherapeutic movement may mean (1) that the client has reconstrued himself and certain other features of his world within his original system, (2) that he has organized his old system more precisely, or (3) that he has replaced some of the constructs in his old system with new ones. This last type of movement is likely to be the most significant, although the behavioral changes may not be as spectacular as in the first type. The second type of movement may be most impressive to those who always look to therapy to produce verbal consistency and "insight."

3. RECAPITULATION OF PSYCHOTHERAPEUTIC PROCEDURES DISCUSSED IN PREVIOUS SECTIONS

In the chapter, "The Psychotherapeutic Approach," a number of psychotherapeutic techniques were discussed by way of illustrating the basic approaches to the problem of psychotherapy. The discussion was preceded by a chapter dealing with the clinician's conceptualization of his own role, his skills, his system of values, and some of his professional obligations. We then dealt with the way in which the therapeutic situation should be set up, including the initial orientation of the client to therapy, behavior of the therapist in and out of the interview room, physical arrangements of facilities and equipment, and scheduling. Techniques for controlling and spacing the interview sequence were described. The important problem of teaching the client how to make use of his therapeutic opportunities was discussed.

Following the discussion of general therapeutic procedures there were discussions of certain selected and important processes and procedures which are likely to be involved in almost every psychotherapeutic case. The definitions, techniques, and proper controlled uses of each of the following procedures were mentioned:

a. Reassurance.
b. Support.
c. Transference.
d. Transference of dependency.
e. Counter dependency transference.
f. Personal-identification transference.

In the chapter "Steps in Diagnosis" we discussed diagnostic procedures. Since diagnosis is the planning stage of therapy, and hence, part of the therapeutic procedure itself, that chapter, too, should be considered as falling, in part, under the topical heading of the present chapter. There we discussed:

a. Normative formulations of the client's problem.
b. Psychological descriptions of the client's personal constructions.
c. Psychological evaluation of the client's construction system.
d. Analysis of the milieu in which adjustment is to be made.
e. Determination of immediate procedural steps.
f. Planning management and treatment.

Under the last topic we discussed the considerations which should govern the selection of the central psychotherapeutic approach, the designation of the principally responsible clinician, the selection of adjunctive resources to be utilized, the designation of an advisory staff, the determination of the client's ad interim status, and the forward planning of dates or conditions under which progress will be reviewed by the advisory staff. All of these discussions are immediately relevant to the topic of psychotherapeutic procedures.

In the two chapters immediately preceding this one we discussed disorders of construction and we sketched a few illustrative psychotherapeutic approaches. We drew simple illustrative treatment sketches in the areas of dilation, tightening and loosening, withdrawal, disorders involving core constructs, aggression, hostility, anxiety, constriction, guilt, dependency, organic deficit, and impulsivity.

Finally, we should say that most of what we have written in each of the preceding chapters has some relevance to psychotherapeutic procedure. The psychology of personal constructs is a miniature system which has been elaborated particularly with an eye to casting its range of convenience around the problems of psychotherapy. The following group of chapters, then, is not an exhaustive discussion of the problem of psychotherapeutic procedures; it is supplemental to much of what we have already tried to convey. With the exception of this review no attempt is made in these next chapters to repeat all the previous discussions which bear upon psychotherapeutic procedures.

4. THE NATURE OF CONTROLLED ELABORATION

A person's processes are psychologically channelized by the ways in which he anticipates events. This is the take-off point for our exploratory venture into the reaches of human behavior. We have envisioned construing as involving, first of all, a series of discriminations which assume the form of dichotomous constructs. The constructs are axes with reference to which phenomena are perceptually fixed and alternative courses of action plotted. A person occasionally finds it necessary to make choices for himself within the matrix of his construct system. Since he is gradually groping toward a comprehensive way of anticipating events, optimally he makes what we have called "the elaborative choice." That is the choice which seems to him to provide the best outlook for developing his system in the foreseeable future. It is the choice which appears to provide the best opportunity for further elaboration.

Yet persons do not always appear to choose the way of adventure. Why? Do they not wish to discover more? Do they not really wish to know what lies over the ridge in the next valley? Are they really not lured by what the future has in store for them? There are, indeed, moments when it seems that way. Those of us who deal with disturbed persons see so many instances of people who pull the bedcovers over their heads that we are tempted to see man as unconcerned with his opportunities. Or we may see him as a skittish creature who is always shying at the shadows cast ahead of him by his own personality. It is not surprising that clinicians are tempted to see mankind as either driven by the inexorable forces of nature or drawn by hunger needs which may never be satisfied. But it is through the historian's vista that we can see mankind so unmistakably on the forward march. It is through the eyes of the aging teacher whose students of yesteryear occasionally return to visit that one becomes convinced that man, the individual, is superbly capable of planned growth.

Perhaps we have said enough to indicate that our position, from Fundamental Postulate on down to psychotherapeutic technique, states that the job of the psychologist is to deal with reconstructive processes. It is not necessary to treat man's processes solely as if they were psychological defenses. This is an important consideration in developing one's psychotherapeutic procedures in a particular case. It is a consideration that the frustrated clinician is likely to lose sight of.

Let us examine man's constructive processes more closely. Since he is basically a creature of curiosity, he tends to pursue the implications of his ideas. That is good. The psychologist is glad to help him. A man says, "Here are the pairings of alternatives as I see them. Now *if* this pair represents the crux of the matter, and *if* I choose this alternative rather than that, what happens? Mind you I said 'if'; I have not committed myself yet!" The psychologist responds in any of three ways. He may say, "You obviously see what you must choose between; now go ahead, choose this!" He may say, "Suppose you do choose this; how is that going to fit in with the other pairs of alternatives in your system? Let's work it out." Or he may say, "Let's take another look at your pairings of alternatives."

Here we are again! These are the three types of psychotherapy that have been mentioned several times before. The first produces the *superficial movement* which, as we have pointed out, may prove to be no more than a seesaw action. It is a matter of sliding a man along his construct slots. If the therapist is not aware of the personal way the man has cut his slots, he may get some rude surprises as a result of his hortatory efforts. The second response represents an effort to produce therapeutic results by the method of *controlled elaboration*. It tends to tighten up the system and produce self-consistency. The third represents *construct revision*. It is the most difficult to achieve and the most likely to produce basic changes in the way a man construes his world.

Let us consider *controlled elaboration* more carefully. The psychologist says, "Suppose you choose this; how is that going to fit in with the other pairs of alternatives in your system? Let's work it out." Of course, any therapeutic program is likely to involve a thoughtfully planned combination of this procedure with others. Sometimes the elaboration of an amorphous set of constructs is necessary before the client can grasp them sufficiently well to act upon them, put them to test, or throw them overboard.

a. *Language as an aid to elaboration.* Language is one of the handiest gadgets ever invented by man to help him elaborate his constructs. Language serves two functions: it serves as a paperweight to keep ideas from blowing away while a man is busy with something else; and it serves, more or less, as a means of communication with other persons, especially with those who have a similar outlook. The latter function permits man to validate his ideas against the experience of other people. It opens vast resources of vicarious experience which he could not begin to accumulate by himself.

In the therapy interview room the use of language permits the client to investigate the implications of his ideas without becoming entangled in their outcomes. It permits him to protect his ventures by means of "ifs." Together with the therapist, he can speculate on outcomes of possible courses of action. He can investigate both sides of his construct without being wholly committed to either.

For example, a *hostile* client complains that his home has never given him a "sense of security." The presence of hostility is established when the therapist determines that the client is unable to accept the natural outcomes of his own experimentation and that he has turned to extortion as a way of confirming his constructs. The therapist seeks to have the client elaborate on what he expected his parents to do in order to give him the "sense of security." The elaboration is pursued down to a very concrete level. As each hypothetical illustration is developed, the client is given an opportunity to view it in the light of the rest of his system to see whether such behavior on the part of his parents is what he really wishes had happened.

Suppose the client describes an incident in which a neighbor once unjustly accused him of stealing a bicycle. His mother, instead of denying the charge immediately, subjected him to a thoroughgoing interrogation in front of the neighbor. He was able to prove his innocence. The neighbor apologized and went away satisfied. His mother did not apologize for her failure to take his part and she failed ever to say explicitly that she considered him absolved from guilt.

Now the therapist, if he is one of those therapists who like to sit in moral judgment of their clients' mothers, may jump to the conclusion that the mother behaved in an unmotherly way. He may say that the client is right; that he was not given the sense of security that he had a right to expect. From the standpoint of the psychology of personal constructs, however, this interpretation, while possibly defensible, is not necessarily profit-able. From our point of view the therapist should withhold his conclusion until he has seriously asked the further question, "So what?"

b. *Illustrative technique.* The therapist starts the controlled elaboration process in such a case by asking such a question as, "What did you want your mother to say?" He follows this up sooner or later with such a question as, "As you look back on the incident *now*, what do you wish your mother had said?" Thus, the therapist is always careful to interweave the elements of the past with the constructs of the present. These questions may be sufficient to start the client on spontaneous elaboration of the implications of his wish. "What would have happened *if* Mother had only done it differently? How would the ensuing days have been different? How would my life have been dif-ferent?"

But before the elaboration can be fully effective, the thera-pist will need to clarify the personal construct which the client invokes to deal with the incident. What is the pair of alterna-tives which the client considers applicable? Perhaps it is that the world is comprised of two kinds of people, those who handicap you forever by rejecting you and those who assist you by believing in you. The client thinks that his mother was one of the former type. The client can then be assisted in elaborating this construct, not only as it appears to apply to his mother, but as it applies to other figures in his personal-social milieu, even as it applies to the therapist.

c. *Bringing new thinking to bear on manifest elements.* As with all forms of reconstruction the ultimate objective of con-trolled elaboration is to bring new thinking to bear upon mani-fest elements. Sooner or later, then, the therapist, or the client himself, should be asking such questions as, "Exactly how would you be doing things differently today if all these things that you complain about had, instead, been the way you wanted them to be? Let's work it through in detail. Take the incident that hap-pened this morning. How would you have handled it *if* . . . ?" In controlled elaboration the client is given every opportunity to pursue the implications of his own construction all the way down to the minute details of his daily behavior. He is helped to spell out his answer to the question, "So what?"

d. *Spelling out alternatives.* Elaboration requires — and this is important — that *both* alternatives of each major construction be spelled out. Every construction involves alternatives. That is just as true of the day-by-day inquiries of the common man as it is in the scientist's carefully wrought experimental designs for testing hypotheses. The task of the therapist is to apply the methodology of experimental design, with its careful consideration of alternatives, to solving the problems of the individual client.

It seems to us to be preposterous that some psychologists who are so careful to design their research around plausible alternatives forget their methodology so completely when dealing with individuals. They go right ahead and expect their clients to "learn" by some happy combination of "motives" and "stimulation" which they would not think of invoking in their own experimental designs. It seems to the writer that psychotherapy which does not encourage the client to put his hypotheses in testable form — in other words, in terms of plausible alternatives — is no less sterile than are scientific efforts which are guilty of the same oversight.

Now it is not always easy to get clients to consider the opposite ends of their constructs. It is not always easy, for that matter, to get graduate students to design their research around alternative hypotheses. Like clients, graduate students are likely to be so bent on "proving" something (a hostile type of behavior) that they cannot *discover* what is under their noses. They have difficulty even in setting up the simplest of all basic research designs, the experimental test of a hypothesis in its experimental versus its null form. Clients, too, often try to keep the opposite ends of their constructs submerged. The therapist who always takes a passive role may find that a client can add elements to the exposed side of his construct for hour after hour and never once seem to add any elements to the other end. Of course, this may be misleading. Sometimes clients are covertly adding elements to the submerged end of their constructs and may even do a little surreptitious experimenting with alternatives. But the therapist who wishes to employ the method of controlled elaboration must see to it that alternatives are explored.

e. *Getting the client to elaborate the alternative pattern.* To come back to our hostile client who has been complaining that he is handicapped because his mother gave him a bad deal! The more he elaborates how he would behave differently *if* all this had not happened to him, the clearer the alternative pattern becomes. Suppose he says, "If I had been given more security as a child I would have had more self-confidence and I would have advanced in my job instead of being fired. Now look at me. I cannot hold a job. I cannot . . . I cannot . . ." and so on, and so on — and the client is back again on the other side of his construction. The therapist may persist: "It is not clear to me what it is that you cannot do. Can you give me some illustrations? . . . Now I am still not clear — just what would you have done in that situation *if* you had had the kind of self-confidence that you failed to acquire? . . . Now is that the way you would like to act?"

Elaboration of the alternatives may so clarify them that the client may start to experiment with them spontaneously. On the other hand, the therapist's efforts to get the client to elaborate alternatives may result in even louder howls of complaint. The therapist should not forget that this client is hostile — we have postulated a hostile client in this illustration — and he should be alert to the fact that the client is trying to protect his investment. What he wants is vindication. If he were to become a successful, well-adjusted person now he would lose the biggest wager of his life. He might lose his role and suffer sharp pangs of guilt. He might find his whole construction system shaken with quivering anxiety.

f. *Exploration of alternatives.* But suppose that the alternatives are sufficiently elaborated to enable the client to try some modest experiments. Ordinarily they should first be tried in the therapy room, although this is difficult for the therapist to control. The elaboration may result in the client's attempting some abortive, but superficial, movement. He may swagger down the street in the manner he thinks he would have if his child- hood had been different. He may indulge in boasting before his friends. The therapist must be alert to the new trends and help the client pursue the implications of his alternative behavior as realistically as possible. The swaggering and the boasting indi- cate that the therapy is entering a new phase. It does not sug- gest that the construction system has been profoundly altered, although the behavior may stand out in sharp contrast to his earlier querulousness. It may or may not get the client into trouble. The therapist, realizing the hostility in the case, will be alert to the possibility that this is a means of extorting con- firmation of some construction that has not yet been clarified and that it may not represent a forward-looking form of aggres- sion.

What the therapist hopes is that the client will unleash his aggression in the direction of exploration. He hopes that the client, with alternative modes of behavior clarified and clearly within reach, will give them a trial. Thus he may be enabled to pick up from the point where he hypothetically would have been if his mother had not disappointed him. The therapist hopes that gradually the client will abandon his investment in the idea that he was saddled with insecurity. This is a big order, for it is likely that there is much structure that rests on that particular idea. The therapist cannot expect that the transi- tion can be made quickly, with unstudied finesse, or without anxiety.

g. *Discovery of incompatibility.* Consider again the obverse side of the construct. Take our client. Suppose the notion that he is a psychological cripple is elaborated in detail. Sooner or later our client confronts himself with evidence which does not support his construct or which he does not care to construe in such a manner as to validate his construction of himself. Now he faces incompatibility of his notion of crippledness with other constructs of his system. Can he accept the incompatibility?

According to our theoretical assumptions his acceptance of the incompatibility will depend upon the permeability of his superordinate structure. If he accepts it and the superordinate structure is fairly *tightly* defined, he will begin to suffer anxiety at this point. If it is *loose* and schizoid, he may not be fazed by the discrepancy. In the latter case controlled elaboration would not be the main feature of the psychotherapeutic design anyway. In the former case the anxiety may lead to revision of the troublesome construction, provided the superordinate structure holds up and does not go *loose*. If the structure goes *loose*, the therapist will know that he has put too much strain upon it. If he is quick enough to note the *loosening*, he may be able to save the situation by discontinuing or altering the elaboration before a break occurs. The same hazard is present when the reverse side of the construct is elaborated, though, in the writer's experience, the likelihood seems not quite as great. Perhaps that is because the alternative construction is subjected only to a little validation at a time and is thus itself held *loosely* at first.

h. *Backward elaboration.* Controlled elaboration can move backward in time as well as forward. Our client was disturbed because his mother did not absolve him from guilt in the incident he cited. The therapist may concern himself with the nature of the guilt that the client felt. Was the accusation of theft leveled at him by the neighbor the only threat to his role status? Had he been dislodged, perhaps, from his role in some other way? Had, for example, an impeccably righteous father displaced him in his relation to his mother? Assuming that the accusation of theft was grossly misplaced, is it still possible that a similar accusation about some other matter could have been substantiated at the time? Was it this *other* dislodgment from role that really called for reinstatement from the mother? Is our client still suffering from *guilt*?

This type of controlled elaboration involves procedures which more closely resemble those of psychoanalysis. From our point of view, such backward elaboration is not always necessary or wise. It has a tendency, temporarily at least, to discourage experimentation with the present and a tendency to place undue emphasis upon that most despondent of all themes — the theme that the client is the victim of his past.

5. IMPLICATIONS OF ELABORATION

What happens when one listens to a person elaborate his complaints? Should "catharsis," "unloading," or "abreaction" ever be discouraged in the interest of the client? These are important questions.

There are some persons who find it easy to air their troubles to anyone who will listen. They do it frequently and glibly. A clinician who accepts a client on this basis may not be building any particularly new relationship in the client's life. But neither is he likely to be establishing a relationship which can ever be psychotherapeutically useful. The client who complains loudly and often is likely to be hostile. We may therefore see him as casting out a dragnet for appeasement. He plays any new situation for what it is worth, collects what appeasement he can, and goes on to the next promising situation. He may even appear to be a responsive client, at first; but, sooner or later, the clinician is unwilling or unable to give him full satisfaction, and then he turns elsewhere for validation of his original construings. While "listening out" such clients is not an appropriate clinical procedure, there is no reason to believe that it is particularly damaging.

But with other types of clients it is a different story. Consider the client, also hostile, who has never expressed her hostility aggressively. She has presented herself to her family and her friends as a compliant affectionate person. She has considered herself as compliant and affectionate — anything but hostile. Recently she has been finding herself indulging in resentful thoughts. The validational material she has needed to retain the use of her original construings has not been forthcoming. She sees herself, as any hostile person does, as having enmeshed herself in a situation from which there is no comprehensive conceptual escape. That being the case, she must somehow extort validation from her social world. She begins to have fantasies of misfortunes befalling members of her family. She begins to realize that these fantasies have a wishlike quality. Her whole construct system is threatened with a shaking up. She is disturbed.

Suppose this client comes to a clinician. Anxiously she reveals her hostile impulses. As she speaks she finds it hard to believe that it is she who is talking. The very thought of herself abandoning the construction of herself that she has so long retained and the role which she has so long enacted in the light of her interpretation of other persons is deeply disturbing. At the end of the interview she has a strange feeling that is a mixture of confusion and relief. She is not sure how she should behave when she goes home, or indeed how she can behave. As she prepares to leave she eagerly awaits a word from the clinician about the next appointment. In her newly established role relation with him she sees some sort of bridge between her old construction of life and the vague new one which is about to thrust itself upon her.

Let us look more closely at what may be happening. The client has built her system of role relationships upon her construction of the construction systems of other people. She has behaved in the light of her own theory of how other people thought and responded in their interpersonal relationships. She has come to see other people as persons who must be humored and served if one is to get anywhere with them. This construction of the thinking of other people cuts two ways. She has been seeing it as providing the only alternative which opens any opportunity for elaboration, and furthermore she now sees it as the construction upon which she has staked her whole life role.

But the compliant role has been offering her fewer and fewer opportunities for elaboration. Why, then, cannot she herself be one of those who requires compliance? In asking herself this question she is not rotating her principal construct axis, she is only considering the possibility of replotting herself with respect to it. To her way of thinking, the question becomes one of justifying herself. How can she protect her original investment in her construct of a world filled with appeasement-seeking people? Perhaps she can best protect her investment by being one of the appeasement-seeking ones herself, rather than one of the appeasement-giving ones. But this, though it is based on the same basic pair of alternatives, may cast her in a new life role. The abandonment of the old role means guilt feelings — a particularly distressing derivative of anxiety.

The client has come to a clinician. She has ventured to express resentment. The clinician has not condemned her as she might have expected. Her first feeble experiment in the appeasement-demanding role was successful! Dare she try it elsewhere? No, only with the clinician!

Now what has the clinician done for her? She feels an excited apprehensive kind of relief. But has he helped her? Our answer at this stage of the relationship would be no. He has only allowed a relationship to develop which may, if properly handled, be turned to therapeutic ends. It may be a long long way from here to the point where the client can resolve her hostility. If the relationship between client and clinician is broken at this point, there may be serious consequences in the area of the client's social relationships. The fact that the clinician has behaved in an accepting manner right at the moment of her most radical departure from her customary role may make life much harder for her than it would have been if he had not listened in the first place. Both guilt and anxiety have been accentuated by her interview-room venture. This is no time to abandon her to her newly aroused impulses.

But what would have happened if the clinician had listened to her and then taken pains to reject or drown out the notes of hostility? Perhaps in this particular case, though not in all, the need for a continuing psychotherapeutic relationship would be less urgent. Yet if the clinician listens to the story and, in his eagerness not to entangle himself with the case, behaves as one of the intransigent members of the client's family, he may, willy-nilly, be acting to validate the client's original construction of her role.

a. *Listening involves a commitment.* What the clinician should always bear in mind is that, regardless of whether he is accepting or rejecting, active or noncommittal, perceptive or obtuse, he creates a professional obligation for himself whenever he lets a person confide in him. This is just as true whether the confiding occurs in a clinic interview room or on a railway train. If the confiding person is aware that the listener is a professional person, greater reliance is likely to be placed upon him, and his professional obligation is proportionally increased.

One way of saying what we consider so important at this point is that the acceptance of elaboration tends to build a strong "transference" relationship. While in the psychology of personal constructs the term "transference" is defined somewhat differently from the customary way, the implication for the issue at hand is the same. If it is dependencies which are transferred, then the listening clinician finds himself in the position of a key element in the newly elaborated dependencies. If it is hostile demands that are transferred, then the clinician is a key datum in the client's new extortive experiment.

Our general rule for listening to people confide intimate matters is that we should do so only to the extent that we are willing to accept responsibility for seeing that the venture works out well for the person who confides. As we have endeavored to show, this responsibility goes far beyond mere acceptance, for acceptance, followed by abandonment of the relationship or by simple indulgence, may do more harm than good.

b. *The academic counselor's commitment.* This issue of how much of a person's story can properly be listened to has some interesting ramifications. Consider the psychological counselor on a university campus. Ordinarily he is not in a position in which he can properly restrict his services to a small number of long-term treatment cases. It is, of course, ridiculous for him to say that he will see only "normal" people. He will see those who come to him! And if he is reasonably alert, he will soon realize that the varieties and degrees of disturbances appearing before him are as great as or greater than those confronting any psychiatrist in private practice. The only abnormal people whom he can be sure of not seeing are those who happen, at the moment, to be institutionalized elsewhere. Sometimes even those are referred by their psychiatrists for part-time university training.

At some point in his interview with a disturbed student, the counselor begins to realize that the case is going to require more intensive services than he is prepared to offer. He must decide where to refer the student. How deeply should he go into the client's problems before making the referral, and what damage may result from his "rejection" of the client after having accepted an intimate type of relationship? The services available in a university community are likely to be varied and highly specialized. The kind of problem one would refer to one service might be badly handled at another. Moreover, the longer one listens the more likely he is to detect underlying problems which are of altogether a different nature from those expressed in the nominal complaint.

The writer has engaged in some spirited discussion with those who believe that a counselor in such a case should pursue his diagnostic inquiry to considerable depth. Logically, this might appear always to be justified, since in a highly specialized professional community there are all too few services which are sufficiently comprehensive to guarantee that the client will be seen in proper perspective. Psychological training should help one see such matters in proper perspective. Indeed, it probably provides better perspective than do any of the other service specialties at the present time, but it is no sure preventive of shortsightedness. Still, a thoroughgoing diagnosis of a person's problem is a major undertaking, and it is one which is not likely to be complete until one is in the last stages of therapy.

It is practically impossible to distinguish sharply between the planning stage of therapy, which is diagnosis, and the treatment stage of therapy. If one's diagnostic system were no more than a set of nosological pigeonholes, it might be feasible for the psychological counselor to continue his interviews to a point where he could tuck his client into one of them and make a routine referral. But a therapeutic relationship is not one in which a therapist applies a specific treatment to a sharply classified fault; it is itself an elaborative procedure and involves a moving relationship. The psychological counselor should not expect to be able to classify the case in two or three interviews. Nor should he be overeager to impose his own set of constructs on all elements in the case. The best that he can expect to do is consider the kind of relationship the client now appears ready to accept and profit from, and hope that the development of such a relationship with a certain person will lead in turn to his use of whatever other community resources are able to serve him effectively.

From our point of view, then, the psychological counselor should exercise great caution against accepting elaboration from, and building relationship with, clients whom he expects to refer elsewhere. There is ample clinical evidence to support the idea that clients who have been passed from clinician to clinician and referred from agency to agency, after having told the intimate details of their story and after having tried time after time to establish a relationship with someone, are demoralized by their odyssey. If one is going to refer the client, he should do so as soon as possible. Referring him to the precise specialist who is experienced with the client's particular type of problem is probably less important than that the client shall have an opportunity to develop a therapeutic relationship with someone who is reasonably competent, even though that person is only partially specialized in dealing with the client's particular type of problem. Once the client is secured in a therapeutic relationship, it should be possible to procure the necessary services of specialists on an adjunctive basis. Certainly our concern with the therapeutic specialty should not cause us to overlook the therapy itself.

B. *The Complaint*

6. ELABORATION OF THE COMPLAINT

Most therapeutic elaboration starts with an elaboration of the complaint or of something which corresponds to a complaint. It is not necessary that a therapeutic series start out in this way; Indeed, it is sometimes preferable to preface the series with one or two tightly controlled interviews in which routine background information is demanded of the client without giving him an opportunity to say what he wants to say or what he considers relevant to his problem. However, if it is expected that the client is to take an active part in developing his own therapeutic program, the clinician should ordinarily not start out by robbing him of his initiative. Many times the client who is most reluctant to surrender his initiative is the one who becomes most helpless once it has been taken away from him. Technically speaking, we may say that his initial struggle to keep the initiative is a struggle to preserve the integrity of his construct system against the sizable *threat* of *dependency*. Psychologists who have observed patients admitted to hospitalization according to standard medical procedures are well aware of the deterioration in morale with the resultant and unnecessary delay in recovery that often follows. The recently discovered advantages of an active program for the patient following surgery or childbirth should serve to make the psychoclinician aware of the value of any client's retaining some degree of initiative.

a. *Uncontrolled elaboration of the complaint.* The client's elaboration of his complaint can be allowed to proceed without specific direction from the therapist. This is the nondirective feature of the "nondirective" — now "client-centered" — school of psychotherapy. When this procedure is used the therapist is by no means a bystander. He may murmur acceptance which the client is free to construe in almost any way he wishes. Or, if he makes no noises, his attentive manner similarly permits him to be used by the client as a target for projected perceptions. The therapist may "reflect feeling" by repeating "feeling words" or "feeling phrases" in a mildly puzzled or questioning manner. Thus the client is invited to restructure his discourse wherever it shows looseness or the characteristics of one of the transitional diagnostic constructs — threat, fear, anxiety, or guilt. The therapist's timing may be such as to allow for circumspection or it may be quickened so as to encourage preemption and control. In the latter case, the therapist will appear to be more spontaneous, though he will scarcely go so far as to whistle, stomp his feet, and pound the table.

With most therapists the phase of undirected elaboration of the complaint is brought to a close when the elaboration becomes repetitive. If the client formulates his problem quite narrowly and refuses to consider "peripheral" issues, the therapist may allow the undirected elaboration to continue to a point where it must be obvious to the client that his discourse is in a rut.

There are techniques for making the client aware of his repetitiousness. The client can be asked to repeat in detail what he said in the preceding interview, with considerable attention being given to recalling the precise phrasing and the precise sequence. He can be asked to compare and contrast today's interview with the last interview or his first interview. He can be asked to enact the part of himself as he was in the preceding interview. He can be asked to enact the part of the therapist in the preceding interview, with the therapist temporarily taking the part of the client. This technique requires delicate sensitivity from the therapist, lest he portray a too sharply drawn caricature of the client.

b. *Contraindications for uncontrolled elaboration.* There are contraindicators for the undirected elaboration of complaint which should be observed by the psychotherapist. We have already mentioned two — the unwillingness of the psychotherapist to "see the case through" and excessive repetition in the client's formulation. Excessive *guilt* feelings are another. As the guilty person elaborates his loss of role, he is likely to perceive himself as more and more cut off from those resources which he needs to sustain himself. He is likely to be confronted with the alternative of checking the process by becoming hostile and demanding appeasement or of trying to conform to his remaining resources by constricting. In the former case he may appear "paranoid"; in the latter, suicidal.

Consider the case of a man, perhaps fifty years of age, who seeks psychotherapeutic help after experiencing some panic reactions. He has started on a trip but soon feels "caught" by the itinerary that he and his wife have agreed upon. He insists that they turn around and drive home. He complains that he gets "nervous" whenever he finds himself in a position which is indefensible in terms of the most legalistic moral standards. He feels his wife is stronger than he, both sexually and intellectually. As he spontaneously elaborates his complaint in the interview room he develops documentation for his loss of role. This brings the guilt features of the case to the fore. How much more undirected elaboration should the therapist accept?

It is reasonable to assume that the client, if he continues to develop the guilt theme, will so document it that he will pre-emptively construe his social situation. This is an invitation to act aggressively. But his aggressive efforts to explore his dependency constructs are hostile because they are appeasement seeking. And they are role destroying because they are incompatible with the obsequious techniques by which he has customarily maintained himself in his role. If his superordinate constructs were somewhat looser, the incompatibility would not necessarily disturb him deeply. He could then become "schizoid." If he were able to systematize his hostility and resolve the incompatibility under some tight, though specious, construction, he might handle the guilt as a "paranoid."

But he has another approach. He keeps his appeasement-seeking hostility but he avoids complete *role* loss by constricting the area in which he allows his aggressive efforts to operate. Thus he compromises. Some childlike dependency structures are kept operational. He keeps the vestiges of his childhood role. Guilt is thus kept within bounds.

Now suppose he is asked to tell his life story and freely elaborate his complaint. His field is momentarily dilated. Constrictive limits are lifted. We may now expect guilt features to become more apparent. The alert therapist may see them alternating with childlike bids for *role* status and momentary recourses to constrictive measures. But suppose the therapist is not alert enough to foresee the outcome of continued spontaneous elaboration of the complaint. Suppose he even lets the client express "insight" into the "childishness" of his bid for role status. Then documentation in support of the client's loss of role soon reaches insurmountable proportions. Constriction by suicide may be the client's only remaining answer.

There are also other types of cases in which the guilt feature would contraindicate continued undirected elaboration of the complaint. But perhaps this will suffice to illustrate the misuse of this important psychotherapeutic procedure in a case involving guilt.

c. *Contraindication in cases of loose construction.* Continued undirected elaboration of the complaint is contraindicated in cases where construction is so loose in the complaint area that the client cannot consolidate his gains. Such a client "goes to pieces" conceptually when he deals with his complaint. Yet suppose — though many clients will not do this — he continues to try to elaborate the complaint area. The continued use of elaboration implies that the therapist hopes to make some gains thereby. He hopes that the client will reach some conclusions upon which he can stand while reaching out for further conclusions. Yet, if every conclusion is so loosely interpreted that what is seen as black today is seen as white tomorrow and it is a tossup as to whether any new experience will be assigned to the black or white category, then the day-after-day reaching of such conclusions is therapeutically unprofitable.

There is even the possibility that continued undirected elaboration of the complaint will lead to further loosening. Elaboration usually produces some dilation of the client's field. The field becomes cluttered up with more elements — an invitation to further loosening of constructs. If the therapist can control the elaboration, both as to content and range, he stands a better chance of helping the client establish some reasonably tight new constructs of sufficient permeability to deal with the immediate future. But this means *controlled elaboration* and we have been talking about contraindications for the *undirected elaboration* of the complaint.

7. CONTROLLED ELABORATION OF THE COMPLAINT

Controlled elaboration of the complaint enables the clinician to circumvent some of the hazards that inhere in letting the client ramble on and on about his troubles. The therapist can steer the client away from the more repetitive features of his complaining. He can avoid the elaboration of complaint areas which are likely to overdocument the client's loss of role. He can set a quarantine against the spread of anxiety by placing certain areas of discussion temporarily out of bounds. He can direct the elaboration to safe areas where there is a reasonable chance of new construction which will be firm enough for the client to stand on during the next succeeding stages of therapy. He can avoid premature completions of the Circumspection-Preemption-Control Cycle (C–P–C Cycle) which might get the client into further trouble with society. He can avoid developing a relationship with his client which will place him under a professional obligation to continue the psychotherapeutic sequence when he is not prepared to do so.

While controlled elaboration of the complaint has all these advantages over undirected elaboration, it involves one important hazard. People have their own ingenious ways of getting themselves into trouble. Until the therapist has heard his client expound his own personal formulas, he will not know precisely how his particular client manages to incapacitate himself. The therapist's efforts to limit the elaboration may keep him out of contact with the client's personal construct system and thus make it impossible to assume a meaningful role in relation to the client.

8. SEVEN BASIC QUESTIONS FOR THE ELABORATION OF THE COMPLAINT

In a previous chapter we mentioned briefly seven basic questions for the elaboration of any complaint. They were:

a. Upon what problems do you wish help?
b. When were these problems first noticed?
c. Under what conditions did these problems first appear?
d. What corrective measures have been attempted?
e. What changes have come with treatment or the passing of time?
f. Under what conditions are the problems most noticeable?
g. Under what conditions are the problems least noticeable?

The formulation of the questions is designed to get the client (1) to place the problems, if possible, on a time line, (2) to see them as fluid and transient, and then to interpret them as responsive to (a) treatment, (b) the passing of time, and (c) varying conditions.

Our basic stand with respect to psychotherapy, as should be clear by now, is that the way problems are construed is a major determinant of whether or not they can be solved. In psychotherapy, as in science, the object is to formulate questions in an answerable as well as in a relevant form. The task of the therapist is similar to that of the research adviser. He must help the client to formulate testable hypotheses. He must help the client conceptualize variables which can be operationally distinguished. He must assist the client in making an experimental design that lets the data — not personal wishes — choose between two or more alternatives. He advises the client how to keep commitments down to a size appropriate to the risks involved. He teaches him how to use laboratory facilities — in psychotherapy the principal laboratory is the interview room.

Our seven basic questions are, therefore, questions as appropriately addressed to the research workers as to the disturbed client. Moreover, they are questions which are as applicable to an industrial-psychology situation as to a clinical-psychology situation. For example, a plant executive asks a psychological consultant to help him install "a training program." The competent industrial consultant psychologist will not immediately rush out to the plant and start thrusting a copy of the last training program he has devised under the noses of supervisors and foremen. Rather, he will go to considerable pains to find just what it is that the plant executive has on his mind — he seeks the *complaint,* and he seeks to have it *elaborated.*

As the complaint is elaborated, he may discover that what the executive is most concerned about is labor turnover. As the executive continues to elaborate, it may become increasingly clear that the factors affecting labor turnover are not likely to be influenced by a training program. Furthermore, an expensive training program may accentuate the costs of the labor turnover. Lest this seem like an attempt to give a pat answer to an industrial problem, let us explain also that it is conceivable that a training program, properly coordinated with a personnel upgrading and an equipment modernization program, could be helpful in a high turnover situation.

This is not the place to discuss the application of the psychology of personal constructs to industrial problems, but perhaps our brief illustration suffices to illustrate the applicability of controlled elaborative methods to a wide variety of complaints and social situations. This is not to say, as we have attempted to explain earlier, that complaints should always be elaborated; there are conditions under which one does not wish to have the issues crystallized prematurely.

9. THE CLIENT'S INTERPRETATION OF CAUSES

It is a common procedure among some clinicians to press the client to explain *why* he has the difficulties he complains about. The clinician interposes such questions as, "Why?" "What do you think caused that?" "Can you imagine why that would be?"

The procedure represents an attempt to force the client to rationalize his behavior. To the clinician who thinks that mental health is an attainment of "the rational man," this seems like a good idea. But from our point of view, verbal rationalization does not necessarily facilitate psychological anticipatory processes nor does it necessarily make a person a better neighbor to live next door to. It may help the client to displace the chaos of anxiety with the cosmos of verbal structure, but there is always the danger that the structure will be a hostile one for which the person will demand vindication rather than one which he submits to the outcomes of natural truth. All too frequently the "rational man" is one who tries to dispel anxiety by serving an ultimatum on nature.

There are limits, therefore, which must be observed by the therapist who seeks to control the client's elaboration by asking him to explain why he feels as he does. Within these limits the procedure is often profitable. It may lead quickly to an understanding of the client's personal construction of life. It may represent an expression of the psychotherapist's interest, a *credulous attitude* which we discussed in an earlier chapter. It may suggest that behavior and feelings must have an explanation and that finding the explanation is relevant to the success of therapy.

Contraindications for this type of controlled elaboration of the complaint include, of course, any combination of extreme anxiety and aggression. They also include any evidence of highly systematized hostility. Moreover, one should not attempt this type of elaboration if he believes that there are some areas which the client might attempt to elaborate and which might fall apart once he started to investigate them in detail. For example, a person whose sex role is only precariously established, and yet who has a great investment in maintaining his present sex role, may be unexpectedly precipitated into guilt and anxiety by this kind of elaboration. Finally, one should not attempt this type of elaboration if he expects the client to develop a dependency role relationship with him as a preparatory step toward later elaboration of preverbal constructs or "deep" therapy.

10. CASTING THE COMPLAINT INTO A SOCIAL FRAMEWORK

The clinician may ask, "Have you known of other people who had this same difficulty?" "What do other people usually do about this type of trouble?" "Do you know of people who have overcome it?" "How?" "Why did some people not overcome it?" "Tell about that person — what was he like?"

This type of control over elaboration helps bring the complaint within the system of axes which the client recognizes as socially valid. It brings the wisdom of society to bear upon the complaint and helps the client to find some firm footing upon which to stand while he surveys his problem. Of course, the social wisdom which is invoked is that which the client himself construes, but generally it represents a better-validated set of personal axes than those with which he privately identifies himself. Furthermore, the approach helps detach the client from his problem and helps place him in a better position to judge the problem as a problem, without trying to judge himself as a person. In a sense, the complaint is detached from the client and identified as the complaint of someone else. There it can be reconstrued without all the threatening implications that reconstruction would have if it were his complaining self who was to be reconstrued.

Not all clients will go along with this kind of elaboration. They may claim that no other person has ever had their complaint or that no other person has had so few resources with which to cope with it. If the former objection is raised, the clinician will make note of the disidentification with the rest of society and the possible guilt implication. If the latter objection is raised, the clinician will make a note to follow up the implications for the client's dependency structure. The very way the client raises his objections to the type of elaboration suggested should throw considerable light upon his personal construction system. Finally, the clinician should not assume, just because the client verbally rejects the suggestion, that there will be no later viewing of the problem in a cultural or societal manner. What a client says he will not do and what he privately attempts to do are frequently in sharp contrast with each other.

This type of approach is usually quite safe, although there are cases where it can lead to trouble. The extremely guilty person may have his guilt feelings accentuated by looking at his problem in this way. He may take it as confrontation with the fact that he is not like other people, that he is not dealing with his problem the way he is expected to, or that he really does not understand other people well enough to maintain a role relationship with them.

11. CONFRONTATION

There is more to the complaint than what the client is willing to talk about. Frequently other people complain about the client. Frequently the client's behavior expresses a complaint that he does not explicitly define in words. Sometimes the trend of events, as for example those of a disease or aging process, causes the clinician to be concerned about complaints that may arise in the future.

There are occasions when it is advisable to confront the client with complaints which he has not mentioned. Ordinarily this is done in order to give him a chance to elaborate them and to profit from the clarification such elaboration may produce. Elaboration is a way of spinning a web of structure. The structure, once it is in place, lends stability and poise to one's psychological stance.

The elaboration which follows confrontation may be either uncontrolled or further controlled by the therapist. The confrontation is itself, of course, a type of control of elaboration. It sets the client down in the midst of a situation which is not of his own choosing. The therapist can then let him swim for it or he can help him find bottom so that he can wade out. Sometimes the therapist has to rescue him outright. He can change the topic of discussion, provide support, or offer reassurance.

a. *Clarifying the diagnostic picture by confrontation.* Frequently confrontation is attempted in order to clarify the diagnostic picture for the clinician. The clinician, in deciding what measures are required, needs to know how the client is likely to deal with issues which he has not yet mentioned. In evaluating the client's response to the confrontation the clinician will examine the form as well as the content. Is the client able to elaborate the new complaint beyond its patent features? Does he limit his elaboration to conventionalized generalities? Are the constructs he invokes to deal with the expanded complaint area relevant? Are they tightly enough construed so that he can make the necessary discriminations? Are they permeable to new experience?

b. *Confrontation to clarify the therapeutic relationship.* Sometimes confrontation is used to provide a broader base for the relationship between client and therapist. If the client has been skirting a problem in hopes that he would not have to discuss it with the clinician, it is possible that his role relationship with the clinician will be too narrowly construed to be useful. The confrontation may give the clinician a chance to demonstrate his wide acceptance of the client, even though "he knows the worst." The client, who may have been waiting for the clinician to "drop the other shoe," may be considerably relieved when the initial shock is over.

c. *Confrontation to produce transition.* Most frequently confrontation is used to produce transition in a therapeutic series. The client may have been elaborating his construction system as it applies to one or two areas only. There is the likelihood that the constructs being evolved will not have sufficient permeability to encompass other problem areas. At a chosen time the therapist adds new problem areas to the client's field of discussion. Will his newly formed constructs have sufficient range of convenience to span the new issues? Will they have sufficient permeability?

When confrontation is used to produce transition, the therapist should not be surprised to find transitional behavior. It is likely that the transitional diagnostic constructs — threat, fear, anxiety, and guilt — will be applicable to what he observes. In "façade" cases he may be perfectly willing to take the risk involved in stimulating transition. In "conversion hysteria" cases confrontation is almost sure to produce marked evidences of hostility. In cases of brain deterioration it usually leads to marked loosening of construction. This is followed by "concretistic" attempts to recuperate — that is, resort to more *impermeable* constructions. The therapist must be aware of the possibility that increasing the client's guilt or anxiety by confrontation will accelerate his compensatory efforts. The client may become depressed and resort to constriction.

d. *Ethical considerations.* Clinicians are frequently asked to see clients on the basis of fictitious complaints. Parents often tell their children that they are "taking them to the doctor to have their teeth looked at, to see how they are growing," and so on. The clinician is asked to "play along" with this deception but at the same time to do something psychologically for the child. The wise and ethical clinician will not accept a client on such grounds. If he finds that a client has been brought to him under deception it is his responsibility to make some appropriate formulation of the complaint and let the client deal with it, explaining that it represents the initial basis for the clinical relationship.

It is not necessary for the clinician to attempt to confront the client with a detailed formulation of a complaint. At this stage such a detailed formulation would be an artifact anyway. He may say simply, "I guess you have been in trouble with the police lately. Perhaps I can help you." Or he may say, for example, "Your parents wanted me to look at your teeth but they seem to be more worried about the way they have had to scold you lately. Sometimes I can help children keep from being scolded so much. Maybe I can help you."

It is not necessary for the clinician to document the complaint or to insist that the client accept it as valid. Sometimes the child will say, "Just what did they tell you?" The clinician does not need to try to substantiate the parents' claims nor does he himself necessarily need to try to judge their validity immediately. The complaint is a matter of construction, and usually a highly personalized construction at that. To try to impose the parents' construction upon the client at the outset of treatment is to miss the whole point of the psychology of personal constructs. The therapist, then, should be careful to make it clear that he understands that the complaint lodged by the parents is a personalized sort of thing. So he says, for example, "Well, they told me something about how *they felt*. They were worried. But I don't know what there *really* is to worry about because I haven't had a chance to talk to *you* about it." This response, while somewhat oblique, represents an attempt to keep the complaint in its place as a personal construct of the person who formulated it. The clinician is careful not to say, "Well, they told me something about what *happened*." That would take the account out of the realm of personal construction.

It is not necessary to follow up the confrontation with probing. The clinician can change the topic or make it easy for the client to do so as soon as the confrontation has been introduced. The client usually comes back to it when he is ready. The purpose of confrontation is not necessarily to get the client to make a deposition. If the therapist is suspending judgment anyway, the deposition may be irrelevant.

12. REFLECTION PROCEDURES

The therapist may confront the client with the client's own complaints. Rogers' approach, in client-centered therapy, is, as we have mentioned before, to reflect "feeling." The fact that it is "feeling" that is being reflected is kept apparent by the way the therapist asks the reflective question.

Deutsch uses a procedure which he calls "associative anamnesis." First, he tries to familiarize himself with the client's vocabulary and the repetitious passages that can be detected in his spontaneously elaborated complaint. He then selects key words and terms which appear to have particular significance to the client. These are then reflected repeatedly in an effort to discover how they can be elaborated by the client. The chains of association which they initiate are taken as indications of the causal linkages by which the client's thinking gets him into difficulty.

The reflection can be repetitive, in order to see what changes the client can ring on the key terms. It can also be sequential, in order to see where the associative chains lead. The client says, for example, "Every time she does that, I get mad." The therapist has noted that "mad" is a key term appearing to have particularly rich meaning for the client. He then says, "Mad?" The client may say, "Yes, she oughtn't to do that to me. She has no *right to*." The therapist repeats, "*Mad?* What do you mean — *mad?*" . . . "I don't understand just how you mean you were *mad*." If the chain association is used, the therapist may say, instead, "*Right to?*" The client may say, "Yes, she is *always* doing that." The therapist says, "*Always?*" and so on.

Deutsch utilizes the technique in connection with a restricted form of therapy he calls "sector therapy." In our terminology this would be a form of controlled elaboration with certain topical areas chosen for elaboration and certain other areas intentionally skirted. As the therapist becomes more and more familiar with the client's key terms, the associations which enrich them, and the linkages by which they are connected with the various areas of the client's life, he begins to interweave the terms into the therapeutic discourse. Thus he seeks to establish new meanings and new causal chains of association.

The reflection of key terms, or simply the client's commonly used terms, is a general technique which can be used in a variety of situations. Indeed, elaboration can be encouraged simply by picking up and reflecting the terminal phrase of the client's last sentence. Ramsdell reports that the technique has remarkable possibilities in ordinary social conversation where one has difficulty keeping his mind on what his companion is saying — and is not particularly interested anyhow. He reports that the technique works so efficiently that one is likely to find himself drenched with more bubbling conversation than he cares to listen to.

There is some formal research evidence to indicate that there are advantages to reflecting the client's own productions rather than confronting him exclusively with stock material. Bixler has shown that nouns selected from protocol produced by the client, when used in an association test, consistently produce a somewhat different type of material from words taken out of the Kent-Rosanoff List. They produce different "feeling tones" and more recollection of past events. Moreover, when used in combinations with words from the Kent-Rosanoff List, they enrich the clinical production.

13. THEMATIC REFLECTION

The "chain association" has long been used in psychotherapy. The use of reflection to develop chains into narratives and narratives into thema may be called "thematic reflection." If the narrative involves a plot or theme which can be abstracted from it and which can be recognized as similar to that abstracted from other contents, the therapist may set about to make a thematic analysis of the client's production. This is one of the ways skilled clinicians interpret the significance of Thematic

Apperception Test protocol, although it should be pointed out in passing that most clinicians appear now to prefer to make "figure" analyses of the TAT. If the therapist takes definite steps to keep the sequence of associations linked up by means of selected confrontations, we have a controlled type of elaboration of the theme.

Thematic development and analysis of protocol, whether it be protocol which is produced in a psychotherapeutic session or in response to the ambiguous pictures of the Thematic Apperception Test, require considerable skill. Not many clinicians have developed that skill sufficiently to be able to use it effectively in psychotherapy. Not only must one be able to construe the client's contextual groupings, but he must be able to follow his *elaborative choices*. That is to say, he must not only be able to see how the client discriminates but, once the alternatives are set up, he must be able to see what the client's elaborative choice is. Following that, he must be able to see how the ensuing experience is construed and what the elaborative choice in each construct dimension is. This means that the clinician must be able to construe the client's life role, an interpretation that requires not only that the clinician subsume the client's separate constructs but that he subsume their superordination-subordination arrangement in the client's construction system.

If the therapist employs reflection in order to tease out the thema in the client's construction system, he can do so by such responses as the following. "You have told me about your mother. You have told me about the incident in your back yard. What comes next? . . . What follows? . . . Can you tell me just why it follows?" The therapist reflects selected elements from the client's previous production in the hope that this confrontation will cause the client to delineate a theme which the therapist can understand or which will lead to experiences calling for revision of the theme. This is similar to the controlled elaboration of the client's thinking about causation, which was discussed in an earlier passage in this chapter.

Thematic analysis, however, involves much more. It involves an organized sequence of transitions specifically involving the

client himself, rather than merely the separate individual constructs that explain certain impersonal types of causal transitions.

14. REVIEW REFLECTION

The review of previous sessions is a form of reflection which
can frequently be used profitably in psychotherapy. The therapist can use it to demonstrate that he has been listening atten-
tively to what has been going on, even though he has not offered
the usual words of approval and disapproval which the client
has been accustomed to expect from interested listeners. The
client may be reassured to learn that he has been listened to.
The review can also be used to set the stage for a series of elaborations which are to be attempted in the remainder of the day's
session.

Review reflection tends to place the subsequent elaboration
at a higher level of superordination than would otherwise be
expected. The client is more inclined to see his performance as
a whole. He is more likely to construe his life role rather than
his role in a certain type of social relationship. He is more likely
to think about the therapeutic sequence than about detailed
incidents. For the moment, this may be what the therapist
wants. The sessions may have appeared to have bogged down
in a sequence of detail which the therapist cannot handle. He
seeks to bring himself and his client together on some superordinate ground and then allow the controlled elaboration to proceed afresh from there.

The procedure may be used to provide a frame of reference
in which the client may construe a changing outlook. Our theoretical position would lead us to believe, not only that our isolated bits of behavior follow constructs, but that the sweeping
changes and evolvements, which are a part of every person's
emerging personality, are themselves personally construed at
some level of cognitive awareness. In an earlier chapter we
emphasized the need for helping the client develop a life-role
construction which would embrace a continuing program of
change in himself. This, then, suggests that it is profitable to

construe change by drawing certain contrasts between the past and the present. The therapist can help the client do this by review reflection. The therapist's choice of what to review, and in what current context to review it, has a lot to do with what contrasts will become obvious to the client and what constructs he will develop to make his changes orderly.

For example, suppose that a client has been voluntarily unemployed for some months. Prior to that, he made several abortive attempts at holding a job, but always gave up after a few days, saying that it was drudgery and that he could not endure it. Suppose that therapy was started after a period of idleness during which there was no effort to secure further employment. Suppose recently in therapy the client has begun to express an interest in the day-by-day activities in a certain job with which he is somewhat familiar. When this spontaneous elaboration has developed some slight measure of structure, the therapist may wish to take steps to exploit the newly awakened interest and help the client to perceive himself as a person capable of changing. He may do this by reviewing, at this juncture, some of the ideas which were expressed in the initial therapy sessions. The array of elements now before the client — the elements produced today and those produced earlier — invites a contrast and a construct to embody it. The same construct, if kept permeable by the addition of appropriate elements in subsequent interviews, may become a valuable movement construct which can be utilized throughout the remainder of therapy, and perhaps through the remainder of life.

The contrast developed in review reflection is sharpened by the selection of elements. Howard has shown that, in a therapeutic situation, there is a sharper contrast in the client's current construction of the past versus the present than there is between the client's current construction of the present and his original construction of what was then "the present." The contrast is, in part, a matter of selection of elements from the remembered past which appear to contrast with the present, and, in part, a matter of reconstruction. In a therapeutically effective situation the client tends to select contrast elements rather than similar elements as he describes his movement. The review reflection is a way of helping him do this.

a. *Hazards of review reflection.* Review reflection has some hazards. If the client is working toward reconstruction, but does not yet have sufficient grasp of potentially contrasting elements, the review may serve only to redocument his old constructs. The therapist may inadvertently have blocked the client in developing new outlooks by smothering him with the old. On the other hand, the therapist may feel that certain old constructs need to be clearly formulated in preparation for testing, invalidation, and eventual abandonment.

The review may threaten the client. If the client feels that he has been moving in recent interviews, the therapist may make the mistake of not construing that movement and of interpreting the client as being as he was several interviews back. This produces a situation to which Landfield's expectancy threat hypothesis is applicable. Under the threat the client may try to take some form of definitive action in relation to therapy and the therapist. The outcome may not be what the therapist would consider desirable.

Again, the therapist may inadvertently betray his prejudices in structuring the review. This too may threaten the client. The more the therapist talks or tries to place verbal structure on what the client has produced, the greater is the likelihood that the sensitive ear of the client will detect harsh notes of criticism and inflexibility. The therapist needs to be particularly careful not to impose upon the reviewed material a theme with which he does not wish to confront the client at this particular time.

Chapter Nineteen

Elaborating the Personal System

WE TURN now from the complaint to the basic task of the psychotherapist: elaboration of the construct system in which his client's difficulties are anchored.

A. Approach to the Construction System

1. ADVANTAGES IN THE ELABORATION OF THE CONSTRUCTION SYSTEM

We make a distinction between the elaboration of the client's complaint and the elaboration of his construction system. The distinction is made largely for convenience in presentation. Actually, of course, the complaint should always be recognized as a feature of the client's construction system and of its relation to the presumed systems of those persons with whom he must get along. There are, however, certain changes in the therapeutic process which take place when one abandons the complaint as a reference point and turns his attention to the client's construction system as a system.

For one thing, when one asks the client to elaborate his construction system he raises the psychotherapeutic issues to a higher level of abstraction. No longer does the therapist deal so explicitly with certain psychological aches and pains. He seeks, rather, to discover what the client has been up to and how the client has been going about it. He seeks to understand the conceptual framework within which the symptoms arose and within which they are currently sustained.

A second outcome of turning one's attention to the construction system is the new emphasis that it places upon seeing alternatives. About the only alternative a client can express in connection with his complaint is that he would like to get well, that he wishes the past had been different, or that people would change their ways of treating him. It is, of course, not quite as simple as this, as a reading of the preceding chapter should indicate; but this much is generally true: the alternatives to the complaint are likely to be unrealistically drawn and oversimplified. The elaboration of the construction system permits the client and the therapist to envision alternatives on a much more comprehensive scale.

A third outcome of turning from the complaint to the construction system is the bringing of more representative elements into the therapeutic picture. This dilation gives both the client and therapist more material to work with in the formulation of new constructs. The complaint picture is likely to be an ideationally impoverished one. Only those ideas which conform to the complaint theme are permitted to arise. In the face of such a biased perceptual field, the therapist is in danger of going down for the count himself. When the client and therapist turn to the construction system as a whole, new features begin to emerge, and both of them stand a better chance of finding a foothold from which to attack the complaint.

A fourth outcome of turning to the elaboration of the construction system is the broadening of the base of the therapeutic relationship. The therapist becomes more than a person who deals merely with one's symptoms; he subsumes more of the client's construction system, and hence has a broader basis for establishing a role relationship with the client. The client is likely to perceive this and, even though he may try to keep the relationship on a limited complaint basis for a time, he will ordinarily respond better to the broad relationship in the end. Such a broadening of the base of the therapist's role relationship thus helps both the therapist and the client.

There are other advantages in the elaboration of the construction system over the elaboration of the complaint, but these we have mentioned are the most conspicuous ones.

2. THE USE OF PSYCHOLOGICAL TESTS IN CONJUNCTION WITH PSYCHO-THERAPY

One approach to the understanding of the client's construction system in psychotherapy is via the use of structured and partially structured tests. Unfortunately, most psychological tests have heretofore been conceived without reference to psychotherapeutic issues. Psychologists have long thought of their task as one of plotting the differences between individuals, as if each person were a fixed body in a galaxy of other fixed bodies and had no rotations, orbits, drifts, or other cyclical movements of his own. Out of this type of thinking all too few reference axes have been developed for plotting the course of individual movement, such as that one seeks to produce in psychotherapy. We have, in short, developed a psychometry of individual differences rather than a psychometry of personal adjustment to life.

Even modern learning theory, with its fresh concern for varying responses to varying stimuli, is severely handicapped by its lack of a suitable system of coordinate axes with reference to which learning changes may be plotted. Only concretistically perceived "responses" are utilized as reference points. That is mere operationalism!

Operationalism is a technical convenience for an experimental science, but it should not take the place of concept formation in the scientist's thinking. Psychologists, and particularly those who are concerned with psychotherapy and social change, sorely need to conceptualize a set of reference axes against which to plot the movement they so ardently hope to produce.

Psychological tests measuring individual differences in intellectual efficiency may provide some service to the psychotherapist by indicating what limitations must be accepted in developing the client's life role. In some measure they may reflect the areas in which competency may be expected — for example, verbal versus performance areas. When carefully observed and analyzed by an experienced clinician, they may give some indication of the presence of anxiety, of constriction, and of the content areas where these handicaps are operative.

Concept-formation tests of the object-sorting type may give, in addition, some idea of the loosening of conceptualization, of preemption, and the like. Their appropriateness for making predictions regarding the client's social adaptations is left open to question by the remoteness of their content from everyday living and the lack of experimental evidence of their relation to personal adjustment. Fundamentally, however, the concept-formation type of testing offers great promise to those who hope that measurements can be made relevant to the psychological variations which need to be compared. The Role Construct Repertory Test, which was described in an earlier chapter, represents an effort to develop a concept-formation test which is directly applicable to the issues encountered in psychotherapy.

Psychological tests relating to perceptual bias, such as the Rorschach Test and the Thematic Apperception Test, may give some indication of the client's position in his world as seen through his own eyes. To some extent, they indicate ways in which his problems can be solved, although they are not always analyzed by psychologists with that issue in mind. The thematic type of analysis of the Thematic Apperception Test may give the therapist some indication of the movement trends he may expect in his client. As yet, we know far too little about what either of these two popular tests show as to what therapeutic approaches can most profitably be used.

Yet with all of these difficulties, the administration of formal psychological tests, as well as informal ones such as those compiled by F. L. Wells, may be an important step toward the therapeutically controlled elaboration of the client's personal construct system. Testing may broaden the perspective of the therapist. It is easy enough to become preoccupied with certain palpable issues during the course of therapy and forget just what type of client one is dealing with. The therapist's own acceptance of his client tends to bias his judgment. The test is a good way to dispel some of the bias and place the case in a well-balanced frame of reference. There are instances in which the test may even point directly to therapeutic content aligned with one of the therapist's "blind spots." For example, testing may show that a client who is undergoing psychotherapy uses the threat of suicide or psychotic break to maintain control of the therapist. The therapist may be unduly befuddled by this ever present hazard in psychotherapy, and may fail to cast his client's behavior in proper perspective.

a. *The test as a form of confrontation.* Testing affects the outlook of the client as well as that of the therapist. The formal structure of the test brings him face to face with issues which he would otherwise reject as irrelevant or put aside as the artifacts of the therapist's misperceptions of his case. Yet here in the prestructured content of the test are these very issues which he has shrugged off. The therapist has not imposed them; they are part of the formal test. They are not issues especially designed to plague him; they are issues raised routinely with many clients. The test has become the vehicle for an obviously impartial confrontation which demands further elaboration.

For example, in taking the Role Construct Repertory Test, clients may make remarks such as, "I can see that this is like telling the whole story of my life"; "I guess my world is just about made up of two kinds of people. That isn't a very intelligent way to look at it, is it?" "I never thought of it before, but I don't seem to see my mother as a human being like other people"; "I'm just saying the same thing over and over on this test. Is that what I do all the time?" "I don't like what I'm doing here. This is terrible"; "I wish I could say that it was the test that is making me put down these things, but it is all my own doing, isn't it?" "I wonder how my friends would sort my name on a test like this." All of these remarks indicate that the test is operating as a confrontation likely to have therapeutic repercussions. The perceptive therapist tries to make sure, through timing and selection of tests, that the repercussions are positively reconstructive.

Morton and others have used the Thematic Apperception Test as a primary psychotherapeutic approach. Morton's procedure was first to elicit the protocol and then make the protocol of each card the basis of a discussion. The client was shown how the protocol could be interpreted and then encouraged to develop his own interpretations of the remaining sections of protocol. Each of the client's interpretations was discussed and alternative thema elaborated. Morton's study was well controlled. Barry followed up both experimental and control cases with a language analysis of subsequent interview protocols obtained some months after the conclusion of psychotherapy. The results indicate considerable success with the procedure.

b. *Threat to the psychotherapeutic relationship.* The psychotherapist who administers formal psychological tests to his client takes some risk with his relationship. Ordinarily, the therapist is less likely to damage the relationship by testing early in the psychotherapeutic series than he is if he breaks into the series with a set of formal tests later. In the latter case he may be genuinely threatening because the client may feel that his gains are being wiped out. Many clients first begin to feel improvement in the therapy room and in their relationship with the therapist. To be sure, it is a very limited and tenuous sort of gain and the client is likely to feel that it does not carry over to the outside. When the therapist administers a test he imposes an outside standard upon the client's behavior and obviously measures the client in relationship to rigid realistic expectancies which are those of society. The client is suddenly confronted with the apparent alliance between the expectancies of society and those of his therapist; and, as a result, the therapist may be seen as just another member of the society which expects too much or expects the wrong things.

The incomplete-sentence type of test, such as Rotter's Incomplete Sentences Test, is perhaps the least threatening type of projective test in relation to what it reveals about the client. Like the personality-inventory type of test, it tends to cover a predetermined range of potential areas of disturbance. However, instead of imposing its own constructions upon these areas, it permits the client to formulate his personal constructions of his problems. Moreover, the standardized list of items guarantees that a maximum of range will be tapped in a minimum of testing time. From reading the protocol one comes very close to the flavoring of a psychotherapeutic interview. As soon as the test is completed, the client's formulations can be made the points of departure for a therapeutically controlled elaboration of the problem areas. The test therefore tends to fit neatly and comfortably into the initial phase of therapy. Later on, if the therapist has been alert to what the client has been saying, it can be expected to add very little to his understanding of the client's personal construct system.

c. *Control of threat.* If the therapist does administer a test to his client, he should do what he can to make the client feel that there is no such thing as "passing" or "failing" the test and that the results have no bearing on whether he *accepts* the client or not. The reassurance will, of course, be only partly successful at best. The therapist may say that the test is to help indicate how the therapy can best proceed and what matters might best be discussed and what matters laid aside until later. He can say, "This test is to help me understand you better, how you deal with your problems in life, how I can help you deal with your troubles. I don't want to misunderstand you; I want to feel that I know you well enough to help you."

It is the writer's observation that the administration of a "projective" type of test is less likely to be damaging to the therapeutic relationship than the administration of an "objective" type of test. In the "projective" test the client may feel that he is being given more opportunity to express his own point of view. In the "objective" test the client may feel that he is being measured against the inflexible standards of society. Of course, in the hands of a well-trained and sensitive clinician, both types of test protocol are perceived as projections of the client's characteristic personality and yet both types are evaluated objectively within a social frame of reference.

d. *Special problems of threat in word-association tests.* The word-association test, in the experience of the writer, is the one type of "projective" test which is frequently damaging to the psychotherapeutic relationship. The client is likely to feel that the therapist is waiting to "pounce" on any slip of the tongue he might make. The client is not given a chance to elaborate the meanings of his response words until the inquiry phase of the test.

The use of the stop watch or any obvious timing device adds to the client's feeling that the purpose of the test is to trip him up. If the therapist does use a conventional type of word-association test, he should be careful to explain that he is writing down the responses and that there will be an opportunity to go back over the responses at the end of the initial presentation. He should be careful not to indicate, during the initial presentation, that some responses are more significant than others.

Yet, while the word-association test usually puts a strain on the relations between client and therapist, there are cases in which it is welcomed by the client. The client may want to bare himself without taking any responsibility for formulating his ideas in communicable form, for selecting problems to be discussed, for actively participating in the relationship with the therapist, or for aggressive exploration of his difficulties. Frequently this is the client who will ask to be "hypnotized."

The word-association test is not wholly unlike other methods of confrontation which play a part in most individual psychotherapeutic programs. This fact needs, of course, to be recognized. The hazard is not that it uses confrontation, not that it seeks to reveal the constructive linkages that a client employs, or that it leads the client to expose himself; the hazard is the way it bludgeons the client with so much diverse confrontation all in the space of a few minutes and gives him so little time to mobilize those defenses which, "unhealthy" as they may be, are still so necessary to the maintenance of his integrity. The rapid pace, the variety of content, the presentation without contextual preparation, all may combine to overwhelm the client. Yet the linkages revealed may be the very same linkages one would expect to have elaborated more informally during the subsequent course of therapy.

The word-association test is not the only kind of projective test likely to throw a client into a flutter. Some clients become disorganized under the impact of a series of Rorschach cards. The sequence of their perceptions may cause anxiety to mount, even though they have more difficulty attributing their anxiety to the stimulus material than one does in the case of the word-association test. The effect upon the therapeutic relationship may be just as trying, but it is harder for the client to rationalize the anxiety that the test has produced and thus harder for the unperceptive clinician to realize what effect the test is having.

e. *Entry material.* It is possible to use test stimulus material in an informal manner as a point of departure for the psychotherapeutic hour. Material used in this manner is called "entry material." Stimulus words from a word-association test, or the responses given at the time it was administered, may be used. A Rorschach card or a TAT card may also be the entry. However, there is no particular advantage in using standardized material for this purpose, since the chain of response is pursued far beyond the point at which any particular card norms would be meaningful. It is just as well for the therapist, who wants the construction system elaborated from a neutral base, to devise his own entries. The procedures for using informal entries in the elaboration of autistic material are discussed in a later section.

In summary, we may say, as we said in an earlier chapter, that the function of testing in any clinical situation is to provide reference points and hypotheses for therapy and client management. One must be particularly alert to the effects the testing has upon the psychotherapeutic relationship, and he must always realize what kind of confrontation, from a therapeutic standpoint, should not be attempted at the particular time the test is administered. By the same token, the test may serve to open up an area which the client is otherwise unwilling to approach.

3. ELABORATION OF THE CONSTRUCTION SYSTEM THROUGH SELF-DESCRIPTION

Self-characterization was discussed in Volume One. We indicated how the self-characterization sketch could be elicited in order to allow maximum opportunity for the client to impose his own organizational construction upon the content. We indicated how such spontaneous material could be approached by the clinician so as to subsume it without losing sight of its personalized features. Finally, because it was an appropriate context in which to do so, we went ahead to describe a formalized therapeutic procedure called *fixed-role therapy*.

But self-characterization may be an important feature of other psychotherapeutic procedures too. Too frequently the initial material elicited in the therapy room is so limited to the client's problems, and so bound up in the implicit assumptions of the client's construction system, that the therapist fails to get a picture of the kind of person he is dealing with. The therapist needs to know what kind of *problem* the client is facing, to be sure. But he also needs to know what kind of *person* the client is. This means elaboration of the construction system as a whole, not just those unfortunate constructions which are applied to the problem areas.

The therapist may say, "You have been telling me about the troubles you have. I intend to do all I can to help you. But if I am to help you I need to know more about *you*. I need to understand you as a person as well as understand the troubles you have. So let's lay aside your problems for a little while so that you can tell me much more about what kind of person you are. What kind of person are you really?"

Some therapists feel compelled to "help" the client by providing him with an outline at this point. They may say, for example, "Now tell me about how your parents reared you." This is a sure way of imposing the therapist's system upon the client. From the standpoint of the psychology of personal constructs it is important that the client himself choose what is a relevant answer to the question. If he does not see the actions of his parents as molding him as though he were a piece of clay, the therapist has no business forcing such an interpretation upon him, even before he has a chance to answer the question. The therapist needs to approach his client wide-eyed and alert. He should not impose his narrower prejudices upon the client before he has heard what the client has to say.

The sudden dilation of the field which this approach presents may cause the client to become temporarily confused. The therapist should not act as if he expected an immediate and facile answer. He may look down and repeat his question meditatively. "Yes . . . that is what I really need to know . . . in order to help." As the first feeble formulations begin to come, he can encourage the flow by interest-revealing responses such as, "Yes . . . I think I understand. . . . Could you go over that again just to make sure that I know what you mean? . . . And could you explain that a little further?"

a. *Difficulties in eliciting self-characterization.* The literalistic client who tries to encapsulate his problem may initially reject this line of controlled elaboration. He may say, "I don't know what you mean. Do you mean you want to know my age, marital status, previous employment, et cetera?" The therapist may say, "Well, yes, if you think that would make it clear to me just what kind of *person* you are. If you don't think it would help me to understand you better you may prefer to describe yourself in other ways instead."

Children in the age ranges below ten years find it quite difficult to respond to this type of questioning. Bugental has developed a diagnostic procedure which he calls the "Who Are You" (WAY) technique. By placing the emphasis upon this type of question he is able, with children, and with adults as well, to elicit a type of self-description. The writer's experience with the technique suggests that the constructs elicited tend to be more in terms of social, institutional, or formal relationships than when the client is asked to describe himself as a person.

b. *What kind of child were you?* The client may be asked to describe himself as he was when he was a child. The therapist, in listening, should be aware of the fact that what the client says is a reflection of the way he, as an adult, *now looks* at his childhood. The content may be out of the past, or the memory of the past, but the constructs — and those are basically what the clinician is interested in — are strictly out of the present. As long as the clinician is careful to examine the bipolar dimensional system which is used for plotting the client's childhood position, and as long as he is careful not to become preoccupied with the events of childhood or the monopolar terms, he may profitably develop the elaboration of the construction system.

For example, if the client says, "I was a dirty little youngster with a runny nose," the clinician can, first of all, envision the "dirt" and the "runny nose." Such a literalistic interpretation of the client's response may or may not be profitable. Secondly, the clinician can accept the client's evaluation and envision him as once being a repulsive child. But if the clinician is interested primarily in the controlled elaboration of the client's construction system he may reason that here is a client who considers dirt as symbolic of an important personality variable, that the client probably has an axis of personality description running from dirtiness and nose-runniness to some kind of fastidiousness. Since the dirtiness was chosen to characterize the childhood period of the client's life, he may suspect, and further investigate, the possibility that the client conceptualizes his maturation process as signified by a change from dirtiness to cleanliness. There is, therefore, the possibility that the client will be threatened by anyone's now perceiving him as "dirty," that he may be threatened by "dirty" people such as children — perhaps his own — and that his efforts to play the role of a mature person may be ineffectual and interrupted by little acts of fussiness.

c. *What kind of person do you expect to become?* The client may be asked to characterize himself as he might reasonably expect to be at the age of sixty-five, the age of retirement. The request can be presented in an unstructured manner similar to that used to elicit the self-characterization described in the chapter dealing with that topic. This is not easy for a young person to do, particularly if the clinician starts to test the limits of the construction system by tossing in unexpected elements such as poor health, limited financial resources, et cetera. Some clients are badly threatened by the very prospect of perceiving themselves as old. Yet this type of elaboration gives the clinician some idea of what kind of experience the client is prepared to face, how his long-range life role is structured, and what therapy must do to prepare the client for the "long haul."

It is frequently a good plan to ask the client to construe himself as he would expect to be at the termination of a successful period of therapy. This is also a way of seeing what kind of time line he can draw through his problems. There are cases in which a whole series of sessions can be spent profitably in elaborating this feature of the construction system. The client can be asked to role play the part he expects to play at the end of therapy. It is possible, and sometimes very efficacious, to design, with the client's help, a fixed role for a two weeks' enactment period around this theme. He will, of course, need to be given the full protection of the make-believe features of role playing, else he will feel that he is being tricked into getting well without having the comfort and absolvement that he expected from therapy. He may feel genuinely threatened by such an enactment if he is not encouraged to perceive it as make-believe, because it will, as we have defined *threat*, represent a major impending dislocation of his core structure.

The client's description of himself after therapy throws considerable light upon what he expects the therapist to do for him. If the description is largely in terms of the changed attitudes and behaviors of other people, the therapist can infer, not only that he himself is expected to behave toward the client in certain ways, but that, somehow, he is expected to make people in the client's environment behave in certain unnatural ways. Thus the client's hostility may burst into view whereas otherwise it might pass unnoticed.

Controlled elaboration includes the testing of constructs for consistency with the construction system as a whole. The therapist can add elements to the client's perceptual field against which the client can test the efficacy of the constructs he has proposed. As the client describes himself after therapy, the therapist can very carefully and gently add certain selected elements to see if the client's design for the future can provide containment for the future's surprises. The addition can be in the form of mentioning possible events which the client may have overlooked, in the form of role enactments in the therapy room, or in terms of suggested ventures outside the therapy room.

d. *Autobiography.* Sometimes it is profitable to have a prospective client prepare an autobiography. Clinicians who place great stress upon the *sequence* of past events as an explanation of present personality structure like this approach. As might be expected by the reader who has struggled this far through this book, our own position is that this emphasis upon the past as an inescapable attribute of the present may actually hamstring the therapist. As we have said before, man need not be the victim of his biography. There is much to be said for the therapist who is careful not to impose such a notion upon his client.

But if an autobiography is used, the therapist should be careful to read it as a historian and not as a chronicler. As a historian he can lift the vibrant themes out of the tumult of context. As a chronicler he can do no more than fall into step with the fateful tread of seasonal events or the patter of little incidents. The therapist should always see the autobiography as a present structure which is, in part, documented by selected memories of the past and is, in part, a viewing screen upon which the events of the past seem to have form and consequence.

First, then, what incidents does the client choose to recount in his autobiography? What do they serve to document for him? What does he find it necessary to prove? Second, what biases does the form of his autobiography impose upon the events of his past? What are the available construct axes against which those events must be plotted?

When the client is asked to describe himself as a person, the clinician is not necessarily looking for a ready-made diagnosis of the case. To be sure, most clients have a version of themselves which corresponds to a "diagnosis." The clinician is interested in this diagnosis, not because it is likely to be "right," nor does he ignore it because it is likely to be "wrong." He is interested in it because he is dealing with a person, not an inanimate object. The person — the client — is the one whose eventual construction of the case will determine what is accomplished. The psychotherapist is never more than a consultant and a live figure in the client's social world. He is not the client, nor the client's conscience, nor the client's intelligence, nor the personification of the client's construction system. It is therefore important that the psychotherapist understand the client's construction system because it is the government de facto of the client's realm.

Yet the therapist must always superimpose his own judgment upon the client's self-description. Unless he does so, he is bound to be ineffectual in helping the client to improve his lot. This does not mean that the therapist hostilely maneuvers the client to fit a diagnostic category. It means, rather, that he takes full account of what the client is, psychologically, as well as what he is physiologically, situationally, and socially. Then he helps the client to exploit his own psychological resources.

4. ELABORATION OF LIFE-ROLE STRUCTURE

We have already mentioned the use of a self-characterization written as the client pictures himself at the age of retirement. The use of an autobiography has also been discussed. Both of these procedures provide an opportunity for controlled elaboration of the personal construct system as a whole. But it may well be that the therapist finds particular need for elaborating the client's life-role structure specifically. This calls for elaborating those constructs having to do with the development of the client's personality over the changing years, his construction of himself in terms of his life cycle instead of his daily cycles, and his view of himself as a gradually aging person.

This type of elaboration is undertaken when the client has problems which might be attributed to lack of over-all purpose and outlook in his life. There may be the case of a young person who is setting the stage for adulthood while trying to appease his parents' ambitions. It may be the case of a person who is undergoing a transition in his domestic life. There may be the problem of occupational adjustment to an unexpected handicap or to changing economic conditions. The therapist finds it necessary to appraise and to stabilize some sort of overriding structure which is permeable enough to contain the fitful uncertainties of the future.

In seeking to have the client elaborate his life-role structure, the therapist may draw upon experiences of the past as well as speculate upon the future. The client is encouraged to see himself in the framework of a structural biography, but not as the product of chronicled events. His biography is projected through the past into the future with the clear implication that where he goes from here is a function of how he holds his compass heading and is not inexorably directed by where he has been. Yet, where he has been is a check upon the heading he has held. As every navigator knows, course, heading, and track are identical only when wind and current can be ignored. One may correct his heading by checking backward on his track. Thus an intentional course may be steered. But only the navigator who is so unfortunate as to lack helm and steerageway is forced to plot his course solely from his track. Thus, when the therapist encourages the client to elaborate his life role in terms of biographical experiences, it is to check the proper relation between heading and course and not to discover what fate has in store for him.

a. *Earlier versions of the life role.* The therapist may ask, "What were some of your plans for the future when you were a child?" "What did you want to be when you grew up?" "What did you think it would be like to be a —— ?" "What led you to change your mind?" "What do you think about it now?" "How do you think it has worked out?" "If you had it to do over again what would you do?" "Why?" "How would things be different now if you had followed this other course?" "What would people think of you?"

Such questions are designed to throw light upon the client's life-role structure. What concessions has he made to fate? In what ways are his experiences incongruous with his over-all view of himself? What long-range wagers does he still have outstanding? What would it take to vindicate himself, to validate his life-role constructs? Does he have a coherent structure for placing the incidents of life in an orderly array? To what sorts of experiences is the life-role structure permeable? What is the client prepared to understand or to make sense out of?

b. *Projective elaboration of life role.* It is possible to have the client elaborate his life-role structure projectively. The client's elaboration of the thema in the Thematic Apperception Test gives some indication of how the life role of the principal figure — himself — is structured. Mahrer has contrived and used an ingenious device for elaboration of the life-role structure. He describes a child in noncommittal terms and then asks the client to complete the story by describing the child as he might be after he grows up. Then he describes a man and asks the client to describe that man as he was when he was a child. Then he repeats the cycle by describing another child, and so on. On the second time around, the client, even though he may be unwilling to talk about himself directly, is likely to give a pretty good life history of himself. The necessity for describing two or more figures forces the client to deal in contrasts. As soon as he does that we begin to see what his construct dimensions are. Even some of the submerged ends are likely to reveal what are the incompatibilities between his own biography and the life-role structure he has attempted to use.

c. *What does the client expect from therapy?* Almost inevitably the controlled elaboration of the life-role structure leads directly into an elaboration of what the client expects from therapy. In an earlier chapter we discussed the client's possible initial constructions of what therapy is and of what kind of person he thinks the therapist is. These can be elaborated. The therapist may ask, "And now what kind of therapist do you think it would take to be of real help to you?" "What do you picture the therapist as saying to you?" "How do you think you would feel about a therapist?" "What would be the therapist's job in your case?" "Now what do you see as your part in this therapeutic program?" "What would be your principal contribution?" "At what point do you think of the therapy as being completed?" "How will we know when to discontinue the therapy?"

It may not be feasible to follow this line of questioning as far as we have illustrated it. Some clients are so discouraged that they act as though — even though they do not say it — they expected the therapist to change all of their circumstances, even substitute a new self. These enacted answers may be perfectly explicit even though they are expressed in terms of wailings rather than syntax. The therapist may, if he believes the client is prepared to face the implications in a more explicit form, attempt to put into words what the client is expressing. He may say, "If I understand what you are trying to say, it is that whatever is done will have to be done without help from you. Is that what you mean? Is that the way you want it to be? Do you want me just to go ahead and take charge of everything in your life?"

The therapist should not attempt such a formulation unless he wants to deal with it in the form in which he has verbalized it. There are times when it is just as well not to let the client's formulation of his life-role structure or his feelings of helpfulness become crystallized in terms of spoken words. If a few hours of rest and a temporary protected environment are likely to make a difference in what the client is prepared to contribute to his treatment, it is just as well not to hurry him into taking a passively defensive position.

5. PROGRESSIVE CONFRONTATION WITH ALTERNATIVES

One way to elaborate the construction system is to keep invoking the C-P-C Cycle. This requires the client to be circumspect in terms of his system, to settle upon some issue preemptively, and to choose one of its alternatives for himself. The therapist keeps asking such questions as, "What does one *do* about such things?" "What could you have done?" "What else could you have done?" "What kind of action does that call for?" "What do other people do when they are faced with that kind of problem?" "Does all of this need to make any difference about the way you go about your daily business? . . . Just what is the difference?" "Having done that, what comes next?" *"Now* what kind of decision would you have to make?" "And suppose you did that—what next?" "And then what?" and so on.

This is a way of cutting through the circumspection and estimating what construction dimensions may be used for preemption and control. The therapist must be prepared to face the consequences of such a line of questioning. The client may decide to act on some of the alternatives he has been forced to choose. If the therapist embarks on this line of controlled elaboration, he should ordinarily pursue it far enough to make sure that the client becomes aware of the principal consequences of his projected actions and will not behave rashly. A good plan is always to back up to the beginning of the sequence after the series has been pursued to some length, and ask the client to pursue one of the alternative courses of action verbally through a sequence of outcomes. Before the exercise is completed, the therapist may wish to point out that the client has pursued only a few of the many alternatives open to him and that part of the task of therapy is to visualize clearly many alternatives before the moment of choice is actually reached.

Again Mahrer has devised an approach for this type of elaboration. He has used a prepared set of questions on cards which are dealt to the client in a fixed order. The fact that the questions are preformulated tends to avoid giving the impression that the client is being pushed by the therapist along one course of action. Such questions as the following are used: "The trouble with most parents is . . . ?" "The reason they are this way is . . . ?" "Another reason is . . . ?" "A good plan would be for parents to be more . . . ?" "Then we might expect that . . . ?" and so on.

6. CONTROLLED ELABORATION BY MEANS OF PRESCRIBED ACTIVITIES

Not all elaboration need be limited to verbalizations in the therapy room. Some of the most important elaborations take place outside, and some of them are expressed only incidentally in words.

The "learning through doing" approach which has had such wide application among American educators is an example of elaboration by means of activities. As the learner puts his ideas to work, he is required to formulate them concisely enough to act upon them. He passes through a series of C-P-C Cycles, each cycle requiring a multifaceted initial approach to his problem, then a temporary preemption to arrive at the issue which is relevant at the moment, and, finally, the choice of an alternative and controlled action. As he repeats each cycle, a whole area of his construction system begins to take shape, and his constructs begin to fall into a tighter organizational hierarchy. Unless he meets too much frustration, he begins to develop an approach configuration which is fairly regular.

In this connection, the therapist should again be reminded that he ought not to lose sight of the possibility that elaboration of the client's construction system, while it may stabilize the client, may also crystallize his approach to his problems. A person who "puts his ideas into practice" within a limited milieu may soon develop highly conventionalized and inflexible approaches. His *level of cognitive awareness* may be reduced. The circumspection phase of the successive C-P-C Cycles is more and more foreshortened until the person begins to behave rigidly all the time. Such are the hazards of nonlanguage thinking and "practical" learning.

a. *Beta Hypothesis.* The practical application of Knight Dunlap's beta hypothesis is another example of elaboration by means of activities. Dunlap pointed out that there are occasions when forced and continued practice of an unwanted impulsive act will eventually enable the person to rid himself of the "habit." The procedure is not likely to be successful unless the act is properly brought under the control of regnant constructs within which the person is able to exercise some choice of alternatives. Practice for practice's sake will not yield satisfactory results.

For example, suppose a therapist is dealing with a twelve-year-old child who has a thumb-sucking "habit." Let us suppose that for good and sufficient reasons he has decided to treat the case "symptomatically."

It is not unreasonable that the therapist should have made such a decision. Sometimes it is more feasible to try to produce personality readjustments by attacking the symptoms than by going directly after the basically faulty structures. Thus some of the cue elements upon which those structures have been resting are removed before the structures themselves are attacked.

Let us suppose that the therapist sets up a program of controlled elaboration by means of prescribed activities. He prescribes five minutes of thumb sucking every hour. The thumb sucking "must take place between the hour and five minutes after the hour." The thumb "must be rubbed across the roof of the mouth exactly fifty times." Then it "must be moved longitudinally along the tongue from back to front exactly fifty times," and so on. At the end of each period the client "must write some notes in her notebook about the experience." "Did the thumb taste salty this time?" "Did the hard palate seem smoother in some places than in others?" "Just how did the experience compare with the experience of the last hour?" and so on. "What did the client think about just before the practice period, during the practice period, after the practice period?" and so on. Nothing is said about not sucking the thumb between periods. The notes are reviewed each day. After the practice has gone on for a time the client is given "a day off" from the prescribed routine. The frequency of "days off" is gradually increased.

It should be clearly understood that this therapeutic procedure is not recommended by the writer for all cases of thumb sucking. We are simply illustrating a type of procedure which may, in some cases, be effectively applied. In others, it is quite likely to do the child more harm than good. For example, it is likely to do more harm than good if the child has already been subjected to too many tight constructions by parents who "intellectualize" the dependency relations between themselves and their child. Of course, the thumb sucking may disappear in such a case, but the possibility of a late-adolescent anxiety break or, more fortunately perhaps, a social revolt is likely to be increased.

What happens in this type of controlled elaboration is that the level of cognitive awareness is raised. The elements underpinning the thumb-sucking structures are brought into sharp focus. In some measure the preverbal constructs are brought into array under verbal ones. The pattern of thumb sucking is regularized; in other words, the constructs are *tightened*. There is even some testing of the constructs, as the client comes to predict precisely what will happen, hour by hour and movement by movement. The whole "habit" is brought under the regnancy of verbalizable constructs and the client begins to find it possible to choose intellectually between being the kind of person who sucks his thumb and the kind of person who does not. Whereas once she felt that she was inescapably branded as a thumb sucker, she is now in a position to decide whether she wants to bear that label or not.

b. *Occupational activities.* Controlled elaboration may be produced by means of prescribed occupational activities. For example, a housewife may be advised to take a part-time job. She may be urged to observe the effect upon her interpersonal relations. Similarities and contrasts can be drawn between what she finds herself doing and thinking while on the job and what happens in her household. The occupational venture may give her a chance to see herself in a new perspective and a chance to deal with different elements by means of her construct system. The organizational scheme underlying the whole may become more apparent to her and to the therapist.

The therapist may help bring about a controlled elaboration of the construct system by prescribing particular kinds and sequences of household activities for such a client. The client may be advised to do some spring cleaning between one interview and the next. The two interviews may elicit some revealing contrasts in outlook. In construing the contrasts the client may succeed in getting a firmer grasp of her construction system, and, moreover, get it at a higher level of cognitive awareness.

c. *Recreational activities.* Prescribed "recreational" activities may be used in a similar manner. Ordinarily, everything possible is done to get the client to verbalize what has happened to his thinking as a result of the prescribed activity. Yet the therapist need not feel that the elaboration has been at a standstill when the client is unable to verbalize his reactions to the assignment.

Elaboration can take place at the preverbal level as well as at the verbal level. Nor is the level of cognitive awareness identical with the level of verbalization. Nearly every therapist who has had experience with "verbalizers" is aware of that. The level of cognitive awareness corresponds more closely to a level of circumspection. Verbalization helps in circumspection but there is such a thing as circumspection without words. The creative artist uses such circumspection in the first phase of many of his C-P-C Cycles. Yet always he strives to put his creations into communicable form. So with the client. The therapist should always strive to help him put his elaborations into communicable form. And that goes even for "recreational" activities, in spite of the fact that most people consider recreation to be essentially an exercise of preverbal constructions.

d. *Social activities.* The therapist may prescribe social activities as a means of developing an elaboration of the client's construction system. The client is encouraged to meet and spend some time with certain people or certain kinds of people. Or he may be advised to meet people in certain types of situations where the social expectancy is different from that under which he usually operates. This is not to say that the client will best elaborate his construction system if he is precipitated into situations which are distasteful to him or which he cannot handle gracefully. The therapist needs to modulate the client's activity program. The more drastic ventures should always be tried out first in test-tube proportions within the protective walls of the interview laboratory before they are attempted in the client's social milieu, where repercussions may mount to catastrophic proportions.

7. ELABORATION THROUGH PLAY AND CREATIVE PRODUCTION

Play is adventure. Its outcomes are always veiled in some delightful uncertainty. When one plays he embarks on a little voyage of discovery — all in the safety of his back yard. He need have no forebodings that he might inadvertently step off the edge of his world. Through play he confidently dispels one little uncertainty after another. Each tidbit of discovery is greeted with surprise and laughter. Thus, through play, one's system of anticipation grows and grows.

It is much the same way with creative activity. This too is a means of shaping up one's anticipations in the midst of foggy uncertainties. But, while play involves discovery within safe limits, creative activity involves taking loose comprehensive structures and tightening them. The creative person ordinarily starts with constructs which can neither be put into words nor communicated with any satisfactory measure of precision. When he is finished, his idea is expressed in a form which is somewhat more communicable, though it may still defy verbal description and it may still look like a shapeless mass to unsympathetic spectators.

a. *Setting safe limits.* The media one chooses, either for play or for art, impose certain natural limitations upon one's accomplishments. Often the media are chosen by the person because of the boundaries they provide. The artist who chooses to copy the Lord's Prayer on the head of a pin may be trying to make sense out of some foggy uncertainties, but he has placed mighty narrow limits upon the bit of fog he seeks to dispel. Not only is the head of the pin small, but he has allowed himself almost no latitude in *what* he is to copy. He may be seeking figuratively to inscribe his religious convictions or his religious charms upon each minutia of his life, lest it fall into the competing realm of secularism.

The person who chooses a competitive game as his recreational medium often sets for himself, through the rules of the game, safe limits for expounding his hostility. The more elaborate the rules, the better protected he is, and the less he has to worry about his hostility's destroying his social role and precipitating him into a state of guilt. Sometimes a person plays a game less to win than to explore the outcomes of certain tactics. To the extent that he does this he eliminates the exposition of *hostility* and uses the game, instead, as a safe field for *aggressive* elaboration.

The therapist who uses play or encourages creative production as a treatment measure should give some thought to the media which are to be employed. He should have in mind what limits the client needs in order to feel reasonably safe from fear, anxiety, or guilt. The client's skills may need to be taken into account, for sometimes, though not always, a client is disturbed when he finds that he is less skillful than his friends in performance.

The social milieu should also be taken into account. With whom will the client associate himself during his activity? What will they expect of him? How will he try to meet their expectations? And finally, above all, the therapist should take into account what the client probably needs to elaborate.

b. *Choosing a medium of expression.* Sometimes clay modeling is used as a therapeutic measure. Psychoanalysts sometimes judge hostility in a certain client to be a symptom of anal fixation and the modeling is thought to be a near-substitute for fecal smearing. They therefore recognize the effectiveness of clay modeling in cases of clients who cannot control their hostility. At the technical level one must agree. Clay modeling does indeed seem to be particularly effective in cases involving impulsive hostility. Within the theoretical position of the psychology of personal constructs, however, the explanation would be formulated on a somewhat more abstract level. Let us remind ourselves of what hostility is. It is an attempt to validate a construction with purposefully distorted evidence. A person who is to elaborate his hostility, then, must have a pliable medium with which to work. Clay, thus, often meets his needs.

Consider an impulsively hostile young adolescent. Suppose a therapeutic program is developed which includes an opportunity for clay modeling. If the client is extremely disturbed, the therapist may have to start with a tubful of mud and a large vacant lot. The usual way is to keep seeking to have the client verbalize what he is doing with the mud. As he passes through the throwing stage and goes into the smearing stage, the therapist is likely to note some clinical signs of depression. The transition has involved some constriction. When the client begins to shape the mud into forms, he is approaching the stage when the project can be taken indoors. At first, the forms will be promptly destroyed. He does not wish to have them stand the test of close examination by others or even by himself the next time he has an appointment. He is not prepared to subject his construction to such a test in the light of reality. He is still demanding appeasement — not truth.

When the client begins to carry over his products from day to day without destroying them, the therapist can usually also note an increased modulation of his impulsive behavior. There is more continuity. The client is beginning to plot his own behavior against a time line. Better clay can be provided. The properties and possibilities of clay can be examined and its limitations accepted. Technical suggestions may be welcomed. Coloring can be introduced. Opportunity for firing in a kiln can be provided. The clay can be accepted in a less submissive form. A theme underlying a series of productions can be introduced. Products can be used as gifts. Interpersonal relations can be developed thereby.

c. *Dilating media.* Consider a somewhat different type of client problem. Suppose we have a person exhibiting what is called a "neurotic depression." The therapist plans a program designed to alleviate the constrictive features of the client's construction system. He sets safe limits on the dilation he seeks to produce. Suppose water-color painting or the use of a long-handled brush with finger-paint pigments is attempted. At first, it may be necessary to limit the painting to the therapy room and to the appointment hours. To dilate the activity to other places, and at other hours, may prove too threatening to the client.

At first, the client may be reluctant to attempt to produce anything at all. He is likely to conceive his task as that of producing fine detail. He is sure that anything that he would produce would be hopelessly inaccurate. Large globs of paint, wide long-handled brushes, the mixing of color, and a demonstration of the grossness of the painting procedure may give him the feeling that his production is acceptable. With an increased feeling of acceptability his strokes become more expansive, his imagination is expressed more overtly, and there is more of a tendency to add constructively each day's achievement to that of the day before. There is dilation, but more than that there is the formulation of a role structure within which he can see his life as having continuity and meaning. Of course, it does not always happen this way, but the approach usually offers some promise of successful outcome for this type of case.

The function of this approach to the elaboration of the construct system is primarily to activate and modulate the C-P-C Cycle for certain *preverbal* features of the client's construction system. The impulsive person is unable, at first, to make use of the circumspective phase of the cycle. The constricted person has such a limited range of choices open to him that he dare not complete his cycle. The opening of additional avenues of expression, through play and creative activity, gives both a chance to put certain preverbal constructs into varying practical forms and to conduct, within safe boundaries, experimental tests of their outcomes.

d. *Difficulties.* Difficulties may arise. The client may not be able to commit his preverbal constructs to experiment, even within these safe boundaries. Or it may be that, having done so, he is unable to capture the meaning of the outcomes his experiment produces. Sometimes he is unable to recognize the boundaries of his field of creative experimentation. Before the therapist realizes it, the client may have launched into a major undertaking that involves too much of his world and is bound to get him into trouble with his friends. The person who lets his creative imagination run riot is likely to scare the wits out of the people who have to live with him.

In the case of most psychotherapy clients the therapist hopes to make large segments of the revised construction system verbalizable. This means that he wants the client to put his revisions into words. While this is not always feasible or desirable, it usually provides some assurance that the client can handle his new-found insights with some measure of precision, that he can continue to put them to test and subject them to revision. The continued use of play and creative activity past the time when the client should be putting more of his experience into words may retard the client's recovery. The therapist will have to judge when it is time to urge the client to become more articulate about what he is experimenting with and more explicit in forecasting his outcomes.

e. *Contraindications.* The use of play and creative activity is contraindicated when the therapist is unable to participate with the client in the experimentation. If the therapist is to be of help, either in the design of meaningful experiments or in providing validational data, he needs to have some measure of contact with what the client is doing. If the therapist is unperceptive, or if the client performs his experiments where the therapist cannot keep in contact with them, the likelihood of therapeutic benefit is minimized. The therapeutic advantage of play and creative activity is not activity for activity's sake, nor play for "release," but is rather a form of experimentation involving design, execution, and genuine appraisal of outcomes against anticipations. The task of the therapist is to assist the client in maximizing the experimental characteristics of his ventures. He cannot do this if he is totally unable to follow the client's line of inquiry or to witness any part of the experimental procedure.

f. *Conclusion.* In conclusion, it should be said that elaboration of the construct system should be conducted with some caution. It is not usually a good idea to try to elaborate the system in a hit-and-miss manner, skipping around from one part of the system to another haphazardly. The elaboration sometimes has a loosening effect, and one does not always want to risk a general loosening of the system. Ordinarily the therapist will want to set limits on the areas he seeks to have elaborated in any one phase of the therapy. For example, if he decides to elaborate the area of the client's construction of female roles, he can expect the client to be confronted with some threat in the process. The client may loosen his construction of women. Ordinarily it is better to help the client come to some tentative conclusions in this area before launching him into a series of construct-loosening experiments in some other area, say the area of vocation, or the area of parenthood. Granted that all of these areas are linked together and the final reconstruction will be an interlocking affair, the therapist should still bear in mind that the client must be kept open for business while the remodeling is going on.

B. Elaboration of Material Arising during the Course of Therapy

8. CONTENT ELABORATION

There is still another kind of elaboration problem. We have discussed elaboration of the complaint as a means of seeing how the client personally experiences his difficulties. We have further discussed the elaboration of the client's construction system in order to see how it functions, regardless of whether or not that functioning is to be judged as disordered. Now we come to the problem of elaborating the various bits of material and behaviors arising during the course of day-by-day therapy. It is necessary to elaborate some of these to see where they fit in the construction system as a whole and to find what relationship they bear to the sequence of developments that occur as therapy proceeds. This is an elaboration problem quite different from the two types we have discussed in the preceding sections.

The first type of elaboration is a matter of exploring the client's areas of anxiety and confusion. The second has to do with the study of the construction system as a whole. The third, with which we are now concerned, is a matter of finding how new material fits into that construction system as a whole and what it signifies regarding impending changes in that construction system.

9. CRITERIA FOR SELECTION OF MATERIAL TO BE ELABORATED

It is not possible to follow up all the clues revealed by the client in a psychotherapeutic interview. Only a very small proportion can be elaborated. The therapist has to keep making a rough classification or *structuration* of what he observes, assigning each item tentatively to a pigeonhole for possible future reference. More precise *constructions* must be limited to such materials as he chooses to have the client elaborate in greater detail. As therapy progresses and the therapist acquires a better overview of the case, he may be able more and more to substitute *construction* for *structuration* of material arising during the course of the day-by-day sessions.

A word of caution. Sometimes a therapist is so rigid in his professional construction of a case that he keeps tossing new and potentially useful material into his pigeonhole system without giving it a second look. Therapists who are guided by a standard lexicon of symbolisms, who are rigidly indoctrinated with a fixed theory of psychodynamics, or who always "live by the book," soon develop an imperviousness to anything new the client may say. There tends to be nothing creative in their therapeutic ministrations, and the only thing new happening to them during the psychotherapeutic venture is that they "discover" further confirmation of their original convictions.

We have said that the clinician who cannot predict what his client will do from session to session probably does not understand his client as well as he should and should therefore proceed cautiously. Contrariwise, we should probably add that the clinician who is never surprised by anything that his client does is not very alert. The psychology of personal constructs lays stress on the need for alertness both to the various ways different clients construe their world and to the varying ways any given client will construe his world during a course of therapy.

We have said that the therapist cannot begin to elaborate all the meaningful cues that arise during a psychotherapeutic hour. Now let us add this. Neither should the therapist always pounce upon the most significant cues the client lets slip. Psychotherapy needs to be conducted in an orderly fashion. It should not be assumed that a disturbed client is psychologically prepared to discuss any topic at any time. What the therapist chooses for further elaboration is determined partly by its suspected significance and partly by the client's readiness to deal with the kind of material the cue seems to represent. All of this means that many of the client's most significant remarks should be filed away for possible future reference without any current comment.

a. *Strange or unexpected material.* Ordinarily when the client starts to discuss something the therapist finds strange or unexpected, steps toward further elaboration should be taken. The steps may be taken immediately or, if there is danger of too much loosening, postponed until an opportune moment arises when the client's thinking seems to be fairly tight. This also applies to the observation of strange or unexpected behavior of a nonverbal nature. As we have said before, one of the informal checks upon a clinician's insight into his client is his ability to predict differentially what he will do. The appearance of strange or unexpected behavior is a sign that the clinician is somewhat unfamiliar with the way his client operates. Elaboration of the material will give the clinician a chance to revise his appraisal of the client or to see how the new material actually fits into already familiar patterns.

b. *Material which is possibly indicative of an expected therapeutic movement or revision of the construct system.* The experienced clinician has some idea of what kinds of developments are to be expected in his client during the course of psychotherapy. He is alert to the signs that these developments are at last beginning to take place. Frequently, though not always, he will seek immediate elaboration of any new material that seems to be a harbinger of such developments. He wants not only to make sure that this is indeed what he has been expecting but also to facilitate the new development and keep the therapy moving along. If the development seems to him to be premature and likely to precipitate the client into areas of elaboration which he cannot yet handle without becoming too schizoid or impulsive, he may choose not to elaborate the new material, even though it is the sort of thing he hopes will come out eventually.

c. *Material possibly relating to an area of the construct system which is under intensive study.* Consider a client whose Repertory Test material indicates a constellation of education, respectability, wealth, and cleanliness. The therapist, in order to be of help to such a client, must know something of how this complex operates, whether it holds together and operates as a single, reasonably tight, comprehensive construct, or whether it is a conglomeration of loose constructions. He needs to know what the critical features of the constellation are and how the client applies it in his everyday living. He will therefore probably place the systematic study of this constellation high on his priority list for therapeutic exploration.

Suppose one day the client reports that he once quit a job because he could not stand to work in association with "cheap, frowzy people." The therapist will immediately recognize the constellation and the possibility that the incident will reveal how it operates in a practical situation. Elaboration of the incident is therefore likely to be profitable. Out of such elaboration may come a much more precise statement of the basic construct or, possibly, the discovery that the constellation can profitably be broken up without damage to the construction system as a whole.

d. *Context material to be utilized in psychotherapeutic experimentation.* Sometimes the therapist asks the client to elaborate material, not so much because it is crucial to the client's adjustment or because it reveals faulty construction, but rather, because it lends itself to experimentation. Suppose the therapist wishes to inaugurate a program of fractional role playing. He cannot, of course, start out immediately with reenactments of crucial situations, such as quarrels with his parents or the expression of resentment toward authority figures. The therapist must first develop the procedure in relation to relatively nonthreatening but socially meaningful situations. In order to provide contextual information for setting up fractional role enactments the therapist may have the client elaborate a good deal of relatively noncrucial material. As we have indicated in an earlier chapter, it is frequently desirable to develop new construction in areas where there is not so much at stake; and then, once the new construction is stabilized and some of its usefulness established, it can be brought into critical areas of the client's life without precipitating a panic. This accounts for the frequent need to elaborate first certain materials which can be used as safe ground on which to erect new structure.

e. *Validational material.* A person uses past experience to validate new constructs as well as experience arising after the new constructs have been formulated. A client formulates the notion that *authority-submission* is not the only dimension along which role relationships can be structured. He begins to perceive that *complementation-dissipation* is another meaningful dimension. But, instead of trying out his new dimensional system today or tomorrow, he may simply cast back into his memory to see whether or not this type of construction would have enabled him to anticipate some of the things which have happened to him in the past. Thus, past experience is frequently invoked as a kind of stale evidence against which to test fresh new constructs. The clinician, realizing this, will need to know something about what kind of evidence the client is going to use in testing out any new constructs that may be developed during the course of therapy. Unless he knows what kinds of tests the new constructs are going to have to meet he may become increasingly puzzled at what seems to be "resistance" in the client.

f. *Documentary material.* This also is a kind of validational material. But here we refer to material which the therapist selects as clearly illustrative of some construct he wants the client to "nail down." It may be a new construct which is tentatively taking shape and which the therapist wants the client to grasp. On the other hand, it may be an old construct which has been rather amorphous. It may need to be given sufficient definition to enable the client to put it to the test and perhaps, as a result of the test, eventually to discard it. The therapist asks the client to elaborate certain material because it is material to which the construct, whether new and tentative or old and amorphous, is applicable. In dealing with the selected material the client makes an arrangement of validational evidence of the sort the therapist believes he should consider at this stage of the treatment.

g. *Material representing an extended range of convenience for constructs already in use.* Suppose a client has a fairly good notion of what *tolerance* means when it is applied in certain restricted areas. The therapist sees some advantage in extending the range of convenience of this particular construct in the client's repertory. He may therefore seize upon the earliest opportunity to have the client elaborate material which is at the fringe of the range of convenience of this construct. Unless the client has some pat alternative construct that he falls back upon when dealing with this fringe area, there is a reasonable chance that he may invoke the *tolerance* construct when he tries to come to grips with the material the therapist has tagged for elaboration.

This type of elaboration is likely to be a feature of the closing sessions of any psychotherapeutic sequence. Therapeutically formulated constructs usually have quite a narrow range of convenience when they are first set up and tested. It is just as well that they do, for if they are too comprehensively formulated they are likely also to be too loose for the client to test and validate. However, after their validity within a limited range has been adequately established, it is well to take steps to extend their range of convenience. Thus, during the later sessions of a psychotherapeutic sequence, the client and the therapist are likely to spend considerable time talking about matters which have not been particularly disturbing to the client but which he is coming to see as falling within the possible range of convenience of new-found constructs.

10. RECAPITULATION PROCEDURE

Reflection and *acceptance* were discussed in earlier sections. Reflection procedures were dealt with in connection with the controlled elaboration of the client's complaint. The implications are broader than complaint elaboration, however. Much of what we said in that section would also be applicable here. Acceptance, discussed in the chapter on basic therapeutic procedures, is also closely related to the recapitulation procedures. The therapist clearly shows acceptance when he demonstrates that he understands the client's point of view well enough to recapitulate accurately what the client has been saying for the past several months. He is willing to see the problem through the client's eyes; although, of course, he should not, in so doing, surrender his professional overview of the client's difficulties. The therapist assumes the position of constructive alternativism, which permits him to see and appreciate simultaneously two variant interpretations of the client's problem — the client's and the therapist's. The recapitulation helps him demonstrate to the client that the client's view is accepted, even though it may be one which the therapist would prefer to see abandoned.

The therapist may attempt to recapitulate what has been discussed in the past several sessions. The client may then be asked to check the recapitulation against his own recollection. This is a type of elaboration requiring the client to consider in an organized manner what he has been saying. It is a test of the internal consistency of what he has been telling the therapist. Sometimes the account obviously presents a confused and incoherent picture. When thus confronted with what he has been saying, the client may be overwhelmed by his incoherency or he may be challenged by it. If he is challenged, he may proceed to elaborate the material as best he can and to check it against validational evidence.

The client himself may be asked to recapitulate what he has been trying to convey during the preceding sessions. He may be unable to produce any coherent overview. He may simply elaborate certain further anecdotal details. The therapist should not be hasty in assuming that the client therefore does not really want to face his problem; the client's behavior may indicate that he simply cannot yet come to grips with it. If the client responds to the procedure and does make a coherent statement of what has been going on, the stage may be set for experimental testing of the emerging central theme.

a. *Diary.* One recapitulation procedure is to have the client keep a diary. Another is to have the client write a summary and critique of each interview and bring it to the next interview. The client may read it to the therapist at the beginning of the session. The latter procedure has been used profitably by the writer in certain types of cases. Both procedures have distinct disadvantages, however, because they take out of the interview room some of the most important developments in the client's thinking, whereafter the therapist has no immediate access to them. When the client sits down to write his recapitulation he may become very much confused, upset, and depressed. Yet this disadvantage may have to be accepted until such time as the client feels safe enough in the presence of the therapist to express himself spontaneously.

b. *Playback.* Verbatim review may be used. A recording of the last interview may be played back to the client. Granted that this is a daring procedure, it may, in some cases, force the client to carry forward his elaboration of what he has been desultorily producing. A client who has attempted to relate himself to the therapist in a dependent manner will find the procedure quite upsetting. Similarly, a client who feels guilty because of his dependency relationship will be disturbed by the procedure. On the other hand, a child who accepts his relationship to the therapist without guilt may be fascinated by the playback, particularly if the therapist does not try to analyze it for him too meticulously. The procedure is strong medicine and the therapist should be very cautious not to allow too much criticism to creep into the ensuing discussion. Most clients will themselves formulate all the criticism they are able to handle.

c. *Group psychotherapy.* Group psychotherapy may be used for recapitulation purposes. The client may discuss in the group some of his experiences in individual therapy. The reporting of such material is not always desirable, particularly if the individual-therapy therapist is trying to keep certain therapeutic explorations confined to the individual-therapy room. Ordinarily, however, group psychotherapy is employed as adjunctive therapy only in those cases where it is deemed advisable to extend experimentation beyond the individual-therapy room. It is to be expected, therefore, that the client will occasionally talk to the group about what has been going on in the individual interviews.

d. *Contraindications.* Recapitulation should never be employed unless the therapist is sure that he wants to deal with therapeutic material in a summarized or recapitulated form. If the client is in a state of flux and the therapist wants to keep him that way, it is just as well not to ask him to formulate any consistent point of view and, by implication, commit himself to it. Often therapy depends upon the client's abandoning many of the hostages he has given to consistency. He relaxes. He allows himself to assume a fresh and novel outlook. He pays less attention to what he has thought in the past and more to what he may appropriately think in the present. It may be quite important that he not be reminded of yesterday's ill-considered commitments, lest he feel obligated to continue to act in accordance with them in spite of his better judgment.

11. PROBING

Probing is a way of controlling the client's participation in the interview. It can be used two ways: to push the client into dealing with certain matters that he might not otherwise mention, and to keep the client from talking about other matters which he is not psychologically prepared to discuss at the moment. The judicious use of probing techniques may save an interview from breaking down into anxious confusion. The client has to keep structuring his answers to questions and that may suffice to keep him from breaking down into tears or from pursuing a hostile line of interaction with the therapist. If the questions are too searching, however, the break may be hastened by the probing.

a. *Misuse of probing.* It is easy for the inexperienced therapist to turn his probing into a kind of inquisition which forces the client to incriminate himself. If the therapist uses his probing to try to prove a point, he has nothing but his own hostility to blame for the resulting therapeutic stalemate. We have defined hostility: it is the attempt to distort data in order to make them conform to prior construction. The therapist who attempts to prove that a client is a certain kind of person by means of probing, rather than trying to discover whether or not he is that kind of person, is acting hostilely. The therapist's probing questions should therefore always provide full latitude for the truth to express itself. They should rarely be of the either-or type. A therapist may ask at a certain juncture in an interview, "Does this mean that you want to divorce your wife?" The client may say yes or he may say no, but the probing question is one to which he might also have given a qualified answer which might better have expressed his ambivalence. Contrast this formulation with the hostile type of question: "Either you want to divorce your wife or you don't — now which is it?"

The object of probing is to give the client a pinpointed opportunity to elaborate his complaint, his construct system, or the notion that has just crossed his mind. The therapist wants to know more about it. He wants the client to explore further what is involved. If properly conducted this is the antithesis of seeking to vindicate the therapist's biases regarding the case.

b. *Types of probing*. One may probe as soon as a cue is given, or he may make a mental note of what the client has said and plan to return to it later. The first procedure may be called the *immediate probe* and the second may be called the *delayed probe*. Ordinarily the latter type is to be preferred during psychotherapy. The client should not be given the impression that the therapist takes advantage of every opening to drive home a point. Rather, the probing should represent a well-thought-out procedure for helping the client to elaborate constructs which are meaningful to him. It is therefore usually much more effective if the therapist follows up a lead only after he is sure it should be followed and that the client is ready to deal with it.

What we are saying here stems from our basic theoretical position. We do not conceive therapy ever to be the mere ventilation of musty ideas. Therapy has to do with construing and reconstruing. The most significant type of therapy involves the formulation of new constructs. If the therapist considers his task merely to be the probing for "emotional" material, he is likely to overlook his central task of helping the client rearrange that material. For this reason we would ordinarily advise the therapist not to be too eager to follow up the client's leads with immediate probes. The delayed probe may be far more timely and more helpful to the client.

c. *Use of the immediate probe.* The immediate probe can be used for making sure the client extends his elaboration to certain fringe material which will enrich the meaning of what he is trying to say. Ordinarily it is used when minor points are involved and the therapist has a pretty good idea of the general nature of the reply that the client is likely to make. It may also be used in diagnostic interviews, where as much significant material as possible is to be elicited in a short time. It is frequently used when a client is being interviewed before a staff and the cues the interviewer detects may be overlooked by other members of the staff unless he makes sure the client elaborates them on the spot. But this type of interviewing is not usually very effective for psychotherapeutic purposes anyway. And perhaps this tendency to "jump down the client's throat" in a staff or diagnostic interview is one of the principal reasons that such an interview often militates against a good psychotherapeutic relationship.

d. *Use of the delayed probe.* An interview in which use is made of the delayed probe is much more difficult for a monitor or a staff group to follow. One needs to have sat in on a number of the interviews of the series in order to see just how the therapist is utilizing his cues and organizing his probes. In any case, one who monitors an interview should first be briefed as to what therapeutic plan is being followed and what kind of material is currently being developed by the therapist. Only if he has this information will he be able to follow the interview intelligently.

12. THE DETECTION OF IMPENDING CHANGES

The therapist needs to be alert to impending changes in his client. Sometimes these involve no more than a reversal of field with respect to some construct. For example, a young woman client whose psychotherapy was recently monitored by the writer had, as one of the structural members of her system, the construct of *objective vs. subjective.* This does not sound like anything very unusual; similar contrasts are used by many psychologists. However, in this woman's case, elaboration revealed that for one to be "objective" was to be rigid, unperceptive, domineering, empirical or nonrational in a philosophic sense, and masculine. These terms are not exactly her own but will perhaps enable the reader to subsume what she meant in terms of his own personal construct system. For her, to be "subjective" was to be imaginative, sympathetic, creative, rational, intelligent, perceptive, receptive, and accepting.

The "subjective" people in her life had, for the most part, been women. Men had frequently, in the end, turned out to be "objective." There was, of course, much more to the construction system than this, but we have cited enough to give some idea of this particular construct dimension.

The male therapist in this case was first approached by the client relatively open-mindedly; that is, she seemed to apply her constructs to him somewhat propositionally and circumspectively. After a few interviews she began to confide some of the difficulties in her "carnal" (sic) relations with both men and women. She also described some marked failures in her social experiments.

In the interview following the one in which she had described some particularly distressing failures, her attitude toward the therapist showed a marked change. She now avoided further discussion of the topics which had been mentioned in the preceding interview and began experimenting with the therapist. She began making personal references to him, using such expressions as "you," "I wonder what *you* think of this," and the like. She now responded to what he said as if she were trying to help him develop his points rather than trying to develop her own, and generally showed the beginnings of what we have called *personal identification* or *primary transference*.

Now, while a therapist will ordinarily want to avoid a full-blown personal-identification type of relationship with his client, what this client was doing was not necessarily antitherapeutic. She had brought to the fore certain aspects of her construct system. She had felt herself somewhat shaken and anxious in revealing what she had in the previous interview. Moreover, her formulations seemed to be subsumed under her *objective vs. subjective* construct. She was ready for a little experimentation. What about her therapist? Was he another figure with respect to whom she would be disillusioned? Was he "objective" or "subjective"? His acceptance of what she had said in the preceding interview suggested that, although a man and a psychologist, he might not be "objective" after all.

In the interview she began responding to him as if he were "subjective." She began presenting herself as an accepting, exciting, exotic person to see whether or not she would strike a sympathetic note. There was much more facial expression, more use of gesture and of nonsyntactical language such as laughter, cooing sounds, and such. She attempted to be warmly responsive to anything he had to say, although it goes without saying that the direction of her efforts prevented her from producing what most therapists would call "new material."

But was she unproductive in this session? Was she merely "acting out"? Here is where the therapist who makes use of the position of the psychology of personal constructs is likely to find himself in disagreement with other therapists. Whereas she had formerly viewed the therapist circumspectively, she now continued through the C–P–C Cycle and tried construing him *preemptively* with resultant *control* of her responses to him. She was experimenting. Her hypothesis was that here was a male who was "subjective." It was worth investigating. In the sense that she was performing an experiment she was not unproductive in this interview.

Was she showing signs of genuine reconstruction? Was this new behavior the signal of impending changes in her construct system? Our answer to both of these questions is maybe. The outcome of the experiment might *lead* to changes, depending upon the kind of validational evidence the therapist provided; but it is highly doubtful whether either the hypothesis or the experimental behavior was actually new. Instead of treating the therapist as an "objective" or as a propositionally construed figure, she was simply trying out the other end of her construct dimension of *objective vs. subjective* on him. It was an experiment which had probably been tried many times before and had probably yielded inconsistent results. It probably represented no more than a reversal of field with respect to the same construct she had been using on men for some time.

Now we come to the next question. When a client behaves in an unaccustomed manner during an interview does it always mean that he is experimenting with the converse side of a well-established construct? No, it may occasionally be a reliable indication of an impending change in the construct system. The client may be behaving in a way he has never behaved or even contemplated behaving before he came for therapy. If so, it means that a new construct is taking shape. Indeed, this is the way new structure usually first reveals itself. We may even formulate a rule of thumb and say that *an impending change in the construct system is usually revealed by new experimentation before it is verbally announced.* The therapist should therefore be particularly alert to the client's experimentation with the therapeutic situation if he wishes to anticipate therapeutic changes in the client. If he waits for the client to come out with a full-blown verbalized formulation of the new structure, the therapy may all be over before the therapist realizes what is going on.

For example, the client mentioned above later revealed an impending change of a more significant type. Her speech became slower. She was more circumspective in her approach to new material during therapy sessions. Her dress was less pretentious and more appropriate to her daily occupation. She was more willing, even though still apprehensive, to discuss elements in the area of her anxieties. This could be taken as indicating an impending change in her construction of the therapist and probably also in her construction of the class of figures with whom she linked him. She was apparently now experimenting with a genuinely *new* relationship which had a somewhat different set of parameters.

About two interviews after this was noted she attempted a more adequate description of her father than she had been able to produce before. She described her "real" father and her "mythical" father. The latter, it seems, was the father she had constructed in her childhood phantasies. In part she perceived the "mythical" father as the "real" father acting in different ways, and in part he was another person. It was obvious that here was the basis of the new relationship which had started to take place two interviews earlier. Shortly after this she said as much. The impending change in the construct system was revealed by new experimentation before it was verbally announced.

13. ELABORATION BY CITING DETAIL

During therapy the client may describe an incident which seems to symbolize something of importance to him. The therapist decides that this is material which ought to be elaborated on the spot. He has various courses open to him. He may ask the client to construe the incident. Or the therapist, instead of asking the client to say what the material means, may ask the client to describe the incident in greater detail. The therapist may use probing questions to elicit finer and finer details. He may say, "Just how did the person look? What was his expression like? Can you remember any little details about his manner?" and so on.

The object of this type of questioning is to discover cues the client can link with other incidents or with repetitive themes which are beginning to manifest themselves in the therapeutic series. The citing of further detail may also surround the tentatively expressed construct with enough content to stabilize it and make it amenable to later experimental formulation. An incident which is described in detail can be more easily recalled in a later session when it comes time to put the subsuming construct up for test. The elaboration of detail may also reveal to the client flaws in the internal consistency of parts of his construct system which are used to deal with the incident. He may also discover that he has been using the incident as validational material for constructs which have outlived their usefulness.

Sometimes the elaboration of detail actually helps control the client's anxiety, though this is not necessarily true. A client describing the incident of his mother's death may express a great deal of anxiety. Yet the therapist may be able to help him dispel some of the anxiety by asking him to attend to some of the minute details of the incident. Anxiety is confusion. The client may be less confused about the details of the incident than he is about his own life role in relation to his mother and the meaning of the incident within the larger context.

14. ELABORATION OF ANTECEDENTS AND CONSEQUENTS

The therapist may, instead of asking the client to describe an incident in greater detail, ask him to describe the events leading up to the incident and the events succeeding it or appearing to be affected by it. This is a way of putting the incident on a time line and possibly subjecting it to time-cycle constructs.

The client's conception of cause-and-effect relationships is important here. He may feel that he caused the incident and his own role is threatened by the part he played. We would then expect guilt feelings to be expressed. Again, the incident may illustrate the turning point in his life beyond which he has no field in which his dependency constructs could operate effectively. Other meanings can also come to the fore as a result of this type of elaboration.

15. CITATION OF MATERIAL WHICH IS CONSTRUED TO BE SIMILAR

This too is a form of elaboration, though the content elicited is substantively different. The client describes an incident or an experience. Instead of asking the client to describe further detail or to describe antecedents and consequents, the therapist asks him to think of some other experiences which gave him the same feeling or which somehow seemed similar. He may also be asked to describe experiences which seem in some manner to contrast with the one cited.

This is an important procedure for exploring the significance of constructions of material arising during the course of therapy. The client may not be able to give his experience a precise verbal definition but often he can cite elements which seem similar and elements which seem contrasting. From the client's alignment of elements the therapist may himself formulate a facsimile of the preverbal construct which the client is apparently using.

a. *Is the therapist ever more familiar with the client's construct system than the client is himself?* Some therapists would be inclined to say that by inference the therapist can gain an insight to which the client is still blind. Granted that the therapist's facsimile construct may be better verbalized than the client's original construct. Granted also that the therapist's version may be more tightly formulated, and hence more easily subjected to experimental test. The therapist may even deal with the client's experience at a higher level of cognitive awareness than the client does. But does this mean that the therapist is closer to the truth, or to reality, or to understanding than the client is? Perhaps not. The client is himself a bit of truth, a bit of reality, and a part of the very substance of understanding. Is the therapist closer to the client than the client is to himself? We think not.

But the therapist's psychological training, if he has any, should enable him to make certain predictions about the client which the client cannot make about himself. He does this, not because he is a better master of the client's construction system than the client is himself, but because he is able to subsume the client's construction system and construe it along with other features of reality which the client does not understand so well. The client, while faithfully representing his own natural bit of truth, is not necessarily wise. The therapist may help him acquire, through the same wisdom-gathering processes that have served mankind so well over the centuries, the wisdom he needs to put his life role into effective operation.

At the conclusion of psychotherapy the client may be far wiser than the therapist. To those who view wisdom as a commodity to be passed only from teacher to pupil or from therapist to client this may seem an anomaly. Among those who are familiar with the scientific methodologies of concept formation, hypothesization, and experimentation the statement will cause no gasp of surprise. It is the client who performs the experiment — why should it not be he who catches the first glimpse of wisdom?

We have digressed at this point in our exposition of the psychology of personal constructs because it seems to us that here is a juncture where the therapist might easily misconstrue his role. It is easy for a therapist to say, "Aha, I see through what my client is doing! Oho, he is deceiving himself but not me! He does not know what he is thinking, but I do!" Nonsense! The client construes as he construes. The most that the therapist can say is, "I can see better than he what this is likely to lead up to." When the therapist asks the client to elaborate by describing another experience which seems to him to be similar to the one just cited — and then another experience which seems to be in contrast to it — it is this latter type of overview which the therapist is seeking to attain. It may lead to better verbalization than the client is able to formulate; it may lead to a better perspective than the client is yet able to envision.

b. *Advantage for the client.* But the therapist need not be the only one to profit from this type of elaboration. Having cited additional experiences which compare and contrast, the client may himself find that he is able to put into words a construct which formerly existed only as a vague feeling or as an impulse. More than that, he may be able to mount some vantage point from which he can see his experiences in better perspective.

c. *Difficulties.* This type of elaboration may fail if the client can cite only additional experiences which seem to have some very concrete elements in common. If the experience initially cited involves, say, a letter, he may go on and on meticulously citing instances in which letters, postage, and mail are involved. While it may well be that the letter, chosen as the symbol of the commonality between experiences, has some very personal value, this approach may not enable the client to express that value in any form the therapist can make sense out of.

Ordinarily the therapist should not give up until he has attempted to get some elaboration via contrast experiences. The client who seems too concretistic to be understood when he is citing similar experiences may reveal the true nature of his construction when he starts to make his constructs clear by citing contrast experiences. Yet even this may fail. In the end, the therapist may have to give up his attempt to get an understandable elaboration by this device.

16. ELABORATION BY CONSTRUING A SERIES OF EXPERIENCES

An approach which is similar to the one just described is to call the client's attention to two or three experiences which he has described and ask him to construe them. That is, the therapist approaches experiences in a manner similar to the way the Role Construct Repertory Test approaches constructs. He says, in effect, to the client, "You have told me about three experiences — A, B, and C. Are there two of these which are alike in some important way, yet different from the third?" In some cases it may be preferable to ask for a less discriminative answer and the therapist may ask, "As you see it, how do all of these experiences seem to be alike?" If the therapist prefers to seek discrimination in order to break up the client's overgeneralization he may ask, "What is the really important way in which you see all of these experiences as differing from each other?" The first method is the one which calls for the most precise expression of a construct.

The approach we have just described differs in this respect from the approach described in the preceding paragraphs: in the former approach we attempt to infer the client's governing constructs inductively by asking him to add elements to the likeness and contrast ends of the context; in the latter approach we direct his attention to elements already cited and ask him to verbalize the governing construct. It goes without saying that the latter approach is better suited to a client who is more articulate or perhaps further along in his therapy.

We can combine the two methods. We can say, "Do not the two experiences you have described seem to you to be alike in some way? ... Now could you tell me about something that happened to you that seems to stand out in contrast to these two experiences? . . . Just what is that contrast? What do you mean?"

17. ELABORATION OF THERAPEUTIC MOVEMENT

As the client begins to alter his behavior pattern he is frequently inarticulate about the changes which are taking place. Sometimes the therapist hears about developments in his client's behavior, not from the client but indirectly, through the client's associates. The therapist may wish to have the client construe at a higher level of cognitive awareness the changes that are taking place in his construction system. Sometimes this can be accomplished by asking the client to construe three experiences, one occurring before therapy, one occurring early during therapy, and one occurring recently. If movement is really taking place, the client will rarely construe the first and third experience as similar. But whether he does or not, the task of construing three experiences which happened at three really different developmental stages in his life is one which encourages him to build a framework for himself in which therapeutic movement can be perceived. At certain stages in the therapeutic series this is a particularly important undertaking.

We have mentioned Howard's study of patients' construction of their movement. He studied the hospital patients' perceptions of the changes which take place in them during hospitalization. Each patient in the study wrote three self-characterizations. The first was written at approximately the time he was admitted. The second and third were written some weeks later. The second was a self-characterization as the patient saw himself at the time of writing, but the third was a self-characterization as the patient remembered himself at the time of admission.

Howard confirmed his hypothesis that there was more similarity between the first and second self-characterizations than between the second and third. One might be tempted to say that the patients overconstrued the movement which had taken place. From our point of view, the question of whether they overconstrued the movement or not is somewhat irrelevant. The relevant point is that these patients, who were presumably under therapeutic pressure to move, did develop constructs enabling them to perceive movement in themselves. This, we believe, is an important feature of therapy.

But Howard's patients did not always perceive themselves as improved. In fact, he found no consistent trend toward their seeing themselves as improved. If he had, of course, he would have had to make some disposition of the possibility that they were merely arguing for their release from the hospital. This may be a subtle point in our theoretical development but, as we see it, it is more important that the client have a framework within which he can perceive changes in himself than that he perceive all of those changes as being for the better.

If one is to travel to the north it is important that he find a highway along which he can travel. The fact that such a highway, when found, would be one which would run south as well as north is no indication that it cannot be used for the journey.

The same is true of the client who is to make a therapeutic journey. He needs to find a highway along which he can travel. The therapist needs to help him. When the highway is found it will, like all highways, lead in two opposite directions. The therapist may hope that the client will see it as a one-way street leading only in the direction of health. But the client's choice of whether to turn to the right or to the left will depend, not upon the highway itself — the construct — but upon the opportunities for further elaboration he is able to see up the road. He will make the *elaborative choice*. He will not turn toward what clearly appears to be a "dead end."

One of the purposes of elaboration of material arising during the course of therapy is to find those highways along which the client is free to travel. They appear in the form of constructs. Some of the constructs can be described in terms of words; that is, their routes can be plotted on surveyors' charts. Some cannot be expressed so abstractly; the client can only demonstrate their presence by means of verbal gestures. The therapist should not always insist upon the client's showing him a precise map. Even gestures have to be accepted at certain stages of therapy and, in some forms of therapy, they may be accepted as the sole means of communication.

18. ELABORATION THROUGH ENACTMENT

One of the simplest and most effective means of helping a client elaborate material arising during the course of therapy is by the controlled use of enactment. Enactment may be used for other purposes too, but here we are discussing it in relation to the problem of helping the client elaborate something he has tried to say.

Instead of asking the client to describe an incident in further detail, or to describe its antecedents and consequents, or to describe other incidents judged to be similar, or to construe the incident, the therapist may say, for example, "Let's see if we can get a clearer picture of how this happened. Suppose I am . . ." The therapist immediately takes the part of the individual with whom the client has described a personal interaction. He speaks some of the lines from the client's description of the incident.

The client may be surprised and may try to break up the enactment. He may be threatened by the possible outcome of the enactment, particularly if he has related the incident primarily with the intention of hostilely manipulating the therapist. Ordinarily, however, the therapist stays in character quite persistently. If the client responds to the therapist qua therapist, the therapist may express his character's perplexity at the client's response in the enactment situation and continue in the part.

In the writer's experience therapists have tended to be more rigid, self-conscious, and resistive to role playing than clients have. Indeed, the therapists have often been more reluctant to undertake the enactments than their own clients have been. This may be a function of their own lack of spontaneity in any therapist role, it may be because they are actually hostile toward the client and are more interested in manipulating him than in helping him elaborate what he has to say, or it may be that they are genuinely threatened by the possibility of outcomes which could destroy the figment of themselves which they think they have created in the client's mind.

If the client says that the therapist is not saying what the therapist's character would say, the therapist may "break character" and ask the client to suggest some lines. He may even do a quick switch in parts and ask the client to enact briefly the part of the character so that the therapist can "get the hang of it." The therapist can then drop briefly into the part of the client in the situation.

a. *First principle: no long preliminary discussions in enactment.* Four principles are important. First, there should be no long preliminary discussions of the enactment or the way the parts should go. The therapist should drop into one or the other of the two parts almost immediately after he proposes the enactment. He takes the initiative, becomes quite active, and makes himself quite responsive to anything the client says as if the client too were playing the part assigned to him. The therapist is aggressive but not hostile. If the therapist allows himself to become embroiled in an "intellectualized" discussion of the incident or of the enactment, he is likely to waste the whole hour. The rule should be, "Don't *talk* about it. *Do* it!" Of course, the therapist ordinarily confines the enactment to a verbal exchange. If the incident involved a fist fight, the therapist will naturally select for enactment only those elements which can be portrayed verbally.

b. *Second principle: make enactment brief.* The second principle to follow is to make the enactment brief. The purpose of the enactment is not to develop and document a complicated and involved "self-insight." Rather, it is to help the client elaborate the construct which governs his recollection of the experience. Enactment may be used for other purposes too, but here we are concerned with its use in the elaboration of material arising during the course of therapy. Ordinarily in the first interview in which enactment is used there will be less than ten minutes' total time actually spent in the enactments. A single passage may last no longer than a minute and still be quite effective. The object is not to elicit a mass of detail but rather to have the client deal with the incident spontaneously as a real incident and not solely as a topic for discussion in the therapeutic session. If, even for a few moments, he can feel and act as if he were again involved in the incident, he will have produced something in the context of the therapeutic session which can be dealt with more realistically than it could otherwise have been. Simply stated, our point is that even a brief enactment serves to turn the client's attention toward the reality that is outside the therapy room instead of allowing him always to confine his enactments to the field of reality which is circumscribed by the therapist, the therapy room, and the therapy hour.

c. *Third principle: exchange of parts.* The third principle is to exchange parts. It is important that the therapist not be cast in an inflexible role. It is also important for the client to perceive the enactment as an experimental procedure and the part he plays as one from which he can extricate himself. He should not feel that he has been cast in the underdog role and that he is expected to stay in it. Most of all, the enactment should introduce the beginnings of genuine *role* relationships. By that we mean that the part should be played out with some measure of understanding of how the other person is construing the situation. All of these essentials are served by having the parts exchanged. The therapist at one moment is seen as portraying one character. The next moment he is seen sympathetically portraying another — that of the client himself. "Aha," thinks the client. "This therapist is both sympathetic and versatile. With him here, this room can become a well-equipped laboratory for experimenting with my life's perplexing social relations, provided, of course, that I dare experiment at all."

The client finds that he too can be versatile. He is permanently cast neither in the one part nor in the other. He plays both parts. But the most important experience comes when he plays the second part. Here he suddenly finds himself playing opposite the character he has just portrayed. Now he knows a little of how that character must be construing the situation and can adapt himself to what that construction is. It is at this moment that a client may begin to enact a role as we have defined role. He now realizes that he is not playing opposite an inanimate threat-

ening machine but face to face with a thinking, perceptive person
— a person through whose eyes, only a moment ago, he himself
was peering out at the world.

d. *Fourth principle: avoid caricature.* The fourth principle is
that the therapist should guard against portraying a caricature
of the client. Some therapists think that therapy consists in getting the client to see himself as others see him, or more particularly, as the therapist sees him. Fortunately, most clients resist
this type of therapist "insight" until they are able to adapt it to
their own construction systems. In a role-playing situation the
impatient-for-insight, or hostile, therapist may not be able to
suppress his impulse to portray the client as a buffoon or a spoiled
brat. It goes without saying that such a lapse on the part of the
therapist is likely to divert the client's attention from the incident
and force him to mobilize all of his resources in a desperate defense of himself in the arena of the therapy room. Just as it is
difficult for the deeply hostile client to participate in certain enactments, it is also precarious for the latently hostile therapist
to try to portray his version of his client.

The choice of an incident for the client's first elaboration by
enactment requires some care. Ordinarily it should not be an
incident in which the client is anxiously involved. Something
relatively innocuous serves much better as a basis for early enactments. Enactment is strong medicine. It may bring the client
so abruptly face to face with interpersonal realities that he cannot handle them. It is much better to deal with anxiety situations
after the therapist is apprised of the client's resourcefulness in
structuring enactments.

Chapter Twenty

Loosening and Tightening

ЛЛЛЛЛЛЛЛЛЛЛЛЛЛЛЛЛЛЛЛЛЛЛ

THIS CHAPTER deals with attempts to move the client along one of our most important reference axes, the axis of loosened versus tightened construction.

A. Loosening

1. THE PROBLEM OF LOOSENED CONSTRUCTION

In the two preceding chapters we have been considering elaboration procedures. Now we turn to another level of discourse and concern ourselves with one of the most delicate issues the psychotherapist has to face — what to do about structural loosening. Instead of talking about ways of bringing personal constructs and their superordinate-subordinate relationships to light, we now take a close look at changes in one of their most important abstracted properties. The diagnostic reference axis for these changes is *loosening vs. tightening*. The definition of this clinician's construct was developed in Volume One, and a simple literal statement of it was repeated at the beginning of this volume. The use of the construct as a reference axis in disturbed cases was discussed in this volume's chapters, "Disorders of Construction" and "Disorders of Transition."

Following the client's elaboration of his complaint and of parts of his construction system, the axis of *loosening vs. tightening* is likely to be the first important line along which the therapist will urge him to move. Loosening is defined as characteristic of those constructs leading to varying predictions, while a tight construct holds its elements firmly in their prescribed contexts. Under loose construction an element classified at one pole of a construct on one occasion is envisioned at the contrast pole on another. Thus a loose construct tends to be elastic, relating itself to its elements only tenuously; yet it retains its identity as a personal construct in the client's system.

How does it feel to think loosely? One thinks loosely in dreams. There the shadowy figures loom large without losing their diminutive proportions; they are black yet they are white; they are alternately ominous and comforting, until the dreamer despairs of telling his tight-thinking therapist anything about them at all. To think loosely? One does it, despite himself, in the daily appraisal of people and things. Today's joy is tomorrow's sadness and yesterday's regret; the failure of the moment is the success of a lifetime; and the inanimateness of stationary things turns into willful intransigence whenever we stub our toe. Yet the wavering construction remains substantially the same: joy is still contrasted with sadness, failure blocks success, and inanimateness precludes willfulness; it is only that they have unstable relationships with the objects they are designed to keep in proper array.

Loosened construction, whether openly indulged in daylight phantasy or secretly wooed behind a thin curtain of sleep, provides the client with a kind of resilience in the face of harsh reality. He realigns his facts in a makeshift way, without ever coming to grips with his inconsistencies. He senses that if his construction were tight it would quickly be shattered by the demands made upon it. With such devastation would come anxiety. The loosening offers him a shifty defense against the world he cannot stand up to.

But loosening is a necessary phase of creative thinking. There is an inevitable cycle to such thinking, one that starts with loosened construction but comes full around to something tight enough to be tested. A construction applied loosely at the beginning of the cycle does not have to be abandoned the moment its elements are discovered out of order; a realignment of facts within the context gives it a second chance to prove itself. Yet the creative cycle is never complete until the idea has taken definite shape and the sturdiness of its structure tested in the rushing torrent of real events. The tragedy of so many of us is that we can perform only half the cycle — sometimes one half, sometimes only the other. What one man can imagine he cannot test, while another goes through life attempting only what others have imagined.

Loosened construction also sets the stage for creative thinking that is to come later. The loosening releases facts, long taken as self-evident, from their rigid conceptual moorings. Once so freed, they may be seen in new aspects hitherto unsuspected, and the creative cycle may get under way.

This is the kind of preliminary stage setting the therapist attempts when he encourages loosening at the beginning of a long and "deep" series of interviews. For the client there are new personal constructs to be created, constructs which will cast his world in an utterly new perspective. Can he complete the necessary cycles? Or will his thinking, once loosened, stay that way, and new constructs always remain just out of reach, too elusive to test? This is the delicate issue the therapist must always face.

2. THE THERAPIST'S PERCEPTION OF LOOSE CONSTRUCTION

Loosening is characteristic of those constructs which lead to varying predictions. Nothing remains firmly in place, even though the construct continues to rest on the same kind of abstraction. To an outsider a client's loose construction seems like an ever shifting accumulation of irrelevancies, miscellaneous fragments, and syncretisms. Undoubtedly it was this feature that led Bleuler to suggest the term *schizophrenia* (fragmented mind) as applicable to a large group of disturbed people whose thinking was characterized by looseness.

From our point of view, loose construction is not to be considered as the same as lack of structure. Ours is a psychology of personal constructs, and it may very well be that a given observer will find it impossible to formulate a parallel construction to the loose thinking of a client. The observer is then without a structure which parallels the client's. But that does not mean that his loose-thinking client is without structure of his own.

The loss of structure is what we have called anxiety. In this case it is likely to be the therapist who is anxious. As he tries to follow his client's varying arrangements of events he may become more and more persuaded that there is simply no organization there. In order to avoid getting caught up in his own anxiety he may even withdraw from the therapeutic relationship, as, indeed, so many therapists have withdrawn from schizophrenic clients in past years.

In another case it may very well be that what appears to be loose to a therapist may actually be tightly and invariably construed by the client. Here it is the therapist who is forced to use loose construction in order to parallel the client's thinking, while the client's own thinking may still be relatively tight. After the therapist understands the client better he may be able to perceive how regular the client's construing actually is.

There is the converse situation. The therapist's interpretations or "insights," which may seem tightly drawn and foolproof to the therapist, may seem either loose or entirely unstructured to the client who tries to follow them. Most therapists can remember times when they have drawn up very neat tight constructs for their clients, only to find that the clients got all mixed up when they attempted to put these little gems of wisdom into practice. If the client paralleled the therapist's constructs with loose construction of his own, he would behave in a varying manner. If the client attempted to parallel the therapist's construction, but without any adequate structure with which to do it, he would likely be too anxious to try anything at all, except as he would possibly grasp frantically for old structures in order to keep his head above water.

There is another type of converse situation. Suppose the therapist imposes loose thinking upon a client who is accustomed to using tight constructions. Since this is a common step in the early parts of a therapeutic program the difficulties arising out of it are also common. The client's first reaction to the therapist may be one of annoyance. Later, as he tries to parallel the therapist's loose constructions, he may feel that his familiar supporting structures are giving way. He may then become too anxious to continue the interviews.

Loose constructs serve important functions in the psychological life of the person. (1) The shifting of elements in the construct context represents an incipient movement in the construction system. The result is that new experience is produced and new responses are elicited from one's associates. (2) The shifting permits certain elements to come into the field of one's attention which might otherwise be firmly ruled out by logic-tight construction. (3) Looseness permits some extension of the construct's range of convenience. (4) Sometimes the loosening tends to make the construct more permeable to new experience.

In psychotherapy loosening also serves certain special purposes. (5) It is a way of getting the client to recall events he would not otherwise think of. (6) It is a way of getting him to shuffle some of his ideas into new combinations. (7) By encouraging loosening the therapist can sometimes elicit an approximate verbal expression of a preverbal construct. (8) Finally, loosening may help release a client from the cul-de-sac of a preemptive construct. As the client loosely applies the preemptive construct, he may find that shifting its context admits new elements to which other constructs are also applicable. All of these functions may be preliminary to the reconstruction which therapy seeks to induce. They may set the stage for rotation of the personal-construct axes, for an eventual tightening of constructions along new lines, for a more spontaneous elaboration, and for experimentation.

3. PRODUCING LOOSENING BY RELAXATION

There are four principal ways in which loosening is produced in psychotherapy: (1) by relaxation, (2) by chain association, (3) by recounting of dreams, and (4) by the therapist's uncritical acceptance of the client. The psychoanalysts, whose technique always includes much loosening, encourage relaxation by means of the couch and the clearing of the room of distracting objects. One may use systematic methods of producing physical relaxation — for example, "progressive relaxation" as advocated by Jacobson. Material produced by the client while he is relaxed is likely to be looser and, because the structure is more resilient, often less likely to be shattered into anxiety. It appears also that the relaxed manner of the therapist may tend to enable the client to employ looser constructions.

The therapist may spend some time in each of the earlier sessions of a series teaching the client to relax. During this period he may be more concerned with setting the stage for loosening construction than he is with the looseness of the material which the client produces. He may explain that this is a skill to be mastered before the client's problems are dealt with. The client may be urged to "relax his thinking" and his voice as well as his muscles.

4. CHAIN ASSOCIATION

The second method of producing loosening is that of chain association. The psychoanalysts also make use of this procedure, although there seems to be less emphasis upon it than there was at one time. The client may simply be told to say whatever comes into his mind. Sometimes this is called "the first rule of psychoanalysis."

Often it is said that the client must say *everything* that comes into his mind. This, of course, is preposterous. It is virtually impossible to keep one's tongue flapping in hot pursuit of all fleeting thoughts and images. What the therapist usually has to do is urge the client to give a running account of what is going on in his mind without trying to decide formally which details are more important than others.

a. *Apparent irrelevancies.* Sometimes a therapist becomes annoyed because his client appears to be taking advantage of the chain-association assignment to produce a smoke screen of "irrelevancies." The therapist, however, may be too hasty in judging the client's motivation. In the first place, what may seem to be a series of "irrelevancies" may begin to fall into a perceptible pattern if the therapist maintains an attitude of acceptance. In the second place, the client may be acting out his loose conceptualization. If so, the therapist needs to attend more to the *way* the client is managing the therapeutic situation than he does to the literal *meaning* of the client's words. As we have already indicated, we do not take such a dim view of acting out as some analysts do. Thirdly, one should keep in mind the possibility that the client's constructions are already too much loosened and that the stock loosening procedure of psychoanalysis is aggravating a pathological condition.

Finally, the "irrelevancies," if they really are selectively chosen, can be examined with an eye to their submerged ends. One of the advantages of seeing constructs as essentially two-ended affairs is the fact that the therapist need not limit himself to the manifest content of the client's constructs, but can discover a great deal by looking for contrast patterns. The therapist can ask himself, "Now what, to this client's way of thinking, stands in contrast to what he is saying or doing?" Sometimes questions of this sort can be put directly to the client. Sometimes the contrasts can be inferred from Rep Test protocol.

b. *Association without report.* Sometimes a client construes the therapeutic situation so preemptively that he cannot imagine himself speaking his thoughts out loud in the presence of the therapist. While one does not like to do so, it sometimes becomes necessary to make some concessions to the client's timidity and tell him to let his mind wander for a time without talking, and then review what he has been thinking about. When this is done, the verbal spontaneity of the loosened elaboration is sacrificed, but there is the greater possibility that the client's thinking will be loosened.

c. *Initial point.* Sometimes the therapist chooses a take-off point for the client's chain of associations. During the early stages of the therapy, when the client is learning how to loosen construction more than anything else, the therapist may start the chain with relatively innocuous words, such as "sky," "thing," "every," et cetera. A stem from an incomplete-sentences test can be used, or a picture, or a street sound which is audible through the window. The client can be encouraged to let his mind wander, or he can be brought back to the initial take-off point from time to time. Sometimes it helps him get the idea of how chain association goes if he is asked to back-track his associations.

d. *Association away from an initial point.* One procedure which is useful in dealing with preverbal material is to give the client an initial point and then suggest that he *associate away from* it. That is to say, he should think about what has been suggested for a short time and then start letting his mind wander away from it. Now, as any experienced therapist knows, it is difficult for the client actually to abandon an important issue. He may skirt it, but his very skirting will tend to trace its outlines. He may deal in contrasts, but these often indicate the nature of the submerged ends of the constructs he is using. He may deal with unexpected material, but it usually happens that the material is asymptotic to the issues he was facing in the first place. *Association away from* therefore does not really take the client very far afield, even though he may have the impression that he is disengaging himself from certain problems.

e. *Breaking up tight construction in chain association.* Sometimes the therapist may find that he has to take positive steps to break up a tightly drawn discourse. He may have to use such comments as, for example, "But how does all of this *feel* to you? What is it reminiscent of? What does all of this vaguely resemble? Does this feel like something you have told or experienced before and yet cannot quite put your finger on? You are telling me facts — let's not deal with facts just now, let's deal with deeper meanings, with pressures, with lurking anxieties, with vague uneasiness, with yearnings, with ideas that are hard to put into words."

f. *Avoid the "important."* Sometimes the therapist can get better results if he cautions the client not to try to say anything "important." The client, in his attempt to stay away from what he thinks is "important," may demonstrate some loose thinking. We can safely assume that what he produces will not be altogether haphazard, that his very attempt to avoid the "important" will bring into play his underlying loose preverbal construct system, as well as reveal its contrast poles. This may well be the theme to which the therapist will want to attune his ear.

5. REPORTING DREAMS

The third technique for loosening construing processes is that of calling for reports of dreams. Dreams represent about the most loosened construction that one can put into words. Sometimes the construction is so loose and preverbal that the client cannot put it together at all. The dream seems to change in the course of its telling. Sometimes at the end of the dream it seems as though the first part of the dream must have happened differently. This shifting context is characteristic of loosening, and the therapist misses the point if he keeps probing to pin the client down in order to find out what the dream *really was*.

For example, a client dreams that he is on a large ship. There is music and dancing. He goes out on deck. He has just boarded a ship. It is a fishing boat. It was not music and dancing that he envisioned. In this sequence the client's construction is loose and shifting. As matters stand at the beginning of the dream, there is music and dancing; from the standpoint of the end of the dream there had been no music and dancing. If the therapist is determined to find out precisely whether the dreamer dreamt about music and dancing his answer has to be yes *and* no. From the standpoint of the beginning of the dream the client did dream about music and dancing. From the standpoint of the end of the dream he did not. If this seems preposterous, we should remember that we are dealing with loose construction. Some therapists might interpret such a dream as one which was being reported out of sequence or as a condensation of a great deal of complex dream material. From our point of view, however, it is usually sufficient to view it simply as loosened construction and go on to elaborate and study the constructs which give it its loose binding.

It is important to keep in mind just what it is about dreams that makes it desirable to deal with them in certain therapeutic programs. From the standpoint of the psychology of personal constructs, it is not the dream as an entity or as a biographical event that principally concerns us. We are more concerned with the loosened construction which it represents. When a client reports a dream, it is what goes on while he reports it that concerns us more than what it was he dreamed about. His act of reporting the dream invokes his loosened construction; that is what we want to see. When we ask a client to recount a dream that means that we want him to engage in loosened construction for a part of the interview hour. Sometimes he seems to be able to remember almost nothing about the dream, and yet what we hoped to achieve is achieved. We wanted him to invoke certain loose constructions which we had not dealt with before. In the course of the discussion of "the dream that he cannot remember" he may do just that. We wanted him to loosen constructs which, heretofore, had been distressingly tight. He may do so. Sometimes we get what we want out of an attempt to recall a dream even though the client is unable to verbalize any of the content at all.

a. *Equivalence of dream content.* In this connection there is a technique which can be used to help the client loosen his construction. For example, the client may say, "I think I had a dream last night but I haven't the faintest idea what it was about." After trying some of the usual techniques for bringing out content, such as asking whether it was a happy or sad dream, whether it seems that there were people in it or not, whether the client was a part of the dream, and so on, and getting no results, the therapist may simply say, "Let's not worry about the dream. Just relax now and think about the dream for a few moments and then let your mind wander. After a little while you can start telling me what you are thinking about." Occasionally this procedure seems to bring out what must have been the essential significance of the dream, even though the content is never mentioned as such.

b. *Tempo in the elaboration of dream content.* The elaboration of dream content nearly always requires a slowing of the interview tempo. Loosening may be thought of as a slightly shifting frame of reference. The rate of talk and the interactions between client and therapist should be at a tempo slow enough to permit this shifting to take place. A severely disturbed "schizoid" client may be able to demonstrate his loose thinking in a rapid exchange with the therapist, but the client who is not so facile with loose construing will tend either to tighten up his thinking or to introduce new constructs altogether when he is pressed for immediate answers to questions. If the therapist wants a client to behave in a "schizoid" manner — that is, to construe loosely — he will ordinarily have to slow down.

But what about the "manic" client's ability to participate in a rapid exchange with his therapist and, at the same time, to produce a "flight of ideas"? Is this not a form of loosening which is readily associated with rapid tempo? We think not. Clinically, this seems to us to be more a matter of leaping from construct to construct than a matter of loosened construction. The "manic's" intellectual process seems to be more kaleidoscopic than elastic. He also characteristically exhibits a dilation in his construing which the therapist has trouble following. The therapist who tries to fall into step with his thinking may himself have to resort to loose construction in order to keep up. But the "manic's" thinking seems to us not to be loose in the sense that the "schizoid's" thinking is.

c. *Suggestion.* Nearly all therapists who make substantial use of dreams will resort occasionally to using suggestion in order to get the client to produce dream material. The technique will not work with all clients. When one uses suggestion he should give some thought to the purpose of the procedure. From our point of view, the purpose is not so much to produce a new kind of content as it is to produce loosened construction in the interviewing room. Of course, the two tend to go together. Loosened structure tends to open the door to new content. New content often demands new types of construction. Yet, in the long run, it is the construction one uses to deal with the new experience that determines his level of adjustment, not the bare record of incidents out of the client's past. When the therapist takes steps to get the client to dream or to recall dreams, he should judge the success of his efforts in terms of the loosened construction produced. The next interview may produce what he wants even though the client claims that he has had no dream. Conversely, the client may report a dream, or a series of dreams, but in such a tightly construed manner that little of therapeutic value can be accomplished.

d. *Standard approach*. The therapist may use a somewhat standardized approach in order to help the client elaborate an elusive dream. Was it a happy dream or a bad dream? Was it simple or complex? Were there many people? Who seemed to be the principal actor? Where were the break points — the points at which the setting seemed to change? The therapist may use the *something like* approach by saying, "What other dream or experience have you had which seems *something like* this one?" Or he may say, "What other dreams come to mind just now?" Another approach which may work when all other methods fail is using one's understanding of the case to raise certain issues which are likely to have been dreamed about at this stage in the client's treatment. Sometimes this leads to the client's recalling his dream later in the same session; sometimes to the kinds of expressions that might, in any event, have followed upon the reporting of such a dream.

It is always important to keep in mind that the plot of the dream is not likely to be a tight expression of the client's conceptual frame. It is more likely to give the "moods" or "affective settings" of antecedents and consequents that the client's conceptual frame generates. It is a mistake to try to force a client to express his dream in terms of tight constructs. The principal purpose in eliciting the dream is to bring loose constructs into the therapeutic exchange — one should therefore not reject them as soon as they are produced.

6. "INTERPRETATION" OF DREAMS

Some therapists like to "interpret" dreams as fast as they are reported. These interpretations often take the form of explanations of the symbolism of the different dream elements. From our point of view, this is usually an attempt of the therapist to impose his own construct system upon the client. Because he is dealing with material which, for the client, has been preverbally construed, he feels that he can communicate better if he uses certain concrete nouns in an abstract or symbolic manner. He may tell the client that one element of his dream is obviously symbolic of a sex organ, that another is an expression of an incestuous impulse, and so on. Because these terms have *symbolic* value for the therapist, he presumes that they have, or should come to have, symbolic value for the client. Therapy conducted in this manner is often successful, although psychologically trained therapists, as contrasted with those whose training is psychiatric only, cannot help but be aware of the incidental nature of the choice of symbol names.

a. *Timing "interpretations."* If a therapist insists upon interpretation of dreams as soon as they are reported, he may block the client's reporting of dreams altogether. The interpretation serves to tighten the construction placed upon the dreams and may provide less freedom for really loose dreaming. Our view would lead us not to attempt to place any interpretation upon a dream until the therapist is sure he wants to move somewhat in the direction of tightening. Our view would also lead us not to insist upon conventional symbolism in the interpretation. The tightening is often better expressed in terms drawn from the client's own experience and vocabulary.

For example, a client, in elaborating the "passivity" which she "discovered" to be a generally threatening element in her life, first presented it in terms of an experience in which she lay in bed without doing anything while a night intruder prepared to enter her apartment. The experience was loosely construed by her in a dreamlike fashion. She said it seemed almost like a dream. The fact that another person saw the intruder and gave him close chase provided clear evidence that the experience was not a dream, even though it brought to the fore some loose constructions of the type one seeks in reporting dreams. Moreover, the experience served to provoke some important dream material as well as some important memory material.

One might, of course, symbolize this client's loose constructs in terms of incestuous desires and a fear of her father. From our point of view, however, it seemed more appropriate to symbolize them as "the night-of-the-intruder feeling." Of course, the therapist in such a case would have to remain alert to the likelihood that "the night-of-the-intruder feeling" embraced some of the early thinking of infancy as well as some of the previously unverbalized constructs which had been governing the client's erratic and ambivalent behavior. Indeed, this proved to be true in this particular case. The client had been slipping back and forth between the contrasting poles of this particular construct.

b. *"Gift" dreams.* Sometimes a client who has adjusted himself to his therapist's interpretations will start producing a regular flow of dreams. These are reported as gifts of what the therapist appears to want. If the dreams begin to follow the stereotype of the therapist's interpretive scheme, one can be reasonably sure that little progress is being made. The client is amusing himself with the infantile constructs which the therapist has helped him name and manipulate verbally. It is probably time for some experimental testing and validation to take place outside the therapy room and in terms of more practical elements.

c. *Dream notes.* We have mentioned asking the client to write down his dream immediately upon waking. While this is a relatively extreme measure for getting loosened construction into the therapy room, it may sometimes be effective. About twenty years ago the writer had as a client a middle-aged professional woman who had done a remarkable job of adjusting herself to a series of hardships. She had been widowed by the accidental death of her husband while she was in her early twenties. She lost her home and suffered other financial difficulties but had trained herself professionally and was giving her son similar educational opportunities. She had come with the complaint that, while she could deal with her problems with very few emotional "ups and downs," she always felt "a little below par." She reported also that she was frequently apprehensive before starting on a trip or committing herself to a new undertaking.

It was very difficult for this client to respond spontaneously in the interview room or to express her looser constructions. We asked for dreams. She reported that she had none. We tried suggestion. She reported that she had a feeling that she might have dreamed, but that was all she could remember. Finally, we suggested that she put a pad and pencil beside her bed and plan to write her dream in the middle of the night as soon as she dreamed it. Thereafter, she recalled waking up but being unable to remember anything that she could write. We then suggested that she write her dream without turning on the light. She brought to the next conference a leaf from her note pad, saying that there was some writing on it which seemed merely to be a jumble of letters and which she could not remember having written. Although she was unable to make any sense out of the writing, it seemed quite clear to the therapist. There was the phrase, "a girl 12 marries a man 37."

The ensuing interviews dealt, in part, with the elaboration of this construction. Of course there was an exploration of her own life when she was twelve years old. Nothing turned up. We then turned to the idea of a man twenty-five years older than herself whom she might have known at any period of her life. A long "forgotten" story then began to unfold. Her mother had died when she was four or five years of age, leaving herself, her younger brother, and her father. This we had known. The father was so grief-stricken that he was unable to give any comfort to the children. It seems that he withdrew from them. A maternal uncle *twenty-five years older than the client* lived in the home, and it was he who took over the mother's role. The client recalled that he took care of their meals, their clothing, put them to bed, and told them delightful stories.

About two years after her mother's death the uncle died. He had been known in the community as a "drinking man," and the preacher decided to use the occasion of the funeral sermon to make an object lesson out of the uncle's death for the benefit of the impressionable younger members of his parish. He preached a long sermon explicitly and vividly portraying the uncle frying in hell because of his sinfulness, particularly his drinking. The client and her brother were shocked to learn that the only person who had shown them kindness since the death of their mother was consigned to hell. For a time they refused to believe that he was dead, and plans were made to go to the local cemetery to dig him up. Death became a daily topic of conversation between the two children. A pact was made that if either should die the other would place a breathing tube in the grave. The elaboration of the loose constructs that surrounded this experience and a later recollection of an experience occurring when the client was twelve provided an opportunity to carry out a successful therapeutic program. It was a dream never actually reported which provided the first entry into the client's system of disturbed constructs.

7. MILE-POST DREAMS

There are some dreams that assume epic proportions. We call them *mile-post dreams*. They are likely to be vivid and to embrace elements from many other dreams and much that has been discussed over the period of treatment. Their vividness is an indication of the tightness with which they structure their content. Yet they arise in dream form, an indication that the structurization is initially loose. The span of material from other dreams suggests the comprehensiveness and the possible super-ordinateness of the construction portrayed. Our experience, as well as our theoretical position, would lead us to believe that they mark a transition in the underlying construction system of the client. There seems also to be a transition in the client's thinking during interviews soon after the report of such a dream. It is our belief that a therapist should be prepared to enter a new phase of treatment whenever such a dream is reported, and that, for the most part, he should not attempt to press an interpretation upon such a dream.

The mile-post dream expresses new behaviors which are about to emerge spontaneously. A certain client who had showed a great deal of hostility and constriction and had enacted her constructs in terms of somatic complaints such as anorexia was beginning to show some therapeutic progress. She dreamed vividly of preparing a meal for her family. It was one that she, her husband, and her son liked. In the dream her husband announced that he was going "off to the races," an expression which had been associated with his going to burlesque shows and with his extramarital adventures. She then threw the whole meal on the floor. This client had had considerable difficulty with the role of housewife and mother. There had been vomiting and a great deal of hostility. There had been difficulty in expressing aggression appropriately. The dream also represented admirably many other features in her construction system. She spontaneously interpreted the dream as a summary of her whole predicament. The interview was soon followed by some changes in her behavior pattern, although, in this case, certain administrative complexities in the therapeutic plans made it impossible to exploit the advantage she had gained.

8. PREVERBAL DREAMS

While we construe many dreams as dealing, in part, with preverbal material, there are some dreams which may be characterized particularly as *preverbal dreams*. They are characterized by vagueness, visual imagery, absence of conversation in the dream, slow unfolding of the content during the interview, and the feeling of the client that it may have been his "imagination rather than a dream." Such a dream may show some of the early origin of constructs which he has been using but which he has not been able to put into words.

A client of the writer's — not the client whose dream was just described — had shown a great deal of passive hostility and constriction in certain areas of interpersonal relations. She reported a preverbal dream. The report followed upon a period in therapy when considerable loosening had been used. During the interview in which the dream was reported she had been asked to relax and various loosening techniques were employed during the hour she was telling the dream. She was not sure she had dreamt at all. She had a vague feeling that she was lying in a crib, that she was feeling isolated from a man and a woman who were in the room. It seemed as though there were a netting between herself and the woman. The woman seemed like a certain aunt who was pretty and to whom she was much attracted when she was a very young child. The man seemed like an uncle whom she remembered as the first person in her life who had seemed to accept her. The most important feature of the setting appeared to be the netting, which seemed to excommunicate her from the persons with whom she had sought or had found a role relationship.

The dream was reported in fragments and the client had the feeling that some of it might have been a memory, a story that she had been told, an old fantasy, or even something which she might be making up on the spot. It was definitely associated with feelings of unworthiness and guilt; indeed, the feeling of loss of role was the principal feature of the dream. This dream, together with other features of the case, established the deep-seated and preverbal nature of the client's guilt feelings as an important fact to be considered by the therapist. Moreover, it threw light upon one of the client's own aggressive techniques, that of excommunicating other people from her own society. This technique had been her principal second line of defense and accounted for many of the constricting measures which she employed. One measure, for example, was the often repeated childhood phantasy of believing herself dead. As a child she had frequently lain in her bed imagining herself comfortably dead.

Such a dream frequently ties up with other dreams. The client who had the preverbal dream mentioned above (we call it a "dream" though of course it is as impossible, as it is unimportant, to discover whether it truly was or not) had reported another dream about a year and a half before. This had been a repeated dream of a woman lying in a casket at the bottom of a grave. The interlacing of the relationships between these dreams and phantasies was, of course, far too complex for detailed narration here. What we have reported is probably sufficient to illustrate the operation of constructs in the preverbal type of dream.

a. *"Repressed" material in dreams.* Some therapists are much concerned with "repression." They see the dream as a means of making contact with the upper layers of the "repressed" material. Our theoretical position would not lead us to place so much emphasis upon what is presumably "repressed." Our concern is more with the constructs which are being used by the client to structure his world. If certain elements have dropped out of his memory it may be simply that he has ceased to use the structures which imbued these elements with sense. We do not see these abandoned elements as covertly operating stimuli in the client's life. As we have indicated at the outset, ours is not a stimulus-response type of psychological theory. Since it is not, we are not necessarily disturbed by a bit of memory which has momentarily dropped out of sight. It need not continue as an undercover influence in the client's life. We are concerned with the operative constructs rather than with all the elements they once embraced or which were once embraced by other constructs long since inoperative.

b. *Submerged contrast poles expressed in dreams.* There are some times when the personal-construct psychologist is concerned with forms of "repression" or "suppression." Our position in this regard has been expounded in connection with an earlier discussion of the diagnostic constructs of *preverbalism, submergence, suspension,* and *level of cognitive awareness.* We have been speaking of the technique of dream reporting as a means of bringing loosened construction into the client's therapeutic program. Since loose constructs are frequently preverbal, their preverbalism making them less amenable to word binding and tightening, the dreams reported by a client frequently throw light upon constructs which are also preverbal. Some of our illustrations have had to do with preverbal construing.

Sometimes dreams enable a person to picture himself at the opposite end of one of his construct dimensions. Here the dream has the effect of penetrating to the submerged end of a construct. While we do not think that such penetration is an indication of any very novel reconstruction in the client's life, it may be an indication that he is getting ready to experiment with contrast behavior. A client who has always insisted he loved everybody may dream that he is fighting someone. This may be an indication that he is ready to deal with the contrast side of his love construct in the ensuing interviews. It is also likely to indicate that some impulsive behavioral experiments are in the offing. The wise therapist will take immediate steps to see to it that the experiments are not abortive.

Therapists who use dream reporting as a technique occasionally speak of the fact that dream elements often appear to represent their opposites. There is nothing surprising about this. Constructs have two poles and one uses constructions in dreams. We see this phenomenon simply as a matter of the dream's representing a construct which has been turned end for end. The dream represents submerged ends of constructs. In most cases the therapist will have already surmised what the submerged ends of his client's constructs must be.

Dream reporting may also be a means of reactivating suspended elements and subordinate constructs. Ordinarily we would not be much concerned with summoning up the ghosts of the past, even to have a curious look at them. Yet some clients, in developing a revised construction of their life role, are determined that their past must be rerationalized as well as their future. They are usually persons whose notion of causality requires them to see themselves as the products — or the victims — of a series of biographical anecdotes. Such clients are vastly impressed by their recovery of memorabilia. While the incidents are likely to be featured as elements in entirely new constructs, the clients see them as anchors in the past for the constructs which are to govern their future.

9. PRODUCING LOOSENING BY UNCRITICAL ACCEPTANCE

We have discussed loosening of construction by the techniques of relaxation, chain association, and recounting of dreams. The fourth technique is that of uncritical acceptance. In an earlier chapter we described acceptance as an attitude which characterizes the role of the psychotherapist. While acceptance is, therefore, not a technique of the same order as the other three which we have discussed, it does have technical implications. From the standpoint of producing loosening of construction in the client's mental processes, the term *uncritical acceptance* is quite descriptive of what the therapist does.

Acceptance has been defined as the willingness to see the world through the client's eyes. It might be more precisely defined as the therapist's attempt to employ the client's own personal construct system. In terms of our Commonality Corollary, acceptance is the movement of the therapist's mental processes in the construed direction of commonality with the client's construct system. If the acceptance is *uncritical*, it means that the client's point of view is passively accepted and there is no tendency to pursue the implications of his thinking to the point of testing them. They are not even tested for internal consistency.

The therapist who uses the technique of uncritical acceptance in order to produce loosening has to be careful not to question the client too closely as to what he means. The loosened construction is a shifting one, and to ask a client to explain at one moment what he meant to say in the preceding moment is to imply that he is expected to be consistent from moment to moment. Rather, the therapist has to say, "Yes," "I understand," "I think I know how you feel," and so on, even when he has only the vaguest notion of what the client's shifting outlook is like. The technique requires a great deal of patience on the part of the therapist as well as great fluidity in his own mental processes.

The therapist cannot expect to produce loosening if he asks such questions as, "Is this what you meant a while ago when you said . . . ?" "I am not sure I understand — could you be a little more explicit?" or "Let's see what this would lead to." Sometimes he can allay the client's criticisms of his own thinking if he says, "I understand that you are telling me how you *feel* about things and that you are not necessarily trying to tell me what is exactly *so* and what is *not so*." Or the therapist may say, "I think I can see. This is a way of looking at things." Essentially the technique of uncritical acceptance provides the client with a passive validation for his loosened construing which is elastic and nonexperimental. No matter how loose his constructions, there are no grounds provided him by the therapist which would require him to tighten up the internal consistency of the system or to subject his thinking to the rigors of experimentation.

10. DIFFICULTIES IN PRODUCING LOOSENED CONSTRUCTION

We turn now from techniques for producing loosened construction to difficulties which the therapist may encounter when he attempts to apply the techniques. Many of these difficulties are in the nature of the "resistances" with which psychoanalysis is so often concerned. We prefer not to use the term "resistance." We do not see the so-called "resistance" phenomena as perverse acts on the part of the client, even though the therapist perceives them as obstacles in the way of therapeutic progress. We see them, rather, in terms of our theoretical assumptions, as an expression of the client's continuing pursuit of an optimally predictive system. We also see these phenomena as being of a variety of sorts. Most of them have to do with avoidance of loosening and an incipient movement away from dependency upon one person; and some do not represent any particular movement at all, but, rather, the lack of a congenial common structure for dealing with the therapist and his interpretations. At this stage in our discussion we are concerned particularly with those difficulties which arise when one seeks to have his client loosen his construction.

a. *The Creativity Cycle.* As we have said before, productive thinking follows a Creativity Cycle. There is a shift to a new topic. The thinking about that topic becomes loose and fluid. The shifting conceptualization begins to fall into place under some new forms of superordinate construction. Now the conceptualization begins to become more precise, more tight. The person begins to construe more explicitly. The constructs become more stable. Elements in the construct contexts become identifying symbols, standing not only for themselves but for the classes of which they are constituent members, or the properties which bind the class into a group. At first, these elements are likely to be objects, such as this particular pen, that particular chair, those particular trees. Or they may be concretistic constructs, such as pen, chair, trees. As construction begins to tighten up even further, the person begins to tailor his symbols to fit his emerging constructs. Words, drawings, gestures, or carvings may be introduced into the new contexts in order to take up a position of symbolic value. Finally, we may have a newly created system in which the elements are themselves all represented by words and, in turn, new words have been introduced as symbols to bind them.

The transition in symbolism we have just described may appear to be nothing more than the induction of a concept in which the movement is, by levels, from concrete to abstract. But that is not what we mean. The movement to which we are referring may proceed from loose to tight and yet remain throughout at the same level of comprehensiveness or super-ordination. But the symbolism employed — that is another matter. As his new construct begins to take shape, the creative thinker is likely to be hard pressed to find a suitable symbol for it. At first he can only point to selected elements in the context and say "this" or "that." The person who tries to understand him can place only a low-level construction upon the "symbol." He naturally concludes that his creative friend is not creative at all but only chattering concretistically about miscellaneous trivia. But the creative thinker, as he tightens up his construction, begins to find more apt symbols. As he does so, his listeners begin to give him credit for being able to perceive matters which are somewhat beyond the end of his nose.

In creative thinking the development of constructs is from loose to tight. Yet, because for a loose construct one must at first use symbols which are commonly perceived concretistically or preemptively, it seems that the thinker is moving merely from the concrete to the abstract. Another way of indicating the same thing is to say that an idea is likely to take shape before a suitable symbol is chosen to represent it; it is born before it is named.

It is important for the therapist who deals with loose construction to understand this relationship between the kinds of symbols a client uses and the kinds of construction they may represent. If the client is feebleminded, the "thing-like" symbols may stand for little more than the bare things they obviously represent. If the client is a paranoid schizophrenic, the "thing-like" symbols may be makeshift representations of constructs for which he has no suitable word symbols. A literalistically minded therapist is likely to be unable to establish communication with the latter type of client.

Aside from the matter of symbolism, the successfully creative person always shows some incipient movement toward the tightening of his constructs. If he did not he would always fail to bring them to the point of experimental testing or to leave them as a legacy to posterity. The therapist who chooses to use loosening as a treatment technique will usually have to navigate against this gentle current. The therapist asks his client to loosen his construction. The client does so, perhaps by reporting a dream. But it is still not loose enough. The therapist tries to get the client to free-associate with the dream. The client steps out on marshy intellectual grounds. He feels the unsteadiness of his ideas. He may become uncomfortable and start his retreat to more steady ground and to more explicit ideas. We can call this "resistance to the therapist" if we like, but we must remember that if the client were never to show any capacity for tightening his thinking the whole undertaking would have a somber outlook.

b. *Two types of difficulties.* Here, then, lie the therapist's difficulties in dealing with "resistance" to loosening. In the first place, he may not realize he is dealing with loosened construction because of the client's difficulty in finding symbols which reveal its truly abstract nature. The therapist may, therefore, think that he is encountering resistance to his loosening efforts when, actually, the client may be far ahead of him, perhaps too far for the client's own good. In the second place, the client's incipient movements toward tightening may be frustrating to the therapist but they represent the very constructive features in the case which in any event will have to be mobilized eventually.

c. *Causes of difficulties in producing loosening.* There are various ways in which the two types of difficulties we have mentioned may arise and there are various ways in which they may be met. One of the most common causes of "resistance to loosening" is a premature attempt on the part of the therapist to offer an "interpretation" of what the client has been saying. If the client is threatened by the interpretation — that is, if the interpretation confronts him with an anxiety-fraught major reconstruction project — he is likely to tighten up his construing processes and have no more of this loosening stuff. The client who loosens his construction is likely to feel vulnerable. The therapist's eagerness to "interpret" makes him all the more vulnerable. The best protection, from the client's point of view, is not to express any more loose constructs while the therapist is around.

In the light of what we have just said it is obvious that one way to avoid resistance to loosening is to avoid expressing interpretations prematurely. But from the standpoint of the psychology of personal constructs, the avoidance of this difficulty is not merely a matter of technique. Rather, it is a matter of the therapist's basic construction of his role. His job is to help the client make discoveries of his own; it is not to shower him with blessed "insights."

Clients can be threatened, and subsequently blocked in their loosening efforts, by certain remarks of the therapist which are not intended to be taken as interpretations. A client who has been expressing loose constructions of sexual matters may find himself threatened when the therapist mentions the client's teen-age daughter. The mere introduction of this new element serves to alarm the client. The loose construction threatens to undermine his parental role structure. In the resultant confusion he is brought to the brink of guilt as well as of anxiety. He may straighten up and start tightening his construing processes. The therapist may view this tightening as a form of personal resistance, but he will do better if he sees it as a defense against anxiety, a defense that was made necessary by his own remark. If a therapist is to avoid resistance to loosening, he must be careful not only in expressing evaluations of what the client produces, but also in his introduction of contextual elements.

d. *Techniques.* As already indicated, we view certain "resistance" to loosening as a difficulty in communication between client and therapist or as a difficulty the client faces in construing certain types of material. We do not, therefore, deal with it as if it were an incipient rebellion against the therapist. Because of the way we view this resistance, our measures for dealing with it cover almost the whole range of psychotherapeutic procedure. Rather than try to introduce a complete résumé of procedure at this point in our discussion, let us suggest a few of the more useful techniques for dealing with resistance to loosening.

The client's loosening of his construction may be thrown into reverse by the intrusion of distracting elements from any source. We have mentioned the possibility of the therapist's introducing an element which makes the loosened construction threatening. But the distracting element may come from other sources also. The distraction may be in the nature of noises intruding upon the therapy room. It may be the gloomy skies the client observed on his way to the appointment. It may be a letter recently received from a member of the family. It may be the accumulation of unpaid bills — perhaps, among them, the therapist's.

e. *Interference.* Another cause of spontaneous tightening of construction is the well-known psychological phenomenon of "interference." Some loosely construed thought bears a superficial resemblance to a more conventional idea. The latter is tightly construed. In the close rivalry ensuing, the client's attention is shifted from the loose construct to the tight construct, even though the former is therapeutically more meaningful.

For example, a client is dealing with a feature of his interpersonal relationships which is only loosely construed. For want of words, and in the absence of precisely formulated enactments, the idea proves to be elusive. Now he knows what he means — now he doesn't. He may try to elaborate his idea in a kind of talking pantomime in which the words are elements in the constructs but in which no one word or sentence has the gathering and holding power of a symbol of the whole construct. He employs verbal gestures; he "acts out." Nothing he says seems quite to express what he means. Yet he is not quite sure what he means. What he means now is not precisely what he meant a while ago. This is loose construction.

Suppose the loosely formed construction seems to be revolving around a construct something like that of a symbiotic relationship to persons. In a loose vague way he sees himself cultivating friends as if they were to be husbanded for their nurturant services. It is as if he saw his mother as a cow to be possessed for the milk she supplies and as if he dealt with society as with a swarm of bees which are to be systematically robbed of a portion of their honey. That strikes a clear note. Now he thinks of bees. He recalls a painful childhood experience with bees. He goes on to describe the incident in precise detail.

Here is a construct which is tightly formed. It *interferes* with the loosely formulated construct with which he was struggling. He abandons the halting attempt to tighten up the construct of his symbiotic-like interpersonal relationships and takes off into a fluent discussion of the painful experience with bees. In listening to this passage in the client's verbalization the therapist may pick up the elements having to do with "mother" and with "nourishment"; but, because of the transition to a painful experience, he may detect only a theme of parental rejection and oral deprivation. Yet, from the point of view of reconstruction, it is more important that the construct of the symbiotic personal relationships be elaborated and tightened. While it is sometimes helpful for a client to see his life as patterned with respect to painful and depriving experiences with his mother, it is more likely that he can replan his future after he understands better just how he is continually milking his friends.

Was our unweaned client, who turned aside to report that he had once been stung by a bee, "resisting" the efforts of the therapist? We do not think it profitable to construe it that way. He was struggling inarticulately with an elusive construct. A tighter construction of some of the same elements invaded his field. He then pursued the more tangible "bees." The therapist must be careful not to overlook the transition. When he detects it he may be disappointed that his efforts to loosen his client's construing have not been wholly successful. But he should not see it as resistance and grounds for feeling hostile toward the client.

f. *Enactment.* The therapist counteracts resistance to loosening, not only by continuing to employ the techniques for producing loosening which have already been discussed, but also by special techniques directed more particularly against the causes of the tightening. The use of enactment techniques sometimes reduces the threat which loosened constructs present. As we have indicated before, the client, when he believes he is "only playing a role," does not see himself as so deeply involved as he would otherwise be. What he produces does not have to be consistent with his core construction of himself.

For example, he can often pretend to enact the part of a person who has a mixed perception of his sex role whereas the least suggestion that he himself has sex-role difficulties may throw him into turmoil. If, during the enactment, he spontaneously produces certain loose constructions which he could not otherwise allow himself to produce, the end result may be nearly as helpful as if he produced them "in his own role." When a person "acts a part" spontaneously and extemporaneously it is still he himself who produces the enacted structure. Since he is "acting," he partly disclaims responsibility for what he says and does. Since he does not feel that his acting must be kept consistent with his core role, he is far freer to produce loosened constructions which he would otherwise have to reject. Another way of stating the same thing, this time in terms of the assumptive structure of the theory, is to say that the "part" or "role" assigned him provides a superordinate structure which is sufficiently permeable to increase his tolerance of incompatibility.

g. *Use of context.* "Resistance" to loosening may sometimes be overcome by the proper use of context. A person who does not dare think loosely about sexual or financial matters may be perfectly capable of thinking loosely about music or social organization. The therapist can set up a context in which loosened construction is possible, launch the client into the kind of free-associative exercise he needs to experience, and then gradually shift the context into the areas where loosened construction can do some good.

h. *Use of role structure.* The role the client adopts in relation to the therapist also has a great deal to do with his resistance to loosening. If he finds the therapist threatening, or if he finds himself beset with threatening constructs when he talks to the therapist, he is likely to throw up the most available defenses against the impending threat. These are likely to utilize a tightening rather than a loosening of structure. It is not an infrequent experience to find a hospitalized patient tighten his structure in the presence of a threatening staff member, or when he thinks he is being considered for a trial visit or release. Conversely, when a client does not feel threatened by the therapist or by the treatment circumstances, he may be more willing to drop his tight structural defenses. The therapist can therefore sometimes overcome resistance to loosening by making sure that the client construes him as someone who will not take advantage of slips of the tongue or force him to make something tight out of a loose construct which he might carelessly let drop. Stated in other words, the client may need to feel that his loose thinking will be accepted rather than challenged or put to test.

We have spoken of the use of loosening in attaining therapeutic goals. We have mentioned techniques, difficulties, and some of the ways of surmounting difficulties. Strangely enough, we should not end this discussion without pointing out that resistance to loosening may sometimes itself be used to attain therapeutic goals. As we shall point out later, there are almost always points in therapy when the therapist's efforts are in the direction of tightening construction rather than loosening it. If the client has "resisted" loosening and the therapist judges that now there has been enough loosening and it is time to start some tightening, he can exploit the very "resistances" which once gave him trouble.

i. *Signs of impending loosening.* There are precursory signs serving to indicate that the client is about to drop his "resistance" to loosening. The voice pitch usually drops. The flow of speech is less rhythmic and paced more to the production of thought than to the emphasis of communication. The syntax becomes less precise. The client looks less intently at the therapist, indeed gazes less intently at any object. He is less quick to respond to the therapist, yet he may still seem willing to orient his discussion to what the therapist has said. He is less histrionic, less concerned with whether or not the therapist gets the "right" idea, less eager to make an impression, less aware of how his words might be construed. He stops making such remarks as, "This is silly," or, "I wonder what you must think of all this," or, "Now why would a person do that?" All of this may be observed as much as several interviews before there is a clear indication that loosening of construction has begun to take place.

11. HAZARDS IN PSYCHOTHERAPEUTIC LOOSENING

The use of loosening techniques in psychotherapy involves some real hazards. The psychoanalytic procedures in psychotherapy, because of their almost universal employment of loosening techniques, frequently get therapists into trouble. The poorly trained therapist, therefore, needs to be particularly cautious about using classical psychoanalytic procedures. To be sure, recent developments in psychotherapeutic procedure among some adherents to psychoanalytic doctrine have made some of the techniques more versatile and less vulnerable to the hazards of loosening.

a. *Relation between loosening and anxiety.* In order to appreciate the hazards of psychotherapeutic loosening we should consider some of the similarities between loosening and anxiety. A loose construct is one in whose context there is some continual shifting of elements from one pole to the contrasting pole. If *breakfast* is loosely construed, then the meal one ate at 11 A.M. might at once be construed both as *breakfast* and as *something other than breakfast,* or as *breakfast* at one time and as *something contrasting with breakfast a moment later.* This is loose construction. It may make some of the person's anticipations

ЛГЛГЛГЛГЛГЛГЛГЛГЛГЛГЛГЛГЛГЛГЛГЛГЛГЛГЛ

misfire; but, if he is as loose in interpreting the validity of his outcomes as he is in making his predictions, he should be able to get along without his world's completely shattering into useless fragments.

But what happens if the system gives him no semblance of prediction? This is what we call *anxiety*. Of course, anxiety is never so extensive as to represent a complete breakdown of the construction system. It can get pretty bad and disrupt even some of the most basic physiological processes, but there is always some kind of structure remaining.

There are various ways of avoiding anxiety. One is to make more elastic predictions and perhaps take a more elastic view of the outcomes of one's predictions. This is loosening. In other words, while loosening and anxiety are somewhat similar, loosening may temporarily help a person stave off the anxiety that might ensue if a tight brittle construction were shattered on contact with reality.

But since loose construing provides some immediate protection from anxiety, it is easy for one to become addicted to it. It is difficult for the person who never commits himself to a precise investment or to admit to a clear loss ever to make any worthwhile discoveries or ever to find any solid ground for reconstruing life. An anxious client may become more comfortable when he is encouraged to sink back into the vagaries of loose thinking. Not all do, as we have pointed out, since some are threatened rather than cushioned by loose thinking. But those who are comforted may become so cut off from reality that progress will become impossible. It is for this reason that most modern psychotherapists are reluctant to use conventional psychoanalytic procedures on clients who already show too much loosening and who might readily abandon their contacts with validational evidence. Sometimes it is said that too much of this type of treatment may make a schizophrenic patient even more so.

b. *Hazards in loosening for the client who depends upon tight construction.* Sometimes, also, it is hazardous to push loosening upon a client whose thinking is compulsively tight. We know that in some persons tight constructs are maintained at the expense of their having very narrow ranges of convenience. A person who tries to employ tight constructions exclusively may be attempting, not only to exclude loose constructions as such, but also to exclude certain elements or contextual material. If he is forced to abandon his tight defenses, he may find himself up to his chin in a clutter of facts and issues which he does not know how to handle. The anxious disarray comprises the contexts of the newly admitted loose constructs. He is overwhelmed, not so much by the looseness of these constructs, as by his inability to deal with the kind of material to which they open the door. A zealous therapist who insists that the client release his tight grip upon precarious fragments of reality may, thereby, inadvertently plunge his client into a state of anxiety so severe as to require immediate institutionalization.

Psychotherapeutic loosening is indeed one of the most important procedures in the psychotherapist's armamentarium. Since it is a feature of creative thinking it may be skillfully employed in the more creative approaches to psychotherapy. But not all therapists are able to follow the procedure skillfully. It requires comprehensiveness and flexibility in one's own viewpoint to follow in hot pursuit, day after day, the twistings and turnings of another person's vagaries. Add to these difficulties the exasperating "resistances" of clients who cannot manage this stage of creative thinking, and add also the hazards of having a client who cannot progress out of it. This is the problem of psychotherapeutic loosening.

B. Tightening

12. TIGHTENING OF CONSTRUCTION

We have described loosened construction as characteristic of the initial phase of the Creativity Cycle. In some respects it is like the circumspective phase of the C-P-C Cycle. However, it seems advisable to view it as different from the C-P-C Cycle, since the latter is concerned primarily with setting in motion a chain of events in which the person is himself actively involved.

In the Creativity Cycle there may be no appreciable personal commitment.

But there are more important differences. The C-P-C Cycle is conceptualized as starting with the circumspective phase. This is the phase when constructs are handled propositionally; the matter is viewed from a variety of angles. It is followed by the P phase, in which one construct is given preemption. This is the selection of the relevant issue. It establishes the alternatives. Finally, the person commits himself to a choice. He chooses sides. He jumps in with both feet. This is the control phase of the cycle. The Creativity Cycle is different. It starts with loose construction rather than propositional construction. The shifting of elements that takes place in loose construction bears a superficial resemblance to the shifting of viewpoint that takes place in circumspection. But in loose construction it is a single construct which is shaping up, whereas, in circumspection, there may be produced an array of fairly tight constructs from which a choice is to be made in the next stage of the cycle.

a. *What cycle was Hamlet seeking to follow?* We might pause here for a moment and become circumspective ourselves. It would be interesting to pose the question of whether Hamlet in his soliloquy was involved in a Creativity Cycle or in a Circumspection-Preemption-Control Cycle. Our answer would be that he was involved in both, neither of which he was quite able to complete. It seems that vague loose constructs had been taking shape in his mind during the preceding hours. These had to do with his affective relationship with both men and women — vaguely conscientious with respect to his father, vaguely incestuous with respect to his mother, and vaguely illusive with respect to Ophelia. His creative mind had contrived the notion of having a play presented which would dramatize, in some way involving his uncle, what he is not quite able to put into explicit terms.

Yet his creation calls for action and action calls for control. At the beginning of the soliloquy he attempts to conclude the cir-

cumspective phase of his C-P-C Cycle by stating the issue —
"To be or not to be." Whatever other issues there may be,
this one now preempts the field. This is the crux of the matter.
Now comes the control phase of the cycle. He must fling himself
to the one side of this slot or to the other; he must live or die —
it is as simple as that. Now he is about to make the elaborative
choice for himself. Yes, death seems preferable until he begins
to elaborate the choice. It then occurs to him that there may
be dreams. He is then reminded

> . . . that the dread of something after death,
> The undiscover'd country from whose bourn
> No traveler returns, puzzles the will
> And makes us rather bear those ills we have
> Than fly to others that we know not of. . . .

We have attempted to embrace this view of human motivation
in our Choice Corollary: a person chooses that alternative in a
dichotomized construct through which he anticipates the greater
possibility for extension and definition of his system. At this
point Hamlet's decision seems momentarily to be postponed
and he falls back into a circumspection which precludes his
taking manly action.

> Thus conscience does make cowards of us all;
> And thus the native hue of resolution
> Is sicklied o'er with the pale cast of thought,
> And enterprises of great pith and moment
> With this regard their currents turn awry,
> And lose the name of action.

But in Hamlet's case the vague constructs which seem to
govern his personal attachments are gradually resolving themselves into definite shapes. They are becoming more and more
tightly construed. Inexorably he is being brought face to face
with a threatening picture of himself which he cannot tolerate.
Step by step he retreats by constricting his field. And gradually the grounds for circumspection give way beneath his feet.

At the last his choice becomes simple and his action impulsive.

b. *Tightening not always desirable.* Perhaps our discussion of Hamlet will indicate that we do not see tightening of construction as always desirable. As we have pointed out before, it is necessary for one to tighten construction in order to subject it to validation. But, as in the case of Hamlet, as well as in cases of clients who reach "insight" prematurely, the outcome of the ensuing test may be overwhelming. On the other hand, some degree of tightening is always necessary if one is to communicate his constructs or share them with others.

In communication, especially with strangers, we rely heavily upon symbols. It is difficult to ascribe symbols to loose constructs. Words keep losing their meanings in the shifting of contexts. Not only does a construct need some measure of tightness in order to be bound successfully by a symbol, but also, once the symbol has been embedded in the context, it tends to stabilize the construct. The same is true when a construct is dated or when it is located in space. Thus we speak of word binding, time binding, and place binding — all ways in which symbolization contributes to the tightening of constructs.

Yet symbolism, too, may not always be desirable. Words too often become semantic chains for the enslavement of thought. They can be inimical to creative thinking. One has only to see certain types of "compulsive neurotic" clients to appreciate this fact. The person who tries to word bind all of his thinking, or who is threatened by anything which cannot be put into words, dries up the reservoir of loose constructs from which he might otherwise draw in the development of new ideas. He finds it difficult both to be creative and to adjust himself to a non-legalistic world. He can only be productive — sometimes not even that!

13. FUNCTIONS OF TIGHTENING

a. *First function of tightening: to define what is predicted.* We can summarize the functions of construct-tightening procedures in psychotherapy as follows: First of all, the broad purpose of tightening, as well as that of any other psychotherapeutic procedure, is to help the client expand the possibilities of making his world more predictable. This does not necessarily mean he is to be consigned to simple routines, although there may be instances in which this is advisable. Broadly, it means that opportunities will be opened up for him to make predictable more and more of the world. This is the direction of movement, rather than that he shall withdraw more and more into a predictable world.

A tightened construct may enable one to make definitive predictions of what is to come, whereas a loosened construct may, by the time its predictions have materialized, have changed so much as to make the outcomes appear strange. The loose-thinking person, when confronted with the outcome of his prediction, forgets what he predicted and remonstrates, "Surely this is not what I bargained for." The tight-thinking person can say, "Ah, there is the clear-cut answer to a clear-cut prediction." He can say, "That is precisely what I predicted and here is precisely what I got. The outcome fits squarely at this pole [or the other] of my construct dimension." The person who casts his prediction in the form of a tight construct has the chance of getting a clear-cut yes or no answer. The loose-thinking person blinks his eyes and mumbles, "What happened?"

We say that the tight-thinking person has a *chance* of getting a clear-cut yes or no answer. He is not assured of such an answer and, if he gets it, it may not, in some cases, be a very intelligent one. Yet the loose-thinking person can only face the outcome of his ventures with vagueness and perplexity. While it may happen that this is the more appropriate way to look at a particular outcome — it may open the door to some creative thinking — looseness does not ordinarily lead directly to definitive experimentation.

b. *Second function of tightening: to stabilize construction.* The second function of tightening construction is to stabilize the client's psychological processes. We are all familiar with the loose-thinking child whose imaginative productions are misleading and therefore sometimes mischievous. His confabulation may include lying, dishonesty, or even cheating. In an older person this characteristic may be viewed as a "lack of integrity." In a sense, this is correct, for there is often a lack of "wholeness" in the person whose constructions are quite loose. The person whose constructions are elastic and internally capricious becomes a puzzle both to himself and to those who rely upon him. He may find, to his surprise, that he has become the source of considerable threat for those who have tried to depend on him — for example, his children.

c. *Third function of tightening: to facilitate organization.* The third function of tightening is to facilitate the organization of the ordinal relationships in the client's construction system. It is difficult to develop superordinate constructs if the lower-order constructs which they subsume continue to be vague and unstable. It is difficult to develop a long-range policy to deal with inexplicitly defined events. If the elements are first more tightly construed or more objectively defined, it becomes possible to step up to a more superordinate level and do something about the client's over-all outlook. Thus, if a client comes in complaining that he has been mistreated by his employer, his neighbors, and his family, it may be necessary, at some stage in the treatment, to become explicit as to the exact instances to which he refers. This is not to say that nothing can be done until the elements are tightly construed; indeed, it may be advisable to avoid crystallization of these matters in the early stages of treatment. But if the therapist decides to try building a systematic construction upon these minor constructs, he may first need to take steps to have them crystallized. If his judgment is good, he may get some matters straightened out simply by reinterpreting the client's situation and the therapy may be completed within a few sessions. If his judgment is faulty, he may find that he has isolated a paranoid psychosis which neither he nor anyone else can handle.

Psychoanalysis appears to view the function of tightening in this light. The psychoanalyst, having encouraged the client to loosen his construction, takes steps to get him to lift certain vaguely formulated ideas into the realm of "consciousness." He asks the client to name them, to express them in verbal symbols, to become explicit about them. We call this *tightening*, whereas the psychoanalyst would perceive it as a matter of bringing the idea itself into an illuminated area of the mind.

Fenichel uses the classic metaphor of steering between Scylla and Charybdis in the strait of Messina. When one steers close to the rock, Scylla, he deals with highly explicit material and runs the risk of shattering the client's personality against the hard rock of reality. When he ventures near the whirlpool, Charybdis, he and the client get caught up in the whirlpool of the client's turbulent unconscious and it becomes impossible to steer. The task of the therapist is to tack back and forth between these two hazards while sailing his way through the straits of therapy. When he moves toward the fixed landmark of Scylla, the client's thinking becomes more explicit, or, as the psychoanalysts like to say, more reality-bound. The whole process of therapy is designed to place the client in such contact with reality that he can build his outlook systematically, or, again as they like to say, that he can acquire conscious insight. This is, as we see it, a matter of using tightening to facilitate the building of an organized construction system.

d. *Fourth function of tightening: reduction of certain constructs to a state of impermeability.* A fourth function of tightening is to reduce certain constructs to a state of impermeability. We have discussed the therapeutic value of closing out the contexts of certain troublesome constructs. This is a procedure often advocated by the general semanticists, whose therapy seems largely to be a matter of reducing the client's thinking to a state of concretism.

We have referred to the reduction of a permeable construct to a state of impermeability as "deterioration." One way to accomplish this deterioration, which is often highly desirable, is to see to it that the construct is very tightly drawn and explicit. In his efforts to tighten the construct, the client is likely to be compelled to resort to concretism. Indeed there are some people who can only achieve explicitness through concretism. The therapist may take advantage of this fact if he wishes to reduce a certain construct to a state of impermeability.

e. *Fifth function of tightening: to facilitate experimentation.* The fifth function of tightening is one which is emphasized within the theoretical framework of the psychology of personal constructs. It is to facilitate experimentation. We have used the model of scientific methodology in conceptualizing the psychotherapeutic process and the client's reconstruction of life. We believe that the way the scientist learns can be used as a way for the client to learn. We believe that science can be used as a methodological model for persons who do not call themselves scientists. We believe it can be used as a model for clients who, like scientists, may well seek to reconstrue life. We believe that the therapy room can be a laboratory and the client's community a field project.

But in taking this view it should be clear that we do not construe scientific methodology as narrowly as some do. Our approach makes considerable use of creative reconstruction, a form of psychological process which some researchers have tried to rule out of the realm of "scientific" endeavor and specify as "art." For example, our description of fixed-role therapy in Volume One made clear to its readers, we hope, our view that the reconstruction of life might well involve a considerable amount of creative imagination. We see nothing incongruous in the notion of creative science.

Just as the research worker has, at one time or another, to make his hypotheses explicit so that he can procure definitive evidence as to their validity, so the client has, sooner or later, to express some clear-cut anticipations. This is one of the important ways in which he can set up his system on the basis of validated hypotheses. When he tightens up a construct it becomes more and more a brittle hypothesis and more and more he must be prepared to perceive it as expendable. He drops his hostility and leaves it up to nature, human or otherwise, to demonstrate whether his prediction was accurate or misleading. One of the functions of tightening procedures in psychotherapy is to enable the client to learn through appropriate experimentation.

14. TECHNIQUES OF PSYCHOTHERAPEUTIC TIGHTENING

We turn now to the techniques for getting the client to tighten his constructs. Tightening is a form of elaboration. What we have already said, therefore, about elaboration in psychotherapy is partially applicable here. The process of elaboration tends to help the client set his house in order with subordinate constructs subsumed in an orderly way under superordinate constructs. As we have already indicated, a hierarchical organization requires a degree of explicitness in the subordinate elements.

a. *Judging or superordinating.* Sometimes psychoanalysts make a distinction between the "judging" and "experiencing" functions of the client's mental processes. While we do not distinguish between processes in these terms, our distinction between loose construing and tight construing, together with our distinction between subordinate and superordinate construing, is somewhat parallel. When one construes loosely and his constructs are not bound by superordinate structures, he may be "experiencing" only. When one construes tightly, it becomes possible, though not inevitable, for his constructs to be fitted into a system. If, indeed, they are fitted into an organized system — an organized system being a group of constructs having well-defined superordinate and subordinate relationships among themselves — he becomes able to "judge" his own behavior.

Now sometimes in psychotherapy we can approach this process in reverse. We can ask the client to subordinate certain constructs. When he is too much on the loose side we can ask him to stop "acting out" or "free-associating" and explain just what he is up to. In the words of psychoanalysis, we urge him to "judge" rather than "experience." What we do is ask him to put a superordinate construction upon a group of constructs which he has been expressing unsystematically. Sometimes the gambit is successful. If the client is to fit what he has been saying into a system, he may have to be more explicit about what he has been expressing. This means tightening.

For example, the therapist may say, "Now just what have you been saying today that you have not told me before?" "Exactly how does this compare in importance with what you said earlier in the interview about . . . ?" "What you have just been saying seems to be different from what you were saying in the last interview but I am not sure how. Could you explain?" "You have told me about a lot of incidents and feelings but it is not clear to me how you see these matters as fitting together. Are they simply illustrations of something?" "Are you trying to get me to sympathize with you or are you trying to explain something to me?" (This remark should not be made unless the client is aware of being accepted.) "You have told me about a number of feelings and ideas today. What should I know about you now that I did not know at the beginning of the interview?" "What was different about today's interview?"

b. *Summarization.* A second technique which is similar to the technique of asking the client to subordinate certain constructs is to ask him to summarize what he has been saying. It is difficult for one to summarize anything unless he systematizes it. And the systematization, as we have indicated, requires some tightening of the subordinated constructs. Nevertheless, some clients seem to be able to summarize only by resampling the loose constructs which they have already produced.

The therapist may say, "Could you summarize what we have been discussing today?" or, "I want to be sure to remember what you said in the last interview. Could you go back over it briefly?" "Now could you go back over what you have been saying; I want to be sure I have it straight," "Let's review what has been happening in the past three interviews. Now what would you say happened last Friday?" "Could you summarize again the last three dreams you have reported?" "You have expressed a series of free associations in the past few minutes. Do you suppose you could retrace them for me, starting with the last one, then saying what led to that, and so on?" The therapist will have to remind himself that the purpose of this exercise is not to test the client's memory but to invite him to tighten up his constructions.

The client may be asked to make, after he gets home, a written summary of each interview. This introduces a tighten-

ing procedure between sessions which may partially offset the
hazards of having a great deal of loose production during the
interviews. The summary may or may not be used in the next
session. If it is used, it may be read either at the beginning
or the end of the interview, depending on when the therapist
wants to introduce tightening. It may be read either by the
client or by the therapist, aloud or silently. Ordinarily, the
tightening will be more effective if it is read aloud by the
client, and if the therapist occasionally stops the reading and
asks for the rereading of some line or for explanation of it.
Incidentally, this procedure sometimes helps the inarticulate
client to express himself in the presence of the therapist. While
one would ordinarily prefer that the client be more spontaneous
in the therapy room, one sometimes has to resort to some such
indirections in order to get suitable material into the immediate
therapy situation.

c. *Historical explanation.* A third way of getting the client
to tighten his constructions is to ask him to explain his thoughts
on a historical basis. "When did you first start having these
thoughts?" "Have you ever felt like this before?" "What does
this remind you of?" "Is this the way you felt that time when
you . . . ?"

d. *Relating one's thinking to that of others.* A fourth way
of tightening is to see whether or not the client can relate his
thinking to that of others. "Do you know of anyone else who
may feel this way?" "Can you remember hearing anyone else
express these kinds of thoughts?" "When you feel this way
whom are you most like?"

e. *Direct approach.* A fifth way of producing tightened constructs is direct. It consists in asking the client to be more explicit, to explain just what he means, to clear up the bewilder-
ment of the therapist. The therapist may say, "I don't understand; could you make it clearer to me just what you mean?" "I
followed you up to the point where you said . . . Now what was
it that you said next?" "Could you explain just how it is to feel
this way? What happens inside of you?"

f. *Challenging the construction.* A sixth way is to challenge the client's thinking. This may be undertaken at any one of several levels, depending on how much threat the client is prepared to manage. The therapist may say, "I don't want to misunderstand you, so could you go back over what you were just saying?" Or, if the client can stand a little more threat, the therapist may say, "I find this a little confusing; first you said . . . and now you say . . . Can you help me understand?" A more challenging statement is, "Can you reconcile what you are saying now with . . . ?" or, "Have you ever had anyone tell you that this sounds like nonsense?" Or he may deliberately misinterpret what the client has said: "If I understand you correctly, this is what you really mean. . . . You say it's not? . . . Then just what do you mean?" Or he may say, "If I took what you are saying seriously, then I would have to conclude that . . ." Finally, there are occasions when it is therapeutically helpful for the therapist to express incredulity in the simplest language: "Bosh!" "When are you going to start talking sense?"

g. *Enactment.* Psychoanalysts usually object to the client's "acting out" instead of "talking." The emphasis that the psychology of personal constructs places upon enactment techniques or "role playing" seems to be in opposition to this view. Perhaps it is because we see psychotherapy as embracing a greater variety of psychological processes at the technical level, no one of which is necessarily of itself either healthy or unhealthy, therapeutic or pathologic. Psychotherapy is the intelligent manipulation and organization of various psychological processes. There are, therefore, times when enactment, instead of producing more explicit communication with the therapist, may interfere. There are other times when enactment may be the most feasible way of bringing certain constructs into the therapy room for examination. Moreover, enactment does not always mean loose construction. There are occasions when the client is forced by the demands of extemporaneous role playing to tighten up certain minor constructions to the point where he can take explicit action on the basis of them.

Our seventh approach to tightening is by way of enactment. For example, a client may express a loose and ambivalent construct such as the following:

"I think my mother hates me. Of course, she is very kind to me. She would be very much upset if she thought I didn't love her. Yet I cannot bring myself to be very demonstrative with her. I think if she really loved me she would try to control me more. She lets me do pretty much what I please — up to the point where it gets in her way. She seems to need me more than she thinks I need her. She seems to accept anything I do but I am not sure I like that. Sometimes I tell people she has put her foot down and refused to let me do something. She hasn't, of course, but it is a nice feeling to pretend that she has."

This is the construction that one eighteen-year-old boy who was undergoing psychotherapy placed upon his stepmother. It is hard to follow. Is it loose or is it simply unusual? We can, of course, take time out to spin several hypotheses about what has taken place. One of the most obvious is that he is threatened by the freedom of home life after ten years of orphanage regimentation. There are others, too, but we are here concerned with the possibility of using enactment to tighten up certain aspects of the construct system.

As the client enacts his mother's part, he is forced to translate his construction of her into specific lines and expressions. If the situations chosen for enactment are simply reportrayals of incidents which have already happened, he may rely principally upon his memory of the incidents. As new situations are set up by the therapist, the client is forced to act the way he thinks she would act in a novel situation. He must improvise on the basis of his construction of her. The therapist can use the old standby situation of pretending that the mother has come to the therapist to talk about her son. This is a rough assignment, but it usually produces important results and tightens up some constructions which otherwise stay loose. When the parts are interchanged and the client plays the part of the therapist and the therapist plays the part of the mother, he is put in a position of having to subsume her point of view in a helpful manner. Again he must tighten up his construction of her.

But enactment provides for tightening up construction in an even more positive manner. As the therapist enacts the part of the client or of his mother, he has occasion frequently to ask the client to evaluate the verisimilitude of his portrayal. The client, in explaining to the therapist just how the part should be played, finds it necessary to be more and more explicit. It is up to the therapist just how explicit he will require the client to become. The therapist, as we suggested before, can even challenge the client's construction of the situation by playing slightly off key. It is frequently in this type of exercise that the client tightens up a troublesome loose construct which no amount of previous questioning, challenging, or cross-examination was able to bring into the open. Sometimes he gives a clear clue when he remarks, "Now I know what it is that I have been trying to tell you about my mother. It was that . . . Therefore, if you are going to play the part like her you will have to . . ." Or he may say, "What I have been saying about my mother doesn't make too much sense. Now here is the way she would have to act. That puts her in an entirely new light, doesn't it?" This latter type of remark indicates not only that there has been some tightening but that the axes have been rotated into a new position.

Not only does instruction of the therapist in how the part of another person should be enacted help the client become more explicit in his construction of that person, but the instruction as to how his own part should be played helps him to become more explicit as to what construction he shall place upon his own role. If he explains, and then illustrates, just how his own part is to be played, the construction usually becomes very tight and probably all the more available to him when he confronts a similar situation at home later. Far from being a procedure which always interferes with tightened construction, enactment is often, instead, a technique which can be used to bring about quite explicit interpretations of what the client has been thinking to himself. Moreover, it helps the client to become explicit *within his own construct system rather than within a construct system superimposed upon him by the therapist*. Perhaps this is why psychoanalysts avoid this type of tightening; it invites the client to use his own terminology rather than practicing the use of theirs.

h. *Concept formation.* In the eighth place, constructs may be tightened by the use of the basic concept formula, *how are two of these alike yet different from the third?* The therapist may say, "You have mentioned this, this, and this. Let's see if we can understand these three things better. Think about them. Are two of them alike in some way that seems to set them off from the third?"

Both the similarity and the difference can be explored. As soon as the concept begins to take shape the therapist can help the client tighten up the construction and establish its range of convenience by asking him to add more elements, both to the likeness pole and the contrast pole of the construct context. "And this, too — is this like one of these? . . . But would you say that this other stands out in contrast the way that does? . . . Can you think of more instances of this? . . . Can you think of more instances of that?" These are elaborative procedures, and we have already discussed elaboration techniques in psychotherapy. We mention them here again because of their implications for the tightening of construction.

i. *Asking for validating evidence.* A ninth way of tightening construction is to ask for validational evidence. The therapist may say simply, "How do you know that?" "What has happened to make you see matters in this way?" "How can you be sure that you really feel this way?" "What kind of evidence would it take to convince you that you were mistaken?" "If this were not so how would you know it?" "Are you sure that this is what you mean to say?"

j. *Word binding.* A tenth technique is to encourage *word binding*. The client is asked to name each of his constructs and stick with the same name. The therapist is careful to use the standard nomenclature when talking about these constructs. The choice of words need not correspond to dictionary definitions; they may be taken from the client's personal lexicon. However, there is an advantage in using dictionary definitions if one wants to go all the way in the direction of word binding. The dictionary brings cultural pressure to bear upon making the construct rigid.

Actually word binding goes further than mere tightening. It tends also to produce *impermeability* in the client's construction. When he accepts a word as a tight symbol, he allows himself to become "stimulus-bound," in the language of experimental psychology. This is a kind of rigidity. Thinking becomes less fluid. New ideas are quickly pigeonholed into word-labeled categories, and resistance is set up against any redefinition of them or refinement of their meanings.

Is this good? Sometimes yes, sometimes no. As we have indicated before, the person who settles on some rigid and precise meanings is free to go on to think about superordinate meanings. He can also communicate with certain objective advantages; those who listen to him can take him literally. He may appear to be a person of intellectual integrity, although, of course, there is much more than this to personal integrity. His meanings are well circumscribed. He seems to be objective and realistic, rather than subjective and impressionistic.

But the word-bound thinker has difficulties too. He has trouble dealing with nameless things. He may be frightened by them. Figuratively he runs to the dictionary whenever he meets anything new or puzzling. If the definition is not there, he is lost. He tends to be rigid to new ideas and insensitive to the wordless thinking of his associates.

Yet one's rigidity may keep him out of trouble. The "paranoid" person who is able to encapsulate his delusional structure with certain fixed terminology may be able to get along in society. If an overeager therapist tries to loosen some of his word bonds, the delusion may spread and get him into all kinds of social difficulty.

k. *Time binding.* The eleventh technique is to encourage *time binding.* The client is asked, in effect, to date his constructs, and thus to eliminate from their realm memberships all elements which occur at other times. This is also a way of narrowing the range of convenience. The client is urged to think, "This is a view which was applicable to what I experienced when I was in high school but it is no longer applicable." As with word binding, this kind of tightening tends to reduce the construct to impermeability.

Our culture provides us with some excellent examples of impermeability produced by time binding. Our ancient ancestors placed great stock in miracles. Much of our religious literature contains accounts of miraculous events. Since many of us are unable to sift out our overriding religious values at a superordinate level, we resort to literalisms and legalisms. We learn rules rather than principles. We read the letter of religious writings and fail to catch the spirit. Or rather, we fail to see the spirit as something which can be conceived as superordinate to the letter. We come to miracles. Shall we try to live by magic in the twentieth century? Obviously not! Shall we try to discard the notion of magic? What would happen to our religious values if we tried to do that? The very prospect appalls us.

Our solution is to resort to time binding and to speak of "the age of miracles." "There *were* miracles but they don't happen any more." The construct of miracle is *time-bound* and thus reduced to impermeability. By embalming it in ancient times we avoid the threat of having to overhaul some of our religious thinking. It should be said in passing that the whole system of religious values is thus likely to get embalmed along with the "miracles," and thus become equally impermeable to current issues. But that is a longer story!

1. *Other forms of symbol binding.* There are other forms of symbol binding. One may encourage place binding, person binding, situation binding, and so on. "This is a construct which we shall consider to be applicable only in this place, that is a construct which is applicable only to that person or in that particular situation," and so on. Thus thinking may be tightened and the construct reduced to impermeability. While it might seem better in such cases to test the construct and discard it

altogether, such a revision, as in the case of a devoutly religious belief in miracles, may have a devastating effect upon the organization of the personality.

15. DIFFICULTIES ENCOUNTERED IN PSYCHOTHERAPEUTIC TIGHTENING

a. *Shifting meanings of a constant symbol.* The therapist's efforts toward getting the client to tighten certain constructions may meet with difficulty. Just as he thinks he has persuaded the client to be consistent in the application of a certain construct, he may discover that the client is consistent only in his symbolization, that the construct itself is still vague and inconsistently applied. One cannot assume that because a client has narrowed down his use of symbols that he is applying them always in the same way.

For example, the therapist may work out with the client a clean-cut notion of what the client means by "respect for my rights." The therapist hopes that, thereafter, the client will use the construct in a tightly delineated manner and thus separate out from it certain other constructs which might better be dealt with independently. There may be much nodding of heads and extended agreement as to what is to be included under "respect for my rights." There may even be clear agreement on what is antithetical to "respect for my rights."

The next day the client uses the term in a manner that seems appropriate; but as the session continues, the therapist develops an uncomfortable feeling that the client is implying more than he appears to be saying. The words are the same, but the meanings have shifted again. The therapist may be exasperated, but he will need to keep in mind that this is the sort of thing the client has been doing all of his life, especially when he has tried to deal with particular kinds of personal experiences.

The therapist will have to decide whether his attempts at tightening the construct of "respect for my rights" were premature, whether the construct should ever be tightened, whether it should be tightened and tested immediately, or whether the "respect for my rights" is a minor element in the context of a more important construction which is shifting from day to day. Perhaps what has happened is that the client is shifting his notion of his field of freedom and the subordinate construct of "respect for my rights" is affected by the shift. The shift may merely represent quotidian looseness in the superordinate structure or it may represent a new and desirable development in the client's outlook.

b. *Tightness at the expense of permeability.* Sometimes tightness is accomplished by a client only at the expense of permeability. If he is incapable of abstract thinking, or superordinate thinking, any attempt to get him to reduce certain constructs to a tight formulation will result in his becoming concretistic or preemptive. Suppose the therapist attempts to get the client to tighten up his notion of "respect for my rights" when the notion of *respect* as a principle or superordinate structure is beyond the client's grasp. The therapist draws on illustrative material produced by the client. The client thinks he sees a relationship between the illustrations which can be termed "respect for my rights." "Let's be definite about this," says the therapist. "Yes, yes," says the client, "this is what I really mean." In the next interview the therapist discovers, to his dismay, that the client can be definite only by becoming concrete, that he cannot distinguish between a certain accumulation of facts and the principle of which they are merely illustrative examples. The result is that the client sees "respect for my rights" as made up specifically of what happens to him in situations A, B, and C — these and no others. The tightening of the construct has reduced it to a state of impermeability. This may not be what the therapist bargained for.

c. *Producing a construct which is too incidental.* Tightening may encounter a similar difficulty in that the tightened construct may become more *incidental* and less *comprehensive,* as we have defined these terms. In other words, even if the application of the construct to situations A, B, and C did not limit it to A, B, and C, the construct might become limited to situations which are narrowly like A, B, and C. If D is seen as like A, B, and C in many other respects, it might be included in the tightened formulation. But if E is seen as unlike A, B, and C in many other dimensions, the tightened construct will not be sufficiently comprehensive to subsume it. The person will simply be unable to see it as being like A, B, and C at all. Here too the tightening of the construct results in concretistic thinking.

Particular difficulty may arise when the client tries to use his tightened construct to deal with everyday situations. If the construct has been rendered incidental by the tightening it will have purely academic or historical value only. It cannot be applied to the business of meeting heterogeneous situations. If it has been rendered incidental, it will have such a narrow range of convenience that it will rarely be applicable. It will be like a bargain accident-insurance policy — good only if one is stepped on by an elephant in the dark of the moon.

d. *Difficulty in producing constructs which are both tight and superordinate.* We can see that a person who has lost his ability to deal in abstractions must frequently resort to loose construction to take the place of abstract or tight superordinate construction. Since he cannot grasp the principle, he resorts to shuffling the facts. The therapist should therefore make sure that his efforts at tightening do not merely reduce the client to a kind of helpless concretism. Usually the client will resist such efforts on the part of the therapist. Indeed, clients often show a robust ability to resist the various misguided efforts of therapists.

e. *Dealing with impulsivity.* The therapist may have difficulty with tightening when he deals with an impulsive client. As we have indicated in an earlier chapter, the impulsive client is one who foreshortens his C–P–C Cycle. Decisions are made and action taken before the client has looked at his situation from all the appropriate angles. Before his therapist knows it, he has precipitated himself headlong into a course of action. Upon reconsideration he is inclined to agree that his decision was rash.

But what does all of this mean? What kind of person is he to consider himself to be? Here are all of these incompatible behaviors. His integrity is threatened. Perhaps he can hold himself together with some sort of loose construction of himself. Whatever rationale he employs to bind together these various impulsive acts must necessarily be loose. If the therapist tries to get him to tighten up his thinking, the client may find himself confronted with too many self-contradictions for comfort. The continuation of loose thinking about himself may be his partial self-protection against the anxiety which would ordinarily follow from his impulsivity.

f. *The client who wants "relationship" only.* The therapist is likely to experience difficulty with a client who wants to constrict his world to the therapy room. Suppose the client wants to have "relationship therapy" with the therapist. Now there is not necessarily anything wrong with a "hand holding" type of therapy, but the therapist should be sure he knows what he is getting into when he undertakes it. The client becomes responsive to the therapist, and he expects the therapist to be sensitively responsive to him. Why be explicit as long as he and the therapist "understand" each other?

If this happens, the therapist may be able to secure tightening only if he shows that the communication between them fails when the client indulges in loose thinking. He may do this by making himself appear less sensitive to what the client is trying to express than he really is. The wise therapist is just as ready to say, "I don't understand," when he thinks the client should tighten his construction as he is to say, "I understand," when he perceives the client's need for acceptance.

A version of this situation occurs when the client insists on acting out what he does not care to abstract explicitly. Perhaps he is expressing his hostility. He berates the therapist for misunderstanding his problem, and yet he does nothing to formulate the problem more explicitly. The therapist, realizing the nature of hostility, looks for the constructs for which the client is seeking to extort validational evidence. Instead of asking merely, "Are you feeling hostile toward me today?" the therapist may go on to say, "Have you given any thought to just how you would like to have me respond to this criticism? What kind of reaction are you looking for?" This may be followed by an inquiry as to the construct which would be validated by such a reaction. For example, the therapist may say, "Now could you explain why you would expect me to do that? This is probably important."

A similar approach may be used when other types of "acting out" occur.

g. *Unwillingness to test.* Tightened construction may be resisted by the client because any opinion definitely expressed is an implicit invitation to make a wager. This is as true of all of one's social intercourse as it is in dealing with an impulsive gambler. Any idea has a predictive implication. If it is explicitly expressed, it invites testing. If it is loosely expressed it defies testing. Many clients resist tightening to the bitter end because they do not dare risk a wager.

Sometimes therapists feel themselves challenged by their clients' evasiveness and bend all their efforts toward making the clients commit themselves. This, of course, may represent hostility on the part of the therapist. Suppose the therapist is successful. The client may be forced to put his construct to test before he is ready to adapt himself to the outcomes. He is caught in his own trap. But before the therapist is halfway through congratulating himself on his psychological skill he finds himself embroiled in the client's hostility. The therapist may win his point and lose his case.

Take, for example, the case of a "conversion hysteria" client. Suppose the thinking is loose in certain areas, as it often is in cases which are given this label. The client claims his health is poor. The therapist tricks the client into formulating more definite claims. Now the client says he is sure that he has cancer. This invites a medical test which the therapist gleefully schedules. Suddenly the client realizes the spot that he is in. He takes the test, but on the night before he is to hear the medical report he makes a suicidal attempt. This illustration, based on an actual case, dramatizes the predicament that tightened construction may present for the client. It is no small wonder that some clients resist tightening in certain stages of therapy. As a matter of fact, if all therapists were able to force tightening whenever they wished they might accomplish a great deal of mischief.

h. *Difficulty with preverbal construction.* One of the principal difficulties in producing tightened construction lies in the nature of human development. Many loose constructs are preverbal. As such, they cannot be readily expressed in words. The therapist finds himself handicapped, not only because of the shifting of the construct context, but also because the client is reluctant to reveal the context and is able to provide him with so few symbolic handles with which it can be grasped. It is like handling a live fish in the dark; not only does it wiggle but it is slippery and hard to see.

16. HAZARDS IN PSYCHOTHERAPEUTIC TIGHTENING

In discussing difficulties encountered by the therapist in getting the client to tighten his constructions we have also mentioned some of the hazards of misapplied tightening procedures. Broadly speaking, there are two principal hazards to be kept in mind. The first is the danger of premature tightening which may bring the client face to face with the implications of his construing. In other words, there is the danger that he will be forced to test his hypothesis before he has any appropriate alternative construction to place upon the world in which he lives. If he has to test his hypothesis against a rival null hypothesis and the null hypothesis wins, he will be confronted by the confusion of anxiety.

If, and this is more likely, the client has to test his present personal hypothesis against a threatening hypothesis with considerable weight of evidence behind it, he may show contrast behavior and precipitate himself into further difficulties. One should not ask a client to put a construct to crucial test unless he has some idea of what the client will be able to do with invalidating evidence. The therapist should be on guard even if he thinks he is sure the client will turn up affirmative evidence. Since tightened construction is an invitation to experimentation, the point at which the therapist should be on guard is at the time he considers asking the client to tighten his construction.

Consider, for example, a client who has construed himself as incompetent in his vocational field. The therapist notes that the thinking in this area tends to be loose, and hence not easily subjected to definitive testing. He tries to make the client become more explicit about his incompetence. Finally, the client settles upon some definitive construction regarding his competence. Here is something which may be tested. In the test the client succeeds where he predicted he would fail. Now, if human life were validated merely in terms of "success" or "failure," as some psychologists have long contended, the client should be very happy about the whole thing; he should pay his therapy fee, offer a modest bonus, and go merrily along his way. Sometimes, indeed, this happens — at least sometimes he goes merrily along his way! But in more deeply disturbed clients this "success" is more threatening than reassuring. As a result of the new turn of affairs, the client is faced with reorganization tasks which are so sweeping in nature that he is flabbergasted.

The therapist needs, from the outset, to keep in mind what it would mean for the client to discover that he was vocationally competent. Would it mean that the client would have to admit that his feeling of incompetence was based on other grounds? Is it perhaps that he sees himself as needing to maintain a front of incompetence lest he be ostracized and suffer the pangs of guilt? Is his claim to incompetence a form of constriction cutting his world down to vest-pocket size? These are the types of questions one should ask himself before tightening up a construct and inviting its subjection to crucial test.

a. *Danger of producing hostility in both client and therapist.* As we have already indicated, part of the hazard of tightening a construct lies in the hostility that may be manifested if the construct is tested and invalidating evidence produced. The hostile client, unable to face the consequences of his own experimentation (cf. our definition of *hostility*), tries to extort validation in favor of his discredited construct. He may try to extort the validation from the therapist. The therapist, finding himself the victim of the extortion, may become hostile himself. He, too, is unable to face the consequences of his therapeutic experiment. With client and therapist hostile toward each other the therapeutic relationship is not likely to be productive.

In a sense, then, the tightening of the client's constructs involves the therapist himself in a testing of his own hypotheses.

He has himself assayed a formulation, even though he has done it through the mouth of the client. Is the therapist prepared to face the outcome of this formulation? What will he do if the experiment backfires?

b. *Loss of comprehensiveness, permeability, and propositionality.* The second principal hazard has also been mentioned in connection with our discussion of difficulties. When some clients attempt to formulate broad concepts precisely, they seem to have to sacrifice their comprehensiveness or their permeability. They find it impossible to state a broad principle in precise terms. They have to narrow it down to a collection of incidental cases in order to state it exactly. They may have to go even further. They may have to deal with the construct preemptively, once they have stated it precisely.

The therapist will perceive this trend as being in the direction of increased "rigidity" of the personality. The movement of the tightened construct from comprehensiveness to incidentalness restricts its application to a narrow range of elements. The movement of the tightened construct from permeability to impermeability prevents its application to new experiences. The movement from propositionality to preemptiveness prevents the client from looking at the same elements from different angles. All of these represent forms of "rigidity." It may therefore be preferable to let certain constructs remain loose, for the time being, in order to preserve their comprehensiveness, their permeability, and their propositionality.

We have dwelt for some time on the functions, techniques, difficulties and hazards both of loosening and tightening in psychotherapy. It is not possible to offer so full a discussion of all of the procedures in psychotherapy as that which we have attempted in the case of these two classes of procedures. Since much of what the therapist does involves tightening or loosening construction, it seems that we can best illustrate the application of the psychology of personal constructs to the reconstruction of life by discussing these two in relatively greater detail. Our subsequent discussions will have to be more sketchy in order to conserve printers' ink.

17. WEAVING BACK AND FORTH BETWEEN TIGHTENING AND LOOSENING

Fenichel's metaphor, often mentioned, of steering between Scylla and Charybdis is an apt one. He also likens psychotherapy to peeling an onion, layer by layer. That, too, is apt. In long-term treatment the therapist takes the client through a series of adjustment stages. He may seek to loosen the client's construction for a time in order to gain permeability and embrace certain elusive constructs. Then he may urge the client to tighten construction and take stock.

After a form of adjustment has been worked out at the tightened level for a time, the therapist may open up the construction again, perhaps dealing with the same contextual elements, perhaps in a new area. The client may then have to reconsider his last set of "insights." After a period of loosened construing, the therapist may move in the direction of tightening again and seek to establish a mode of adjustment at a new level. The cycle, which is essentially a Creativity Cycle, may be repeated many times in the course of protracted treatment.

It is important for the therapist to realize he should not insist that the client "embrace the true faith" before he lets him tighten and test. Therapy, like any scientific venture, proceeds by successive approximations. The therapist seeks only to have the client work through a series of stages of "insight," partly so that he will attain a particular better mode of adjustment, partly so that he will learn *a way* to develop better and better modes of adjustment. The therapist teaches the client how to be creative in reconstruing his life. As one starts a new loosening and tightening cycle, what the client learned in the last cycle may be pulled apart for reconsideration. The welcome "insights" emerging from the present cycle may become the irritating "resistances" of the next. Thus, if one may use a pair of badly mixed metaphors, one peels his onion by tacking back and forth between the whirlpool and the rock.

a. *Hazards in weaving.* There are hazards in weaving too. Especially in the early stages of therapy, one should be careful not to ask the client to alternate too rapidly between judging and experiencing. He may lose the ability to do either. This is a common error among young psychotherapists. When a supervisor finds his student psychotherapist running overtime on interviews, the chances are pretty good that the psychotherapist is trying to do too much loosening and tightening both in the same interview. The therapist may come away feeling that he understands a great deal more about the client's problem and knows just how the client should approach it, but the client is likely to have made little real progress. Therapy needs to proceed a step at a time. The objective for one session is, ordinarily, not just to give the client one hour's worth of health-giving personal magnetism, but rather to accomplish one step, if possible, in a well-conceived course of treatment.

While one should avoid too much weaving in the early stages of therapy, there are minor cycles of loosening and tightening in the course of any single interview. Usually the judging, or the tighter construing, comes at the end of the interview, though sometimes one needs to have some tightened construction at the very beginning. When one asks for tightened construction at the end, he is keeping in mind that the client has to get along in a real world between this interview and the next, and cannot be expected to get along in it by "free-associating" for the next two or three days. The tightening gives him some measure of solid structure to bridge the gap between interviews. Sometimes the tightened structure is nothing more than a sketchy summary of what has gone on in the interview, just enough to enable the client to set limits on the loosening process. When tightening is attempted at the beginning, it may be in the nature of a review, again to set safe limits on the loosening which is about to be attempted in the interview.

b. *Cycles in various stages of treatment.* In the early stages of treatment, there may be a considerable succession of interviews at the "experiencing" or loosened level. Ordinarily the therapist will attempt this only after he has made sure that the client places considerable reliance in the therapist's ability to keep the loosening in hand. The psychoanalysts describe this as an aspect of "transference." We have defined transference somewhat differently but we do recognize that the transference of certain dependencies to the therapist may serve to protect the client during loosened or anxious stages in his treatment. We do not insist that the therapist be seen in a father role in order to make the client secure enough to loosen up his construction. As we mentioned in our chapter on the role of the psychotherapist, the earlier therapeutic efforts are more in the nature of teaching the client how to be a patient than of putting certain crucial constructs immediately to test. When loosened construction is first attempted, it is more likely to be attempted as an exercise designed to show the client what sort of thinking is anticipated by the therapist. The elements subsumed by this practice loosening may better not be threatening elements and the therapist is well advised to stay away from especially confusing material.

In the later stages of therapy the weaving between loosening and tightening ordinarily takes place in shorter cycles. Eventually there may be a considerable degree of both loosening and tightening in the same interview. This is when the client's thinking about himself becomes more and more like normal creative thinking. In fact it *is* creative thinking — all therapy is!

Chapter Twenty-one

Producing Psychotherapeutic Movement

THIS CHAPTER deals with techniques to be employed in those stages of therapy when the therapist is urging the client to experiment with new ideas and new behaviors.

A. Interpretation, Movement, and Rapport

1. THERAPEUTIC "INTERPRETATION" AND PROCEDURES FOR INCREASING THE PERMEABILITY OF PERSONAL CONSTRUCTS

The psychology of personal constructs does not take a conventional view of therapeutic interpretation, although many of the procedures we would use for helping the client reconstrue life are identical with those used by therapists who think they can provide their clients with new concepts served up on a platter. But even though the moment-by-moment techniques are often the same, the contrasting systematic viewpoint makes a world of difference to the client. Principally the difference shows up in the way certain emergencies are handled and in the tolerance the therapist shows for deviant outlooks among his clients.

From the systematic point of view we are attempting to expound, a construct is a psychological process of a live person. It is not an intangible essence that floats from one person to another on the wings of an uttered word. A therapist can fill the air with the words that symbolize his own notions, and succeed only in annoying and confusing his client. The therapist must help the client develop new constructs out of the materials that the client is able to furnish. The words passing between them need to be valued in terms of what they mean to the client and not in terms of any natural symbolism or in terms of any magic properties of their own. Always the therapist is working with the client's personal constructs. Constructs other than these are for the therapist alone — for helping him keep his own thinking straight, as in the case of the diagnostic constructs we have proposed. Or they may be merely for his own amusement.

Not only is a construct *personal*, but it is a *process* that goes on within a person. It thus invariably expresses anticipation. It is easy to forget this point and to start thinking again, as men thought for centuries, of a concept as a geographic concentration of ideas. When one attempts to communicate with a client, he is attempting to direct a process in the client's mind; he is attempting to generate certain anticipations.

a. *The basic principle in "interpretation."* But what the therapist anticipates, and the chain of subsequent anticipations which he sees stretching beyond it, may differ radically from what the client sees. Logically, for example, the concept of *punctuality* may mean nothing more to the therapist than that one customarily turns up at a given place at a given time. To the client, however, punctuality may mean that his life is to be ticked off in unison with a clock, that he will have to spend a great deal of his life waiting for people who are not punctual, that he cannot make any dramatic "entrances" to already filled rooms, that he is doomed to listen to a great many "introductory remarks," or that he can never linger with a friend, an idea, or a comfortable chair that has momentarily caught his fancy. The therapist who tries to sell the client on *punctuality* had better take into account both the personal nature of the construct, as it appears in the client's repertory, and the freight of anticipations with which it is burdened.

This brings us to a principle governing therapeutic interpretation. *All interpretations understood by the client are perceived in terms of his own system.* Another way of expressing the same thing is to say that it is always the client who interprets, not the therapist. If the therapist is to be effective, he must take into account what the interpretation will mean to the client and not depend solely on the natural "correctness" of the interpretation he offers.

As we have indicated in our discussion of tightening, it sometimes helps the client stabilize a construct he has come across during loose thinking if the therapist suggests a name for it. That is a way of tethering the idea to a symbol so that it will not trot away the moment the client turns his head. Furthermore, the therapist can set the stage for the client's formulation of interpretations by laying selected elements side by side for the client to construe, if he is able. But it is always the client who interprets, while the therapist can only do what he can to help the client interpret wisely.

b. *Basic interpretive formats.* There are some fairly simple techniques which can be employed by the therapist to facilitate interpretation. The following types of sentences illustrate the forms which may be used:

1. Is this like A? How is it like A?
2. You have been talking about A. I recall that once you talked about B.
3. You have been talking about A and C. But how are A and C alike? And how are A and C different?
4. Is this what you meant by . . . ?
5. Let us see if we can state the general formula.
6. Now try this on for size.
7. If you had wanted A, then I presume it would have meant that you would . . . and . . . and . . .

All sentences of this type represent invitations to the client to conceptualize in some new or more generalized form what he has been talking about.

c. *Extending the range of convenience.* Sometimes the therapist's principal task is not so much to get the client to formulate a construct as to get him to see the extended applicability of one which he has already formed. This is a matter of extending the range of convenience. If the range of convenience is extended, there is a greater possibility that the construct will be utilizable in dealing with brand-new experience — will become more permeable.

This function often arises in cases where the therapy has dealt largely with historical material. The client finally has a satisfactory formulation of "how he got that way," but his "insights" are not sufficiently permeable to carry implications as to "what he can do about it." Clients who are inclined to see themselves as victims of their biography are more likely to limit their understandings to impermeable constructs. For them, history presents a rationalization of the past, but no alternatives for the future. Therapists are often circumscribed by the same limitations in outlook. Yet actually the psychotherapist's task is not to interpret the past for the sake of having it rationalized, but to find suitable reconstructions for the future.

Here is the point where the therapist should get his head out of the past and his nose out of the therapy room. He can bring up new situations and he can encourage the client to bring up new situations in order to demonstrate the possibility of subsuming new experience under a new construct. He can use enactment to indicate how the new structure can fit new experience. He can anticipate experiences which are likely to arise between the present interview and the next. He can demonstrate his own permeable use of the construct in order to take it out of the realm of the impassively concrete and into the realm of the alive. He can encourage the client to explore the present implications of the new structure.

d. *Use of elaboration.* We have already discussed techniques of elaboration. Many of these, as was indicated, have the effect of producing greater permeability in constructs already formulated. There is the technique of documentation or "working through." There is the weaving back and forth between the loose and the tight which we discussed in a later section, and which has implications for building permeability. There is the technique of isolating certain features which stand in the way of extending the range of convenience of a given construct. By isolating certain elements from the construct context the whole construct may, in some cases, become more permeable. All of these may be used to increase the permeability of a construct.

2. JUDGING MOVEMENT IN PSYCHOTHERAPY

How does the therapist know when the client is making progress in reconstruing life? Actually it is impossible to measure precisely each minor bit of progress and assess its portion of the whole. Certainly we know that some interviews seem to be much more profitable than others and that there are sometimes interviews which the therapist feels might better not have occurred at all. Certainly no experienced therapist is so naïve as to believe that progress can be measured by the total minutes of interviewing time. Much of what takes place to help the client reconstrue life takes place outside the interview room. Much of what takes place in the interview room is a matter of an occasional apt remark, a flash of insight, a choice of a word, a well-timed silence.

The length of the single interview is certainly not a measure of progress. While the conventional interview is about forty-five minutes in length, that is probably determined more by convenience of scheduling than by any natural psychological cycle. Some therapists believe that all interviews might better be placed on a half-hour basis. They note that much of the important exchange comes after the client notes that the clock is pointing to the end of the session or even after he is on the threshold. That being the case, they figure that the sooner the clock points to the end of the session, or the sooner the client gets to the threshold, the sooner he will get down to business, and the less time will be wasted in preliminary sparring.

a. *Surprise.* Short-term movement is usually judged by the way the client seems to handle new constructs or his revisions of old ones. How does the therapist know when his client has formed a clear conceptualization of some area of puzzlement?

There are some cues which he can note. First we can mention the surprise that the client shows when puzzling elements seem to fall into place. This is the "Aha!" phenomenon made famous by Lewin.* Sometimes the surprise takes the form of laughter, but the therapist should be careful not to take the client's laughter too literally. Sometimes it represents sudden withdrawal from the problem, derision, or the sudden recurrence of a construction which has been causing difficulty all along.

b. *Spontaneous documentation.* A second cue to an adequate reconceptualization is the client's tendency to provide spontaneous documentation. The new elements he supplies indicate more clearly than his repetition of symbols just how the construct functions. The comprehensiveness of the new structure is indicated by the variety of elements which the client suggests in his spontaneous documentation. If his interpretation of the new construct permits him to subsume, in a meaningful fashion, a considerable variety of new elements, and if this subsuming is not too loose, the therapist can be reassured as to the level of insight which has been attained.

c. *Use of current experience.* A third cue is similar to the preceding one. It refers, however, to indications of the new construct's permeability. If, in a subsequent interview, the client spontaneously includes elements from the intervening daily experience, the therapist can take this as evidence of permeability. The therapist can be particularly reassured if the client indicates that he has used the construct in producing new responses in social situations. The therapist will want to know, however, whether the behavior is getting the client into additional trouble or whether it is opening up important new vistas

---

* While it has been the Gestalt psychologists who have emphasized the importance of the *ah ha phenomenon* in connection with insight and closure in learning, Harriman's *Dictionary of Psychology* credits the origin of the expression to the English political scientist Graham Wallas in 1926. Wallas did mention a "click" or a "flash" phenomenon in his discussion of the art of creative thinking. N. R. F. Maier has probably come closer to putting his finger on the origin of the term when he notes *"Aha Erlebnis"* in an article published by Carl Bühler in 1916. In any case, the term is a modernization of Archimedes' bathtub exclamation, "Eureka!"

for him. If the client is getting into trouble, the difficulty may be with the construct which the therapist helped him generate rather than with the client's misinterpretation of the construct.

d. *Mood change in relation to behavior.* A fourth cue is a change in the client's "mood" without too marked a change in his daily behavior. This criterion may appear to be in contradiction to the one we have just cited and to the whole practical nature of our theoretical position. However, moody behavior is principally contrast behavior; the client swings from one end of some of his principal construct dimensions to the other. After the client has structured his life in new ways, he may show superficial signs of changes of mood, but the swings are not as pronounced, nor do they appear to take place in the same construct orbits. It is as if the moods lost some of their governing power and have become more like ripples on the surface of the personality. The client may say, "I seem to keep on doing about the same sorts of things each day but now I *feel* less upset about them. The change seems to be more of a change in *feeling* than a change in *behavior.*" Or he may say, "As far as I can see, I am facing the same sorts of problems I always faced, only now they don't seem quite so overwhelming. I don't know exactly why it should be, but now I seem to *feel* differently about them." Or he may say, "The only difference seems to be that *now I meet emergencies differently.*"

e. *Perception of behavior contrast.* A fifth cue, though a misleading one in the case of a person who is engaging in a "flight into health" because of the threat inherent in treatment, is the tendency of the client to perceive his present behavior as contrasting in many ways with his earlier behavior. We may cite again Howard's interesting study of this perception that the client has of his own movement. He asked hospitalized patients, at the time of their admission, to write self-characterizations according to a formula similar to the one we described in an earlier chapter. Call this self-characterization A. Later, after these patients had been in treatment for about six weeks, Howard asked them to write another self-characterization. Call this self-characterization B. At this time he also asked them to write a characterization of themselves as they remembered being at the time of admission. Call this self-characterization C. There are three comparisons which can be made: A with B, A with C, and B with C. One can also compare the comparisons. For example, one can take the contrast between A and B and see whether it is as marked as the contrast between B and C, the latter two having been written at the same time — B with respect to the moment and C in retrospect.

Howard found that the tendency was for the patient to express a greater degree of contrast between B and C than between A and B. The contrast was not always expressed in favor of improvement; it was simply more exaggerated than the contrast between A and B. The patient tended to inflate the change in whatever direction it seemed to be. Howard points out that, in part, this is a function of construct formation, that in making any kind of comparison we tend to accentuate the differences even beyond what they actually are. This accentuation tends to highlight what the person is trying to describe.

Howard's study throws light upon the client's conceptualization of his own movement. He tends to see his present self as contrasting with his former self. He may do this even though he keeps making complaints about the troubles that beset his life. He says, in effect, "Look, I've got all these troubles that haven't been solved yet! . . . Me? Oh, of course, *I* have changed. *I* am very much a different person from what I was when I started coming here. But, so far, I haven't solved my problems. That is why I keep telling you about them! Tell me, just when will I reach the point where I will have no more problems?"

Some clients consider the goal of therapy to be "peace of mind," and "peace of mind" they consider to be synonymous with a monastic unconcern for human problems in the flesh. The therapist may be so busy trying to make his client comfortable that he does not realize what he has on his hands. Sometimes he needs to take stock by asking the client to contrast his present outlook with his outlook at the beginning of therapy.

f. *Change in complaint.* A sixth cue to the adequacy of new conceptualization is the dropping of certain complaints, or even the substitution of new complaints for old ones. Frequently clients will neglect to tell the therapist that their principal "symptom" has disappeared. Sometimes it is because the symptom, like an unpleasant memory, drops out of the field of awareness as a function of changing conceptualization. Sometimes it is because they do not want the therapist to stop the treatment just when such promising results are being obtained. Sometimes it is because of the dependency relationship which they do not want severed. Sometimes, it seems, it is because of lingering hostility; they do not want to admit they were in the wrong about the nature of their symptoms. This cue is first perceived by the therapist when he suddenly realizes that it has been a long time since the client has mentioned a once familiar complaint.

g. *Summarization.* A seventh cue is in the client's own summaries of what has happened in a previous interview. The summary may be either written or oral. The way the client summarizes in his own words gives some indication as to whether he has taken a new "insight" to heart.

h. *Change in autistic material.* The eighth cue is one of the most interesting ones. It is a change in the autistic or loose material produced by the client. While the client may not specifically elaborate new constructs, the therapist realizes that something has happened when he notes that dreams, free-associative material, loose constructs, and the like are beginning to include new content. There may be an unusual vividness in the dreams produced following the suspected new "insight." These are the "mile-post" dreams which we discussed in an earlier section. The thematic development of the dreams may be in contrast to those produced earlier. Even the chain of free associations produced in the therapy room may show a markedly different course of development. While we have not experimented with changes in Thematic Apperception Test protocol, we suspect that in these cases there would be changes which could be detected in a thematic analysis, even though a figure analysis might not reflect the new structures.

3. CUES TO INADEQUATE NEW CONSTRUCTION

a. *Loose construction.* Just as there are cues to adequate new construction there are cues to inadequacies in supposedly new construction. First of these is erratic or loose verbalization of the new construct — for example, the client keeps expressing new opposites. This is not to say that the client should always be articulate about his new construction. It is to say, rather, that his verbalization may be sufficiently fluent to make it clear to the therapist that he does not yet know precisely what he is talking about.

b. *Bizarre documentation.* The second cue is bizarre documentation. The client may insist that he has a new "insight," but, as he documents it, the therapist may be horrified at what it contains.

c. *Oversimplification.* The third cue is oversimplification. The client may tend to lump everything in a preemptive fashion as if his new "insight" were some sort of magic mumbo jumbo. Manic clients sometimes show this oversimplified construction. It amounts to a kind of psychological incantation which they hope will solve all of their problems.

d. *Contrast behavior.* A fourth cue is in the nature of sharp behavior changes or "flight into health." The behavior shows simple contrast qualities rather than evidences that new axes of reference are being developed. Whereas the client was reserved yesterday he becomes ebullient today. Whereas he was depressed he now becomes euphoric. Yesterday he was hostile; today he loves everybody. Last night he was a sinner; today he is sanctimonious. These overnight changes are not the changes one expects to emerge from a revision of the dimensional system with which life is construed. Often these contrast shifts are nothing more than a client's flight to escape the threat of going through further therapy. Sometimes a client makes a desperate effort to behave like a well person in order to avoid facing what is coming up next in the course of his treatment.

e. *Legalistic applications.* A fifth cue is the client's tendency to make rigid or legalistic applications of his new "insight." He applies his insight like a lawyer reading the fine print.

4. CHECKING THE CAUSES OF THE FAILURE TO PRODUCE ADEQUATE
RECONSTRUCTION

Whenever the therapist finds that the client appears to have accepted a new construction and his check shows that the new construction is inadequately formulated, he may need to check the possible causes of the failure.

a. *Check anxiety.* First, one checks whether there were signs of excessive anxiety in the client just before the new construction was formulated. The client may be grasping at a straw, or bringing a new "insight" to his therapist, in just the same way that an insecure pupil brings an apple to his teacher. A very anxious client may grasp at new interpretations in sheer desperation. The therapist might better have given him support, or even reassurance, than to have caused him to cling so frantically to a construct which he is not able to understand.

b. *The therapist may be "taken in" by a loose construction.* Secondly, the therapist should check his own overeager concurrence in some of the client's loosely exploratory formulations. Perhaps he seized too eagerly on what appeared to be an "insight" produced by the client, when actually the client had only the faintest glimmer of a useful idea.

c. *The therapist's anxiety.* Finally, the therapist should check himself to see whether he may have been betraying his own anxiety and confusion. When that happens, the client sometimes seizes upon an "insight" because he feels the therapist is going under and can no longer support him. Clients frequently sense the insecurity of their therapists and often make valiant efforts to keep both heads above water. The writer has seen cases in which it seemed to him that the client was doing more to support the therapist than the therapist was able to do to support the client. The client seemed to be carrying the two of them, sometimes with profit to himself as well as to the therapist.

5. "RAPPORT," "TRANSFERENCE," "RESISTANCE," AND
"INTERPRETATION"

These four terms ordinarily occupy major positions in a psychotherapist's working vocabulary. Because they do, it seems advisable to summarize our position with respect to all of them.

a. *"Rapport."* With respect to the term "rapport" we have no special technical sense in which we would wish to use the term. We have therefore not attempted to give it any particular systematic definition within the psychology of personal constructs. In fact, it would not be absolutely necessary for us to use the term at all, since most of what it subsumes we have conceptualized in terms of *role*. The term *role*, however, is one to which we have given a very particular definition — a definition which may cause the reader some difficulty until he gets used to it. Our point of view regarding *role* is anchored in our Sociality Corollary: to the extent that one person construes the construction processes of another he may play a role in a social process involving the other person. The elaboration of the definition of *role* is offered in connection with our first discussion of this corollary.

With respect to "rapport" we would then believe that the therapist places himself in a position to play a *role* in relation to his client as soon as he is able to subsume a part of the client's construction system and when he is ready to conjoin his efforts with those of the client in undertaking a social process. In contrast, the client's assumption of a role relationship to the therapist may not amount to much until some time later. In other words, the therapist can adopt a role relationship to the client long before the client adopts one in relationship to the therapist. Of course, in a minimal sense, each adopts *some* measure of role relationship as soon as he perceives that he is in the presence of another human being who, because he is a human being, presumably has some characteristic outlook.

As the role relationship develops, these two persons, client and therapist, take considerable account of each other, especially during their face-to-face contacts. Their interaction may not be happy, as some therapists insist that it must be if there is "rapport." From our point of view, the happiness in the interaction is not always necessary in a profitable relationship. We emphasize the role relationship between client and therapist rather than the mere comfort in the relationship between them. What part of each other's construction systems are they able to subsume? What is the nature of their construction of each other? These are the important issues in determining how effectively the two of them are carrying out the social process we call psychotherapy.

Other features of "rapport" we would subsume under such technical terms as *anxiety, guilt, threat,* and *acceptance.* All of these are terms for which we have prescribed rather tight definitions within the system of the psychology of personal constructs. It is probably not necessary to resummarize these definitions at this point.

b. *"Transference."* "Transference," as it has been expounded by the psychoanalysts, is a complicated concept. Basically, they see it as a form of biased perception in which a patient misidentifies the therapist as one of his parents. They do not stop here, however. They go on to subsume under transference many behaviors and attitudes which they believe must always follow from this misidentification.

The psychoanalytic use of the term seems altogether too loose for our purposes. We have therefore tightened up our use of the term to refer precisely to the tendency of any person to perceive another prejudicately as a replicate of a third person. In this sense, "transference" is not necessarily pathological, nor is the prejudgment necessarily antipathetic. The client in therapy may transfer various perceptions upon his therapist. At some stages of treatment he may not seem willing to grant the therapist any individuality whatever and may insist on relating himself wholly and indiscriminately to the therapist as he must have related himself to his father when he was a youngster.

The psychoanalysts like this kind of transference — up to a point. They believe — and we agree — that such a preemptive perception of the therapist may eventually be used to provide the client with an opportunity to reconceptualize his relationship to an important earlier member of his society. Most psychoanalysts, however, place more emphasis upon historical "causes" than we would; and hence they are likely to be more insistent that the client get his infantile relationships with his father all straightened out. Whereas the psychoanalysts would be inclined to speak of a client as being in a state of transference, including being dependent upon the therapist in a childlike manner, we would be more concerned specifically with *what preemptive constructs* were being applied to the therapist and specifically with *what dependencies* were being placed upon him. We would not consider it mandatory that an indiscriminate transference of childlike dependencies be applied to the therapist by the client in order for a therapeutically profitable role relationship to be established between the two of them.

c. *"Resistance."* "Resistance" is not a term for which we reserve any special definition. Since we do not employ a defensive theory of human motivation, the term does not have the important meaning it must necessarily assume for the psychoanalysts. Instead, we recognize necessary limitations in various persons' construct systems. We recognize threat and anxiety. But we do not see "resistance" as a special type of process designed to defend the person against anxiety. When we use the term, as we have in our discussion of the difficulties in loosening and tightening, we employ it in a literary or common sense, rather than in an intradisciplinary sense.

The client who exasperates the therapist by his failure to deal with what the therapist wants him to, or by his refusal to see things the way the therapist so clearly sees them, is not necessarily warding off the therapist as a person; more likely he is demonstrating the fact that his construct system does not subsume what the therapist thinks it should. If the client is hostile he may, indeed, be making a whipping boy out of the therapist; but even this, we feel, is more profitably seen as an effort to retrieve some bad bets on which the client wagered more than he could afford. If the therapist has no more enlightened construction of what is going on than to insist that the client "is being stubborn," it would seem that the therapist is hostile too. Here we are using the term *hostile* in the very special sense which we have reserved for it in the psychology of personal constructs.

d. *"Interpretation."* "Interpretation" is a term for which we have no particularly limited definition. As we have pointed out, interpretation, in order to do much good, has to be an act of the client rather than an act of the therapist. The therapist does not so much present interpretations as attempt to get the client himself to make helpful interpretations. Of course, the more the therapist offers interpretations, the more the client gets the idea that the therapist is a peculiar kind of person and the less he perceives the therapist as like anyone else he has ever known. Thus the therapist's offering of many interpretations tends to break up the client's *transferences* upon him. If the therapist's interpretations are generally incomprehensible, the client soon realizes that he cannot rely upon the therapist to make much sense out of anything. He will therefore stop *depending* upon him. As a consequence he may find it more and more difficult to establish a role relationship for himself with the therapist. Thus there is an important relationship between the therapist's "interpretations" and the role relationship which the client is able to sustain in the therapeutic situation.

e. *Interpretation of transference.* Now it is often claimed by the psychoanalysts that the transference relationship must eventually be "interpreted." Fenichel insists that the "interpretation of resistance" must precede the "interpretation of content." Since the "interpretation of resistance" usually means the interpretation of transference, the orthodox psychoanalytic view is that the client must see something of how he has prejudged the therapist before he can fully appreciate the uniqueness of some of his attitudes.

Again we agree, as we so often agree, with the broad technique of psychoanalysis. But our approach is somewhat differently conceptualized and thus somewhat differently executed in the therapy room. We try to help the client formulate and express the constructs which govern his role relationships. The Rep Test protocol gives us an opportunity to see these role relationships as prejudged perceptions. Often the client begins to see them that way from the moment he takes the test. Yet the full realization of how much he depends upon transference may not dawn on him until after months of therapy. The fact that he applies such prejudgments to the therapist in the therapy room provides him with a palpable instance to examine. But it is not the only instance of transference, and it seems to us that the therapist is constricting the client's "insights" when he concerns himself with these transferences upon himself only. From our point of view, the reconstruction of transferences can start almost with the first interview — long before the therapist ventures to point out that he too is the victim of the client's prejudgments.

f. *The transference cycle.* There is another matter we should mention. In an earlier section on this topic we spoke of the weaving between loosened and tightened construction. We said that the cycle of loosening and tightening tended to be longer in the earlier stages of therapy and shorter in the later stages. There is the same cyclical quality to transference relationships and to the dependencies which often characterize them. The client transfers certain ready-made perceptions upon the therapist. These involve, perhaps, certain types of dependencies. The client gets things figured out. He begins to see the therapist simply as a professional man doing his job and his dependencies as something he can allocate more discriminately. He no longer feels he must dump all of his troubles into the lap of the therapist. We may then say that a transference cycle is coming to an end.

This transference cycle, and the cues to its phases, have been discussed in an earlier chapter. We have also mentioned the fact that the therapist may precipitate another cycle if he feels that the client is still not ready to discontinue treatment. What we should point out here is that these cycles may become quite short during the closing stages of therapy.

Sometimes therapists become frightened at what we like to call "terminating flare-ups" in a client who they thought was about to go merrily on his way. These short cycles, sometimes lasting only a few days, or even during only part of an interview, are often resolved by the client with very little help from the therapist. It is as if he were saying, "Oh, yes, I almost forgot.

There was one frame I had once wanted to try on you for size and I never got around to it. Let's see what happens!" Then he trots out something so fantastic that the therapist sits aghast. Yet the client is only half serious, and he may be clearing out the last vestiges of a psychotic structure which he had not ventured to present for examination before. The experience is likely to be one the therapist will not soon forget, and perhaps one he dares not confide to his professional friends, lest he be accused of overlooking the psychotic substructure of his client.

g. *Therapy is threatening.* We should not conclude this section without pointing out that therapy is likely to be threatening to any client. This fact has important bearing upon the role relationships between client and therapist. Here we use both the term *threatening* and the term *role* in the systematic sense in which they have been defined in an earlier chapter. The client who is not threatened by the prospect of therapy is either very willing to assume a childlike dependency relationship, or he has very little belief that therapy will change his outlook. We can say that the magnitude of the threat the client perceives in connection with his relationship with the therapist is a measure of his perception of how much is at stake and how distressingly plausible are the changes which he thinks are imminent.

We may say that the client's feeling of threat in this situation is a measure of his guilt, but that common belief is misleading. It is, rather, a measure of his feeling of being out of tune with the society with which he sees the therapist identified. In part, this is guilt, as we have defined guilt. But, in a larger sense, the client may feel amply secure in the particular society in which he ordinarily plays his role. This is an important point for a therapist to keep in mind when dealing with a client who belongs to a group having unusual intrasocietal controls.

6. CRITERIA OF THE CLIENT'S READINESS FOR NEW VENTURES IN PSYCHOTHERAPY

The principal reason for assessing rapport, transference, and so on, is to determine whether or not certain topical areas may be discussed and whether certain experiments may be attempted.

How does the therapist know when the client's role relationship to him will sustain a certain type of inquiry? This is an important question, and the failure to find a satisfactory answer to it is a frequent cause of breakdowns in therapeutic relations. Let us consider some of the criteria which can be used.

a. *Relaxation.* The commonest criterion is the client's appearance of being relaxed. It is difficult to judge how relaxed a client is, because some clients do not give any obvious motor expression to their tension or guardedness. Usually, we have to depend upon our observation of posture, freedom of movement, modulation of speech, smoothness of little motor acts, appropriateness of facial expression in relation to interview content, eye movements, coloration — particularly of the neck and knuckles — smoking pattern, intertonal sounds, breathing pattern, pulse rate — where it can be observed in the neck — irregularity in blink rate, and so on.

b. *Spontaneity.* The second common criterion is the client's spontaneity. Does he move freely from impersonal material to personal material, or is the personal material set aside and expressed in more stilted language? Can he use ejaculations in his speech? Does he use slang? Is the flow of speech appropriate to the content or is it paced as with a metronome? Are the final consonants of words all carefully pronounced? Are the articles *a* and *an* separated from the words which follow them? Does he alternately talk and listen, or does he tend to make speeches or demand that the therapist make speeches? Can he, if necessary, carry on a rapidly moving conversation with the therapist in which each makes only a brief statement in units of less than a sentence?

c. *Control of loosening.* A third criterion is the client's ability to loosen his construction, at will, in the presence of the therapist. Usually the client who reports dreams to his therapist feels more secure than one who cannot report dreams. If he can produce free-associational material, it is usually a sign that the relationship is developing.

d. *Dropping of guards.* A fourth criterion is the client's dropping of guards. There are various ways in which a client sets up obvious guards. The most common guard is the compulsive addition of qualifying phrases to everything he says, particularly what he says about personal matters. If he seems unwilling to take a chance that the therapist will misunderstand him it suggests continuing defensiveness. The secure client does not mind too much if the therapist misunderstands what he is trying to say. The insecure client is disturbed if he suspects that the therapist is drawing any inferences other than precisely what he intended.

e. *Present vs. past.* A fifth criterion is the client's tendency to contrast his outlook in the present with his outlook in the immediate past. In applying this criterion the therapist must distinguish carefully between contrast in outlook or construction and contrast in circumstances. The client may feel that circumstances have altered radically for him recently, but that may not imply that his point of view has undergone any recent revision. It is the recent revision of the point of view, and the client's ability to express it, that suggests that he would not need to be threatened by any move which will lead to a further change in point of view.

f. *Present vs. future.* A sixth criterion is the client's tendency to contrast his present outlook with some future outlook. Of course, he cannot express the nature of the future outlook except in the most general terms; if he could, it would already have arrived in the present. Again, it is important to keep in mind that it is a personal point of view that we should note and not merely circumstances. The client who is able to conceptualize movement, either from past to present or from the present to the future, is less likely to be threatened by the investigation of a new topical area. He conceives himself as a changing person anyway, and does not need to feel that his whole world is crumbling if a particularly flimsy structure is examined closely. Here we may remind ourselves of Howard's thesis that the client who is undergoing accelerated movement has a construction of change that outruns the actual changes in his construction.

g. *Optimism.* A seventh criterion is the client's optimism. If the client indicates that he thinks matters will soon be better and that therapy will have some part in the improvement, the therapist has some evidence that it is safe to move a little more rapidly. Even if this optimism is more concerned with an improvement in circumstances than an improvement in outlook, it is still a positive sign.

h. *Flexibility.* An eighth criterion is the client's ability to alter his construction in the presence of the therapist. A client may say, "A few months ago I said that . . . I am not so sure that I really think that way." Or a client may say, "I seem to be making quite a point of this. I wonder if that means I am defensive about it." He may say, "When I came here, I was determined that I was not going to let you have anything to say about . . . Well, I suppose I've changed my mind."

i. *Dropping of defensiveness.* A ninth criterion is the client's ability to reject an interpretation offered by the therapist without being defensive about it. The client may say, "Oh, of course not!" Or, "No, I think you've got the wrong idea!" Or, "That sounds simply ridiculous!" If the client seems to feel that he must go further and apologize for his difference of opinion, if he passively subsides after making such a remark, or if he tries to test the therapist by making him explain what he meant in great detail, there is reason to believe that the relationship will not sustain inquiry into difficult areas.

j. *Aggressiveness.* A tenth criterion is the client's ability to enact an aggressive role with the therapist. The client who is not prepared to deal with a particular area is the one who feels himself vulnerable in the therapeutic relation. Sometimes one can be reassured if the client is able to act aggressively, not necessarily hostilely, toward the therapist. There is reason to believe that he has some adequate defenses against a premature encroachment upon a problem area or that he can quickly get to work and erect such defenses.

One of the best ways of applying this criterion is by means of enactment or "role playing." The therapist can structure a situation for enactment which requires the client to act aggressively toward the therapist. The parts can be reversed after a few moments of enactment. If the client can "dish it out" as well as "take it," the therapist has some evidence that he will not allow himself to become too vulnerable. If, on the other hand, the client finds it impossible to play the aggressive part, or if he cannot defend himself against the aggressive part when it is enacted by the therapist, there is evidence that he is too vulnerable to deal with all the topical areas which the therapist might consider important.

k. *Construction of therapist.* An eleventh criterion is the client's ability to construe the task of the therapist. In a sense, this criterion subsumes the others, since the client's subsuming of the outlook of the therapist is the very basis of his own role relationship to the therapist. What does the client consider the job of the therapist to be? What does he think the therapist is trying to accomplish? What does he expect the therapist to be concerned with? The answers to these questions may indicate whether or not the client is ready to have the therapist open up a particular new line of inquiry.

l. *Patient role.* A twelfth criterion is the client's ability to subsume many constructs under his construction of his role as a patient. This is a rather subtle criterion but, nonetheless, a useful one. If the client can say to himself, "Here is an attitude that I have which seems to be related to the fact that I am undergoing therapy," or, "I suppose all patients feel this way at times," he is in a better position to deal with troublesome material. Sometimes it is simply expressed when the client says in the midst of an interview, "I suppose I feel this way because I'm in therapy." Or he may say, "Will I have this kind of attitude when I get out of therapy?" He may say, "This is probably related to the fact that we discussed . . . last time." Or he may say, "I think I expressed that idea last time more because I thought you wanted me to than because it was something I would have thought of myself."

One should be careful not to confuse this type of expression with anything that might be in the nature of a delusion of reference. If the client says petulantly, "I didn't have all of these ideas before I started coming to you," or, "Is this the way you make all of your patients think?" the therapist will have grounds for suspecting that, in addition to subsuming many constructs under his conception of his patient's role, the client is perceiving the therapist as a hostile person with an ax to grind.

m. *Portrayal of therapist.* A thirteenth criterion is the client's ability to portray the part of the therapist sympathetically. A good plan is for the therapist to set up some enactment situations calling for the client to play the part of another patient coming to the therapist for help. In the chapter on the role of the psychotherapist we mentioned a particular form of this type of enactment in which the client plays the part of one of his parents coming to the therapist for assistance. When the parts in this role-playing situation are reversed, the therapist also gets an opportunity to see the client enacting his conception of a therapist. Realizing that this is what the client is prepared to see in a therapist, he may then be able to judge whether or not this conceptualization will sustain the type of inquiry he has in mind.

n. *Lack of impulsivity.* A fourteenth criterion is impulsivity in the client's decision to talk about a certain topical area. This is an important criterion. It is a reverse criterion or danger signal indicating that a certain area is *not* ready to be opened. One of the most important speeches in the therapist's repertory is, "This is something that we shall want to consider thoughtfully before these sessions are finished. Just now, however, you do not know me well enough to talk about this without wishing afterward that you hadn't. Let's save it for a while."

The writer recalls the case of a client who was disturbed in the sexual area. She seemed utterly prudish and unable to discuss the topic with her therapist during the first two or three sessions. Then one day when the therapist, who was a physician, was completing a physical examination, she suddenly expressed strong sexual feelings toward him. He neglected to evaluate the impulsive element in her approach and allowed her to continue her discussion for a few minutes in a somewhat informal manner while he completed his examination. Within a few hours she had become so threatened by him that it was impossible for him to continue in a therapeutic relation with her.

Always the therapist should keep in mind how the client will react when he looks back on his discussion of a certain topical area. Will he be able to face the therapist again? Certainly the therapist should be careful to distinguish between a secure spontaneity and an insecure impulsivity in his client's remarks.

o. *Lack of obliqueness.* The fifteenth criterion is a rather obvious one: the client's obliqueness in dealing with certain topics during the interviews. This too is a warning signal rather than an indication that the client is ready to deal with these topics. The fact that the client approaches the topics, and then shies away, suggests that there is some incipient movement toward what needs to be discussed. The fact that he cannot bring himself to set foot on tabooed ground suggests that his defenses are not yet adequate for dealing with the material which might be produced. At some point in such a series of asymptotic discussions the therapist will probably have to decide to move in and start a more frank discussion and inquiry. His evaluation of the other criteria we have mentioned should help him determine when to take the step.

Presumably it is obvious that no one of the criteria we have suggested is alone a sufficient guarantee that the therapist may safely turn his inquiry into forbidden paths. The therapist who senses that a certain line of inquiry is likely to have widespread repercussions will want to check the situation against several of the suggested criteria. Even so, he will make mistakes. No therapist can develop an infallible judgment of what inquiries his clients are ready to face and what would be premature. Sometimes he is amazed to discover that it is he who has been skirting the important issues and wasting the client's time.

B. Control of Anxiety and Guilt

7. SIGNS

Neither our theoretical position nor our clinical observations would lead us to believe that anxiety and guilt are necessarily evil. Freudianism, probably because it was formulated in a milieu of disturbed people, views human motivation largely in terms of the avoidance of anxiety, either by escape or by binding the psychic energy whose ungoverned discharge is presumed to account for it. If the psychology of personal constructs were primarily a psychopathological theory, it too might express its view of human motivation in terms of the avoidance of anxiety. In that case we would be concerned primarily with the alleviation of human suffering, and hence of anxiety. But the psychology of personal constructs turns its attention in the other direction and concerns itself primarily with the affirmative processes in man's ongoing quest. It is neither a theory of psychological sedation nor a theory of surgical extirpation. Some measure of anxiety is seen as a correlate of adventure. When anxiety stifles adventure, then it is time to do something about it.

Nor is the psychology of personal constructs a moralistic system. It does not see guilt as necessarily detrimental to life. It does not conceptualize human motivation solely in terms of the avoidance of guilt — even more particularly it does not see men as seeking only to escape "punishment." Yet it recognizes that mankind pursues its quest by means of collaborative effort and that the maintenance of role relationships is therefore crucially desirable. Guilt, representing as it does within our system the perception of loss of core role, may serve either to restore teamwork or to stifle initiative.

Our view, then, is that anxiety and guilt are not necessarily things to be dispelled whenever they arise. The task of the therapist is to assess them, take account of their functioning in his client, and deal with them in the light of the welfare of the particular personality. In dealing with anxiety and guilt it is important to keep in mind the systematic definitions we have attempted to give them. Anxiety is the awareness of failure of structure in a situation. Guilt is the awareness of dislodgment from one's core role structure. The procedures we suggest for assessing and controlling them arise directly out of these definitions.

How does the therapist know when the client is anxious or under what conditions he would become anxious? First of all, we may refer back to the preceding section, in which we discussed the criteria for determining whether or not to open a particular inquiry. Most of these criteria have to do with the assessment of the client's likelihood of becoming anxious. Second, we get some cue from the client's own statement regarding his anxiety. As we indicated in an earlier chapter, the client can tell us a great many things we want to know if we will take the trouble to ask him. Third, we may infer anxiety from our knowledge of the client's experienced events. A client who has recently lost a member of his family toward whom he had ambivalent feelings may ordinarily be assumed to be both anxious and guilty. Fourth, we may use our knowledge of common anxieties to infer the presence of anxiety in the client. For example, most adolescents are anxious about sex. If our client is an adolescent, it is a good plan to keep in mind the possibility that he, too, is anxious about sex.

Fifth, we can observe behavior which seems to be designed primarily to protect the client against anxiety. This suggests that there is an urgent reason for the protective gesture. If the client keeps structuring a certain topical area beyond what the situation would appear to demand, the therapist may infer with some confidence that the client is anxious in the immediately adjacent areas. For example, if the client keeps reiterating that he does not want the therapist to concern himself with anything except vocational guidance, it seems likely that he is potentially anxious in some area which is closely related to the vocational area. Further exploration may show, of course, that he simply does not trust the therapist's competence in any area except that of vocational guidance. In that case it may be that the area of anxiety is limited to a combination of topical area and a particular social relationship with the therapist. Yet, whenever a client overstructures a situation, the therapist may take that as a warning that an area of anxiety is just around the corner.

Sixth, the therapist may observe self-reassuring devices on the part of the client. This is the "whistling in the dark" cue. The client may do some boasting of his sexual exploits. He may engage in such lusty pursuit of certain objects that the therapist begins to suspect he is attempting to reassure himself that they are still available to him. Or the client may make a show of his composure in a stressful situation. Or the client may overstate his confidence in his marital security. Or the client may be particularly demonstrative of his independence of the therapist. Or he may loudly assert that he "doesn't give a damn" what a certain person thinks. All of these and others would suggest that the client is taking particular steps to reassure himself — a pretty good sign that he thinks he has need of reassurance in the area covered.

Seventh, there is weeping. This is a familiar sign of anxiety. In assessing its importance, the therapist should not make the mistake of assuming that a person who cries is necessarily more anxious than another person who does not cry. Nor is the person necessarily more anxious when he sobs openly than when he sits in stunned silence. The therapist is usually safe in assuming, however, that a person who cries is experiencing more anxiety than usual.

8. TYPES OF WEEPING

a. *Diffuse-inarticulate weeping.* There are types of weeping which can be distinguished clinically. Perhaps the purest expression of anxiety is diffuse-inarticulate weeping. There seems to be no topical area in which the client recovers enough structure to bring the weeping under control. He cannot express himself coherently nor even say what he is crying about. He does not verbalize fear except to imply that he is afraid of everything. He does not even verbalize guilty feelings. He cannot formulate a determined protest. This is the kind of weeping that one expects to find in a "decompensating compulsive neurotic." It may be preliminary to a "schizophrenic" type of break — sometimes a matter of only a few days' duration, sometimes something more serious. This type of weeping is always a danger signal, not so much in that the weeping itself is damaging, but that the weeping may be a sign of a rapid deterioration in the psychological structure. The therapist will ordinarily take immediate steps to get the client on his feet. This may mean the need for temporary institutionalization to protect the client from the threat of suicide.

b. *Infantile weeping.* Here the weeping seems to be an attempt to express oneself emphatically without the words to do so. This is the familiar "organic cry" which is sometimes mixed with wailing laughter. It occurs in some cases involving thalamic lesion or intracranial distortion. It also occurs in some cases of feeblemindedness, particularly in severely handicapped cerebral-palsy cases. It is similar to "hebephrenic" weeping — both represent infantile levels of organization. It has an animal-like whimpering quality. The client may be able to keep it up for hours on end, but there is a real danger of exhaustion that the clinician should take into account. Its presence specifically suggests the need for neurological collaboration in dealing with the case.

c. *Regressive weeping.* This is accompanied by childlike overtures. The client is likely to talk "baby talk," to grimace, whine, and generally make an effort to employ the devices of a winsome child. This kind of weeping is often found in the "hebephrenic." It represents an attempt to simulate childlike distress signals, but without the signs of neurological disturbance one notes in infantile weeping. It does not seem that this type of weeping is necessarily injurious to the client. Indeed, it may indicate that he is ready to relate himself to the therapist, but in the role of an infant. In that case it may even be behavior which can temporarily be encouraged, provided the therapist is prepared to build something out of it.

d. *Loose weeping.* This usually involves ideational content which seems to be inappropriate to the behavior. The structure both of the ideas and of the behavior is loose; that is, it varies from time to time. The clinician may recognize it in "acute schizophrenia." There is not likely to be much that the therapist can do to bring it under immediate control. If there is too much agitation involved he may wish to conserve the client's energy.

e. *Situational weeping.* A student cries for hours before an examination. The moment it is finished or he is excused from it, he is ready to celebrate. The specific situation the client faces seems to define the limits of his area of disorganization. As soon as he extricates himself from the situation, he seems to recover necessary structure. While the therapist knows that the problem is not as simple as this, the client operates as if it were. If the therapist is sure that this is the type of weeping that he has on his hands, the therapist need not feel that he has to stop it. The client will withdraw from the situation of his own accord when he gets tired weeping. Moreover, the therapist may wish to use the situational anxiety to get the client down to business in treatment.

f. *Histrionic weeping.* This is the kind one expects to see in "conversion hysteria." It may also be exhibited in cases of "psychopathic personality." The client is acting out his confusion in order to put on an exhibition. If he is skilled, he can use conventional stage tricks to make his acting convincing. The type of weeping is betrayed by his use of "hammy" devices and artistry. The client, in the words of Janet, "suffers beautifully." If he is clever, he may enact the part of a martyr. About the only disadvantage in letting this type of weeping go on is its distracting effect on the course of treatment.

g. *Hostile weeping.* Sometimes this, too, is exhibited in cases which carry a diagnosis of "conversion reaction." It is more characteristic of those cases which some clinicians call "hypochondriasis." This weeping seems designed to embarrass the therapist. There is a protest quality to the weeping. It is often observed in "conversion reaction" patients whose physicians have attempted to disillusion them. This invites the hostility. The client cries in such a manner as to make it clear that he is being misunderstood and abused by his therapist. If someone is within hearing distance, he makes sure that his voice and complaints will carry. If he is hospitalized, and has several visitors, as in a ward round, for example, he puts on a show that makes it clear that his therapist is a demon.

In this case the client combines hostility with histrionics. Many times a client cannot express himself aggressively in relation to the therapist except by weeping in this manner. While the weeping itself may not be particularly destructive, it is quite inadequate as an aggressive approach to the client's problems; the task of the therapist in such a case is to help the client explore aggressively along more productive lines.

h. *Constrictive weeping.* This is revealed by withdrawal tendencies on all fronts. The longer the client cries, the more he tries to "hole up." He perceives everything as dangerous, himself as completely guilty, and no venture as either worthwhile or safe. The client, as in the case of diffuse-inarticulate weeping, becomes less and less able to verbalize, his sobbing becomes more convulsive, ideas deteriorate as the weeping continues, and even in his constricting field he finds no firm ground to stand on. If the weeping is allowed to continue, the client may become exhausted and disoriented. There is danger of suicide in severe cases. This is the type of weeping one expects to find in "depressed" cases, either psychotic or neurotic, and in "involutional melancholia."

i. *Agitated weeping.* In this type there is incipient movement toward adventure and aggressive exploration. The client cries and tries. There is more bodily action. There is some tight formulation of constructs and some obvious movement in the C–P–C Cycle. The exploratory efforts may not be very well conceived and they may be sporadic, but the confusion of anxiety does not wholly paralyze the client. This type of weeping is like that of the bride's mother who cries at her successful culmination of several years' surreptitious effort. Instead of clapping her hands, jumping into the air, and clicking her heels, the mother cries. When a client shows this type of weeping, the therapist may be encouraged because at last the client seems to be "getting over the hump." He should temper his enthusiasm, however, by the realization that such anxiety may be accompanied by impulsive behavior which both he and the client will later have cause to regret.

j. *Façade weeping.* This is one of the most interesting types, from the standpoint of those who deal with less deeply disturbed clients in a "counseling" situation. It is somewhat similar to histrionic weeping and to hostile weeping, except that its function seems to be both to persuade the therapist and the client himself that he has a "real" problem. The client magnifies his confusion in one area as a façade against exploration in another area where he might have some real cause to be upset. This often happens in students who come to a professor to wail about their academic problems. The more they wail about these problems the more of a smoke screen they set up against the fear that they have made a bad investment in their choice of career.

One may suspect façade anxiety whenever the client is too specific about what is bothering him or when he keeps turning the interview back into the same cul-de-sac. If the therapist is sure that he is dealing with this type of anxiety, he may take bold steps to tear down the façade — at least up to the point where he begins to see how severe is the real anxiety which is being uncovered. The therapist may even attack the façade by pointing out that it does not make sense, that not much can be accomplished until the client is ready to talk about what is really bothering him, or that the client appears to be trying to fool himself as well as the therapist.

In extreme cases, after some measure of role relationship has been established, the therapist may even venture to put the client under tension — that is, instead of asking him to relax, asking him to tense himself, to grip his chair tightly, to keep talking, to remember that he is "on the spot." This is radical treatment and should not be attempted unless one is prepared to deal with the outcomes. Of course, as soon as the client has opened up the real problem area, the therapist changes his approach.

9. TECHNIQUES FOR REDUCING ANXIETY DURING AN INTERVIEW

How does one reduce anxiety during an interview or sequence of interviews? Of course, one of the eventual outcomes of a therapeutic series as a whole is to diminish or increase anxiety to a size where it is both provocative and manageable. Here we are concerned only with the temporary devices one uses to keep anxiety under control. Much of what we have to say on this subject has already been said in the chapter on basic therapeutic procedures under the headings of Support and Reassurance. We shall not attempt to repeat or to summarize what was said there. Both support and reassurance are devices which, among other things, may be used to reduce the client's anxiety temporarily. They may also be used to reduce his guilt.

In addition to support and reassurance we may mention other devices for bringing structure to bear upon an area of the client's life, or for bringing the client into an area where he has sufficient structure to ward off confusion. As a particularly important device, we might also mention *acceptance*, as it was discussed in the chapter on basic therapeutic procedures.

a. *Leading the interview into structured areas.* This means that the therapist has already determined what the structured areas are before he allows the client to get into the anxious area. He is therefore prepared to move quickly and effectively back into the structured area as soon as he has determined that the client should be extricated from the anxiety area. Simply changing the topic is not always enough. He must be sure that the structured area is both tightly structured enough to withstand the encroachment of anxiety from the area just abandoned and that it is one which will elicit constructs which are sufficiently comprehensive to keep the client on his feet after he has left the interview.

b. *Allowing sufficient time to complete reconstruction.* After dealing therapeutically with one area of anxiety the therapist should allow the client sufficient time to complete restructuration before opening up another problem area. He must remember that restructuration is not merely a matter of one or two apt verbalizations of "insight" but that it requires considerable documentation and experimental elaboration before the new structure is bound into place. This is the kind of control of anxiety we had in mind when we discussed the advantages of delayed or circular probing in connection with elaboration procedures.

c. *Use of binding.* Another device comes from our section on tightening. The client who is manifesting more anxiety than the therapist believes advisable may be partly protected by time binding, word binding, or place binding. The therapist may point out that "all this happened back in 1936 when you were a child." Or he may say, "Oh, yes, now this is technically what we may call a 'situational anxiety' " — as though this were some particular type of experience which could be separated off from other anxiety experiences by means of a label.

d. *Differentiation procedures.* The therapist may say to the client, "Let's be sure to keep this straight: this is *not* the particular kind of anxiety we were talking about a while ago; this is different; note that it is . . ." This tends to fractionate the anxiety and keep it separated into chunks of manageable size.

e. *Introspection.* The therapist may ask the client to introspect the "feelings" that he has. The therapist may say, for example, "I would like you to step out of your own shoes for a moment and give me a careful appraisal of the kind of experience you have been going through for the past few minutes. Let's review. Just how did you feel at the beginning of this passage? Then you said . . . How did your mood change at that point? Now trace the rest of the passage as if you were to make an appraisal of just what is going on in J——'s mind."

f. *Anticipation of hurdles.* When a therapist knows that he is going to have to go through a number of severe anxiety areas in rapid succession, he may prepare the client by setting up successive hurdles for the client to use in judging his own progress. He may say, "Now first you are going to feel very uncomfortable with me. You still wonder what I think of you and whether you are making a fool of yourself. Now this is a stage of treatment in cases like yours. I shall ask you from time to time if you feel you have passed through this stage yet. Then there will be another stage in which you will probably be anxious about . . ." This procedure tends also to fractionate the anxiety and help the client feel that what he is going through is a stage of therapy which it is his task to complete as soon as possible. This is similar to one of the techniques of reassurance discussed in an earlier chapter.

g. *Encouraging dependency.* Some therapists feel that they control anxiety by keeping the client dependent upon them. This works in some cases, but the therapist should not be too sure that when a client feels dependent he also feels secure. We have already spoken of the hazards of this type of thinking. If the client does accept the dependency and construes such a role relationship to the therapist, he may be able to keep his anxiety under control by reminding himself that "the doctor knows best." This type of dependency is, however, likely to be habit forming, and the time may come when the therapist will fervently wish he had never suggested that the client's fate should be "left in the doctor's hands."

Another means of controlling anxiety is to encourage preemption by urging the client to be specific about what is worrying him. This calls first for tightening, a measure which automatically tends to keep the anxiety from spreading. Furthermore, when pushed hard for specificity, most clients are forced to become concretistic or preemptive in their thinking. This also tends to encapsulate the anxiety, although it may make the material hard to reinterpret when it comes time to incorporate it into another structure. They may become so literalistic about their anxieties that they become unable to see them in any new light.

h. *Structuration of the interview.* A neat way to handle anxiety in early interviews is by the rigid structuration of the interview form itself. The clinician can use an obvious outline, take notes conspicuously, keep his questions flowing, keep professional "props," such as printed questionnaires, in sight, and speak frequently of the "routine questions which have to be covered before the therapy proper can be started." The interview may be kept on an impersonal basis and the movement can be kept rigidly structured. This approach requires careful and detailed planning. A therapist may keep such an interview plan in a standby status.

Some therapists fear that if they start their contacts with a client by doing diagnostic work they may destroy the appearance of acceptance which is necessary for most therapeutic interviewing. For this reason some psychologists refuse to do psychodiagnostic tests on clients whom they are to treat psychotherapeutically. There may be occasions when this separation of diagnostic and therapeutic activities is advisable, but for the most part it can be handled satisfactorily if the therapist explains the nature of his diagnostic interviewing. He can describe it as routine and explain that the type of interviewing to come later will be much different. Furthermore, this type of approach via psychodiagnostic testing will give the therapist an opportunity to find the anxiety spots, and to control them through structured interviewing until he gets around to dealing with them therapeutically. Thus, he need not be stumbling into confusion areas during his psychotherapy when he might better stay clear of certain ones until others have been dealt with. When the time comes for him to discontinue the psychodiagnostic testing and start the therapeutic interviewing proper, he can make clear the change in the type of interviewing not only by describing it, by his manner, by the removal of "props," but also by his chosen line of inquiry.

i. *Control of tempo.* The final ad interim means of controlling anxiety is by regulating the tempo of the interview. This has been discussed in an earlier section. The client is kept moving along so rapidly that he does not have an opportunity to generate a lot of anxiety about one topic. The therapist keeps invading his field with responses, with requests for additional material, and with shifts in topic. The slow unstructured interview is more likely to disorganize the client than the rapid-fire "less sensitive" interview. Of course, there is the danger that this technique may put strain on the clinical relationship.

10. CONTROL OF GUILT

a. *Reconstruction of core role.* Many of the suggestions regarding techniques for controlling anxiety are also applicable to the control of guilt. Since guilt is specifically an awareness of the loss of core role, the most prominent addition to our list of anxiety-prevention techniques would be reconstruction of core role. The therapist can help the client work out a line of behavior which is based upon his interpretation of the thinking of other persons. This means helping the client see how his part in life meets the needs of other people, how he can relate himself to them, and how he may be perceived by them as meeting their expectations.

b. *Finding alternative role structures.* The second procedure for controlling guilt is to help the client find alternative roles to replace the one which he feels he has lost. This means assigning the client tasks to do; putting him to work; helping him decide upon a vocation, select a job, choose a major course of study, undertake a community responsibility. Occupational guidance and placement have more to do with the control of guilt feelings than most therapists realize. Perhaps that is because the usual conceptualization of the nature of guilt is quite inadequate.

c. *Interpretation of persons.* The third procedure for the control of guilt is the interpretation of figures and actual persons with respect to whom the client would normally delineate his role. This is sometimes called "interpretive therapy" and it is not often suggested as a means for controlling guilt. Yet, from our point of view, it is a focal approach to guilt. The interpretation can be either didactic or demonstrative. For our own part we like the use of role-enactment procedures for this type of interpretation.

d. *Broadening the base of the role relation to the therapist.* The fourth procedure for the control of guilt is to broaden the scope of the client's role relation to the therapist. This means essentially that the client is given a more comprehensive role relation to the therapist to replace temporarily that which he sees himself as having lost. This means frequent therapeutic contacts and contacts which cover many topical areas and many aspects of the client's life. The client must feel that his relationship to the therapist is an important one and one which is sufficiently broad to justify his continuing to stay alive. Furthermore, he must feel that it is highly enough structured not to be likely to fall apart, as have other all-out role relationships with which he may have previously experimented. Of course, this type of laboratory replacement of a lost role has to be a temporary one; sooner or later the client must establish a sufficiently comprehensive role relationship to a variety of other persons.

Except in the paragraphs on façade weeping, we have discussed specifically only those procedures which have to do with *the reduction of* anxiety and guilt. Yet there are occasions when the therapist must expose the client to a calculated additional amount of anxiety or guilt in order to challenge him. How does he do this? Usually by moving into an area where the present structure is weak. Sometimes he accomplishes it by encouraging experimentation, knowing that there is a likelihood of unexpected results. Sometimes he simply starts withdrawing some of the temporary supports. Not infrequently the therapist finds, to his surprise, that the summer vacation he took with some misgivings with respect to his client's anxiety was just what the client needed.

C. Psychotherapeutic Experimentation

11. THE CLIENT'S EXPERIMENTATION

The relationship we see between psychotherapy and scientific research is more than a mere analogy. We believe there is a fundamental similarity. The discoveries one makes in therapy are similar to the discoveries one makes in the laboratory or in the field. Both are forms of personal progress. The client is a creature very similar to a scientist. The major difference is that the client has no technical vocabulary, such as the scientist has, nor are his problems always so easily formulated. But we see this difference as superficial only. Therefore, we believe that it is appropriate to make available to the client the means by which the scientist learns. Thus the client cannot avail himself only of *what* scientists have learned but he can discover *how* scientists learn. The latter should prove to be the more useful of the two if he can apply it to his personal problems.

It would be a mistake to presume that a person trained in one phase of scientific methodology can always apply his methodological skill to his personal problems or even to another "area of science." We have seen too many examples of physicists who tried to say something "scientific" in the field of sociology and too many examples of psychologists who tried to import "scientific" methodology from physiology. The task of translating scientific psychological methodology into psychotherapeutic terms is not to be underestimated, even though both are concerned with psychological discovery. We would therefore not assume that a research-minded psychologist would necessarily be either a competent therapist or a promising patient. But we do believe that the clinician who has an appreciation of the principles of scientific psychological inquiry may gain a deeper understanding of his client's quests.

Our present chapter is concerned with psychotherapeutic procedures. As in research, these procedures involve elaboration. We discussed elaborative procedures in an earlier chapter. Like the scientist who must first explore the implications of his theoretical system before he can design a meaningful experiment, the client often needs to explore the implications of his construing system before he plans venturesome activity for himself.

In the next chapter we turned to problems of loosening. If the scientist is to be creative he must not allow himself to be tied to literalistic thinking. The same is true of the client. Then we discussed tightening. At some point before he launches out on an experiment the scientist must formulate precise and testable hypotheses. So must the client.

We discussed some of the problems of communication between the therapist and his client. Scientists, too, if they are to collaborate, have to solve their communication problems. We discussed some of the problems of confusion (anxiety) and loss of role (guilt) which arise. And now we come to the problems of experimentation.

As in all scientific methodology, experimentation has important functions. It was, of course, some time before man found this out. Aristotle did not believe in experimentation, yet he contributed much to scientific methodology in his day. Many scholars still have only a half-hearted belief in experimentation. Some even believe that one should never experiment in the field of the psychology of human relations. There is a great deal of public prejudice against making "guinea pigs" of human beings.

Yet everyone experiments. Timid persons may think that if they close their eyes to the possibility of unexpected outcomes or if they set their minds against learning anything from experience they can prevent their ventures from becoming "experiments." In this way they try to protect themselves against the threat of unexpected outcomes. In some cases, where the outcomes can no longer be ignored, the perseveration takes the form of hostility.

We see this hostility particularly in the case of certain rigidly held religious convictions. Indeed, it often appears that there is no hostility quite so brutal or quite so insensitive as religious hostility. The more the devoutly religious person tries to fight off disillusionment, the more hostile he is likely to become.

The client is also likely to object to the idea of experimentation. Or, if he is hostile, he may rig his experiments so as to validate his complaints. Sometimes it seems as though the client has but a single purpose in life — to drag the therapist down to his own level of despair. But now we are ahead of ourselves in this discussion!

12. FUNCTIONS OF PSYCHOTHERAPEUTIC EXPERIMENTATION

a. *Framework of anticipation.* The first function of experimentation is to give the client a framework for anticipating what would otherwise be incredible. An experiment is a venture for which alternative outcomes are conceptualized. The experimenter recognizes, first of all, that there may be more than one result. He is willing to face the alternatives, to accept them for what they are, not to rebel against them, and to stand ready to make something out of them.

b. *Touch with reality.* The second function of experimentation is to place the client in touch with reality. The psychology of personal constructs is based upon a notion of there being a real world. It holds that this real world is subject to many alternative interpretations. It holds also that the real world is open to experimental inquiry. When a person's experiments yield negative results, that amounts to a clear invitation for him to reconstrue the nature of things. Thus, he may keep his eye so fixed upon reality and his mind so alert to its various possible meanings that he will never need to be victimized by it.

c. *Test of system.* The third function of experimentation is to test the client's construction system. Neither the client nor the therapist can tell for sure just what the client's construction system implies until it is put to test. The verbal exposition of the system is not itself enough to indicate clearly what the implications are. Too much of the system is subverbal; too many of the words are impoverished of practical meaning or enriched with meanings not assigned them by the dictionary. Only when the client puts his system to experimental test can he be really certain of what all his thinking and talk amounts to.

d. *Check on therapist.* The fourth function of experimentation is to test the therapist's construction of the case. The client is not the only one who can make mistakes in construing. The therapist makes mistakes too. The experiment gives both the client and the therapist an opportunity to see how appropriately the therapist has construed the client's situation. Because of this, some therapists are just as threatened by the prospect of experimentation as their clients are. They are afraid that their clients will lose all confidence in them if the results turn out unexpectedly.

This is a matter for some soul searching on the part of the therapist. Has he tried to represent himself as an infallible father? Would it not be better if he represented himself as a fellow inquirer and alerted the client to the various possible outcomes of the experiment?

e. *New vistas.* The fifth function of experimentation is to open new vistas of experience. The person who experiments usually raises as many questions as he settles. New vistas of experience are opened up to him. He discovers realms he never knew existed. If he is not frightened by the experience, he may find it highly stimulating and provocative. The decision to make an experiment should not be a final gamble with life or death but should be a truly elaborative choice which opens up the possibilities of further development of the predictive system. Thus a good experiment leads to another, and that to another, and to another in a lively sequence. Indeed, this is life.

f. *Putting the client in touch with other people.* There is one function of experimentation in psychotherapy which is a particular case under the second function mentioned above. *It is to put the client in touch with other people.*

Here lies an interesting issue. Which is the more important, for the client to see himself as others see him or for him to see how others see their world? Some therapists believe that the client should see himself as others see him. This presumes that others have a more realistic or a more valid perception of him than any private perception he might have of himself. But from our point of view, this is no more than a way of making a client the victim of his social circumstances. Our experience in dealing with clients whose perceptions of themselves appeared only to be a reflection of others' views has led us to believe that this is an unhealthy state of affairs. Such persons are very much at the mercy of their reputations. They may fit neatly into a "socialized" society but they tend to lack integrity when an unpopular issue is at stake. They behave more like sheep than like men.

From our point of view, it is more valuable for the client to learn to see how others see their worlds. This, rather than the conformity theme, was the basis upon which we developed our conceptualization of *role*. In a sense, subsuming the constructs of others, as one must do to play what we call *role*, includes a measure of understanding how others see oneself.

But a more fundamental issue is involved. If the emphasis is placed upon being able to see the world as others see it, albeit from the vantage point of one's own system, the client sees ways open to him for adjusting his role to a more effective relationship to others. If his aim is only to see himself as others see him, he becomes caught in their expectancies and must either adjust to them by conforming to their expectations or break out in hostile revolt against them. It seems far more healthy for all concerned for one to play out his part through a critical understanding of others' outlooks than by trying to conform to their expectations.

13. TECHNIQUES FOR ENCOURAGING PSYCHOTHERAPEUTIC EXPERI-
MENTATION

There are various techniques by which the therapist can encourage experimentation. Some of these have to do with experimentation inside the interviewing room and some with experimentation outside. As we have indicated before, we look upon *enactment* or "role playing" as one of the most useful clinical devices for clarifying experimental hypotheses and putting them to test. We are reserving our discussion of enactment procedures for a succeeding chapter. Our present section, therefore, deals exclusively with other procedures.

When a client meets his therapist for the first time, he is likely to be uncomfortable, unless he is able to develop some kind of role structure to govern his interaction with the new personality. To be sure, he employs such ready-made transferences as may appear to be reasonably relevant. Yet there is always a distinctly experimental quality to the client's first interactions with the therapist. This the therapist should always recognize. He should treat the client's overtures in such a manner that the client will continue to be willing to experiment with the therapeutic situation. The time may come when the therapist looks back on this stage with nostalgia and deeply wishes that he could once again get the client to try just one wee little experiment with the therapeutic situation.

Children, especially, are likely to explore the therapeutic situation and keep the therapist on the jump. Frequently their exploration is centered primarily on discovering the various conditions under which the therapist will say no. This is exploration dealing with dilation and constriction. Ordinarily, the therapist who deals with a child should not fool himself into thinking that he will never have to face the issue of setting limits. An active child will see to it that the therapist faces the issue whether he wants to or not. The therapist should decide in advance where he will draw the line if he is tested. Ordinarily, he will want to draw the line in response to the child's experimentation rather than constrict the child before he has had an opportunity to raise an issue.

a. *Permissiveness.* We now turn to techniques for encouraging the client to experiment. Within the therapy room, the first technique is an attitude of permissiveness on the part of the therapist. While it may at first seem inappropriate to call an attitude a technique, it is true that we can generalize a series of techniques by embracing them with an attitude. The therapist removes the obvious limits upon what the client can say and do.

Sometimes the therapist can express this dilation of the field by saying, "This therapy room is to be an unusual kind of place. Here you will be able to say many things, express many feelings, think many thoughts which you might not ever consider on the outside. Here you will find that we can dispense with some of the rules for good manners in order to get down to your real feelings and attitudes. You can laugh, when otherwise you might not laugh; you can cry, pray, swear, and experiment in many ways in order to find out how you really feel about things, about yourself, about people, or about me."

The therapist has to be careful in expressing this permissiveness, for the client may start testing the limits immediately and the therapist may have to say, "It is important, too, for us to understand *why* you want to do this; but if you go ahead and actually do it, you may think differently about it later and wish you hadn't. Besides, even though I am your therapist, you will have to recognize that I have to stay alive and reasonably healthy if I am going to be of any help to you."

b. *Responsiveness.* The second technique applies both to experimentation within the therapy room and to experimentation outside. It is to provide the client with a responsive situation. If the client works up his courage to try something, then something should happen as a result of his venture. In a research situation the director has to do what he can to provide a situation in which data are available, if the researchers are to get down to business and start experimenting. The same is true of a therapist and his client. The client needs to be in a situation where he can try out some of his old ideas as well as his new ones experimentally. A therapist with a dead-pan face is hardly worth talking to if one is seeking validational evidence for his constructs. A hospital situation which is so regimented that no subtle changes in the client's behavior would ever be noticed is certainly no place to stimulate the experimental attitude. When the client makes one of his half-hearted furtive attempts "to see what will happen" there should be the possibility of something lively happening, something more than the clock ticking on in the silence of a lonely hospital room.

c. *Novel situation.* The third technique is one which is commonly used under the guise of "a rest" or "a vacation." It is to project the client into a novel situation. We have already mentioned the fact that a person who goes into a novel situation is inclined to experiment, even if it is merely a transference of his old constructs. A new situation almost inevitably requires a person to check his perceptions, as if, for no other reason, to assure himself that they still provide a defense against anxiety. When a young lady whose social adaptation has been particularly inept has progressed far enough in her treatment to be able to conceptualize a number of new social behaviors for herself, it is often helpful for her to spend a summer in a new setting where she will be with new companions. She can experiment with them and not feel that she is bound by their previously formed expectancies of her. Sometimes a more disturbed client even finds a hospital sufficiently novel to enable him to try out behaviors which he would not otherwise dare or care to attempt.

The same technique can be applied in the therapy room. The therapist can change the ground rules from time to time, thus making the situation new. If he changes them too radically, or without warning, the client may be precipitated into anxiety; but a planned change in the therapist's manner, properly announced, keeps the client "on his toes" and encourages him to experiment with the emerging situation, when otherwise he might settle back into his well-tried manner.

Sometimes it takes a combination of certainty and uncertainty to elicit experimental behavior in a client. He needs to feel certain that the experiment will not get out of hand. This can be done if the therapist uses the concept of test-tube exploration and that of the laboratory with protective walls. He may also need to feel, for the time being, that the therapist will not get out of hand, that the therapist will provide a firm and steady hand while he ventures, ever so little, into the unknown. Yet the time may come when he will need to see that the therapist is presenting himself in a new way and that he will need to experiment afresh in order to discover how to maintain a role relationship.

d. *Tools.* A fourth technique is to provide the client with the tools of experimentation. A researcher often needs laboratory or field equipment if he is to obtain meaningful data. The same is true of the client. A woman who has no attractive clothes to wear, no permanent wave, no vocabulary, no setting in which to be seen, is not likely to do much experimenting with social interactions, no matter how much "insight" she is able to muster. A musician needs an instrument if he is to recover his self-respect. A mechanic needs tools. A child needs paints and plastics. A motor-minded client — for example, a "catatonic" — needs a ball or a swimming pool. Even a therapist needs an interviewing room.

e. *Hypotheses.* The fifth technique is to get the client to make specific predictions. If an interpersonal situation is involved, the therapist may say, "What would Mary do if . . . ? What would she not do? What are some of the other alternatives?" The client, having "called the shot," can be encouraged to check his prediction. More and more, the therapist can pose alternative forms of behavior to be enacted by the client following the "ifs" in the first question. If the client tries them out, he launches himself on his experimentation. So with other types of situations; if the client makes a wager in the form of a prediction, or if he begins to wonder which of two or more outcomes is to be expected, it becomes harder and harder to refrain from finding out how accurate his prediction was. It is an unusual person who, having laid a well-planned wager on a race or bought a raffle ticket, does not take steps to find out whether or not he won.

f. *Interpretations.* The sixth technique is to ask the client to make interpretations of others' outlooks. This also is a way of getting the client to commit himself to wagers. But it goes further. It invites the client to find out more about the points of view of others so that he can fill in some of the gaps that appear the moment he tries to make interpretations. Of course, one of the best methods of raising these issues is by enactment procedures — but we shall discuss those later. It is like asking a painter to paint the portrait of a famous man, and then, after he has made some ill-defined sketches, giving him an opportunity to interview that man in the flesh. It is not likely that the opportunity will be rejected, even though the subject has a most forbidding reputation.

g. *Portrayal.* The seventh technique is to encourage the client to portray how another person views himself. This is an extension of the preceding technique. The client is urged to express the way in which a certain other person might secretly view himself. The therapist can help the client work out the portrayal in a sympathetic manner and, from it, infer what kind of social interaction would reassure the subject and what kind would bring forth defensive reactions. This suggests that the subject's behavior is modifiable and that the client himself might elicit varying and contrasting behavior from the subject. If the opportunity for dealing with this person should then arise, the client will find it difficult not to make some effort toward seeing for himself what the person's response will be.

h. *Portrayal of how another person views the client.* The eighth technique is to encourage the client to portray how a certain other person perceives the client. This is a further extension of the two preceding techniques. Again, the client is asked to elaborate the perception that the other person might have of him, in a way that seems plausible and consistent with human nature. This suggests what behaviors in the client will seem to the other to confirm his opinion of the client. It also suggests what behaviors in the client will serve to invalidate the other's perceptions and surprise him. Armed with these hypotheses, the client is ready to experiment. Whether the client's experimentation proves him to have been right or wrong is of less consequence than that he can discontinue his hostile attitude toward the other person and set out to explore the possibility of role relationships with him.

It will be noted that the sixth, seventh, and eighth techniques for eliciting exploratory or experimental behavior are in the area of role constructs. That is to say, they have to do with the client's interpretation of another person's outlook and its implications for his own behavior. The techniques have to do with subsuming the other person's outlook in general, his view of himself, and his view of the client. It is important for the therapist to get the client to construe these outlooks in sufficient detail to produce testable hypotheses about what the other person might do under certain circumstances. If the therapist is contented merely with letting the client express broad attitudes of an evaluative nature, the hypotheses will probably not be available to the client in testable form and he will see no tangible way of experimenting with them. It is when the client's interpretations are translated into collectable bets that he begins to get the itch to find out how nearly right he was.

i. *Negative predictions.* The ninth technique is to encourage the client to make negative predictions as well as positive ones. Benjamins, in a study of the effect of induced changes in self-perception on performance, was able to demonstrate that frequently the self, and the goals set for enhancing or maintaining the self, are described in a negative way. A subject may say, "I am predicting that I will make a low score in the hope that I won't." This is like the scientist who formulates his experiment in terms of the null hypothesis which he hopes the results will discredit. Sometimes it helps for the therapist to assist the client in visualizing what would constitute an undesirable outcome to his social experiment. The client, having structured "the worst" in considerable detail, enters the experiment with some protection against anxiety, in case "the worst" actually happens to him. If the experiment proves him wrong, he and the therapist can take a second look at the situation with a view to reconstruing it.

j. *Biographical hypotheses.* The tenth technique is for the client to elaborate the biographical conditions under which he would behave differently. This requires considerable skill on the part of the therapist, and the results are likely to be slow in forthcoming; but, in some cases, this procedure will get results when others will not. Suppose the client insists that he cannot attempt certain things because of the way he was reared, because of traumatic experiences in the past, or for other biographical "reasons." The therapist can then start working through the kinds of biographical antecedents which would have made it possible to experiment with new behavior forms. The particular way the antecedents would have contributed to the new behaviors can be delineated in some detail. Also, the new behaviors can be explicitly illustrated by the client and therapist working together. All of this is "as if" speculation. As the structuration of the new behavior becomes increasingly clear, and the more plausible it becomes, the more likely the client is to forget himself and actually do what, supposedly, he "cannot do." The therapist can be reasonably sure that it will be some time after the client has let himself slip into the new behavior before he will sheepishly confess what he has been up to. When the client first does let the therapist know what he has done, the therapist should be careful not to make an issue of it immediately. He should let the client be the first to point out that the theory of biographical causation had not worked out.

k. *Direct approach.* The eleventh technique is direct: "See here, why don't you do this and see what happens; we'll go over the results in our next interview and decide what ought to be done next." This formula in various forms is the most forthright of the approaches to experimentation. As we have phrased it, it is almost identical to what the research director has to say to his more timid graduate students time after time. We would class with this technique any attempt to set the client about a particular task, encouraging him to take a job, or helping him select a vocation.

l. *Social example.* The twelfth technique is to place the client in a social situation where his companions are enthusiastically attempting what he could do well if he had a mind to. It is difficult for an expert bridge player to look over the shoulder of a novice without making suggestions or participating actively. When a person is immersed in a situation for which he has some structure and in which he finds it easy to subsume the outlooks of the other participants, he is much more likely to start playing an active role. His exploration does not threaten him with anxiety; the personal structure is there and ready for use. Sometimes the therapist can induce experimentation by getting the client into a group which has interests in which he might also be expected to become involved. For example, he can encourage his client to go to the Iris Growers' Annual Convention, the Wednesday night exhibition of the Model Railroaders' Club, or to an antique auction.

14. OBSTACLES TO EXPERIMENTATION

a. *Hostility.* There are some difficulties which the therapist can expect to face when he launches his client into the experimental phases of treatment. The first obstacle the therapist is likely to face is hostility. If the therapist thinks that hostility is always accompanied by aggressiveness or rebelliousness he may underestimate the difficulty he is facing. The hostile client is unwilling to sit at the feet of nature and learn. He does not perform experiments; he tries only to stage demonstrations. He does not try to discover what is right; he seeks only to prove that he was right in the first place. When the therapist asks him to experiment, he approaches the exercise with the attitude that he will use the experience to show the therapist just what happens. It is not hard to imagine what the outcome of such a venture might be. This hostile attitude can cause the therapist all kinds of difficulty and make him wonder whether he himself has any idea of what human nature is like.

b. *Anxiety.* The second general obstacle to experimentation is anxiety. Frequently a very anxious client will accept the therapist's first invitation to experiment. The structuration that goes with the invitation to experiment gives the client some stability and reduces his anxiety temporarily. He performs the experiment. But as soon as the experiment is over he is confronted with the outcomes and their implications. If the outcomes are comprehensively meaningful, the client is threatened; that is, he is faced with the prospect of making a major revision in his construct system. The system is already shaky; if he is to dislodge more of it the whole structure may fall down.

The response of an anxious client who has been prematurely thrust into meaningful experimental situations may be very puzzling to the therapist. Why does the client go to pieces when seemingly the experiment was so successful and the client reaped such "rewards"? The answer often lies in the extent of the implications, not in their "rewarding" features. For example, a student who has long considered himself to be dull, and who is anxious, may be encouraged by his counselor to use a certain new approach in his studies. This is by way of an experiment. The student, seeking any kind of new structure that will serve him, agrees to cooperate. The experiment turns out "successfully," or so the counselor thinks! The student gets a mark of "A" in his course. But then the student begins to show great anxiety and confusion. The counselor, still believing that human nature is governed by rewards and punishments, is at a loss to explain the student's reaction.

What has happened is that the student begins to see the far-reaching implications of his experiment. For a long time he has conceptualized himself as a stupid person and has organized a great deal of his life around that conceptualization. The organization has been disintegrating lately, and he has been faced with larger and larger areas of chaos in his construct system. In the midst of this teetering structure he finds that one of the major beams, his construction of himself as being a dull student, is faulty. Perhaps he never "liked" the idea of being stupid but nevertheless a great deal of reliance had been based on that postulate. Worry, worry, what is he to do now that he is "bright"?

Perhaps this illustration seems implausible, yet anyone who has dealt intimately with distressed students is likely to have had a similar experience. Perhaps the point can be made in a way which the reader will find more understandable. Perhaps the reader, a long time ago, failed to accomplish something which meant a great deal to him. Let us suppose that twenty years ago he had tried very hard to be a musician and was forced to abandon his efforts because of lack of "talent." Suppose he then built much of his life around the idea that he had no musical talent, although he continued to live in a world where the *talent-no talent* construct seemed always to be significant. He made an adjustment, somewhat unhappy, of course, but, nonetheless, an adjustment.

Now suppose, in addition, he has recently been faced with considerable anxiety, not necessarily related in any obvious fashion to his lack of musical talent. The reader goes to a friend for advice. The friend suggests that he reconsider his musical career. The reader, ready to try anything that offers even the remotest possibility of solution to his spreading anxieties, becomes the pupil of a distinguished teacher whose judgment of musical "talent" is generally unquestioned. Before long the teacher informs him that he definitely does have "talent." Does this make the reader comfortable? Probably not. It is likely to make him feel even more confused.

Now it is essential that the two most important considerations we have imposed on our illustrations not be overlooked. In each case the person who had the unexpected "success" was quite anxious. In each case a major construction was involved in the experimentation. What would have happened if only one of these conditions had been involved? For example, would the unexpected "success" be disturbing to a person who was not already upset, even though it implied that a major reconstruction job was at hand? Perhaps not. Would the unexpected "success" be disturbing to a person who, even though anxious, was not staking a major personal construction on the outcome? Probably not.

c. *Threat of outcomes.* Our illustrations lead us to the third difficulty which the therapist may encounter in seeking to have his client attempt experimental behavior. That is the threat of facing outcomes having far-reaching implications. All psychotherapy is likely to be threatening if it undertakes a major revision in the client's construct system. When the client is advised to undertake an experiment, it may suddenly become obvious to him that there is more at stake in the experiment, and perhaps in the therapy itself, than he is prepared to risk. When that thought strikes him he is likely to try to wriggle out of doing the experiment or to try to muddle it so as to produce equivocal results. The therapist should always think twice before encouraging a client to undertake a definitive experiment.

d. *Dependence.* The fourth difficulty is the client's dependence upon the therapist. A client who has developed a dependency transference upon the therapist may seek to obtain all of his validational evidence directly from the therapist. He does not want to discover how other persons think or act; he is concerned only with determining how the therapist thinks and acts. When the therapist suggests that he relate himself to others, or to matters outside the treatment room, he fails to generate any interest. Such a client may experiment with the therapist, of course, but he will avoid experimentation elsewhere. When the therapist suggests that he try to discover something outside, the client replies, in effect, "No, you just tell me and we will work it out here. You are the only person whose opinion I am interested in."

e. *Guilt.* The fifth difficulty may be the client's guilt. When urged to undertake an experiment, the client may say, "I don't see any use in trying that; it really doesn't make any difference, no matter what the outcome. Everything seems so empty and so futile." What the client means is that he feels himself dislodged from his role and that nothing that he can do seems relevant to its reestablishment. In such a case, the therapist may need to make sure that the client feels himself in some role relationship to the therapist before asking him to undertake experimental ventures outside the room.

f. *The nonelaborative choice.* The sixth difficulty is the client's belief that he will be trapped by the results of the experiment. Perhaps he believes that negative results might place him in a position where no further elaboration would be possible. Or it may be that either negative or positive results will leave him with no apparent further place to turn. He may feel that the experiment is equivalent to committing suicide; that is to say, it is an experiment which produces irreversible and terminal outcomes. Such a prospect runs counter to the basic tenet of constructive alternativism and to the principle of the elaborative choice.

15. HAZARDS IN EXPERIMENTATION

Some of the difficulties we have mentioned also constitute hazards. In that case, they are not only annoyances to the therapist, but also involve the possibility of injuring the client. This is particularly true in the case of the client who is too anxious to be asked to experiment or for whom the experiment would have too far-reaching implications. The outcome may be a client who constricts, becomes hostile, or who disintegrates in anxiety altogether.

Sometimes parents, and therapists too, try to teach children by letting them "burn their fingers." The parent feels safer when he is able to get the child to constrict, to stay off the street, to retreat to safety, to do nothing venturesome. He therefore lets the child get hurt a little as a result of some venture "in order to teach him a lesson." The child becomes anxious and perhaps constricts his field in order to reduce it to manageable size.

The same may be true of a client. He may constrict as an outcome of the experiment which the therapist has urged him to perform. Increased hostility may also be an outcome of ill-conceived experimentation. The client is unable to abandon his hypothesis as a result of the experiment, and so he rigidly adheres to the hypothesis and keeps trying to demonstrate rather than to discover its validity.

Another hazard is the loosening of conceptualization which may come about as the result of ill-timed experimentation. The client, unable to assimilate the outcomes of his venture in any tight structure, resorts to loosening. He may invoke mystical explanations for what happened. He may seek to overgeneralize old constructs in order to make them permeable to the new data, thus making them loose.

A further hazard is in attempted experimentation in an inappropriate milieu. The therapist, not realizing what the client's situation is, may urge him to perform an experiment in a group of people who will respond in a manner which the therapist is not prepared to interpret. The therapist will then find that he has confronted *himself* with a problem which he is poorly prepared to face. This happens particularly in an institutional setting where the patient is sent out to his home community on a trial visit. The therapist who has a misconception of the folkways and mores of the home community may ask the patient to attempt certain exploratory moves. The outcome may be disastrous to the patient and perplexing to the therapist.

The reader will recognize that our approach to therapy places great reliance upon experimentation. But in therapy, as in science, experimentation can contribute to progress only if the experimenter keeps his experiments within a conceptual framework, formulates adequate hypotheses, designs his procedures so that not too many factors will become variables at once, and prepares himself to construe the outcomes. If he fails to follow such good scientific procedure, he will not be experimenting systematically, he will only be puttering.

Chapter Twenty-two

Special Techniques in Psychotherapy

⊓⊔⊓⊔⊓⊔⊓⊔⊓⊔⊓⊔⊓⊔⊓⊔⊓⊔⊓⊔⊓⊔⊓⊔⊓⊔⊓⊔⊓⊔⊓⊔⊓⊔

THIS CHAPTER deals with techniques which serve special purposes, such as enactment, group psychotherapy, and the clinical training of psychotherapists.

A. *Enactment*

1. ENACTMENT PROCEDURES

While we have already discussed elaboration and experimentation procedures, both of which include enactment, we have reserved our detailed discussion of enactment for a special chapter. The psychology of personal constructs leads one to place particular emphasis upon enactment as a means of achieving therapeutic goals. We might have used the term "role playing" instead of "enactment," except that we have defined *role* in a manner which tends to exclude some forms of enactment. Ordinarily, of course, we see enactment as a more potent therapeutic procedure if it is based upon role constructs. A great deal is accomplished in any therapeutic series when the client develops a more adequate understanding of how the others with whom he lives are viewing their worlds. His enactment of a revised role follows immediately upon this reconstruction.

But enactment of a role is more than merely an outcome of one's understanding of others; it is also a way to arrive at a further understanding of them. Thus it is not always necessary that the first enactment venture be based on a very profound understanding of other persons. The role-like features can come later. The client may simply be asked, at first, to play a part, to do a job, to portray something, to involve himself in an experiment. In the course of elaborating the part he will soon find it necessary to construe another person's outlook; from that point on, his enactment will assume the properties of a role enactment.

a. *Classification.* It is possible to classify psychotherapeutic enactment procedures into certain broad groups, some of which are not specifically limited to a therapeutic setting. Let us suggest the following scheme:

A. Fixed patterns of enactment
 1. General cultural patterns
 2. Occupational patterns
 3. Institutional patterns
 4. Fixed-role therapy
B. Casual patterns of enactment
 1. Recreational patterns
 2. Creative patterns
 3. Teaching patterns
 4. Sociodrama
 5. Psychodrama
 6. Assessment
 7. Time sampling
 8. Task sampling
 9. Group psychotherapy
 10. Individual psychotherapy

This classification is a rather loose one, since not all of the suggested categories are at the same level of generalization. The pie is cut to serve our purposes, however.

We can quickly dismiss the four categories in the first group. We do recognize that there are cultural determinants which have a great deal to do not only with the way one patterns his life but with what he discovers about life. Shifting a person from one culture to another may, if he is able to reidentify himself and assume a role relationship with members of the new cultural group, enable that person to achieve a therapeutic readjustment. Occupational and institutional patterns of enactment are also frequent bases for therapeutic readjustment. Sometimes all a client needs is to involve himself in a new job or identify himself with a new organization. The fourth category in the group, fixed-role therapy, was discussed in Volume One. We inserted it there in order to give the reader a preview of the practical implications of the psychology of personal constructs as early in the exposition as possible.

If this were intended to be a complete discussion of psychotherapeutic procedures, we would have to include a discussion of the use of recreational and creative activities, such as games, painting, writing, designing, and so on. We have chosen not to try to cover all the implications of the psychology of personal constructs with respect to the therapeutic implications of these enactments, however.

b. *Enactment in teaching.* Enactment may be used in teaching. When so used it involves more than the classical "teaching demonstration." The student learns by playing the part of someone who is deeply involved in the problem which is being studied. For example, a student of American history might be asked to take the part of George Washington at the Constitutional Convention of 1787. By putting himself in Washington's shoes and carrying the "role play" through some episode, he might be able to reach a level of understanding of that phase of history which would otherwise seem contradictory or quaint. If we were to attempt to write a chapter on the application of the psychology of personal constructs to educational-psychological problems, we would have a good deal to say about supplanting the conventional approaches to teaching. Enactment could be shown to have important implications, not only for "learning," but for measurement of the results of the teaching effort.

c. *Sociodrama.* Sociodrama is a form of enactment procedure which has recently been the subject of a number of interesting studies, including those by Jennings. The procedure has been used in governmental agencies as well as in schools and in industry. It has been used both for the purpose of teaching skills required on the job and for straightening out frictions which have arisen in a group as a result of misunderstandings or ambiguities in the organizational structure. Sometimes it permits the psychologist to arrive at a quick appraisal of a confused organization which would be impossible if he relied upon more formal methods of trouble-shooting.

d. *Psychodrama.* Psychodrama, as developed by Moreno and his colleagues, is more specifically directed at what is presumed to be the client's inner emotional life. The presence of other persons during the enactment is supposed to help the client keep in contact with reality by providing him with "auxiliary egos." The procedure is partly conceptualized in the form of the classic Greek drama, with participant spectators having an opportunity to express and develop their souls. In this connection we shall reserve our discussion of group psychotherapy, as viewed within the psychology of personal constructs, for a later section of this chapter.

e. *Assessment.* Assessment is a form of enactment which attracted attention in this country as a result of the work of Murray and his associates in the U.S. Office of Strategic Services. It was adapted from the procedures of the British War Officer Selection Boards, which, in turn, had derived the idea from the German military psychologists. Both group and individual enactments are included under assessment. They include a great variety of tasks, some of which are highly structured, some quite free, and some quite anxiety producing. The enactments give the observers an opportunity to make relatively unstructured diagnostic observations. These may be used as a basis for planning treatment, although, for the most part, assessment is used as a criterion-building procedure for the selection of personnel for particular assignments, or for research requiring the formulation of a comprehensive dependent variable. So far, no one has used assessment procedures extensively in connection with psychotherapy.

f. *Time-sampling procedures.* Time-sampling procedures have been with us for some time. When the term is used, it is ordinarily intended to refer to a particular kind of time sampling — the intensive observation of a person's behavior during an intermittent series of short intervals. The intervals are chosen to sample a certain defined population of the person's behaviors. The procedure is ordinarily applied to children only, although there is no systematic reason why it cannot be applied more extensively to the observation of adult behavior.

g. *Task-sampling procedures.* These procedures are often used in industry, both in connection with personnel selection and in connection with criterion building. The subject is given a task which is a reasonably representative sample of the kind of job for which he is an applicant. His performance on the sample is taken as an indication of how he might be expected to perform on the job as a whole. Such measures have to be validated, of course, and sometimes the research gets pretty confused with a great deal of uncertainty as to what is the "predictor" and what is the "criterion." Is the "predictor" a standard against which the "criterion" is to be validated, or is the "criterion" a standard against which the "predictor" is to be validated?

2. THE FUNCTIONS OF CASUAL ENACTMENT PROCEDURES IN INDIVIDUAL PSYCHOTHERAPY

Since group psychotherapy is to be discussed in a special section, we next find ourselves at the last item in the list, casual enactment procedures in individual psychotherapy. Here we refer to informal role-playing techniques which can be used in the interview room with client and therapist enacting the parts. The parts can be structured with the two of them agreeing in advance as to how the parts are to be played out. Alternatively, the parts can be attempted with a minimum of pre-structuring and the enactment allowed to develop spontaneously. The therapist can furnish such guidance as he considers necessary, through a careful control of his enactment of his part.

The function of enactment procedures is to provide for elaboration of the client's personal construct system, to provide for experimentation within the laboratory of the interview room, to protect the client from involving core structures before he is ready to consider abandoning them, to free the client from preemptive constructs too tightly tied to actual events and persons, and to enable the client to see himself and his problems in perspective.

We have already discussed elaboration and experimentation and the functions these procedures have in the psychotherapeutic process. In our earlier chapter on fixed-role therapy we discussed the advantage of allowing the client to hide behind role playing when he is dealing with precarious issues. If the client feels that he is "being himself," rather than "acting a part," he is likely to feel threatened by any development in the enactment which appears to invalidate his core structures. If, on the other hand, he considers that he is "only acting a part," he thereby disengages his core structures from the enactment and may proceed to explore the implications of his thinking more freely. He knows that he can always "return to being himself." One may say that the enactment procedures in psychotherapy correspond to the projective procedures in psychodiagnosis.

The freeing of the client from preemptive constructs is one of the interesting functions of casual enactment procedures. Suppose a therapist has a very literalistic client. The client describes, in detail, incident after incident and seems unable to express any generalized attitude or principle which might transcend the endless succession of anecdotes. We may say that he is "stimulus-bound."

Now suppose the therapist sets up an enactment situation. The client is now on his own; he cannot refer back to a specific set of events to determine how he should act. He simply has to do the best he can. The principles which he was unable to discuss in the previous therapy session must now be invoked as a guide to be followed spontaneously in the rapidly moving enactment. The therapist, through his own portrayal, can pace the enactment so as to bring into play either the client's planned strategies or to force him to fall back upon makeshift tactics. Thus, parts of the client's construct system can be brought into the therapeutic situation which, otherwise, might remain elusive and utterly inaccessible to treatment.

The enactment provides both client and therapist with material for immediate discussion. Here the client and the therapist have both observed the client's handling of a problem. The data are clearly remembered; they are only a few minutes old. The discussion which follows is based on common perceptual ground. This is what the client meant; that is what the therapist meant. The client has seen himself in action and now he can immediately look at his performance with some detachment and perspective. He has not held anything back from the therapist, as he may have held back in reporting events occurring on the outside. The discussion which follows an enactment session is likely to have relatively few gaps and relatively few misperceptions.

3. THE TECHNIQUES OF CASUAL ENACTMENT

a. *Unverbalized enactment.* There are some points to be kept in mind by the therapist who uses enactment procedures for the first time. First he should remember that much of the enactment takes place on a nonverbal basis. The verbal fluency of the client and therapist is not a measure of the success of the procedure. Sometimes a client can get a great deal out of an enactment session, even though he seems utterly unable or unwilling to express himself. Just sitting there and feeling that he is cast in a certain part, or that he is perceived as being in a certain part, is, in itself, a form of adventure which he is not likely to pass off lightly. As the therapist, enacting his own part, keeps insinuating that the client is cast in the opposite part, the client is forced to do some thinking. How can he respond? How can he defend himself? How is this different from "real" life? What words would he like to say? How strange it is to be perceived in this fashion! What would happen if anyone really saw him in this light? All of these are questions which may urgently arise in his mind, even though he never says a word during the enactment period.

b. *Brevity.* The second point to be remembered is that the

enactment may be very brief and yet quite effective. Therapists who are used to the enactments of sociodrama, psychodrama, or group role playing may be surprised at the brevity of some of the enactments which can be used effectively in individual treatment. In the writer's practice most of the separate enactments vary from about two minutes to about fifteen minutes. The average is probably about five minutes. In the earlier sessions the enactments are much longer, since the therapist does not plunge into difficult material until the client is well ensconced in his part.

c. *Exchange of parts.* The third point is one on which we find it necessary to place increasing emphasis. It is the exchange of parts. Recently we have come to the conclusion that a less experienced therapist should never fail to exchange parts with his client and reenact the scene. Enactment has some hazards, as we shall point out presently, and the immature therapist is likely to find that the client feels the therapist has taken advantage of him in the choice of parts. The exchange gives the client a chance to equalize the score, as well as take advantage of what he has learned from the therapist's portrayal. The switch also gives the therapist an opportunity to portray both parts in the scene comprehensively and sympathetically. This is just as important in portraying a figure in the client's social world as it is in portraying the client's self.

d. *Protective use of enactment.* The fourth point to keep in mind is that the therapist must always be ready to use the enactment to protect the client when he gets into trouble. This requires alertness and skill. Enactment therapy moves very rapidly and the therapist who is used to dozing in his chair at the head of a couch may find that he is not up to it. Certainly he cannot take notes while he enacts his part. The therapist simply must be prepared to adapt his part, moment by moment, so that the client does not get beyond his depth. Furthermore, it is not a good plan to stop the enactment as soon as the client gets into trouble. Rather, the enactment should itself be used to resolve the situation. If the enactment is called off every time the client starts to get into trouble, he may develop considerable anxiety. So may the therapist.

e. *Selection of scenes.* What situations should be used as scenes for enactment? In the first place, most of the scenes should be adapted from the client's own reports of incidents. They need not be exact portrayals of the incidents reported by the client, as is sometimes required in psychodrama, but they can often be based on these incidents. When the scenes are chosen from reported incidents, the enactment becomes more of an elaborative procedure. When the scenes are designed to anticipate incidents, as in most of the sessions in fixed-role therapy, the enactment is more of an experimental procedure.

As the therapist prepares to move into the area of superordinate constructs, he may set up scenes in which he and the client portray the parts of hypothetical persons. This tends to disinvolve the client and permit him to attempt to portray a part which he might presently consider incompatible with the personality of any person about whom he has made a prior judgment. Thus he is freer to try to express any new conceptualization that might have been developing recently in therapy.

Later the therapist and the client may portray the parts of persons who are closer to the client, and for whom the portrayals suggest reinterpretations. At a later time the therapist may set up a hypothetical scene in which the client, and then the therapist, play the part of the client's self. Some of the most dramatically effective enactments the writer has known have come about as a result of the client and the therapist playing out a scene between the client's self and one of his parents, or between his parents. The roles, of course, must be exchanged in such crucial enactments and the scenes replayed.

There is another type of scene which brings the client face to face with the need for revising his construction of his parents. The therapist suggests that the client play the part of the therapist and the therapist play the part of the client's father who has come to the therapist for help on his own problems, particularly in relation to his son. The client, if the exercise is undertaken at a time when he can allow himself to enter into the enactment, may be somewhat shaken by the experience and the therapist may need to provide him with some support later in the interview. Again, of course, the parts must be exchanged, and the scene reenacted immediately. The discussion should mostly be postponed until after the reenactment.

The enactment scene may be built up around a hypothetical situation occurring in the client's childhood. Following the reenactment, it may be set up around the client's old age. Frequently it is advisable to work out a scene portraying one of the client's parents when that parent was younger than the client now is. Sometimes it is quite helpful to realize that the parent he is describing, through the eyes of his childhood, was a person younger and less experienced than the client is now. This perspective rarely fails to make a profound impression on the client and usually makes him more ready to view his relations with his parents in better perspective.

Another type of hypothetical scene is one in which the client is expected to comfort someone who has suffered a bereavement. This situation puts the client into a supportive role and usually forces him to select positive approaches to the hypothetical problem. If his efforts at support are not sufficiently outgoing, the therapist, through his playing of the opposite part, can point out just how the support is failing. When the parts are exchanged, the therapist can vary his portrayal of the supporting part, first playing it somewhat the same way the client did, then in a more effective manner. The ensuing discussion will enable the client to say what he found supportive in the therapist's portrayal.

A scene can be set up in which the client has already suffered all the terrible things that he has been apprehensive about. This is a way of getting the client to imagine the worst, and then to see what resources he might have available for meeting the emergency. If he is one in whose personal construct system all guilt requires atonement, the imagined punishment in the situation will tend to permit him to look beyond the atonement to see what can be done in the way of reconstruction. In theological terms this is simply stated as looking beyond atonement to repentance. "Repentance" is used here, not in the popular sense of self-abasement, but in its etymological sense of reconsideration or reconstruction.

Sometimes the therapist finds it advisable to set up a situation in which the client is expected to behave in an aggressively hostile manner toward the therapist. Experienced therapists may complain that such artificial aggressive hostility is not equivalent to the real thing, and that one cannot expect the client to profit from the experience as much as he might if he genuinely showed aggression to the therapist and was able to get by with it. We would have to agree; in fact, none of the enacted roles is equivalent to the playing of a role with which the client genuinely identifies himself. Yet the enacted parts provide a basis for experimentation, a test-tube approach to the problems of living. Thus the client, like a child behind a Hallowe'en mask who expresses his aggression toward an awesome figure, edges himself a little closer to adulthood.

One form of enactment procedure, sometimes helpful, is for the therapist to structure a situation in which the client first plays the part of a psychotherapist and the psychotherapist plays the part of a hypothetical client who has many of the same problems the client has. The psychotherapist may structure his part deliberately so as to show that it is not actually the client he is portraying, but a person who happens to have some, but not all, of the same kinds of problems the client has. From such an enactment the psychotherapist may learn just how the client hopes the therapist will behave in relation to him. He may find, for example, that the client expects him to be dictatorial and inflexible. Or he may find that the client expects him to be indulgent and uncritical.

Another approach is to ask the client to play the part of a hypothetical close friend who has come to talk to the psychotherapist about the client. This gives the therapist a chance to ask some rather direct questions which might otherwise threaten the client. For example, the therapist may say, "Do you know whether your friend Mary is secretly afraid that she will lose her husband's affections, or has she ever confided in you to that extent?" The therapist may also use the enactment as a vehicle for the client to express some of her feelings toward him. He may say, for example, "When I talk to your friend Mary, are there any special attitudes or feelings that I should be particularly sensitive to? What is likely to be her response to me?"

There are many useful variations of this technique, and the therapist who is able to improvise, while remaining sensitive to the client's "need for distance," will be able to build the client's sense of security, even in a case in which the client is very much afraid to have the therapist move in close to him. In the case of a very fearful client, the therapist may conduct all of the first several interviews in this manner. When the time comes for the client to stop "playing peek," the therapist may suggest, "Do you suppose you could persuade Mary to come with you to the next interview and perhaps let us talk to her directly for a little while?" This may seem like a technique to be used with children only, but the writer's experience indicates clearly that it is extremely valuable for certain adults, even quite sophisticated ones. A client, particularly a professional person, often feels uncomfortably naked and vulnerable when he comes for treatment. The use of this type of enactment may be just what he needs to protect himself during the early stages of treatment.

Another type of scene is one in which the client portrays the part of the therapist while the therapist plays the part of a consultant to whom he has gone for consultation regarding his case. The client's portrayal indicates something of his interpretation of the therapist's outlook, and hence reveals something of the role the client is playing. When the parts are exchanged, the client's portrayal will indicate some of his feelings of hostility toward the therapist by the manner in which the consultant is portrayed.

4. OBSTACLES TO ENACTMENT PROCEDURES

a. *Reluctance of the therapist.* Among the obstacles the therapist may meet when he approaches therapy via enactment procedures is, first of all, a reluctance in himself. He will be likely to fear that he cannot assume as much initiative as the enactment requires of him. The procedure is not one that a passive therapist can be comfortable with. He cannot expect the client to do all of the work.

The therapist may be afraid that he will make himself look ridiculous. Some therapists are so busy maintaining their pomposity that they cannot stoop to explore life on equal grounds with the client. Sometimes they are afraid that if the client ever sees them enacting a humble part he will thereafter lose all respect for them.

b. *"Insincerity."* Another obstacle is the client's complaint that he would feel "insincere" if he enacted a part. Persons who make a fetish of "sincerity" often turn out to be people who are so narcissistic that they cannot do a job; they can only "express themselves." One finds this to be true of adolescents who use the term "sincerity" frequently in their Rep Test protocols.

Sometimes the therapist feels he is being "insincere" when he enacts a part. Our answer to that is a short one! The sincere therapist is one who will do whatever is necessary to help the client, and do it without self-consciousness. If it were necessary, the sincere therapist would stand on his head to help the client get well. The client comes to the therapist, not to watch him be "sincere" for an hour, but to get help!

c. *Breaking role.* One of the therapist's most persistent technical difficulties is getting the client to stay "in cast." The client is likely to drop out of role and start discussing his difficulties in the part, his poor performance, his reluctance to carry through the enactment, and so on. The more the client is inclined to "acting out" his difficulties in relation to the therapist, the more he is likely to drop out of cast in the enactment situation. This may seem incongruous, yet the explanation is probably very simple. The client is so busy "putting on his own act," and using the therapist as a "straight man," that he becomes disturbed when he is cast in another part or when his behavior is pre-labeled as "an enactment."

The therapist can often control this tendency to drop out of cast by staying in cast himself. If the therapist is playing the part of the client's mother and the client is playing the part of his father, whose name is John, the therapist may say, for example, "But John, I didn't realize you felt this way; I knew our son did, but not you. I have sometimes worried about our son's feeling this way. Now what do you think about . . . ?" and so on. By keeping considerable initiative, staying in cast himself, and interpreting everything the client says as if it were spoken in cast, the therapist can often keep the situation in hand.

, d. *Other difficulties.* In addition to these difficulties we should call attention to those we previously mentioned as interfering with elaboration and experimentation. Many of them apply also to enactment, since enactment is often used for elaboration and experimentation.

5. HAZARDS IN ENACTMENT

There are some hazards which ought to be mentioned. First of all, there is a real danger that the therapist may reveal more of himself in the enactment than the client ought to see. As we have said before, things happen in rapid succession in the enactment and the therapist finds himself behaving spontaneously under the regnancy of his own personal constructs, as well as under his professional system. If he is hostile toward the client, he is much more likely to reveal it than when he uses more circumspective therapeutic methods. It may show up in his stubbornness, his slowness to pick up the client's leads, his attempts to fence the client into a corner, or his portrayal of a caricature of the client. Of these, the last is the most likely to occur, and is also the most destructive. The client will not be slow in sensing his therapist's hostility in an enactment situation, and if he has any self-respect he will set up defenses against it. The defenses may protect the client — fortunately — but they may also prevent the therapy from getting anywhere.

In the writer's opinion the development of enactment techniques holds great promise in psychotherapy. Basically they turn the attention of the client toward what is to be done and away from the redundancy of trying to find out what there is within himself which is trying to be expressed. They emphasize the role a man is to play and the conceptualization of others upon which it is based. They turn the client toward the world around him in an effort to understand it and let him stop considering himself a psychological spastic cripple with a libidinal birth injury.

B. Group Psychotherapy

6. FUNCTIONS OF GROUP PSYCHOTHERAPY

In an earlier chapter we discussed one particular type of group psychotherapy — group fixed-role therapy. Let us turn now to other types and some of the procedures which they involve. It will be impossible to present an exhaustive discussion of this topic, but here, as elsewhere, perhaps we can present enough to indicate the principal implications of the psychology of personal constructs.

The functions of group psychotherapy are broadly the same as those of any form of psychotherapy — to assist the person to develop more effective channels through which he and others may anticipate events. Since such a large portion of the events to be anticipated are human events, group psychotherapy, like most psychotherapy, deals particularly with the improvement of one's anticipations of his fellow man. This is not only because our fellow men are such busy inventive people — always making unexpected things happen — but also because each of us has dispersed his dependencies so widely among his neighbors. Keeping up with the world has become a very complicated business, altogether too much for a person who relies upon antiquated ideas.

Group psychotherapy has some functions for which it is particularly well adapted. These are not as restricted in scope as some therapists are inclined to believe. We see group psychotherapy as a procedure which need not always be considered merely an adjunct to individual treatment. Indeed, group psychotherapy may often represent the focal psychotherapeutic effort and, in some cases, the sole psychotherapeutic effort. Moreover, the effectiveness of group psychotherapy is not limited to mild or transient disorders. It may be the treatment of choice for seriously disturbed clients. In fact, group psychotherapy may represent the only access to a particular client, until such time as it has prepared him for individual treatment.

a. *Base for experimentation.* One of the advantages of group psychotherapy is that it gives the client a broader initial base, both for experimentation and for his new role. There are more persons with whom he can try out new ways of behaving. And there are more individuals whose construction systems can be intimately interpreted. Yet all of this can be accomplished within the protective walls of the therapy room, with a therapist present to keep matters from getting out of hand. It is like having a large, well-equipped social laboratory with a variety of figures in it, in contrast to a small laboratory with only one other figure in it. The better-equipped laboratory affords an opportunity to perform a greater variety of social experiments. The contrasting personalities of the fellow group members give the client an opportunity to develop a more comprehensive role for himself.

b. *Discrimination.* Because there are several other people in the therapeutic situation the client has an opportunity to discover that some of his constructs can be applied successfully to several persons, hence are permeable, while others are applicable only to certain persons, hence are best managed as impermeable. The group type of laboratory also gives the client an opportunity to see which constructs can be applied comprehensively — in other words, to persons and situations which are otherwise quite dissimilar — and which constructs apply only to persons and situations which are identical.

c. *Approach to preemption.* Perhaps, most of all, the group situation provides a way of shaking out preemptive constructs. Preemptiveness is a particular kind of rigidity which causes therapists a lot of trouble. For example, a client views a certain person as "Mother" and, because she is seen as "Mother," seems unable to construe her along any other dimension except "Mother." In Steinesque language, "a 'mother' is my 'mother' is my 'mother'"! In the group-therapy room, the client gets to see how other mothers are portrayed and, to the extent that he is able to share other clients' mother figures with them, he has occasion to make discriminations and generalizations along dimensional lines which would otherwise have been ignored.

d. *Approach to constellatory construction.* Not only does group psychotherapy seem to be more effective in dealing with preemption than individual psychotherapy, but it also seems more effective in dealing with a similar, but slightly different, type of rigidity — namely, stereotypy. Our term for this type of construction is *constellatory.* By it we imply a little more than is usually implied by "stereotypy." For example, a client who has been inclined to think that all fat people are happy-go-lucky, self-satisfied, materialistic, and lazy may have an opportunity to find out that his fat companion in group psychotherapy is by no means so simply construed. Furthermore, both constellatory and preemptive constructions are more likely to be reconsidered by the client if the group within which he works out his role is heterogeneous.

e. *Variety of validational evidence.* The use of a group-psychotherapeutic situation also makes available a greater variety of validational evidence. The events in which several persons jointly participate are more complex, and hence more fertile. There are more ways in which the client's experimental explorations can turn up validational evidence, both positive and negative. The therapist who believes that the client is always threatened by negative evidence ("failure" or "negative reinforcement") may feel he has to control the situation so as to prevent such evidence from turning up. In a group-therapy situation he is likely to become quite anxious, lest something "negative" should happen. This attitude toward negative evidence probably accounts for many therapists' reluctance to venture into group psychotherapy.

f. *Dispersion of dependency.* The group situation provides an opportunity for the client to disperse his dependencies in an early stage of therapy. In fact, the dispersal of dependency is an important feature of the first stage of a group psychotherapy series. The therapist leader needs to be able to handle this dispersal of dependencies and must never be jealous of them. He must realize that the ultimate object of therapy is not to make each client dependent upon the therapist, but rather, to help each client find how he can discriminate between his dependencies and to distribute them appropriately among other persons. When the therapist sees this taking place in the group-therapy room, he should not feel that he is being ignored or that the group is necessarily getting out of hand.

g. *Economy.* Finally, group psychotherapy tends to be more economical in its demands upon the therapist's time. This is particularly true in an intramural setting where patients can be made available at any hour of the day. Extramural group psychotherapy is likely to be much more difficult to schedule, especially when it must be fitted to clients' working hours. It is extremely difficult to get a group of men together during the day, and the therapist usually ends up scheduling his group psychotherapy in the evenings. Sometimes a group of women can be scheduled in the morning or early afternoon. By the time scheduling problems have been met, the therapist may find that some of the economic advantages of group psychotherapy have been canceled out.

7. TECHNICAL PROBLEMS IN GROUP PSYCHOTHERAPY

The first technical problem that a therapist faces, after it has been determined that a certain client or group of clients should have group psychotherapy, is that of deciding what the composition of each group should be. Ordinarily, he will want all of the group to start the treatment together, since latecomers are often put to a serious disadvantage and may never be accorded full group support. The therapist must also face the problem of how much heterogeneity the role relationships can be expected to sustain. There are two ways to approach this problem. If all members of the group share a common threat — for example, if a group is composed of mothers whose children are feebleminded, or of husbands and wives of hospitalized patients — the group supports, about which we shall have something to say presently, are likely to appear almost immediately. If the members of the group represent age, sex, and cultural variations, the group supports may be slow in appearing, but the constructions which finally emerge are likely to be more comprehensive, and the clients are more likely to graduate without need for supplementary treatment.

Verbal facility is not particularly important in choosing clients for membership in a psychotherapy group. Rather, the most important consideration is the client's readiness to perceive others' points of views — in other words, his readiness to develop role relationships. Because of our theoretical position regarding guilt, we are led to believe that a client who feels guilty, because he is aware of his displacement from role, is often a good candidate for group psychotherapy. We have to exercise some caution, however, in applying this selective criterion. If the candidate has overconstricted, or if he has developed an extended system of tight literalistic constructs, he may be prevented from establishing a useful relationship with more than one person at a time.

Usually the Rep Test will give the therapist some idea of the advisability of inviting a client to become a member of a psychotherapy group. The protocol should show one or two good permeable constructs which are sufficiently comprehensive to enable him to deal with dissimilar personalities. There should also be some indication of dependency in the protocol — for example, a construct of "people who like me versus people who are cold." There should not be too many physical-situational constructs such as "people who live on a farm versus people who live in the city." Persons who structure all their worlds in this manner are not prepared to change their view of a person until that person packs up and moves.

8. PHASES IN THE DEVELOPMENT OF THERAPY IN A GROUP

We find it convenient to identify six phases in the development of a psychotherapy group. They are:

1. Initiation of mutual support.
2. Initiation of primary role relationships.
3. Initiation of mutual primary enterprises.
4. Exploration of personal problems.
5. Exploration of secondary roles.
6. Exploration of secondary enterprises.

As a group develops, one can often see these phases clearly developing in sequence. The phases do overlap, however, and there are some sessions which seem somewhat to exhibit all six phases at once.

9. INITIATION OF MUTUAL SUPPORT

The group therapist should ordinarily start the group with a series of activities which are designed primarily to introduce the first phase of the program, the initiation of mutual acceptance and support. We are fully convinced that no member of the group should be encouraged, or even allowed, to put himself in a vulnerable position before the group until supports have become apparent in the group's interactions and those supports are obviously available to the person who confides. This is, as we have explained before, important in individual treatment; but it is doubly important in a group situation, in which a client can feel threatened by several people all at once, not just by one.

We have defined *acceptance* as the readiness to see the world through another person's eyes — that is, readiness for commonality. *Support,* in turn, was defined as a broad response pattern in relation to which the client successfully experiments with a variety of constructs and behaviors. In a group situation, support is necessarily based upon acceptance. For a member of the group to feel supported he must feel that at least one other person in the group is trying to see matters the same way he does. Therefore, it seems to him, there is at least one person with whom he can successfully experiment. This is what the therapist works for. He checks carefully for evidence that each person feels he is supported from some quarter. He keeps the discussion away from deeply disturbing material until he has satisfied himself that the supports are operative.

a. *Enactment.* There are ways of initiating this support. We prefer enactment, or role playing, just as we prefer enactment as a procedure for accomplishing a number of other psychotherapeutic objectives. Partially structured parts can be set up for certain members of the group to enact and develop. The enactments can be quite brief at first. As soon as the first enactment is completed, the therapist can ask each member of the group which of the participants he found himself identifying with. Then the parts can be exchanged and a reenactment attempted. Again, the members of the group can be asked to indicate which of the two participants they identified with, and why they have made their choices.

This exercise is not so much to force participation on the observers as it is to give participants in the scene a clear perception of being supported by other members of the group. This point is important. The therapist must be quick to note an instance in which a participant fails to enlist any support for himself. Usually a participant's feeling of lack of support is immediately reflected in his behavior.

The fact that participants in the enactment have been supported will not escape the attention of candidates for future enactments. Thus, during the first phase of the psychotherapy program, the awareness of the possibility of receiving support tends to spread among the membership with each enactment. As support is being built within the group, the therapist should not himself succumb to the temptation to seek support of his own, nor should he indicate his own preference identifications. He will get any support he needs in due course of time.

b. *Use of stressful scenes.* In order to strengthen the supports, the therapist can propose stressful and guilt-laden enactment situations. These should always be academic at this stage. He should still avoid situations which come too close to the biography of any one of the clients. Here the supports become more apparent, and observers tend to express sympathy for the participants in the enactment.

At this time the therapist can turn the attention of the group to changes the members perceive taking place in it. He can help them verbalize their feeling of being supported by other members of the group. It will also help if he tells the group near the outset that role playing can be threatening until group support has been established.

c. *Cliques.* During this period the therapist needs to be alert to the formation of cliques. While, ideally, all members of the group should support each other without prejudice, in actual practice, particularly with deeply disturbed clients, there is a considerable tendency for cliques to form and re-form. At first, these cliques tend to be pairs, each composed of a follower-leader relationship. Later they take on more complex and transient characteristics.

d. *Exchange of parts.* In group therapy, as in individual therapy, the exchange of parts is important. The therapist ordinarily does not want one of the members to feel he is being "typed" in his parts. If he always exchanges parts, this feeling tends to be avoided. The reenactment usually takes only about half as long as the initial enactment, hence the therapist need not be concerned that the exchange of parts will seriously slow down the group's movement. Ordinarily, it is better to carry out most of the discussion of the enactment after the reenactment, rather than immediately following the original enactment. If the group is fairly large — for example, more than eight — the situation can be enacted, reenacted, then new players substituted with a second enactment and exchange of parts. This can then be followed by a discussion.

e. *Length of enactment.* How long should the therapist allow an enactment to continue before he breaks it off? A rule of thumb is to continue the enactment at least until all participants have had to resort to obviously spontaneous behavior — that is, until it becomes apparent that each participant has had to abandon his original plan and deal with an emerging situation he had not anticipated.

f. *Number of participants.* Ordinarily we prefer to limit the number of participants in an enactment situation to two. In a later stage of therapy, more complex interpersonal relationships can be explored. During the initiation-of-mutual-support phase the therapist may set up the enactment situation and assign parts. If he can control his anxiety and hostility he may occasionally take a part himself, but he should not attempt to participate too often in the enactments. Rather, he should keep himself more of a peripheral figure so that most of the supports and role relationships will be established among the members of the group.

g. *Illustrative scene.* This is not an appropriate place to attempt to expound psychotherapeutic techniques in great detail. However, the following illustrates the type of enactment situation which can be used during the later part of the first phase of group psychotherapy. This is a situation which involves considerable threat to the participants but which tends to build intragroup supports. The situation is set up as follows.

Two participants are involved. The scene is the living room of the person played by the first participant. This person is the parent of a ten-year-old son. The time is 9 P.M. The participant playing the part of the second person knocks on the door of the house. The enactment starts at this point.

After the therapist has structured the situation, as described above, each participant is asked, in turn, to leave the room until the other participant has been briefed before the group as to the background of his part. Thus, when the enactment starts, neither participant knows the background of the part being played opposite him, but the nonparticipant members of the group all know the background of both parts. Following is the background structure given the first participant.

"Your ten-year-old son is generally considered to be a 'problem child'. He has been in trouble with the police, and the neighbors have complained to you about his impudent behavior. This evening the two of you had a quarrel and he became quite angry over your refusal to give him some money. He stamped out of the house, slamming the door behind him. You have not seen him for several hours."

Following is the background structure given the second participant.

"About four hours ago you unexpectedly ran across an old companion whom you had not seen for several years. You have spent the early part of the evening together having a good time. While driving home your car struck a child who was crossing the street in the dark between intersections. You stopped, an ambulance was summoned, and the child was taken to the hospital in an unconscious state. A bystander identified the child and gave you his home address. You are about to knock on the door of his home to inform his parents of what has happened."

This is a difficult situation and the therapist will not set it up for his clients unless he is reasonably sure that they are able to meet the situation without becoming loose or uncontrollably aggressive. It is important for all members of the nonparticipant group to know what the background information is and for each participant to know that they know the background for his own part. This is the reason for briefing each participant in front of the group. In this manner the participant may feel supported from the outset. He will need the support and will be inclined to accept it. As we have emphasized before, the parts should be exchanged, even though the reenactment does not involve the element of surprise that the first enactment does. The reenactment provides some protection for the second participant and it tends to emphasize the impersonal nature of the experiment.

h. *Staying in cast.* One of the difficulties the therapist experiences in using enactment is that of getting the participants to stay "in cast." This is not quite as difficult here as it is in individual psychotherapy, but the problem does often arise. Since the therapist is ordinarily not himself a participant, he cannot control the situation by staying rigidly "in cast" himself, as he may in the interview-room situation. One device we have used is to set aside two chairs at the front of the room or at the head of the conference table to be used exclusively for enactment. When members of the group sit in these chairs it is assumed that they shall enact only the parts assigned them. Before discussing the enactment they vacate the chairs.

i. *Extracurricular enactment.* The therapist should caution members of the group against role playing among themselves or with others outside the supportive framework of the group. Sometimes a person who gets enthusiastic about enactment can get himself into a pretty anxious state by attempting it without supports.

10. THE THERAPIST'S UNDERSTANDING OF ENACTMENT

The therapist's own conception of the function of enactment will have a great deal to do with what happens in the enactment situation. As we have indicated in our earlier discussion of fixed-role therapy, the assignments should not be conceived as parts each client should "learn" to play in real life. If the therapist takes this "learning" point of view, he is almost certain to get himself and his clients into difficulty.

The purpose of enactment is to give the client a chance to experiment, not to indoctrinate him. The client tries a part in order to see what it is like. He may deliberately try a part that neither he nor the therapist would predict would be "right" for him. Certainly the idea of enactment, under the psychology of personal constructs, is not to accumulate a backlog of pleasant "reinforcements," but to discover something. This, as we have so frequently said before, is the model of science. The scientist who attempts only to accumulate a backlog of reinforcements is likely to become rigid, timid, opinionated, and generally inert. The scientist who is inventive, curious, receptive, and progressive is the one who is as happy over negative results and the enlightenment they offer as he is about positive ones.

The therapist and the clients in a group situation should seek out the latter point of view. The parts they play are to enable them *to discover,* not *to demonstrate.* The therapist wants each client to have a chance to observe something. The enactment is designed, like a good experiment, to give the experimenter and his colleagues a chance to observe its outcomes. The client may be given a chance to do considerable experimenting with parts that he will eventually reject for himself, or, perhaps, has already decided to reject. No matter! It may be as important for him to know what he is rejecting as it is to know what he is accepting.

We would emphasize, therefore, that the therapist should take an experimental point of view toward the enactments used in group psychotherapy. He should design and propose them in collaboration with the group. He should not limit the assignments of parts to those which he thinks the individual group member should adopt permanently, nor even to those which he thinks the person should find acceptable. He, together with the members of the group, should consider himself free to reconstrue. This freedom should be limited only by the structure of the individual personality and the societal implications of the experiment.

Our discussion of the mutual-support phase of a group-psychotherapy sequence has thus far dealt primarily with enactment procedures. The therapist can also pursue the objectives of this phase by other means. The kind of discussion he initiates following an enactment is important. Ordinarily, he will ask for a show of hands, followed by spontaneous comment, on which members of the group identified themselves with each participant. He will make sure the participants take notice of this. He will ask individuals to indicate the points at which they began to feel their identification and the points at which they shifted from one participant to the other.

Even without enactment procedures the therapist can take steps to initiate mutual support in this first phase of the sequence. He can encourage members of the group to tell of experiences they have had. He can then urge others to indicate how they might have felt if they had been in the same circumstances. This is acceptance, as we have defined it, because it tends to indicate a willingness to see something through the eyes of the other person.

The therapist himself can indicate support during the early part of this phase. However, he should keep in mind that his primary task is to develop mutual supports between the client members of the group so that no member of the group will have to rely wholly upon the support of the therapist.

11. INITIATION OF PRIMARY ROLE RELATIONSHIPS

Let us turn now to the second phase of the group-psychotherapy sequence. We have called this the phase in which there is an initiation of primary role relationships. We used the word *primary*, since the role relationships in this phase are established wholly within the face-to-face therapy group. We use the term *role* in the special sense in which we have defined it, a course of activity pursued in the light of one's subsuming the construction system of another person. This is the phase of treatment in which the advantages of group psychotherapy over individual psychotherapy may begin to pay off.

Let us suppose an enactment has just been performed. The therapist judges that each member of the group is prepared to support some or all of the others and that each member of the group feels himself supported by some or all of the others. It seems to be time to move into the next phase of the series, hence the therapist starts proposing a somewhat different kind of problem. Now he may ask each of the nonparticipants to indicate just how they think the participants felt at certain points in the enactment. This, of course, means asking the nonparticipants to subsume the constructs of the participants and hence sets the stage for role relationships on the part of the nonparticipants. The participants can indicate how well they think their own feelings were anticipated by the nonparticipants. Hence there will be some immediate validation of the role constructs which the nonparticipants are beginning to put into shape.

The discussants can also indicate what they believe their own feelings would have been if they had been one of the participants. This gives the alert therapist an opportunity to make some important evaluations. The contrast that a client sees between the way another person appears to feel and the way he thinks he would feel in the same situation is a measure of the commonality the client perceives between himself and others. If he sees his own outlook as differing quite markedly from that of another it does not necessarily mean that he cannot play an effective role in relation to that person. It does mean, however, that the role he plays in relation to that person, if he does play one, may not be wholly spontaneous.

The therapist can begin to look for combinations of parts and participants which will give this particular member of the group a better opportunity to identify with someone. He may even try an enactment himself in order to get the identification process started. Often he may ask the noncommonality-perceiving member to participate in a reenactment of the incident, in order to see for himself just how he would feel in the part. He can also ask others to play the part, as this person appeared to play the part, in order to help him conceptualize the similarities and differences between his own outlook and that of others. The task, of course, is not necessarily to break down the "barrier" the therapist thinks the client has erected — that might be a hostile thing for the therapist to do — but to have the group explore together the similarities and differences between their outlook and the outlook of this particular person.

a. *Threat.* As the therapist moves into the role phase, in which he asks members to construe each other's outlooks, perhaps by portraying them through enactments, he must be alert to the threats involved. Both the participant and the person whose behavior is being portrayed are likely to be threatened. The participant may portray a caricature of the original. He may do this, not so much because he dislikes him, but because he feels threatened in the part. Perhaps the part seems to require him to reveal a facet of his own personality which he has tried to abandon or which threatens to engulf him. The person whose outlook is being portrayed may also feel threatened. He may see enactment as uncovering a facet of his personality he has hoped to keep covered, attempted to stave off, or tried to abandon.

If the therapist is insensitive to these threats he may lose considerable ground at this point. He should, of course, first make sure that his supports are in place before he proposes this type of enactment. Second, he should be able to use the situation to help the group understand, in a general way, why an enactment of this type is threatening, both to the participant and to the person who is portrayed. This is an important lesson. As the members of the group begin to grasp it they may also begin to understand each other in a way that will enable them to develop role relationships with each other.

b. *Alternative versions of parts.* One approach is to ask for an exchange of parts immediately, and suggest that the non-participants pay particular attention to the two different versions of the original which are portrayed by the participants. This not only suggests that there are different ways of interpreting the person whose personality is being portrayed, but it also helps the group conceptualize the nature of the threat the participants are feeling when they try to portray a fellow member.

The ensuing discussion should also serve to indicate to all, including the object person, that there are still other versions and conceptualizations possible. The therapist may, if he wishes, select some member of the group who seems to have a particularly sympathetic version of the object person to participate in a third enactment. During the discussion, the object person may also make comments which tend to have the force of validating evidence as to what his outlook is. At the end of the passage, someone may attempt to portray the object person as he has described himself during the discussion. Thus the emphasis is kept upon the task of understanding faithfully the outlook of the person portrayed.

c. *Clarification.* The discussions held during the primary role-building phase of therapy tend to emphasize the clarification of the group members' remarks. John makes a comment. Fred responds. Jim suggests that what John really meant was . . ., and so on. Or there may be an elaboration sequence such as the following. John makes a remark. Fred responds. Jim says that he is not sure he understands what John meant and asks John to elaborate. There may be an anticipatory sequence such as the following. Fred makes a remark. Jim turns to John and says, "Isn't this the way you would respond to that . . .?" In each of these three types of role-building sequences it is Jim who is developing his perception of John so that he can establish a role relationship with John.

d. *Hostility.* Often there is genuine hostility to be dealt with in this phase of group psychotherapy. As in the case of threat, it may show itself most clearly in enactments of a caricature. The hostility may be general, or it may be expressed, more particularly, when one of the clients is confronted with the task of developing a role relationship with a certain other client in the group.

First of all, it is important for the hostile client to feel supported before too much of his hostility has a chance to be revealed. Next, his caricatures of other persons can be allowed to prove themselves invalid. After a discussion he may be permitted to reportray a part which, at first, he portrayed in caricature. Sometimes a more positive check on the hostility can be provided by asking him to play the part in two contrasting ways. If his caricature in the first portrayal represents one end of an important construct dimension in his system, the enactment of the second version is likely to have to be at the opposite end of the same dimension. Thus he is urged to experiment with both ends of the construct, and in this way it becomes clearer to him, the therapist, and the group just what it is that is bothering him and what alternatives he is able to perceive.

12. INITIATION OF MUTUAL PRIMARY ENTERPRISES

The third phase of the sequence, as we see it, is that in which mutual primary enterprise is initiated. This is the phase in which the members of the group use their understanding of each other to propose and execute experiments. It starts when members of the group begin to suggest that the group ought to explore a certain kind of situation, or attempt to discover the answer to a certain kind of problem.

When the therapist detects this note in the discussions, he should always take steps to make sure that it involves role relationships, not merely individual hobby rides. He can do this by asking one client how he thinks the proposed enterprise might meet the needs of the other clients. The therapist can also ask how he thinks the other members of the group can help him by participating in such an enterprise. The preliminary discussion can become more specific, with the therapist suggesting that each indicate what positive contribution he thinks certain other clients will make to the enterprise.

As the term "primary" implies, this third phase of the group-psychotherapy sequence has to do with enterprises undertaken and completed within the group. It does not include those enterprises involving outside persons or those enterprises in the group which are attempted in preparation for situations arising outside the group. Ordinarily the tasks are completed within the session and are not envisioned as having immediate implications for life outside the sessions. The latter we call *secondary enterprise*. We envision it as the last phase in the sequence. While the therapist need not be rigid about the matter, it ordinarily seems to be a good plan to postpone secondary enterprises until after the group has passed through the fifth phase of treatment.

13. EXPLORATION OF PERSONAL PROBLEMS

The fourth phase of treatment deals with matters of the type which individual psychotherapy explores intensively. It should be noted, by way of contrast, that in group psychotherapy much more has been done beforehand. The client has been shored up on several sides by the supports which the therapist has helped the group put into place. He has already developed several role relationships involving other members of the group. He has gone even further; he has conjoined with the others in enterprises of a minor nature. He is presumably prepared to undertake problems as a member of a team. Now we shall see whether he can use the team approach to problems of a highly personal nature.

If enactment is used, this is the phase in which members of the group enact incidents from their own and each other's lives. These enactments may resemble the procedures used in psychodrama. However, it should be apparent that we envision the process somewhat differently than do Moreno and his colleagues. We would agree with them that there is validation or "reality testing" involved. However, we would place somewhat greater emphasis upon the value of the experience to the person who serves as an "auxiliary ego." It reestablishes him in a role relationship, a fact which should help him deal with his own guilt feelings. It shows him how a team approach can be used to solve personal problems. It helps him place his own problems in a social frame of reference by observing their similarity to the problems that other persons have.

During this phase various members can enact their versions of a particular client's predicament. They can also indicate, at a concrete level, just how they would deal with his problems. Suggestions and specifications for each enactment situation can come more from members of the group than from the therapist. The enactments are likely to be briefer, more spontaneous, and rapid moving.

If discussion is used primarily during this phase of treatment, the therapist must be alert to the rapid transitions which are likely to take place. Sometimes individual members of the group will find themselves seriously threatened by an unexpected turn in the group's discussion of their problems. When tensions develop and the hostile expressions of one member threaten other members of the group to a dangerous degree, the therapist may resort to the protective screen of enactment. The hostile client can be invited, not to portray "himself," but specifically to portray the hostility or the aggression he felt at a particular time or in connection with a particular type of incident. Both he and his friends are then partly protected by the make-believe of the enactment situation, yet he is free to express what he feels like expressing. This also helps the others see that, in expressing aggression, a member of their group is actually working out his own personal problem, and that what he says does not necessarily call for their defending themselves. Furthermore, the casting of the client's behavior into a structured part helps him set boundaries on his impulsivity and enables him to disengage himself whenever he begins to feel that he is losing self-control. It also helps protect him from the guilt reactions which so frequently come over a person after he has expressed himself aggressively; he can remind himself, quite appropriately, that he was enacting a part, expressing a point of view, clarifying a position. His role relationship as a member of the group is therefore not so much endangered.

If the use of enactment does not immediately bring necessary controls into effect, the therapist may use the exchange of parts to help the client keep his aggression or his anxiety within bounds. Another limiting device is to have another person act as the client's surrogate in the portrayal of aggression. The disturbed client can coach the surrogate, but in doing so he must describe and define in word-bound constructs the basis and nature of the aggression which is to be expressed in the scene.

14. EXPLORATION OF SECONDARY ROLES

The fifth phase of group psychotherapy is one of the most interesting. It is the phase in which the clients begin to try to establish roles for themselves outside the therapy group. Within the therapy room, this phase appears when clients begin to try to interpret the points of view of outside persons. The therapist will have to judge whether such efforts at interpretation represent real attempts to discover how certain other persons think, or whether they constitute merely hostile evaluations of the other persons. Usually he can assume it is the former if there seems to be any flexibility or tentativeness in the construing of the outside person. He can also judge that there is the beginning of role relationship if the client starts to deal with the person *propositionally* rather than *constellatorily* or *preemptively*. He can also be encouraged if the client starts to apply some variety of permeable constructions to the outside person.

It is in this phase that the therapist may begin to employ the procedures of sociodrama most effectively. Sociodrama requires the participants to construe some outside situation with reasonable accuracy; moreover, it is expected that the participants will learn to conform to the requirements of the situation. In any case, whether sociodrama is employed in this late phase of the treatment or in an earlier phase, it should not be attempted until the therapist is reasonably sure that adequate group supports have been established. In sociodrama it is not quite so important to use an exchange of parts.

During the establishment of secondary roles the therapist will need to do what he can to help individual clients generalize the role relationships they have developed within the group. There can be free discussion of the respects in which outside figures are like or unlike individual members of the group. Thus the therapist helps individuals make their role constructs more permeable. When this takes place, the client finds that he can relate himself to people as well as to certain persons.

Some parenthetical observations are of interest here. One of the features of communal living, whether on the Soviet model, the monastic-ecclesiastic model, or the collegiate-fraternity model, which is attractive to some persons, is the opportunity to establish secure and highly specific role relationships with certain other persons. In this respect, these forms of communal living are like the early stage of group psychotherapy. Indeed, one is impressed with the similarity of the devices used by communists, monks, and fraternity brothers to those used successfully in the early stages of group psychotherapy. The communal form of role is based on relatively impermeable constructions. The individual relates himself *to certain persons* and to them only. The constructs he uses to govern his role relationships to them do not seem to be applicable to anybody else. Not only may his constructs show the rigidity of impermeability but they may also tend to be preemptive and constellatory. If so-and-so is a "bourgeois-capitalist-imperialist," he is nothing but a "bourgeois-capitalist-imperialist"; if he is a "worldly disbeliever" he is nothing but a "worldly disbeliever"; if he is a "barb" he is nothing but a "barb."

The same kind of outlook is implied in an extreme nationalism which prevents one from making discriminations and generalizations. A person may find it impossible to see a fellow citizen in any terms except "loyal" and "disloyal." He cannot discriminate between liberalism, democracy, Stalinism, Trotskyism, or the principle of academic freedom. Thus it is that there are so many who espouse all the principles of "Soviet tyranny" and still represent themselves as the archenemies of "Communism."

But there is a certain sharp difference between this type of group acculturation and that which, under the psychology of personal constructs, we perceive as producing a healthy society. The difference lies in whether one can be loyal to certain persons only or whether he can be loyal to humanity. Can he govern himself by principles or can he respond only to labels, flags, uniforms, names, places, and passwords? In brief, the loyalty to principles, in contrast to loyalty only to facts, is the basis of that much prized quality of personality — personal integrity!

Back to group psychotherapy! The task of the therapist is, then, to help the client extend the lessons he has learned about role relationships with a particular group of persons and apply them to other persons outside the group and to humanity in general. The therapist needs to be able to lift the role language the group has developed in the therapy room and help them apply it outside the therapy room. This is the point where he must show broad perspective in his own viewpoint. He cannot be jealous of the contacts his clients make outside the group or of the new loyalties they try to establish. He must also help other members of the group not to be jealous of these extensions of principle.

15. EXPLORATION OF SECONDARY ENTERPRISES

Finally, the sixth phase of group psychotherapy is that which is characterized by the exploration of secondary enterprises. When a member of the group comes in and says that he has embarked on an enterprise involving an outside person, the therapist may assume that he has entered this phase of treatment. The entry may be premature and ill-conceived, but it is, in any case, the sort of undertaking that the client should eventually attempt if he is to graduate from the status of a patient.

A client should not be ejected from the group as "disloyal" when he embarks on this kind of venture. The therapist will have to be careful to maintain and verbalize an appropriate evaluation of this turn of events. The group can continue to supply its supports, and the venturesome client can capitalize upon these supports by discussing some of his outside experiences. During this phase, the client may keep his membership in the group, primarily as an insurance policy against outside failure. He may also keep it through a sense of obligation to the other members "to help them see their own problems through."

16. SPECIAL PROBLEMS IN GROUP PSYCHOTHERAPY

A special problem arises in group psychotherapy when a client joins the group late. Ordinarily the therapist will want to avoid this. The client may be treated as an outsider and hence have no feeling of support. If the role relationships have already been established on fairly complicated bases, he may not be able to follow the interplay of ideas and actions. Ordinarily, the therapist's first step is to let the new man show that he has himself identified with a participant in an enactment. The therapist may deliberately select the most insecure other member for the sympathetic part in the enactment, and may call on the new man only for an expression of identification. The participant thus has his attention focused upon the new man as the person who has most obviously supported him. The participant should therefore come to accept the new person more rapidly, particularly if the participant was threatened in the enactment.

If one combines enactment with discussion, it is a good plan to differentiate between the functions of the two different procedures. Ordinarily he will use the discussions to generate hypotheses and design experiments. The enactments, in turn, provide the experimental data. Finally, a discussion of the enactment provides a basis for determining the validational implications of the data and the grounds for further hypotheses.

A word of caution to those who have had dramatic experience! The enactments in either group or individual therapy are not theatrical productions. They are not designed to entertain, nor are they to be used as a vehicle for propaganda; their purpose is to provide members of the group with factual information about themselves, and the creatures among whom they live — information which none of them, not even the therapist, would be able to acquire otherwise. The enactments are therefore sheer adventures, not cut-and-dried exercises. For this reason, the participants may seem to be weary or inept entertainers, who sometimes act without conviction, who often muff their lines, who break out of character, and who cross each other up. The voices may drop to inaudibility. The gestures may contradict the argument. The actors may hide behind their props. Yet often the enactments which are the poorest "theater" turn out to be the most significant psychotherapy. The task of the therapist is not to improve "the production," but to let the enactments reveal faithfully the human nature which lies beneath the exterior surface of each participant.

Is the enactment artificial? Our answer is an emphatic no! The only thing artificial about therapeutic enactment is the pretense that it is artificial. The play of the participants is no more unnatural than the actions of a year-old youngster who plays "peek" behind his hands. Yet it provides a transparent mask behind which the actor portrays, not a false self, but the true self which is so often hidden by daily conventions and manners. The mask is therefore not a disguise, but a screen behind which the person can divest himself of his customary pretenses.

As we said at the outset of our discussion of group psychotherapy, the phases we envision do not necessarily fall into a precise order nor are they mutually exclusive. While two or more of them may appear to overlap in any one session, it is helpful for the therapist to see this particular passage as belonging to one phase and that passage as belonging to a later phase. Furthermore, the classification of phases provides the therapist with a basis for planning the therapeutic sequence and for pacing the group's progress.

C. Training Problems

17. QUALIFICATIONS OF PSYCHOTHERAPISTS

Psychoanalysts usually make a great to-do about no one's attempting to be a psychotherapist until he has been psychoanalyzed. This doctrine has provided psychoanalysis with a form of direct professional lineage from Freud. It corresponds to the apostolic succession from St. Peter claimed by certain ecclesiastical groups. Ordinarily, scientists find this kind of argument intellectually unacceptable and are likely to reject any system whose authority presumes to rest solely upon such a casuistical aristocracy. They think a great idea should be allowed to stand in its own right in the minds of men; it should not have to base its claim to validity in the persons of its sponsors. Moreover, it should be communicable in terms of the written language if it is to withstand the ravages of time and the vagaries of cultism.

But there is another issue which separates itself from the specious arguments of the successionists. This is the question of how adequate the psychotherapist's own subsuming construct system needs to be before he can properly understand the construct systems of others. There are perhaps two levels at which the issue should be faced: (1) how adequate should the therapist's verbal constructs be, (2) how adequate should the therapist's preverbal constructs be? In more common phrasing: (1) what should be the therapist's capacity for "intellectual insight," (2) what should be the therapist's capacity for "emotional insight"?

a. *Professional constructs.* Our own position has, in part, already been stated in our chapter on the role of the psychotherapist. We believe, first of all, that the interests of the client are best protected when the training of the psychotherapist has been primarily directed toward the formation of systematically sound professional constructs. This means more than indoctrination with a working knowledge of a particular psychological system. It means that the psychotherapist should have some more profound understanding of the principles of scientific methodology and of scientific evidence. It means that he should be prepared to keep his system open to investigation and revision. His professional training should not be concerned solely with the exploitation and "application" of scientific knowledge — the notion of the "professional practitioner" — but also with the nature of that knowledge and of the processes by which it assumes its various shapes. This latter is the notion of the *professional scientist,* the notion we prefer to espouse.

Having said this much, it must become clear that we would take a dim view of the current practice of turning loose upon the public psychotherapists who have only the most elementary understanding of psychology. A medical education, a psychiatric residency, and a personal analysis are poor substitutes for advanced training in scientifically oriented psychology. Yet relatively few of the psychotherapists being trained today have anything more than the most meager background of psychological information. Most of our psychotherapists are being trained like witch doctors, with reliance placed primarily on long apprenticeships, unquestioned doctrines, and empathic "relationships."

This is harsh criticism. It needs to be tempered with a recognition of the fact that if it had not been for the adventuresomeness of certain psychologically unsophisticated medical men, such as Freud, Meyer, and Sullivan, the field of psychotherapy might not have been opened up to exploration at all. It needs also to be tempered with a recognition of the fact that psychologists have shown only a tardy interest in the recovery of the mentally disturbed person or, indeed, in any of the humanitarian values. Be that as it may, we are able to generate little more than a passing interest in the question of which of the professions has squatter's rights to psychotherapy. What is more important is the matter of what today is the best way to train a psychotherapist so that his clients will get well. As we have indicated, we consider that the primary approach should be to help the therapist develop a professional construction system which is printable, psychologically informed, systematically intact, scientifically supported, amenable to searching inquiry, and in process of continuing revision.

b. *The therapist's system as a whole.* Having made as clear as we know how what we believe should be the primary consideration in the training of psychotherapists, we may turn now to an important secondary consideration: the therapist's construct system as a whole, and especially those preverbal substructures which need to be approached through psychotherapeutic channels. Just as a good deal of the client's behavior is organized under constructs which are not symbolized by him on a verbal level, so the psychotherapist, being a person too, also lives under the aegis of a personal construct system not always clearly marked by names and guideposts.

In those instances where the student therapist's constructs are explicit and are communicated, it is possible for his teachers to come to grips with them. Those outlooks of his which are obviously invalid or hostile can be checked. The teacher can then help the prospective psychotherapist revise his explicitly communicated constructs; and, if his outlook continues to threaten the well-being of his clients, the teacher may exercise his moral obligation to deny the student professional status. This calls for a kind of interchange of ideas between student and teacher more comprehensive than that which characterizes the usual classroom. It means that psychotherapists need to be taught in very small groups, that the teacher should inquire more deeply into the preprofessional student's thinking than he usually does, and that he should be ready to make inferences from the student's behavior which go far beyond a literalistic reading of examination papers.

18. FUNCTIONS OF PSYCHOTHERAPY FOR PSYCHOTHERAPISTS

a. *Illustration of technique.* But what about the constructs which the student does not express in explicit form? To deal with these it is often desirable, though the writer is convinced that this is not always so, for the prospective psychotherapist to undergo a psychotherapeutic sequence himself. This may serve several functions. First, it may enable the supervising psychotherapist to illustrate psychotherapeutic technique. Sometimes psychotherapeutic techniques are more easily perceived when one is a bystander to psychotherapy, sometimes more easily when one is a participant. The function of support, for example, and the effectiveness of its various techniques can often be appreciated only when one is himself in a precarious spot and badly in need of it. Other procedures may be too obscure for the psychotherapist-client to follow at the moment they are employed, yet may be deeply appreciated at a later time when the supervising psychotherapist recalls for the psychotherapist-client's benefit just how a certain passage was handled.

b. *Grounds for role relationships.* A second function of psychotherapy for the psychotherapist is to give him better grounds upon which to establish role relationships with his clients. Since a role relationship requires the subsuming of some part of the construct system of the person with whom the role is played, the more the therapist can understand about how it feels to sit at the other side of the table, the more appreciative of his own client's position he is likely to be. Even experienced therapists are likely to be surprised at how different the therapeutic situation looks when one is in the role of a client.

c. *Discovering parallels.* A third function is to give the prospective therapist grounds for seeing parallels between himself and his clients. This involves a delicate issue. Will a therapist do a better job if he does see the client as resembling himself?

In answering this question we would make a distinction between seeing the client as like oneself and seeing him as having the same unsolved problems. From our experience it appears that something can be gained by a therapist's being able to see his client as passing through a stage of development which he himself passed through at one time in his life. But if the therapist has never satisfactorily resolved the problems of that stage, he is likely to have trouble with certain features of the treatment. In such a case it works better to have a therapist who has never personally faced those problems at all. For example, a male client may do well with a male therapist who has experienced and solved the kinds of problems he faces. If such a male therapist is not available, it may be better to assign the client to a female therapist who has never faced such problems than to a male therapist who has faced them but not solved them. This is true even though the male therapist might initially be the more accepting and "understanding" of the two.

The therapist who sees parallels between himself and his client may use this perception as grounds either for accepting the relationship or rejecting it. If he has solved his own problems in the area, he may use the perceived parallels as evidence that he may be able to help the client. If he has not, and from his own experience as a client knows that he has not, he may use the perceived parallels as evidence that he should not undertake the treatment of this particular person.

Sometimes the premature perception of parallels between one's own solved problems and the client's unsolved ones causes difficulty. The parallels may be only superficial in nature. Because of the confusing similarity, it may take the therapist some time to wake up to the fact that the client is only superficially like what the therapist used to be, and that his route to recovery is not the same as that which the therapist followed. This, of course, involves the familiar phenomenon of interference, so commonly observed in "learning" experiments. The similarity between the client's problems and the therapist's former problems interferes with proper differentiation between the problems.

d. *Discovery of self-appearance.* A fourth function of psychotherapy for the psychotherapist is to enable him to discover what roles clients may be able to perceive in relation to him. It is important for clients to play roles in relation to therapists as well as for therapists to play roles in relation to clients. Sometimes a therapist is unaware, until after he has experienced the intimate relationship of psychotherapy, just how clients are likely to perceive him and how they may most conveniently cast their dependencies upon him. A male therapist may find, for example, that female clients are likely to perceive him as a certain kind of father figure. His own therapy should give him a preview of how his clients will perceive him in this way, and what roles they are likely to play opposite him.

There is a special consideration which applies to the third and fourth functions of psychotherapy for psychotherapists. The kind of understanding one has of himself and of the way he is likely to be perceived by clients depends upon the construction system he employs. There is very little value in having a psychotherapeutic experience entirely structured in one system if one, in his own practice, expects to employ an entirely different system. "Insights" are meaningful in terms of the system in which they are cast; they may lose their poignancy when one is confronted with personal issues couched solely in terms of another system. Thus, if a person is preparing to practice psychoanalytic therapy, he will get more out of his own therapeutic experience if he has a psychoanalytically oriented therapist. If he is to practice another form of therapy — client-centered, for example — he will do much better to seek out a client-centered therapist for himself.

e. *Self-improvement.* The fifth function of psychotherapy for the psychotherapist is to help him put his own house in order. As the psychotherapeutic sequence progresses, the importance of this function alternates between a primary and a secondary position in the minds of the participants. If the therapy is seen as bearing only on the psychotherapist-client's professional life, he will take a much too constricted view of the problems arising during the course of treatment. If the psychotherapist-client's intimate problems are allowed to displace the problems of being a psychotherapist, he may fail to appreciate fully the importance of examining his own psychotherapeutic process in order to anticipate what his own clients will be going through.

As we have indicated before, we do not feel that psychotherapy has yet reached the stage of perfection when it will sanctify its clergy and give them clean hands and pure souls. No amount of brain washing will erase the individual character of the prospective psychotherapist. No matter how deeply he explores himself in the course of therapy, there are always unknown impressions lying just below the last layer he has uncovered.

There is always a problem in judging where psychotherapy should leave off, as well as in knowing where it should begin. Some persons may find that their treatment has left off at a point which unsuits them for doing certain types of therapy themselves. It is utterly impractical to try to resolve all of a person's psychological problems; indeed, it is mildly horrifying to speculate as to what such a changeling would be like if he were set loose in the neighborhood.

In brief, then, our position on purification is this: psychotherapy may be of inestimable personal help to the psychotherapist but, as for making his personality more suited to the responsibilities of the profession, it is frequently irrelevant. The writer has seen some instances in which it appeared that psychotherapy, while of real personal help, made a bad therapist out of a mediocre one.

19. PSYCHOTHERAPEUTIC PROCEDURES FOR USE WITH PROSPECTIVE PSYCHOTHERAPISTS

a. *Use of summaries.* There are some procedures which are particularly applicable to the psychotherapeutic treatment of prospective psychotherapists. Ordinarily the client-psychotherapist should be urged to write a summary of each interview within a few hours after it has been held. He should be encouraged to indicate what his feelings were during the interview as well as giving a factual account of what was said. He should also be encouraged to express his reaction to the interview and to keep an account of his experiences between interviews. These summaries may or may not be reviewed in the psychotherapy sessions, depending on what seems best to fit the needs of the particular client-psychotherapist.

In some cases it may be advisable also to keep recordings of the interviews and turn them over to the client-psychothera-pist at the end of the series. The recordings are not as valuable, however, as the person's written comments. The latter will be particularly revealing of his reluctance to discuss certain matters with the supervising psychotherapist. As he reads them months later, he will be more appreciative of his own clients' inability to come to grips with their problems in the therapy room.

b. *Judging.* Sometimes the supervising psychotherapist can terminate an interview with a suggestion that therapist and client-psychotherapist step out of their roles as client and therapist and review, as two professional men, the interview which has just been concluded. This may seem artificial but it often works surprisingly well, even when the client is going through an actively hostile period. The review can be on a factual level; that is, it can deal with what was explicitly said, what topics were dwelt upon and which ones were touched upon only lightly, and with the sequence or manifest "process" of the interview. Both participants should contribute to this account.

As the client-psychotherapist begins to be able to participate in the review as a professional person, the supervising psychotherapist may also comment on the techniques he has used, the topics he moved away from, or even some of the passages he was unable to evaluate and will need to study further. He may comment on the feelings of the client-psychotherapist, although this is somewhat precarious. If he does comment he may say something like the following, "During the discussion of . . . it seemed to me that I observed in the client some indication of mounting anxiety, though of course I could not be sure. I decided to deal with it, for the time being, if indeed it was anxiety, by the use of tightening procedures. I therefore asked for a more explicit statement about . . . If what I observed was a mounting anxiety associated with some aspect of the topic we were discussing, I am inclined to believe that it will come up again before long, perhaps in a context which will give us a better frame for dealing with it. Do you, as a psychologist, agree that this was an appropriate decision on my part, or do you believe that I should have handled the matter somewhat differently?" This latter is a rather extreme example of frankness, perhaps too extreme ever to be used with certain client-psychotherapists, even in the advanced stage of treatment. Yet one of our criteria for a good prospective psychotherapist is his ability to respond to this type of review, even when he has expressed annoyance at the therapist during the interview proper.

c. *Aggressiveness.* One of the problems in this type of treatment is that of getting the client-psychotherapist to deal with his problems spontaneously. It may seem that he is going through the motions of being treated without coming to grips with "real" problems. The supervising therapist may have to move in more aggressively than he would in the case of an individual who had sought help for personal rather than professional reasons. Sometimes this means threatening the client-psychotherapist, not with hostile violence, of course, but with the prospect of personal maladaptation or of professional ineptitude. The principal trouble with this approach is that the client-psychotherapist may get the wrong idea of how therapy should be handled. He may think that he has to treat all his own clients aggressively.

d. *Dependency.* Sometimes this kind of interrelation produces an undesirable dependency situation. As we have indicated before, we are not so much concerned with greater or lesser amounts of dependency in persons as we are with the way in which they differentiate and disperse their dependencies. When a client-psychotherapist is under treatment from his training supervisor, he has a complex dependency relationship on his hands. The supervisor is not the disinterested external adviser that a therapist should ordinarily be; he is himself a hurdle to be cleared. This means that the client-psychotherapist must not only depend upon him for personal clarification, but that he must also win and hold the therapist's approval as a professional man.

One of the advantages in an ordinary psychotherapeutic relationship is that the client's dependencies are not permanently vested in the psychotherapist; always the client can look upon the therapist as someone who, in the end, he can take or leave. Ordinarily clients who are well handled prefer to leave, not because they find the therapist repugnant, but because they enter into a new stage of life with new interests and new personal relationships. Not so the client who is preparing for admission to the profession which the therapist represents. He is stuck with his therapist. The dependency is difficult to disperse. The problem becomes all the more acute if the supervising therapist is a member of a staff which has to pass upon the client's professional qualifications. The kind of professional person produced under these conditions is likely to be narrowly dependent upon authoritative figures within his own profession, covertly resentful of administrative organization, and ambivalently militant in his doctrinal position.

e. *Tandem treatment.* A special problem arises when a psychotherapist undergoes treatment while he is himself treating clients. This kind of tandem treatment situation is quite common in psychoanalytic circles. While there is something to be said on both sides, our experience indicates that there is more counter dependency transference in the psychotherapist's response to his clients than there would otherwise be. The course of psychotherapy is likely to be rocky, even for an experienced professional person. It is likely to be characterized by impulsive decisions, inconsistencies of judgment, guilt, great feelings of need for quick success, or for the warm approval of one's associates, alternating with insularity, loose thinking alternating with literalism, and the sudden opening of large areas to the confusion of anxiety. A person who is undergoing these experiences is bound to work out his problems with his own clients as experimental subjects. Even if he practices psychotherapy only in the later stages of his own treatment, his professional outlook is likely to continue to be unstable.

f. *Finding a therapist.* Some psychologists encourage graduate students or psychiatric residents to undergo treatment while they are still in the pretherapeutic stage of their training. This too presents problems. The first problem is that of finding someone who is not a member of the training staff to conduct the therapeutic series. A very messy situation arises when a person accepts treatment from his teacher or employer. In most cases the difficulty extends to accepting employment under one's psychotherapist, even after the psychotherapeutic series has been terminated.

g. *Interference with other aspects of training.* Psychotherapy with a graduate student presents another kind of problem. Our experience with this situation strongly suggests that little educational progress can be expected from the student during his period of treatment. Psychotherapy produces new outlooks; so does graduate education. The difference is this: the new constructs developed in psychotherapy are *core constructs* — that is, constructs vital to one's personal identity; the new constructs developed in the training program are ordinarily presented and experienced as *peripheral constructs* — that is, constructs which are utilized more impersonally and objectively.

Yet, for the psychologist, both sets of constructs deal with similar elements; both have to do with intimate psychological matters. When one attempts to conduct a discussion of a psychological principle of personality in a group where several of the members are currently undergoing psychotherapy, every remark that he makes strikes at the core of the students' construct systems. The discussion, while often stimulating and "vital," takes on a subjective and personalized hue which is inimical to the kind of critical thinking one expects of scientifically oriented students.

One may argue, of course, that all perceptions are biased anyway, and that every peripheral construct is more or less rooted in a person's core structure. But this is a relative matter; it should be possible, and is often extremely desirable, to keep intellectual discussions on an intellectual plane and not let them sink to emotional levels. Thus the student is able tentatively to accept, reject, or test each new idea without vaguely feeling that his whole life structure is involved.

h. *Group psychotherapy.* There is something to be said for group psychotherapy on a more or less superficial level while students are in training. It does involve the same hazards that we have just mentioned, but to a lesser degree. The student in a properly managed group is more widely supported. Because of the need for more explicit communication, the thinking in a group situation tends to be less loose or "schizoid" than in individual therapy. This tends to protect the core structures and keep the construction on a more "intellectual level." However, if there are rival theoretical systems being vigorously propounded in the training program, the internal supports of the group may not be wholly adequate to withstand the pressure caused by the collision of such comprehensive systems.

When and how, then, can a psychotherapist receive psychotherapy? The answer to this question is not yet clear. At the moment it seems to the writer that the best time for a psychologist is during a postdoctoral year, before he has undertaken psychotherapeutic responsibilities with clients. Another possibility is during the intern year, when systematic thinking tends to be less turbulent and the learning is more concretistic. As we have indicated before, we believe it is neither necessary nor desirable for all prospective psychotherapists to undergo psychotherapy, provided, of course, that their personal preparation for psychotherapeutic duties is otherwise carefully assessed. In most cases, we would be inclined to vote for group psychotherapy with a minimum amount of didactic treatment on an individual basis. Yet we must keep in mind that the psychotherapist needs to know a great deal about the treatment situation. If the training program does not make liberal use of one-way screens and monitored interviews, it may be necessary for the trainee to acquire his intimate picture of what psychotherapy should be from across the table in the role of a client.

20. NOTES ON THE TRAINING AND SUPERVISION OF STUDENT PSYCHOTHERAPISTS

This, of course, is not intended to be a book on the training of psychologists. The writing of such a book is a major undertaking in itself. However, there are some particular procedures which are relevant to a discussion of the psychology of personal constructs.

a. *The historical fallacy.* Most clinicians seem to be of the opinion that therapeutic practice should not be undertaken until after one has mastered the theory and techniques of diagnosis. This view is probably related to the fallacy which permeates so much of current psychological thinking, the *historical fallacy:* Since diagnosis chronologically precedes treatment, in dealing with the client the clinician should therefore master it first.

b. *The fallacy of realistic determinism.* The preceding view is probably also anchored in a more subtle fallacy: that of realistic determinism. This is the view that one should never attempt to treat something until he knows precisely what it is. This seems such an utterly reasonable statement that it is difficult to see how it could possibly be challenged. Yet the view of constructive alternativism, and hence of our psychology of personal constructs, is that there are many different ways to cut a pie, and the way one selects depends largely on how he expects to eat it. Similarly, there are many different ways to structure the diagnosis of a client, and the way one chooses depends largely upon what he is able to do with the client after he has him all neatly wrapped up in a "diagnosis."

Diagnosis, as we have emphasized repeatedly, is the planning stage of treatment, and what one plans has to be tempered with an appreciation of what he is able to do. The writer doubts that any clinician can perform adequately as a diagnostician until he has had some well-structured experience as a therapist. Certainly he has seen some instances of highly sophisticated diagnosticians who had to change their diagnostic point of view drastically when they came face to face with the problems of treatment. This experience applies particularly to clinical psychologists, whose doctoral training has generally tended to emphasize measurement and diagnosis to the partial exclusion of treatment. Clinical psychologists whose training has been emphasized by the client-centered school of thought are less affected by this fallacy, since they are plunged into treatment experiences during an early stage of training. Originally the followers of this point of view tended to deprecate diagnosis altogether, although more recently there has been the tendency to plan treatment more systematically, though not in conventional nosological terms.

c. *Therapy "more complicated"?* The third fallacy which accounts for the delay in training clinicians to perform therapeutic functions is the view that therapy is inherently more complicated than diagnosis. Here again our systematic point of view throws new light upon the issue. Nature is itself neither complicated nor simple; it is man's ideas about her that range from the complicated to the simple. Because clinicians tend to be confused about problems of psychotherapy, psychotherapy is judged to be "complicated." Because they think they are less confused about problems of diagnosis, they presume that diagnosis is "simpler." But the construing of a client before treatment, in a way which will predict how he will respond to treatment, may very well prove to be vastly more "complicated" than construing what his responses will be during the course of treating him. After all, the categorization of psychopathological conditions has reached vast arborescent proportions, while the techniques of therapy remain relatively undifferentiated. Indeed, some of those who are most insistent that psychotherapy is a complicated matter are the very ones who use the same undifferentiated procedure hour after hour.

There is, however, one legitimate reason for attempting psychotherapy only after one has reached an advanced stage of training. That is because of the risks involved. Unfortunately, treatment efforts sometimes do the client more harm than good. Even though we do not yet know much about the differential effects of various forms of treatment, the stakes are so high that we should exercise great caution to avoid whatever mistakes may arise out of ingenuousness. But this argues with equal force against the uncritical acceptance of the findings of an ingenuous diagnostician. What it argues for is the judicious and continuous evaluation of everything the student does which might have far-reaching effects upon the client's life.

d. *The student's first case.* It goes without saying that a clinician's first psychotherapeutic cases should be undertaken only with competent supervision. Prior to undertaking a case of his own, he will have profited from assisting others in dealing with their cases and from participation in staff conferences in which treatment has been discussed and evaluated. He will do better if his first interviews tend to be structured — for example, if they involve case history and psychometric examination. He should not go into the freer types of psychotherapeutic interview until after a good diagnostic construction of the case has been formulated. He can participate in this diagnosis, but he should also have the help of others who not only are familiar with the diagnostic instruments and the test protocol but who also understand what kind of diagnostic preparation is needed by a therapist.

e. *The student group.* The writer prefers a setting in which three or four student psychotherapists make up a staff under the close supervision of an experienced teacher of psychotherapeutic procedures. Moreover, as one would infer from what we have said about constructive alternativism and personal construct systems, it is highly desirable for the teacher to be prepared to structure each case in terms of the system with which each student is familiar. Otherwise, the learning experience will degenerate to a very low technical level and the students will learn no more than rules of thumb for dealing with specific kinds of clients.

f. *The interview report.* Interviews should be observed, monitored, and recorded. The most satisfactory way is to pair off the students and have each member of a pair monitor all of the other's interviews. During the group staff meetings the teacher can ask for oral reports of the interview, both from the interviewer and his monitor. In addition, the teacher should observe some of the interviews.

Each interviewer should prepare a detailed report to present in staff. This should include four parts: (1) the student's plan for the interview, (2) a factual account of what he considers to be his more important observations, (3) his interpretation of the interview at a professional level of abstraction, and (4) his prediction as to what the client will do between interviews.

The first part of the report should indicate how the student has incorporated the last staff discussion into a plan of action. The second part indicates both how well the student was able to anticipate the client's behavior — thus measuring his understanding of his client — and what new facts are now available for interpretation. The second part, since it is at a low level of abstraction, permits other members of the staff to place their own constructions upon the information. There is nothing more exasperating than to have a case presented wholly at an interpretative level; the presentation provides no grounds for checking the therapist except against his own logical consistency.

The third part is, of course, always somewhat controversial, and it is this part that is the most likely to be redrawn as a result of the discussion. Next to having a presentation made wholly at the interpretative level, it is exasperating to have it made wholly at a factual level: the discussion may flounder in a sea of anecdotes. The final part of the report provides the therapist with a series of specific hypotheses which can be tested at the time of the next interview. It represents, of course, the scientist's kind of thinking, applied to day-by-day clinical practice.

In the second part of the report, material is usually presented more or less chronologically. The student should prepare this part of the report on the basis of listening to the recording of the interview and discussing it with his monitor. He should enter in the margin the time at which each passage occurred. When the case is staffed, it is a simple matter to turn to any passage in which the staff is particularly interested and play it back through the conference speaker.

g. *One case at a time.* Ordinarily we prefer the student to see his first psychotherapy case through to its conclusion before he takes on additional cases. This permits him to follow the case more intensively, although the supervisor must recognize the danger to the student if he has a particularly unfortunate case on his first try. The writer recalls one instance in which he believes he lost a reasonably promising clinician largely because his first and only treatment case was too much for him. At this stage in his career, however, the writer believes that he could prevent the reoccurrence of this particular type of mistake.

While the student starts by handling a single case, nevertheless the arrangement for monitoring and for staffing permits him to follow more than one case and to see other students struggling with professional problems similar to his own. There are other ways of generalizing his experience. One of the best is for him to enact a passage from one of his interviews with his monitor, first taking the part of the client and then exchanging parts. The monitor's portrayal of the student during the interview is likely to be strong but effective medicine for the student therapist. Ordinarily this should not be undertaken until the student group, like a psychotherapy group, has developed mutual supports and the student has a fairly firm initial construction of his client. The student's therapy experience can be further generalized by discussions of his own feelings of identification with the client. Care should be exercised not to make these discussions too intimate, since we do not want a student therapist thinking about himself rather than the client during the course of an interview.

h. *Self-involvement.* One of the things that need to be faced by the student during his early practical training in psychotherapy is his overwhelming desire to compel the client to get well. To the extent that this represents a general optimism and an acceptance of the client's outlook, it is good. In some instances, however, it may have the flavor of hostility, particularly if the student has laid some private wagers which he has not confided to the supervisor, or if he finds that his own obstinacy has started to lead him into trouble. Often the teacher has to remind the student therapist that the client has a full set of human rights, including the right to remain ill. The student, then, must be prepared to accept the client as the person that he is, to respect him and his errors, and not demand that the client get well just to appease him.

i. *Assigning the initiative.* It is important that the supervisor leave the clinical initiative clearly in the hands of the student therapist. He should never tell the student that he should do a particular thing in the next interview, without also indicating that the tactical decision at the time of the interview is in the hands of the student. A therapist should never feel that his hands are tied when he is face to face with a client; he should always feel that he has the initiative. The supervisor will often say, for example, "This appears to be the way to set up the next interview; but of course, if the situation when the client arrives does not appear to warrant carrying it out, it is your responsibility to modify the plan." Clients seem to sense very quickly that something is wrong when their therapist comes to them with his hands tied by a supervisor.

j. *Jealousy.* Beginning therapists develop jealousies involving their clients. Almost universally, a beginning therapist will be upset when his successfully treated client begins to show healthy signs of resolving his dependency transferences upon the therapist. This happens even when the student has been forewarned. It is a particularly acute problem when the student is under therapy himself. In that case he is likely to be jealous or rejecting of all the client's other acquaintances. The tendency of therapists to blame all the client's ills on the client's mother is a well-known phenomenon of this type — one which shows up with embarrassing clarity even in the writings of some distinguished clinicians. Other therapists, in looking for scapegoats, seem to concentrate on their clients' spouses or their clients' teachers. Needless to say, the teaching supervisor should do what he can to help keep his students from falling into this kind of trap.

k. *The therapist's anxiety.* Student therapists show their anxiety in various ways. A common sign of anxiety in a student therapist, or in an inexperienced therapist, is shifting the "diagnosis" to "paranoid schizophrenia." Some therapists lose control of themselves to such an extent that they communicate their new suspicion directly to the client, as if to say, "Stop behaving this way or you'll go crazy and I won't be able to help you." As we have indicated before, just because a client loosens up a little, is hard to understand, and shows a little hostility, there is no reason to believe that his construct system has fallen apart. It may only be that the therapist's construction is confused — in other words, that he is *anxious*.

Sometimes student therapists show their anxiety by becoming either extremely active in the therapy session or extremely passive. Sometimes they show it by floundering around in the third part, the interpretation part, of their interview reports. Often they show it by pointing out scapegoats in the client's social milieu. They also show their anxiety or their hostility toward their clients in the same ways that clients show anxiety or hostility: by rigidity, by "using" the client, by being late for appointments, by badgering the client, by ignoring evidence, and by avoiding important issues.

1. *Interpersonal relationships.* The training of student therapists is a fascinating task. The dynamics of interpersonal relationships — the relationships between the teacher and the student, the student and his fellow students, the student and his client, the student and client's colleagues, and the client and his colleagues — weave a complicated pattern that cannot fail to challenge the psychologist. Moreover, the far-reaching social implications of the undertaking can be most satisfying, even to the most dilated personality.

21. CONCLUSION

Our discussions of psychotherapeutic procedures have not been intended to provide an exhaustive coverage of the topic. They are meant, instead, to indicate where our theory of personality, the psychology of personal constructs, leads us when it is pursued down to a practical level, and how its reflections highlight the incidents of everyday clinical practice. Some of the things we have said about psychotherapeutic technique might be said from other viewpoints too. No matter! A belief in constructive alternativism would lead us to expect that.

Perhaps some of our observations have seemed more like outgrowths of clinical experience than inferences from a theoretical postulate. We think it is a matter of their being both. What we saw was there all right, but our unique pair of spectacles accounts for the way we saw it. The reader has now been offered a look through the same spectacles. We hope they fit.

Index

client's assets and, 778, 806–807

Sociology, 834

Solutions, psychological, significance of, 887–888

"Somatic" symptoms, inaccessibility of, 921–922

Something like approach, 1040

Speech, therapist's, 642

Spontaneity, client's, readiness for movement and, 1105

Spontaneous activity:
conceptualization of, 732–738
description of, 738–742
observation of child in group, 742–747
vocational choice as, 747–752
see also Experience

Spontaneous elaboration, 778, 874, 875, 924
areas to be opened to, in client management, 817–818

"Spread," 899

Stalinism, 1175

Status examination, 784, 785

Stereotypy, 563, 666, 1157

Stimulus-bound, meaning of term, 1076, 1146

Stimulus generalization, 875

Stooge, therapist as, 580–581

Stress, 745, 792

Strong Vocational Interest Blank, 733

Structuration, of material in therapy, 1004–05, 1120–21

Structure:
areas of, 1118
of client's experience, 769–773
looseness and loss of, 1031–33
see also Superordinate structure

Styller, Harold, 690

Submergence, 564, 818, 1047–48

Subordinate constructs, 564, 1048

Subsuming construction system, 595–596, 600

Success, client's, therapist and, 606–608

Suicide, 637, 730, 872, 1114, 1116

Sullivan, H. S., 1179

Summaries, in therapist-training, 1184–85

Superficial movement, 945

Superordinate constructs, 564, 895, 927, 960, 1068

Superordinate structure, 847–848, 851, 1044, 1068

Support, 773, 813, 942, 1117–18, 1160
mutual, initiation of, 1160–67
as a response pattern, 657–662
techniques of, 658–661
in transference control, 679
uses of, 661–662

Surprise, movement judged by, 1092–93

Suspension, 564

Symbol binding, 1076–77

Symbolism, 563, 763, 770, 1089
loose-tight construction, 1051–52, 1063
psychotherapeutic use of, 878–879
shifting meanings, 1077–78
verbal, 602, 645

Symptoms, 614, 763, 976
adjustments to illness and, 759
climate of opinion and, 770–771
gains and losses to client through, 795–797
levels of formation, 922
reinstating, for reassurance, 654–656
therapeutic attack on, 995–996
see also Diagnosis *and* Manifest deviant behavior

Taboos, religious, 702

Task sampling, enactment procedures, 1142, 1145

Teachers:
attitude toward tests and records, 711–716
child's problems as stated by, 722–726
in school appraisal, 704–710
significance of salaries of, 703
therapist's interview with, 710–711